Righteous Warrior

ALSO BY WILLIAM A. LINK

A Hard Country and a Lonely Place:
Schooling, Society, and Reform in Rural Virginia, 1870–1920

The Paradox of Southern Progressivism, 1880–1930

William Friday: Power, Purpose, and American Higher Education

Roots of Secession: Slavery and Politics in Antebellum Virginia

RIGHTEOUS WARRIOR

*Jesse Helms and the
Rise of Modern
Conservatism*

WILLIAM A. LINK

ST. MARTIN'S PRESS
New York

www.stmartins.com

Book design by Mary A. Wirth

LIBRARY OF CONGRESS CATALOGING-IN-PUBLICATION DATA

Link, William A.

Righteous warrior : Jesse Helms and the rise of modern conservatism / William A. Link. —
1st ed.

p.   cm.

ISBN-13: 978-0-312-35600-2
ISBN-10: 0-312-35600-5

1. Helms, Jesse—Political and social views.   2. Legislators—United States—
Biography.   3. United States. Congress. Senate—Biography.   4. Conservatism—United
States—History—20th century.   5. United States—Politics and government—
1945–1989.   6. United States—Politics and government—1989–   7. Southern States—
Politics and govenment—1951–   I. Title.

E840.8.H44L56 2008
328.73'092—dc22
[B]   2007039411

First Edition: February 2008

10 9 8 7 6 5 4 3 2 1

For Steven and Nancy

Contents

Preface

This study of Jesse Helms grew out of a long-standing interest in southern public life during the nineteenth and twentieth centuries. Less a personal biography than a public one, this book seeks to unwrap the tangled history of the South and the nation, and the rise of the American right, through an examination of a single individual. Helms has long intrigued me. Growing up in New Jersey to parents who were North Carolinians, I spent summer months in the South during the 1950s and 1960s, and it was, for me, an exotic and fascinating place of hope and despair, failure and promise. It was also a place of powerful traditions of regional identity. I began college in North Carolina in September 1972, just about the time Helms's first Senate campaign was heating up. I paid little attention to the campaign, had no knowledge of his background as a conservative television journalist, and was unimpressed when he was elected in the Nixon landslide of that November. Observing him as senator in the mid-1970s, I regarded him as out of the political mainstream and of little importance: most people, especially in student circles of the 1970s, regarded him as something of a buffoon who would almost certainly not last longer than a single term. Along with my contemporaries, I was not only badly mistaken but had seriously misread the political culture of the 1970s. Helms had, in fact, become a major figure in a rising tide of modern conservatism.

After graduate school, I returned again to North Carolina to my first job as an academic historian in 1981. Helms, in my absence, had not only been reelected but had achieved extraordinary power in the political revolution ushered in by Ronald Reagan in the presidential election of the previous year. In the subsequent quarter century in North Carolina, I lived through Helms's last three senatorial campaigns, watched hundreds of his political television ads, read scores of newspaper articles and editorials about him, and observed his activism on the Senate floor. Although I disagreed with him profoundly, I was struck by the degree to which he inspired loyalty among supporters in North Carolina and around the country. Helms articulated a strong sense of traditionalism that existed in North Carolina political culture, and Bill Friday, president of the University of North Carolina system and the subject of a biography that I published in 1995, represented a very different, progressive/liberal tradition in North Carolina public life.

Deliberately, I have tried to achieve some distance between myself as biographer and Jesse Helms as my subject. As a political observer at the time, I subscribed to his demonization: he represented everything that I dislike in modern politics, his policies represented polar opposites of everything I believed in. But I also recognized Jesse Helms's significance, and I see in him a figure of extraordinary importance. In order to write a full and fair study, which has been my intention, I have had to abandon my own preconceived idea of Helms, and judge him on his own terms. This was made more difficult by my lack of access to him. I discovered early on that interviewing Helms was impossible because he was afflicted with dementia, a disease that had, by 2004, overtaken his mental processes and affected his memory. Although I regret not having the opportunity to talk to him, I am the beneficiary of an ample record of past interviews by journalists and historians. Not interviewing Helms provided me, perhaps, with additional distance to fashion a biography that fairly treated my subject.

In addition, I am also the beneficiary of an extraordinary documentary record left behind and preserved at the Jesse Helms Center in Wingate, North Carolina. This record includes his voluminous correspondence beginning in 1951 and proceeding to the end of his senatorial career in 2002. Helms was an avid letter writer, and he loved the process of correspondence. He also loved words, and he used them nimbly and profusely. In the 1960s, his words came in the daily WRAL editorials; in the Senate, he learned to use rhetorical devices to his political advantage. His opponents and supporters alike agree that Jesse Helms possessed a certain sort of transparency: he meant what he said, and he said what he meant. And his words have survived in abundance, a rich source for a biographer.

WILLIAM A. LINK
Gainesville, Florida
August 2007

INTRODUCTION

In September 2005, nearly three years after retiring from thirty years in the United States Senate, Jesse Helms published his memoir, *Here's Where I Stand*. Helms had served as an iconic figure in American life, first as a North Carolina television editorialist and then as the most assertive spokesman for modern American conservatism in the Senate. Like many other conservatives, he opposed big government, believing that the expansion of federal controls presaged a creeping socialism. Helms favored reversing the accelerating growth of government that began during the New Deal and continued in the post–World War II era. Jesse's conservatism encompassed other issues. An outspoken opponent of the 1964 Civil Rights Act and efforts to end Jim Crow segregation through federal intervention, Helms spoke for millions of southern whites who resented the rapid changes of the 1950s and 1960s. Helms's conservatism was defined in reaction to the tumultuous 1960s: he resisted the sexual revolution, opposed feminism and the Equal Rights Amendment, and championed old-fashioned morality against the American counterculture. Opposing the secularization of public life, Helms embraced the reassertion of traditional Judeo-Christian values as a central feature of his brand of conservatism. During the 1960s, his viewing audience as a television editorialist extended no farther than eastern North Carolina, but, after his election to the U.S. Senate in 1972, he attracted a large, national constituency.

Helms's political message had a powerful resonance among Americans.

Unquestionably polarizing, Helms struck hard against his enemies, using cleverly constructed language. Over the years, his enemies remained the same: the liberal press, academics, homosexuals, blacks and minorities, organized labor, and urban cultural elites. Right and left along the political spectrum, Helms became a symbol. Both sides used him to define their position and message, but both sides have also demonized each other through him.

LEAVING THE SENATE in December 2002, Helms steadily declined physically and mentally, and his memoirs were finished only with considerable assistance from the Jesse Helms Center. By the time the book appeared in September 2005, Helms had deteriorated to the point that he had ended nearly all public appearances and, with few exceptions, no longer granted interviews. He was barely active in Republican Elizabeth Dole's senatorial campaign of 2002 and Republican Richard Burr's campaign two years later; in a few campaign commercials that were broadcast in 2002 and in limited appearances in 2004 he remained seated and seemed frail. On September 10, 2005, Helms attended a Raleigh bookstore event to promote his memoirs, and he appeared confused and befuddled. Ten days later, Helms attended a gala dinner in Arlington, Virginia, where five hundred people gathered to celebrate his book's publication and to hear tributes to Helms from Senator Elizabeth Dole and a videotaped message from President George W. Bush. These were, however, his last public appearances: already problems with memory and vascular dementia had overcome his usually forceful personality, and he was not recognizing old associates. In the fall of 2005, when two conservative journalists, Fred Barnes of *The Weekly Standard* and Sean Hannity of Fox News, visited Raleigh to do interviews to promote the memoirs, they found him in bad shape. Barnes ran a fluffy story, but Hannity chose not to air the televised interview. By the spring of 2006, Helms had deteriorated to the point that he entered a Raleigh convalescent home.[1]

The reaction to Helms's memoirs in 2005 suggested that the powerful ideological polarization that he inspired remained an important part of his legacy. Only a few observers confronted the truth about *Here's Where I Stand*: that, even in the self-serving genre of memoirs, it contained little substantial information about his experiences and only faintly represented the rich and detailed content of Helms's life. Even Jesse's former associates privately acknowledged that the book did not reflect Helms's authorial voice. Most of the press, however, ignored the book and focused instead on Helms's legacy. Conservatives greeted its appearance. R. Emmett Tyrrell,

Jr., wrote in *The American Spectator* that Helms was a figure who had "braved liberals' indignation to create the politics that now prevails on Capitol Hill and in the White House, namely, modern American conservatism." Liberals, predicted Tyrrell, would not like *Here's Where I Stand*, and they would, in "another grotesque image of the conservative public figure," try to portray him as a "bigoted, small-minded, not very intelligent, provincial" person. Helms would be interred in the special burial place that liberals reserved for leading conservatives, Tyrrell predicted.[2]

Months before the book appeared, in June 2005, the *Raleigh News and Observer*, long Helms's most consistent critic, obtained advance proofs of the book. Rob Christensen, longtime political reporter for the *N&O*, wrote a story emphasizing Helms's unchanged views on race. Unlike most southern segregationist politicians, said Christensen, Helms had never recanted his views on the civil rights movement or admitted that segregation was wrong.[3] The reviews of *Here's Where I Stand*, appearing in the fall of 2005, followed Christensen's lead. Barry Yeoman of The *Independent Weekly*, a progressive-liberal tabloid with a loyal following in the Raleigh–Durham–Chapel Hill area, denounced Helms's memoirs as a "curious exercise in political whitewash" that offered "no introspection, no sense of fallibility—not even the basic elements of good storytelling." Helms had become a "lover of all humanity" in this retelling "of Helms' own words, or perhaps those of a second-rate ghostwriter."[4] Historian Tim Tyson, reviewing the book in the *N&O*, described *Here's Where I Stand* as an "uncompromising plate of North Carolina barbecue, served up hot with red pepper vinegar" but delivering a "broth so thin" that it was, quoting Illinois senator Paul Douglas, "like soup made of the shadow of a crow which had starved to death." Where Helms claimed that he had been misunderstood on race and segregation, Tyson asserted that the former senator had embraced a "segregationist backlash" as "his ticket to the top." Jesse would be remembered, said Tyson, as "one of the most able and relentless adversaries of the South's homegrown freedom movement." But Tyson's review, by far the most biting denunciation of Helms's legacy, became subsumed when the *N&O* editors decided, presumably in the interest of "balance," to run it next to Tyrrell's laudatory piece.[5]

IN 1994, ONE of Helms's Senate colleagues, Bill Bradley, gave Jesse a copy of Bradley's recently published memoir, *Time Present, Time Past*. Bradley was elected to the Senate from New Jersey in 1978, and, although the two men spent more than fifteen years together in the clubby, highly

personalized environment of the Senate, Bradley and Helms occupied opposite ends of the political spectrum. Although Jesse was always courtly
and courteous to him in personal encounters, the New Jersey senator objected to Helms's raw political style, his willingness to "take the scabs off"
in order to accomplish his political objectives. Helms's conservative positions, Bradley recalled, represented the "personification of everything that
I didn't believe in." Not long after he gave Helms a copy of the book, he
heard from him by telephone. Helms thanked Bradley, politely suggesting
that he enjoyed the book even while he disagreed with it politically. But
Helms then went on to ask a favor. Jennifer Knox, his granddaughter, a
basketball fan, would be visiting Washington, Jesse said, and he wondered
if Bradley, a former Princeton and New York Knicks basketball star,
would be willing to meet her. Bradley agreed, but suggested that they
meet on a blacktop basketball court in Washington. Arriving with Jennifer
in a "ridiculously old car," Jesse and Dot, his wife of five decades, watched
as Bradley and Jennifer shot baskets, and he immediately realized that she
was "a player." Bradley took a larger message from the encounter, as he
watched two proud grandparents "beaming" on the sidelines. This was a
"big lesson for me," said Bradley: after that experience, he recalled, he
found it difficult to regard Helms as "the personification of evil." Rather,
he saw him as a grandfather, a person, something other than a "cardboard
cutout."[6]

This book represents an attempt to see Helms as something more than
a "cardboard cutout." Perhaps because of the tendency to view Helms in
ideological terms, he has been widely underestimated, misunderstood, and
even ignored by journalists and historians. During his career and after, there
has been a tendency to dismiss him as an ineffective right-wing crank. In a
gross misunderstanding, many of his opponents have ignored his facility
with language and clever argumentation—though they have done so at their
peril. I hope to avoid the ideologically charged caricatures of the right and
left, and instead to understand and assess the impact of Helms during the
last third of the twentieth century. As such, this biography enjoys the approval of neither side of the polarized political environment. Many of my
colleagues are astounded that anyone could abide writing such a book. On
the other hand, this book has been written without the approval of Helms
and his supporters; as mentioned, about the time that I started work on it in
earnest, his dementia prevented him from granting any interviews, nor have
I have ever met Helms. This work is not, in any sense, an authorized biography. The Jesse Helms Center, which houses Helms's papers, has been exceptionally gracious in making materials available to me, but I cannot say

that they will agree with my emphases or interpretations of the senator's life. I have gotten to know him well, nonetheless, through the millions of sentences that he wrote in editorials, speeches, and correspondence; I have also met him, in a sense, through numerous interviews with his contemporaries, both opponents and supporters.

THERE ARE FEW figures more important than Jesse Helms in the emergence of the American right in recent years, more forceful in articulating a conservative agenda and ideology, more effective in fashioning a message with wide popular appeal, and more successful in implementing a political strategy to gain power. Despite the outpouring of work by recent historians about modern conservatism, remarkably little attention has been paid to Helms. Ernest Furgurson's biography of Helms, *Hard Right: The Rise of Jesse Helms,* appeared in 1986, midway through Helms's Senate career. Furgurson's study has remained the standard account.[7] Recent scholars of modern conservatism have raised a number of important questions. While some have emphasized the central role of racial politics in modern conservatism, others have stressed the potency of anti-Communist and anti-statist ideology. Still others have stressed that the emergence of conservatism as a national movement was less important than developments at the local level. This study makes a slightly different case. Even while the grass roots are crucial in understanding the emergence of modern conservatism, its emergence cannot be properly understood without comprehending developments at the national level: conservatism was a well-coordinated movement that looked to national organizations. The leaders of modern conservatism, such as Helms, helped to forge a national constituency, to communicate with it effectively, and to mobilize it politically. Suggesting that individuals do matter, I argue that Helms was a central figure in modern conservatism. I further argue that the rise of the new American right cannot be properly understood without coming to terms with Helms's role.

Between 1950 and 2002, Helms had many careers, all of them significant, as radio broadcaster, congressional aide, banking lobbyist, television broadcaster, and United States senator. From the 1950s on, Helms waged a righteous war that sought to upend the political status quo in America. In all of these careers, he was consumed by an ambition to reverse a liberal consensus that, he believed, dominated government, the media, academic life, and public affairs generally after World War II. Helms advocated an attitudinal revolution that would seal the doom of liberalism. During the 1950s and 1960s, he became a conservative ideologue, opposing the further expansion of federal power, supporting a reversal of New Deal policies in labor, agriculture, and social welfare, and criticizing the leftward shift of national politics. During the 1950s and 1960s, Jesse also vigorously defended the racial status quo. He opposed the *Brown v. Board of Education* requirement that segregation in public schools should end, and he resisted federal mandates to end segregation. Helms also strongly attacked the black-led civil rights movement and its white allies, and he maintained that the uprising that they had ignited would lead to the social deterioration of the South. Helms's conservatism combined attributes of opposition to government intervention with resistance to integration, but these positions fell under a general umbrella of anti-Communism.

As a television editorialist who enjoyed a strong following in eastern North Carolina, Helms had expanded his message by offering a critique of the 1960s. During this decade, he initiated a long-standing cultural war against the sexual revolution and the triumph of secularization in American public life. Connecting Helms's message during the 1950s and 1960s was his message about race. He opposed federal intervention, and African American activism, to Helms, was itself a cause of social breakdown. Jesse became very effective in expressing a message of racial politics that transcended the crude segregationism of many of his contemporaries. Translating the debate about civil rights into a debate about individual rights as well as about social decline, in the 1960s Helms played a major role in the racial politics of the post–Civil Rights Act South. These views would remain largely unchanged over the years: Helms was rigidly consistent, and unlike most southern segregationists he never renounced his opposition to the Civil Rights Act. Indeed, he remained as passionately opposed to the civil rights movement's historical legacy.

Helms joined the U.S. Senate on the heels of a rightward turn in American politics occurring during the 1970s and 1980s.[8] Helms occupied a prime seat in this political transformation. Joining the Senate in 1973, for the next seven years he carved out a niche for himself as the most important conservative spokesman in the Senate—and, as a leader of a coalescing right. Opposed to expanding government and what he saw as the liberal establishment, Jesse earned a reputation as "Senator No"—a designation that the *News and Observer* gave him but one that he eagerly embraced—because of his obstructionist parliamentary tactics that led to few victories but considerable publicity about conservative issues. Helms's tactics forced his liberal opponents in the Senate to engage in recorded votes, and he used their votes against them in subsequent elections. As a senator, Helms embraced the agenda of the New Right. In the 1970s, he not only opposed federally mandated school busing for desegregation but also became an unrelenting opponent of legalized abortion and court-enforced bans against prayer in public schools. Rarely did Helms achieve legislative victory: in the 1970s he had little interest in enacting legislation or making policy. Rather, his political strategy was to publicize issues and rally a national conservative constituency.

With this successful political strategy, Helms's message and rhetoric reached new constituencies. Beginning in the 1970s, he encouraged the mobilization of Christian evangelicals, a group that had long remained politically inactive. Raised in a conservative Southern Baptist tradition, Helms believed in traditional Christian values, and his conservatism was rooted in religious fundamentalism. In the senatorial election of 1972, Helms experienced a religious conversion that made his faith and his conviction that God was guiding his actions a central element in his subsequent three decades in the Senate. He had little trouble communicating with Christian evangelicals; he spoke their language. Using issues such as school prayer, nonprofit status for private Christian schools, homosexuality, and the general rubric of "secular humanism," Helms helped to nurture the political organization of Christian evangelicals. He attracted evangelicals' support, and by the late 1970s he had become their most important leader in the Senate. The organization of the Moral Majority in 1979 and the Christian Coalition about a decade later at least partly resulted from Helms's sponsorship, and in North Carolina the mobilization of Christian evangelicals formed a crucial part of his electoral strategy.

Helms rallied his conservative constituency not only because he possessed the forum of the Senate but because he assembled a formidable political machine that succeeded in fund-raising, using broadcast media, and communicating a political message. The North Carolina Congressional Club supplied the muscle for Helms to win elections and to become a national conservative leader, and it pioneered new methods of political communication. Beginning in 1978 and culminating in 1984 and 1990, the club attracted an assortment of committed conservative, youthful ideological, and, most important, creative innovators in a new style of politics that depended on opinion polls, targeted political advertising, and slash-and-burn attacks against their opponents. Between 1978 and 1990, the club became a full-time operation that was constantly engaged in the conservative revolution. It ran Helms's political campaigns and constructed an unequaled fund-raising machine, while it also made Helms substantially more effective than his political enemies in using the media to his advantage. The club and Helms had different interests, but both were bound together by a common desire to promote a conservative revolution nationwide and to obtain and secure political power. The Congressional Club and Helms became known for a bruising, take-no-prisoners political style that relied on character attacks and negative advertising. Helms's political advertising also relied on wedge issues to divide the electorate, most especially issues emphasizing race and sexuality. His political organization pioneered these techniques, which were widely duplicated by political managers on all sides of the ideological spectrum around the country.

After Ronald Reagan's election in 1980, Helms became the American right's leading congressional spokesman. During the subsequent twelve years of Republican control of the White House, Helms usually occupied the right flank, fighting pragmatists and urging purity on conservatism. In the early 1980s, Helms unsuccessfully promoted the New Right's early political agenda on school busing, school prayer, and abortion. Later in the decade, Jesse became the most important opponent of gay rights and public toleration of homosexuals. His war against gay people focused on the AIDS crisis, and Helms maintained that gay rights leaders were attempting to legitimize homosexual behavior in their efforts against the disease. Further, Helms blamed gays for spreading the disease, which he asserted had its origins in what he considered their "disgusting," irresponsible social behavior. Helms waged an ongoing war against homosexual groups into the 1990s, and he became their most important enemy and symbol of public currents of homophobia. Helms's shift to culture war in the late 1980s also included an attack against cultural elites. In 1989, he led a campaign against federal funding for "obscene" art.

While Jesse Helms waged war at home for conservatism, he also opposed the consensus that shaped American foreign policy after 1945. Soon after he arrived in the Senate, he became a persistent opponent of détente and Richard Nixon's attempt to negotiate with the Soviet Union. Believing that détente was a morally bankrupt policy, Helms ardently believed in the destruction of Soviet Communism. Helms's foreign policy positions remained on the margins until the late 1970s, when arms control failed and when Reagan's election ended détente. In the 1970s and 1980s, Helms remained an unrelenting anti-Communist, and his foreign policy increasingly focused on the developing world, where he saw the most potential for Soviet expansion. With little concern for democratic development, Helms backed white minority regimes in southern Africa and authoritarianism in Latin America. Up until the collapse of apartheid, Helms continued to urge American opposition to black-majority governments. Helms remained a loyal supporter of repressive right-wing regimes in Chile and Argentina, where the military seized power through coups and where military govern-ments ruthlessly suppressed the left. In Central America, especially El Sal-vador and Nicaragua, Helms supported anti-Communist authoritarianism because he saw it as preferable to left-wing triumph.

By the late 1980s, Helms's interest in foreign policy was consuming more of his attention. In 1987, he became ranking member of the Senate Foreign Relations Committee, and from that position a subtle transforma-tion came over his approach to foreign policy. During his early years in the Senate, he had been more interested in ideology than policy; after 1987, policy became his main goal. In Latin America, he shifted attention from unremitting support of rightist regimes to a focus on democracy, human rights, opposition to political corruption, and the drug trade—subjects that made Mexico and Panama important in his thinking. Helms's shift coin-cided with the collapse of the Soviet Union. For most of the 1990s, Helms attempted to define America's position in the post–Cold War world, and his positions were squarely at odds with traditional American foreign pol-icy and the positions of the administration of Bill Clinton.

The final phase of Helms's righteous war was thus waged over foreign policy, and he occupied center stage after November 1994, when Republi-cans swept to control of Congress and Jesse became chair of the Senate Foreign Relations Committee. For the next six years, Helms promoted a muscular American presence in the world and laid the basis for at least some of the attributes of post-9/11 American unilateralism. Rejecting arms control and multilateralism, he opposed the Clinton administration's diplo-macy in Haiti, Bosnia, and the Middle East. Believing that it was ineffective and only benefited America's enemies, Helms opposed the last significant attempts at arms control of the twentieth century. Blocking the Chemical Weapons Convention, in 1999 he helped to lead the successful fight against the Comprehensive Test Ban Treaty. A longtime opponent of foreign aid, Helms sought to alter the diplomatic bureaucracy. He led congressional ef-forts to cut the United States's financial contribution to the United Nations, and he insisted on changes in the international organization's structure.

THIS BOOK EXPLORES the various ways in which Jesse Helms, as a righ-teous warrior, left a permanent stamp on late-twentieth-century American public life. Much of his success and failure lay in Helms's unswerving ad-herence to principles and his unwillingness to change with the times. An architect of the emergence of the American right, he served as an uncom-promising ideologue who helped both to assemble a rhetorical message with wide appeal to ordinary Americans and to fashion a strategy to obtain political power. A majority of North Carolina voters admired Helms's tenacity, and they elected him to the Senate five times. Conservatives nationwide relied on him to energize the movement. In the end, the conservative movement was wrapped up in Helms's career, and his life charts the emergence of modern American conservatism.

THE TWO FACES OF JESSE HELMS

Although Jesse had earned a fearsome reputation for his slash-and-burn political tactics, there was also a softer side. Within his political circle, Helms was compassionate and caring; his Senate staffers uniformly remembered him warmly. By the late 1980s, Helms was well known for his personal style and his conscious rejection of the imperiousness of some of his colleagues. In 1998, when the *Washingtonian* surveyed 1,200 staffers and Capitol Hill employees, Jesse was rated among the nicest senators.[1] Garrett Epps, a columnist for the liberal *Independent Weekly*, published in Durham, interviewed Helms in 1989. He was surprised at what he found. "The Helms I expected," he recalled, "was a sizzling-hot, angry, defensive ideologue." The person he found instead was "relaxed, friendly, funny and genuinely curious about ideas and people."[2] Don Nickles, one of Helms's closest allies in the Senate, later reflected that the common caricatures of Helms as mean and vindictive were "misplaced." Nickles described him as "probably the nicest person serving in the Senate," certainly "the most gentlemanly of any of the senators," and a person who "epitomized the Southern gentleman." In his dealings with other senators he was "always very pleasant, never disagreeable." He was also unpretentious, according to Nickles. During Reagan's inauguration in January 1981, Nickles recalled, Helms objected when police stopped traffic so that a bus with senators could pass through.[3]

Helms' personal warmth extended beyond senators. The third floor of the Dirksen Office Building, where Jesse's Senate offices were located,

contained two public elevators, which were old and slow, and three private
elevators reserved only for senators. Staffers and visitors that snuck on the
senators' elevator were routinely evicted. The public elevator, located just
outside of Helms's office, was often crowded with tourists. If he noticed
them waiting, Helms delighted in gathering tourists and taking them on the
senators' elevator, or for a ride on the Senate subway shuttle that ran between Dirksen and the Capitol, even when votes were about to occur and
the shuttle was reserved for senators. Sometimes, on the spur of the moment, Helms ushered tourists to the family gallery, on the third floor of the
Senate, and provided seats for them to watch the proceedings. The Senate
guards were so used to Jesse's routine with visitors that they often chuckled
when they saw him coming with an entourage in tow. He considered himself a sort of unofficial host of Capitol Hill, and he personally felt that it was
his duty to ensure that tourists enjoyed their visit.[4]

Helms was especially kind to children, and he liked nothing better
than speaking to visiting schoolchildren. According to his own estimate,
between 1973 and the mid-1990s, he visited with some 60,000 children
from North Carolina. He sometimes disappeared, and staffers would later
discover him with a group of children. To "countless small children who
have visited the Capitol with their parents," wrote a *New York Times* reporter in 1987, he was "simply the friendly man who let them pretend to
drive the Senate subway train." Once Helms gathered up one little girl,
seven-year-old Lindsay Rogers of Denver, asking her: "How would you
like to sit in the driver's seat?" Like many other children, he put Lindsay at
the controls of the subway, which ran automatically. In 1987, he received a
letter from a college student who remembered similar treatment when his
sixth-grade class visited Washington, and the Senator let him "drive" the
subway.[5] Helms was also known for welcoming visitors into his office, especially visitors from North Carolina, and many of them were escorted to
the Senate floor for a personal tour from the Senator. He loved seeing a
"sparkle" in their eye, he recalled, when they received this sort of treatment from a United States senator. Once he hosted a student group while
the president of Argentina was waiting to see him. When an aide interrupted him, he told her to visit with the Argentine. "What do you think I
have you for?" he asked.[6]

Helms's office was also known for unusual staff loyalty and dedication,
despite low pay: the senator paid some of the lowest salaries on Capitol
Hill, and he always made it a point to return money to the Congress. He
scrupulously avoided excessive overseas travel himself; his staff traveled at
private expense. Very often they made phone calls at their own expense

because they realized how carefully he scrutinized the phone bills. But his staff was, nonetheless, fiercely loyal. Partly, staff loyalty came from ideological commitment, partly because of the personal bond they felt with the senator, who was warm and avuncular within his circle. He established warm, personal relationships with staffers. After aide Deborah DeMoss lost her father in 1986, Helms became a sort of surrogate father. When she became engaged to Honduran René Fonseca in 1992, Jesse insisted that he meet him in order to look him over. He spent half of a day, taking Fonseca around Washington. After the visit, the Senator informed DeMoss that he approved of the match. In many other instances, he reached out to staffers, keeping up with their health and the welfare of their families. According to DeMoss, Helms, on a personal level, was a "complete opposite" of his public image.

Helms's office was known through Washington for its efficiency and responsiveness to constituents. Darryl Nirenberg, who served as Helms's chief of staff between 1991 and 1995, described Jesse as a superb manager who would have made, Nirenberg thought, an excellent lawyer or small businessman. Jesse often mentored staffers by projecting high standards and expectations, by carefully editing their prose, and by permitting them to pursue initiatives on their own under his supervision. His standards included an impeccable ethical sense, and Helms could never be accused of crossing lines or seeking shortcuts. As a former journalist, Jesse took great pride in effective communication. He was a "fabulous writer," Nirenberg recalled, and "nobody could write like him." Helms exhibited an unusual work ethic, and he did not expect others to do things that he was unwilling to do; he personally involved himself in many issues.[7]

The senator made it a point to instruct staffers that solving constituents' problems was the office's primary mission; the first thing new staff were told was the need for responsiveness. He expected phone calls to be answered within an hour and all mail to be answered promptly; and periodically he checked up on things by investigating whether phone calls and mail were answered. Although most Senate offices did not treat mail in this careful fashion, Helms insisted on this level of service, and if problems remained unsolved, said one staffer, "we heard about it." Mail consumed a large portion of the time of his entire staff; all of them worked on it, and unlike other Senate offices there were no legislative correspondents whose sole duty was the mail. Helms himself personally answered a large bulk of the correspondence, taking a stack of letters home with him at night and returning with typewritten drafts for his assistant to retype. Scott Wilson, who worked as a staffer in the early and mid-1980s, remembered that

everyone in the office spent much of their time on mail; everyone had type-
writers at their desk. One day Wilson was in the senator's office and he suggested the need for additional staff support to handle the mail. "Well, son,"
Helms responded, "if Friday afternoon gets here and you've got any left
over, just bring it in, and I'll take it home with me over the weekend and
answer it." Embarrassed, Wilson spent the weekend catching up with his
mail. He was impressed with how the senator "never asked anybody to do
anything that he wasn't prepared to do." Jesse considered the mail a vital
lifeline to his constituents. "Some of the best ideas I got from back home,"
he would later tell an interviewer, "came from the average working guy
who saw a need and suggested it." Staffers were constantly on the lookout
for information and ideas that emerged from the large volume of constituent mail.[8]

Helms often took up causes of individuals, sometimes even individuals
not from North Carolina, in cases as diverse as overseas property that was
confiscated or efforts at foreign adoptions. Constituent services were "real
important" to Helms, recalled his chief of staff Jimmy Broughton, and he
instructed his staff to "never say no" to requests for help. It was his "second
nature," according to Broughton, "to help people." Helms's constituent services maintained state offices in Hickory, serving the western part of the
state, and Raleigh, serving the eastern half, with Frances Jones coordinating
eleven caseworkers. Broughton recalled one case of a Raleigh resident who
lived near N.C. State who was having problems with Social Security in dis-
posing of the estate of her husband. When things reached a dead end, a
friend, a faculty member at N.C. State, advised her: "I hate the sonabitch,
but it's time to call Jesse Helms." When Helms left the Senate in 2003, his
successor, Elizabeth Dole, kept his constituent services operations intact.[9]

FOR MOST OF his political career, Helms used the "liberal media" as a
foil. Charging that the mainstream press was against him and other conservatives, he argued that he was unfairly portrayed and that liberals controlled most outlets of newspaper publishing and broadcasting. Interestingly,
even while he attacked the liberal media, Jesse nurtured relationships with
reporters, especially those from North Carolina who were reporting from
Washington. He "got a kick out of speaking to reporters" because he enjoyed the banter, recalled staffer Scott Wilson, and the North Carolina reporters had to "run him down" in the hallways in order to get an interview.
"If I told you everything I know," Wilson recalled his telling one reporter,
"then you'd know everything you know, plus everything I know."[10] John

Monk, who covered Helms for the *Charlotte Observer's* Washington bureau during the 1990s, later said that it was "hard not to like him." Although he was not a "photogenic image of a politician," he had an engaging personality with a voice that was "resonant and rich." Once Monk visited Helms's office to discover the senator singing happy birthday over the phone to an elderly woman in a nursing home. He was, recalled Monk, a "personable, kind person." When Helms was "on," said Monk, "no one could be more gracious and kind and decent."[11] In some respects, Helms even liked the abuse from the North Carolina media. On the wall of his Senate office, he kept framed newspaper cartoons, most of them unflattering.

Helms had less regard for the national media, and he felt little hesitation about refusing interviews or not returning their calls. Once, when a North Carolina newspaper reporter was in the senator's office, an aide came in and told him that the *New York Times* was trying to reach him. "I don't care," he said. "I'm not talking to the *New York Times*." This was typical: there was little to be gained by interacting with the national media. Most North Carolina print journalists covering Helms in the Senate found him accessible and friendly, and always what Chuck Babington, the *N&O's* Washington correspondent in the late 1980s, called a "great source of news" and "my rainmaker." For many years, Helms refused to hire a press secretary, which was unusual for Senate offices. Reporters often called Helms at his Arlington home, and he usually took their calls. Babington so often depended on Helms for stories that he sometimes felt that the relationship was too easy. "Chuck," he told himself at the beginning of some days, "you are going to have do something other than Helms today." Still, he remembered that Helms could be manipulative. He praised Babington for favorable stories, but on those occasions that he was displeased, Helms "would kind of pounce" in a phone call or letter. The ultimate effect "could have been that you were intimidated," something that Babington resisted.[12]

Other reporters also experienced a different side to Helms. Most of them eventually discovered that the senator and his staff worked hard to manipulate the North Carolina press. John Monk later said that he was on-again, off-again in his relations with Helms. If he wrote a story that offended Helms or appeared to cast him in a bad light, he would be denied access for his "transgressions." Access was the lifeblood of reporters, but Monk realized working in a Washington bureau for a major North Carolina daily made his job high-profile. All of his stories were faxed into Helms's office after publication and carefully scrutinized. On occasions when he wrote stories that displeased Helms, the senator or his staff would get on the phone to complain to Monk's *Observer* editors. In 1993, for example, when Monk wrote a story describing Helms's staff as among the lowest paid in the Senate, Helms took offense. Monk wrote that Helms paid staff bonuses as compensation for low pay; Helms insisted that no such bonuses existed. He further believed that Monk had told staff members about their low pay, hoping to "cause problems among my staff members." Helms became so furious, according to Monk, that he refused to take his phone calls for months.[13]

Reporters for the most important newspapers in the state, the *N&O* and the *Charlotte Observer*, were often singled out as purveyors of the liberal media. In eastern North Carolina, Helms complained to his audiences about bias in the *N&O*, in the west it was the *Observer*. But most of this was playing to his audience. During the 1984 campaign, Helms approached Ken Eudy before a rally at the Country Adventures Barbecue House in Hickory. The senator warned him that, in his speech, he would single out his presence as a *Charlotte Observer* reporter. "Don't get upset," he said, "don't take it personal; it's just politics." But on other occasions, Eudy noted that Helms could be intimidating. He recalled that Helms's press conferences on the campaign trail were usually held with reporters encircled by hostile Jesse supporters, and he sometimes felt "physically threatened." Helms himself, at six foot two, had a presence and a way of wagging his finger at reporters. He was especially combative during the election season, when tensions and tempers were short. Bob Rosser, who traveled with the senator during the 1984 campaign, believed that Jesse was claustrophobic, and the press crush that followed often provoked him to lash out at reporters, especially if he believed that they were asking stupid questions. Still, Eudy remembered him as exceptionally skillful in anticipating and deflecting reporters' questions.

On one occasion during the 1984 campaign, Eudy recalled, Reagan had visited the state aboard Air Force One; Helms rode with him from Washington. Eudy cornered Helms at a press conference in Shelby. The Helms campaign, he pointed out, had made much of the fact that Hunt traveled aboard state aircraft, at public expense, while campaigning. Helms then interrupted him. "I know what you're getting ready to ask," he said. "Should taxpayers pay for Ronald Reagan's campaign travel?" Helms had "preempted" his question: now he proceeded to answer it. This was no double standard, he said. Reagan worked on behalf of national security; Hunt could make no such claim. Even if there was a double standard, it was acceptable because of the greater interest of the country. Eudy recalled this as yet another manifestation of Helms's ability to manipulate the media.[14]

Helms had long used the *N&O* as a whipping boy for the liberal media.

Its reporters were frequently singled out at political gatherings as representing a bastion of the liberal media, but he realized that the newspapers served as a political symbol. Babington recalled that Helms realized the difference between the highly partisan editorial page and the less political reporters, but he made no such distinction before political crowds. During the 1984 campaign, which Babington covered briefly at the end when he joined the *N&O*'s staff, he remembered that Helms would needle the newspapers only within their readership area. In the western Piedmont, he said nothing about *News and Observer* liberalism. Reporters served as a prop for Jesse, who, Babington thought, was "very clever" in his use of the symbolism of the liberal media.[15]

Jack Betts, who covered Helms for the *Greensboro Daily News* and the *Charlotte Observer*, provided another example of the senator's complex relationship with print journalists. En route to a campaign appearance in March 1978, Helms told Betts that he intended to serve only two terms. Betts, who later described himself as stunned by this admission, told Jesse that he would write a story about it if he was serious about not running. "My inclination is to let 'er go," Helms responded. "I could change my mind but I doubt that I will." After political adviser Tom Ellis "hit the roof" over the interview, Betts wrote to Helms suggesting that perhaps he had not meant what he said and providing an opportunity for him to back off. Although Helms would later assert that "my intent was to make it as irrevocably unqualified as it apparently sounded," Helms continued to insist that Betts had reported the interview accurately. But then Helms's versions of events changed. In October 1979, after winning reelection to a second term, Helms told Gene Marlowe of the *Winston-Salem Journal* that he had written a reporter (Betts) to correct the story, but the correction never appeared in print. A day later, Helms told an *N&O* reporter that he had commented about not running in response to a question about term limits; he had said that he would abide by a constitutional amendment providing restricting time in office, but he had not ruled out running for a third term.

Soon after Helms announced that he would run for a third term, in February 1984, Betts revived the issue in a column entitled "Where Do You Stand, Jesse?" Reviewing Helms's zigzagging about running for reelection, he suggested that Helms had been less than consistent about the issue. Helms's inconsistency, Betts later observed, "seemed at odds with the general belief that Jesse Helms says what he means and means what he says." About a week later, on February 21, 1984, Betts received a pointed letter from Clint Fuller. Helms had read Betts's column, Fuller reported, and had stuck it in the outbox without a word. "He just shook his head," Fuller

wrote. Helms had been criticized by the media so often that he was not upset by the account. "But it did puzzle him," Fuller explained, "because he
has always liked you," and Helms had often referred to him as a "fair and
objective newspaperman." Clearly, Betts had let him down. "Wonder why
Jack didn't at least ask me?," Helms later said. "He didn't even call." Fuller
suggested that Helms should stay to protect North Carolina tobacco farmers; without him at the Agriculture Committee, it was a "goner." There
were, as well, "other reasons" why Helms decided to run again, "but I'm not
at liberty to discuss them." Nonetheless, Fuller admitted that he was "not
without prejudice when somebody lays the wood to my boss and *our* friend."
Reflecting on the episode, Betts later reflected that this was "when I learned
Jesse was an equivocator."[16] Helms thoroughly understood modern media,
and he was a master practitioner of employing the media to his political advantage. Most reporters saw him as a real person, beneath the stereotypical
image that prevailed—and which, to a large extent, he had promoted. But
this was, Betts observed, a "love-hate relationship." In his experience, he
found Helms's "personal touch" compelling, and there were two or three
instances in which Jesse reached out with some gesture that "touched me."
He was not, to be sure, a "one-dimensional character."[17]

Chapter 1

A BOLL WEEVIL IN THE COTTON PATCH

Early Years

In October 1992, about a half century after he left his hometown of Monroe, North Carolina, Jesse Helms returned to speak to the home folks. Experiencing feelings of nostalgia, he recalled the small North Carolina town as "remarkable" and "not typical." Growing up in Monroe, he was bound to his hometown by a "sense of community, compassion, resourcefulness, courage, pride and self-reliance." The Depression and a looming world war, he remembered, decisively shaped his attitude toward the world, as they did for all Americans growing up in the middle of the twentieth century. Fundamentalist Protestant Christianity, with its unyielding view of reality and its unwillingness to tolerate opposing views, also helped to form his outlook on life. Helms developed a strong sense of faith and a belief in the value of struggle against adversity, and this worldview remained virtually unchanged for the rest of his life. The experience of growing up in Monroe determined Jesse's views about himself and his world. "Because I was *when* I was and *where* I was," he said, "I have such deep feelings about our country."[1]

Helms's larger "country," reflecting the world in which he grew up, was insular, suspicious of outsiders, and traditionalist in its views on race, class, and gender and sexuality. The small-town values that he imbued included self-reliance, discipline, and hard work; his "country" scorned efforts by outsiders to alleviate social problems through charity and welfare. This value system also required strict probity, rectitude, and obedience to a code of ethical behavior, and its cornerstone was strong family ties. Monroe residents were conservative "in everything we thought," remembered one contemporary.[2] Despite living in the worst of times, through depression and war, the town offered a happy childhood for Jesse that included an intimacy and closeness. But the small-town environment of Monroe also offered life lessons about society, culture, and politics. In his early years, he acquired well-defined characteristics: his father, in teaching him that ambition was good, instructed him that he could accomplish things and achieve recognition by following a strict work ethic. His teachers provided life lessons that stressed independence and achievement. Individual enterprise, not the assistance of others, brought results; character was all-important.

Jesse's highly developed sense of individualism fit in with a southern small-town ethos. This ethos stressed civility, but it regarded those outside the code—including black people—suspiciously, and, in a rapidly changing world, the small-towners were quick to see enemies around them. Helms internalized these values, developing in his childhood and adolescent years bonds of affection toward family, church, and neighborhood. Outside of this circle of affection, he learned, lay adversaries that challenged his small-town ethos. He later discovered that combating enemies required aggressive tactics. Energetic and clever, Helms gained a facility with words that would serve him well over the years in facing these enemies. Not until young adulthood did he discover the power of communication in modern politics, and his political awakening in the senatorial election of 1950 coincided with a realization about the ability of modern media to shape public opinion. Achievement, he had learned, did not come easily. Recognition, influence, and power came through struggle.

Born on October 18, 1921, Jesse Helms grew up in Monroe, a growing small town of about four thousand inhabitants twenty-five miles east of Charlotte, the state's largest city. Founded in 1844, Monroe, named for President James Monroe, was the county seat of Union County, organized only two years earlier. At the center of the North Carolina's Gold Rush of the 1840s, Union County was one of several cotton-producing counties of the southern Piedmont. The town included a black population that composed about a quarter of the county's population; numerous cotton gins throughout the county; a prevailing racial attitude of white supremacy; high rates of tenancy and sharecropping; and rural poverty. As Union County's leading town, Monroe housed a railroad repair shop for the Seaboard Air Line Railway, and the town included some manufacturing, finance, and retailing operations, two textile mills, a Belk department store and a J.C. Penney's, two drugstores, and five churches. Most of the town's social, business, and economic life revolved around the courthouse and the adjacent retail district.[3] The town served as the county's center of local government; the old City Hall, built in 1849, was located in the middle of town. On Saturdays, local farmers came to town to shop and to sell their produce. By 1916, the town boasted its first paved streets; by the time Jesse was born, some residential areas were also paved. Electricity and running water had been available in town for about twenty years: electric lights were first switched on in January 1900, and a water system served the town beginning in 1907. Compared to surrounding rural districts, the town also enjoyed superior schools, and Monroe High School was constructed in 1915. As Jesse grew up, Union County's movie theaters, the Pastime, State, and Center, dominated local residents' leisure activities.[4]

Like most Monroe and Union County residents, the Helmses descended from English and Scots-Irish immigrants who settled the region during the mid-eighteenth century. Sometime in the late 1740s, three ethnically English brothers who were born in the colony of West Jersey— Tillman, Jonathan, and George Helms—migrated to the booming Carolina backcountry. They settled in the western reaches of Bladen County, along the southern boundary separating North and South Carolina. Over the succeeding seven or eight generations, Helms descendants continued to occupy the Pee Dee and Catawba River valleys. Born on a Union County farm on July 19, 1893, Jesse's father, Jesse Alexander Helms, was the son of Joe Clayton (1861–1918) and Sarah Ellen Moore Helms (1863–1949). Like many of his contemporaries, Jesse moved to town in search of a better life.[5] Soon he courted his distant cousin, Ethel Mae Helms (b. August 17, 1896),[6] and on Christmas Eve 1912, they married. Their marriage produced two boys, Wriston Alexander (b. December 13, 1916) and Jesse Jr., and a daughter, Mary Elizabeth (b. May 9, 1929).[7]

Quiet, reclusive, and devoted to her children, Ethel Helms rarely extended beyond her immediate environment, which included family and church, and she communicated a worldview deeply suspicious of outsiders. Jesse recalled that his mother focused on activities at the First Baptist Church of Monroe and was there when it opened its doors; she and her family regularly attended Sunday church service as well as Wednesday prayer meeting. Ethel fostered a conservative Southern Baptist credo on her children, a credo that emphasized biblical literalism as a cornerstone tenet of Christianity. Southern Baptists in small towns such as Monroe were restrictive in their concept of the social contract. They emphasized and encouraged individual behavior, strict morality, and mutual responsibility to fellow Christians within their community.[8]

Over six feet, four inches tall, with huge, powerful hands, Jesse Helms, Sr.—"Mr. Jesse"—became one of the town's several constables in 1920, and, in the same year, worked as assistant fire chief. For three decades he served in these deputy positions. Although his son liked to say that his father was Monroe police chief, only in 1951 did he rise to this position, and, three years later, at age sixty-one, become fire chief. Subsequent historians have described Jesse Sr. as a domineering figure: his son certainly maintained a healthy respect for him.[9] Although his friends called him "courteous but firm as a rock," he was not a man easily trifled with.[10] Mr. Jesse exercised an especially firm hand with Monroe's African American population, and as a police officer he was expected to maintain the racial hierarchy through intimidation and, if necessary, brute force. The black population of the town more than doubled in raw numbers between 1920 and 1940, from 1,049 to 2,203, while the percentage of the town's African American population increased from 26 to 34 percent. The town was strictly segregated along racial lines.[11]

Like many southern whites of his generation, Jesse Helms, Jr., subsequently convinced himself that segregation was not a bad system and that African Americans remained contented. "Nobody thought it was terrible," Jesse told an interviewer years later, "not even the black folks." The reality was, however, far different. Black people of Monroe were less happy with the racial status quo than resigned to the reality of their circumstances. Segregation meant that the African American Newtown community, located across the railroad tracks from Monroe's downtown business district, had substandard housing, outhouses rather than flush toilets, no sidewalks, inadequately paved streets, and inferior schools. White supremacy meant blatant inequality in public services, and government did little to help black residents.[12] "On our side of the fence, it was different," recalled African American Herman Cunningham. Black people, he said, attended segregated schools, were excluded from restaurants, and used separate bathrooms. To African Americans, according to one black woman, Mr. Jesse operated unfairly, using "his power to the fullest, in the wrong way." Openly favoring whites, Jesse dealt with blacks with authority, and, if anyone crossed the line, "he'd rough them up." This same observer saw a strong resemblance between Mr. Jesse and his son: both had a "big head, pop eyes, deep voice," and were "loud and bossy."[13] As a symbol of white supremacy, the elder Helms was widely resented among Monroe African Americans.[14] Civil rights leader Robert F. Williams, who grew up in Monroe, remembered his hometown as "loyal to its southern traditions in almost every aspect" and "predominately white, Protestant and racist." Mr.

Jesse represented, to Williams, a visible symbol of the town's oppressive racial atmosphere. Helms was a "hard core racist," according to Williams, with a "well-deserved reputation for his brutal treatment of Afro Americans." A "mere approach by him struck terror in the hearts of our people." Williams recalled an incident when he was a young man when he witnessed Mr. Jesse, who he described as a "a big over-six-foot brute of a cop," dragging a drunken black woman by her heels, pulling her along as if she were "a log or a sack of potatoes" and roughly shoving her into a police car. The incident demonstrated to Williams how black males under white supremacy were "impotent and seemed so useless in moments like these."[15]

His father's influence also loomed large in young Jesse's development. Like his father, he was extroverted and effusive, and enjoyed the company of people. "I like to study people," he later told an interviewer. Like his father, Jesse believed in constancy, loyalty, and respect for order. Young Jesse also inherited some of his father's characteristics. His friends nicknamed him "grasshopper" because of skinny, long legs and bug eyes, and his habit of walking with big, leaping steps; his sister called him "telephone pole."[16] Tall and lanky, as an adult Helms measured six feet, two inches tall—two inches shorter than his father. The captain of the Monroe football team, Jack Porterfield, remembered Jesse as "tall and skinny and very frail." It seemed, he remembered, "like you could blow him over with your breath."[17] His large head was Jesse's most prominent feature: with a hat size of 7⅝, he later described his head as shaped like "an enormous gourd."[18] And then there were those eyes: his Baptist Sunday School teacher said that she had "never seen such enormous eyes in such a thin child."[19]

Helms grew up in a clapboard house that his family rented a few blocks from the courthouse. Two doors down from his house lived James W. "Bud" Nance, who became a lifelong friend.[20] The Helmses were not affluent; Monroe residents remember them as living in a modest rented home. Nance's declaration that he and Jesse were "as poor as you could absolutely be" was perhaps an exaggeration, when set against the prevalent rural poverty of the Depression-era South.[21] But Helms shared an experience of deprivation with many rural and small-town Southerners, an experience that was worsened by the Great Depression.[22]

Attending elementary and high school in Monroe, Jesse remembered three teachers who had a particular impact. Helms described Lura Heath, who taught him in the first grade, during the 1927–28 school year, as "the kind of soul whose life has been dedicated to tender personal relationships with the people around her."[23] In his high school years, others shaped his development. His English teacher, Annie Lee, helped Jesse hone his writing skills by insisting on strict adherence to precision. Matronly and heavyset, she was a nurse and ambulance driver during World War I. Miss Annie taught tenth- and eleventh-grade English, but she also insisted that her students know the world around them. Years later, as United States senator, Jesse once halted action on a bill because it contained a split infinitive; the amended bill went through in her honor. When he called Miss Annie to tell her, she responded, "Good boy."[24] Probably the greatest influence on Helms by the time he reached high school, however, was Ray House. Born in Cooleemee, a mill village in North Carolina, House worked his way through Duke University, taught science in Statesville, and became principal of Monroe's Walter Bickett High School in 1932. House began a band program, although he could not read music and lacked formal training. He insisted on a regimen of discipline, hard work, and character building. According to Bud Nance, House "cracked a mean whip." Band members were required to attend daily practice from 3:00 to 6:00 in the afternoon, plus thirty hours of practice. The hard work paid off, and there was a waiting list to join the Monroe band. House's bands won seven consecutive state championships and two national trophies. House devoted himself to his students and was dedicated to helping them "make good."[25]

House took a special interest in Jesse. Although House recalled Jesse as "a regular old boy," he recognized potential in the gangly, awkward youth and treated Jesse as he did many of Monroe's other young boys: despite adversity and economic depression, he told them that they could succeed through discipline and hard work.[26] After he entered high school, House recruited Jesse and his peer group to join the band. These included Henry Hall Wilson (who later became White House Congressional liaison in the administrations of John F. Kennedy and Lyndon B. Johnson), Hargrove "Skipper" Bowles (who ran as a Democrat for governor of North Carolina in 1972), Bud Nance (who became rear admiral, military adviser to the National Security Council, and Helms's chief of staff on the Foreign Relations Committee), Will Henson, and Jack Menius. House urged Helms to become a tuba player—and, when needed, to serve as a drum major—because everyone would "be able to see you with that thing around your neck, Jesse, even when you're sitting down." Playing a borrowed tuba, Jesse used, as a uniform, his white jacket that he wore as a soda jerk at Wilson's Drug Store.

From a young age, young Jesse worked at several jobs to bring in extra income. Like most other children, he picked cotton during the fall, when school let out during harvest season, and he usually earned about a dime a day. Along with his friends Nance and Henson, Helms delivered newspapers twice a week for 50 cents and distributed advertising circulars for a dime. Jesse also worked behind the soda fountains at Wilson's Drug Store and Gamble's Drug Store. Beginning at age nine, he swept floors and folded newspapers at *The Monroe Journal*, as well as at *The Monroe Enquirer*—the town's two newspapers, which were published twice weekly on alternate days.[27] At the *Journal* he met R. F. "Mr. Roland" Beasley, who founded the paper and who, in his calm and unexcited manner, loaded his pipe with Prince Albert tobacco and wrote newspaper copy with ease, punching out editorials with two fingers. Mr. Roland's brother, George M. "Buck" Beasley, was the *Journal*'s Linotype operator during the 1930s, but he would later run the newspaper.

Buck Beasley taught Helms how to set type and make up the newspaper's page forms. Mr. Roland not only became a role model, he also provided Jesse with the opportunity to write stories about local high school sports. After his experience at the *Journal*, he later wrote, he never managed to get a zest for journalism "out of my blood."[28] While he was in school, his columns on subjects such as baseball, tennis, football, car racing, and boxing began to appear in the *Journal*. Schoolmates called him "the scribe" because he was always carrying a notebook and scribbling down notes for a story.[29]

When Jesse Helms graduated from high school in May 1938 at the age of sixteen, he was a restless and ambitious young man. The school yearbook, the *Senior Mohisco*, described Henry Hall Wilson as "tall" and Bud Nance as "lucky," while for Jesse it reserved the designation "most obnoxious." Ray House later admitted that he predicted that Wilson, not Helms, would make the biggest mark in the world.[30] For financial reasons, he decided to attend Wingate Junior College. Jesse received a small scholarship, lived at home, and worked at various jobs—including digging postholes for the Rural Electrification Administration for 25 cents an hour—to save money.[31] But he possessed higher aspirations, and Jasper Memory, a family friend from nearby Marshville who worked at Wake Forest College, urged Helms to consider transferring to study journalism. Memory, a legendary Wake Forest figure who performed an assortment of tasks at the college—including overseeing the athletics program—recognized Helms's potential, and he promised to hire him on National Youth Administration money to write sports copy for the Wake news bureau under football coach Walter "Dynamite" Holton for $18.75 per month. Jesse eagerly accepted the chance to leave Union County for greater opportunities in the wider world.[32]

WHEN HE LEFT Monroe to attend Wake Forest College during the 1939–40 academic year, Jesse had $60 saved. The leading Baptist college in

North Carolina, Wake Forest was, until 1956 (when it moved to Winston-Salem), located north of Raleigh, in the village of Wake Forest. The campus offered a lively liberal arts environment, along with small medical and law schools, that produced a large portion of the state's lawyers and political leaders. Most students lived in local boardinghouses directly across from the campus, and Jesse secured a job as a dishwasher at Lizzie Harris's boardinghouse, in exchange for room and board. Helms subsequently told an interviewer that he "washed every dish at Wake Forest 100 times."[33] Though eager to get there, Jesse's year at Wake Forest seems to have been unmemorable. He also had little intellectual curiosity, and many of his ideas and values were firmly established. An indifferent student, the academic environment bored him, and he looked for alternatives. In part because of his need for money, his restless energy forced him to work at several jobs.[34] One of his part-time jobs was at the *Raleigh News and Observer*, the state's largest and most prestigious newspaper, which hired him in the fall of 1939 as an overnight proofreader for 50 cents per hour. Every night, Helms rode eighteen miles by train to Raleigh and then returned in time for an 8:00 A.M. class.

By the end of his year at Wake, Helms was consumed by the world of newspaper writing. During the spring of 1940 he did stringer work in sports stories about Wake Forest for local newspapers such as the evening *Raleigh Times* and the *Henderson Daily Dispatch*, his stories were sometimes picked up nationally.[35] Helms worked closely with the *N&O*'s sports editor, Anthony J. McKevlin, a one-eyed native of Charleston, South Carolina. An even more important figure for Helms's later life was the *N&O*'s patriarch, Josephus Daniels (1862–1948), who had made the newspaper into an important force in state politics during the 1890s: Daniels was an architect of North Carolina's notorious White Supremacy campaign of 1898–1900, which overthrew a ruling coalition of white Populists and black Republicans from state government, culminating in bloody violence in Wilmington in August 1898. Influential in the national Democratic Party, Daniels subsequently served as Woodrow Wilson's secretary of the navy during World War I and, under Franklin Roosevelt, as ambassador to Mexico. Although by the 1940s Josephus's son Jonathan Daniels controlled the *News and Observer*, the "Old Man" remained a presence. At the *News & Observer*, Jesse—who lived across the street from the Old Man—regarded him with deep respect.[36]

Helms's opportunities remained limited at the *N&O*, and he continued to explore other possibilities.[37] Sometime in the autumn of 1941, John A. Park, the publisher of the capital's evening newspaper, *The Raleigh Times*, offered him a job as a regular news reporter and assistant city editor. He eagerly embraced the opportunity.[38] In three years' experience with the *Monroe Journal*, at Wake Forest, and at the *News and Observer*, Jesse had developed an easy, conversational writing style that alternated between hard-hitting and personal. At the *Times*, the twenty-year-old Helms found a newspaper that was smaller than the *N&O*, with more opportunity for advancement. Helms wrote for the *Raleigh Times* on a wide variety of subjects, including doings at City Hall, the police department, local crime, and automobile and railroad accidents. Jesse reported all of these stories enthusiastically; vigorous, accessible prose became his trademark. After two years in Raleigh, Jesse's star was rising: in January 1943, the North Carolina Press Association recognized him for spot news reporting in the state.[39]

A few years earlier, not long after he began working at the *N&O*, Jesse met Dorothy "Dot" Coble, a Raleigh native who attended Meredith College and then graduated from the University of North Carolina's journalism school. In 1940, after Jesse started as a proofreader, Dot began writing for the newspaper. Her office was located between his and the water cooler. She eventually reported for the newspaper's society pages—the first woman, she later claimed, the newspaper had hired since 1924. Dot was the daughter of Jacob L. Coble, a Raleigh traveling shoe wholesaler for Craddock-Terry Shoe Corporation in Lynchburg, Virginia. Walking by Dot on his way to his desk, Jesse often brought her a cola and a bag of fried peanuts. In what amounted to a first date, he "chaperoned" Dot when she reported on a Frank Sinatra appearance at a college dance at North Carolina State College. Dot and Jesse, after work, sometimes had a steak dinner at the Hollywood Café, which was about a block from the *N&O* offices. Smitten, Jesse actively pursued Dot. Sometime in the next few months, Jesse and Dot met each other's families in Monroe and Raleigh, indicating the relationship's seriousness. Newspaper colleagues teased them about looking alike, both with tall, slender frames, dark complexions, and large eyes.[40]

While working in Raleigh, Dot and Jesse witnessed the massive defense mobilization that swept up their generation into war. On December 7, 1941, Jesse heard the news of the attack on Pearl Harbor on his way out of church. Afterward he went to work at the *Raleigh Times* and put that day's extra edition to bed. He then walked up the street to the city post office, which was serving as a recruiting station and was crowded with young men eager to serve. Volunteering for the Navy, he was rejected because of hearing loss in his left ear due to a childhood disease. The naval officer suggested an alternative job for him as a recruiter in the Bureau of Navy

Personnel: the officer had a friend there, and would seek a waiver for Jesse.[41] Helms's application as a naval recruiter was hurried along by a letter from Governor J. Melville Broughton, who wrote the commandant of the Sixth Naval District in Charleston, South Carolina, in late January 1942. Describing Jesse as a "young man of character and integrity" with an experience that revealed him to be a "diligent, efficient, and industrious newspaper man," Broughton called Helms "one of the most promising young newspaper men of this city."[42] Accepted into the Naval Reserve as a recruiter, Helms was sent to basic training at the U.S. Naval Training Station in San Diego on March 18, 1942, where he completed his course (with a grade average of 80.3) on April 25, 1942.[43]

Like others in their generation, the war sped up the pace of Jesse and Dot's relationship. On August 9, 1942, after more than a year of courtship, the two bought an engagement ring, and the wedding took place at Raleigh's First Baptist Church at 4:00 P.M. on October 31, 1942.[44] The bride's attendants were dressed in autumn green and dusty rose. Serving as one of Jesse's groomsmen was John Marshall, the *Times*'s city editor and Dot's brother, while Jesse's brother, Wriston Helms, served as best man. Doris Goerch, Dot's best friend and roommate at UNC, was maid of honor, and Jesse's sister Mary Elizabeth was bridesmaid. While Dot wore a white wedding dress, Jesse donned his blue naval uniform, looking, as he recalled, "like a beanpole." Julius W. Whitley, a minister from Albemarle and Dot's uncle, presided. Jacob Coble gave his daughter away.[45] The couple then left for a brief honeymoon in New York City, where there were nightly blackouts to ward off a potential attack. Staying at the Hotel Taft, at Seventh Avenue and Fiftieth Street, the newlyweds attended big band orchestras in the city, Radio City Music Hall, and again saw the young Frank Sinatra perform. The couple then returned to Raleigh to take up residence at the Capital Apartments.[46]

Immediately beginning work as a Navy recruiter, Jesse moved frequently. Following basic training, he entered service at the rank of naval specialist first class and began work for the Navy's recruiting program in his home state of North Carolina, at the substation in Wilmington. He was "tied up and down with a damned drive which netted us at the finis with 79 men in one day," he wrote one friend from Wilmington; he described his recruits as "good crispy, crunchy cannon fodder."[47] Using his skills as a reporter, Jesse wrote a column, "Navy Notes," that appeared in the morning editions of the *Wilmington Star*.[48] Helms also acquired two additional experiences as a naval recruiter that would later prove invaluable. First, by delivering frequent talks to local groups, Helms became a polished orator, learning how to speak easily and succintly and to craft an appeal to reach his audience. Second, Helms gained experience with radio broadcasting and became entranced by the power of the media.[49]

Originally anticipating a longer stay in Wilmington, Dot and Jesse made arrangements to live in a home on South Third Street.[50] But on September 12, 1942, he was transferred to Raleigh, where he headed up Navy recruiting publicity statewide. Helms, gaining a reputation as one of the best (and certainly the youngest) naval recruiters in North Carolina, successfully participated in the recruitment of more than one thousand North Carolinians. Advancing through the ranks, in May 1943 he returned to Wilmington and became a petty officer in charge of its recruiting station. In the spring of 1944, Helms moved again, taking charge of the recruiting station in Elizabeth City, in northeastern North Carolina. Jesse and Dot lived in an Ahoskie boardinghouse. While Jesse served as a recruiter and also helped the Navy track down AWOL sailors, Dot worked as a newspaper reporter for the *Gates County Index* and the *Hertford County Herald,* both weekly newspapers. In September 1944, he moved once again, as chief naval recruiter in Charlotte. During the last six months of the war, Helms was stationed as a recruiter in Columbus and Macon, Georgia. While there he also wrote articles for the *Columbus Enquirer.*[51] Before his discharge in December 1945 in Norfolk, Virginia, Jesse and Dot became parents of their first child, Jane, who was born on October 5, 1945. Hearing the news of her birth on a Sunday, Jesse borrowed $20 from a friend in order to rush home.[52]

Once demobilized, Jesse returned to the *Raleigh Times* as its city editor. His experience with the Navy was far removed from harm's way; he later described himself as having "the most colorless military career."[53] But his wartime experiences were life-changing. No longer content with newspaper journalism, during his Navy stint Helms had been swept up by the war's excitement. He had learned about the art of persuasion in motivating young men to enlist and in convincing the public of the war's rightness. He also gained exposure to the world of radio broadcasting, and as a recruiter he did some broadcasting. By the 1940s, it was already becoming evident that radio (and later television) held tremendous promise, and Jesse found himself attracted to its possibilities. As he explained in his memoirs, during the war he came to realize that radio broadcasting had "real potential as a source for broader news coverage" because it offered an "immediacy," captured emotions and feelings, and reached a broader audience. The future, he believed, lay in broadcasting.[54]

After a little more than a year back with the *Raleigh Times,* in April 1946, Jesse resigned his position to become program director and news editor with radio station WCBT in Roanoke Rapids, North Carolina. Involved in press relations during the war, he made contact with radio stations in many of the state's small towns, and he realized that radio could do much more than what it was currently doing with news coverage. Most of radio's airtime was occupied by syndicated radio shows, with little of it used for local news. Returning as a newspaper reporter, he remembered that he "couldn't get that idea out of my mind" that radio had "a greater responsibility than just to entertain." He wondered why radio stations did not expand their news coverage, and, after pitching the idea to WCBT, they hired him, giving him a blank check to run a different sort of programming.[55]

During his work as wartime recruiter, Helms became acquainted with Roanoke Rapids, where he had struck up a friendship with Ellis Crews, owner of the WCBT, the town's 250-watt station. Located about fifty miles northeast of Raleigh, Roanoke Rapids was a textile mill town that was riddled with deep class divisions and social tensions. With the local radio station then in its infancy, Jesse started up news programming. He was part of a small news staff and hauled around a large, heavy wire recorder to conduct interviews. His most important innovation was to develop WCBT's first early morning news show, with himself as its "wake-up man." Airing between 6:30 and 8:45, *Rise and Shine* reached over 100,000 listeners in North Carolina and southern Virginia. A newspaper announcement of the show, informing potential advertisers of the program's sizable following, told how listeners woke up to "hear the drawling ramblings of Jesse Helms on his morning show." With an "infectious wit," *Rise and Shine* offered "timely comments" about the news while serving as a sort of "alarm clock" for listeners in search of "good music, the latest news, the weather report and the temperature analysis each morning as they dress."[56] *Rise and Shine* also provided a forum for the airing of Helms's views about local events. Although the show was only a part of his primary news responsibilities, according to a contemporary, he used the show as an opportunity "to get over his own—and usually the community's feeling—about local situations." Helms's views were sometimes controversial—Helms told a reporter that he liked to get local people "riled"—but his message contained few political overtones.[57] In his eighteen months in Roanoke Rapids, Jesse became a local personality and community booster. For the first time in their marriage, the Helmses sank roots in a community. Jesse was elected as a deacon in the town's First Baptist Church and became active in the Rotary Club and in the local Jaycee chapter, where he helped to establish a minor league baseball team.[58]

IN JANUARY 1948, bolstered by his radio experience in Roanoke Rapids, Jesse returned to Raleigh to become news director for WRAL radio in Raleigh. When he decided to leave Roanoke Rapids, he announced in the local newspaper, it was "like losing my right arm." He would "feel the stub many times, and remember the wonderful folks here—because no matter where I go I never hope to find better cooperation or more friendliness."[59] Fifteen years after he left, he described Roanoke Rapids as "a sort of second hometown."[60] Certainly, his postwar experiences in Roanoke Rapids were critical, as he successfully made the jump from newspapers to radio broadcasting—even while keeping his hand in print media. In 1948, his return to Raleigh, in charge of the news operation of a larger radio station, would vault him further forward in terms of access to the state's political power structure. By working under WRAL's owner, conservative lawyer A. J. Fletcher, Helms had now moved more decidedly into the political realm. Heretofore, there was little indication of his political philosophy: his journalism had been iconoclastic but nonpolitical. In Roanoke Rapids during the late 1940s, he experienced a community in the midst of the transformation of the postwar South, and it would have been scarcely possible for Helms not to have observed these changes. During World War II, labor organizers—including the more radical Congress of Industrial Organizations (CIO)—had organized many of North Carolina's textile mills and tobacco factories. African Americans, in North Carolina and elsewhere, were meanwhile challenging white supremacy. Across the South, these tensions were about to erupt, and soon Jesse would choose sides.

As WRAL news director, Helms oversaw the far-flung Tobacco Radio Network, which broadcast news, sports, and entertainment across eastern North Carolina. With the legendary broadcaster Ray Reeve as their sports director, sports fans often turned to WRAL for coverage of their favorite teams.[61] After Helms's arrival, WRAL moved more aggressively into news broadcasting. At the station he joined his old Navy commanding officer, Charles Neely, who was a local WRAL newsman. With Carolina Power and Light sponsoring their broadcasts, and with feeds to as many as twenty radio stations, Helms's newscasts reached a broad market.[62] He began airing a news program, the *News of Raleigh*, which Raleigh residents could hear every evening at 6:15. Helms's news broadcasts, which used clips of interviews obtained on a twenty-five-pound wire recorder, soon became the most popular in the Raleigh area.[63] During his early months on the job, Helms reported on local affairs, while he became a booster of the local

March of Dimes fund-raising efforts. He also found himself in the middle of state politics.[64]

In 1948, W. Kerr Scott was swept to office as an insurgent in the Democratic gubernatorial primary, and his campaign left the political system profoundly shaken. In 1900, most African Americans lost the vote through the adoption of a constitutional amendment that required a literacy test for voting, and, because most blacks were then Republicans, the GOP no longer competed in statewide elections. Like the rest of the South, North Carolina became a one-party political system, in which winning the Democratic primary became everything; general elections were an afterthought. Not until the 1970s did Republicans win any statewide offices. Organization Democrats, generally conservative in their views toward race and labor issues and sympathetic to urban and industrial interests, dominated politics until the advent of Scott, who ran as a left-leaning populist, a political outsider promising reform. An Alamance County dairy farmer and commissioner of agriculture, Scott challenged the political establishment—the famous "Shelby Dynasty" that had run the state since the 1930s—and he appealed to a broad coalition of farmers, organized labor, and urban African Americans. Defeating organization candidate Charles Johnson in a runoff, Scott upset the applecart.[65] His election was a turning point for Helms. He would face a fundamental choice about his political future: would he become a Scott Democrat, or would he support the conservative Democrats who were coalescing against the governor?

During the early months of Scott's governorship, Helms left this question unanswered. According to some accounts, he unsuccessfully sought a position in the Scott administration, but by 1950 he had allied himself with its conservative opponents, who sought to roll back the growth of the federal and state government, limit changes in the Jim Crow system, and reassert unregulated free enterpise.[66] His Monroe background, he later recalled, was "apolitical." Politics was rarely discussed in his family's household, and Jesse's father was "far from being politically minded." Helms's politicization occurred in the late 1940s. Dot was a strong conservative Democrat, and she exerted an influence on her husband. In Raleigh, Jesse's two most important political mentors were his father-in-law, Jacob Coble, and WRAL chief A. J. Fletcher. Coble, whom Helms later described as the "original conservative," opposed New Deal liberalism, and, like many of the new, anti-liberal conservatives, avidly followed national anti-Communist radio commentator Fulton Lewis, Jr. When Coble died in April 1962, Helms remembered him as a person possessing "a great many old-fashioned virtues which ought never to go out of style." Out of step with a society "that sometimes seems to believe that nothing can be accomplished without regimentation," Coble believed in individualism—that in order to "be equal, or better than equal, a man had to make himself so." As Helms remembered, Jacob had "no other hobbies other than keeping up with politics." On Dot and Jesse's return to Raleigh in 1948, they lived for three years with Jacob, who had become a widower, and Helms's political attitudes began to take shape. While Jesse was "anxious to get on his good side," Coble was "glad to have a listener," and he passed along information from news magazines. Coble introduced Jesse to conservative political ideology, and he became intrigued by it. "I learned the important differences between liberal and conservative philosophies," he recalled, and "I began to think in political terms." Jesse later said that Coble's conservatism was critical in the evolution of his political philosophy, and Helms reflected that he would not have "been interested in the conservative cause had it not been for him."[67]

Alfred Johnson Fletcher was another decisive influence in Helms's political evolution. Known as "A.J." and originally from Ashe County, in the North Carolina mountains, Fletcher, the son of an itinerant Baptist preacher, enrolled at Wake Forest Law School. When he ran out of money, he operated a weekly newspaper in Apex, earning money to return to school in order to learn enough of the law to be admitted to the bar (though he never graduated from college). Serving as administrative assistant to Congressman Robert L. Doughton, Fletcher acquired useful political connections. With a successful Raleigh law practice, in July 1938 he obtained a Federal Communications Commission (FCC) license for AM radio station WRAL, broadcasting at 1240 kilohertz with a power of 250 watts. After the war, Fletcher saw the potential for further expansion, and in September 1946, he obtained an FM license, which boosted the station's power to 250,000 watts. Meanwhile, Fletcher created the Tobacco Radio Network, which reached most of eastern North Carolina and included stations in New Bern, Rocky Mount, Kinston, Goldsboro, Fayetteville, and Durham. An advocate of free enterprise, A.J. opposed the federal government's expansion under the New Deal during the 1930s and 1940s. But he also feared the erosion of segregation. Realizing the political power of broadcasting, Fletcher believed that radio, and later television, could promote conservatism and combat liberal domination of the print media, especially of the *Raleigh News and Observer*. Helms and Fletcher were "like father and son," one of Helms's friends recalled. Fletcher recognized Helms's abilities—his trenchant wit, his presence on the airwaves, his sense of audience—and he recruited him as his lead news person in order to make WRAL into a political force. While Jesse presented straight news, Fletcher hired a highly ideological and mercurial figure, Alvin Wingfield, Jr., to deliver weekly editorials.[68]

Scott's election as governor in 1948 galvanized conservative opposition. His "Go Forward" program promised a significant expansion of state government into highway construction, hospitals and public health, and education. Inaugurated in January 1949, Scott soon proposed a $200 million highway bond issue. The new governor wanted to make an appeal for the bond issue on the airwaves, and Helms arranged a WRAL broadcast in which Governor Kerr Scott promoted this program. Lasting fifteen minutes, the program was picked up by a number of radio stations around the state. Attracted to his energy and enthusiasm, Helms lent his help to some of the governor's efforts, but Jesse had an ambivalent relationship with the governor.[69]

In March 1949, only a few months into his governorship, Scott faced a decision: whom should he appoint to the U.S. Senate seat to replace Helms's old friend J. Melville Broughton, who died suddenly on March 6, 1949?[70] In a surprise announcement on March 22, Scott chose longtime UNC president Frank Porter Graham. "Dr. Frank" was much loved, a gentle soul, but he was also known as an active supporter of controversial causes in labor and race relations. Although Graham did not favor integration—he preferred a more cautious, gradualist approach—many North Carolinians branded him a turncoat on white supremacy.[71] Graham remained vulnerable politically, and his appointment to the Senate galvanized the anti-Communist and segregationist wing of the Democratic Party, which rose up in revolt.[72] Before he was appointed to the Senate in January 1949, conservative radio commentators attacked Graham, charging that his associations with liberal groups with Communist connections should disqualify him from his security clearance. In Frank Graham, the opponents of New Deal liberalism had found a target that embodied their fears about labor relations and race; these joined with anxieties about Communist subversion in the administration of Harry S. Truman. Since Governor Scott was closely associated with Truman and his Fair Deal, attacking Graham struck a blow to Scott's populist coalition. Like so many others, Helms considered himself an admirer of Dr. Frank's. With her friend Doris Goerch, as a UNC student Dot had visited Graham's home on Sundays, when he opened his doors to all students on campus. The president's house was across the street from their dormitory, and both of them "loved him to death." After Dot and Jesse were married, according to what Helms told an interviewer in the 1980s, they visited Graham in Chapel Hill six or eight times. Although by the late 1940s Jesse disagreed with Graham politically, he saw nothing personal in his opposition, and he considered him as a "charming and dear man."[73]

Appointed to office in 1949, Graham faced a special election to retain the seat. In the Democratic primary of May 1950, although former Depression-era senator Robert "Our Bob" Reynolds would challenge him, his more serious opponent was Raleigh attorney Willis Smith. Anti-Graham organizers unsuccessfully attempted to persuade others to enter the race; Smith, a World War I veteran, respected attorney, and former legislator, was their last hope. A tall, large man, Smith exuded a commanding and self-confident presence. His Raleigh law firm, Smith, Leach, and Anderson, represented many of the state's largest business interests, and he held views typical of the conservative wing of the Democratic Party. After deliberating for several weeks, on February 24, 1950, Smith decided to run. Smith's announcement was a Rubicon for Helms.[74]

What happened thereafter is somewhat murky. Helms's version, which he has repeated numerous times, runs as follows. Sometime in late January 1950, Helms was summoned to a meeting with Governor Scott and Senator Graham. There they attempted to persuade Jesse to serve as Dr. Frank's publicity director. Scott urged Helms to get out of radio broadcasting—there was, he said, "no money in radio"—and he urged him to enter politics as Graham's aide. After the end of their pitch, Helms was torn between his personal devotion to Graham and his new dedication to conservatism. "Dr. Frank," Jesse told Graham, "you know I love you, and Governor, I appreciate your thinking about me." But he could not accept their offer. He then explained that he had recently met Willis Smith and intended to support him if he ran. Helms was then overcome, becoming "choked up," and his eyes welled up. Standing up, Graham moved toward Helms and put his arm around him, assuring him that he understood.[75]

Whatever the truth of this encounter, Jesse had reached a key decision sometime in early 1950. He was already a devoted admirer of Smith. A. J. Fletcher backed him, as did all of his political circle. Some months earlier, while working for WRAL radio, Jesse heard Smith give a speech at the American Legion Luncheon Club. Smith's high sense of integrity, his devotion to conservative principles, and "the way he thought" impressed Jesse. The two men immediately established a rapport, and Helms offered to help his campaign on his own time, outside of his WRAL employment. In Smith, Helms found another older man he could emulate, another in the series of father figures he had earlier found in Ray House, Josephus Daniels, Jacob Coble, and A. J. Fletcher. Helms and Smith became fast friends; Jesse admired him, he recalled, and he "respected his principles, and Smith knew it." His first political campaign became a defining moment. Helms was an unofficial campaign worker, though he tried, for the sake of the radio station, to preserve a nonpartisan appearance. Smith's inner circle included Colonel William T. Joyner, a Raleigh attorney and former chairman of the State Highway Commission; attorney and son of a former governor J. C. B. Ehringhaus, Jr.; Smith's law partner, John Anderson; stockbroker Jim Thompson; Carolina Power and Light publicist Bill Sharpe; and Raleigh Democrat Banks Arendell. Smith's staff also included a cadre of enthusiastic young people: Charles Green, a youthful Louisburg lawyer and war veteran, who would serve as campaign director; Dunn, North Carolina, newspaperman Hoover Adams, who served as his publicity director; Raleigh attorney James H. Pou Bailey, who was son of the longtime senator Josiah William Bailey; and attorney Thomas F. Ellis and radio broadcaster Alvin Wingfield, both of whom served as researchers and key political operatives. Ellis and Colonel Joyner's son, attorney Billy Joyner, researched Graham's past Communist associations and found material to use against him. Jesse claimed that he played a small role: although he did some political writing for Smith and, on some occasions, sat in on a number of strategy sessions, he has frequently suggested that he was on the margins of the campaign.[76]

ONE OF THE bitterest elections in modern North Carolina history, the 1950 contest defined Helms politically.[77] Early on, Smith ran an aggressive campaign that accused Graham of subversion for his connections with liberal/left organizations and Communists.[78] Smith further suggested that Graham favored federal intervention through a revived Fair Employment Practices Committee and questioned his devotion to white supremacy. Graham responded defensively—and, in general, ineffectively—to Smith's attacks, though he carefully documented his denunciations of Communists and his support for gradual and voluntary, not compulsory, desegregation. Smith linked Graham with the left-wing tendencies of the unpopular Truman administration on the issues of race, labor, and taxes. With the Smith campaign in full throttle, by its conclusion in May 1950 the primary election had turned nasty. Smith supporters ran ads and circulated handbills that emphasized the race issue and Graham's weakness on segregation. In one of the most notorious incidents, a handbill was distributed to rural North Carolinians reproducing pictures of black soldiers dancing with white women in England during the war, with the suggestion that Graham approved of such interracial contact. In another example of smear tactics,

Smith's operatives sent out postcards from New York City, supposedly from the National Association for the Advancement of Colored People, to heavily white areas urging voters to support Graham because he had "done much to advance the place of the Negro in North Carolina." Meanwhile, rumors were circulated that Graham had appointed an African American to West Point. (In fact, Graham had turned such appointments over to a selection commission, and it had named the black student, Leroy Jones, as a second alternative, and he never received the appointment.) On May 27, Graham earned a decisive plurality of 53,000 votes (nearly 49 percent to Smith's 40.5 percent), but since he did not receive a majority, under North Carolina's election laws Smith was entitled to call for a second, runoff primary.[79]

Smith deliberated for the next few days. With his campaign funds spent and exhausted from the rigors of the campaign, he seriously considered withdrawing from the campaign. Tired of the strenuous campaign schedule and the bitter conflict, and urged by many Democratic leaders to end the bloodletting, Smith was fed up. According to Helms's recollection, Smith felt rejected by the electorate and "wanted to be free from the burden of more campaigning." On June 6, Smith instructed Hoover Adams to send a telegram on his behalf congratulating Graham on his win. But Smith's enthusiasts were insistent, and on June 6, Helms, James K. Dorsett, Jr., Joyner, Adams, and Ehringhaus met and decided to urge Smith to continue the fight. They sent a smaller delegation to meet with him. Jesse did not participate, but he learned that evening that Smith had again refused to call for a runoff. Swinging into action, Helms telephoned A. J. Fletcher and asked if he could purchase airtime on WRAL to run thirty-second spots, every ten or fifteen minutes, during the recorded music segments in the 6:00–9:00 time slots. Although contemporary accounts claimed that an organization known as the "Citizens Committee for Willis Smith" financed these spots, in fact Helms and Fletcher paid for them. In the thirty-second advertisements, an announcer read a statement that Helms drafted, urging supporters to go that night to Smith's Raleigh home, at the corner of St. Mary's Street and Glenwood Avenue, and urge him to seek a second primary. By 9:00, 120 people had arrived at the large lawn in front of Smith's house. Later that night, Jesse and Dot went to Smith's house and found the street "jammed with cars," with as many as four hundred people in his yard. The rally was decisive, and Smith announced that he would reach a decision by the next day, adding that "I don't believe that you are going to be dissatisfied." After nine days of indecision, saying that he had acquiesced to massive public support, Smith on June 7 called for a runoff.[80]

A seventeen-day campaign then led up to the second primary. In this campaign, as in the first primary, Smith went on the attack, suggesting that Graham was soft on Communism, sympathetic to the relentless expansion of federal control under Roosevelt and Truman, and only a weak defender of segregation. As was true in the first primary, local Smith campaign committees emphasized the race issue. A fictitious "Colored Committee for Dr. Frank Graham" placed an ad announcing their support. Handbills and circulars reproduced photographs of the black-majority South Carolina legislature of 1868. In the most outrageous of these circulars—a copy of which has not survived—a photograph of Graham's wife, Marian, was superimposed on the picture of a white woman dancing with a black soldier during World War II. Only verbal reports have survived about many of these race-based materials, which were flashed from wallets and pockets, representing what the historians of the 1950 election have called "political pornography." The pace of the second primary led to an even more frenzied use of the explosive issue of interracial sex designed to fan white fears. "WHITE PEOPLE WAKE UP," read one ad. "DO YOU WANT Negroes working beside you, your wife and daughters in your mills and factories? Negroes eating beside you in all public eating places? Negroes riding beside you, your wife and your daughters in buses, cabs and trains? Negroes sleeping in the same hotels and rooming houses? Negroes teaching and disciplining your children in school?" Radio ads reinforced the message: voting for Graham meant a vote to end segregation. Despite efforts by Graham supporters to counterattack, the Smith campaign relentlessly pursued the race issue. For example, Smith supporters frequently reminded white voters that a "bloc vote" of African Americans composed an important part of Graham's coalition. Despite denunciations of these tactics—including a column by *Baltimore Sun* and former *Greensboro Daily News* reporter Gerald W. Johnson describing the "sewer rats" of the Smith campaign and the "filth" that "inevitably sticks"—the charges against Graham were effective.

The Smith campaign successfully fused the race issue with anti-Communism. In a final campaign rally on June 23, 1950, Smith supporters reminded voters that big government—and federal intervention in matters of race—had become the campaign's most important issue. Smith opposed "all unnecessary encroachments of big government upon the lives of all the people." Nell Battle Lewis, speaking at the rally, also framed the issues in terms of unnecessarily expanding government. Lewis, a crusading liberal journalist for the *News and Observer* during the 1920s, had now become a strong anti-Communist. Did voters want to follow a trend to the left, she asked, "or do you want to preserve that way of life which despite its many obvious imperfections gives to both individualized nations and states the maximum of freedom and initiative consistent with stability and order?" In the end, voters agreed with Lewis, and, in a large turnout, Smith carried the state by nearly twenty thousand votes.[81]

Helms was subsequently accused of participating in, indeed instigating, the viciousness of the 1950 campaign. But Jesse and his supporters strenuously maintained that he had nothing to do with it. In 1981, Jesse described attempts to make him chief dirty trickster a "canard." At other times, Jesse has declared that he had no "formal connection" with the campaign and that he had nothing to do with creating the political ads. But in his memoirs he admitted that, though he had no official role in the Smith campaign, he visited the campaign office every day as a WRAL newsman and sat in during some staff meetings "as an observer."[82] On the specific charge of race-baiting, Helms suggested that he never even saw the racially charged literature, though he admitted that there might have been some "free-lancers" responsible.[83] Then and subsequently, partisans such as Hoover Adams vehemently disputed charges of Helms's nefarious influence. Adams pointed out that both sides employed attack politics; the Smith campaign simply responded in kind. In 1984, Adams declared that Helms had "absolutely nothing" to do with the Smith campaign and that he "came in and out of my office like any other reporter and sometimes was one of the last to know what was really going on." Adams's memory was dimmed by the passage of time, however. In late May 1950, he declared that there was not "another single individual who has done more for Mr. Smith" than Jesse. In June, once the campaign had ended, he wrote to Jesse that "I know of no one who made a greater contribution of time and assistance."

Despite these recollections and Helms's own denials, it's clear that he had a great deal to do with the Smith campaign: as one journalist who covered the election later recalled, the press corps regarded Helms as "a part of Smith's headquarters, working in the campaign, not officially, but as part of Smith's retinue."[84] Pou Bailey said that Helms was "up to his neck" in the campaign, that there was "no substantive publicity that he didn't see and advise on," and that he "contributed to practically every ad that was run." A. J. Fletcher had lent "his best writer to the campaign." "Maybe Jesse didn't create any of those ads," Bailey recalled, "but I'm pretty sure he saw them all." Bailey's account did not suggest that Helms masterminded the Smith campaign's smearing of Graham, however, and Smith and his staffers long contended that any excesses that transpired did so without his knowledge. But in a later interview, R. H. Carson, the N&O's advertising manager, claimed to have seen Helms cut and paste the notorious doctored photograph showing Marian Graham dancing with black soldiers. Helms, however, vigorously denied being the author of the doctored photograph— or ever having seen it.[85]

Despite these denials, the Smith campaign ruthlessly used the race issue to win. By linking anti-Communism with fears about racial change and interracial sexuality, Smith strategists were seeking white votes. Helms certainly believed that the election could help reverse the country's path toward socialism. Jesse emerged out of the 1950 election a hardened ideologue, a true believer in his cause, but a true believer armed with potent weapons of wit, skill in new media, and an uncanny ability to sense popular sentiments and public opinion. Helms had used these skills effectively on behalf of Willis Smith's victorious efforts in the spring of 1950.

THAT HELMS HAD crossed over politically from an apolitical observer to conservative activist was demonstrated by his deteriorating relationship with Governor Kerr Scott. The 1950 primary battle marked a change, and thereafter Helms became what Pou Bailey described as a "horse fly constantly being kicked at by the Governor."[86] On June 7, 1950, the same day that Smith called for a runoff, Helms broadcast charges on WRAL that Scott's state prison director, J. Brice Moore, was illegally using prison trustees without any compensation to build a two-car garage and apartment next to his home. Helms visited Moore's home and interviewed prisoners, and his reports prompted a State Bureau of Investigation inquiry. On June 30, Moore resigned, and a few months later he was convicted of malfeasance in a Wake County court.[87] Animosity between Helms and Scott—aggravated by Helms's partisanship during the primary campaign— remained. In November 1950, at a Raleigh press conference, in an extraordinary exchange, the governor and Helms sparred heatedly. Referring to the Moore case, Scott told reporters that though some "deep-rooted and well-concealed" graft persisted in the prison system, he was attempting to reform the system. The Moore case, Scott claimed, was merely "baby stuff" compared to larger problems existing in the prison system. At the end of the news conference, reporters watched as Scott blurted out—in a reference to Helms's misplaced coverage of "baby stuff"—that "the trouble with Jesse is that he does not give us credit for things we have done." When Helms replied that he was happy to mention instances in which Scott had "broken up" graft, Scott compared Jesse to conservative radio broadcaster and *High Point Beacon* editor Robert L. "Battlin' Bob" Thompson and other administration critics. Although Scott said that he could "stand constructive criticism and I think it is healthy," he complained that Helms had made himself into a political opponent. "I call my shots as I see them," Helms said in response, and if these were "interpreted as critical of the administration, then it's too bad." The news conference abruptly ended, and, as reporters left, Helms turned to Scott and said, "You certainly gave me a spanking, Governor." "You have spanked yourself, Jesse," Scott responded.

Helms later described the 1950 campaign as the moment when North Carolina began to emerge from a "self-imposed...narcosis that had set in from an overdose of public apathy and unconcern about what was happening at the national level."[88] On election night, as a measure of Willis Smith's confidence in Helms, he called him while Jesse was reporting Smith's victory to the WRAL audience in order to offer him a job as a Senate staffer. Helms initially refused, though he remained a dogged Smith admirer. In February 1951, he broadcast a *News of Raleigh* report on WRAL that defended Smith against his critics. Smith had criticized Truman, and Jesse noted that as a "general yardstick" opponents of Smith were also supporters of Truman. Smith kept in contact with Helms over the next few months, and, after repeated entreaties over the next months, Jesse relented, and in January 1952 the twenty-nine-year-old political enthusiast became the administrative assistant in Smith's senatorial office in Washington. Scott, said Pou Bailey, was glad to see Helms leave North Carolina because he had become a "boll weevil in Scott's cotton patch."[89]

By the time Jesse went to Washington, his family had grown with the birth of a second daughter, Nancy. In 1952, while establishing Smith's broadcast network and setting up his Raleigh office, Jesse commuted back home, but after January 1953 he and his family moved into a furnished apartment in southeast Washington, where they stayed until the following summer.[90] His family saw little of Jesse, who had received under Smith "a much broader cloak than most administrative assistants" normally enjoyed. Dot spent a good portion of time in Raleigh with her family, and Jesse returned to North Carolina when he could. Working as a chief of staff, he oversaw and edited Smith's speeches, supervised his legislative activities, and worked on public relations. The year and a half that Helms spent in Washington solidified his political conservatism. Although a Democrat, he sympathized with the Republican surge that occurred with the election of Dwight D. Eisenhower and a Republican Congress in 1952. A few days after the election, in November 1952, he described himself as "utterly astonished" about Ike's win, and he predicted "a few interesting years ahead of us."[91]

One of Smith's new freshman colleagues was Richard Nixon, recently

elected from California after a bitter campaign in which he used the anti-
Communist issue to defeat incumbent Helen Gahagan Douglas. Like
Helms, Nixon had two young daughters; like Jesse, he was a self-made
man; and the two sometimes went out for lunch. Senators in the 1950s had
smaller staffs, composed of only about five people, and the various offices
helped each other, while senators and staffers often ate together. Nixon,
sworn in four days after Smith on December 1, 1950, occupied Suite 341 in
the Senate Office Building, with Smith on one side (in Suite 345) and longtime North Carolina senator Clyde R. Hoey occupying the other side
(Suite 337). Across the corridor from Nixon and Smith were Georgia senator Walter F. George and New Mexico senator Clinton Anderson, while
around the corner was "Mr. Republican," Ohio senator Robert A. Taft. "A
young fellow, now grown older," Helms would write later of himself, "had
gone to Washington to try to be of assistance to Willis Smith." He admired
all these senators, all of them good conservatives, and they told him stories,
he later reflected, that "I'm still telling."[92] But Smith remained a role model
for Jesse.[93]

Helms proved to be of a great value to Smith especially in using broadcasting to solidify Smith's political base. Helms helped to create a radio
broadcasting network of eighty-seven stations that carried messages from
Senators Smith and Hoey. Beginning in February 1952 and continuing into
1953, Helms began the broadcasts, overseeing and introducing them. The
programs lasted twelve minutes, with time for two one-minute commercial
breaks. WRAL provided an FM radio signal that transmitted the broadcast
to the stations. They made thirteen copies of the program each week and
distributed these to radio stations. The broadcasts were taped at the joint
House-Senate Recording Facility in Washington. Once these broadcasts
became established, Helms recalled, "there was very little to the operation
of the program." One woman in Smith's office checked in the tapes and
kept track of broadcast times. For both Hoey and Smith, this system of
reaching their constituencies succeeded. According to Helms, they performed a "splendid service in getting basic factual information to the people."[94] His broadcast experience was vital in this operation; Jesse served as
a moderator, introducing Smith and Hoey and sometimes injecting some
commentary. He occasionally felt frustrated by his "dual role" of moderator and senatorial assistant, and he chafed a little at having to restrain himself from adding political commentary.[95]

Smith was a dedicated anti-Communist and, in international affairs, a
nationalist. He served on the Senate Internal Security Subcommittee
(SISS), which was established in late 1950 and became one of the most

important Communist-hunting and anti–civil rights committees in Congress. Like Richard Nixon, in 1951 Smith co-sponsored the Bricker Amendment, which sought to limit the treaty-making powers of the presidency.[96] He participated in the writing of the McCarran-Walter Immigration Act of 1952, which extended the racial quota system established by Congress in 1924 and provided that "subversive" foreign nationals could be barred entry or deported. Smith also became aligned with southern conservative Democrats who resisted the Truman administration's efforts to desegregate. Like many of them, Smith had become actively hostile to the Truman White House. As one indication of the growing alienation between Smith and southern conservatives from the national Democratic Party, Smith was only lukewarm toward the candidacy of Illinois senator Adlai E. Stevenson, the darling of the party's liberal wing. Smith announced his support, but, speaking to a reporter in October 1952, he explained that he was "not enthusiastic about it." Smith would not, he said, "engage in a tirade of abuse" against Republican candidate Dwight Eisenhower.[97]

Senator Smith had only halfheartedly supported Stevenson, and although he campaigned for the Democratic ticket, he refrained from mentioning Stevenson by name. Smith had supported Georgia senator Richard B. Russell, who in 1952 ran an unsuccessful campaign for the Democratic Party's presidential nomination. Helms, with Smith's blessing, took leave to work for Russell's campaign, taking charge of his media. Although Russell had little chance of winning the nomination, this was Jesse's first experience with big-time national politics, and he attended the Democratic National Convention in Chicago in July 1952. Helms was greatly impressed with Russell, who, he said, "made men think" and whom he later described as the "best qualified man in America for the Presidency of the United States."[98] He was not a crass politician, which appealed to Helms's concept of political purity. Favoring an America where people could succeed on the basis of merit alone, according to Helms, "he rejected absolutely the kind of politics that preaches that the world *owes* anybody anything."[99] By working for Smith, Helms not only learned about Washington but also continued to maintain contacts with business leaders, journalists, and others in North Carolina. He opened a North Carolina office in Raleigh to deal with constituent business—something that Jesse would imitate after he was elected to the Senate twenty years later.[100] He sometimes gave speeches in Smith's absence, and he weighed in state politics, some controversially so.[101]

Smith's sudden death on June 26, 1953, forced Helms to take stock of his position. Only a few days earlier, Jesse, substituting for Smith, delivered a speech in Hickory, North Carolina, and when he returned he discovered the senator had been hospitalized in Bethesda Naval Hospital, suffering from several heart attacks and coronary thrombosis. At Smith's deathbed, Helms wept as he realized that the senator would not survive.[102] Smith's death was a "tremendous shock," he wrote to a friend, because he "looked upon him something like a son regards a father." In his files, Helms saved his page from his daily calendar, on which he wrote, in large block letters, "WILLIS SMITH DIED."[103] At age thirty-two, Jesse had experienced Washington and gained contacts with anti-Communists such as Richard Nixon and southern segregationists such as Richard Russell. But he never regarded his stay as more than temporary. His relationship with Alton A. Lennon, who succeeded Smith as senator, was cordial, and Lennon regarded Helms's knowledge and experience as invaluable. Born in Wilmington, North Carolina, Lennon was a Wake Forest College graduate who practiced law in southeastern North Carolina and served as judge and state senator before Governor William B. Umstead appointed him to the Senate on July 10, 1953, to fill Smith's unexpired term. But Lennon—who later went on, after 1956, to serve as an eight-term congressman from southeastern North Carolina—was a colorless figure who lost his seat in a special Democratic primary in May 1954.

Helms exhibited none of the affection and respect for Lennon that he had for Willis Smith, and he was unimpressed by Lennon's support for the 1952 presidential candidacy of liberal Democrat Adlai Stevenson.[104] Regarding Lennon as inferior to Smith as a conservative, he voiced criticisms among his closest friends, concluding that the best approach with Lennon was to "keep quiet ... and pray." Lennon's "worst enemies" would now admit that "Lennon is no Smith, and probably never will be." He later commented, in a letter to Senator Joseph R. McCarthy, that Lennon was "not interested in taking a flat-footed stand with respect to ferreting out Communism in America." After his time with Smith, Helms found that he lacked "sufficient enthusiasm to do justice to him." Most likely, as well, Helms shared widespread doubts about whether Lennon would be reelected in the 1954 primary.[105] Sometime during the summer of 1953, Helms informed Lennon of his plans to leave Washington.[106] Helms had had some discussions with Carolina Power and Light about working for them in public relations, but the company president, Louis Sutton, worried about offending Lennon.[107] In September 1953, the North Carolina Bankers Association (NCBA) was looking for a new executive director, and Jesse soon became a candidate. The bankers organization, in existence since 1936, was interested in revitalizing itself by becoming a more effective force in state policymaking.[108] For Jesse, accepting the NCBA position posed risks, for he had no experience with banks or banking. Still, the job offered Helms a chance to return to North Carolina and to hone his skills at public relations, journalism, and politics, and on September 13, 1953, NCBA president John P. Stedman announced that Helms would become the organization's new executive director to replace Joseph H. Wolfe, who left to become an executive with the American Bankers Association.[109]

HELMS'S ARRIVAL BACK in Raleigh in September 1953 attracted the attention of old friends and foes: state politicos remembered Helms's raw style during the election of 1950. No shrinking violet, Jesse sought out the media's attention. Only four days after he became the NCBA executive director, on September 17, 1953, Jesse set the new tone in a speech to the Raleigh Civitan Club by sharply criticizing the Democratic Party's "left-wing" direction during Harry Truman's presidency. Helms also attacked the North Carolina liberal establishment, composed primarily of the *News and Observer* and most of the state's major daily newspapers. Jesse always believed that the *News and Observer* had treated Willis Smith unfairly during the 1950 campaign and while he was senator. While Smith was in office, he stood against left-wing "pygmies," but "their world came tumbling in around them" with Eisenhower's election in 1952. Moreover, Helms saw it as a "matter of common knowledge" that the Daniels family, which controlled the *N&O,* had been "selling out the south at least two generations earlier." Jesse defended Joseph McCarthy, who was known for his exaggerated attacks against supposed Communists. Describing him as "a great deal better American than some of the newspaper men who are so free with their abuse of him," Helms said that McCarthy had never violated good taste or brought "harm to any innocent person." He was a "great deal more truthful" than most of his newspaper critics. The McCarran-Walter Immigration Act was a good piece of legislation, despite what the "pinks & the punks" said about it. Liberal forces and "Trumanism," he said, had caused the Democratic defeat with the losses of the presidency and Congress in 1952.[110]

Helms's Civitan speech evoked a sharp response. Jesse himself admitted that this was a speech which he "probably ... should not have made," but he had scheduled it before he realized that he would be working for the bankers association. The speech represented, he said, a response to Smith's critics, and he now had "most of the bitterness out of my system," and promised Stedman that he would not make another speech "even remotely similar to that one again."[111] Nonetheless, Helms attracted fire; in the aftermath of the bitter 1950 campaign, he already had a reputation as a conservative hatchet man. Norman B. McCulloch of the *Bladen Journal* wrote that Helms, in this political speech, had left bankers "holding an empty bag" in which "the word 'empty' is stressed." He wondered why Helms had affixed the left-wing label on venerable Democratic institutions, and he suggested that Jesse had adopted McCarthy's tactics of political smear and innuendo. To McCulloch, the *News and Observer* was a "right good newspaper" that advocated the cause of common people.[112] Later, in November 1953, Roy Parker, Jr., then editor of the *Hertford County Herald,* described Helms as a "a dirt digging columnist" and a "political hatchet man." Helms had a history of engaging in "scurrilous, degrading and slime pit type of stuff," said Parker, and he should be especially remembered as the "same said hatchet man" who was "so well broadcast in the closing days of the Smith-Frank Graham campaign in 1950."[113]

Helms's job with the North Carolina Bankers Association thrust him into a new role that was quite unlike his work in the U.S. Senate. He was attracted to the NCBA position in part because of his growing and close family. With daughters Jane, age seven, and Nancy, age four, he wanted a position that had a secure income and did not have the late hours associated with work on Capitol Hill. Jesse successfully mixed work and family, and he often took his family with him on NCBA business trips. In the summer of 1956, for example, he and Pou Bailey took their families to Disneyland, which opened only a year earlier, while they attended a meeting of the American Bankers Association in Los Angeles.[114] Bailey remained one of Jesse's better friends. Not only was Bailey legal counsel to the NCBA, he and Jesse often got together on Thursday nights with five or six other friends for a steak and nickel-and-dime poker at Bailey's house or at his cabin outside town. Bailey recalled that Jesse was a bad poker player because he was "completely honest" and never bluffed. The Poker Club went on fishing trips twice a year. Helms remained close to Dot's father, Jacob Coble, and the Helmses built their first and only house, a colonial on Caswell Street, next door to Jacob's home, in Raleigh's tree-lined Hayes-Barton neighborhood.[115]

As the NCBA executive director, Helms managed a trade association that sought to improve the influence and image of the banking industry in the state. Part of his job was to lobby the legislature, which he did successfully. During his tenure, banking laws were liberalized, and, partly as a result, North Carolina banks during subsequent decades emerged dominant in the nation.[116] As part of his job, he was expected to promote conservative free enterprise ideas in speeches to small groups across the state. Jesse was granted, in effect, a blank check: managing the NCBA as a trade association, he also could become a leading spokesman for resurgent conservatism. Although there were limits to Jesse's conservative activities, he obtained wide latitude in projecting his and the bankers' presence in the political affairs of the state. His most important mouthpiece for espousing conservatism was the *Tarheel Banker,* which he transformed from a sleepy trade publication into a slickly produced publication with an appealing, folksy tone. By the time he left the NCBA in 1960 it had become the most widely read state banking magazine in the United States, and the quality of its writing and analysis was clearly a notch above the typical trade publication. the *Tarheel Banker*'s main appeal was to those North Carolinians looking for conservative commentary.[117]

In a regular editorial column entitled *By Jesse Helms,* he insisted on the dangers of an expanded federal government. He criticized agricultural policies that had, since the New Deal, relied on massive federal intervention.[118] As he wrote in the *Tarheel Banker* in February 1958, the federal government should "get out of the crutch business—for agriculture, for business, for everybody." Farmers only wanted a fair chance, and they refused to become "an albatross around anybody's neck."[119] The *Tarheel Banker* expressed Jesse's political philosophy of anti-Communism. A great admirer of FBI director J. Edgar Hoover, Helms, in an editorial entitled "Hoover—A Fine American," described him as "a man totally dedicated to his country."[120] A 1958 editorial warned its readers that Lenin's prediction that Communism would force the United States to spend itself into destruction was coming true in the uncontrolled growth of government. State and local governments were, he wrote, "scheming at every turn of the road" to take people's money. Helms suggested that Americans were perhaps heading toward the "abyss the founder of communism predicted for us."[121]

Helms's attitudes about the press became fully antagonistic during the 1950s. The *N&O* and the state's liberal media would continue to be objects of Helms's scorn for most of his public life, although he belonged to "the media" himself and more thoroughly understood its political significance than anyone in North Carolina. For Helms, "the media" meant his liberal opponents. Raleigh suffered from a "newspaper monopoly," Helms wrote in 1958, in which he saw himself as "Public Enemy Number One."[122] Jesse had a long history of conflict with the *N&O*, and the newspaper opposed the NCBA's attempts to rewrite North Carolina's banking legislation. Helms blamed the *N&O*'s position toward bankers on "venom," and to him this exemplified the larger problem of how only one side appeared in print.[123] Helms believed that Daniels's media machine monopolized public information and dominated the state newspapers, which, he explained in private correspondence, were "spoon-fed" a "party line." Newspaper editorialists such as Pete McKnight of the *Charlotte Observer* and Bill Snider at The *Greensboro Daily News* provided examples of liberal bias.[124] The "ultra-liberals" used "two sets of rules—one for themselves, the other for their opponents," Helms declared on another occasion.[125]

Helms shared these attitudes with his inner political circle, which included the old warhorses of 1950, conservative hard-liners such as A. J. Fletcher, Alvin Wingfield, Jr., and Hoover Adams.[126] Editor of the *Dunn Daily Record,* Adams maintained his connections with Jesse and remained a stalwart friend. Wingfield, a conservative ideologue whom Helms befriended in the late 1940s, became a conservative Don Quixote. District manager of the Royal Typewriter Company in Charlotte, he was an activist, writer, and radio broadcaster. He was also a devotee of the ideas of Ludwig von Mises, an Austrian émigré who—like the more influential Austrian Friedrich Hayek—constructed an anti-statist, libertarian critique of liberalism and the social welfare state that postwar conservatives found attractive. A strong nationalist, Wingfield was deeply suspicious of liberal internationalism and the United Nations. Too much of an ideologue to enjoy much political appeal in the 1950s, he remained on the political margins. But, with his doctrinaire conservative views, he became a sort of ideological mentor for Jesse.[127] In April 1954, Wingfield stepped forward to run for the Democratic nomination for the U.S. Senate; the party's primary would occur in May.[128] From the start, Wingfield's 1954 Senate primary campaign was hopeless. His entry into this race coincided with a persisting split between the progressive and conservative political traditions of the North Carolina Democratic Party. Although conservative Willis Smith had vanquished Frank Graham in 1950, four years later the candidacy of former governor Kerr Scott rallied the Democrats' progressive coalition. From the outset, Scott was the front-runner, and Wingfield's best hope was to force a runoff and rally conservatives. With very little name recognition, virtually no money, and no organization, Wingfield's candidacy had little chance. Unable to keep his job with Royal Typewriter, Wingfield confronted a dire financial situation. Before announcing his candidacy, he traveled to Raleigh and consulted with A. J. Fletcher and Helms, who advised against running.[129]

The 1954 Wingfield candidacy highlighted two facets of Jesse's political persona—the pragmatist and the ideologue. His career ran parallel to Wingfield's: both were ideologues, both pioneers of conservative broadcasting, and both resolutely unwavering in their principles. But major differences lay in their political paths. Unlike Wingfield, who lacked necessary instincts and skills, Helms was thoroughly political in his instincts. Although personally loyal to Wingfield—as he was to all his life-long friends—the political calculus was such that any close association, given Helms's public position, would damage his political influence. By March 1954, when Wingfield announced his candidacy, Helms was already committed to supporting Senator Alton Lennon's reelection. Asked by a political ally in private correspondence if he supported Wingfield, Helms responded cautiously. He explained that he was "completely mixed up, due to my high personal regard for Alvin" and a "personal commitment and obligation which I will not disavow." Yet Helms also admitted that he would be "less than candid" if he suggested that Wingfield enjoyed "even the remotest chance of getting anywhere in his latest venture."[130] Writing to Wingfield, Helms explained that he did not want to endanger their friendship. While promising his help in the campaign, Jesse provided little support.[131]

From the beginning, Wingfield ran a quixotic campaign, which he managed himself without any real financial support. He advocated unqualified opposition to government, supporting the privatization of both public schools and the state highway system. He often called himself the only candidate in the senatorial primary who favored liberty, while he also told voters that he was the only true conservative, anti-government candidate. On other occasions he described federal management of agriculture as a first step toward enslaving farmers, comparable to measures that the Nazis took in the 1930s to construct a totalitarian state. The United Nations, Wingfield argued, was a "trap" dreamt up by the Russians. During the campaign, Wingfield complained to the FCC when radio stations gave Lennon free airtime, and he forced stations to give him equal time. But Wingfield's effort made little difference, as Kerr Scott won decisively.[132]

By the late 1950s, Wingfield had become something of a crank. In increasingly shrill and paranoid communications, he warned of the threats of socialism and Communism in the expanding federal state. In 1957, he ran for Raleigh City Council, advocating radical reductions in the size of government—he proposed eliminating, for example, the use of parking meters and opposed fluoridation of the city's water supply—and he finished twelfth out of fifteen candidates. In 1959, Wingfield wrote to President Eisenhower—with copies to the CIA and Air Force intelligence—claiming that Soviet intelligence agents were making use of the recently launched Sputnik satellite.[133] Correspondence with Helms in the late 1950s suggested further deterioration in Wingfield's emotional stability, and when he requested work from A. J. Fletcher as a broadcaster, he was turned down.[134]

Matters came to a head in November 1960, when Wingfield was discovered dead in his typewriter sales truck, along with a suicide note. Helms was "remorseful" at this turn of events because he did not "anticipate what he planned and thus did nothing to avert it." If he had known, Jesse said, he would have "made any financial sacrifice personally to dissuade him from such a course." The tragedy of Alvin Wingfield, he confided in December 1960, had been deeply troubling. Six months after his death, Helms remarked to a friend that he found it "difficult, even yet," to realize that Wingfield was gone. When the *Asheville Citizen*, in an editorial, associated Wingfield's suicide with the demise of the conservatism that he advocated, Helms sharply disagreed. Wingfield took his own life primarily because of "extreme financial difficulty during the past several months, most of which had nothing to do with his philosophy of government."[135]

BY FAR THE most important issue of the 1950s facing North Carolina's white leadership was the future of de jure segregation. Under attack as early as the 1930s, the legal basis of segregated public education ended in May 1954 with the U.S. Supreme Court's landmark decision in the *Brown v. Board of Education* case. While federal courts intervened, Congress during the 1950s enacted new civil rights legislation that began to chart a new path in federal-state relations. Helms greeted these changes unenthusiastically. He often commented that civil rights activists did not truly represent the mass of black people, who, he said, remained satisfied with the status quo. He claimed that Raleigh African Americans told him privately that they wished that the Supreme Court had not issued the 1954 landmark decision. They were worried, he told *Tarheel Banker* readers, about the ruling's consequences and were not "taking this thing *nearly* so seriously as the Supreme Court thinks they are."[136]

Although refusing to use racial epithets of any kind, Helms shared the racial prejudices common to whites of his time. He believed that he was enlightened, yet he saw no inconsistency in opposing the end of segregation, which he saw as beneficial to black people. He saw no contradiction in his professed commitment to black improvement and his alliance with segregationists. He enjoyed racially and ethnically stereotyped jokes, he explained to *Tarheel Banker* readers in August 1956, and he wondered whether anyone was truly offended. When some civic clubs attempted to limit the use of racially offensive jokes, Helms argued that restricting them deprived white audiences of the "down-to-earth philosophy of the Negro." Eliminating racially stereotyped jokes, he wrote, was equivalent to saying that blacks did not have a "natural instinct for rhythm and for singing and dancing." Helms then offered a broader point. There was no race issue in North Carolina, he asserted, except a "phony one" that a "few outside rabble rousers" kept alive. White Southerners rightfully resisted intrusions on their freedom and the "finger-pointing from other sections." If left alone, the white South would solve its problems to the satisfaction of everyone, rather than by government edict. Instead of using governmental coercion, he preferred that "men of good will" reach solutions through "patience and understanding." People outside the region who wanted to impose desegregation, he asserted, knew little about the hearts of Southerners of both races.[137]

In the 1950s, Helms also opposed the integration of churches. As an usher and deacon at Raleigh's First Baptist Church, he refused to seat black people and warned other ushers about this as a "potential problem." He even threatened to resign, should the church seek to seat black visitors. Helms's rationale—at least in the matter of seating black people in his church—was complicated: if black people sincerely sought to worship in a white church, he explained, he would sit with them. The same God created both races; it was, he wrote, "no personal accomplishment of mine that I am white." But he believed that nearly all black visitors to white churches were primarily interested in causing "strife and dissension." In a curious analogy, Jesse compared himself to Jesus driving away the money changers from the temple. Integrationists were using church as a "potential bartering place."[138]

Jesse's posture toward the integration of white churches was, however, quite clear: he opposed it. Some years later, in 1966, he led opposition when an African American applied for membership, and eventually he would leave the church. His experience in the church exemplified his posture toward race elsewhere: he was utterly confounded that anyone would consider him racist, and he was convinced that he had the best interests of black people in mind. But he made a distinction between "deserving" blacks, those that went along with the system, and "undeserving" blacks, those that challenged it. Ultimately, in this and other incidents, he was self-indulgent about race: he considered any insinuations about his racial attitudes profoundly insulting, any suggestions of hostility toward black people as offensive.

In response to the *Brown* decision, in 1954 Governor William Umstead appointed a Governor's Advisory Committee on Education, chaired by State senator Thomas Pearsall, to recommend legislation. From the beginning its true purpose was to evade compliance. After Umstead's death in 1955, Governor Luther Hodges reappointed the committee as the North Carolina Advisory Committee on Education, and a year later it produced the infamous Pearsall Plan.[139] Enacted into law as a series of state constitutional amendments, the Pearsall Plan complied only nominally with the *Brown* decision. First, it provided for voluntary desegregation in those few, mostly urban communities willing to tolerate it; second, it extended various forms of state support—including publicly supported private academies—to resisting communities. In a speech in Asheville in 1955, a Wake Forest law professor and vocal segregationist, I. Beverly Lake, urged the decentralization of public education through state subsidies for private schools. Lake described his proposals as a sort of "GI Bill" serving to protect segregated schools. Helms enthusiastically embraced Lake's ideas. While the Pearsall committee deliberated, he wrote a controversial *Tarheel Banker* editorial suggesting alternatives to desegregation. Helms anticipated the Pearsall committee's eventual remedy—and the "massive resistance" approach of segregationists. Rather than destroying the school system, Helms suggested, there existed "another way": privatizing the public schools by providing state support for all-white schools. Long before conservatives embraced public support for private education through devices such as voucher plans, Helms was suggesting that integration might require a breakup of the traditional model for public education.[140]

Helms's editorial prompted a sharply negative reaction among North Carolina's daily newspapers.[141] The *News and Observer* called Helms's proposals the "silliest school suggestion yet," saying that the *Tarheel Banker* editorial went further than any other segregationist school plan; it amounted to "a camouflaged state school system under the guise of subsidies to private schools and their students." The *N&O* wondered whether Helms spoke for all bankers, and it urged those who disagreed to express themselves.[142] Hiden Ramsey, editor of the *Asheville Citizen,* described Helms's proposals as "reckless talk" that threatened "real tragedy to our children through hysterical wrecking of the school system,"[143] while *Charlotte Observer* editor Pete McKnight called Helms's ideas "over-reaching extremism."[144] Refusing to bend to criticism, Helms enjoyed the attention, telling his readers in the October 1955 issue of *The Tarheel Banker* that he was not "in the habit of running." The *N&O* had "frothed at the mouth," he declared, at the *Tarheel Banker* and bankers generally.[145]

The *Brown* decision, Helms privately admitted, by itself was of no "particular consequence," and he considered the battle on school desegregation lost.[146] Provocative, even goading to his liberal opponents, Helms asserted that he was no supporter of white supremacy—even while his entire message sought to protect segregation. Crude racial appeals, he advised in December 1957, would not "be effective with people who have a sincere misunderstanding of the South's problem."[147] In the 1950s Helms offered a more effective way to oppose the civil rights movement. This approach relied on an ideological approach—strong anti-Communism and opposition to federal intervention; he also suggested that racial mores would change only through slow, voluntary action by whites and self-help by blacks, who, he claimed, were not yet ready for leadership.[148] Helms continued to take aim at what he believed was the increasingly "socialist" federal government. He worried less about integration, he wrote in December 1958, than about "the destruction of the fundamentals that made this government unique in all history."[149]

School desegregation remained a flash point in the civil rights struggle during the 1950s. After Arkansas governor Orval Faubus blocked court-ordered integration of Central High School in Little Rock in September 1957, President Eisenhower federalized the Arkansas National Guard and dispatched paratroopers to provide for the safety of the black children. Helms, like many other white North Carolinians, was appalled at Eisenhower's intervention. He neither supported nor opposed Governor Faubus, he wrote in the *Tarheel Banker*. Nor did he impugn Eisenhower's integrity. But integration could not occur at "the points of bayonets," he argued, and the Little Rock crisis had set race relations back for at least a decade. Helms condemned northern liberal hyprocrisy about southern race problems and the media's condemnation of the South. Federal intervention in the South, he wrote in the *Tarheel Banker,* was "exactly in tune" with Karl Marx's predictions: government-required integration amounted to socialism. "The cackles you hear," Jesse wrote tellingly in the *Tarheel Banker* editorial, had "a Russian accent."[150]

On November 21, 1957, in a speech to the Western North Carolina Conference of the National Association of Bank Auditors and Comptrollers in Waynesville, North Carolina, he called for a "Truth Campaign" that would make the white South's case to a national audience. Race relations meant human relations; governmental coercion undermined both. There had been no problem in race, he said, until federal authorities, "aided by meddlers and extremists, manufactured one." National public opinion was able to hear only one, liberal perspective. Segregationists should communicate their views; white Southerners had been "negligent not so much in our *human* relations as in our *public* relations." Jesse proposed creating a $1 million fund designed to provide the "plain, unvarnished truth" to non-Southerners, provided by respectable southern whites who could not be "tagged as racists." He then repeated the fiction that most black people preferred segregation: responsible blacks, he said, joined whites in deploring the unrest that politicians and outsiders created by relying "more heavily on bayonets than on balance, who believe more in force than in fairness." The mistakes of the segregationist South were "of the head rather than the heart." Whites should communicate more effectively to a national conservative constituency, which, armed with the truth, would oppose governmental intrusion and meddling in southern affairs. The only "shame in the Southland" was that Southerners had failed to organize themselves against the distortions and slanders of outside critics.[151] Segregationists from around the South thus applauded Helm's Truth Campaign speech.[152]

While maintaining a public distance from militant segregationists, Helms privately provided support. He remained in regular contact with various white supremacist organizations, such as the White Citizens' Councils, and local offshoots, such as the North Carolina Defenders of States' Rights. One such organization, the Federation for Constitutional Government, was headquartered in New Orleans, with branches across the South. Hearing from one of their leaders in late 1958, Helms promised that he would cooperate with the organization "in any reasonable way." But he also insisted that he not have a public association with white supremacists: his name, Helms wrote, should "be held in confidence for reasons that will be obvious." From his days as Willis Smith's assistant, Helms had known Mississippi senator and avid anti-Communist segregationist James Eastland, a backer of this organization. He also pointed out that "I know each of the North Carolinians connected with your organization, and I believe they all know me." Helms promised to help the segregationist organization as long as they "understand my position."[153]

In the final analysis, the Truth Campaign remained a rhetorical exercise: no organization emerged, nor did Helms seem to have much interest in one. Rather than sustaining an organized campaign, Jesse wanted to attract attention to the segregationist cause and rally supporters by fashioning a language of opposition to federal intervention. Although Helms was not confident that his views commanded majority support, he believed that persistence—qualities that characterized his entire public life—might eventually carry the day. As would be true for much of his career, he created an oppositional role for himself with long-term objectives. Rather than immediately defeating integrationists, he sought to force his opponents to put their views on record. This strategy of political exposure was on his mind during the Truth Campaign. Helms acknowledged that his Truth

Campaign received a cold reception in North Carolina, but he blamed this on the state's liberal press.[154] Although Jesse realized that he and his supporters were outnumbered, he wrote to an ally in December 1957, "I would like to call the roll, somehow," and determine if there were "enough people who understand state sovereignty to have some political effect."[155]

By the late 1950s, nonetheless, Helms had become fully aligned with white resisters of integration. He corresponded with the White Citizens' Council leaders, met with their president, William J. Simmons, and helped with their media program. Starting in the 1960s, the council's main publication, *The Citizen,* began publishing portions of his television editorials, and they even described Helms as "our favorite media master."[156] Jesse remained a critic of the "moderate" segregationism of the North Carolina political mainstream, and he preferred hard-line resistance. But his contacts with a variety of segregationist groups was off the record, and he was also careful not to become identified with extreme segregationism, rejecting violence and methods that would alienate the white middle class. Helms's decision to ally himself with opponents of the *Brown* decision reflected a larger political evolution: in the late 1950s he worked to wed opposition to segregation to a larger conservative appeal that criticized federal intervention. Ultimately, his fusion of anti-statism and segregationism would reap big political benefits.

HELMS'S FIRST EXPERIENCES with running a campaign occurred in 1957, when he vied for the Raleigh City Council. He entered the race indifferently, remained vague on the issues, and barely campaigned.[157] Promising to donate his salary of a few hundred dollars to charity, Jesse advocated limited government, suggesting that city government should not force water fluoridation on residents who opposed it. His campaign included little media, with the exception of a newspaper ad publicizing Georgia senator Richard Russell's support of his candidacy—something that Helms feared might have an adverse effect.[158] Helms ran a low-key campaign in part because he realized that some of his bankers in the NCBA worried about the propriety of his entry into politics. He needed his NCBA job for a regular salary, and, in deference to his employers, only campaigned during evenings.[159] Nonetheless, in May 1957, Helms won office, placing fifth out of the seven elected candidates.[160] Rejecting business as usual, he made it clear that he would, as a fellow member of the City Council remembered it, stand up "for those people who were against anything the city [government] was doing."[161] As one reporter would later describe

it, he often threw "rocks at the playhouse" of Raleigh civic life. He sided
with the local bus company in favor of parallel parking along Fayetteville
Street, despite the city manager's intention to eliminate it. He angered local building and loan associations when he claimed that there was a legal
conflict in having the city invest their funds in these financial institutions.
Employing obstructionist tactics that he would later perfect, Jesse stalled
appointments to the planning commission and the school board in order to
make a statement. Described as "shrewd," he was also capable of delivering
biting public critiques of the mayor and the city establishment.[162]

Helms, as city councilman, opposed federal intervention in local communities, the worst example of which, he believed, was urban renewal. His
father-in-law, Jacob Coble, was a landlord in some of Raleigh's poorer districts and exemplified the small-scale real estate entrepreneur most
threatened by urban renewal. Jesse expressed his opposition as a matter of
principle. In an example of government run mad, Helms wrote in the
Tarheel Banker in October 1957, urban renewal empowered "government
to condemn your property, force you to sell it to the government, which in
turn resells it to *another* private citizen." Liberals who worshipped an "all-
powerful government" wanted to confuse things with "high-blown plati-
tudes," but, to Helms, urban redevelopment exuded a "distinct odor of
tyranny."[163] But he realized that this was a losing battle.[164] Despite Helms's
lone opposition, on April 21, 1958, the Raleigh City Council voted to participate in federally sponsored urban renewal. Two years after his lost battle in Raleigh, he wrote in the *Tarheel Banker* that urban renewal, like
other "governmental hand-out schemes," had encouraged increased public indebtedness, expand government controls, and reduced individual incentive.[165]

Helms attracted attention in other battles. In the 1950s, Raleigh's in-
terdenominational Institute of Religion, a group sponsored by the local
United Church—along with the Raleigh Woman's Club, the League of
Women Voters, and the Raleigh PTA Council—had a long history of hosting controversial and often liberal visiting speakers. The United Church
was known for its controversial positions on race; in the 1950s, it became
one of the first Raleigh churches to integrate. In early 1958, the institute invited civil rights leader Martin Luther King, Jr., who was now a national
figure because of his leadership in the Montgomery, Alabama, bus boycott.
A. J. Fletcher was incensed. On January 27, he wrote a memo to his lieutenant at WRAL-TV, Bill Armstrong, suggesting that he obtain a list of the
institute's speakers over the past fifteen years and to send that list to Jack

Spain, North Carolina senator Sam Ervin's administrative assistant, to see if any of these speakers could be identified as "subversives." The audience might arrive with a Bible, Fletcher wrote, and leave with an "emblem of hammer and sickle." A.J. sarcastically suggested that a more appropriate name for the the organization would be the Institute of Socialism.[166] With Fletcher's encouragement, Jesse seized on the Institute issue.[167] On January 30, he wrote to city manager W. H. Carper indicating that he was "somewhat concerned" about the institute's programs. Anonymous phone callers, Helms claimed, had warned of possible anti-King violence. Though he favored free speech, Jesse warned that King's visit, and violence, might become "a blot on the good name of Raleigh, which has a reputation of tolerance for the expression of views contrary to those of the majority of our citizens." Jesse urged Carper to ensure that the police force was "inconspicuously available to keep order and to protect the rights of people with whom we may be in disagreement."[168]

Helms's letter, which was made public, created a furor. Carper declared that no violence would be tolerated, and he promised to dispatch the entire Raleigh police force, if necessary, to maintain order.[169] Some charged that Helms's institute letter was a publicity stunt—an attempt, according to one Raleigh resident, to "gain some free publicity at the expense of one of Raleigh's outstanding civic projects."[170] Others claimed that Jesse wanted to intimidate the institute and its white liberal supporters. Since his letter to Carper was written on NCBA letterhead, still others questioned the propriety of Helms's role. The normally conservative *Raleigh Times* declared that it was a "little difficult" to understand Helms's concern about the institute, which was admittedly liberal about race. But the institute series had always been liberal on race, and if there ever had been "any great public outcry or other manifestations of civic dismay about it, such has not been shouted from the housetops before."[171] But the sharpest criticism came from Helms's adversaries at the *News and Observer*. In an editorial entitled "Pious Incitement," the *N&O* questioned Helms's intentions. This was the same Jesse Helms who had participated in the "race-baiting campaign against Dr. Frank Graham" in the Senate race of 1950, and Jesse was engaged in an "effort to stir up trouble where none existed." The institute had previously hosted speakers whose views were "well to the left of Councilman Helms." The *N&O* challenged the propriety of Jesse's attempts to undermine the institute while making the *Tarheel Banker* "the journal of his personal prejudices." Now he had gone too far. On NCBA letterhead, Helms's letter to Carper was a "pious epistle" indeed; he had circulated copies around town like handbills. This was a "slippery incitement of trouble in a sanctimonious stunt" of the worst kind. The institute needed "the protection of Jesse Helms like they need holes in their heads."[172]

Helms vehemently responded that he had not intended that his letter to Carper be published. The *News and Observer* had obtained the letter without his knowledge or permission, he wrote a few days later, and if he had known this he would have requested that they not publish it. Jesse had received numerous phone calls warning him about violence, and he claimed that he was genuinely concerned. Some of the callers protested the use of a white school auditorium for King's appearance; others threatened to show up and throw eggs. According to Helms, his letter went only to Carper, with a copy to his close friend and NCBA chief counsel Pou Bailey. When Bailey learned that the *N&O* had obtained a "smattering" of the letter's contents, he released the entire letter—but did so without Helms's permission. On January 31, the *N&O* ran its story without consulting Helms, and a day later the "Pious Incitement" editorial appeared.[173]

Helms's denials notwithstanding, in fact he welcomed the controversy—and especially the opportunity to do battle with the *News and Observer*. A few days after the appearance of the "Pious Incitement" editorial, Helms interrupted a City Council meeting to denounce the *N&O*'s "false and misleading" assertions. Demanding a retraction and threatening a libel lawsuit, he described the editorial as "totally false" and "an intentional reflection upon my character and reputation." Jesse charged that the *N&O*'s contention that he was involved in race-baiting during the 1950 campaign was also untrue: although he had disagreed with Frank Porter Graham's political philosophy, Graham was still his "personal friend." The *N&O* had "constantly defiled and besmirched" Willis Smith during the 1950 campaign, and its attempt to tie Helms's views to the NCBA reflected its opposition to the banking industry. The City Council then passed a vote of confidence on Helms's behalf.[174]

The Institute of Religion affair fulfilled one of Helms's goals: to focus publicity on himself and his stand against liberalism. Fellow conservatives such as Bill Sharpe, segregationist and outspoken editor of Raleigh's *The State*, enthusiastically followed his fight with the *N&O*. Sharpe believed that Helms was "100 per cent right" in his criticism of the "type of people" that the institute was hosting.[175] Once he drew the *N&O* into conflict, Helms realized, he had transformed the issue into a broader, and potentially winning, conflict. "I've had a considerable amount of fun with the *News and Observer*," he wrote in March 1958 to Erwin A. Holt, a Burlington segregationist, and Jesse thought that he had "won this round." His main accomplishment was that he had forced liberals "into the open on another aspect of integration."[176] About a year and half after the Institute of Religion affair, in August 1959, Helms, writing to a Statesville white supremacist, concluded that the real issue had become how "ultra-liberals" and the Raleigh press had targeted him.[177]

Helms's style of opposition on the City Council earned him some admirers. Helms was a different kind of Raleigh city councilman and a different kind of politician, commented the *Laurinburg Exchange* in June 1959. A person who often bucked majority opinion, Jesse refused to "bend with the prevailing winds," though this meant that sometimes he walked "a lonely road." Despite his intransigence, he gained voters' respect, according to this analysis, for this was a "man who has convictions and the courage to express them, even if he is on a contrary course." People admired political consistency, even though he was "an unregenerate non-conformist."[178] Helms's City Council experience helped to shape a distinctive conservative rhetorical style. An opponent of the liberal mainstream on matters of race, he also preached fiscal conservatism and minimal government. Neither Democrats nor Republicans were facing up to the nation's needs, Jesse believed. "We are being swept along in a tidal wave of so-called political liberalism," he warned in a speech in Monroe in May 1959, which threatened to wash away "our individual rights, one by one and two by two." For Jesse, as for other southern segregationists, "rights" meant the codified privileges of white supremacy, a system that had, after all, been imposed on African Americans. His insistence on white "rights" as a sort of natural right would become a consistent theme in his rhetoric about race. The message also melded into an anti-Communist appeal that tried to link any forms of governmental intervention with socialism—an appeal that appeared most commonly when Jesse was on the attack.[179]

Helms's presence on the City Council made him difficult to ignore, and, although disliked by many, a growing constituency avidly followed him. Jesse realized that his impact was polarizing voters. In 1957, as he later wrote, he ran for Raleigh City Council with the "full knowledge that my views and my statements would be subject to public examination and criticism." Helms also knew that the local press, especially the *N&O*, would "use every opportunity to portray me in an unfavorable light," something that he attributed to his "close relationship" to Willis Smith.[180] As he privately wrote to A. J. Fletcher during the campaign, the "hounds" were "really after me in this City Council race," though he was "troubled by the fact that I had mistakenly assumed that some of them were hares."[181] Announcing his candidacy for re-election in March 1959, he admitted to Raleigh voters that he did not have "all the answers." Nor was he foolish enough to believe that all of his positions had been popular. The themes of his council career, he said, were his defense of individual rights and his support for limited government.[182] This political consistency—a characteristic that Helms exhibited throughout his political career—became a prominent campaign theme. If reelected, he promised voters in a campaign letter to "continue to do and say those things which I believe to be right." Not all of his positions would be popular, but he promised to "try to take positions which are honest and fair, and consistent with my fundamental philosophy of economy in government."[183] Helms was easily reelected in the May 1959 elections, again placing fifth out of the seven candidates elected to City Council, with 69 percent of all voters choosing him. His re-election, he wrote, occurred despite the *N&O* having portrayed him as the "blackest reactionary ever to crawl from beneath a rock."[184]

When his second two-year term concluded in 1961, however, Helms decided against running for reelection. A contemporary described him as "pretty much a loner on the council." Jesse was frustrated about his outsider status and "quite depressed," as he told one friend, at being "flattened" by the City Council majority. Helms also complained (referring to Raleigh mayor William G. Enloe) about the "Enloe Steamroller" and the council's inclination "to operate as a private club."[185] Although he liked his fellow councilmen individually, he was unable to understand their positions, and he foresaw the same majority, interested in the same status quo, would remain in power and outvote him.[186] Helms had another reason for leaving the Raleigh City Council in March 1961: he intended to run for North Carolina State Senate in 1962. As early as December 1960, he was telling friends that he might be interested in this office.[187] Then, in March 1961, Jesse announced his intention to step down from City Council, and he told voters that he would seek the State Senate seat.[188] Jesse even considered leaving the Democratic Party, and he conferred with local Republicans, who promised in a reference to Arizona conservative senator Barry Goldwater to make him "our Goldwater."[189] But the political fates intervened, thwarting his ambitions to hold additional political office. Raleigh attorney John Jordan, Jr., who held the seat, had privately assured Helms that he would not run again. Under pressure from Democratic governor Terry Sanford, however, Jordan decided to run again in August 1961. Deeply disappointed and resentful toward Sanford, Helms chose not to challenge Jordan. Although he was not holding any grudges, Jesse admitted to a friend that he believed Jordan "did not play entirely fair with me regarding the 1962 State Senate race," since Helms had withdrawn from the City Council race based on Jordan's "absolute statement" that he would not seek reelection.[190]

Speaking to a Siler City, North Carolina, Rotary Club in February 1960, Helms declared that the "road to socialism in America" had been "paved on a non-partisan basis." Jesse was a registered Democrat, and he would remain so until 1970, but he had embraced a new brand of conservatism that rejected mainstream politics. Neither the New Deal nor the Fair Deal was to blame. Nor was the "recent strange era of modern Republicanism, whatever in the world that was," at fault. Rather, America's slide toward socialism was "chargeable to both parties, and to all citizens."[191] Politics held an intrinsic appeal to Helms during the 1950s. Although everything that he did in public life pointed toward political office, in other respects the time was not right for a political move. The elections of 1960, which brought John F. Kennedy to the presidency and Terry Sanford to the North Carolina governorship, suggested a new era of liberalism at the state and national levels. Conservatives such as Helms were isolated. As Helms's political ambitions came to an end, for the time being at least, he moved wholeheartedly in a new direction, back into the business of television broadcasting.

Chapter 2

TRAVELING THE LONG, DREARY ROAD

TV Conservative

During the 1950s, in various settings, Helms wedded segregationism with anti-Communism and anti-government ideology, and this matured into a full-scale critique of New Deal liberalism. Helms thus anticipated an important phenomenon: how southern resistance to change in the Jim Crow system became part of an emerging national conservative movement. In expressing his opposition to desegregation as a part of the defense of individual "rights" against governmental tyranny, Helms anticipated the transformation of racial messaging in politics. In the bracing changes of the 1960s, moreover, Helms found ripe material, because the Kennedy and Johnson presidencies brought a new period of expansion for the federal government. In this conservative rationale, Helms linked liberalism to a broader disorder and disintegration in American society. Criticizing the direction of change, Jesse in particular focused on civil rights and university campuses as examples of a wider disintegration.

EVEN WHILE HE worked with North Carolina Bankers Association, Helms never abandoned his connections with broadcasting. Those connections depended on his friendship with A. J. Fletcher, whom he described in 1958 as "one of the best friends I have" and "a sort of second father."[1] Fletcher was also an astute businessman with a keen eye for the bottom line, and his penurious ways resembled Helms's own inclinations to pinch pennies.[2] A.J.'s conservatism matched Helms's philosophy. A segregationist, Fletcher advocated limiting federal power, and he favored further limitations over organized labor by eliminating existing New Deal protections.[3] Fletcher realized television's power, and he knew that it would soon supersede newspapers as the most important communications medium.[4] Like Fletcher, Helms saw television as a tool to advance the conservative cause.[5]

Helms lent his influence when Fletcher successfully lobbied for a Federal Communications Commission (FCC) television license for WRAL in 1956 over its main competitor, WPTF. In January 1954, Helms appealed to Joseph McCarthy for support.[6] Subsequently, after Fletcher obtained the FCC license, Jesse continued to ward off political attacks. In 1957, when the FCC threatened to downgrade WRAL's frequency level from VHF to UHF frequency, Helms wrote on Fletcher's behalf to Senator Sam Ervin, requesting his help.[7] Jesse saw these FCC maneuvers as reflecting efforts of the *News and Observer* to maintain its media stranglehold and to prevent Fletcher from presenting "the *other* side of the story insofar as government and politics are concerned."[8] Meanwhile, Helms continued to dabble in broadcasting, and in early 1957, he conducted a short television program for WRAL that interviewed members of the state legislature.[9]

In the late 1940s, Fletcher had put Alvin Wingfield on WRAL as a conservative radio commentator. Wingfield, however, did not make a successful transition from radio to television: impulsive and reckless, he did not have a good visual presence. Fletcher considered using Bob Thompson, a conservative High Point broadcaster Helms had strongly recommended.[10] But Fletcher really wanted Helms to return to broadcasting. In July 1957, his son, WRAL official Fred Fletcher, lunched with Helms, proposing that he join the television station full-time. Declining the offer, Helms kept the door open to working on a "sideline" basis. In September 1957, A.J. proposed that Jesse broadcast a weekly news commentary and add his own "editorial flavoring."[11] Eventually, Helms agreed to this format, and Fletcher convinced him to begin a new, once-a-week TV editorial entitled *Facts of the Matter.* Jesse explained his entrée into television as an attempt to "lick these guys"—referring here to the liberal media—by fighting them "with their own weapons."[12] The show, which was taped in advance, first aired on July 20, 1958, and it was broadcast every Sunday afternoon at 3:45.[13]

The inaugural airing of *Facts of the Matter* marked Jesse's first appearance before the television cameras. "I have never been so terrified in my life as I am at this moment," he admitted to his audience. Radio broadcasters could "dash into a studio at the last minute"; it mattered little whether they were smooth-shaven, or how they looked. Radio broadcasters' only concern was to "sit down, watch a clock, wait for an introduction by an announcer, look for the red light to flash on, and then—start talking." Television broadcasting required that Jesse appear in a studio "roughly the size of Reynolds Coliseum"—which was North Carolina State's sports arena—and produce five copies of a manuscript for "various directors, producers, announcers, el[e]ctricians, plumbers and cage cleaners who are necessary in order to put this show on the road, or beam, or whatever they put it on."[14]

Over the next twenty-seven months, between July 1958 and October 1960, the *Facts of the Matter* editorials aired regularly. Repeating the themes appearing earlier in the *Tarheel Banker*, Jesse stressed hostility to the liberal establishment, opposition to the growth of federal power, skepticism about internationalist foreign policy, and support for the southern white segregationists. But while his *Tarheel Banker* editorials sporadically considered political topics, in the *Facts of the Matter* editorials Helms was able to express a much fuller conservative agenda. His television program's purpose, he explained to a viewer in October 1960, was to challenge liberals without fear of the consequences.[15]

In his *Facts of the Matter* broadcasts, Helms also communicated familiar themes about integration and individual rights—at least, rights for middle-class white people.[16] The civil rights struggle, for Helms, was really a fight over expanding governmental coercion. The struggle over integration, he told viewers in October 1958, had become a "happy stroke of fortune" for advocates of "an all-powerful government." Liberals, he charged, had manipulated middle-class revulsion about racial injustice. They wrapped themselves in "cloaks of self-styled purity," while they attacked with "pious epithets and confusing accusations" those who disagreed with them. But liberal propaganda about civil rights had clouded the true issues, Helms maintained. The liberal North Carolina media, he claimed in his TV editorials, was duplicitous: unable to support integration openly because of its unpopularity among whites, it opposed political leaders who favored segregation.

Black activists, Helms asserted in his broadcasts, bore responsibility for inflaming racial conflict. The NAACP, Helms claimed, could have accomplished more if it had exhibited "good faith" by assuring southern whites that they would not "push this thing too fast." Black militancy led to federal intervention, Helms claimed, which would bring disastrous results. The Supreme Court was inflicting far more damage by altering the nation's constitutional structure; the radical tilt of Chief Justice Earl Warren's Supreme Court, he suggested, had aided Communism.[17] In other *Facts of the*

Matter editorials, Helms contended that the civil rights issue was not primarily a matter of justice. The more important concern, for Helms, was individual rights, the power of the federal government, and liberalism's destructive effect on the constitutional structure.[18]

Black activism, Helms claimed, led to a clash between civil rights and individual rights. In February 1960, black college students in Greensboro launched a sit-in movement against Woolworth's that quickly spread to other North Carolina cities, including Raleigh. In a *Tarheel Banker* editorial, Jesse described the Raleigh sit-ins as creating "an emotional mess" that was leading to a "racial crisis." Black demonstrators were fighting for their rights, but, asked Helms, "what, really, is a right?" Black protesters and their white liberal supporters were violating the rights of lunch counter operators, who had a right to serve whom they pleased. Protesters wanted their rights, he declared in a broadcast on February 14, 1960, but they had little concern for private property. Store owners could rightfully refuse service; the dime store was not, after all, a "socialistic enterprise." The sit-ins threatened to destroy "whatever remains of a kindly feeling between the races in North Carolina."[19] Like other segregationists, Helms diminished, underestimated, and fundamentally misunderstood the black freedom struggle: although he often asserted that sit-ins resulted from the intervention of outsiders, the movement sprang from local roots and community activism. But Helms blamed northern liberal whites for misleading southern black protesters. He was especially suspicious of crusading white ministers. "I hardly give a damn about *who* drinks coffee or eats lunch *where*," he wrote privately, "but I cannot permit my pastor or yours to dismiss the fundamental principles of private property with a mere wave of a pseudo ecclesiastical wand." Liberal ministers, he said, should pay greater attention to the social problems of the black community, where "illegitimate children and immorality and irresponsibility abound."[20]

The Greensboro sit-ins provided Jesse with the opportunity, in his *Facts of the Matter* broadcasts, to recast issues of segregation and desegregation. Reiterating his larger points about the civil rights movement, he stressed the conflict between individual rights and the ability of outsiders (such as liberals) and outside institutions (such as the federal government) to control individual behavior. Using this argument, Helms claimed that he did not oppose racial justice, but rather sought to protect ordinary people from tyranny. In Greensboro, several days after the Woolworth's sit-ins began, the chancellor of the Woman's College of the University of North Carolina, Gordon Blackwell, discouraged students from participating in the sit-ins. Eight N.C. State faculty members responded by signing a protest statement. On March 27, 1960, Helms devoted an editorial to the professors' manifesto. Only one of the eight faculty was a native North Carolinian, Jesse pointed out; N.C. State faculty were criticizing a UNC campus as well as the governor of North Carolina. It might be "good business to integrate," or it might be "unwise, from a business standpoint, NOT to integrate." That, said Helms, was not the primary issue. Rather, the most important question was whether the "proprietor of a privately-owned store" should still possess the "right to use his own judgment, or must he surrender to the will of others, such as out-of-state professors who may not know as much about another fellow's business as they *think* they know."[21]

Helms adopted an adversarial style on the TV airwaves that welcomed controversy. He especially sought to engage his liberal adversaries, including the media, college professors, and government bureaucrats. Jesse's strategy, honed as *Tarheel Banker* editor and City Council member during the 1950s, was to push hard on issues, attract public attention, and depart the scene having made his point. He was clever in his choice of combat and effective in the way he responded. By comparison, however, other conservative broadcasters, though agreeing with Jesse's mixture of race and anti-Communism, were far more reckless. Beginning in 1958, Earl LeBaron, a faculty member in the Social Sciences Department at East Carolina College, broadcast a television commentary on Greenville's television station WNTC, *History Behind the Time,* that was conservative and segregationist.[22] But these broadcasts were too extreme even for an eastern North Carolina television audience to tolerate, and after some East Carolina faculty complained, in December 1958 the station took him off the air. Like many other broadcasters, WNTC worried about the FCC's regulations about equal time, which required that politically controversial broadcasts provide the opportunity for rebuttal. In 1958, Charlotte TV station WBTV had its license suspended over the equal time issue. The station managers also worried that LeBaron's excited broadcasts might provoke violence and that "we would have another Little Rock on our hands."[23]

Although Helms and LeBaron were both conservative broadcasters with weekly shows, there were profound stylistic differences. LeBaron was a committed obstructionist who charged that NAACP leaders had Communist associations and favored the "mongrelization of the white race by intermarriage with blacks."[24] Helms's differences with white supremacists such as LeBaron emphasized the distinctiveness of his approach as an opponent of integration. LeBaron was a crude segregationist, Helms a sophisticated one. LeBaron had little comprehension of his audience, Helms understood it thoroughly. And while LeBaron had only a

vague understanding of the larger issues and their implication for the future, Helms favored a softer, more media-savvy segregationism. Writing
to LeBaron in the middle of his fight with WNTC, in December 1958,
Jesse offered words of advice that indicated his own notions about politics
and media. Considering himself a "very poor one to give such advice," he
said that he had "learned the hard way" that his liberal adversaries
wanted to provoke him into an overreaction. Helms and LeBaron had lost
the "so-called racial fight" and it was time for a realistic assessment. What
Jesse described as "forced integration and socialism" fed on each other.
Some might argue that public schools were not socialist, but, Helms said,
the only real issue was whether public schools were "a form of socialism
which we desire and can live with." Dispatching "children to government-
controlled school buildings" was one thing, educating children another.
He did not disagree with LeBaron's ideas; both of them were "voices in
the wilderness." Nonetheless, Helms disagreed with LeBaron's methods.
"Both of us must take care in our zeal to protest that we do not entirely
destroy our means of being just a little effective," he wrote. The most
they could hope for was that "we may keep the spark of imagination
alive" by stating the "truth as we see it" and by offering a "tiny guidepost"
for future generations, when and if they decide to "turn back down the
road to freedom."[25]

Helms's broadcasts were only on a part-time basis, which, early on, he
found frustrating. "Occasionally I have some encouraging comment, but
mostly I feel that I'm just wasting my time," he wrote in November 1958.
He was scheduled at a time slot, Sunday afternoons, when people were "out
in their cars, or else are taking naps."[26] But the bug of television had bitten
him hard—and he was drawn to the possibility of reaching a mass audience
on behalf of the conservative cause, of mixing politics and media. Helms
himself saw a thin line between these two realms, and his desire to create a
television mouthpiece enjoyed Fletcher's full support—despite the risks
that existed in the FCC's equal time requirements. What conservatives
needed to do was "get organized," Helms wrote to a friend, and this was the
"main goal of what we're trying to do at this television station."[27]

IN 1960, THE divergent political forces in North Carolina came together
in that year's gubernatorial and presidential campaigns. The contest for the
Democratic gubernatorial nomination pitted segregationist I. Beverly Lake
against Terry Sanford, former FBI agent, Fayetteville attorney, and Kerr
Scott's campaign manager in the 1954 U.S. Senate race. Inheriting Scott's

legacy, in 1960 Sanford was a moderate segregationist who reassembled North Carolina's progressive-liberal coalition that had been in existence since Scott's election as governor in 1948. Although he claimed impartiality, Helms was actually a strong Lake supporter: the two men had had a close association since the *Brown* decision, when Lake became the most forceful legal and intellectual opponent of desegregation in the state.[28] Sanford, in contrast, represented much that Helms disliked about North Carolina politics. Despite his position as a television broadcaster, Jesse abandoned any pretense of neutrality and supported Lake. In a *Facts of the Matter* editorial that aired in August 1959, Jesse observed that Lake was unquestionably the best-qualified candidate. Although newspapers had black-balled him as an "absolute racist, a hell-for-leather segregationist," Lake, said Helms, simply opposed integration on constitutional grounds.[29] As the Democratic gubernatorial primary neared in May 1960, Helms continued to include pro-Lake remarks in his broadcasts. According to one reporter, Helms, on occasion, actively participated in Lake rallies in which Jesse raised a bucket and urged the crowd to donate to the campaign.[30] Jesse covered Lake's headquarters for WRAL on May 28, the evening of the first primary, and Sanford supporters claimed that his coverage was overtly pro-Lake. Helms maintained strong associations with the Lake campaign, which forced a second primary but then lost in the runoff.[31]

As disappointed as he was about Sanford's election, Jesse found the presidential elections even more discouraging. Helms described the choice in the presidential election of 1960 between John Kennedy and Richard Nixon as "like going to a house of assignation to pick out a wife." Although he considered himself a friend of Nixon's, Helms criticized him for rejecting an openly conservative agenda. The Richard Nixon of 1960 scarcely resembled the fierce anti-Communist of the late 1940s. An "imitator rather than a leader," he had somehow lost his bold imagination. Statesmen, Helms argued, were those people who could "pick their side, stay on it, and defend it—not men who stand spraddle-legged in pretense of being on both sides at once." A true leader could not "go both directions at once" but should "choose his direction and his destination and stick with them." Nixon, Helms thought, "fell short of statesmanship."[32] The presidential elections proved that "you can't win by promising less," for GOP presidential candidate Richard Nixon refused to face the true issue of whether Kennedy's campaign promises would lead to a socialistic United States. Jesse wondered whether it was possible that American voters might embrace the largely untested proposition of "looking for a man who would rather be right and lose, than be wrong and win."[33]

HELMS'S PART-TIME INVOLVEMENT with WRAL in the late 1950s
drew him back to broadcast journalism. Although he would remain in his
post as North Carolina Bankers Association executive director until October 1960, after 1958 the position held less interest for him. He discovered
that the most effective instrument of promoting his political message
would not be the pages of the *Tarheel Banker,* but across WRAL's television
airwaves. The *Facts of the Matter* broadcasts were controversial, hard-
hitting, and aimed at liberal enemies. They stirred up more controversy
and attracted a large, and potentially expanding, audience. Jesse did not
mind the controversy. Indeed, throughout his career in public life he came
to see controversy as advantageous to the conservative movement, and he
thrived on the attention that it focused on himself and his causes. Television, Helms realized, was the future of politics, and he intended to master
the medium.

In November 1960, Helm agreed to join WRAL as an executive vice
president, a job that gave him considerable influence over the day-to-day
operation of the station, including operations and news programming.
Fletcher provided him with a free hand to upgrade the news coverage and
alter its program structure; A.J. wanted to use WRAL to destroy the liberal
monopoly over news in North Carolina.[34] WRAL became a beacon for
conservatives: Fletcher had the station sign off by playing "Dixie," rather
than "The Star-Spangled Banner."[35] Conservatives, he thought, could
overthrow the liberal monopoly only if someone took the step of "standing
up and crying out against the oppressor." Fletcher was dedicated to providing a conservative media outlet, and he wanted Jesse to expand his *Facts of
the Matter* broadcasts in a new series of daily television editorials known as
Viewpoints that were only several minutes long and were broadcast twice a
day, five days a week. Reaching WRAL's large viewing area, between
November 1960 and February 1972, Jesse would eventually air 2,732 *Viewpoint* editorials.[36]

An editorial board consisting of Jesse, A.J., his son Fred Fletcher, and
the WRAL comptroller reviewed the *Viewpoints,* but Helms enjoyed unrestricted freedom in choosing his topics and writing about them. The review board, in twelve years of *Viewpoints,* rarely intervened.[37] Focused,
hard-hitting, and always containing a political message, the *Viewpoints*
stirred up controversy, exciting conservatives and enraging liberals. Soon
after his first *Viewpoint* aired, he told a friend, the "liberals began to howl,"
for they maintained "control of the majority of the press in this state."[38]

Helms's style of delivery was all-important, and there was a difference between hearing Jesse and reading the transcripts. The *Viewpoints'* tone, said one later critic, was "frequently sarcastic, mean-spirited, and vindictive, and their content provided a voice for 'responsible' racism and insistent intolerance."[39] Jesse experienced some discouragement about the criticism—he admitted to friends that the *Viewpoints* prompted a regular "battering" from what Helms and his friends liked to call "libruls"—but he wrote that things were "not as bad as I had imagined" and that "he was "picking up some friends along the way."[40] When he was told that his editorials were "sneering," he took exception. It was not in his nature, he wrote, "to be unduly unkind."[41]

From the airing of his first *Viewpoint,* on Monday, November 21, 1960, in which he attacked President-elect Kennedy, Helms used his broadcasts to assault liberalism.[42] Americans needed to return to basic principles, he said in October 1961, and they had too frequently ignored those "distinctions between socialism and freedom." Jesse's conservative message stressed the threat of an ever-growing government, which had become so large that ordinary people no longer understood its size, while its complexity became a "a sort of justification for more bigness."[43] Government, he explained to a civic group, could either "be man's servant—or his master": it could not be both. The "sacred cows" of "subsidies, controls, and federal aid" all consumed freedom.[44] A cornerstone of the liberal state, Helms always believed, was the media, but resistance here was like "fighting an octopus."[45] Liberal newspapers in North Carolina—especially the *News and Observer, Charlotte Observer,* and *Greensboro Daily News*—dominated information and expressed, he believed, "unfairness, partiality and bias."[46]

Helms's strong anti-Communism provided a broad umbrella for his conservative, anti-liberal message.[47] Helms's anti-Communism meant that his earliest broadcasts dealing with foreign policy—about which, up to this point, he had said very little—were steadfastly anti-Soviet, and his unqualified hatred of the Soviet empire would remain a defining characteristic. An inveterate Cold Warrior, he opposed expanded trade with the Soviet bloc, and he believed that any assistance for Russian economic development supported the worldwide Communist conspiracy.[48] For the developing world, Helms urged American resolve. In the early 1960s, he sporadically expressed support for Latin America's authoritarian, anti-leftist regimes. A thin line separated liberalism and Communism; too many front organizations disguised subversion. Who were those who argued that Cuba's Fidel Casto was not a Communist but instead a "sort of Robin Hood of the Caribbean?" Who had insisted on U.N. membership for the People's Republic of China?[49]

The struggle against Communism required vigilance against subversion at home. Before condemning conservatives as super-patriots or claiming that there was no danger of Communist subversion, Jesse declared, liberals should check their "license to hurl such epithets."[50] Helms maintained regular communications with congressional investigators at the House Un-American Activities Committee and the Senate Internal Security Subcommittee, and they fed him information about supposed subversives. He regularly corresponded with staffers at Senator Sam Ervin's office, which provided a steady diet of information. Jesse endorsed the vestiges of political anti-Communism of the late 1940s and 1950s; like most conservatives, he saw no contradiction between opposition to government and support for loyalty oaths and Communist registration laws.[51] Into the late 1960s, Helms continued to defend HUAC—long after most public figures had abandoned it—and regarded its opponents as belonging to "left-wing oddball" political groups who were repeating what he called the "same old dreary, unfounded charges" about HUAC's persecution of innocent Americans.[52] Jesse also maintained contacts with the FBI and its director, J. Edgar Hoover.[53]

When a group of University of California–Berkeley students protested HUAC's hearings in San Francisco in May 1960, police responded by arresting and fire-hosing them. The police overreaction prompted even larger anti-HUAC demonstrations. Subsequently, HUAC produced a documentary, *Operation Abolition,* which claimed that Communist infiltrators operating on the Berkeley campus had organized the protests. According to one historian, *Operation Abolition* was "so addlebrained that it strengthened the case of liberals against HUAC" and, over time, even became a cult classic.[54] Helms enthusiastically endorsed the documentary; he considered HUAC chairman Pennsylvania congressman Francis E. Walter a personal friend.[55] In February 1961 and on several subsequent occasions, Jesse arranged a WRAL broadcast of *Operation Abolition* that attracted criticism. Rather than abolishing HUAC, Helms thought that it should be strengthened.[56] Helms's defense of HUAC ultimately became an attack on liberalism. Because of liberals' squeamishness, Jesse said in a *Viewpoint* editorial in October 1961, many Americans believed that there was little danger of subversive infiltration. Liberals participated in a "calculated campaign" to depict anti-Communists as "something sinister," Helms further charged, and even J. Edgar Hoover had not been "spared in the assaults."[57] Liberals' opposition to loyalty oaths was "pitifully artificial" and "pious nonsense," Helms told viewers in March 1963. A free society possessed a right to protect itself against infiltration.[58]

BEGINNING WITH THE lunch counter sit-ins of early 1960, African Americans revolted against segregation and, using methods of nonviolent resistance, challenged the racial status quo. Helms's *Viewpoints* opposed the civil rights uprising; these "professional agitators," he wrote, had no interest in "logic or truth."[59] There was little doubt where Helms stood regarding civil rights, but he urged white resisters to adopt more effective strategies against integration. Alabama governor George Wallace's style of opposing federal authorities and civil rights protesters, he said in a September 1963 *Viewpoint*, was "all liability." Although Jesse agreed with Wallace's goals, he disagreed with his noisy methods, describing him as "absurd," "not impressive," and "ludicrous." The Alabama governor had become a comical figure; he evoked nothing more than "head-wagging incredulity reserved for the fool." The Birmingham street demonstrations in the spring of 1963, Helms declared, had become a lost battle, and, because of Wallace, the white South had become a "butt end of ridicule." White Southerners should communicate their case against integration more effectively, Helms declared. Despite the "sound reason" of segregation, he said, Wallace had squandered an opportunity to explain the white South's position to a national audience.[60] Wallace practiced "no strategy," Helms complained in correspondence, but was "simply doing what Martin Luther King is doing—except that King is smart enough to conduct himself so that *his* followers will stay united." The only way that the white South could reverse things was to show that it was the "*other* side, not ours that is stepping out of line in our free society."[61] Helms's opinion of Wallace would subsequently change: when he ran for the Democratic presidential nomination in 1964 and began to attract northern working-class votes, Helms recognized a kindred spirit. In June 1964, Helms hosted Wallace when he made a WRAL appearance, and he pronounced the Alabama governor "intelligent, adroit, honorable and courageous." Describing him in a May 1966 broadcast as "not perfect, by any means," Jesse called Wallace as "obviously a vastly better and more competent man" than his liberal critics portrayed him. Even more important, Helms recognized that Wallace was a transitional figure whose populist appeal that mixed race and anti-government rhetoric could potentially reshape the electoral balance.[62]

Helms strongly opposed the Kennedy adminstration's attempts to expand the federal role in southern affairs. The president's proposals to expand federal aid to public education—a centerpiece of his early domestic agenda—encountered the resistance of southern Democrats in Congress because they feared that federalization would become an opening wedge toward school desegregation. Opponents of federal aid, Jesse said, were not against education per se but were resisting national control. Jesse wrapped his opposition to integration in the mantle of home rule: control and financing of schools belonged with local communities. The "malignant myth of all federal aid," he argued, was that federal government possessed a "sort of magical power" by which it could "produce money out of nowhere." Only at tax time did people realize that "every dime" the government spent came either from "present taxpayers or from a mortgage placed on the productive capacity of generations yet unborn."[63]

Jesse encouraged white Southerners to obstruct Kennedy's domestic proposals, while he also defended senators' right to filibuster against civil rights legislation.[64] When Lyndon Johnson became president after the Kennedy assassination in November 1963, Helms soon became a strong critic. Any conservative who could swallow LBJ, he said, had a "somewhat larger mouth than brain."[65] In 1964, he supported Barry Goldwater's campaign for the presidency as a conservative who would undo the big government policies of the past decades—as the "last hope of the capitalistic, free enterprise system."[66] Although he often "doesn't do things the way I'd want them done, or say them the way I would hope I would say them," Goldwater was a "good deal more honest than many of his critics." He had certainly been much maligned, Jesse believed, with the liberal label of "right-wing extremist." Yet Helms realized, as he wrote in September 1964, that Goldwater would get "the dickens beat out of him" in the upcoming presidential campaign against Johnson. On election day, as returns of the Johnson landslide came in, the Helms family was a "rather disconsolate and apprehensive group." Ultimately, however, Goldwater's defeat reflected, Helms thought, the "moral decay in our country."[67]

While Helms blamed white liberals for the civil rights movement, he also began to identify what he considered to be the deficiences of the black-led movement.[68] Jesse charged that sit-ins and demonstrations marked a turn toward lawlessness that imperiled the social order, revealed northern hypocrisy, and demonstrated contradictions within modern liberal ideology. He contrasted "responsible" African Americans, who accepted segregation and sought to advance themselves within the status quo, with "irresponsible" blacks, who spawned social disorder and chaos. In some of his *Viewpoint* editorials, he related conversations with blacks who disagreed with civil rights militance. In September 1964, Jesse told viewers how a Raleigh "negro mechanic" confided that "fighting and fussing" was imperiling good race relations. In a community in which "we helped them pick their cotton and they helped us pick ours," said Jesse, blacks and whites took care of each other. Helms reassured his white audience that most blacks did not want the racial system changed, and he reported his black friend as against a "pulsating bitterness" that was "being coldly and calculatingly promoted throughout the nation."[69] Despite the anecdote, there is little evidence that black skepticism about the civil rights movement had any basis beyond Helms's own imagination and misperceptions. He was not alone, however, for many southern whites were convinced that "their" blacks would have little to do with the civil rights uprising.

This tension between "good" and "bad" blacks dominated Helms's descriptions of race. The discontent of the 1960s, he said, resulted not so much from a heritage of racism and white supremacy as from problems within the black community. The main task for the future, according to this analysis, was not guaranteed individual rights but black leaders' willingness to confront their own, systemic problems. Although integration was possible, Jesse explained to viewers, "forced" integration was disastrous and could only lead to a breakdown in racial communication. The "irresponsible Negro" penalized the "responsible Negro" when the latter failed to exert leadership requiring a "higher level of respectability among others of his race." The roots of African Americans' social problems, said Jesse, lay not in racism and discrimination, but in deficiencies in family structure and personal responsibility. Civil rights leaders, Helms said, ignored this reality at their peril—and to the "immense disservice to the hopes and dreams of responsible Negroes not only in the South but everywhere in the nation."[70] Whether black leaders admitted it, Helms told viewers in July 1962, crime and black "irresponsibility" were a reality.[71] Black people should rely on "hard work, self-reliance and moral behavior" rather than street demonstrations.[72]

Helms's emphasis on the lack of personal responsibility was part of a larger attempt to discredit the civil rights movement—and to blame the victims. The attempt was subtle and sophisticated, but it was directed at the heart of what the movement meant for black freedom. What this view ignored was the prevalence of urban poverty, racial discrimination, and a legacy of white supremacy, all of which contributed more to rising crime than the civil rights revolution. Social disintegration threatened to make meaningless the issue of black rights, Helms suggested. Were civil rights available only for blacks, he asked in a March 1963 *Viewpoint,* or did they exist for white women threatened by assault? Other examples of violent crime, he said, reflected the "same situation, the same question." The liberal response—"handouts" and welfare—only encouraged "idleness." Helms raised the matter of African American deficiencies "not to disparage the Negro or to offend him," but to make the point that it was "past time for Negro leaders to take note of the fact that for every effect there is a cause." Helms believed that blacks were achieving little progress by "political force and government handouts," and certainly not by ignoring their weaknesses. What really mattered was mutual respect and understanding, and "no court, no Congress, no President, no Governor" could create and sustain it.[73] "Negro agitators" were pushing white Americans to a "breaking point"; if this were reached, it would be a "black and regrettable day in the nation's history—and, most of all, for the Negro."[74]

In this way, Helms was beginning to transform the debate from a discussion of white oppression to a discussion of black deficiency. It was a skillful argument that potentially carried considerable appeal as an explanation that was fundamentally racial, though to respectable white audiences it disavowed any association with the old style of white supremacy. On a basic level, he thus not only opposed the civil rights movement but also suggested that it brought on social decline. During the early 1960s, younger African Americans, mostly students, led a new nonviolent revolt that sought to topple segregation. In April 1960, black students organized SNCC, the Student Nonviolent Coordinating Commitee, and, working with an older interracial group, the Congress of Racial Equality (CORE), in the spring of 1961 organized the famous Freedom Rides, which challenged the segregated policies of interstate bus companies. Black and white students rode buses across the segregated South, deliberately challenging the law. In Montgomery and Birmingham, Alabama, angry mobs assaulted and beat the Freedom Riders. Where civil rights protesters suffered violence, Helms usually blamed the victims. These were "two dangerously silly groups of people," he said, who both sought trouble and who "found what they were looking for in Alabama." Helms condemned mob violence but laid responsibility at the demonstrators' feet. Protesters violated the law rather than seeking redress within the system. Despite their "pious pretensions," the Freedom Riders were not promoting a "mission of peace and brotherly love—and they knew it when they started." Both the mob and demonstrators deserved "cracked skulls." Possessing little sympathy for Alabama whites who lost control of their temper, Jesse also felt little affinity for the Freedom Riders, who wanted martyrdom and chose to flout the law.[75]

When President Kennedy supported federal intervention by endorsing a new civil rights bill in June 1963, Helms strenuously opposed it. In high irony, he conjured an image of mob violence that would have been startlingly familiar to African Americans. "The way things are going," he said, "we'll all be hanging on lamp posts pretty soon"—at least, those who "dare to lift a finger."[76] The implementation of the new act, in early 1964, would bring federal intervention and faceless bureaucratic controls, he warned. He wrote in January 1964 that the civil rights bill was a "fraud," the "most far-reaching, dangerous piece of legislation I have ever read," and it would be "destructive of everybody's liberty."[77] Helms responded similarly to the South's worst anti–civil rights terror in Mississippi. In July 1964, after three civil rights workers were murdered in Philadelphia, Mississippi, he denounced the killers as besmirching "the name of the South." The killings were the work "not of sane men but of men without reason or logic or decency," he told viewers, and "no amount of rationalizing can make of it anything other than utter savagery." Still, Helms appeared less concerned about the justice of the matter, or the welfare of the victims, than about long-term strategy. White terror, in the age of modern media, was simply bad public relations. The Mississippi murders dealt a blow to the South's efforts to "present its case in the forum of public opinion in this country and abroad," and southern whites stood "indicted for a crime that no rational Southerner can stomach." Having condemned the murderers, Helms once again blamed the victims. The murdered civil rights workers, he claimed, were at least partly responsible for their own deaths: they "went in search of trouble amidst a rolling tide of resentment in the delta country, even though no reasonable man would at the outset have denied such a conclusion."[78]

HELMS'S OBJECTIONS TO black and white student activists formed part of his case against nonviolent civil disobedience. Reasserting points that appeared in the *Facts of the Matter* editorials—that demonstrators were violating the property rights of white merchants—he also questioned the movement's threat to order. Privately, he urged his supporters not to lose heart. The "inflammatory activities" of civil rights activists, he wrote to a fellow opponent of integration, meant that "all we need in North Carolina is just a little more courage than we have demonstrated in the past."[79] Americans could not choose which laws they obey,[80] and he was fed up with "piety in this matter."[81] Respect for the law and property rights should never become debatable, he said in an April 1961 *Viewpoint*, and no right of civil disobedience existed.[82] In March 1964, Jesse complained about the "long, dreary road that we are travelling" in which, "at every stop along the way there are those who would have us surrender to mob rule." Protesters who deliberately violate the law, he told viewers, should expect justice "equally applicable to all."[83]

Focusing his attack on the movement's leadership, Helms targeted Martin Luther King, Jr. In numerous *Viewpoint* broadcasts, Helms tied King to Communism, a connection that Jesse for many years would insist existed. The FBI subjected King and his associates to extensive wiretapping and surveillence, to little avail. In December 1964, when J. Edgar Hoover described King as the "most notorious liar" in the country, Helms defended the FBI director and criticized King's "wild statements." King failed to realize that the FBI was "an agency of law-enforcement and not an adjunct to any organization of social reform." King disliked Hoover, Helms suggested, because of his persistence in establishing connections between civil rights and Communism. The entire civil rights movement, he wrote, was "shot through with Communists and fellow travellers," and it did not "take much imagination" to realize that Russia was "behind all of it."[84]

For Helms, the case of Robert Williams illustrated the relationship between subversion and black activism. An NAACP leader from Helms's hometown of Monroe, Williams had achieved national notoriety for his unequivocal rejection of white supremacy. In the late 1950s, Williams led a movement in Jesse's home, Union County, that defied local authorities, challenged the local Klan, and advocated armed resistance to white authority. Wrongly charged with kidnapping a white couple, Williams fled arrest to Cuba in 1961, spending much of the next decade there and in the People's Republic of China. In late August 1961, Helms visited Monroe just before Williams's flight, and he drove to Williams's house "to see firsthand what manner of man he was." On Williams's porch he discovered a group of thirty or forty African Americans, along with some sympathetic white college students. Helms called Williams a "hostile, often belligerent individual" who avoided questions "with a sweep of the hand." Condemning his "disregard for the law" and his advocacy of violent resistance, Helms suggested that Williams's activism arose from past associations with alleged Communists. Like Williams, civil rights activists were "Trojan horses," Helms maintained, which would assist international Communism in its "hope to defeat us by dividing us." Citing a Senate Subcommittee on Internal Security staff report about Williams, he described him in 1964 as Fidel Castro's "paid hireling." Helms used the case of Robert Williams to provide evidence of his larger assertion that Communists had infiltrated the civil rights movement. Although not everyone in the movement was Communist, he contended, the SISS document offered a warning. Those "true friends of the Negro's search for advancement" should realize that "many of those who chant about 'freedom' while advocating violence and disregard for the law are not really friends of the Negro, but agents for a conspiracy to destroy America."[85]

On the eve of King's March on Washington in August 1963, Jesse repeated a smear about Jack O'Dell, New York director of King's Southern Christian Leadership Conference. The FBI had spread unsubstantiated rumors about him to suggest that he was a Communist; Helms repeated these in a *Viewpoint* that aired in August 1963. Recounting a story that was published in the southern press, Jesse asserted that O'Dell was not only a Communist but had been an organizer for the Party. Helms wondered why O'Dell was in the higher echelons of King's organization. Echoing J. Edgar Hoover's warnings about the civil rights movement's ties to Communism—warnings that never gained any substance—Helms claimed that racial unrest was providing a "spawning ground for Communism." Only if these charges proved untrue could King and other leaders of what Helms called "the agitation" be "cleared of suspicion."[86]

Helms also tied subversion to sexual immorality. In a November 1963 *Viewpoint* editorial, he claimed that King's "outfit" was "heavily laden at the top with leaders of proven records of communism, socialism and sex perversion, as well as other curious behavior." Jesse pointed out that one of King's "Negro agitators" was found in a Norfolk, Virginia, motel with a woman not his wife. This incident prompted him to describe the movement—in what became a major theme of his editorials—as rife with immorality.[87] In April 1965, Helms repeated approvingly the charges made by Alabama Republican congressman William L. Dickinson, who, on the floor of the House of Representatives, criticized the "beatniks, prostitutes and communists" who infiltrated the movement. Blacks and whites, Dickinson claimed, engaged in "sex orgies of the rawest sort, including burlesque shows advertised by handbills in advance." Helms told viewers about a Chapel Hill civil rights activist who pled guilty to charges of sending obscene literature through the mails. The Guilford County, North Carolina, sheriff, Helms also said, reported "incredible details" about sexual immorality among black and white demonstrators who were arrested in Greensboro. There were an "uncommon number of moral degenerates"—meaning homosexuals—in the movement. Black novelist and activist James Baldwin, who was gay, was described as a person who "cannot get his mind out of the sewer, if one may judge by his literary efforts." Helms also cited the case of Bayard Rustin, whom he described as a "self-confessed homosexual who served time in jail for a sordid offense."[88]

In Rustin, Helms identified a link between liberalism, subversion, and perversion. Despite what he called Rustin's "perverted" past, Helms said, he was "idolized by vast segments of the political spectrum as a great leader." Openly gay, a Quaker pacifist, and having numerous Communist connections, Rustin's example supplied Helms with concrete evidence of the moral bankruptcy of the black insurgency. As the March on Washington's mastermind, Rustin, according to Jesse, was a "convicted sex pervert" who had "neither denied nor apologized for his past Communist connections." Somehow, however, the mainstream media remained silent about Rustin, even while ample information documented connections between this "self-confessed sexual pervert" and subversion. Liberals embraced Rustin's leadership; Lyndon Johnson extended him a "warm handclasp." What would have happened, Helms wondered, if information such as this had become available about George Wallace?[89] About a week before the March on Washington, on August 20, 1963, Helms detailed how Rustin had been arrested eleven times for "sexual perversion." Condemning him further for draft evasion and "perversion," Helms informed viewers that Rustin had belonged to the Young Communist League, attended a Communist Party convention in 1956, and visited the Soviet Union in 1958. According to Helms, along with O'Dell, Rustin comprised the Communists who belonged to King's inner circle.[90]

Jesse regarded both the Civil Rights and Voting Rights acts of 1964 and 1965 as terrible mistakes, blows to states' rights, and examples of how an unwieldy liberal government had run amok. Lenin "had it sized up right," Jesse said. "If his movement could divide, it could conquer."[91] When the civil rights bill passed the House in early 1964, he condemned it as an "unspeakably bad piece of legislation" that violated the Constitution in "a dozen different ways." Although Helms predicted that future historians would depict the bill as an example of "questionable statesmanship," most scholars have subsequently disagreed with this assessment. Indeed, federal intervention was a key ingredient in ending segregation and white supremacy.[92] Few commentators understood the civil rights bill's constitutional dangers, Helms feared, which he called the "single most dangerous piece of legislation ever introduced in the Congress." Opposing the civil rights bill was not "anti-Negro," Helms believed: rather, its supporters were too willing to sacrifice individual freedom for political gain.[93] In April 1964, on the verge of Senate passage, he described the civil rights bill as "extremely dangerous" and as something "that the communists would very much like to see enacted." It deserved defeat because of its "very bad principles."[94]

ALTHOUGH FOR MOST of his career Jesse had had little to say about college campuses, beginning in the early 1960s he targeted higher education, especially the University of North Carolina. Like the civil rights movements, colleges and universities, he charged, were becoming safe havens of what he called "too much concealed infiltration." Why should Americans, Helms asked in May 1961, provide Communists such a convenient hiding place?[95] In 1961, Helms expanded his attack to the Chapel Hill campus of the University of North Carolina. Since the 1930s, UNC had been the best public university in the South; out of its intellectual ferment came a tradition of political activism. There were Communists at Chapel Hill in the 1930s and 1940s, but by the early 1950s, in the wake of the nationwide purge of suspected subversives occurring in the McCarthy era, the campus had rid itself of Party members. No Communists served on the faculty; Communist speakers were prohibited. By the 1960s, Chapel Hill's liberalism was thoroughly sanitized and anti-Communist. Because of its reputation for racial liberalism, however, UNC remained suspect to North Carolina conservatives. A network of anti-Communists in Chapel Hill reported suspicious campus activities. One was Colonel Henry E. Royall, head of the local American Legion chapter; another was Sarah Watson Emery, an anti-Communist Chapel Hill resident. Both were certain that subversives ran the university. Royall and Helms shared a common interest in the case of Junius Scales. Son of a prosperous Greensboro family, Scales joined the Party in the 1940s while a UNC student and ran the Communists' activities in the Carolinas between 1947 and 1956. Joining the Party because of its unequivocal opposition to segregation, Scales was tried and convicted in 1955 for Party membership and was sentenced to six years in federal prison. His conviction was then reversed on appeal, but, after a second trial, he was again convicted, with the same sentence. Although Scales recanted his Party membership in 1957 and appealed his conviction, the Supreme Court eventually denied the appeal, and he was ordered to surrender to prison authorities in October 1961. Scales supporters campaigned to persuade President Kennedy to commute his sentence. Helms and Royall denounced their efforts. Reminding North Carolinians of Chapel Hill's tradition of subversion, Royall said that commuting Scales's sentence would be a "miscarriage of justice." Noting that his supporters included Jonathan Daniels and Harry Golden, the liberal gadfly editor of Charlotte's *Carolina Israelite,* Jesse urged viewers to shed no tears for Scales as a victim of injustice. Scales owed the "nation an apology—not the other way around." In spite of Helms's opposition, Kennedy commuted the sentence in December 1962, after Scales had served a little more than a year in prison. Nonetheless, Jesse used the Scales case as evidence of Chapel Hill Communism.[96]

Sarah Watson Emery, married to UNC philosophy professor Stephen Emery, sent a steady stream of letters to Helms charging campus subversion.[97] In 1963, Emery published *Blood on the Old Well,* which claimed the existence of a UNC Communist conspiracy. UNC administrators tolerated left-wing subversion, Emery claimed, and permitted sexual degeneracy. Young men came to UNC with "high ideals of service to mankind," but while on campus they became exposed to left-wing faculty or visiting speakers such as J. Robert Oppenheimer, whom she described, in a burst of anti-Semitic language, as a "limp, elegant Jew." Along with the corruption of subversive ideas, Emery described another threat: how male students might be converted to homosexuality. Swayed by Chapel Hill's Franklin Street beer joints and the "seductive message of the disaffiliates," the young male student became "a proper subject for the homosexuals waiting to solicit him." While UNC was infiltrated by Communists, she claimed that it was also a "notorious haven" for homosexuals, who were "particularly susceptible" to Communist ideology.[98]

Helms described *Blood on the Old Well* as "fascinating," and despite "a tendency to pooh-pooh her statements," he suggested that her assertions had some basis. In reality, however, Emery's charges about the university were exaggerations and entirely fictitious.[99] A Chapel Hill resident who described herself as a conservative said that Emery had a "habit of accusing various persons of all sort of perversion and injustice."[100] But conservative critics of Chapel Hill enabled Helms to use UNC as another symbol of institutionalized liberalism. In September 1962, Henry Royall's American Legion chapter adopted resolutions condemning left-wing subversion at Chapel Hill and calling for measures to regulate the academic environment there. Warning of the "mortal danger" arising from the Communist threat, the Legion's resolutions charged that UNC tolerated left-wing activities, criticized recent appearances by visiting subversives, and maintained that UNC authorities had not properly denounced Junius Scales. The Legionnaires were especially aggrieved about the connections between Chapel Hill left-wingers and the brewing civil rights revolt that was sweeping through North Carolina in 1962–63. They were incensed that the UNC Progressive Labor Club—a Marxist-Leninist organization—had sponsored visiting civil rights speakers. The appearance of speakers defending Robert Williams made a lasting impression. Nearly three years after the event, Hoover Adams, Helms's old warhorse, asked why the principle of academic freedom should permit "two Negroes charged with kidnapping a white woman" to speak on the Chapel Hill campus.[101] Claiming that the Progressive Labor Club was "furthering the Communist cause," the Legion resolutions demanded that the North Carolina General Assembly investigate UNC subversion and propose "remedial legislation" so that "freedom loving North Carolinians may be saved from a possible academic Frankenstein."[102]

Helms worked in close coordination with Royall. As was often the case while he was a television editorialist, he exuded a spirit of conspiracy and secrecy. He nurtured a network of contacts, even as he assured that his participation in this network would be out of public view. In October 1962, Jesse asked for Royall's help in producing a sixty-minute documentary about Chapel Hill Communists: although Jesse wanted others to help with research, he asked that Royall keep Helms's involvement in "absolute confidence." After completing the documentary, he continued attacks on the university.[103] In January 1963, Royall delivered the Legion's resolutions to the legislature, and Helms sent an encouraging note saying that he hoped that "our combined efforts will bear fruit." Royall, meanwhile, obtained information from HUAC that he shared with Helms about supporters of Junius Scales.[104]

Endorsing the Legion's resolutions, Helms incorporated them into a general critique of university liberalism. Many North Carolinians, Helms said, perceived UNC as a spawning ground for Communists, and he thus saw nothing wrong with the Legion's call for a legislative investigation.[105] UNC liberals, he said, had "unknowingly and unwittingly and foolishly" aided Communism. Although "all of the known, card-carrying Communists in Chapel Hill could meet comfortably in a broom closet," Jesse charged that campus left-wingers advocated expanded federal power, governmental centralization, and a "downgrading of capitalism and free enterprise."[106] Helms's editorials fueled a mounting anti-UNC political backlash and a widespread perception among the state political leadership that white university liberals were encouraging the African American revolt. Jesse's *Viewpoints* cemented anti-Communism, segregationism, and anti-university sentiment, and he continued to criticize the presence of campus New Left groups. In December 1962, he objected to a concert by folk singer Pete Seeger, whom Jesse described as a "known Communist," and a visit to campus by Progressive Labor national chair Milt Rosen. Both were sponsored by UNC's New Left Club. The UNC campus was "plagued ... by the activities of the extreme left," Helms told viewers, and developments there demonstrated how academic freedom had reached a "stomach-turning point."[107] In an early April 1963 *Viewpoint,* he asserted that the Legion's resolutions "never got very far beyond first base" in the legislature because UNC administrators had "quickly and rather summarily shushed up" the issue. Questions about UNC subversion "ought to be cleared up—or the University cleaned up," he said, and it was now up to legislators to take the lead. The reality was that Communists wanted to impose their ideology by force, and where that was impossible, they sought to undermine freedom through subversion, espionage, and "poisoning the intellectual climate and the educational system." American campuses were susceptible to infiltration, and foreign enemies realized this, Helms alleged. UNC administrators had ignored the Legionnaires' resolutions; their concerns deserved better.[108]

Bubbling beneath the surface in the anti-UNC dialogue of 1962–63 were white anxieties about the African American freedom struggle, which by June 1963 had erupted into a full-scale revolt in urban North Carolina. Raleigh experienced daily demonstrations while the legislature sat in session, and angry legislators blamed Chapel Hill liberals. Helms was only too happy to reaffirm the connection between liberalism, subversion, and the civil rights revolt. He privately wrote friends that he knew UNC professors who participated in civil rights demonstrations, though this McCarthyite "list" never materialized.[109] "When you start unraveling the threads of discord in this unhappy era, you run across some rather startling coincidences," he announced in a *Viewpoint* on June 14, 1963. Many white UNC faculty actively promoted protests, he claimed; many also participated in subversive activities, including efforts to abolish HUAC and support for the international, anti-nuclear "Ban-the-Bomb" movement. According to Jesse, these UNC liberals were the same people who had pressed for the release of Junius Scales, and they hated American immigration legislation that limited foreigners entering the country. Liberals favored increased taxation and spending by government and a larger federal government, while they had little concern about the mounting national debt. The United Nations was their "dream world." Pull one thread in the "torn fabric of the structure of America," and the thread crisscrossed "from one stormy issue to another." Was this part of some larger plan, Jesse asked, or was this "one weird, monstrous coincidence?" UNC subversion was another thread that should be "unraveled carefully and objectively to see what's at the other end."[110]

Helms was more explicit in his message to the legislature in a June 21 *Viewpoint.* He cited the example of Ohio State University, where President N. G. Fawcett had banned alleged Communists from speaking on campus. When faculty and students sued in federal court, Ohio legislators enacted a law forbidding Communists from speaking at any state-supported campus.

In Ohio, Helms told viewers, the legislature did not "pussy-foot with issues." There was real danger here, he argued, and North Carolina legislators should not assume that college students heard these speeches "merely out of curiosity." The university, he claimed, was tolerating and to an extent even lending support to subversion. Fawcett might lose his case in court, but at least the Ohio legislature supported him—something that might give the people of Ohio "some comfort" and provide a "lesson for the rest of us who have been too timid, or too disinterested, or both to take a stand."[111]

With Helms's active encouragement, on June 25, 1963, the North Carolina Speaker Ban law was rushed through on the legislature's last day of its session. The law prohibited speakers at North Carolina's public colleges and universities who were "known" members of the Communist Party, who had advocated the overthrow of the constitution of North Carolina or of the United States, or who had pled the Fifth Amendment about questions regarding Communist subversion. The Speaker Ban's sponsors were obviously inspired by Helms's attacks: state representative Ned Delamar of eastern North Carolina's Pamlico County persuaded Secretary of State Thad Eure to obtain a copy of the Ohio bill mentioned in Helms's June 21 editorial, and the Speaker Ban sponsors used it as a model. Although there is no evidence that Helms directly participated in the writing of the law, his television editorials successfully connected UNC liberalism with both the civil rights revolt and campus subversion, and provided a basis for legislative intervention. Attacking UNC was a centerpiece in Helms's larger attack on liberalism and its North Carolina supporters, and it exposed what he claimed were its connections with social disorder. Helms quickly found that his attacks on UNC, which were either exaggerations or untrue, were politically popular, for they fed on common anti-intellectual and anti-liberal suspicions that had always existed in the state.[112]

While newspaper editorialists and UNC supporters condemned the Speaker Ban, Helms in a *Viewpoint* on July 1, 1963, praised the law as "a firm blow for freedom." Helms maintained that the Speaker Ban reflected a reasonable response to Communist subversion on campuses, which, he claimed, the FBI and congressional investigators had documented. There was no reason why a forum should be provided to Communists any more than one should be provided to rapists and murderers.[113] Rather than being pushed by legislative sleight of hand, Helms said in November 1963, the Speaker Ban was democracy in action. In the months following the law's passage, Helms used the airwaves to ridicule Speaker Ban opponents. He dismissed its detractors as worms "on a hot brick" who were hurling "epithets at those who had passed the law." As defenders of Communism, UNC liberals were painting themselves into a corner. The main issue, Helms said, was not free speech: no one would argue that "thieves, murderers and vice lords ought to be furnished a respectable forum on our campuses."[114] The law simply reflected the need for academic responsibility to accompany academic freedom. UNC had already received due warning about subversion; these warnings were ignored, and the university's own "laxity and poor judgment" had led to the law's enactment.[115] The "two-word catechisms of 'academic freedom' and 'civil rights'" were, he thought, meaningless: academic freedom had "little to do with freedom," while the "rights we hear so much about are not very civil."[116]

In defense of the law, Helms emphasized the distance that had grown between public opinion and Chapel Hill liberals. He hoped that UNC supporters would make the Speaker Ban into a political issue, as he wrote, because they would experience a "jolt when they get a reading on the attitude of the people."[117] UNC trustees, faculty, and administrators had become "insensitive to the feelings of the people of this state," he said, and they ignored objections to the use of publicly supported facilities for "propaganda purposes." If UNC had properly regulated itself, legislative intervention would have been unnecessary.[118] For Helms, the Speaker Ban issue—whatever its outcome—was a political windfall. Still, as with so many of Helms's battles, the war with UNC was mostly rhetorical, and he remained skeptical about the Speaker Ban's effectiveness. In December 1963 he wrote to conservative columnist James J. Kilpatrick that the controversy was "largely humorous." "I would like to see the darned thing repealed," he wrote, because the law created "no penalty for disobedience." Whether he actually believed what he wrote is debatable; Helms's letter was probably tailored to Kilpatrick, who as a civil libertarian told him that he regarded the Speaker Ban as an unconstitutional limit on free speech.[119]

What was important for Helms was that he and his legislative allies kept UNC in a bind. Realizing that public opinion had rallied against the university, as he explained to a fellow conservative, he could "label the whole affair as a battle between the professors and the people."[120] Even UNC supporters realized that repeal became politically impossible soon after the Speaker Ban's passage, and during 1964 and 1965, opponents wanted modification of the law. Should they attempt repeal, UNC supporters would be "in for a surprise," Helms said in a *Viewpoint* in December 1964. All the Democratic gubernatorial candidates in 1964—I. Beverly Lake, Dan Moore, and Richardson Preyer—favored the law, and any attempt to repeal it would amount to a "breach of faith." What was needed instead, Helms declared, was a "housecleaning...throughout our university system" that the legislature did not "have the guts nor the leadership to undertake" when they originally passed the Speaker Ban.[121]

He had great hopes for Dan Moore, who he thought belonged to Willis Smith's conservative political tradition and who was elected governor in 1964. Acquainted with governors for many years, Jesse wrote Moore, he had "never felt as comfortable with any of the rest of them in office as I do with you."[122] But Moore would soon prove disappointing. Only months into office, the governor faced a crisis when the Southern Association of Colleges and Schools (SACS) informed UNC officials in the spring of 1965 that the Speaker Ban imperiled the university's accreditation.[123] Moore's response—to organize a special legislative commission chaired by Representative David M. Britt to study the Speaker Ban law in light of the SACS accreditation threat—immediately raised doubts in Helms's mind. After the commission was appointed, he complained that it was "stacked" against the law with UNC supporters.[124] While the Britt Commission deliberated during August and September 1965, Jesse continued to express reservations. Was higher education "travelling a one-way street in North Carolina?" he asked in a *Viewpoint* on September 2, 1965. Was "political liberalism always right, to hear the professors tell it, and political conservatism always wrong?"[125] The "crux of the matter," he declared a few days later, was the "difference between academic freedom and academic responsibility."[126] The commission, issuing its report in September 1965, recommended that the legislature amend the law and return oversight of speakers to university authorities, and a special session of the legislature enacted these changes into law in October. Outraged, Helms voiced his disappointment. In a November 1965 *Viewpoint*, he called the revision of the Speaker Ban law as reflecting a "curious judgment" by Moore, who, he thought, was "carrying water for a Trojan Horse that had galloped into their stable." The legislature's decision, he believed, was no victory for the governor. In effect, the Speaker Ban law had been repealed. Moore, he complained, should "take care, lest he stumble over some of his own rose petals."[127]

What ended the Speaker Ban was not these legislative revisions but a student movement that tested the amended Speaker Ban system, which maintained a ban over subversive speakers but required that UNC administrators police campus speakers. Nationwide, the Students for a Democratic Society (SDS) became, after its founding in 1962, the most important student radical organization. At Chapel Hill, SDS leaders invited two controversial speakers, historian and Communist Party member Herbert Aptheker and anti-HUAC activist Frank Wilkinson, who had taken the

Fifth Amendment in congressional testimony. After a tumultuous trustees meeting in early February 1966, UNC administrators banned the two speakers, but the students hosted the talks off campus anyway. Students, including mainstream campus leaders, initiated a legal challenge to the law. Their efforts culminated in February 1968, when a federal court struck down the Speaker Ban law as an unconstitutional violation of the First Amendment. For Helms, the anti–Speaker Ban student movement at UNC reflected essentially the "same crowd and the same tactics" that had overrun the University of California at Berkeley during the Free Speech Movement in 1964. He condemned Carolina student activists whose actions, he thought, threatened to "produce another Berkeley, this time in North Carolina."[128] A "small group of asinine students" had arrogantly invited Aptheker and Wilkinson; "such a motley outfit" as the SDS should not be intimidating.[129] Although "stout hearts" were needed, Jesse found "not very much stoutness" in the UNC board of trustees, which served, he believed, mostly as "a social organization to rubberstamp the slightest whim of the University administrators."[130]

What had happened at Berkeley in its Free Speech Movement was instructive: there, a relatively small group of students was manipulated by a larger, worldwide Communist conspiracy that was "too clear, and too consistent, for it to be mistaken by other than simpletons." A group of "student misfits" struck at the "jugular vein of the nation," but they were "ready-made instruments to be used by forces which seek to undermine and destroy our nation and all it stands for." UNC authorities should "deal sternly with those students and faculty members who insist upon playing trick-or-treat with constituted authority." The SDS had led a "pipsqueak rebellion" whose participants would "do well to skip a protest meeting in favor of a trip to the barbershop." Helms also noted that student body president Paul Dickson, who played a leading role in the anti–Speaker Ban movement, was nearly expelled after spending the night with a female student at his fraternity house. According to UNC's "curious standards of morality," Dickson was slapped on the wrist, while the female student was sent home. Although he should have been turned over to his parents "for a spanking," Dickson remained on campus "to inflict upon us his asinine declarations of philosophy." University leaders, Jesse believed, were asleep at the switch.[131]

Nine months after the federal court's decision invalidated the Speaker Ban, in November 1968, SNCC head and Black Power advocate Stokely Carmichael visited UNC. In a television editorial, Helms described him as a "highly-publicized advocate of violence" whose visit to UNC demonstrated how university leaders who had "loudly condemned" the Speaker

Ban had failed in their responsibilities. Although UNC leaders claimed that Carmichael's visit amounted to little, some five thousand people cheered him with a standing ovation. His appearance at Chapel Hill demonstrated the Speaker Ban's tangled history. In 1965, the legislature had unnecessarily diluted the original Speaker Ban law, in Helms's opinion; the state's political leadership surrendered to pressure from a "gaggle of leftwing editors and educators." Overturning the Speaker Ban in 1968, a federal court had simply set aside the law's "tattered remnants." Now it had become possible for "anybody—no matter how violent, or crude, or treasonous—to make free use of facilities created and maintained by the taxpayers of this state." A new chapter, he believed, had unfolded in the disintegration of the liberal university campus.[132]

IN OCTOBER 1966, six months after the UNC student revolt about the Speaker Ban ended, Helms was at the center of another furor on the Chapel Hill campus. On the afternoon of October 17, WRAL ran a report claiming that a UNC instructor had assigned his students to write a paper on seduction using seventeenth-century English poet Andrew Marvell's poem "To His Coy Mistress." The instructor of the class, Michael Paull, a modest, unassuming graduate student from Detroit, suddenly came under intense media scrutiny. Supposedly receiving a complaint from a student who was offended by the poem, WRAL reached UNC administrators with the story the previous Friday, October 14. Chancellor J. Carlyle Sitterson, returning from an out-of-town weekend, on Monday, October 17, declined comment, saying he needed to investigate. In Sitterson's absence, UNC provost Hugh Holman had convened an ad hoc committee composed of Holman, the dean of arts and sciences, and the English Department chairman. They read the student papers in the class and determined that the contents of some were "vulgar." Conferring with Paull, they informed him that they were recommending his reassignment. Returning to campus on Tuesday, October 18, Sitterson accepted this recommendation after conferring with his advisory committee. He then informed the press that he was removing Paull from the classroom and reassigning him to nonteaching duties. Although Sitterson described "To His Coy Mistress" as a poem that was "widely anthologized and almost universally praised," he concluded that a "normal teacher-student learning relationship" had been disrupted and that Paull's reassignment was in UNC's best interests.[133]

Twenty-four years old in October 1966, Michael Paull had received his BA from the University of Michigan and his MA from Cornell, and had

arrived at Carolina a year earlier on a prestigious Woodrow Wilson graduate fellowship. Described by the *Greensboro Daily News* as "soft spoken," Paull
was shocked by the accusation of classroom impropriety. He had assigned a
routine English composition paper that was based on Marvell's poem, and
some of the students had misunderstood both the assignment and Marvell's
poem.[134] Students backed up his version; two days after his suspension, all
the students in Paull's class petitioned to Sittterson to reinstate him. Contrary to WRAL's news account, Paull asked students to write a paper—as
required by the course syllabus—describing six elements of style in "Coy
Mistress." Paull, according to his students, did not assign a paper on seduction. Disagreeing with Sitterson's conclusion that the teacher-student relationship had been disrupted, the students uanimously demanded Paull's
return to the classroom.[135]

The "Coy Mistress" affair became yet another manifestation of Helms's
anti-UNC campaign. His immediate quarry was not "To His Coy Mistress" but the fall issue of the UNC literary magazine, the *Carolina Quarterly,* which Paull edited. It contained a short story about a love affair in an
ice house, a subject that is tame by today's standards but that Helms
considered obscene. Writing to UNC president Bill Friday on October 3,
1966, Helms relayed a parent's complaint that the *Carolina Quarterly* had
become required reading in some freshman English classes. Helms agreed
with the parent's assessment. Although obscenity had become commonplace, Jesse feared that there was a "trend towards decadence rather than
towards creative art forms." On October 13, Helms broadcast a *Viewpoint*
criticizing the publication of the *Carolina Quarterly.* Helms intended to use
the *Quarterly* as an example of UNC's loose moral standards, but the eruption of publicity associated with "Coy Mistress" soon overshadowed the
issue.[136]

What was known as the "Coy Mistress" case soon became a national
sensation. As what the *Charlotte Observer* called the "more-or-less guardian
of the morals of the Coastal Plains, the Sandhills and a minor part of the
Piedmont,"[137] Helms had pounced on Paull, a victim of his all-out war
against UNC. Mortified by UNC administrators' ready willingness to offer
him as a sacrificial lamb, Paull subsequently described his "great disappointment" in Holman, a noted literary scholar. Soon after the news broke,
Anne Queen, the longtime head of the campus Y and a friend, telephoned
Paull; they knew each other because Paull had been involved with Upward
Bound, a program for low-income high school students, and he continued
to be involved in Chapel Hill. Queen advised him to speak with UNC law
professor Dan Pollitt for help, and they met for dinner at the Ratskeller, a

local haunt on Franklin Street, across from the campus. A noted free speech lawyer and president of the campus American Association of University Professors, Pollitt immediately took charge. Recognizing that Paull's plight was primarily a matter of public relations, he did not pursue a legal strategy. Instead, he instructed Paull to get a haircut and abandon his contact lenses for glasses in order to appear more professorial. He further advised him to be agreeable and not bitter. Soon, reports appeared in the *New York Times, Life* magazine, and CBS television news documenting the affair; the *Life* story appeared because its editor was a "boyhood chum" of Pollitt's. Meanwhile, the media circus consumed Paull. He was, in his words, "swept along in a celebrity that I never quite understood," as local notables embraced his cause, and he was invited to the homes of literary luminaries such as novelist Reynolds Price. The Canadian Broadcasting Corporation even telephoned to ask about his ten favorite poems. Paull felt unequipped to deal with the explosion of publicity, and he simply wanted all of this to "go away."[138]

In a difficult position, Sitterson was sensitive to any political attacks in the Speaker Ban's aftermath. He had acted hastily to head off Helms, hoping to avoid negative publicity. As he later wrote to Helms, matters such as the Paull case could be handled "more calmly and more thoughtfully" if they stayed out of the newspapers.[139] The UNC chancellor could do little that would satisfy Jesse. Meanwhile, Sitterson faced the same student groups that had mobilized behind the Speaker Ban issue during the previous spring. The SDS chapter took up Paull's cause, as did the Committee for Free Inquiry, the broad-based student group that had led the anti–Speaker Ban movement. Fellow graduate students and younger faculty were poised to conduct a pro-Paull sympathy strike. In the campus community, Sitterson was seen as acquiescing to Helms. In a biting editorial appearing on October 20, 1966, entitled "Who's Afraid of Jesse Helms? The University— That's Who," the UNC student newspaper, the *Daily Tar Heel,* declared that the Paull case had become "a monumental tribute" to Helms and his anti-UNC campaign. For a teacher, there was nothing more humiliating than to be removed from the classroom, while there was no greater threat to the faculty to see this occur unjustly. The *Daily Tar Heel* editors had resigned themselves to accepting Jesse as "one of the unavoidable evils in our society." Why, asked the editors, had this "rasping tongue" proved "so powerful as to cut through the respected walls that protect academic freedom from an often misunderstanding citizenry?"[140]

Other editorialists spoke out in Paull's defense. In the *Greensboro Daily News,* editorialist Edwin Yoder (himself a former *Daily Tar Heel* editor) described Sitterson's decision to reassign Paull as a response to a "bully television pundit" and a television station that devoted itself to "poisonous innuendoes against the university." Only "minimal literacy" would reveal that "To His Coy Mistress" was about mortality, not seduction. "Let WRAL-TV's guardians of public morality," advised Yoder, "devote themselves to their proper business; and let the English departments instruct students in literature and writing—even at the price of disclosing to their sheltered students that literature is about life."[141] If there was any seduction "in this bizarre bit of emotional inflation," said the *Raleigh News and Observer,* "the class and the system of free inquiry seem to be the seductees."[142] The *Southern Pines Pilot* described a "coyness" that existed "all over the place"— in the poem, in the "incredibly prissy coyness" of whoever had relayed the story to WRAL, and in the "unexpectedly coy" Sitterson. Students and faculty objecting to Paull's treatment were not coy, the *Pilot* thought, and they provided the "first solid, meaningful words spoken in the matter." "Have a good laugh, Andrew," the editorial concluded, "wherever you are."[143]

Sitterson faced pressure from all sides: from angry students who regarded him as having no backbone in confronting Helms and from graduate instructors whose words were "laced with outrage." On October 21, one student group even picketed South Building, which housed UNC's administration, with a sign that read: "Jesse Helms for Chancellor: Eliminate the Middle Man." As one angry UNC supporter wrote Sitterson, he had surrendered to WRAL, which opposed "this university and what it stands for." Stuck in an untenable position, Sitterson reversed course. Instructing the English Department to investigate the matter fully and "clarify and amplify" his original ruling on the case, he announced that the determination of Paull's status belonged with the department.[144] Sitterson's handoff of the Paull case did not solve his problems immediately. The next day, the *New York Times* published a report describing how WRAL—which it described as a Raleigh television station "with right-wing views that has been a frequent critic of liberalism at the university"—had brought on a furor on the Chapel Hill campus.[145] While Paull went into seclusion, moreover, CBS News and *Life* both prepared stories.[146]

The criticisms of liberal editorialists only encouraged Jesse. In a *Viewpoint* airing on October 25, he reviewed the case. In this "fuzzy, superficial world of misguided academic freedom," all the world was "mostly a stage" and a "good many of the people" were actors. Then he connected the *Carolina Quarterly* and the "Coy Mistress" cases. Noting that Paull, as the *Carolina Quarterly*'s editor, had permitted the publication of a "bit of fiction which spells out details of a sordid bit of fornication on a 100-pound block of ice," he said that the university should not defend Paull on the basis of academic freedom. Sitterson, Helms believed, should abide by the original decision to remove Paull from the classroom.[147] Despite abundant evidence to the contrary, he continued to believe in Paull's culpability. There was little question about what had occurred in his classroom, Helms told a friend on November 1. A "great cover-up" existed in which the news media was trying to "alibi and excuse the young instructor."[148]

Helms stubbornly stuck with a version of events that for many years he would continue to defend. In another *Viewpoint* on November 3, he again asserted that Paull had assigned a paper about seduction. Seventeen of eighteen class papers, he claimed with no basis whatsoever, concerned the subject of how to seduce a girl, and the eighteenth was a girl who refused to turn in a paper. Once again, he denounced attempts to make Paull's case into a matter of academic freedom. Subsequent investigation would prove that Helms's assertions were completely unfounded: only two of the papers concerned seduction, and these were papers that Paull never read because of his insistence that the students immediately rewrite them. The students who participated in a "juvenile protest meeting" supporting Paull, Helms said, were a small minority—despite the existence of a petition signed by all the students in the class. In Helms's version, Paull's student supporters were composed of a "few bearded, stringy-haired students who scrawled some words on placards and began to picket their chancellor." The "left-wing press" had "moved in"—CBS News, *Life* magazine, and the *New York Times,* along with the state newspaper press—and transformed Paull into a hero with various "concoctions, distortions, misrepresentations, alibis and excuses." Their approach was to "vindicate the instructor and intimidate any student suspected of having blown the whistle on what had been happening in the classroom." "To heck with the facts," he continued, "gut the chancellor, if necessary, and whenever possible—attack the television station that dared to report the incident in the first place."[149]

On November 10, the five-man English Department committee that reviewed the "Coy Mistress" case released its report with what one commentator called "all the solemnity of a royal commission."[150] The report cleared Paull of any misdeeds. After speaking to him and all nineteen students individually and reading the original papers and their revised copies, they concluded that Paull had abided by English 1's general syllabus. The paper assigned toward the end of class on October 11 was in no sense about seduction. Male students were not asked "to tell how to seduce girls"; female students were not "assigned to tell how either to seduce or to resist seduction." Indeed, the students and Paull both denied that there was any assignment that required students to "write on how to seduce anybody." Paull asked students, instead, to write a paper about "To His Coy Mistress" that explained Marvell's imagery and six figures of speech in the poem.

The committee then provided its version of events. Paull gave out the paper assignment hurriedly, at the end of the October 11 class, and it was not well understood by the students. Several began asking questions. One complained that the subject was vague, while another asked if he could write about seduction. Paull apparently responded: "You might call it that. If you want to write on seduction, go ahead." When another male student asked if he wanted "us to give away our best lines," Paull responded, "You could put it that way." A female student then asked: "Where does that leave us? What if you are a girl and don't have a coy mistress?" "Pretend that you are a boy," Paull responded. No single student remembered all of these conversations, but most agreed that Paull was being "playful" in his responses. When the class resumed on October 15—Paull had canceled the scheduled class on October 13 due to illness—he decided to have students read their papers. Paull read the first two: these were "playful treatments" about youthful love, but they said nothing about seduction. A third paper, by a female student, also said nothing about seduction. When called on, a male student warned Paull that his paper's language "might be a little rough." Paull told him to proceed, but to use his judgment. The boy's story contained a word in its last sentence that the committee regarded as "language that would make one uncomfortable in a mixed group." The offending language appeared to have been the word "ass," along with the student's use of "laid" as a pun on the word "made." But even in this essay there was no reference to seduction. Taken aback, Paull said: "Is anybody embarassed? Well, I am." Paull then returned the papers to the students and asked them to revise them if their language was too blunt, or if they had failed to consider the main assignment about figures of speech. Those students who had written about seduction were required to rewrite their papers. Although there were two papers that did consider the subject of seduction, Paull never saw them.

Much of the difficulty in "this whole lamentable affair," the committee believed, resulted from the conflation of the *Carolina Quarterly* controversy with Paull's class. In late September, a parent had complained about the *Quarterly* to Governor Moore; he turned the complaint over to President Bill Friday, who, in turn, gave it to Provost Hugh Holman on October 14—the same day that word reached Chapel Hill about an upcoming WRAL story about a teacher requiring a paper about seduction. The director of freshman English questioned Paull that Friday, and once WRAL identified him as the "Coy Mistress" teacher, he was critically interrogated. But "what sounded to early investigators like hard information," the report read, "was sometimes erroneous." In the end, the review committee found that Paull had been truthful and candid in his answers, that he should be completely exonerated, and that he should be returned to the classroom. The same day, November 10, the English Department and Sitterson fully accepted the committee's recommendations. Michael Paull came back to the course "in triumph." Interestingly, the person who had substituted for Paull in the classroom, then a lowly graduate student, was Doris Betts, who later became an acclaimed novelist on the Chapel Hill faculty. Subsequently, Pollitt led a successful effort to provide regular appointments—with legal protections and greater security—for graduate students teaching in UNC classrooms.[151]

Helms's conservatism would later embrace public uncertainties about sexuality more fully: for now, this marked only an initial foray, joining fears of subversion on campus with anxieties about loose morals among young people. During the Speaker Ban controversy, he had suggested that campus protesters were also sexually immoral: in the fall of 1965, Helms had reported that student body president Paul Dickson had been caught with a female student in his fraternity house. Privately, Helms chided Dickson's father, who edited the *Raeford News-Journal*, that no one could "tell those Dicksons anything about seduction!"[152] Later, in the "Coy Mistress" affair, Jesse engaged in a highly publicized struggle over the atmosphere of sexual permissiveness that, he argued, prevailed on college campuses. Just as university faculty were leading students into questionable left-wing politics, Helms suggested, they were also encouraging the new immorality that seemed to be sweeping college campuses. His larger point, to be sure, hit home with his television audience, and the issue of sexuality would, in the coming years, occupy much of Helms's message. And the case created publicity—for the first time in his career—on the national scene. A day after the appearance of the review committee's report, on November 11, *Life* magazine published a cover story about the "Coy Mistress" case, describing Helms as an "ultraconservative who thinks academic freedom has gone too far."[153]

But Michael Paull was the real victim of Helms's anti-UNC campaign. Unsuccessful in making the *Carolina Quarterly* into the subject of controversy, the "Coy Mistress" affair at best was a case of excessive exaggeration and, at worst, a case of character assassination. In either event, Michael Paull was an innocent bystander who was dragged into an emerging cultural war, in what can only be described as an unjust slander. Paull was humiliated by his suspension and removal from the classroom, according to a friend of his, and things were never quite the same. Indeed, he decided to pursue a career in continuing education because of his bitter experience in the classroom. In nearly twenty years of conservative journalism, the "Coy Mistress" case became the first instance in which Helms played such a role in a controversy with human consequences.[154]

Paull was profoundly disappointed by the failure of his academic mentors to protect him. Elder UNC academic statesmen such as Hugh Holman were "people who I had always really respected and really aspired to be." Sadly, for a variety of reasons beyond his control, Paull remained undefended by UNC administrators until the damage had been done. The university's actions reflected "no credit on an administration admittedly gun-shy after numerous unfounded Communist allegations and other moves by detractors through the years," concluded the *Durham Morning Herald*.[155] In another biting Yoder editorial, the *Greensboro Daily News* blamed Helms's attack machine. The committee report was "far more tolerant of the serious injustice done Mr. Paull, and far more cautious about the larger issues of the case, than strict patience requires." Yoder contrasted the committee report's "quiet, temperate language" to WRAL's "university-baiting" attack, which charged him "with making an assignment he did not make" and "embroidered its inaccurate reporting with a tasteless personal attack." Yoder believed that Helms and WRAL owed Paull "an apology and a retraction."[156] This was not the first time that Helms had "shot from the hip and I dare say it won't be the last," wrote *Fayetteville Observer* columnist Gibson Prather, but he urged UNC administrators to defend the "young English instructor who was almost crucified, even though innocent."[157]

Despite overwhelming evidence to the contrary, Helms remained convinced of his version of events. On November 11, 1966, he denounced the review committee's report as a "miserable whitewash." "So Michael Paull goes back to the classroom," he said. "What a victory for 'academic freedom'! What testimony to the backbone, or perhaps lack of it, among administrators at Chapel Hill."[158] Rather than dealing with the truth of the charges and innuendo against Paull, Helms returned to the familiar theme of how a liberal media had distorted his case. In his fifth and final *Viewpoint* on the case, which aired on November 14, 1966, Helms reasserted how the *Carolina Quarterly* had published obscene fiction, how a parent had complained that she had never seen "such trash" in her home. For bringing the matter to public attention, Jesse and WRAL were tarred with being "right wing." Let the mainstream media "put up or shut up," he declared, daring them to publish the *Carolina Quarterly*'s story. If this was "fit study material for freshman students at Chapel Hill, then it certainly ought to be fit to grace the pages of our 'liberal' newspapers."[159]

Fourteen years later, in late July 1980, the "Coy Mistress" affair again surfaced. As Republicans were nominating Ronald Reagan as their presidential candidate in their convention in Detroit, Ed Yoder, now a columnist for the *Washington Star,* wrote a piece about the Religious Right's dominance of the party platform. Describing Helms as a "flaming Savonarola of the GOP," Yoder recalled his days as a "video prophet" and his attempts to obtain Paull's dismissal. Helms responded to Yoder's column vehemently, describing his characterization of the Michael Paull affair as a "falsehood" that exposed his journalism. Offering to contribute $100 to Yoder's church if his column was accurate—and challenging Yoder to contribute $100 to Helms's church if it was not—Jesse asserted that the "young instructor" was "obsessed with discussing the clinical aspects of sexual intercourse in at least one of his classes which contained both young men and women, mostly freshmen." Paull assigned a paper on the topic of "How to Seduce a Girl," according to Helms, and "enjoyed the discomfiture of the young women" in his class. Parents of three different students complained, Jesse said, and WRAL reporters obtained affidavits from each, and the "similarity of the accounts given by these people was persuasive that the reports were probably authentic." Helms claimed that he called Bill Friday, that two of the parents visited with Chancellor Sitterson, and that following these visits Sitterson ordered Paull's suspension, and his contract was not renewed. What Helms called the "Andrew Marvell fantasy" was later invented as an explanation embraced by the North Carolina liberal press, which did not bother "even to attempt to get the full story." Marvell's poem was not mentioned on WRAL until Paull offered his "absurd defense."[160]

Yet Helms's recollection of the "Coy Mistress" episode runs contrary to the evidence. All parties agreed that Paull did *not* assign a paper on seduction; all of the students interviewed testify to that fact. Paull, personally modest and unassuming, took no special delight in embarrassing the young women in his class, and he was embarrassed by the students' off-color discussion. There is no evidence in Helms's own files that three parents complained, no evidence whatsoever of affidavits taken from the three students, and if such affidavits existed, they were never provided to UNC authorities. Nor is it likely that Sitterson ever met with these parents: such a meeting was never mentioned anywhere in any account, or anywhere in Sitterson's papers. Sitterson did not order Paull's suspension, but instead reassigned him—a minor but important distinction—while Paull's contract was certainly renewed.

Nowhere in Helms's account does he seem to realize that Paull was a graduate student. If there was a fantasy, in short, it is in Helms's rather curious version of the chain of events.

The "Coy Mistress" case marked a significant departure in Helms's career as a television journalist. Using the *Viewpoints* as a political tool to mobilize public opinion against liberalism, the episode provided an opportunity to explore Helms's belief that a subversive college environment was also an immoral environment. Linking a politics of anti-Communism to a politics of morality, Helms explored new questions that the sexual revolution raised—and succeeded in linking sexual immorality with the permissive qualities of liberalism. The strategy worked, for it carried a strong appeal to his constituency. But Helms had also crossed a line. The "Coy Mistress" affair, in distorting and manipulating the truth with abandon, engaged Helms in a politics of character assassination.

Chapter 3

BLACK IS WHITE, AND WRONG IS RIGHT

Backlash Politics

By the mid-1960s, Helms had become North Carolina's leading conservative voice. His *Viewpoint* editorials reached perhaps a million viewers in the eastern half of the state, and his daily barrage defined issues in a way that polarized opinion and challenged the state's media establishment. While rallying his audience around a new conservatism that rejected interventionist government, resisted integration, ridiculed student protesters and campus revolt, and opposed changes in morality and sexuality, Jesse also enraged opponents. Helms's polarizing style fit well into the highly charged environment of the 1960s, as the liberal consensus that had dominated national politics since the New Deal began to unravel. At home, the civil rights revolution stalled as the movement's coherence dissipated into infighting, the revolt turned violent in cities, and racial fears grew among whites. Jesse Helms came to articulate a growing national backlash against liberalism, and he rode this backlash to a new position of prominence.

ONE OF THE contradictions in Helms's life was how his fierce combativeness toward his enemies contrasted with his affection toward members of his family and immediate circle of friends. There were at least two sides to Helms: the tough, hard-hitting fighter and the soft, avuncular patron, the mean Jesse and the nice Jesse. Most were familiar only with the latter and had little knowledge of the former. Helms's stridency contrasted with his "personal demeanor," journalist Ferrell Guillory would later write, and Jesse was a "man of almost impeccable personal manners." Describing himself as "plain as an old shoe," he did not belong to a country club, preferred the company of ordinary folk, refused alcohol, led a subdued social life, and only occasionally watched movies. Although avidly interested in ideas that he could use in his television broadcasts, Helms rarely read fiction. With few hobbies, Helms devoted all of his time to work and family.[1] An interviewer for the conservative magazine *Human Events* called him the "soul of Southern courtesy" whose chief concern was to make people comfortable. "He's the kindest human being I ever met," said one WRAL worker. "Whenever there was a problem of any kind, you could always get in to see Jesse." But the *Human Events* interviewer also noted that Helms was "nobody's pushover," and beneath his chivalrous exterior lay "fire and iron."[2] He was a loving father to daughters Jane and Nancy, both of whom went through high school and college in the 1960s. Though Jesse was a workaholic, the Helmses vacationed regularly and, by the late 1960s, constructed a vacation home at Lake Gaston, about an hour's drive north of Raleigh.[3]

Dot managed life at home, though she also provided personal—and sometimes political—ballast. As Helms told an interviewer in the mid-1980s, Dot was a "pretty wise lady who's a conservative."[4] The softer side of Helms's personal life emerged with the adoption of Charles Helms. In 1962, after reading a newspaper article about a nine-year-old Greensboro orphan struck with cerebral palsy who said that all he wanted for Christmas was a mother and father, Dot and Jesse arranged to meet him at the zoo. For a long time, since her own childhood, Dot had wanted to adopt. With a couple of teenage daughters, Jesse later recalled, "we figured this little boy deserved a chance." The entire family agreed.[5] Charles came to live with the Helmses as their adoptive son in June 1963. Passed over for adoption by others because of his condition, Charles was, as Jesse reported, a "joy to all of us."[6] Over the next few years, Helms doggedly pursued medical treatment for Charles, working closely with Lenox Baker of Duke Medical School and the North Carolina Cerebral Palsy Hospital. First approaching Baker in July 1963, Helms described Charles as "bright as a dollar, but his legs leave something to be desired." Dot and Jesse were immediately impressed with Baker; Jesse reported in August 1963 that he could "not recall Dorothy's ever having been so impressed with anyone as she was with you."[7] Baker promised a series of operations; Helms was hopeful that if this "very fine youngster" could "get his walking a little nearer normalcy," he could "grab the world by the tail."[8] The surgeries occurred in December 1963, October 1964, and July 1967, with some success in improving Charles's ability to walk.[9]

Helms and Baker became close friends, and Baker persuaded Jesse to serve on the board of the North Carolina Cerebral Palsy Hospital. Developing a close relationship with the older man, Helms described their friendship as "among the most meaningful experiences of my life."[10] They struck a bond that was as much political as personal: a vocal conservative, Baker regularly complained to Jesse about liberalism. In a typical comment in 1963, Baker denounced the "pussyfooting" North Carolina legislature, whose actions made Baker "want to throw up."[11] In national politics, he supported Arizona senator Barry Goldwater for president in 1964 and called Lyndon Johnson "that sanctimonious thieving s.o.b. from Texas."[12] Like Helms, Baker was a strong Speaker Ban supporter who believed that UNC had become a place where "off-beat, homosexual, bearded beatniks" dominated student life.[13] Both men also seemed to share common racial views: Helms agreed, for example, with Baker's suggestion that African Americans with a low IQ should be disenfranchised.[14]

IN THE 1960s, Jesse Helms was helping to create a new conservative politics. Since the late 1940s, he had stressed an anti-government ideology, and he subsequently added the themes of opposition to integration and the civil rights movement. But by the mid-1960s, with his attacks on the University of North Carolina, Helms articulated resentment—and a message of backlash—toward the civil rights revolution as the core of a political message that stressed the excesses of liberalism and the adverse consequences of change in social disintegration, disorder in family life, race relations, and crime. Helms presented his own version of reality, in which the African American freedom struggle had brought racial conflict rather than racial progress. How could one measure the cost of the "sullen though restrained hostility between the races," he said in August 1966, which had "gradually taken the place of what once was an atmosphere of understanding and affection?" What had become of the lost "sense of values" that once guided most Americans? When would Americans again respect government and its leaders "in what was once a government of laws instead of a government of men seeking the political support of pressure groups?"[15] In December 1964, Helms reviewed the chaotic developments of what he called a "year of daffy definitions," a time during which Americans clamored to "be persuaded that black is white, and ... wrong is right." Liberalism had produced an "incredible insanity" that had damaged the "posture of the nation" and the "stability of its people."[16]

At the core of Helms's message was race. In 1972, the *Raleigh News and*

Observer would call him "the most notable antagonist of Negro rights in the last 10 years in North Carolina."[17] Unreconciled to federal intervention in the Civil Rights and Voting Rights acts of 1964 and 1965, he continued to oppose the revolution in civil rights that occurred as a result of federal intervention. Civil rights protest, he believed, had spun out of control in the black urban uprisings that erupted for four summers after 1964. Urban violence seemed to confirm Helms's general assertions about the civil rights movement's disrespect for law and order and its abdication of "responsible" racial leadership. Too many African American leaders wanted "open and violent conflict with their white neighbors," he told viewers in April 1964.[18] Black people deserved a "right to pursue progress, and to strive for opportunity," but their leaders wrongly encouraged them to "misbehave and violate the law in demanding what they vaguely call 'freedom.'"[19] The civil rights revolution's main legacy, Helms suggested, was social disorder. Martin Luther King, Jr.'s, civil disobedience campaign had created a climate that encouraged "riots and anarchy in the streets in recent years." King was joined by white liberals, a "gaggle of preachers and professors" who joined in flouting the law, and these liberals had created a "condition in which the vicious and the irresponsible have gone to war with all society."[20] In Helms's world, legal and social order were disintegrating. The nation raced toward anarchy, he warned in June 1964: in their disrespect for the law, civil rights protesters enjoyed the tacit support of federal authorities.[21] When they took the law into their own hands, suddenly legal wrongs became civil rights, and the law was violated "deliberately and repeatedly."[22]

In the mid-1960s Helms sensed an atmospheric transformation that was gripping white America. The pendulum of public opinion, he told viewers in April 1965, had begun, "ever so slowly," to swing the other way.[23] Future Americans might conclude, Helms observed about the black uprisings, that "in the hot July of 1964 that the mood of America began to change." The first of a series of urban revolts occurred in New York City on July 18, 1964, when black Harlem residents, outraged by the shooting of a fifteen-year-old boy by a white policeman, rioted for two nights. For the rest of the 1960s, violence broke out in major cities across the country—in Los Angeles (1965), Chicago (1966), and Newark (1967)—in response to conditions of poverty, racism, and neglect. Helms regarded black violence through the lens of nervous whites, and he saw it as a telling reminder of the chaotic consequences of African American insurgency. Harlem's violence, he told viewers, had changed national attitudes toward race, which was no longer solely a problem of the white South's bigotry and discrimination. African American leaders had had an opportunity to win "a war of responsible citizenship," but they had failed. This was a "wretched day" for black leadership.[24] The Kerner Commission, which Lyndon Johnson appointed to examine the urban black rebellion, and which issued its findings in 1968, concluded that racism, embedded racial discrimination in housing and police treatment of black people, and poverty had led to "two societies, one black, one white—separate and unequal." These structural problems, the Kerner Commission concluded, were the main causes of black uprisings in northern cities. Not surprisingly, Jesse saw the report as yet another expression of the liberal analysis of race. The Kerner Commission's findings, he told viewers in March 1968, sounded like "nothing so much as a black power manifesto." Noting that nine of the commission's eleven members were pro–civil rights, Helms rejected the commission's main conclusion: that racism caused the black rebellion. Black Power advocates such as Rap Brown and Stokely Carmichael "could not have said it better," he declared. "It was, in short, all the white man's fault." When the second part of the commission's report appeared in July 1968, he described it as concluding that those who "pillage, burn and destroy" were not criminals but instead were acting out a form of social protest. This, Helms thought, was simply "insulting nonsense."[25]

HELMS OFTEN RAISED a double standard in racial politics in which blacks were treated one way, whites another, and which encouraged black leaders to ignore lawlessness and even Communist infiltration.[26] Helms pushed this double standard concept even further. Some viewers were outraged when he suggested in May 1966 that Klansmen in Lumberton, in eastern North Carolina, enjoyed as much right to march as did civil rights demonstrators. When North Carolina state government officials ran an anti-Klan campaign that year, Helms objected because, he said, it violated their constitutional rights.[27] He complained that the South was traveling on a "one-way street": black leaders could violate the law "or participate in mayhem," while whites were scolded for not doing enough.[28] Were racially based killings in Watts during the summer of 1964 any different than racially based killings by whites? What about a double standard in which black protesters camping out in Lafayette Square, across from the White House, remained unprosecuted for trespassing? "Do we believe in equality or not?," he asked in a May 1966 *Viewpoint*.[29]

The Civil Rights Act of 1964, which included new federal mandates for schools, stimulated new momentum toward desegregation. U.S. Commissioner of Education Harold Howe and the Department of Health, Education, and Welfare (HEW) pressured school boards in the South to develop "free-dom of choice" plans. Helms focused his opposition to school desegrega-tion to the federalization of educational policy. School integration, he told viewers in September 1966, fed a "federal octopus grown fat on human greed and political expedience and public indifference."[30] The NAACP pressed its case for even more stringent desegregation suits that led to a se-ries of Supreme Court decisions—including the *Swann v. Charlotte-Mecklenburg* decision (1971)—that required busing to achieve racial balance. Helms remained vociferously opposed to this "rolling tide of federal con-trols" that placed Washington "squarely" in charge. Accepting federal funds meant that decisions occurred only at the pleasure of Washington bureau-crats, he told WRAL viewers, and that local schools were forced to abide by "every jot and tittle of every federal regulation already in existence," along with "any and all future regulations dreamed up in Washington." Federal control also meant acceptance of desegregation plans that included crosstown busing, along with a racial balance of teachers and administrators that was approved in Washington and that fed a "constant chain of sworn reports." If local schools displeased "their masters in Washington," federal funds would be cut off.[31]

As school boards struggled with HEW administrators about accept-able school desegregation plans, Helms continued to criticize federal in-tervention. When HEW officials rejected the Raleigh school board's plan in April 1968, Helms denounced "federal tyranny." The Supreme Court, he complained, lacked any constitutional authority to empower "faceless bureaucrats" to make these decisions. Black parents, Jesse correctly pointed out, were unhappy with desegregation: in eastern North Carolina, in Franklin County in 1966 and in Hyde County in 1968, African Americans objected to desegregation plans closing black community schools. Black opposition to desegregation, he said, was a "dismaying jolt" to the Wash-ington bureaucracy. Federal officials had rejected local plans in "arrogant disregard of the rights of Negro students and their parents" because they had not "produced a degree of integration satisfactory to the bureaucrats."[32] Although school desegregation was advertised as a "great panacea" for blacks, Helms believed that they had become its chief victims.[33] After 1971, the Supreme Court's requirement of crosstown busing and massive relocations of students evoked Helms's strong opposition. In the summer of 1970, he warned of the chaos that busing would bring to public educa-tion. The path to desegregation, he asserted, had become a "long road of vascillation [sic] and tyranny."[34]

For Helms, U.S. Commissioner of Education Harold "Doc" Howe II

became a symbol of federal intervention. Howe joined the Johnson administration after the adoption of the Elementary and Secondary Education
Act of 1965, which infused federal funds and controls into the nation's public schools. Regarding Howe as the front man for HEW's freedom of choice
desegregation efforts, Helms derisively called him the "Commissioner of
Integration."[35] Howe wanted to centralize control of education, Helms
charged. Writing guidelines for the schools' freedom of choice plans, he
threatened to cut off federal funds if they were not followed.[36] Describing
Howe as a career bureaucrat, Helms charged that he engaged in harassing
tactics to overcome local resistance. "Children will go to school where
Harold Howe chooses," he told viewers in December 1966, "by federal direction and dictation, or the federal purse will be snapped shut." Jesse further suggested that Howe had revealed his hypocrisy by insisting on
integrated schools while he sent his own son to a private boarding school in
Connecticut.[37]

Helms saw the coming conservative backlash as the backbone of the
new anti-liberal revolution. Among left-wingers, these were the "days of
whines and neuroses"—a pun that Helms offered on "wine and roses." The
liberals' "dream world of phony slogans and broken promises" was collapsing, and they had brought the American republic to the brink. Taxes, inflation, rising federal debt, foreign adventurism, billions sunk in foreign aid,
racial conflict, crime, and violence had undone liberalism. There was a
"restless stirring through the land," Helms believed. Sooner or later, he
predicted, a conservative revolution was approaching: "the dam will burst,
and a tidal wave of pent-up resentment may well spread from coast to
coast."[38] Soon, Jesse warned, the "law-abiding citizens of this republic"
would "push aside all of the phony political doubletalk about 'movements'
and 'marches' and 'non-violence' and 'civil rights.'" When that occurred,
the "blanket of deceit and intellectual dishonesty woven by men who are
supposed to be our leaders" would become exposed.[39] "These long-hairs
keep talking about a revolution," he wrote a friend in 1970. "One of these
days they may get one—but not the kind they expect."[40]

DURING THE KENNEDY and Johnson administrations, the Federal
Communications Commission closely scrutinized political practices of local broadcasters in license renewal proceedings. In response to the inability
of civil rights groups to gain access to the airwaves, the FCC developed the
fairness doctrine, which required that broadcasters provide equal time for
opposing points of view. In late 1963 and early 1964, the FCC considered

WRAL's license renewal, and its investigators spent more than two weeks in Raleigh, a week going through WRAL's files and another week, as Jesse put it, interviewing "those who dislike us." In private correspondence, he described the struggle with the FCC as "hell," an "exercise in nit-picking, [em]barassment and intimidation."[41] The FCC focused on editorials that Helms delivered in 1963 attacking SCLC officials Bayard Rustin and Jack O'Dell—Rustin for his homosexuality and Communist connections, O'Dell for his Communist associations—without providing either the chance to respond. Jesse and WRAL claimed that the *Viewpoints* balanced the liberal perspective offered in the national news broadcasts, but the FCC rejected that argument. Meanwhile, Helms had angered the Democratic Party establishment, including Governor Terry Sanford, and he and his political circle lobbied to block WRAL's license renewal.[42]

By late July 1964, WRAL received word that its license would be renewed, and soon after the decision Helms aired a *Viewpoint* that mused about the past eight months of "red tape and the expense and the torment of proving ourselves innocent, before an unseen jury, of vague charges made by accusers whom we were not permitted to face." He complained about the fairness doctrine, which he described as "vague beyond comprehension" and as imposing something that came close to an "attempt at censorship." This was yet another attempt of the federal government to intervene, and broadcasters should remain free to conduct their business. "When one is denied any part of his rightful freedom, then every man's freedom has been lessened."[43]

Prior to WRAL's license renewal hearings, however, Helms had delivered his editorials with little regard for the opposing point of view.[44] FCC scrutiny forced Helms to take the fairness doctrine seriously, and after 1964 the commission expected broadcasters to be proactive in seeking out editorial responses. Under strict direction from WRAL's attorney (and A.J.'s son) Frank Fletcher, Helms routinely sent a *Viewpoint* transcript to any subject of his editorials, with an offer to broadcast a response. The fairness doctrine permitted opposing groups to contest Helms's politicization of the airwaves, and after 1964 the FCC received a number of complaints from his political opponents. In various editorials, Helms criticized eighteen-term 4th District congressman Harold D. Cooley, who served as chairman of the House Agriculture Committee. In 1966, Republican Jim Gardner of Rocky Mount challenged Cooley and engineered an upset victory in which a last-minute attack broadcast on WRAL played an important role. The Gardner campaign aired a paid political program that included a portion of a televised debate held at N.C. State on October 3, 1966. Gardner's campaign televised another political tape that was scheduled to be broadcast on October 31, the day before the election. Cooley stormed into the WRAL offices that afternoon, demanding that the Gardner film be pulled. Meeting with Fred Fletcher and Helms, Cooley claimed that WRAL had made available a videotape of the debate so that it could "be distorted and used as a political document." According to his account, by making the tape available, WRAL violated the fairness doctrine. Though they admitted they had provided the tape, Helms and WRAL officials refused to halt Gardner's broadcast.[45]

Cooley and his supporters continued to object following Gardner's victory. About a week after the election, two N.C. State professors—including political scientist Abe Holtzman—telegrammed the FCC. WRAL permitted Cooley to respond, but Helms on November 7 delivered an editorial that served as a rebuttal to his response.[46] Cooley's "agents," Jesse claimed, had attacked WRAL for political reasons, the N.C. State professors' telegram constituted "nothing but a bald attempt at intimidation of this station."[47] On November 18, 1966, Cooley filed a complaint with the FCC. Helms's November 7 *Viewpoint,* Cooley charged, was a "vicious attack on my candidacy," impugning his integrity as a public servant. Receiving no notice of Helms's editorial until 6:15 P.M.—*Viewpoints* aired at 6:25 P.M.—Cooley's telephone calls to WRAL remained unanswered until 9:30 that night. It was obvious, Cooley charged, that the television station was making Cooley's ability to respond impossible and that it had served as "an integral part of the campaign machinery of my opponent." He demanded that the FCC hold public hearings.[48] On November 29, 1966, Holtzman also filed an FCC complaint, asserting that Helms never provided any opportunity for response.[49]

For the next six months, the Cooley case consumed much of Helms's time. His mother died in December 1966, and arranging her affairs and managing the Cooley complaint, as he wrote a friend, kept him "from doing anything that I really wanted to do."[50] Nonetheless, Helms realized that there was little real threat of FCC intervention. Earlier, in June 1966, in cases in California and Mississippi, the FCC had narrowed the fairness doctrine by saying that it would not rule on the merits of broadcast material but would instead focus on whether all parties had received a fair opportunity to be heard. That meant that defamatory or even false statements were not covered by the doctrine; the FCC would intervene only in cases in which good-faith efforts were not made to extend equal time. Unless it could be demonstrated that WRAL had clearly denied Cooley an opportunity for equal time, his complaint had little future.[51] Advised by WRAL of these legal parameters, Helms thoroughly documented his attempts to make the airwaves available. Cooley and Holtzman, Jesse maintained, had been provided with ample opportunity to respond. In Holtzman's case, he said, Jesse personally photocopied the relevant *Viewpoints* because his secretary was hospitalized. He also composed and sent a letter inviting Holtzman's response. On December 6, 1966, according to his account, Helms again offered Holtzman the chance to appear on the air.[52] Nonetheless, that WRAL had skewed its coverage toward Gardner is without question: Helms became closely associated with Gardner during the campaign, and remained so as he emerged as a potential Republican gubernatorial candidate. The FCC investigation, while essentially confirming WRAL's prejudicial coverage, found insufficient evidence of a "conspiracy," and by a 3–2 vote in July 1967 it declined to hold public hearings.[53]

After the resolution of the Cooley case, Helms, in an artful dance around FCC doctrine, routinely offered equal time to all those he attacked in his editorials.[54] In November 1969, Helms took on the subject of Angela Davis, who was hired for a temporary position by UCLA's Philosophy Department. Charging that she was a Communist and member of the radical black group, the Black Panther Party, he endorsed California governor Ronald Reagan's attempt to have her fired. When the University of California regents stood behind her (though later her contract was not renewed), Helms described her as "one of numerous Negroes on the university faculty" with a "very predictable campus protest movement" organized around her. Noting that federal courts protected Communists' ability to teach at universities, Helms observed that faculty, once hired, could now teach any way that they chose and, if critics objected, they were "shouted down with that old 'academic freedom' argument." Davis claimed that the University of Calfornia regents were seeking to fire her for racial reasons; Helms responded that she was black when she was hired, but what was now different was the knowledge that she was a Communist. There was no inherent right to teach, and permitting Communists in the classroom was a "strange and dangerous contradiction of national purpose."[55]

In November 1969, David Paletz, a young junior faculty member at Duke University who had arrived on that campus two years earlier with a UCLA Ph.D., taught political communication. With some awareness of Davis's case, he considered Helms's editorials, which he watched regularly, to be outrageous—and especially so because so often they went unanswered. After hearing Helms's *Viewpoint*, he wrote to Davis, who declined to respond but authorized Paletz, in a letter to Helms, to serve as her spokesperson. Paletz had little interest in broadcasting a response, despite

Helms's repeated invitations. Because Davis was black and "because your editorial was a personal attack on her," he wrote, he did not "feel qualified in this particular case to reply on her behalf." Events kept the issue alive: on August 7, 1970, several armed men burst into a Marin County, California, courtroom and shot and killed the sitting judge in order to free "Soledad Brother" George Jackson. Davis, who had led an effort to free Jackson, was charged with supplying the murder weapons and renting the getaway car. A fugitive from justice, she was eventually apprehended and, in a subsequent trial, acquitted. Helms brought up Angela Davis's case as an example of black extremism that was encouraged by liberal permissiveness. The "usual gaggle of leftwing news media and politicians—and professors" had provided a "chorus of praise for this young woman," said Helms, even though she had openly expressed contempt for America. Helms then named Paletz as a "leftwing" professor who had been designated as Davis's spokeman but was refusing to appear on the air.[56]

Now the object of a Helms attack, Paletz considered a response. Further negotiations followed: Helms offered to tape Paletz in WRAL's studios; Paletz responded in January 1970 that he was "extraordinarily busy." Even after they agreed that Paletz would tape his broadcast in the studios of WTVD, the Durham television station, further sparring ensued. Paletz listed conditions—he insisted that his broadcast appear on the same stations that broadcast the *Viewpoints,* that it air at the *Viewpoints'* regular time, that his words be aired in full, and that he be notified in advance when it would be broadcast. Although neither man agreed to any ground rules, Paletz taped his broadcast on February 19, 1970, and it was broadcast on February 25. Helms provided Paletz equal time, but in no sense did he extend unfettered access to the airwaves. In what amounted to a rebuttal of Paletz's comments, Jesse prefaced the broadcast with his own commentary. Reviewing the sequence of events, he reminded viewers about his original November 1969 *Viewpoint,* how Davis had subsequently been jailed for murder. Paletz, Helms said, had taken "strong exception" to this and subsequent editorials and had been extended numerous invitations to speak on Davis's behalf.

In his statement, Paletz said that he was not defending Davis's ideas, most of which he disagreed with. The more significant issue was power— and, in particular, the power of media over politics. Who, Paletz asked, possessed more power: a professor teaching a few students with a "commitment to facts and to presenting every side of an issue," or Helms, who, "careless with the facts," regularly spread his message throughout North Carolina? Paletz listed Jesse's distortions: in November 1969, Helms claimed that Davis was one of "numerous Negroes" on UCLA's faculty, while in fact blacks comprised less than one percent of all faculty. Helms said that Davis remained free to teach anything, while in fact she taught only those courses that were approved by a faculty curriculum committee. Helms said that she lectured only about Marxism and Communism, while in fact she taught other political philosophies. Rather than a subversive faculty member twisting the facts and threatening young minds, the real distortion of ideas had occurred on WRAL, and Helms's editorializing exemplified the political power of that media—and how that power was abused. Had WRAL been exercising its unchecked power responsibly? Paletz's answer was a "categorical no."

Paletz had been eloquent, and, while saying little about Davis and her case, had turned the discussion toward Helms's editorializing. As a young Duke faculty member—and as a student of mass communications—Paletz's main motivation was to respond in such a way that would highlight the nature of Helms's political communication. Years later, he recalled that in his "academic innocence" he believed in a "marketplace of ideas" in which the truth would emerge after public discussion. He further believed that he had an obligation, as a public intellectual, to offer a reasoned response to Helms's editorials. Helms wanted Paletz's participation in order to have a real, flesh-and-blood liberal professor who would tie himself to Davis's radicalism. His appearance at WRAL, Paletz later realized, was a "setup": his name sounded strange and foreign, he was not from North Carolina, and he taught at Duke. His broadcast thus played into Helms's plans.[57] In his encounter with Paletz, however, Helms had the last word. Jesse broadcast Paletz's comments only after providing an introduction; he closed them by reminding viewers that WRAL stood "upon the facts as stated in our editorial 15 months ago." Ignoring Paletz's larger point about WRAL's abuse of its public responsibility, Helms reasserted his general critique of universities, left-wing radicals, and liberalism. The "tragic events of the past year," he said in a reminder about the murder charges against Davis, had illustrated the difference between academic freedom and academic license. There was "great risk" in having Communist faculty in the classroom.

Helms had been eager to broadcast Paletz's response because he considered him a useful target, but his treatment of him demonstrated the way in which he disregarded the spirit of the FCC's fairness doctrine. Soon after the broadcast, Paletz complained that Helms's editorial introduction and closing were neither "fair" nor "factual." No wonder, he concluded, that dissenting opinions on WRAL were "so rare."[58] Even WRAL's attorney, when he reviewed the case, concluded that Paletz's treatment was "an abuse of the power and position of the TV station" and that steps should be taken in the future "for this not to occur any more."[59] Helms, possessing few worries about the FCC, dared Paletz to review the station's files on the matter.[60] One of Paletz's undergraduates at Duke, R. Scott Lynch, complained in a letter to the FCC, but his efforts had little effect. Helms was astute enough to realize that, so long as he invited those he attacked to respond—even if he limited their ability to respond—he could escape FCC pressure. He also realized that political pressures, and his own popularity among his North Carolina audience, effectively insulated him from external pressures.[61]

AS A STUDENT of modern media and politics, David Paletz was impressed with Jesse Helms. Often providing commentary about Helms's subsequent political career, Paletz was struck, from this first encounter, by several qualities. Although disagreeing with almost everything that Jesse said, Paletz recognized that Helms was a masterful television performer who understood how to convey a political message. Helms remained clear and consistent about his political positions. According to Paletz's analysis, in his understanding of politics and the media, there was "not anyone...in the country" like Jesse Helms. Understanding what journalists needed and how they functioned, he skillfully targeted his audience and communicated in such a way as to appeal to them. To Paletz, these ingredients pointed toward something inevitable in Helms's career: a move into politics.[62] As events would show, Paletz proved correct. Jesse had always been interested in a political career, and since the 1950s journalism was but a vehicle toward political communication and the development of a new, revitalized conservative political message. Helms had never lacked political ambition, and his election to the Raleigh City Council whetted his appetite. The timing now seemed right for a political move.

There were, however, some remaining obstacles. Although Jesse was a registered Democrat—as were most white North Carolinians of his generation—he had little faith in the party. Converting to the Republican Party, which could claim no statewide officeholders until 1972, was not yet an option if he wanted a political future. Among Democratic gubernatorial candidates of the 1960s, Helms felt comfortable only with Dan Moore, whose election in 1964 over Greensboro congressman and Sanford ally L. Richardson Preyer, he thought, marked the reassertion of the conservative coalition of 1950. Although Moore was not "the most articulate person in the world," he wrote one friend, "he has character."[63] But Jesse soon became disillusioned with Moore, who had compromised on the Speaker Ban and who proved less conservative than Helms hoped he would be. In July 1965, Jesse privately expressed doubts. Moore had already made "some asinine small mistakes"; Helms worried that it was "only a matter of time until the big ones begin to happen."[64] Moore, he wrote in August 1967, was like Dwight Eisenhower. Both were elected "as a result of the people's rejecting 'liberalism,' yet both surrendered to their enemies."[65] In national politics, Helms believed that the Democratic Party remained under liberal control, and he had voted Republican in every presidential race since 1948. Although Helms remained politically close to Senators B. Everett Jordan and Sam Ervin, he expressed strong disagreement with both over time.

There was another consideration in Helms's potential political moves: the opposition of his boss, A. J. Fletcher. In July 1967, while visiting Raleigh, Helms's old friend Earl Butz urged Helms to consider running for governor. But when Helms floated this suggestion to Fletcher, his response was decidedly negative. According to Butz, A.J. "did not take to the idea too well" and was "rather inflexible" in his opposition.[66] Sensing that the timing for a move into politics was right, Jesse wrote Butz that he found A.J.'s attitude "a little deflating." Butz, who knew both Fletcher and Helms well, believed that a gubernatorial run would be "great for North Carolina." But he described A.J. as a person who had been "used all his life to having his way." Helms, meanwhile, wondered whether Fletcher resented him for the attention he received as a media figure. Jesse considered trying out a candidacy despite A.J.'s opposition, but at this point he was unwilling to challenge Fletcher. Jesse also worried about employment: "If worse came to worst, I suppose that I might find some sort of employment elsewhere that would keep body and soul together—even at my age," he wrote. There was no solution to his predicament, he wrote later, as Fletcher was "beset by a number of apprehensions compounded with a determination that all things shall go precisely as he wishes."[67]

Although confined to the political sidelines, Helms was moving ever closer to political involvement. Opposing Lyndon Johnson and the Great Society, he welcomed Richard Nixon's election as president in November 1968, and supported his presidency on the air. When Nixon was nominated at the Republican National Convention at Miami Beach in August 1968, Helms in a *Viewpoint* praised his "masterful speech" while he dismissed attacks from the "leftwing crowd."[68] Helms was heartened by Nixon's choice of Maryland governor Spiro T. Agnew for vice president.[69] When Agnew subsequently attacked liberals in the media and universities, Jesse applauded him. After Agnew visited Raleigh in October 1970, Jesse described him as the "country's most memorable Vice President," a "tough, competent man who has won the admiration of the country" for "speaking the minds of millions of Americans" by daring to "tell the truth about the giant national news media" that misled public opinion. Agnew had "refused to tremble in fear and compromise at threats and jeers shouted by campus radicals and violent revolutionaries."[70]

Yet Helms worried that the Nixon White House included too many liberals and was too moderate in its domestic policies. He bitterly opposed Nixon's willingness to permit the school desegregation process to play out during his administration. Although he knew Nixon from his days as Willis Smith's aide in the Senate, he had distrusted him since the Eisenhower presidency, which he considered too compromising with liberal opponents. Helms believed that Nixon should fashion a conservative backlash against liberalism into a political majority. In November 1970, he told viewers that Nixon should "get out among the people for a few days" in order to "gain a new perspective, and a new determination to try to set the country straight again." Scanning the mail that came in to WRAL, Helms found the "people speaking—frustrated, disillusioned, often bitter people." Nixon agreed with Helms's political strategy: early in his presidency, he and his political advisers appealed to a "silent majority" that was coalescing against the excesses of the 1960s. Nixon campaigned to capture this vote, though in office he moderated his policies. Helms advocated fashioning the Silent Majority into a permanent governing coalition. They were searching for "answers, solutions," and they yearned for "just a word of comfort."[71]

During Nixon's first term, Helms pondered his alternatives. In 1969, he rejected feelers about a lower-level presidential appointment, though he promised to help Nixon's effort on a voluntary basis.[72] Shortly before Nixon's inauguration in January 1969, Jesse privately admitted that he needed some time away from Raleigh because he stayed "so clobbered with meaningless meetings that serve no purpose other than the killing of time." Helms continued to complain that A.J. remained opposed to his entry into politics, but he remained determined to maintain his Washington contacts.[73] On September 17, 1970, Helms took a turn toward direct political involvement by changing his political affiliation from Democrat to Republican. In an interview in 1989, Helms described his decision. His younger daughter, Nancy, was planning her wedding, but because John Stuart, her husband-to-be, was away in the Army, he was unable to get home to get a marriage license. Nancy asked Jesse to go to the courthouse with her, and on the elevator she told her father that she intended to register to vote. When Nancy registered as Republican, he asked her why she had made that party choice. Smiling at him, she said, "I'll tell you why if you'll tell me why you remain a Democrat when you are as conservative as you are." With that comment, he recalled, he registered as Republican. "The little child," Helms would later recall, "shall lead."[74]

Like many of Helms's stories, this contained only part of the truth: rather than acting on impulse, his political switch was a calculated move that reflected his desire to obtain elective office. The day after he changed parties, Helms wrote to Nixon, saying that he would "not try to suggest a course of action without demonstrating my willingness to be a part of it."[75] In another interview in 1974, he explained that he had considered himself on the "perimeter" of politics all of his life. Although a Democrat, he had never voted for a Democratic presidential candidate. The party, he believed, had "veered so far to the left nationally, and was taken over by the people whom I'd describe as substantially left of center in North Carolina" that he no longer had faith in it.

Confident that two-party politics was returning to North Carolina, he became convinced that his political future lay with Republicans.[76] It remains unclear what office Helms was seeking. The only elective office that interested him, he told an interviewer in 1966, was the U.S. Senate, but "that's never going to happen." He was close to both Sam Ervin and B. Everett Jordan, but he believed that both were too beholden to the national Democratic Party structure. Jordan, who had served in the Senate since 1958, had become ill—he would die in March 1974—and faced a spirited primary battle, which he would lose to Durham congressman Nick Galifianakis. Helms was approached by leading North Carolina conservatives, including Wachovia executive and Winston-Salem resident Archie Davis, to run for Jordan's seat. Although Helms subsequently claimed that this would be "fire insurance" in the event that Jordan lost renomination, Jesse had a score to settle: in November 1971, Jordan, siding with his Democratic colleagues, had voted against the nomination of Earl Butz for secretary of agriculture, though Helms had made a personal appeal that Jordan at least refrain from voting. In late November, he wrote a bitter letter to Jordan denouncing him for his vote against this "fine and decent man who deserved better treatment than he received." "You are traveling," he wrote, "with the wrong crowd, Senator."[77] In early December 1971, Helms aired a *Viewpoint* that attacked Jordan as a person whom liberals now regarded as "*their* man in the Senate." He observed that Jordan attended the 1970 Democratic state convention flashing a peace symbol, something that "originated with the protesting mobs then clogging the streets of America, threatening to take over the government of the United States." Siding with "top union bosses" and "various minority groups," Jordan had opposed Butz's nomination. Helms concluded that the "contradictions of the Senator's political career hover like a cloud."[78]

Helms would write to Jordan, in a letter that was made public, that his disappointment in him had "nothing to do with the friendship I continue to feel for you." But the breach was permanent—and indicated that he had reached a decision about running for the Senate.[79] When more entreaties came forward about a Senate candidacy, Jesse became more receptive. According to one account, the person primarily responsible for the effort to elect Helms was Tom Ellis, a Raleigh conservative and attorney who had known Jesse since the 1950 campaign. Helms, after his two terms on the Raleigh City Council, had toyed with the idea of running for various offices: in addition to a possible run at John Jordan's State Senate seat, he had also considered running as a Republican against Congressman Harold Cooley in 1962–63.[80] In 1966, Ellis had attempted unsuccessfully to persuade Helms to challenge Jordan. Facing an apparently entrenched incumbent and the strong opposition of A. J. Fletcher, Helms had demurred; he "didn't give me the time of day about it," Ellis recalled. Now, Ellis returned with the same message, and others, noticing that Jesse had become a Republican, urged him on. In late 1971 and early 1972, Ellis implored Helms to run, but Jesse remained dubious. He thought that the idea of his candidacy was "farfetched," and he worried about the financial insecurity of giving up his job in order to campaign. Earlier, sometime in 1971, when political commentator John Kilgo had asked him about running, Jesse laughed and said, "Come on, John." In early January, after a poker game at Pou Bailey's, Ellis recalled, he and Jesse chatted in the driveway as they stood by his car. "You've just got to do this thing," Ellis told him, in order to save the country from liberalism. This was part of his effort, Ellis recalled, to "beg and prod" Helms into running.

Helms was noncommittal, but said that he would consider if Ellis could meet three conditions. First, Jesse wanted Ellis to determine whether James T. Broyhill, scion of a wealthy Hickory furniture family who had served five terms in Congress, was planning on running. If he was, Helms would not campaign, out of respect for Broyhill. Second, he would need the blessing of A. J. Fletcher—and his assurance that, should he lose the campaign, he could return to his WRAL position. Jesse, Ellis remembered, was "very tight," and Dot "tighter," and both were concerned that he not give up a regular paycheck. Finally, Helms wanted some assurance that he would likely win the Republican nomination. Ellis met all three conditions. Writing Broyhill, he received no response; he took this as an indication that

Broyhill would not enter the race. In an effort that Ellis orchestrated, supporters sent out about four thousand letters to test the waters, and within
two weeks they received about fifteen thousand pieces of mail and about
$20,000 in campaign funds.

Next Ellis organized a delegation composed of A.J.'s former law partner Beverly Lake and Ellis's law partner, Tee Taylor. Ellis had known
Fletcher since the 1950 senatorial campaign, and he had supported his
quest for an FCC license in the 1950s. As A.J. sat in his big office at WRAL,
Ellis made his pitch, urging Fletcher to support Helms's candidacy as an
act of patriotism and dedication to the conservative cause. Taylor and Lake
joined in, and Fletcher told the group that he would discuss the matter with
Jesse and think about it. Sometime in December 1971, Fletcher agreed that
Helms would step down as television commentator but would continue at
WRAL—and that he would have his job back if he lost the election. A.J. believed that Helms had little chance of winning, Ellis realized; Fletcher was
a "bottom-line guy and a dedicated conservative," and these two impulses
worked in tension with each other. A.J. then dropped by Helms's WRAL
office, and told him that he believed that Helms should run in order to get
the "conservative message" out to voters. "As far as your contract is concerned," he told Jesse, "we will suspend that but it will be renewed the day
after the election, and I will sign it to that effect." Helms would step down
as *Viewpoint* editorialist but would continue to work as WRAL vice president. Between February and August, A.J. permitted Helms to campaign
only on weekends. In mid-January, Fletcher formalized these terms in
writing. For Helms, Fletcher's approval and willingness to guarantee his
future employment sealed his decision to enter the race.[81]

But Helms remained coy, still undecided, and he waited until the
eleventh hour before declaring his candidacy. On February 1, 1972, he
wrote Jordan that there was a "fairly good chance" that he would run for
Senate. If he ran, "I shall be seeking to win the office, and not to bring personal defeat to you."[82] A few days later, he told a reporter that he was "95
per cent ready" to enter the race, but he noted that "the other 5 per cent is
the tough part." Ellis, at the same time, told the press that the odds were ten
to one that Helms would run.[83] Three days before the Republican primary's filing deadline, on February 18, 1972, Helms announced his candidacy for the United States Senate. His announcement was modest: deciding
against a news conference, Jesse instead issued a press release promising a
campaign "free of pretense, from start to finish." His experience of nearly
twelve years in television broadcasting, Helms said, had convinced him to
accede to the effort to draft him into running for the Senate. "I have tried to

level with the people," Helms said, "and, in turn, they have leveled with me." Along with the apparently enthusiastic reponse to Ellis's draft-Helms movement, over the years he had received over 300,000 pieces of mail at WRAL, and viewers' response had convinced him that North Carolinians shared his conservatism and yearned for "political forthrightness among our leaders, for a return to sanity, honesty and economy in their government, and for a meaningful two-party system that will give [them] a choice."[84]

Thus began a highly successful, two-decade partnership between Jesse Helms and Tom Ellis in which, according to one account, they were "almost as close as brothers, both politically and personally."[85] Ellis was "absolutely indefatigable," Jesse later recalled, and in the 1972 campaign took responsibility for ushering Jesse around the state, driving Helms's car. Taking leave for a year from his law practice, Ellis continued to work on Jesse's behalf without compensation. In 1972, his law partners—many of whom had joined Ellis in urging Jesse to run—agreed that, while campaigning, Ellis would continue to receive his share of the income from the law firm. Ellis never enjoyed any financial benefit from his relationship with Helms. Instead, his main interest was in helping the conservative cause and to expand its political power.[86]

In running for the Senate, one chapter of Jesse's life would close while another would open. He realized the significance of the decision, but it was a limited risk, since he was assured of his WRAL job should his campaign fizzle. Announcing his intention to run for Jordan's seat, he immediately took leave from WRAL. A. J. Fletcher delivered a *Viewpoint* on February 21, 1972, informing viewers about Helms's departure. Since his arrival in November 1960, Helms had delivered 2,761 WRAL television editorials: this was, Fletcher said, the "end of an era." The WRAL *Viewpoints* would continue, he said, and would include appearances by various guest columnists. He regarded Helms's departure with "sadness"; the *Viewponts* had made "a contribution to public awareness" by stimulating the public to "think, to consider, to evaluate."[87] The senatorial campaign of 1972 occurred in the midst of major changes in the national and regional political landscape. Four years earlier, in 1968, Richard Nixon had won the White House by campaigning on civil rights, crime, urban riots, and moral permissiveness—all issues that Jesse had explored in his *Viewpoints*. Despite Nixon's narrow win, his vote, combined with that of independent presidential candidate George Wallace, constituted an anti-liberal mandate. Seeking to capture the Wallace vote after 1968, Nixon focused on a southern strategy that depended on a reinvigorated Republican Party, which, despite a post-1945

revival, remained anemic in the former Confederacy. Fundamental to
Nixon's strategy was an attempt to capture southern conservatives and attract them to the Republican Party.[88]

In his quest for a Senate seat, Helms mounted two very different campaigns. In the Republican primary campaign, he sought Republican votes
in the Piedmont and western North Carolina, rather than in the Democratic eastern part of the state, the home of the WRAL viewing area and the
heart of his strongest following. There were geographical, factional, and
ideological divisions among Republicans that shaped the primary campaign. North Carolina Republicans clustered in the Piedmont and west, but
a rich potential for votes existed in eastern North Carolina, which was
filled with conservatives who voted for Republicans in national elections
but remained registered Democrats. Tensions existed between newly converted Republicans such as Helms and Jim Gardner, whose political base
was in the east, and more traditional Republicans, whose base was in the
Piedmont and west. Much of this conflict reflected ideology, but some of it
was personal: party regulars perceived recent converts—known as "Jessecrats"—as demanding newcomers. These tensions were also race-based;
Helms and Gardner articulated a hard-hitting conservatism on issues of
culture, race, and government. Identifying with moderates in the national
party, traditional North Carolina Republicans emphasized limited government and lower taxes.

In the three-month campaign leading up to the May 6, 1972, primary,
Helms danced around these tensions. He said little negative about his opponents, and there was little of the sarcasm and hard-hitting wit that were
so typical of his television editorials. Neither of his two challengers
mounted a serious campaign. William Booe, a Charlotte lawyer and school
board member, opponent of crosstown busing, and recently converted Republican, enjoyed the early blessing of party leaders but never acquired
momentum. Jesse's most serious primary opponent, James "Jimmy" Johnson, another Piedmont Republican who was a three-term legislator from
Cabarrus County, ran a spirited campaign in which he criticized Helms's
lack of experience and recent political conversion. Appealing to traditional
Republicans, Johnson reminded them that only a moderate stood a chance
of winning statewide office; Helms, he said, was "a strong, strong, ultraconservative." Not long after Helms joined the race, Johnson predicted that he
would "whip Jesse."[89]

But Republican Party regulars, who regarded Johnson as a maverick,
rallied behind Helms. An important endorsement came from Republican
congressman Charles R. Jonas of Lincolnton, a ten-term congressman first

elected in 1952 who was known as the state's "Mr. Republican." On March 28, Jonas endorsed Helms in a letter to former Duke football coach Wallace Wade (who had also endorsed Jesse), noting that he was "widely known and respected in Eastern North Carolina," the weakest area of Republicanism.[90] Jonas's endorsement legitimized Helms among Piedmont Republicans, and very soon some thirty party regulars, including Asheboro's Worth Coltrane and Davidson County Republican and former state party chair Sim Delapp, joined the bandwagon. As one reporter noted, Helms had "pulled off a coup when he won the endorsement of Congressman Charles Jonas."[91]

Armed with these endorsements and facing weak Republican opposition, Helms and his senatorial campaign essentially laid low. So secure was Helms's political position that he refused various televised debates—Republicans, Helms told audiences, could not "afford the luxury of division and disunity"—pursuing what one reporter called a "late blooming public candidacy" that concentrated on his Democratic opponents. Rather than headline-grabbing speeches, as one reporter wrote, he "stuck instead to handshake and a 'bless your heart.' "[92] With the best-financed and -organized campaign of the field—he would eventually outspend Johnson by four to one—Jesse devoted his time to thirty Piedmont and western counties.[93] A strong supporter of Nixon, Helms attacked liberals, the Democratic Congress, and student antiwar protesters.[94] "Liberal do-nothings" dominated the Democratic Congress, he told one Guilford County audience, for these were people who knew "how to ruin a government." "If we don't get away from this liberal, left-wing kick," he continued, "the country is going to go down the drain."[95]

Though running as a Republican, Helms told voters that he was primarily a conservative, and he portrayed himself as wedded to principle rather than political advantage. He contrasted his ideological clarity with his liberal enemies' moral ambiguity. Massachusetts senator Edward M. Kennedy became a favorite target, and Helms reminded voters of Kennedy's role in the death of aide Mary Jo Kopechne at Chappaquiddick in July 1969. While he described himself as "not like Teddy Kennedy, who tries to cross a bridge before he comes to it,"[96] he also quipped that if Kennedy was defeated someday he would "make a good driver's ed instructor."[97] When Jimmy Johnson claimed that Jesse "loves Barry Goldwater," Jesse was unapologetic, and he declared that Goldwater was "a very good candidate in 1964."[98] Like most other candidates, he condemned the comprehensive, court-ordered school busing that arrived across the South and in North Carolina in the 1971–72 school year as "unnecessary and chaotic." Describing busing as the most important issue concerning Americans, Helms even favored the drastic step of an anti-busing constitutional amendment.[99] He was "nobody's yes man," he told an Asheville audience in April; he was, first and foremost, a conservative. With never much doubt about the outcome, Helms decisively won the May 6 Republican primary, capturing nearly 60 percent of the vote.[100]

In the Democratic primary, Durham congressman Nick Galifianakis's upset of B. Everett Jordan, incumbent senator since 1958, seemed to mark the emergence of a new political order. Helms had been increasingly critical of Jordan since 1970 because of the incumbent senator's opposition to Nixon and his position on the Vietnam War (by 1972, Jordan favored ending American involvement). Jesse had expected to run against Jordan; Galifianakis's upset was a surprise. Nick's father, Mike Galifianakis, immigrated to the United States from Crete before World War I, eventually settling in Durham and opening a restaurant. Mike became an American patriot, flying two flags and always ending the dinner table prayer by saying, "God Bless America." Nick attended local schools and Duke University, served three years in the Marine Corps, and then returned to Duke for law school. Practicing law in Durham, Galifianakis was elected to three terms in the state-house and then won a seat in Congress in 1968. Affable, energetic, and outgoing, Galifianakis loved retail politics—the press of flesh in meeting and greeting voters. Reporters covering him rarely saw him "miss a hand-shake, whether in an elevator, on a sidewalk, or in a restaurant," and moving past him "without being greeted requires pretty fancy footwork." Behind in the polls in the primary campaign at one point by thirty points, Nick ran an aggressive effort that delivered sharp attacks on Jordan.[101]

Galifianakis's upset victory created an opening for Helms. Entering the campaign, according to campaign worker Charlie Black, no one believed that Helms could win, except for Tom Ellis.[102] Now the Democratic primary results changed things, and, in the general election campaign during the summer and fall of 1972, Helms created a finely tuned organization that would overwhelm the opposition with superior strategy, organization, and financing. Ellis, his campaign manager, set up a two-person campaign office with Helms's secretary, Frances Jones, in the Sir Walter Hotel in downtown Raleigh. Once the campaign expanded, Ellis moved his head-quarters to the College Inn Motel, near the N.C. State campus. Ellis was a native Californian whose father, a manufacturing representative, moved his family to Delaware when he was thirteen. Meeting some Carolina students at Virginia Beach when he worked there as a teenager, Ellis attended UNC, served in the Navy during World War II, graduated from the University of Virginia Law School in 1948, and then practiced law in

Raleigh. Ellis was legendary for his ability to organize, raise money, focus a campaign message, use the media effectively, and, when necessary, wage merciless political combat. As a UNC undergraduate, he knew Frank Graham—like Helms, Ellis recalled that he "loved Dr. Graham," though he considered him impractical about the ways of the world. Ellis first got to know Helms in the 1950 senatorial campaign, when they both supported Smith, and Ellis ran as a political candidate only once—in 1956, when he lost a race for the State Senate. Thereafter, he became consumed with conservative politics.

Deeply ideological, Ellis, like Helms, opposed integration. In 1958, he served as legal counsel to the Pearsall committee, which devised North Carolina's attempt to resist compliance with the Supreme Court's *Brown v. Board of Education* decision. Ellis was also a hard-core anti-Communist who was convinced that liberalism was leading the country astray. After participating in I. Beverly Lake's gubernatorial campaign in 1960, four years later Ellis became prominent in Barry Goldwater's presidential campaign in North Carolina. Like Helms, Ellis changed his party affiliation to Republican in 1970 because he believed that the Democrats were "taken over by the libs." Communism, he told a reporter, was a "whole lot closer than ... ever," and he was unwilling to turn the country "over to the liberals, commies or anybody else." Rather than seeking any personal gain, Ellis, said another contemporary, was "simply convinced that the commies are going to take over the world." Described as professorial, Ellis was a person for whom "laughter comes easy; humor is self-deprecating." For him, salty language was confined to an "occasional hell or damn," while his remaining spare time was devoted to family and golf. Over the years, Ellis became Helms's conservative conscience, and when Helms encountered the realities of politics and governing, Ellis, as a true believer, reminded of him of conservative priorities. Ellis, recalled his longtime associate Carter Wrenn, "always had a pure heart, and he always tried to do what was right, even when it was wrong." He was an idea person. Wrenn said that Ellis possessed one of the three most brilliant political minds of anyone he had ever met, while Charlie Black, another acute commentator, described him as possessing "the best political mind in North Carolina."[103]

Ellis was dedicated to Jesse's political success, but from the outset their political partnership had tensions. While the two men were extremely close, they frequently sparred. Much of it had to do with ideological purity and Ellis's utter devotion to the conservative cause. He was a man whose political ideology approached a sort of religious fervor and fanaticism, according to Wrenn, and this meant not only an insistence of purity but also, sometimes, ruthlessness and cruelty. Ellis saw politics as a war, and he waged it mercilessly. "I play hardball," Ellis told one reporter, "because I think it's a hardball game." Ellis would lead many campaigns, observed Wrenn, that were "mentally and physically brutal." Helms, though himself also very ideological, was the more practical and politically sensitive of the two men, and occasionally willing to compromise principle to necessity. For the next two decades, these two men needed each other, but they sometimes diverged in their goals. Their "mutual need for each other," observed Wrenn, "strapped them together," but the relationship remained contentious. According to Wrenn, the two men were constantly in conflict, with the conflict easing as elections approached and accelerating after elections had occurred.[104]

In campaigning, Ellis was usually the bad cop, Helms the good cop: Ellis would do whatever it took to win.[105] He recruited young, smart, political fighters, many of whom came from College Republican and Young Americans for Freedom (YAF) ranks around the country. One reporter described Helms's headquarters as resembling "a Young Americans for Freedom convention." Helms would recall that his Senate campaign was "delightfully infiltrated by YAF people." YAF, founded in 1960, had inspired a new generation of conservative activists. Ellis found one YAF enthusiast in Harold Herring, a recent graduate of Atlantic Christian College in Wilson and formerly southeast director of YAF in Atlanta. In the spring of 1972, at the urging of a friend, Ellis met Herring in Charlotte. Describing him as a "great, big heavy fella" with a high-pitched voice, Ellis was immediately impressed, and he named him campaign director. Herring recruited other YAF members from all around the country as field-workers, including, at various points, George Dunlop, Bill Saracino, Tim Baer, Jim Minarik, Fil Aldridge, and Pat Reilly. David Adcock, who had been active in the conservative student movement in North Carolina through groups such as YAF, Students for America, and College Republicans, organized Youth for Helms groups across the state. Other YAF activists periodically arrived in order to help out the campaign. In 1968, Dunlop, who, while still a student at Catawba and a YAF organizer serving as vice chair of the North Carolina Students for Reagan, had visited Helms with Herring. Later, Dunlop entered a Ph.D. program in history at Lehigh University, and soon after finishing his qualifying exams, Herring called him to join the Helms for Senate campaign. He drove from Bethlehem, Pennsylvania, but when he arrived and learned that Helms was running as a Republican for the United States Senate—rather than for the State Senate—Dunlop became so discouraged that he nearly returned to Lehigh.[106]

Perhaps the most important Young Americans for Freedom recruit was Charlie Black, whom Herring hired in May 1972 as the campaign's field director. A native of eastern North Carolina, Black was a University of Florida graduate who became active in the campus YAF chapter. While throngs of UF students were attracted to campus radicalism, Black led a hardy band of conservatives who supported American involvement in the Vietnam War. Attending YAF conferences in the late 1960s, Black met Jesse. Later becoming state YAF director in Florida, in 1971 he moved to Washington to work as director of the organization's chapter services and national director. At Herring's suggestion, Ellis and Helms visited Black in Washington and hired him on the spot. Attracted to the Helms campaign as a "sort of Don Quixote–type operation," Black became Ellis's campaign aide-de-camp. His first task, when he arrived in North Carolina, was to read five thousand pages of Jesse's *Viewpoint* editorials in order to find anything damaging—a task that took Black about a week's worth of seventeen-hour days. But, from this experience, he learned something about Jesse: "Helms does not make mistakes," he recalled, and if he said something controversial, it was calculated, and he knew "exactly what he's saying." Although Black found a number of issues that his opponents might be able to "take out of context" and use against him, the basis of his success was that he could make "the most conservative case for things" in "a moderate, reasonable tone."

With a statewide organization that included twenty-five paid workers, Black organized Citizens for Helms committees in all of North Carolina's one hundred counties. Meanwhile, Ellis also proved an exceptionally skillful fund-raiser. By the end of the campaign, Helms would outspend Galifianakis by four to one, and Jesse succeeded in attracting support from out-of-state donors, as well as in-state contributors, especially textile, furniture, and banking executives. These funds made possible a statewide campaign organization, but they also paid for an ambitious media campaign. Ellis and Helms turned to outside expertise: New Yorkers who had participated in conservative New York senator James Buckley's successful 1970 campaign, political consultant Cliff White, advertising by Phil Nicolaides and his New York City film production company, the Agora Group, and public opinion polling by Arthur Finkelstein. Between June and late October 1972, the Helms campaign spent $100,000 in television advertising and about $16,500 on radio spots. In the 1972 campaign, radio was especially important in the Helms strategy, as ads were run on the Tobacco Network (where his WRAL *Viewpoints* had run for many years) and the Carolina News Network. In the early 1970s, political advertising relied especially on newspapers, and a substantial portion of resources went toward more traditional forms of media, about $14,000 on billboards and $80,000 for two thousand newspaper ads, mostly in small-town newspapers.[107]

In the Senate race, Jesse benefited from the long coattails of the 1972 Nixon landslide over Democratic presidential candidate George McGovern. The vote for George Wallace also helped Jesse.[108] In August, Helms attended the Miami Republican National Convention, telling reporters that he was "proud of MY presidential candidate"—in contrast to Galifianakis, who by then was avoiding the unpopular McGovern. Subsequently, Jesse benefited from visits from prominent Republicans such as South Carolina senator Strom Thurmond, New York senator James Buckley, Arizona senator Barry Goldwater, Vice President Spiro Agnew, and Agriculture Secretary Earl Butz. Helms campaigned with Thurmond, who joined him for four appearances in a day. Ellis remembered the day Thurmond visited as "hotter than hell," but in each appearance Thurmond would speak for thirty minutes, Helms only for about five minutes of introductory remarks. While Jesse complained that he was "counting the minutes til I could get to sleep," Thurmond "bounded to the podium like it was his first speech of the day." About 11:00 that evening Helms and Ellis noticed Thurmond, then in his sixties, jogging by the hotel. The Nixon campaign, and national Republicans, provided little help and no money to the Helms campaign; the gubernatorial campaign of Jim Holshouser attracted their resources. In general, recalled Ellis, the Helms people had "nothing to do with the Republican party." Only late in the contest, when Nixon's pollsters showed Jesse pulling ahead, did the president visit Greensboro. Still, the president's visit attracted huge crowds and brought considerable momentum to the Helms campaign.[109]

That momentum was evident by the last month of the campaign. Ferrel Guillory, who came from Louisiana in 1972 to join the News and Observer as a political reporter, remembered that the rough-and-tumble campaign was not unlike what he had left behind: Louisiana's gubernatorial election of 1971, Edwin Edwards's first campaign, was a bruising battle. Guillory was struck by the adversarial attitude of the Helms campaign toward reporters, especially those from the N&O: at one press conference, he watched as Helms threw "verbal darts" his way, while his supporters cheered. Late in the campaign, Guillory attended a press conference convened by the pollster for Skipper Bowles, the Democratic gubernatorial candidate, and he was given a poll showing Bowles maintaining a lead over Holshouser. But Guillory and other reporters noticed that each page of the poll had a large section cut out, and they quickly concluded that Jesse was in the lead.[110]

Throughout his political career, Jesse never enjoyed campaigning, and the election of 1972 proved no different. For campaign appearances Ellis often drove Helms; if the trip were long enough, Jesse slept most of the way, and while awake he frequently complained.[111] Those people expecting a "stem-winding, rock 'em sock 'em orator" would be disappointed, Helms admitted to a reporter late in the campaign. Naturally introverted, he did not enjoy the rough-and-tumble of elections: on the campaign trail, he nodded awkwardly to voters, who would "nod back as they would to any polite stranger." Yet he succeeded in connecting with the electorate, a connection that he had already established in twelve years of television broadcasting. Repeating the familiar *Viewpoints* message, he told voters in 1972 about an expanding and intrusive federal government, the threat of socialism, the excesses of the welfare state, rising crime, deteriorating moral standards—all problems related, he said, to an out-of-control liberal state. The welfare system, he explained to an audience in the eastern North Carolina tobacco town of Smithfield, was a "mess," beset by "loafers and parasites." Helms fashioned a populist appeal that was targeted toward ordinary people and toward the frustrations of white, rural, and small-town North Carolinians. His message, Helms said, was directed toward "the person who pulls on his clothes in the morning and grabs his dinner pail and goes off to work."[112]

Helms freely mixed religious faith and politics during the campaign. He grew up in a strict Baptist background, and, as a regular churchgoer and deacon, his faith infused his political rhetoric. He often reminded voters of his Baptist background, but during this election he came to consider his faith and political future as intertwined. Long before the political mobilization of Christian evangelicals that began during the late 1970s, he described a born-again experience occurring during the campaign. Flying aboard a small plane across the state, he departed from an evening appearance in the coastal town of Manteo to an early morning appearance in the western mountain city of Asheville. As he flew across North Carolina, he looked out on a "darkened landscape with only a light here and there" while listening to the drone of the plane's two engines. Watching the lights in houses below, he thought of a "thousand little vignettes," with alarm clocks ringing and parents rising to get their children off to school. He wondered about the worthiness of seeking political office. Could he really solve the nation's problems? "What can you do," he asked himself, "that can make their lives happier, and less frustrating?" What was he "doing up here in this airplane by myself going to speak to a crowd of people I don't even know," not knowing "whether they like me or dislike me or care or don't care?"

For the first time in his life, Jesse said later, "I asked the Lord to help me because I sure needed it." He began praying. "Lord, you know that there's not much to me," he remembered saying. "But let this campaign count for something, win or lose. Guide me, even in defeat, to do and say the things that will be useful to you. Please keep me from being a phony." "Help me," he asked in prayer. As the sunshine crept through the window of the plane, he "felt a sense of serenity I had never felt before." He was accompanied by aide George Dunlop, who recalled that he saw Helms looking out the window when a tear rolled down his cheek. Asking him what was the matter, Jesse told him that the "Lord just spoke to me" in response to his prayer. "George," he said, "the Lord said to me, you tell them that what we need . . . is to have a spiritual rebirth—we need to get back to the roots of morality." Helms told Dunlop to put away all his briefing papers, and when he reached Asheville, without any notion of what he was going to say, he described his recent spiritual experience, exciting a positive reaction among his audience. When his talk had ended, remembered Dunlop, "you could have heard a pin drop." "These people care," he recalled, "and I think we're on to something." At this point, he realized that political progress could occur "not by myself—only with God's and the people's help." The Asheville audience—whom Helms expected would receive him indifferently—greeted his message of spiritual rebirth enthusiastically, leaping to their feet and waving their breakfast napkins. Helms called the experience a "defining moment for me" and a "turning point in my life." For the remainder of the campaign, as he later told an audience in Smithfield, he would describe a "crying need for a spiritual rebirth." Americans, he said, had "drifted away from the faith of our Fathers." Priorities were "all wrong": if people gave God "top priority," he said, "our problems would fall into place." Helms agreed with Benjamin Franklin: "A Providence that lets no sparrow fall unnoticed was unlikely to be an idle spectator when a nation was born."[113]

Helms's Christian rebirth was a critical part of his political persona. In the future, he would remain convinced that divine guidance had led him to politics, that his political purpose was tied to a higher calling. "Who in the hell would have thought that Jesse Helms," he later reflected, "son of a damn good guy who worked hard but who didn't get beyond the fifth grade in school" would achieve high political office? Somehow, he believed, he needed to "live up to what the Lord is trying to tell me." In subsequent years in the Senate, he would slip away to a hideaway off the Senate Chamber and pray before important decisions. "I'm not making this up," he remembered, "I have almost felt a hand on my shoulder" instructing him on how to act; he even felt that divine instruction led him to specific pages in the Senate rulebook. This, he believed, was no accident. On many occasions, following prayer and inspiration, Jesse opened the Senate rulebook "just to see what I could see," and "all of a sudden there it was."[114]

Jesse's born-again experience did not, however, make him into a more forgiving or charitable campaigner; and, as election day approached, his contest with Galifianakis grew bitter. There was no love lost between the two men: Galifianakis had already been a target of several *Viewpoint* attacks. A column appearing in the *Greensboro Daily News* quoted Galifianakis as saying that he detested Jesse. The press, encouraged by the Galifianakis campaign, raised questions about Helms's attitudes toward race during his broadcasting career. As the *Charlotte Observer* bluntly expressed it, Helms had "consistently supported white supremacy, opposing every significant effort to remove the old barriers and backing the illegal efforts of segregationists to maintain them even after clear Supreme Court rulings." Galifianakis, who won an uphill primary campaign by describing Jordan as an aging millionaire (Jordan was then seventy-five years old), already had his gloves off. His staff compiled what one reporter called the "most extensive file of Helmsiana in the state," including transcripts of the WRAL *Viewpoints,* and they diligently circulated materials to editorial writers across the state.

In August 1972, Helms charged that Democrats were spreading rumors accusing him of leaving Raleigh's First Baptist Church in protest after an African American joined. In a speech to the North Carolina Associated Press Broadcasters Association on August 5, Helms's voice trembled as he claimed that his opponent was circulating innuendo portraying him as a racist and "hatemonger." The specifics of this assertion were incorrect: when Helms left the church in 1966, it had no black members, and the ostensible reason for his leaving was that his son, Charles, who was physically impaired from cerebral palsy, wanted to join a Boy Scout troop at the Hayes Barton Baptist Church, only a few blocks from his home. But the charge that Helms opposed the integration of First Baptist was true: in 1963, Helms was strongly opposed to integration, and he offered a motion for a congregational vote denying membership to a black man when he attempted to join the church. And in October 1964, he wrote to a fellow church member expressing unhappiness with the "deteriorating interest and spirit of unity in our congregation." Like other members, he worried about liberal tendencies infecting the congregation.[115]

Benefiting from North Carolina's overwhelmingly Democratic registration, Galifianakis maintained a double-digit lead in early polls: in order to whittle down that lead, the Helms campaign went on the attack. Jesse had promised soon after winning the primary that he would run a "high-level campaign," and his newspaper ads during the summer promoted Helms as hardworking and compassionate, with small-town values. He was not a politician, according to these ads, but a "citizen candidate" who promised to become a "citizen senator." But as the campaign wound down, Jesse's managers struck hard.[116] In September, newspaper ads reminded voters that Helms had been "against busing since the beginning" and that he favored an anti-busing constitutional amendment. In mid-September, Helms's campaign published a round of anti-Galifianakis newspaper ads. In an ad entitled "Where was Nick?," the Helms campaign criticized Galifianakis for missing votes on drug enforcement legislation, suggesting that his absence reflected an indifference to problems of drugs and crime. In a pattern that later became a preferred tactic, Helms informed the press that he disapproved of the "Where Was Nick?" ad, telling reporters that he wanted no anti-Galifianakis ads "printed in any newspaper without my specific written approval." Although these ads were nominally sponsored by a group known as "Doctors Against Drug Abuse," the Helms campaign paid for and designed them. But Jesse did not disavow the notion of such ads, only that he had not seen them in advance; his disavowal was meaningless, and even more aggressive ads appeared during the last month and a half of the campaign.[117]

On October 4, new, full-page newspaper ads identified Galifianakis as a liberal, tying him to the McGovern campaign as a unified "McGovernGalifianakis ONE AND THE SAME" ticket. Both men, the ad claimed, had voted to override two recent Nixon vetoes that sought to limit welfare spending and were adopting a "cut-and-run" approach to the Vietnam War. In reality, neither bill had anything to do with welfare: Nixon vetoed appropriations of hospital construction and education, and they were overridden by large, bipartisan majorities.[118] Nonetheless, the Helms forces relentlessly portrayed Galifianakis as a liberal. More than that, however, they suggested that his Greek-American ethnic heritage was out of place in North Carolina. In more full-page newspaper ads, Helms forces employed the slogan "He's One of Us." Helms's managers later explained this as part of an attempt to persuade eastern North Carolina voters that Galifianakis was excessively liberal and it was "socially acceptable" to cross party lines and vote for Helms, a person that they knew well through his WRAL *Viewpoints*. Democrats saw things differently, asserting that this amounted to an ethnic slur against Galifianakis. Years later, Galifianakis remembered that the Helms campaign employed ads, signs, and even word of mouth to convey this message. One sign, he recalled, read: "This is not Greece." By election day, the 1972 Senate race had become, according to political commentator John Kilgo, "so bitter and so hotly contested" that it had "all but overshadowed other political races in this election year."[119]

During the final weeks of the campaign, with the impending Nixon landslide and Helms's attacks having an effect, Galifianakis's lead dwindled, while Jesse's supporters grew more confident. Not long before the election, Dot's brother ran into Jesse. "You may as well pack," he said, "you're going to Washington." Riding on Nixon's popularity and on what the *Charlotte Observer* described as "heavy advertising and frequent slashing attacks against his character and record," Helms pulled slightly ahead a few days before the election. At the last minute, pollster Arthur Finkelstein urged a media blitz; emphasizing the close connection between Nixon and Helms, he argued, would assure Jesse's election. In September, Ellis had published new newspaper ads that tied Helms with Nixon, and now that point would be made more explicitly in a new round of ads. Harold Herring visited Elkin textile magnate Hugh Chatham and persuaded him and several other supporters to co-sign a $100,000 bank loan. Ellis doubted whether Chatham would agree, but he knew that Herring had the "hutzpah" to ask him. Chatham agreed to endorse the loan, and the new media paid off.[120] Nixon's massive landslide—he attracted nearly 70 percent of North Carolina's presidential vote—swept Helms to office. Overall, he captured 54 percent of the vote, defeating Galifianakis by more than 120,000 votes, a margin that substantially exceeded that of fellow Republican Jim Holshouser, who narrowly captured the governorship. Learning of the news, Jesse went off by himself and prayed. In his victory statement, Helms announced his determination to return America "to the principles that made her great."[121]

Chapter 4

STANDING AGAINST THE PREVAILING WIND

Leading the New Right

In the 1960s, using modern media and communications, Jesse Helms fashioned a broad and generally effective attack on liberalism. Although his opponents have frequently underestimated him, Helms was highly effective in the use of language, and he learned how to turn words to a political purpose. In the 1940s, it was newspaper and radio; in the 1950s, television became the arena in which he did combat. Fighting liberal dragons in North Carolina, the media-savvy Helms articulated a timely critique of modern liberalism and its bastions among intellectuals, the press, universities, government, and policymakers. He further questioned liberalism's accomplishments and legacies—the civil rights revolution, the growth of the federal government at the expense of state and local power, rising taxes and bloated bureaucracy, and campus unrest and bohemian counterculture. Helms became supremely effective in using words, in his ability to play with words, fashion a language of opposition, create a competing, conservative narrative, and, above all, to use the levers of the media.

Helms's decision to run for the Senate in February 1972 moved this powerful political message onto a national stage, and when he arrived in Washington he became a leading spokesman for the conservative movement. Years of rhetorical combat had trained him well for conflict with liberalism in Washington, and in some respects, he was ahead of other conservatives in his understanding of how to use modern media for political purposes. In Congress, where many Republicans had long accommodated to a minority status, Jesse's confrontational approach isolated him within his own party. But Helms's primary goal in the 1970s was not to practice politics as usual. Rather, he wanted to upend the status quo, rally and mobilize a national conservative movement, and overturn liberals' domination. By 1980, after less than a decade in Washington, he had succeeded in these objectives to a remarkable extent.

IN THE MONTHS following his election to the Senate, Jesse began the move from Raleigh to Washington. All three children had left home; Charles started that year at Western Carolina University in Cullowhee. Patches, the six-year-old hound that Jesse called the "Lolita of Caswell Street" because she had puppies when she was a year old, was Dot and Jesse's only companion. Moving to Washington coincided with other personal transitions, including the death of Jesse's father, after a series of strokes, in January 1974. Jesse and Dot rented an unpretentious suburban home in Arlington, Virginia, for $325 a month. Subsequently, the Helmses bought a nearby house, which remained their Washington residence for the next thirty years. They also maintained their Caswell Street house in Raleigh and their vacation home at Lake Gaston, which they had purchased a few years earlier with Dot's inheritance. The Helmses judiciously avoided a lavish lifestyle. In an interview published shortly after their Washington move, Dot noted that they both were "quiet, rather reserved people"; Jesse said that they were not especially sociable people. "I came up here to work," he told an interviewer. "I feel more work and less socializing is what's needed."[1] He promised to "work hard, pray a lot, and leave the socializing to the others," he wrote, and no one had ever come to the Senate "caring less about the personal aspects" of this office than he.[2] Rather than attend evening occasions, Helms told an aide, he preferred to have dinner with some North Carolinians: "One is named Dorothy, and the other is named Patches."[3] But he remained convinced that conservatism was misunderstood; his views were so contrarian, Helms told a reporter, that some warned he might end up as a "village crackpot." His role as a leader was to explain his views and to communicate the message of those who "have been ignored and disregarded through the years" by standing "against what may be the prevailing wind."[4]

Inaugurated into the Senate on January 4, 1973, the first North Carolina Republican elected to that body in the twentieth century, Helms was escorted down the aisle by North Carolina senator Sam Ervin. Along with three other new senators, Jesse was sworn in by Vice President Spiro Agnew while his father watched from the gallery. Joining Jesse as his administrative assistant was Harold Herring, who, at age twenty-five, was reputed to be the youngest administrative assistant in Senate history. Assigned a Senate desk previously occupied by Warren Harding, Olin Johnston of South Carolina, Harry Byrd, Sr., of Virginia, and J. Melville Broughton of North Carolina, Helms refrained from carving his initials, as was Senate custom, inside the desk drawer. Instead, he waited until the Senate was out of session, as he explained to a friend, and then "crept in and did the deed."[5]

Jesse, as was his habit, wrote his own material for the press: in what were described as "offsprings" of the *Viewpoints*, on weekends he wrote weekly columns that were distributed to more than a hundred small-town North Carolina newspapers (these continued into the 1980s).[6] One of his first appointments was Clint Fuller, friend and editor of the *Franklin Times*, to serve as communications assistant, who had first met Jesse when he republished the *Viewpoint* editorials as a newspaper column. During the 1972 campaign, Fuller resigned his post as Franklin County Democratic Party chairman in order to support Helms. After the election, Jesse persuaded Fuller to come to Washington, and he began work on March 1, 1973.[7] His first responsibilities included helping the senator prepare taped five-minute radio broadcasts three times a week in which he answered prerecorded questions from reporters; Fuller also laid out Helms's newspaper pieces in two columns of camera-ready copy. Helms would insist on not having a press secretary until the 1990s, and until then staffers rarely spoke on the record and never on his behalf. Both Herring and Fuller were key aides, as was Charlie Black, who returned to Washington to coordinate political matters, supervise constituent services, and help Helms on the Agriculture Committee. During the first year of his Senate term, Helms also hired future columnist George Will as a staffer; he later described him as "shy and quiet" and looking a "great deal like Mr. Peepers of television fame a few years ago."[8] Within a year, however, Jesse's staff changed significantly. Herring left in 1974 when it was alleged that he had sold mailing lists of contributors to direct mail operators. John Carbaugh, who replaced Will, and James Lucier, both of whom came from Strom Thurmond's staff (Lucier in 1973, Carbaugh in February 1974), quickly became dominant players in Helms's office. Both men would play significant roles in the early years of Helms's senatorial operations.[9]

From the beginning, Jesse's office was legendary for its attention to constituent services. Soon after his election, Helms hired George Dunlop, one of the youthful conservatives who had been active in his 1972 campaign, to create and run home-state offices in Raleigh and Hickory for the constituent services operations. Helms, perhaps because of his experience as a Senate staffer under Willis Smith, realized the value of creating such a system. In the early 1970s, it was highly unusual for senators to offer constituent services; most would refer requests for help to local congressmen. But Helms embraced this as an opportunity to extend his network of contacts, so he ordered Dunlop to create a system that was second to none.[10]

Dunlop's operation was soon working efficiently. When North Carolinian Tom Boney came to Washington to work for Helms as a Senate intern in 1976, he found a smoothly running office. A conservative recent UNC graduate, Boney worked in the mail room for the next two years and "basically got hooked." Working out of the Carrol Arms Hotel, behind the senator's suite in the Dirksen Office Building, Boney recalled a finely honed system that produced form letters that Helms closely supervised. Rather than straight, generic letters, he and other staffers produced personalized responses that drew from Helms's letters and other writings. Before anything went out, the letters were subjected to the editing of Helms's blue felt pen. In many cases, Jesse rewrote his own prose several times in order to insure that it contained his own voice and expressions. He often took this occasion to teach writing. When staffers argued that split infinitives could be used for emphasis, he would quote his old teacher, Miss Annie Lee: she had told him that the only thing a split infinitive emphasized was "your ignorance."[11]

After only a year in the Senate, Jesse had become, according to one *Human Events* reporter, a "shining star in the conservative galaxy."[12] Helms encountered a discouraging environment in the Senate. Although in 1972 Richard Nixon had just won reelection in one of the largest landslides in American history, Democrats remained in control of both houses of Congress. For nearly twenty years, Republicans had occupied the minority side of the Senate aisle, and their leadership, for the most part, had accommodated itself to the majority. The GOP, Jesse complained to a friend in January 1973, was "*almost* as 'lib'rul' as the other side."[13] As an ideological conservative among Senate Republicans, Helms was a minority within a minority. In August 1973, he spoke to one thousand "clean-cut, well-dressed and overwhelmingly white" members of the Young Americans for Freedom in Washington who greeted enthusiastically his attacks on welfare recipients, Democrats, and the news media. His comments had a sarcastic bite. He described George McGovern, rumored to have fathered a child out of wedlock, as "probably using [an] ink eradicator on a birth certificate somewhere," while—in a reference to the car accident and death of Mary Jo Kopechne on July 18, 1969—Jesse called Edward Kennedy the

"Chappaquiddick car boy." Kennedy, Helms said, was probably "off teaching morality somewhere to a driver's education class." In a joke with distinct racial overtones, he described how welfare recipients drove north on Interstate 95 in a jalopy with a squirrel's tail hanging on its antenna and then mistook the highway number for the speed limit. Although the joke "hung silently"with the YAF crowd, Helms had become, according to one reporter, a "pop hero" among youthful right-wingers.[14]

Helms also earned a reputation as one of the Senate's hardest-working members. "The man's got a lot of charm and a genuine sense of humor," said one midwestern Democratic senator. This senator also noted that although he respected Jesse's work habits he disagreed with "every darn thing he thinks."[15] In September 1974, Jesse told constituents that he worked seventy hours a week, arriving at his desk at 7:00 A.M., rarely leaving before 7:00 P.M., and usually taking work home with him on weekends.[16] Constantly in his Washington office, Helms earned an excellent attendance record: he was present for 97 percent of the 2,200 roll calls between 1973 and 1976. He preferred the Senate to the campaign trail, and whenever he campaigned, he insisted on paying back his salary; when flying on Air Force One, he paid the cost of first-class airfare. His staff, one of the smallest in the Senate (in 1976, he returned $591,000 of congressional funds appropriated for staff), absorbed Jesse's work ethic. He refused to take the overseas junkets that most senators considered one of their perquisites. Instead, he and his staff traveled abroad only at private expense.[17]

Helms soon realized that in the Senate, minorities, even isolated minorities, could still shape Senate business. Years earlier, in the 1950s, Georgia senator Richard Russell told him that a senator without knowledge of Senate rules was "a 50 per cent senator, at best." Soon after his election, Helms obtained a copy of the Senate rulebook and studied it for six weeks. He also followed another bit of Russell wisdom: the most effective way to learn its rules, he realized, was to preside over the Senate as often as possible. He gained other useful advice from southern conservative Democrats. On occasion, Mississippi senator James Eastland would invite Helms to chat in his office, where he would offer him a bourbon. A teetotaler, Jesse declined, but he sat at Eastland's feet for advice about the Senate. Helms also relied on Senator James Allen of Alabama and Independent Senator Harry F. Byrd, Jr. On the day that Jesse was sworn into the Senate, Allen made a point of being the first senator to greet him. Subsequently, the Alabama senator mentored Jesse, and during his first months in Washington, Helms visited Allen's office on the sixth floor of the Dirksen Building twice a week.[18] Knowledge of the rules was especially important, Jesse realized, for Senate insurgents like himself. For those senators who would not "do anything difficult," he remembered, "you don't need to know the rules all that good." "But if you are willing to take over some things with intricate implications, you got to know the rules."[19]

Becoming a master of parliamentary procedure, Helms adopted a strategy of obstructionism. The Capitol press corps, according to one account, saw Jesse as a "glib gadfly, adept at tossing 'legislative smoke bombs' amid dozing Senators in the near-deserted chamber."[20] According to Senator Bill Bradley, Jesse in the 1970s pioneered the use of legislative amendments to push his agenda. Unlike other senators more skilled in thinking on their feet, however, Helms usually made his maneuvers after a great deal of preparation; his moves were not spontaneous but were well planned. Almost always, according to Bradley, Helms was out to stop something.[21] Helms became one of the Senate's most able tacticians, and he perfected the hit-and-run attack in which he would spring amendments on unsuspecting legislation. Timing was crucial. By Senate rules second-degree amendments—an amendment that followed another amendment—required a vote without further amendment, and Jesse's staff became adept at informing the senator about when he needed to rush something to the floor. Richard Shelby, a Democratic senator from Alabama who switched parties and became a Republican in 1994, once claimed that the "most feared words" in Democratic Senate ranks were "Helms has an amendment." It was said among Jesse's staff that Democratic staffers monitored the whereabouts of Helms and his staff in order to determine whether any Helms surprise attack was imminent. When Helms entered the Republican cloakroom, there was often speculation that something was afoot.[22]

Realizing that he was part of an isolated conservative minority, Helms introduced legislation that had little chance of consideration, let alone adoption. "Defeats don't discourage me," he told an interviewer in 1976, because it was "good to get people on the record" and make his fellow senators "feel the heat so they'll see the light."[23] By attracting attention, moreover, Jesse could mobilize national support for the conservative cause. His main objective, concluded one observer, was to become a "rallying point for the national conservative movement of which he sees himself as a leader." During his early years in the Senate, he thus quickly became a leading spokesman for the new conservative movement.[24] By March 1973, two months into his term, he had sponsored or co-sponsored seventeen bills and four resolutions, with the most prominent of these being two proposed constitutional amendments—one that would permit school prayer and one to end school busing. Although neither of these measures made any progress, they drew a clear line in the sand between liberals and conservatives by forcing senators to go on record.[25]

This legislative strategy became apparent early on. One of Helms's first actions as senator was to vote against confirmation of Nixon's appointee as labor secretary, Peter J. Brennan; he was only one of three senators to vote no, and the only Republican. On January 29, 1973, he reluctantly voted to confirm Elliot L. Richardson as defense secretary. Helms considered both Nixon appointees insufficient—Brennan because he was an "acknowledged strong advocate" of organized labor, Richardson because of his support for easing tensions with the Soviets through détente. In rejecting both men, he told supporters that he would not become a "yes man" for the Nixon administration.[26] Later, in September 1973, he opposed the nomination of détente's main architect, Henry Kissinger, as secretary of state; he was one of only two Republicans in opposition.[27] In addition to opposing presidential nominations, Helms often delayed them in order to pressure the White House: for example, over several weeks in 1973, he blocked forty of Nixon's sub-cabinet appointees.[28] Helms also opposed many of Nixon's measures in Congress, including emergency aid to Israel, revenue sharing, home rule for the District of Columbia, mass transit, and emergency energy legislation. He also disapproved of Nixon's wage and price controls.[29]

Yet, during the Watergate crisis, Helms remained one of Nixon's most loyal supporters, and, unlike many of his fellow Republicans, he refused to abandon the president. After the details of the Nixon administration's Watergate cover-up emerged and leading advisers resigned in late April 1973, Helms blamed the liberal media in a Senate speech. The press had distorted the Watergate scandal, Helms claimed. Did Nixon not have a constitutional right, like any other American, to be considered innocent until proven guilty? While illegal activities could not be condoned, Americans should not permit "irresponsible and venomous reporting based on half-truth and allegations."[30] The liberal media, he later wrote to a friend, had "hated Nixon ever since he exposed Alger Hiss, and they will never forgive him."[31] In late April and May 1973, Jesse met with Nixon four times in three weeks and tried to bolster his spirits, while in July he would describe the matter as a "vendetta." As the Watergate crisis progressed and fellow North Carolina Republicans such as Congressmen Jim Broyhill and Jim Martin criticized Nixon, Helms remained loyal, urging the White House to take on the president's critics.[32] Although he voted in favor of creating a Senate select committee to investigate the scandal, he supported an unsuccessful move to include an investigation of Democratic activities during the 1964 and 1968 campaigns. In the summer of 1973,

Jesse objected to the expense of the Senate investigation—though it was chaired by his colleague Sam Ervin—and denounced it as a Democratic partisan ploy to discredit and oust the president.[33] Helms described the Nixon administration's appointment of Archibald Cox as special prosecutor as "some sort of death wish."[34]

In March 1974, he refused to join in a chorus of congressmen calling for Nixon's resignation. It was a mistake, he thought, to force the president from office in order to "appease a hostile press, or even a majority of his countrymen."[35] Even as late as May 1974—only a few months before Nixon resigned, in August—Jesse declared himself "surprised and disappointed" by Nixon's use of profanity on the transcripts of his taped conversations in the White House. Still, he called the congressional impeachment inquiry "one of the greatest campaigns of smear and slander against conservatives in the history of the nation."[36] In August 1974, just before Nixon left office, Helms was one of thirty-four loyalist congressmen and senators who were summoned to the White House for a final meeting with the president just before he announced his resignation in a televised address. During the coming years, Nixon called Helms on a regular basis to chat and offer advice, and as late as February 2000 Jesse brushed Watergate off as a "silly mistake."[37]

Oppositionism became Jesse's trademark—and a way to establish himself as a leading Senate conservative. In March 1973, Helms was only one of a handful of senators who unsuccessfully opposed an $850 million federal highway appropriation. Later that year, he introduced legislation—that met an early demise in the Senate—permitting automobile manufacturers to produce cars without any pollution controls, as a way to increase gasoline efficiency.[38] In his first year, Helms proposed some ninety-six bills, none of which passed. The measures that he opposed included increases for Social Security and emergency medical benefits, federal funding for biomedical research, programs to combat child abuse, veterans training, emergency farm loans, and programs to expand aid to the elderly. Opposing a $90 million federal appropriation to establish a national center on child abuse and neglect, he denounced such an effort as "yet another step in the direction of further centralizing power and responsibility in Washington."[39]

Early in his Senate career, Helms discovered the power of the Senate filibuster, which would become perhaps the most intimidating weapon in his arsenal. In late 1973, the Nixon administration and Congress compromised on legislation to establish the Legal Services Corporation, which would provide a federally financed system of legal counsel for the poor. Federal legal services for the poor dated to the Economic Opportunity Act of 1964, and the Nixon administration, seeking to abolish the Office of Economic Opportunity, agreed to retain government-financed legal services. Helms opposed the bill, saying in a speech on the Senate floor that it would "contribute to social disruption and serve to encourage would-be rioters." The Legal Services Corporation, he warned his constituents, would "finance federal lawyers who run around the country stirring up riots and protest movements." To oppose this bill, Helms, in cooperation with Tennessee senator William Brock, launched a filibuster. He lost this battle: by a vote of 68–29, the Senate invoked the cloture rule for only the fifteenth time in its history. But cloture did not end Helms's obstruction, and he was able to delay final consideration of the bill for several months. The bill eventually passed the Senate in July 1974, despite Helms's opposition.[40]

Helms became the best-known filibusterer of the 1970s Senate—what one reporter in November 1975 called a "master of the filibuster."[41] Throughout the decade, he filibustered; he did so, he said, because this remained the "only way a minority has to work its will."[42] In August 1977, even though sorely outmatched on his filibuster against a Senate campaign finance bill—he was eventually outvoted 88–1—he was unafraid to pursue this guerrilla strategy. "No big thing," Jesse said. "Just sort of a protest."[43] Usually losing filibusters, Helms sometimes resorted to other measures. In June 1976, he filibustered a bill that would have strengthened the federal government's antitrust powers by extending a state's ability to participate in class action suits. After losing the cloture vote, Jesse used up the remaining allotted time for debate and slowed consideration by offering amendments and then demanding roll call votes on each of them. Helms ultimately lost the cloture vote on the antitrust bill, but he obtained concessions that altered the character of the bill. Helms's obstructionist tactics alienated him from the Senate leadership. In 1975, the Senate changed its cloture rules by requiring sixty votes (or three-fifths) to end debate, rather than sixty-seven (or two-thirds). In addition, in May 1977, Majority Leader Robert Byrd proposed new rules that would limit Helms's ability to make frequent quorum calls, demand a full reading of reports and daily journal, and use minor amendments to require roll calls. Helms supported Byrd's changes in order to maintain the sixty-vote cloture rule.[44]

When Gerald R. Ford succeeded Richard Nixon as president in August 1974, Helms became noticeably more aggressive in dissenting from Republican leadership. For the next two years, he worried that, in the post-Nixon years, party moderates might gain control of the party, and he was fully prepared to organize an independent conservative third party. When Ford nominated New York governor Nelson A. Rockefeller for vice president in

September 1974, Helms strongly objected. As soon as the day after Nixon resigned, Helms, along with other conservative Republicans, urged Ford to choose someone else. An old-line northeasterner, Rockefeller represented everything that Jesse objected to in mainstream Republicanism. Jesse preferred, rather than Rockefeller, a conservative such as Ronald Reagan or Barry Goldwater. Although Helms the next day disavowed having said this—"I don't fight this way," he declared—the *Observer* reporter, Paul Clancy, remained certain that he had correctly reproduced the quotation. In an interview with the *Charlotte Observer* in mid-August 1974, he called Rockefeller a "wife stealer" who was disqualified, for moral reasons, from serving as vice president. (More than ten years earlier, in 1962, Rockefeller had divorced his first wife and then, in May 1963, remarried the recently divorced Margaretta Fitler "Happy" Murphy.)[45]

Over the next few weeks, Helms continued to attack Rockefeller. On September 26, he took the extraordinary step of testifying against his nomination in hearings conducted by the Senate Rules and Administration Committee. Saying nothing about Rocky's private life, he identified the dangers of putting an extraordinarily wealthy person, with liberal inclinations, in the vice presidency. Jesse wondered whether Rockefeller would be able to place the national interest ahead of a "dynasty and wealth and power unequalled in the history of the United States." Did Americans really want one of the nation's highest offices to "be identified with one of the highest concentrations of private power in the land?" Helms emphasized that he was not so much attacking Rockefeller's wealth per se as he was the "ingrained dynastic values" that were associated with Rockefeller philanthropies that embraced abortion rights, improved relations with Communist totalitarianism, and other liberal positions. He repeated charges that Rockefeller had tampered with state funds while governor of New York and had received information from wiretaps conducted by the Nixon White House about Secretary of State Henry Kissinger. Several weeks later, Helms raised questions about the propriety of a $500,000 gift that Rockefeller had made to William J. Ronan, ex-chair of New York City's Metropolitan Transit Authority and one of his advisers while governor. In the end, however, the full Senate voted to confirm with only seven dissenting votes, despite Jesse's shrill opposition.[46]

Much of Helms's unhappiness with the Ford administration focused on the ascendancy of Secretary of State Henry Kissinger and the policy of détente that Nixon and Ford both pursued to ease tensions with the Soviet Union. Détente, Helms believed, meant compromise with the evils of Communism. The "spirit of détente" might be "on the wind," he told a meeting of the Peace Through Freedom Conference in London in September 1973, but "cold reality" would "have its day." The assumption that the Soviets wanted peace was folly, he said, for they had placed "more energy into war-like capability than ever before."[47] Negotiating with tyrants, he told an audience in June 1974, was "like caressing a rattlesnake, except that a rattlesnake is honest enough to give fair warning of what to expect."[48] Détente, he said two years later, was "nothing other than a name for a protracted period filled with negotiated settlements of many kinds" that became a "rationalization of surrender."[49] In 1973, he criticized Kissinger's handling of the Soviet wheat deal—in which, he said, the Soviets effectively cornered the market and forced up food prices in the United States. He also questioned whether Kissinger's negotiations in Vietnam had led to anything but failure. Although Jesse favored "honest agreement and… mutual concessions," he disagreed with a "paper peace" that disguised "the real power relationships in the world."[50] A former associate of Rockefeller's, Kissinger represented the foreign policy professionalism of the northeastern liberal elite that Helms despised. When Ford eased out Defense Secretary James Schlesinger in November 1975, apparently because of his anti-Soviet attitudes, Helms voted against the nomination of Ford chief of staff Donald Rumsfeld to replace him.[51] Helms remained suspicious of Kissinger's efforts at negotiating an end to the Arab-Israeli war, and in October 1975 he opposed further American involvement in monitoring Israeli withdrawal from the Sinai.[52]

Helms dramatized his conflict with Kissinger and the Ford administration during the visit of the dissident Russian author and Nobel Prize winner Aleksandr Solzhenitsyn, who in 1974 was stripped of his Soviet citizenship and exiled to Switzerland. For Jesse, Solzhenitsyn's struggle against Communism exposed the bankruptcy of détente. Americans, he wrote in his newsletter, had been "lulled into a false sense of security" in which Communism was portrayed as "no longer brutal and oppressive." Solzhenitsyn had faced hardship in order to tell the truth about the Soviet regime's brutality. On February 18, 1974, Jesse introduced a Senate resolution making Solzhenitsyn an honorary American citizen; the House turned back the resolution. In March 1974 he invited the Russian dissident to visit the United States. Helms then dispatched his Russian-speaking foreign policy adviser, Victor Fediay, to meet with Solzhenitsyn in Zurich.[53] Hearing that he was planning to visit the United States in the summer of 1975, Helms called him in Switzerland, and spoke using Fediay as interpreter. During Solzhenitsyn's subsequent visit to Washington in late June and July 1975, Helms became his unofficial sponsor and host. Because Solzhenitsyn did not like to fly, Fediay drove to Albany and ferried him by car to Washington, where he arrived on June 27. His first stop was Helms's house in Arlington; Fediay stayed at Solzhenitsyn's side as his translator during the visit. Maximizing publicity from the visit, Jesse persuaded Solzhenitsyn to visit North Carolina and telephoned UNC president Bill Friday and Wake Forest president Ralph Scales to set up campus visits. Later complaining of fatigue, the Russian author backed out of the North Carolina trip. Jesse also tried to set up a White House visit, and he and Strom Thurmond sent Ford a letter proposing a meeting when Solzhenitsyn was in Washington on June 30 addressing a meeting of the AFL-CIO.

Although Ford's aides were initially enthusiastic, Secretary of State Kissinger vetoed the idea because it might offend the Soviets. The State Department prohibited its employees from attending the AFL-CIO dinner, though some White House advisers attended nonetheless. Those who did, such as United Nations ambassador Daniel Patrick Moynihan, were criticized by the State Department. White House press secretary Ron Nessen offered various excuses for Ford's snub of Solzhenitsyn, including the claim, during a press conference on July 1, that Ford wanted to see his daughter, Susan, who was apparently about to leave for the summer. But since the son of Helms's aide Clint Fuller was then dating Susan Ford, they knew that this was not accurate. Nessen later asserted that Ford avoided a meeting for image reasons: the president liked to have some substance in meetings, and it was "not clear what he would gain by a meeting." On the same day that Ford could have seen Solzhenitsyn, he visited with the Brazilian soccer star Pelé; the Maid of Cotton; the 1974 National Farm Family; Alaska senator Ted Stevens, who delivered a map of Alaska; Representative Delbert Latta (R-OH), who gave the president a wood carving of a 33rd degree Masonic seal; and Representative Guy A. Vander Jagt (R-MI), who gave him a Bicentennial quilt and pillow.

Helms was outraged at this rebuff by the White House, and on July 7, 1975, he took his case to the Senate floor. In a "sad day for our country," Jesse declared, the president had exhibited "cowering timidity for fear of offending Communists" by refusing to meet with Solzhenitsyn, a "dedicated exponent of freedom" and a "dedicated Christian." The president's attitude constituted a "slap in the face to all the freedom-loving people throughout the world who understand the nature of communism." Ford had always extended a "lavish welcome" to visiting Communists, while he had plenty of time to meet with actors and soccer players, Helms wrote in his weekly newsletter. But he had no time for Solzhenitsyn, "one of the most remarkable men of our time." Détente had lulled Americans into complacency. It was nothing more than a "deceitful device" for Communists to promise peace while they continued to "throttle and enslave countless millions of people all over the world." American presidents now traveled to the Soviet Union and to China "with hats in hand," Helms charged. Little wonder the United States was widely regarded as a paper tiger.[54]

Turning the tables on Ford, Helms's Senate speech resulted in an outpouring of support for a Solzhenitsyn visit. While the White House received 488 negative letters, all but one correspondent to Helms was critical of Ford.[55] Conservative Republicans, a constituency most alienated from the president and least likely to support him in his 1976 reelection bid, were furious. The chairman of the Mississippi Republican Party wrote angrily to the White House, wondering whether James Schlesinger would be fired for attending the AFL-CIO dinner and for expressing "détente deviationism." Ronald Reagan, commenting in his weekly newspaper column, attacked the president. On July 11, the White House instructed press secretary Ron Nessen to tell reporters that the president would meet with Solzhenitsyn if he requested a meeting. But no reporter asked a question about Solzhenitsyn, and that evening, though Ford issued a statement, the press ignored it. The White House then called Helms's aides to assemble a meeting. Feeling the political pressure that the Solzhenitsyn affair was generating among his party's right wing, Ford attempted to repair the damage.[56]

Solzhenitsyn arrived at the Capitol in triumph on July 15, 1975, to an enthusiastic reception. Helms sponsored a Senate reception for him at the Russell Office Building, and in his remarks Solzhenitsyn urged the United States to abandon détente and to "come and interfere" in Soviet internal affairs. After the Senate reception ended, Helms and Democratic senator Henry "Scoop" Jackson—a determined critic of détente—escorted Solzhenitsyn to Jackson's office. There, at about 3:00 P.M., White House aides Russ Rourke and Max Friedersdorf, head of congressional liaison for President Ford, reached Fuller and Helms. The White House would agree to a Solzhenitsyn visit, but aides refused to issue a written invitation—something that Solzhenitsyn insisted on. Fuller showed Helms the message, and he "sort of grinned," realizing what a difficult position the situation had created for the White House. When Fediay translated the White House's message, Solzhenitsyn's response was unequivocal. Offended by the White House snub, he said firmly: "Nyet."[57]

Later reports claimed that the decision suggested the extent of

Kissinger's dominance over Ford's foreign policy. Kissinger, on July 16, confirmed that he had recommended against a meeting, insisting that Solzhenitsyn's views were a "threat to peace" and would prove disadvantageous to American foreign policy.[58] *Washington Post* columnist team Rowland Evans and Robert Novak maintained that none of the White House advisers in favor of a Solzhenitsyn meeting—Chief of Staff Donald Rumsfeld and Defense Secretary James Schlesinger—was consulted, and the matter was not brought before the National Security Council. Ford's decision also reflected the White House's "low regard" for Helms. The Solzhenitsyn affair of July 1975 was a public relations triumph for Helms and marked his divergence from Republican moderates on foreign policy issues. Helms emerged from this clash with the Ford White House with a greatly strengthened reputation as an opponent of détente and as a conservative with national stature.[59]

SOON AFTER HELMS'S election to the Senate in 1972, Tom Ellis, Jesse's closest political confidant, established the North Carolina Congressional Club as the basis of what became a Helms political machine. It was founded in order to retire a $160,000 debt that the Helms campaign owed from the 1972 Senate campaign. At first, Helms was unenthusiastic: a "direct effort" to retire the debt, he wrote in early 1974, "would have been more effective."[60] The club grew slowly. Carter Wrenn joined the organization in December 1974, at the recommendation of some of his UNC classmates who were involved in Young Republican politics. Charlie Black, serving as the political liaison on the senator's staff, persuaded Ellis to hire Wrenn. As a high school student in Durham, Wrenn remembered watching Jesse's *Viewpoint* editorials and thinking that they were "mean." He seems to have had a change of heart in college. While a UNC student, Wrenn worked as a volunteer for Helms's 1972 campaign and then, two years later, for a congressional campaign in Asheville, and following that election joined the Congressional Club as one of its few employees. Beginning in the spring of 1975, Wrenn ran things under Ellis's direction.[61]

The Wrenn-Ellis partnership dominated the club's subsequent history and, for the next two decades, provided the basis for Jesse Helms's political power. Ellis envisioned an organization that would not only retire Helms's campaign debt but would, over the long term, finance and elect conservatives to political office in North Carolina and around the country. "He was basically setting up a political campaign vehicle that would recruit and elect conservative candidates that shared Helms' philosophy or the conservative philosophy," remembered Wrenn. That was his primary goal; paying off the debt was "simply the first piece of business that had to be taken care of."[62] During the first year or so of the Congressional Club's existence, it raised money by recruiting new members and by holding dinners with well-known conservative speakers. The donor base was small, composed of people identified by Helms or Ellis. That most of them were conservative Democrats rather than Republicans was perhaps not surprising: Ellis deliberately sought to convert Democrats, showing less interest in traditional Republicans. On January 19, 1974, the club held a $25-a-plate dinner at the Royal Villa on Durham Road in Raleigh, with Senator James Buckley of New York as the featured speaker; with one thousand attending, the dinner netted $25,000. The event featured Buckley's speech and videotaped comments from fellow senators who praised Helms as a "citizen senator."[63] The club moved steadily to erase the 1972 campaign debt. By February 1975, it had raised $108,000; one thousand people had bought $100 memberships; and the club operation continued to expand with the addition of three more staff—a total of five—who sold memberships. In the summer of 1975, all that remained of the debt was a $2,000 bank note.[64]

In the 1970s, through direct mail fund-raising, the Congressional Club became one of the most powerful political action committees in the country. Direct mail, which involved using computerized mailing lists to identify, mobilize, and seek funds from a constituency, was in its infancy. In the late 1950s, conservative activist Marvin Liebman had used direct mail to organize support for his anti-China Committee of One Million. Liebman later worked for the Young Americans for Freedom, where Richard Viguerie, a conservative activist who served as the group's executive director during the early 1960s, immediately grasped this new technology's potential. Fascinated with direct mail, Viguerie had begun to identify donors by recording the names of people who had given at least $50 to the Goldwater campaign in 1964. In January 1965, only a few months after Goldwater's disastrous defeat, Viguerie organized his own company and created a business model to deal exclusively with direct mail political fund-raising. Using this model, he raised funds for conservative candidates with increasing success. He also identified a national conservative base that could be used to transform American politics. Direct mail proved successful in California, where in 1968 conservative Max Rafferty, in the Republican primary, upset incumbent senator Thomas H. Kuchel (and then lost the general election). In addition, in 1969, Viguerie used direct mail to help elect conservative Philip Crane to Congress from suburban Chicago. Three years later, he used his expertise for George Wallace's

1972 presidential campaign. Viguerie pushed conservative issues through "persuasion mail" sent to a national conservative constituency, and their mostly small donations financed conservative causes. Viguerie ran his operation as a business: he charged his customers by renting his extension mailing list—one of the largest in the country—and by processing and mailing the appeals. Direct mailings contained a long letter, often twelve pages long, that hammered away on a controversial issue. Viguerie assembled a larger master file, and, by the mid-1970s, he had created a national database of conservative donors.[65]

Viguerie met Ellis through Charlie Black, who knew him when he worked for Young Americans for Freedom in 1971–72. Although Ellis was dubious about direct mail, he arranged a meeting between Viguerie and Helms in the Senate. However, Jesse had little interest in fund-raising, and Viguerie soon realized his main contact would be Ellis. In the summer of 1975, Viguerie used Helms's name in a direct mail solicitation, while the club sent out its first appeal in order to retire its remaining debt. This early foray into direct mail yielded an avalanche of mail and checks that helped to extinguish what remained of the campaign debt. Ellis's eyes "got real big," recalled Viguerie, when he saw the fruits of direct mail. Ellis and Wrenn immediately realized the possibilities: using Viguerie's expertise, not only could they raise large amounts of money, but through direct mail they could also unify and sustain a national conservative constituency. Helms's stature as a national conservative—and the leading voice of conservatism in the Senate—would help to rally this constituency. The Congressional Club would no longer be confined to a North Carolina audience, no longer dependent on the whims of local politics. For now, Ellis and Wrenn kept this in the back of their minds, and, about a year later—following the presidential campaign of 1976—they turned their attention to exploiting its potential.[66]

The culmination of the club's campaign to retire Helms's 1972 debt occurred on July 25, 1975, when Ronald Reagan spoke to a crowd of two thousand at Raleigh's Kerr Scott Pavilion, reputedly one of the largest fund-raising events in the state's history. This was the second occasion on which Reagan had spoken at a club dinner; in October 1974, he had appeared before one thousand club supporters in Charlotte. But the scenario was now completely different, as Reagan was about to challenge Gerald Ford for the GOP presidential nomination in 1976. Ellis was an enthusiastic Reagan supporter; Helms was less sure. He had first met Reagan in the early 1960s, when he visited the WRAL studios—Helms later remembered him as a "smiling, soft-spoken, likeable youngish gentleman"—and in 1972 Reagan filmed an endorsement for the senator's campaign. Assuming that Nixon would finish his term, he saw Reagan as Nixon's successor. But Helms tried to follow a policy of never endorsing anyone in primaries. Ford's succession to the presidency in 1974 complicated matters. According to Carter Wrenn, despite Helms's aversion to supporting candidates in presidential primaries, Ellis was seeking to "marry up" Jesse and Reagan, and he lured Jesse into supporting Reagan. Ellis orchestrated a lunch visit at Reagan's Los Angeles home in August 1973, at which time Helms promised his support in a future presidential run. Helms's sparring with Ford over Rockefeller, Kissinger, détente, and Solzhenitsyn continued through most of 1975, and, along with Paul Laxalt of Nevada and James A. McClure of Idaho, he became among Reagan's most important supporters.[67]

Helms also flirted with organizing an independent conservative party. In May 1974, at a dinner honoring Clarence Manion, conservative legal expert and the dean of the Notre Dame Law School, Jesse declared that both parties were "in a state of confusion." "Could it be," he asked, "that it is time to forge new political parties, fashioned along the lines that the people are thinking, not along the existing lines of political power-seeking?" He proposed that this political realignment might be oriented around an "honest and workable conservative platform."[68] At a meeting of about five hundred people at a conference sponsored by Young Americans for Freedom and the American Conservative Union in Washington in February 1975, Helms called for an "injection of new life into our political system through the realignment of political action into philosophically consistent parties." Pointing out that low Republican voter turnout had accounted for the Democratic sweep in the congressional elections of 1974, he advocated a grassroots effort to organize conservatives and to mobilize new voters—such as Christian evangelicals who were "not presently part of the political process." He saw two possible alternatives—either that conservatives dominate the Republicans or that they form an independent party.[69] Earlier in the year, Helms was appointed chair of the Committee on Conservative Alternatives, which explored the possibility of a third party.[70] In April 1975, Helms visited Ford, warning him that the Republican right wing might defect, either to a third-party candidate, or to Reagan, should he decide to run. He urged him to move to the right and to abandon Rockefeller as vice president. By the summer, Helms had informed Ford, who announced his reelection campaign in early July 1975, that he could not support him if Reagan decided to run. Helms was "astonished" at Ford's decision to seek reelection; the president had told him earlier in his administration that he would not run. Reagan's July 1975 Raleigh speech was designed to consummate the Helms-Reagan alliance.[71]

Wrenn was assigned the task of assembling a crowd, and he gathered a list of twenty thousand names into a database. Ellis dispatched Elizabeth "Lib" Smith to put together a mailing, and she organized a team of volunteers to do a "blizzard of mail." As Wrenn remembered it, "pretty soon we were snowed under" with checks pouring in.[72] Ellis instructed Wrenn about table arrangements in order to squeeze more people into Scott Pavilion. When Wrenn told him that they could fit 1,200, Ellis responded "Cram more in," and eventually the audience contained two thousand people. Meanwhile, Ellis contacted WRAL-TV and borrowed the services of Earl Ashe—later the club's media production specialist—to provide for a live telecast of Reagan's speech. Ellis had other, strategic hopes pinned on Reagan's visit: portraying the candidate as a major force in North Carolina, thereby cementing the alliance among his campaign, the Congressional Club, and Jesse Helms.[73]

Joining Reagan in Raleigh that day were other conservative Republican senators, including Laxalt, Scott, and McClure. Scott—who had joined Jesse as a freshman senator in 1973—told the audience that the senator reminded him of Stonewall Jackson. "Your Jesse" stood "like a stone wall in the Senate for the things he believes are best for North Carolina and the United States." Introducing Reagan, Helms described him as a man who would "rather be right than president"—though adding that there was a "very good chance that he can and will be both." Opposing the formation of an independent third party for conservatives, Reagan urged true believers to work within the Republican Party, but he stressed that the party banner should be blazing with "bold colors," with "no pastels." Republicans, he warned, had no future in "blurring philosophies to make the two parties indistinguishable," and the party should not try to "be all things to all people": Reagan had switched from the Democratic Party because he believed that Republicans would be different. The United States should not "buy peace at the price of freedom" and, in a clear reference to the American defeat in Vietnam, stated that if "ever again our young men are called on to fight and die, our goal will be victory." Laying out a solidly conservative domestic agenda, Reagan declared that Americans had now "repudiated the welfare state." They had remained prosperous, he said, in spite of an interventionist federal government that had imposed high taxes on the electorate. He told his southern white audience that the recent extension of the Voting Rights Act had been "pure cheap demagoguery."[74]

Reagan's speech was the smash hit that Ellis had hoped it would be. Hundreds waved "Reagan for President" posters, and the crowd gave him a standing ovation. More important, in the summer of 1975, in fully backing the Reagan presidential challenge, the club had emerged as an independent political force. The stage was set, as well, for a power struggle for control of the North Carolina Republican Party. Traditional Republicans, located in western and Piedmont North Carolina, had run the party for most of the twentieth century; the GOP was, as Ellis recalled, "their baby." They regarded Helms's supporters—"Jessecrats," who drew on Democratic voters and whose power base was the non-Republican eastern part of the state—as interlopers. While traditional Republicans were moderate and nonideological, Jessecrats were committed conservatives. These "two political traditions," according to Carter Wrenn, were presently "thrown into the same party," but they were fundamentally uncomfortable with each other. Jessecrats were conservatives first, Republicans second. They "weren't really interested in electing a lot of moderate Republicans," and they "didn't really care if you'd been a Republican for five minutes or forty years. If your philosophy was right, that was what mattered." Helms's supporters were acutely aware that Jesse's margin of victory in 1972 was significantly greater than GOP governor Jim Holshouser's.[75]

Republicans had been divided into moderate and conservative wings since the Goldwater campaign of 1964, and these bitter feelings were worsened by Helms's arrival on the scene. In addition, Jesse had supported the establishment of an independent medical school at East Carolina University since the 1960s, while Holshouser persuaded the GOP congressional delegation to oppose it. Jesse responded by writing to Republican executive committee members, requesting their support. According to one account, the two men had words about the East Carolina University issue. There were also reports that Holshouser was contemplating challenging Helms for his Senate seat in 1978, and what was a personality conflict became a power struggle. Six months after both Helms and Holshouser were elected, in June 1973, a spat erupted when Holshouser aide Gene Anderson fired from state offices conservative Democrats aligned with Helms. Anderson had advised Holshouser since the 1960s, but many perceived him as brash, arrogant, and devious. Nonetheless, Anderson and the governor now controlled the party. Opposing Anderson was state Republican Party chairman Frank Rouse, who was allied with Helms and had supported Jim Gardner rather than Holshouser for the 1972 Republican gubernatorial nomination. According to one report, Rouse and Anderson detested each other. At one point in 1973, Rouse went to the governor with a yellow legal pad listing complaints about Anderson, and Holshouser responded: "Frank, it's a closed issue. He's here and you've got to work with him." While Holshouser and Anderson became determined to oust Rouse from the party chairmanship, Rouse allied himself with Ellis and Helms. Although subsequently it became apparent that Rouse was not a Helms loyalist, he fully accepted Jesse's support. But Rouse's campaign was no match for Holshouser's patronage powers, and in the fall of 1973 the governor succeeded in electing Carteret County's Tom Bennett as state chairman over Rouse.[76]

The Helms-Holshouser conflict was related to the club's support for Reagan, as Holshouser aligned himself with Ford. In early August, when the governor announced his support for the president's reelection bid at a large press conference with one hundred members of the state GOP, Helms was noticeably absent.[77] Jesse continued to urge Ford to move to the right: in the spring and summer, he informed him that Rockefeller was a political liability, and in July he told a reporter in an interview that the president would be committting a "serious error" if he retained Rocky.[78] In early November, Rockefeller announced that he would not serve as vice president if Ford were reelected. Helms claimed that, as early as July 1975, the White House had informed him about Rockefeller's decision because he would be a drag on the ticket.[79] Helms urged Reagan to enter the race officially; although he had effectively decided, his campaign managers delayed the decision until November 20, 1975. Helms began active involvement in the Reagan campaign in August 1975. In mid-August, he complained that Betty Ford, the president's wife, had made "appalling" and "unwise" comments in support of abortion rights, the Equal Rights Amendment, premarital sex, and the use of marijuana. He believed that she might become a political issue in North Carolina. Meanwhile, Helms fought it out with Holshouser.[80] At the North Carolina Republican convention in mid-November 1975, Helms broke protocol by turning a portion of the meeting into a "minirally" for Reagan; in an eighteen-minute speech, Jesse called him "our party's most articulate and exciting spokesman." Holshouser, who spoke after Helms, was caught flat-footed. He was forced to scrap his prepared speech and deliver an impromptu appeal for Ford.[81]

Reagan's campaign in the North Carolina primary soon assumed critical significance. The campaign's national managers hoped to win a primary or two initially and then begin a strong showing in the South. By August, Ellis took charge of the North Carolina campaign. By September, he and Wrenn, along with several other staffers, were working full-time, with many late nights. The campaign became a battle between the political organizations of Helms and Holshouser: while Ford's campaign, according to one account, was a "warmed-over group of Holshouser campaign workers from 1972 who have floated in and out of state government and on and off the staffs of other candidates since that time," Reagan's campaign was "primarily a warmed-over group of Helms campaign workers from 1972 who have worked either for the Senate staff or the senator's sideline political fund-raising organization since that time." But a crucial difference was that the Reagan campaign in North Carolina took on the aura of a crusade.[82]

For Governor Holshouser, a strong showing promised to lead to a position in the Ford White House, possibly even the vice presidency. For Helms, the election battle reduced to whether conservatives could achieve what he often called "philosophical unity" and a "rebirth."[83] Helms and Ellis's focus on ideology meant that they were generally unconcerned with party building and that they were very willing, even eager, to bypass normal procedures in order to acomplish their objectives. In North Carolina, Helms and Ellis essentially ignored the party organization. In 1974, Jesse did little to help the Republican senatorial candidate, William Stevens, who was allied with Holshouser's moderate Republicans, and he openly sympathized with Democratic candidate Robert Morgan. He also did little to recruit candidates, either for statewide offices or for the legislature. Nationally, Ellis and Helms also sought to create an extra-party basis for the conservative cause. Helms held "only a slight personal feeling of attachment to the party," noted one reporter. Helms's political history indicated that he was "interested in a cause, but not the cause of the Republican party as such," and his primary concern was furthering the "Reagan philosophy" rather than party interests. Reagan's candidacy thus became a vehicle for Helms and Ellis's attempts to create an ideologically conservative political party.[84]

In contrast to Helms and Ellis, Reagan campaign manager John Sears and other advisers wanted Reagan to run a nonideological campaign focused on leadership issues and to avoid alienating the political center. Ellis fundamentally disagreed with this strategy for ideological and practical reasons. Convinced that Reagan could win only if he made a strong conservative appeal, Ellis wanted an aggressive campaign that directly took on the president. In October 1975, Charlie Black, at the recommendation of his Young Americans for Freedom friend David Keene, joined the Reagan campaign staff; Sears recruited him, and Reagan called Jesse for permission to borrow Black. But Black's participation in the national campaign exposed larger tensions. Ellis perceived Black, according to Wrenn, as "part spy, part advocate." Clint Fuller believed that Ellis was "planting" Black, perhaps hoping eventually to obtain a vice presidential nomination for

Helms. By early 1976, as Ellis saw things, Sears had "turned Charlie into his spy," and Ellis excluded him from the club's inner circle. Clint Fuller, who lived in the same apartment complex as Black and considered him a friend, later observed that Black was "caught in the middle" of the Sears-Ellis conflict. Because of tensions with Reagan's campaign managers, recalled another staffer, it was generally agreed that it "would not be comfortable" for Black to return to the Helms operation.

In early 1976, Helms and Sears gathered with Ellis and Wrenn in Washington in what one attendee described as a "pretty hot meeting." The meeting in Washington not only indicated tensions between political professionals like Sears and ideologues like Ellis, it also suggested the dynamic of the Helms-Ellis relationship. Helms had, for the most part, stayed out of Ellis's struggle with Sears. While Ellis pushed hard to get Reagan to make his campaign more ideological, Sears maintained that in the upcoming New Hampshire primary Reagan enjoyed a large lead, and that their cautious strategy would result in a knockout punch without dividing the party. Helms initially backed off from the discussion and remained noncommittal. According to Wrenn, Jesse "didn't really want to push himself into the Reagan campaign." Although he supported Ellis's position, Helms "didn't really break anybody's arms to do what Ellis wanted him to do," and refused to take his case over Sears's head directly to Reagan. Ellis left that meeting thoroughly disgusted, and communication with Sears became limited.[85]

In fact, Reagan was badly prepared for the early primary season. In late 1975 and early 1976, Ford regrouped by moving to the right, and the strategy seemed to pay off.[86] By the March 23, 1976, North Carolina primary, Reagan had lost to Ford in New Hampshire, Vermont, Massachusetts, Illinois, and Florida, and his campaign appeared headed to an early defeat. Party leaders called on Reagan to withdraw, while his campaign laid off workers and the candidate flew on commercial airlines because of a lack of funds. In desperation, Reagan's managers turned over control of the North Carolina campaign to Ellis. The one exception to Ellis's autonomy occurred when the North Carolina campaign reprinted a newspaper article suggesting that Edward Brooke, the African American senator from Massachusetts, might become Ford's running mate. The reprint, many believed, was an obvious ploy to use the race issue against Ford. The national Reagan campaign wanted nothing to do with this, however, and Keene told Ellis to destroy the flyers or to expect a disavowal from the Reagan campaign. Somehow, however, *News and Observer* reporter Ferrel Guillory walked into a campaign headquarters and found the flyers. Thereafter, the story made its way into the press. At a press conference, Reagan denounced the reprints—an obvious racial appeal—and Ellis blamed the Reagan managers for undermining his effort.[87]

To run Reagan's campaign, Ellis relied entirely on the Congressional Club. For data management and polling, Ellis used Arthur Finkelstein, a Columbia University graduate college libertarian who had once participated in a radio show with fabled libertarian Ayn Rand. Starting his career as a pollster with NBC News, in 1970 he worked on James Buckley's mercurial but successful campaign in New York as an independent Conservative Party candidate for U.S. Senate. Ellis sought to model the 1972 Helms campaign on Buckley's victory. After he heard about Finkelstein, he recruited him. Carter Wrenn, who worked with him in numerous campaigns, described Finkelstein as able to "take a poll and look at numbers, and see emotions." Finkelstein, who was gay and would later break with Helms because of the senator's anti-gay positions, was casual; Ellis was rarely without a tie. But the two men developed and sustained a creative energy. Ellis appreciated Finkelstein's intelligence and ability to understand politics. "Just knock on his head," he said once, "and he'll give you an idea." Being in a room with Finkelstein and Ellis was like watching a "wrestling match . . . at the Coliseum," according to Wrenn, but Ellis "absolutely just challenged him, pumped him." The Finkelstein-Ellis partnership provided a creative synergy for political ads and strategies.[88]

In the 1976 Reagan campaign, at Finkelstein's insistence club workers painstakingly gathered lists of Republican voters off local registration rolls, which they recorded on index cards and entered into a computer. This system of voter identification, according to Wrenn, was the "whole Reagan organization" in the 1976 North Carolina primary. The club dispatched volunteers to obtain lists from boards of elections; using these names, the club assembled the list, and "we mailed it and we phone-called it." Later, Wrenn constructed a political organization composed of workers who received a minimal salary but who were responsible for mobilizing voters in key counties. The club was at the cutting edge of a new approach to political mobilization. The club's efforts at assembling what became known as "The List"—a roster of eighty thousand voters—would also provide essential data for future efforts at voter mobilization. At the same time, the club also built up a contributor list of 350,000 names that provided a national fund-raising base.

Under Ellis's direction, the Reagan campaign in North Carolina was hard-hitting, aggressive, and heavily dependent on media exposure. For months, Ellis had pressured Sears to broadcast a complete Reagan speech. In the 1964 Goldwater campaign, Ellis had bought airtime to broadcast

"The Speech," the legendary address that Reagan made in October 1964 in support of Goldwater, and the results demonstrated Reagan's ability to reach audiences on television. Ellis had originally thought of rebroadcasting "The Speech," but his media people discouraged using it because it was on black-and-white film. Instead, Ellis instructed Wrenn to play "The Speech" before private audiences. Although this ran contrary to conventional wisdom, which called for short, one-minute or thirty-second clips, Ellis was convinced that extended television exposure was a key to making Reagan's case. When Ellis sought a more recent Reagan broadcast, the national campaign was uncooperative, and he "kept raising Cain and getting nowhere." Only after Helms intervened by calling Nancy Reagan did he receive a copy of a thirty-minute speech Reagan had given in Miami. Although Ellis wanted to have a North Carolina background the tape was obviously shot in Florida—with palm trees in the background—but Ellis's media people were able to edit these out. The telecast of the Reagan speech, which aired for five consecutive days before the election, was a "smash hit," as Wrenn recalled it. The heart of the Reagan broadcast— which Ellis also distilled to a thirty-second campaign commercial— criticized "the collapse of the American will and retreat of American power" that détente represented. Reagan's managers permitted Ellis to use the tape only if he would raise the money to air it. Ellis agreed on the condition that all money he raised would be spent in North Carolina. The Reagan campaign concurred if they received the federal matching dollars on these funds. Ellis's fund-raising produced a cash flow, according to one account, of about $10,000 to $20,000 per day. During February and March 1976, club organizers transported the checks to Washington, and every day the Citizens for Reagan treasurer, Angela "Bay" Buchanan, would cut a new check to Ellis's couriers, either Alejandro "Alex" Castellanos or Mark Stephens.

Castellanos was quickly becoming a rising star in the Helms organization. Having fled Cuba as a child, he grew up in North Carolina's Harnett County, and attended UNC–Chapel Hill on the coveted Morehead Scholarship. Involved in conservative politics, he went to Raleigh to volunteer for the club while still a student. A member of the Morehead selection committee, George Coxhead, called and told Wrenn that Castellanos was interested in taking some time off from school to work on the campaign. He was interviewed by Wrenn and another club staffer, Paul Reynolds, and they were immediately impressed. Castellanos was also impressed with the club. He met Wrenn, whom he described as a "big heavy kid" who was wearing Converse Chuck Taylor All-Stars and smoking a cigar. As the

1976 campaign geared up, Castellanos began playing a larger and more critical role in club operations.[89] He joined a crew of young activists who were working in the club's campaign for Reagan that included, along with Wrenn and Castellanos, Rick Miller and Reynolds. All four lived together in an apartment at the intersection of Oberlin Road and Glenwood Avenue in Raleigh. Castellanos remained with the club until 1978, when he joined Finkelstein in his political consulting business. As the club grew, the core group of young activists closely bonded, and often ate together and socialized within their circle.[90]

As the North Carolina primary approached, the level of distrust between Raleigh and Washington remained high. Reagan's campaign directors remained wary of the Helms organization, and they feared alienating traditional Republicans who supported Holshouser. Despite tensions between the Helms and Reagan operatives, the senator and Reagan maintained very cordial relations.[91] More important, Ellis's efforts turned the tide for the Reagan campaign in North Carolina—and nationally. Helms threw himself into the campaign, touring the state on Reagan's behalf—though he paid back his Senate salary at a rate of $123 per day while he was on the campaign trail. Meanwhile, Ellis persuaded campaign leaders to commit Reagan to nearly a week of campaigning in the state. When the Ford managers pressured Reagan to quit the race, Helms appeared in Goldsboro four days before the election and declared that Reagan was "not a loser, and he's not quitting!" Reagan was, he thought, the "best chance we have to elect a president who will stand up for traditional American values, free enterprise, strong national defense, and prosperity without inflation."[92] At the same time, the campaign became much more aggressive in its attacks on Ford. The American Conservative Union joined the effort by sponsoring radio spots criticizing Ford for his policy of détente. Ellis persuaded Reagan to spend the week before the primary exclusively on the stump in North Carolina, where he hit Ford hard, especially on foreign policy issues.[93]

Highly visible in the Reagan campaign, Jesse served as a surrogate for Reagan in the attack strategy. He criticized Ford for the "horrendous inflation," which he tied to a rising federal deficit. Helms also warned of a possible agreement to relinquish control of the Panama Canal, which, he said, meant the decline of American economic and military power. Helms further portrayed Reagan as an anti-Washington outsider—a successful theme that had already worked for Democratic candidate Jimmy Carter. Helms also attacked Governor Holshouser, whose unpopularity was growing among North Carolina Republicans. In a speech in Wilmington, Helms ridiculed a report that Holshouser might become Ford's vice presidential nominee, describing this as a "politics as usual" maneuver that sought votes from liberal Republicans. He also sarcastically transposed Holshouser's name with his chief political aide Gene Anderson, calling them "Governor Anderson" and "Gene Holshouser."[94] Campaigning in the Florida primary, which occurred a week before the North Carolina election, Helms directly attacked Ford. "Let there be no mistake," he declared. "The Jerry Ford who is today President is not the Jerry Ford who was a U.S. representative from Michigan." Ford, Helms charged, had accepted Kissinger's policy of dé-tente, "hook, line, and sinker." The president was on the verge of establish-ing diplomatic relations with Cuba and Castro and was now ready to give away the Panama Canal.

With the Panama Canal the Reagan campaign discovered a particu-larly useful issue for voters. Reagan had first broached the subject in Florida; by the time of the North Carolina primary, it had become a full-blown issue. There had been leaks that Kissinger was negotiating what might become a treaty to turn the canal over to the Panamanians. Helms also warned that Kissinger would attempt to transfer the canal by executive order rather than by treaty. As early as April 1975, Helms helped to gather signatures from thirty-seven senators and 245 members of the House against a treaty, effectively scuttling the negotiations.[95] Helms felt strongly about the canal as a test of American strength. Americans had a right to keep sovereignty over the canal, Helms said, and now Kissinger was seek-ing to "give it all away." Ford, Helms claimed, was being "led around by his nose" by advisers, chiefly Kissinger.

Encouraged by Helms's political managers, Reagan tapped into values that many North Carolinians held dear. George Dunlop, who worked for the Reagan campaign with Helms, recalled that a turning point came in a visit to a rural school auditorium in Alamance County in March 1976. Ellis insisted that the candidate reach out into the hinterlands, and Dunlop arranged logistics. After his speech, Reagan turned to the audience for a question-and-answer session. Commonly, Dunlop recalled, North Car-olina audiences wanted to know two things of candidates: what was their favorite hymn, and what was their favorite Bible verse? A questioner asked Reagan the latter, and he was prepared with a successful answer. Without hesitation, he responded: Second Chronicles 7:14: "If My people which are called by My name shall humble themselves, and pray, and seek My face," the verse read, "and turn from their wicked ways; then will I hear from heaven, and will forgive their sin, and will heal their land." Easily reciting the verse from memory, Reagan told the audience that he included it in daily prayer. According to Dunlop, the word then went out among North Carolinians: "Ronald Reagan is with us." Reagan's remarks, remembered Dunlop, were interpreted by the audience as "standing up for Jesus."[96]

The appeal to values worked. On March 23, Reagan carried the North Carolina primary by 53 percent to Ford's 47 percent, a margin of slightly more than twelve thousand votes. Reagan's win in North Carolina immediately revitalized his campaign, which went on to major victories and continued to challenge Ford through the Kansas City Republican National Convention. The North Carolina win also revived Reagan's lagging fundraising, and money started pouring in. Although Reagan would narrowly lose the presidential nomination, he had positioned himself well for his subsequent run at the presidency four years later. This was, according to one of Reagan's biographers, the "turning point of Reagan's political career."[97] But Reagan's primary win in North Carolina also marked a turning point in Helms's career. The primary, observed *Washington Star* editorialist Ed Yoder, had become a proxy war between Helms and Holshouser. While Helms represented a new face to the southern GOP voters that the party had "recruited in droves in the suburbanizing South since the Democratic party cast its lot with civil rights," Holshouser appealed to "old-fashioned" Republicans.[98]

No one doubted that the victory was the result of Jesse's political organization, which succeeded in identifying and turning out the vote. Before the primary, Ellis had predicted that if Republican turnout reached 200,000—an increase of thirty thousand voters from the 1972 Republican gubernatorial primary—Reagan would win. In the end, about 194,000 Republicans showed up at the polls.[99] The larger turnout helped Reagan to carry the urban Piedmont cities of Raleigh, Durham, Greensboro, and Winston-Salem by large margins, and to win Charlotte by a narrower margin. Reagan carried all of the state's congressional districts except for the 11th, in the far western mountain counties. Some asserted that Reagan's win reflected Helms's personal popularity and prestige. This was a "Jesse Helms victory," said conservative activist Phyllis Schlafly, and "if all our conservatives would just tend to their knitting—and do the job in their own states—we could win nationally." In truth, the credit for Reagan's win lay with Tom Ellis and his strategy of expanding Reagan's exposure and emphasizing conservative ideology. Post-election polls of key precincts in North Carolina found that an overwhelming number of those Republican voters disturbed about détente voted for Reagan. The Holshouser team had managed Ford's campaign poorly, and they failed to get their voters to the polls, and post-election reports suggested a voter backlash against the governor. Ford's loss effectively ended Holshouser's political career, and he would never again run for public office. The governor was "now dangling from a broken limb," said the *Winston-Salem Journal*, with his influence in party affairs shattered.[100]

Now indisputably in charge, the Congressional Club solidified control of the state Republican Party. In 1977, their allies elected Fayetteville Republican Jack Lee, a Helms stalwart, as party chair, and the club maintained firm control over the party for the next decade. Ellis did not "give a whip" about the party in 1976, he recalled: what governed him was his desire to elect Reagan. In the months after the primary, Ellis and the Congressional Club filled Republican district conventions with their supporters, outhustling Holshouser and the Ford campaign and refusing to seat Ford delegates in proportion to the primary vote. By July 1976, the race for the nomination remained extremely close, and both sides scoured for delegates. With Ellis in control of the North Carolina Republican state convention in June 1976, Holshouser and other moderates such as Charlotte congressman Jim Martin demanded that they be sent as delegates to the Kansas City convention. But Ellis, with Helms's approval, refused to seat any moderate Republicans, including Holshouser, unless they pledged to vote for Reagan. Although Helms and Holshouser conferred in late May in a meeting that textile magnate Hugh Chatham brokered, no resolution occurred, and at the party's state convention the governor was denied a slot as delegate-at-large. When Holshouser spoke before the convention, he was booed. This marked "the moment at which Sen. Helms completed his conquest of the N.C. Republican party," wrote *Charlotte Observer* columnist Reese Cleghorn. Holshouser's humiliation indicated not so much a "personal sting" as the solidification of "right wing control of North Carolina's struggling Republican party." Helms, Cleghorn concluded, exhibited a "scorn for the Republican party, except when it is a vehicle for his rigid ideology." Even some of Helms's supporters later described Holshouser's treatment as a "gratuitous slap." Helms's partisans regarded any notion of fostering party unity as "nonsense," remembered a reporter who attended the convention, and they despised the "very notion" of compromise.[101]

By the end of the primary season, with Ford possessing a narrow delegate majority, Ellis pursued a two-sided strategy that sought to maximize the exposure of the conservative cause before a national audience. Like other Reagan supporters, he argued that Reagan should continue the fight, and he searched the country for delegates who might switch sides.[102] Ellis also fought to keep the Reagan campaign ideologically pure. Campaign manager John Sears had frequently clashed with Ellis about whether Reagan should define himself as a conservative ideologue, or whether he should seek to move to the middle. The Sears approach failed in the early primaries, while the Ellis approach succeeded in the North Carolina primary and after. Reagan's manager, meanwhile, sought to smooth over differences between Helms and Holshouser, hoping, perhaps, to attract moderate Republican delegates to their cause. Reagan aide David Keene thus visited North Carolina in mid-June 1976; after his return to Washington, he told Holshouser that he had urged Ellis that "reasonableness is not a sin," though he admitted that "only time will tell if he agrees."[103]

With Reagan about a hundred delegates short of the nomination, Ellis pursued a strategy that, with or without the cooperation of the national campaign, tried to make the platform the centerpiece of the conservative struggle. Ellis appealed to conservative Ford delegates by pushing campaign planks that were further right than Ford. With the help of East Carolina University political science professor John East, Ellis constructed an alternative party platform and ordered Wrenn to summon Reagan's state party chairmen to meet in Atlanta, before the convention. When Reagan's advisers tried to block the meeting, Ellis instructed Wrenn to convene it anyway, "Sears or no Sears." In the end, about thirty of Reagan's state chairmen attended, with Reagan aides Charlie Black, Lyn Nofziger, and David Keene reluctantly present. East drafted alternative platform planks and served as the insurgents' representative and advocate. Ellis announced his plan: using a platform fight to polarize the convention ideologically and to attract conservative Ford delegates to the Reagan cause. The meeting ended with general agreement, although the Reagan managers, urging patience, told the meeting that a "surprise" would soon occur.[104]

Reagan managers had already concluded that, without a radical change in strategy, the fight for delegates was lost. Within days their "surprise" became public: immediately after the Atlanta meeting, Charlie Black returned to Washington and met with Helms at his house about 8:00 in the evening to brief him about an important decision: the next day, Reagan would announce the selection of moderate senator Richard Schweiker of Pennsylvania as his choice for vice president. Schweiker was no movement conservative; the strategy sought to capture the ideological center and thus sway Republican delegates. Although Helms disagreed with Schweiker on many issues, Black told Helms, they agreed about the abortion issue and school prayer. The Schweiker strategy might succeed or fail, but if the Reagan campaign did nothing they would almost certainly lose the nomination. It was worth the risk, Black declared, because "this is our one chance." Helms, by the end of the meeting, had "half talked himself into it." He understood the strategy, though doubts remained. Helms's chief of staff, Clint Fuller, who heard about Black's phone call from Helms, recalled things a little differently: he said that Jesse "blew his cool" about the Schweiker selection. Whatever the senator's immediate reaction, Black swore Helms to secrecy, and, although the meeting ended without any firm commitment, Black hoped to have him present at a noontime Washington press conference the next day, Monday, July 26, when Schweiker would be introduced.

After Reagan, in California, read a statement choosing Schweiker, the Washington press conference proceeded. Helms attended, but his concerns about Schweiker remained. Sometime Sunday evening, Helms had spoken with Reagan, and, according to his account, expressed his doubts. At the press conference, he was placed prominently in a front row—as a way, perhaps, of signifying the Republican right's acceptance of the Schweiker nomination. While waiting for the press conference to begin, Fuller ran into Reagan aide Peter Hannaford. "Clint," Hannaford said, "I don't think your man has any business at this thing." "I don't think so, either," Fuller replied, and he then approached Helms. "Everybody thinks I'm going to give you an urgent message," Fuller whispered to Helms. "I am: get out of here." Helms then quickly left the press conference before it began, and the cameras started rolling. The entire proceeding, as Fuller later remembered it, was a "bummer."[105]

According to Wrenn, Ellis did not learn about the Schweiker decision until it became public, and—along with the other Reagan chairmen—Ellis was "livid" about the choice and angry at Helms for not informing him ahead of time. This was "throwing a match on a barrel of gasoline," remembered Wrenn. Ellis remembered that the only time Reagan ever called him on the telephone was on July 27, the day after the Schweiker announcement. "Have you talked to Jesse Helms about this before you did it?" Ellis asked angrily. "I can't believe that you all would leave us hanging." Ellis's wife, passing in the hallway, was shocked that her husband would speak this way to Reagan. For Ellis, Schweiker's selection seemed to him a capitulation to the party's liberal wing—as much, perhaps, as Ford's selection of Rockefeller in 1974 had been. In the twenty-four hours following the Black-Helms meeting, Helms realized that the choice of Schweiker would arouse a conservative revolt, and he swung against it. According to Wrenn, Helms never "gauged how livid the right wing was going to be," and the revolt of his conservative supporters over the Schweiker selection forced him to reassess his position. Although previously he had believed that the decision might help gain some additional undecided delegates, he was now forced to take a strong anti-Schweiker position. Jesse told reporters that when Reagan called him the evening before the announcement—during which he had tacitly approved of the nomination—this was "the shock of my life." Moreover, in what Wrenn described as a "tactical repositioning," Helms now became Schweiker's strong opponent. Interviewed at the convention, Rockefeller described Helms as "terribly upset" with Reagan's vice presidential choice, and he predicted that the senator would try to "do the same thing to Schweiker that he tried to do to me." Helms had an abiding distrust of Rockefeller Republicans: Rockefeller and Helms, said a *New York Times* reporter, were like "mismatched bookends at opposite ends of a long shelf." At one point, at a pre-convention party, when they ran into each other, they "studiously ignored each other's presence, carefully avoided each other's eyes and masterfully used a clump of indoor greenery to maintain their proper ideological distance."[106]

Even before the Schweiker decision, Helms and his supporters were concerned about the apparent drift toward the center, and they worried that Reagan had become so absorbed with chasing delegates that he would ignore the platform. "A lot of people think this will help balance the ticket, but I didn't think we were looking for balance," declared Ellis. He preferred presenting voters with a "clear ideological choice—a liberal Democratic ticket against a totally conservative Republican ticket." Helms informed reporters that the North Carolina delegation might not support Schweiker. Although his support of Reagan was "firm," Helms said, "I have never committed to Mr. Schweiker." In early August, there were rumors that Helms might be nominated as vice president as a conservative alternative.[107]

The conservative rebels arrived a week before the Kansas City convention opened in order to marshal their forces, and on August 8 they met with about fifty conservative delegates from around the country. Arriving with a package of twenty-two hard-core platform items, Helms now became fully involved in the fight. Rather than a "Reagan operation," said Ellis, he and Helms were "just enunciating some principles that we think the Republican party should stand for, and we are encouraging like-minded delegates to go along with us."[108] Helms's operation was semiautonomous: Reagan aide Lyn Nofziger told a reporter that there were three groups at the convention, Ford supporters, Reagan supporters, and those "crazy SOBs from North Carolina."[109] On August 11, Sears brokered a compromise in which two Reagan aides, Martin Anderson and Edwin Meese, met daily with the Helms forces to plot strategy—and to monitor their activities. Helms's platform battle occurred to the "obvious chagrin" of the Reagan team, according to veteran *Washington Post* reporter Jules Witcover, and they had little desire to wage a floor fight. Helms's "mini-rebellion" against Ford, they feared, was also directed against moderates in the Reagan campaign.[110]

Despite attempts to restrain him, Helms continued to attract media coverage. On August 11, speaking to the full platform committee in its three days of hearings at Kansas City, Helms delivered a speech that roused up the conservative faithful. Although some saw politics as the art of compromise, he viewed it as "a challenge to provide principled leadership." A political party that could not follow "a forthright course of action to inspire the nation to rise to greatness is a political party that will wither and blow away." "Our people believe in God, and they see government as threatening the moral order," he said. Conservatives worried about the secularization of education, opposed school busing, saw abortion as "destroying the most important elements of family life," and wanted to "work when and where they please, without dictation by government or union monopoly." Welfare, conservatives believed, destroyed the work ethic. Republicans should not avoid the difficult task of "stating precisely the principles in which we believe." Why, he asked, should conservatives "shrink from truth in the pursuit of expediency?"[111]

Helms's pressure tactics soon paid off. On August 11, the same day, the platform committee voted to reject a pro–Equal Rights Amendment plank, which had been part of the Republican platform since 1940.[112] Helms supporters continued to raise the stakes. While the platform fight was occurring, a rumor surfaced that New York conservative senator James Buckley might announce himself as a third candidate for the Republican nomination, with Helms's support. The move came from Arthur Finkelstein, who saw it as a way to draw delegates away from Ford.[113] The Helms forces sought further leverage by circulating reports that the senator might bolt from the Republican Party if he lost the platform fight. "As long as the Republican party offers a hope for conservative positions," Jesse told one reporter, "I will stick with it." "And I still have hope." Ellis hinted that Helms might become disenchanted with the Republicans; the senator would be "awfully disappointed" if his platform proposals were not adopted. Other reports suggested that Helms might accept the presidential nomination for a new national conservative party that was being organized in Chicago later in August.[114] Although Helms denied reports that he might lead a third-party exodus, he was applying maximum pressure in order to exact concessions.[115]

There was little likelihood that Helms would leave the Republicans: he had already gained considerable influence within the party, and his forces were riding on the crest of a conservative wave in public opinion. In the end, Helms lost on the foreign policy plank, which sought to repudiate the Nixon-Ford-Kissinger policy of détente and conciliation on the Panama Canal, but won on the domestic issues plank, which was more conservative as a result of his pressure tactics. Although he threatened to take an omnibus platform to the convention floor, these were empty threats. Ellis's strategy was based on a platform fight, by which he hoped to polarize the convention and entice wavering delegates into Reagan's camp. Realizing Ellis's strategy, Ford's supporters responded by conceding virtually everything on domestic issues. Helms's platform negotiator, John East, returned with concessions, not realizing that Ellis wanted confrontation. In the long walk from their hotel to the convention center, Ellis pushed East in his wheelchair—East had long ago been paralyzed by polio—and tried to make him understand the necessity of maintaining conflict with the Ford forces. Ellis needed an issue around which he could write a minority plank to take to the convention floor—something, according to Wrenn, that the Ford campaign would not be able to "choke down." He found it on foreign policy issues. East had proposed a foreign policy plank entitled "Morality and Foreign Policy" that repudiated Kissinger and détente; it was voted down by the platform committee. Hoping to expose fractures in Ford's support among the delegates, Ellis tried to force a roll call vote on the plank. Convention rules provided that if three state delegations requested a roll call, the chair had to permit it; Ellis had gathered the support of five states. But after Ellis tried to force a vote, Ford supporters, with the complicity of Reagan's managers, adopted the majority plank by acclamation at 2:00 A.M. Ellis's microphone was turned off when he tried to protest. He was hoarse for a week, he recalled, because of his futile efforts to be heard. Yet the final platform was decidedly more conservative as a result of Helms's and Ellis's efforts. In addition to eliminating the pro-ERA plank, the Republican platform called for a constitutional amendment banning abortion, endorsed legislation that would defend the "traditional American family," called for military superiority in the arms race with the Soviets, and condemned "Marxist" activity in Central America.[116]

At Kansas City, Helms's main accomplishment was in attracting attention to himself and to the conservative cause. Mainly interested in building a movement, said one columnist, Helms was "busy pulling apart the Republican party like a man pulling apart the wishbone of a chicken." He believed "the same thing about political parties that he believes about wishbones: It doesn't matter if you tear them apart, just as long as you get the biggest piece." Jesse was "uncontrollable by any faction of the party."[117] Helms also served the conservative cause by attracting media attention, and he became, according to Wrenn, a "press star." Both Ellis and Helms were "pretty damned delighted" about this attention. With the platform fight over, Ellis pushed another publicity stunt: a last-minute effort to nominate Helms as Ford's vice presidential candidate. The idea had been dreamed up in a brainstorming session of Helms's advisers, in the last of a series of publicity efforts by Ellis. A Helms vice presidential candidacy, Ellis admitted to reporters, was a symbolic move seeking to anoint Jesse as the "incumbent leader of the conservative movement in the country." After his supporters put his name in nomination on the last day of the convention, August 19, Helms quickly agreed to withdraw, in exchange for a prime-time speaking spot. Waiting until the nomination was submitted, Helms pulled out—though he nonetheless tallied 103 votes.[118] Speaking before the convention in prime time on August 19, he seconded Reagan's nomination, but his speech became a manifesto for a conservative revolution. Urging Americans to follow Solzhenitsyn's advice that "we place our trust in God, not politicians," Jesse sharply criticized Ford's policy of détente. Americans were not prepared to "give away" the Panama Canal, nor were they satisfied with a national defense that was not first in the world. The Helsinki Accords of August 1975, which provided for détente in Europe, had slammed the door "on freedom for captive nations," while the United States was preparing to "sell her Chinese friends on Taiwan down the river—just to curry favor with the Communists in Peking."[119]

FOLLOWING HIS NOMINATION in 1976, Gerald Ford would narrowly lose the White House to Democratic candidate Jimmy Carter. But the Republican defeat, for Helms, merely set the stage for the advancement of the conservative cause. With Reagan's 1976 campaign, according to Wrenn, Helms had taken a "huge big step" toward emerging as a national conservative leader.[120] In large part because of his efforts, Jesse and his conservative allies had achieved substantial gains during the previous four years. Because of his "remarkable consistency on the issues," said *Human Events* editor M. Stanton Evans, Helms had emerged "as a conservative leader in almost every sector of political combat."[121] In the Senate, Helms had fought hard to obstruct his liberal enemies and to publicize conservative issues. His critics frequently noted that his noisy efforts bore few fruits in the form of legislation. As usual, his opponents underestimated Jesse Helms: during his early Senate career, his most important accomplishment was the construction of a new, more unified national constituency. The causes that Helms embraced became the mobilizing issues cementing together a new conservative coalition—opposition to abortion, the Equal Rights Amendment, the Supreme Court's banning of mandatory school prayer, and crosstown busing to achieve racial integration. While he offered himself as a figure who would advocate these causes, he embraced Ronald Reagan as the presidential candidate who would unify a diverse coalition. Ford's defeat was but a prologue to a larger development during the late 1970s, as this conservative coalition came into full fruition.

Chapter 5

CONSERVATISM HAS COME OF AGE

Organizing the Movement

A little over a month after Gerald Ford's defeat in the presidential election of 1976, Jesse Helms delivered a major speech to conservatives in Dallas. The lesson of the past presidential election, he said, was that Ford had not drawn a sharp enough distinction between conservatism and liberalism; most Americans believed that both Ford and Carter were equally conservative. In Senate races across the country, Helms declared, conservative challengers who ran forthright campaigns against incumbent liberals won their contests. Most Americans were conservative, according to public opinion polls; successful candidates simply had to draw distinctions and persuade voters that they provided a conservative alternative. The Republican Party needed to embrace conservatism and unite "workers and producers into one camp, leaving the special interests and self-seekers to the liberals." Republicans should devise a strategy designed to take power. Spokesmen should be appointed to speak clearly, and with one voice; as an alternative to Jimmy Carter, conservatives should offer a "shadow government," including an array of "coordinated spokesmen" ready to communicate information generated by a "revitalized national committee." The transformation of Republicanism should take the war to liberalism. Conservatives should "take heart from the gains they have chalked up, and they must be ready to win over voters who thought they were voting conservative this time. Conservatism has come of age, and the task of leadership must begin."[1]

In the four years after November 1976, Helms helped assemble the pieces of a new conservative ascendancy. In the four years after his election to the Senate in 1972, he had positioned himself as one of the most important leaders of what was becoming known as the New Right. Although he remained in a hopeless minority in the Senate, he had learned how to exploit senatorial privilege, cleverly criticizing liberalism while he promoted conservative alternatives and helped to construct a national constituency. In the Congressional Club, which relied on the political brilliance of the take-no-prisoners approach of Tom Ellis, Helms possessed a powerful political tool that could identify voters, promote conservative issues, and, as events would prove, raise large amounts of money to further conservatives' drive for power. In Ronald Reagan, Helms found a telegenic, articulate, and popular leader who could advance national conservatism. Although in 1976 Reagan lost his challenge to Ford, he did so only narrowly, and he left the Kansas City convention with his reputation intact. When Ford lost the White House to Jimmy Carter in November 1976, Reagan almost immediately became the front-runner for the Republican nomination four years later.

HELMS ALSO REMAINED an uncompromising opponent of the legacy of the civil rights movement. Soul City, North Carolina, provided a target that Jesse pursued relentlessly in the 1970s. Founded in 1968, Soul City was the creation of former Congress of Racial Equality head Floyd McKissick, who sought to create a self-sufficient, largely African American community located in the heart of impoverished and rural Warren County, about fifty miles northeast of Raleigh. Soul City's original plans called for a town of more than 50,000 residents and 13,000 homes, including 5,180 acres, a 928-acre industrial park, and jobs for 8,200 people. It initially attracted the support of Lyndon Johnson's Great Society new cities program, which sought to create thirteen "new towns" across the country. Soul City was the only one of these new, multiracial communities that was located in a rural area. McKissick, who became a Republican on July 21, 1972, attracted the support of Richard Nixon in the early 1970s and succeeded in obtaining a $14 million bond issue guarantee from the Department of Housing and Urban Development (HUD) and a $500,000 bank loan. According to one estimate, by the mid-1970s various federal agencies had contributed a total of $19 million toward Soul City and five affiliated nonprofit organizations and four for-profit organizations that were under McKissick's control. But by 1975, a year after it officially opened, Soul City had little to show for itself: the Soul City Health Company treated no patients, no companies had been recruited, and very few people called Soul City home. After six years, according to the *Raleigh News and Observer*, "there still is no Soul City," only an office and industrial park still under construction and a few mobile homes scattered around the site. McKissick maintained federal support, it was charged, as a result of his support for Nixon's reelection campaign in 1972 and his new Republican affiliation. In an investigative series, the *N&O* found "political impropriety, apparent conflicts of interest, mismanagement of federal funds and nepotism." McKissick's wife was manager of the sanitary district, director of the parks and recreation association, and part owner of Soul City's store. Floyd McKissick, Jr., was planning director. A better name for Soul City, said a local newspaper editor, would be McKissickville.[2]

Helms used Soul City as an example of the civil rights movement and Great Society social engineering gone wrong. He had attacked it in a *Viewpoint* editorial on January 17, 1969. When McKissick used the term "free enterprise," Helms said, he meant that "taxpayers are supposed to give him, free of charge, millions of dollars so that he can set up an enterprise to his own liking."[3] Soon after he was elected to the Senate, Helms brushed off McKissick's overtures and, on March 5, 1975, requested an audit by the federal government's watchdog General Accounting Office (GAO). Federal support of Soul City was a "gross waste," Jesse declared in a Senate speech on July 26, 1975, with funds spent for health care but no patients, for art and culture without any evidence of its presence, for industrial development but no industry and workers, and for roads and infrastructure but no people. The conclusion, Helms said, was obvious: Soul City was "the greatest single waste of public money that anyone in North Carolina can remember." Most important, it served as an example of an "intellectually and morally bankrupt doctrine, a doctrine that suggests that enough money thrown at any problem will make it go away, or thrown at any proposal will make it happen." Sadly, Helms pointed out, there was "no such thing as a free lunch." Somebody would pay the price, and that somebody would be the American people.[4]

In December 1975, when the GAO released its audit of Soul City, its report provided further grist for Helms's critique. Calling on Attorney General Edward Levi to conduct a criminal investigation, Jesse described the Soul City project as "just an expanse of bare land that has been somewhat tarnished by the most massive, wasteful boondoggle anyone in that area can remember." Citing a "confusing maze of corporate and other entities, with...interlocking directorates and nepotism" that governed Soul

City, he called for an end to federal funding.⁵ Urging that the GAO recommendations be carried out, Helms also wrote to the heads of various federal agencies that had supplied more than $19 million in grants and loan guarantees to Soul City, including David Mathews of Health, Education, and Welfare, C. B. Morton of Commerce, and Carla A. Hills of HUD. Helms asked that each of these agencies account for Soul City expenditures within two months.⁶ After months of bureaucratic inaction, Helms again went on the attack in June 1976, arguing that Soul City exempflied the corruption and ineptitude of anti-poverty programs and was "an insult to the hard pressed taxpayers of North Carolina and the nation."⁷

Despite Helms's attack, for the next four years Soul City survived. In May 1979, after federal officials ended the new cities program and canceled seven out of the thirteen original communities, Soul City survived, but still had little to show for its continued existence: in the spring of 1979, only 220 people inhabited the community. All but four of the families were black, and they inhabited thirty-three houses and thirty-three trailers. Although McKissick told a *Wall Street Journal* reporter that Soul City was "almost a religious idea" that could not be "judged in white man's terms," Helms saw matters differently. This was an example of wasteful spending, he believed, and the squandering of public money by federal bureaucrats, Helms declared in a Senate speech. The problems of Soul City were not unique: according to one estimate, the federal government lost $200 million in the entire new cities program. In 1979, after spending approximately $28 million in support, federal authorities, despite McKissick's protests, announced an end of federal support for Soul City, and federal authorities took most of its remaining assets in 1981.⁸

For Helms, Soul City provided a ripe opportunity to show how civil rights and federal anti-poverty programs had gone wrong. In fact, the experiment had been given little chance of success, and it was barely in existence before it suffered his political attack. Although the project suffered from mismanagement, it was not as disastrous as Helms suggested, and its legacy still awaits a balanced assessment by historians.⁹ Because of McKissick's alliance with Republicans, he enjoyed little political support among North Carolina Democrats, and little support among liberal whites. Soul City thus became an easy target for Helms, and his noisy opposition figured prominently in its failure.

HELMS SUCCESSFULLY RAISED the issue of "forced" busing, which resulted from the Supreme Court's insistence, in a series of decisions leading to the landmark *Swann v. Charlotte-Mecklenburg* case (1971), that public schools must be affirmatively desegregated. No longer was the integration of a few black students into white schools adequate: school systems would have to achieve a unitary system of education in which proportions of students and teachers approximated the general racial character of the surrounding population. In practical terms, the *Swann* case required that southern school systems bus white and black students in massive numbers, often away from neighborhood schools. Once busing began during the 1971–72 school year, it was greeted with widespread anxiety and opposition, though over time it took hold in much of the South.

Soon after his election to the Senate, Helms became a leading national opponent of busing. In 1976, he laid out his rationale in his polemic against liberalism, *When Free Men Shall Stand,* a brief book published by the Congressional Club. The insistence on using busing to achieve racial balance was liberalism gone crazy, he said, an example of the "destructive application" of a "fanatical" quest for equality perpetrated by "social engineers" in the federal government. The liberal establishment cared little if forced busing treated "human beings as if they were robots or the components of some kind of machine." School busing was, Helms thought, a form of "cultural imperialism" that was accompanied by "contempt for the ordinary parent." Opponents of busing were waging, in effect, a struggle for self-determination in which parents exerted their rights to choose their schools and to determine the control of the classroom.[10]

During his first few years of office, Helms consistently opposed school busing. In August 1973, he offered a bill in the Senate that would define the limits of school desegregation, require that juries review decisions to desegegrate schools, and mandate that pupil assignments not be made on the basis of race.[11] In November, Jesse offered an amendment to an emergency energy bill that would limit busing as a way to save gasoline. The important issue, he explained to his constituents, was how "federal judges and federal bureaucrats continue to impose arbitrary and arrogant power over the lives of little children," and, in the process, continue to waste "scarce and precious fuel." Because of a popular backlash against busing, Helms gradually began to enjoy more support in the Senate: in late 1973, his amendment failed by only one vote.[12] Helms's anti-busing efforts, for the first time as a senator, became an issue where other senators took him seriously, and he persisted. In September 1974, he offered an amendment to the HEW appropriation bill prohibiting that agency from intervening in school desegregation cases. The measure passed the Senate by three votes (45–42), and, although it was subsequently defeated, busing had become a potent political issue.[13]

School desegregation also had national implications. With the support of Delaware senator Joseph Biden, the Senate, in September 1975, again adopted a Helms anti-busing measure that prohibited HEW from cutting off federal funds to school districts that disobeyed desegregation orders. Supporters of busing mounted a counterattack by attempting, unsuccessfully, to close debate and pass the HEW appropriations bill without the rider. These parliamentary maneuvers transpired over nine days of Senate debate, in what Jesse called "an endurance contest which demanded constant alertness in terms of parliamentary procedure." Debate was so intense that Helms stayed at his seat, and he kept tubes of glucose as a food substitute. Helms's amendment survived and was enacted, though Biden amended Jesse's original resolution to say that HEW could not enforce busing plans "unless such transportation is specifically required by a final decree of a court of law." Most commentators agreed that the measure would have little effect; the Biden-Helms amendment, as the *Washington Star* noted, was "mostly symbolic," for there were few important instances in which HEW initiated desegregation without a court mandate. Nonetheless, this was an important political victory for Helms. He described it as a "turning point in our history" that indicated a decided change in the mood of the Senate. This "sorry business" of busing, he said, was coming to an end. Americans had had enough of "statistics and racial percentages" and of "hostility and violence." "Let's return our schools to the people, and to the purpose of education—before it is too late to salvage our public schools."[14]

Helms's anti-busing campaign continued for the rest of the 1970s, as he sought legislative restrictions over busing and even a constitutional amendment to prohibit it.[15] Much of his campaign focused on the Department of Health, Education, and Welfare, with which he was conducting a larger war. Helms's anti-HEW campaign encompassed two other issues: the desegregation of the University of North Carolina and the federal government's efforts to curb smoking. Since 1973, HEW, under the pressure of an NAACP lawsuit, pressured southern public universities to desegregate and achieve what the courts called "unitary" systems that would fully integrate white and black students, faculties, and institutions. Using public school desegregation as a model, HEW favored coercive measures that would compel students to attend integrated institutions. HEW focused much of its attention on UNC, which possessed both the most extensive system of historically black institutions and the best public multi-campus university system in the South.

It is thus perhaps ironic that Helms, a bitter critic of the university during the 1960s, became a steady friend and ally in the 1970s. In May 1974, on the Senate floor, he described HEW's efforts at higher education desegregation an "absolute absurdity" and argued that they constituted a "yoke of Federal arrogance" and an "abuse of power."[16] In September 1975, in another Senate speech, he objected to HEW's pressure tactics as efforts by "faceless bureaucrats" who were "ignoring the educational needs of the students, and seeking solely to serve their own illegitimate and illegal purposes." Calling the HEW higher education desegregation efforts "affirmative discrimination," he introduced legislation in April 1977—in another rider placed on an HEW appropriations bill—to relax affirmative action policies in higher education.[17] The following June, Jesse, along with California Republican senator S. I. Hayakawa, unsuccessfully tried to strip HEW's ability to use affirmative action as part of its policies.[18] Subsequently, he denounced "quotas" for UNC or any other American university.[19] This legislation was important because it helped Helms politically as an opponent of arbitrary federal bureaucrats: he was, as he said all throughout his career, not opposed to black civil rights, only against federal intervention. But most of his efforts focused less on quotas than on HEW's effort to compel desegregation. In 1977, for example, Helms offered a bill that would end federal court supervision over any state's public university system after it had complied for one year. Helms, in a speech to the Senate, praised UNC officials for the "excellent job they had done during the past eight years in providing equal opportunity for the students of North Carolina while maintaining high academic standards."[20]

Similarly, HEW became a political symbol for Helms when HEW secretary Joseph Califano, announcing in January 1978 that tobacco was the nation's most important public health enemy, introduced an ambitious $20 million effort to reduce smoking among Americans. Helms later described Califano's program as "absurd," and he denounced HEW as a "bureaucratic monster." Congress, he thought, should consider cutting off its funds.[21] Back home in North Carolina, the response to Califano's anti-tobacco campaign was adverse. Califano, said the *Henderson Daily Dispatch,* was "making war on tobacco" that could "devastate North Carolina's economy." It called on President Jimmy Carter to "instruct Califano to desist from his latest efforts against tobacco, or else, better still, insist that the Secretary resign his office."[22] Tom Ellis, reflecting the anger that prevailed among North Carolina's political leadership, was prepared to exploit the tobacco issue to Helms's advantage. Califano was "Jimmy Carter's man," and Democrats would have to live with him. Nixon was, similarly, "our boy," he said, and Republicans "had to live with him." "Now let them live with theirs." Tobacco, he believed, would "definitely" be a future campaign issue.[23]

For much of the late 1970s, Helms waged a high-visibility war with HEW. In a speech in Lumberton, North Carolina, in February 1978, he told an audience of supporters that he was "appalled" at HEW's threat to terminate funding to UNC.[24] Congress, Helms told a Hickory group about a week later, should inform Califano that "if he wants to talk about cutting off funds, we can cut off his funds." Helms promised to "tie up the Senate for a number of days if Califano persists in what he is doing to the University of North Carolina."[25] Helms proposed the Academic Freedom Act of 1979, which would restrict HEW authority only to those academic programs receiving funds from HEW, limit its power to terminate funds to those parts of the university not in compliance, require federal officials to prepare an "education-impact statement" that would assess how much time and effort HEW mandates would require of universities, and exempt institutions with less than 5 percent of their total budget coming from federal funds. As the *Greensboro Daily News* concluded, this was primarily a political document rather than a serious proposal; Helms's anti-HEW campaign was mostly rhetorical. Nonetheless, Jesse's efforts placed UNC officials in a delicate position: Helms, long their critic, was now their defender. How seriously should they accept Helms's help, and to what extent did this mean getting in bed with the enemy?[26]

After mounting political pressure, in July 1979, Carter fired Califano and replaced him with Housing and Urban Development secretary Patricia R. Harris. Helms used her confirmation hearings to publicize his war with HEW. Writing to her prior to the hearings, he announced that her views about the tobacco and UNC desegregation issues were of "immense interest" to him. Two years earlier, in her confirmation hearings as HUD secretary, Harris had announced her strong support for civil rights. As the daughter of a black Pullman car porter, wryly noted the *Fayetteville Observer*, it seemed "unlikely" either that she would "back away from that commitment," or that a president "aiming for re-election will ask her to do so." When Harris refused to answer Helms's letter directly, he threatened to put her confirmation on hold. But after a meeting with Harris, he permitted the confirmation to go through. The meeting was "cordial and encouraging," and Harris made clear that she did not have the "obsession about tobacco that led Califano to refuse to listen to opinions and facts contrary to his own position." Nonetheless, Helms warned that Harris would "have problems if she attempts to follow in Mr. Califano's footsteps. In that case, I will be one of her problems."[27]

Nearly all of Helms's sparring with HEW was rhetorical flourishes, though they contained political value. The clash between Harris and Helms, noted the *Raleigh News and Observer*, was "thankfully, brief." For the *N&O* editors, historically Jesse's most consistent adversaries, Helms's tactics proved little: if all of the Senate's members approached nominations as he did, the editors declared, "the process of organizing a government would be utterly chaotic." If adopted by all one hundred senators, his approach would create a "nearly impossible obstacle course for each senator to insist that prospective Cabinet members commit themselves in advance to the special interests of 50 different states." The fact of the matter, which Helms surely realized, was that Harris was constrained by federal policies, which committed whoever became secretary to seek to limit smoking. At the same time, HEW was under the constraints of a court order in the UNC case. The *N&O* believed that North Carolinians should not expect a "180-degree shift in federal policy on either desegregation or smoking."[28]

Helms was Jimmy Carter's most consistent opponent in the Senate; a *Congressional Quarterly* report in 1979 found in that year that he opposed the administration 75 percent of the time.[29] Meanwhile, Helms also obstructed many of the president's appointments. Soon after Carter's inauguration, Jesse voted against confirming Cyrus Vance as secretary of state, Andrew Young as United Nations ambassador, and Michael Blumenthal as secretary of the treasury.[30] Opposing the choice of Paul Warnke to head the Arms Control and Disarmanent Agency, he threatened to filibuster the nomination.[31] Later, he voted against the confirmation of Maine senator Edmund Muskie as Vance's successor, while in May 1980, when Carter chose David Jones as chairman of the Joint Chiefs, Helms threatened a filibuster against the nomination, claiming that Jones was a "political general" whose policies—as a supporter of SALT II and the Panama Canal treaties, and as an opponent of the B-1 bomber—had been "disastrous for this country."[32] While Helms also blocked or slowed Carter's ambassadorial nominations, he did the same with judicial appointments.[33]

IN THE LATE 1970s, what became known as the New Right mobilized thousands of Americans around a conservative agenda. Since the 1930s, conservatives drew support from voters opposed to increased intervention and regulation by the federal government, high taxes, and bureaucracy. In the South, conservatism was oriented around the race issue, and it drew support from a white backlash that occurred in the aftermath of the civil rights revolution. But what forged a new conservative ascendancy was a cluster of new, powerful issues that mobilized still more voters into an enlarged constituency. The New Right issues of the 1970s drew in large part from an expanded reaction against the main features of the 1960s—youth rebellion, sexual permissiveness, and expanded rights for women. A newly mobilized, highly organized, and highly politicized movement of conservative evangelicals provided additional energy and leadership. Some of these elements were present in Barry Goldwater's presidential campaign of 1964, still more in Ronald Reagan's campaign of 1976, but they expanded and solidified during the late 1970s.

Among the most important issues appealing to conservatives during the 1970s were abortion and school prayer. In both instances, the Supreme Court altered the status quo by prohibiting the states' requirement of prayer in public schools (in 1962) and their decriminalization of abortion (in 1973). Both issues, to conservatives, suggested a wider moral decay. The elimination of prayer marked the dominance of a "totally secularist philosophy" in public schools, Helms wrote in *Where Free Men Shall Stand,* that had led to permissiveness, the drug culture, pornography, and crime. The school prayer ban meant "freedom *from* religion."[34] He became the Senate's leading advocate of restoring school prayer to the schools, and, though unsuccessful, he attracted attention to his cause—and made school prayer prominent in the conservative agenda. In his first Senate floor speech, he called for a "rededication" of Americans' "traditional right to public prayer." For much of the 1970s, Helms introduced legislation and a constitutional amendment that would permit school prayer; that amendment, by 1980, suffered defeat in Congress five times.[35] He intended to fight against the Supreme Court decision, he told constituents in November 1975, in order to restore the "physical and moral strength of the American Republic." In the past decade, he wrote, increased crime, drugs, pornography, and obscenity flowed from the Court's intervention, and Congress should limit its authority. When his school prayer amendment gathered little support in Congress, Helms attempted to introduce it by legislation.[36]

Helms also became the Senate's most important opponent of legal abortion. Abortion, he said, could never be a "moral way to solve a problem of immorality—or, for that matter, a population problem," and it was "a few steps away from the reasoning that Hitler used to exterminate people."[37] In the September 1975 issue of *Human Events,* Jesse declared that it was "terribly wrong...to kill these children in order to serve the convenience of those who may not want them around." Abortion, Helms thought, was "murder—and no other face can be put upon it." Raised to believe that human life was sacred, Jesse wanted no part of any national policy—including a "strained" Supreme Court decision—that asserted that convenience justified murder. Jesse would resist such a conclusion.[38] Only five months after the Supreme Court issued its decision, in June 1973, Helms proposed a right-to-life, anti-abortion constitutional amendment. Although the amendment made little progress, as with school prayer, Helms sought to force his fellow senators to put themselves on record. In January 1975, at a national March for Life conference in Washington on the second anniversary of the *Roe v. Wade* decision, in which the U.S. Supreme Court provided for legal abortion under certain circumstances, Helms denounced the ruling as reversing "our moral traditions and our national sense of the dignity and uniqueness of each human life." In April 1976, he succeeded in obtaining a vote on an anti-abortion constitutional amendment; although he lost, the full Senate considered the measure. Thereafter, he continued to promote a right-to-life constitutional amendment.[39]

Helms's outspokenness about these issues endeared him to the newly energized Christian Right. Although American conservative evangelicals had remained politically quiescent since the evolution controversy of the 1920s, they reentered politics in reaction to the tumult and turmoil of the 1960s. Outraged about the intervention of federal courts in abortion and school prayer, conservative evangelicals became mobilized by the apparent triumph of secularism during the 1960s—and by what they believed as moral degeneracy, sexual permissiveness, and a weakening family structure. While resisting new roles for women, conservative evangelicals opposed the legitimization that gay people sought in expanded civil and political rights.

Helms became a key figure in incorporating the Christian Right into a wider conservative coalition. Possessing impeccable Christian credentials, from the beginning of his Senate tenure Jesse actively participated in the Senate Prayer Breakfast, and he claimed during the 1972 campaign that he had undergone a born-again experience. He regularly called for a spiritual revitalization. There was a common tendency to view "Christian witness as something which should be separate and apart from our Nation's political life," he told the Concerned Christian Citizens for Political Action in Lynden, Washington, in September 1974. Helms had been motivated to run for the Senate by "some unseen force," and it was this divine power that would lead Americans back to redemption.[40] Some sought to "destroy freedom in the name of freedom," he told a Kinston, North Carolina, audience in June 1975, and these people, under the cover of freedom of religion, wanted to "strip from our public life, the spiritual allegiance upon which our nation was founded."[41] America's days were numbered, he said while campaigning for reelection to the Senate in July 1978, without a "genuine, natural, spiritual birth." There was "nothing wrong with this nation that prayer and a return to spiritualism will not cure."[42] Helms communicated with a new breed of religious broadcasters: for example, in October 1978, he appeared on Jim Bakker's *PTL Club* in Charlotte, where he called for spiritual rebirth. The Lord, he said, was "giving us only one more chance" to restore the country. "I really, truly think that if we had the faith of our fathers we could work out all of the problems we have," he told Bakker.[43]

With Helms's support and participation, Jerry Falwell, an evangelist from Lynchburg, Virginia, organized the Moral Majority in the spring of 1979. Tom Ellis had long been intrigued with the possibility of mobilizing Christian evangelicals and attracting them to an active role in the conservative cause. Ellis, Wrenn, the Conservative Caucus's Howard Phillips, and Viguerie had discussed the political potential of evangelicals, and a delegation of conservatives, including activist Paul Weyrich, drove to Lynchburg to visit with Falwell. Weyrich, telling Falwell that a "moral majority" of evangelicals existed in the country, urged him to become involved, and Falwell immediately seized on the name. The movement took off, and Viguerie obtained the direct mail contract for the new organization. Although Ellis was annoyed by Viguerie's freelancing, he soon realized Falwell's ability to mobilize voters. Evangelicals, Ellis realized, could provide the shock troops of the conservative revolt.[44] In April 1979, the organization held its first big "Decency Rally" in Washington, and Falwell proclaimed this event as the beginning of a "moral revolution." The meeting attracted more than ten thousand supporters, with Helms as one of its featured speakers.[45] In North Carolina and elsewhere, Helms helped to incorporate the Christian Right into the conservative mainstream. Organizations such as the Churches of Life and Liberty and the North Carolina chapter of the Moral Majority used the resources of the Congressional Club to organize and to establish themselves as viable entities.[46] By 1980, Jesse had become the Christian Right's most important advocate in the Senate. The Religious Right had long wanted church schools to be freed from federal interference, and in August 1978, objected to a new IRS regulation that would eliminate tax-exempt status for private schools that practiced a form of racial discrimination. The ruling placed the burden of proving nondiscrimination on the schools. Arguing that independent Christian schools were imperiled, Helms led an effort in the Senate to enact a measure prohibiting the enforcement of the new regulations—a measure that had already passed the House. Helms's measure received Senate approval, and, a year later, he strengthened the ban with another amendment. The IRS regulations had important political implications, and they were a major factor in the political mobilization of the Christian Right. According to Viguerie,

"Jimmy Carter scared the dickens out of the Christians," and the tax-exempt issue became a crucial force that thrust evangelicals into politics.[47] As the Moral Majority's executive director Ron Godwin said, the IRS issue became a "galvanizing, unifying issue" that brought together evangelicals and mobilized them politically.[48]

Helms spoke language that evangelicals understood, and he was particularly critical of the impact of secularization and "secular humanism." When Congress established the U.S. Department of Education by separating it from HEW, Helms objected to the confirmation of its first secretary, Shirley Hufstedler. In a Senate speech on November 30, 1979, Helms described the new Department of Education as an "enormous and expensive bureaucracy" that would increase the federal government's "oppressive intrusion" into education. But Helms had other objections. Because she had served on the board of the Aspen Institute—whose full title was the Aspen Institute for Humanistic Studies, a well-known, nonpartisan leadership training center in Colorado—Helms claimed that Hufstedler belonged to an anti-Christian "secular humanist" movement. "Secular humanism" had become a code, a term that the Christian Right recognized as describing the erosion of Christian values. Humanism, said a North Carolina fundamentalist, was an "all-encompassing philosophy and ideology" that placed people above God; secular humanists maintained that there were "no absolutes, no right or wrong." All ethics to them were relative, and sexual freedom, sex education courses, abortion-on-demand, euthanasia, suicide, alternative lifestyles, and "building a global community independent of the Creator" were their goals. Three years earlier, in 1976, Helms had outlined his views about secular humanism in *When Free Men Shall Stand*. Liberalism, he wrote, was the "political creed of a pseudo-religion known as humanism," which, arising from the Renaissance, had attempted to "create a heaven on earth—a heaven with God and His law excluded from it." Secular humanism had become a kind of "state religion" in which traditional Christianity had been replaced by Karl Marx, John Maynard Keynes, John Dewey, and Sigmund Freud. This state religion was "collectivist, totalitarian, and implacably hostile to the family, the church, and free institutions." With allies among the liberal establishment, advocates of this state religion favored making "a god of government."[49]

Helms connected Hufstedler to this wider conspiracy. The duty of Christians, he said, was to "resist the secular humanists who are taking over our schools, our society, our businesses, our institutions at every level." He saw a natural connection between Hufstedler and secular humanism, and, voting against her confirmation (she was overwhelmingly confirmed nonetheless), Helms declared his opposition to the "abomina-tion" of an expanding federal bureaucracy. But he also objected to Hufst-edler because her Aspen Institute connections meant that she was a secular humanist. She might be a "fine lady," said Jesse, but "one of the things wrong" with America was "too much humanism," which disavowed "spiri-tual values as a priority."

The Aspen Institute, despite Helms's claims, had nothing to do with a humanist conspiracy: rather, it was an institute that used corporate and foundation contracts and grants to promote executive leadership training. Most of this leadership training focused on two-week seminars in which corporate and government leaders underwent networking and interaction. The Aspen Institute was itself perplexed, even slightly confused, by Helms's charges. "I don't think we should honor this by getting mad," said Aspen trustee Douglass Cater. Others noted that Helms had perhaps con-fused the Aspen Institute's humanism—which grew out of University of Chicago philosopher Mortimer Adler's call to return to the classics—with a vaguely defined secular humanist movement. Terry Eastland, editorial page editor of the *Greensboro Record,* was a conservative who later worked in the Justice Department of the Reagan administration. Eastland objected to Helms's muddling of the fundamentalist version of humanism with the broader notions of the study of the humanities. For Eastland, the country, if anything, needed more humanism.[50]

Nonetheless, in this instance and others, for Helms the reality seemed less important than the rhetoric and symbolism: although his charges against Hufstedler were a fantasy, they surely struck a chord with his Reli-gious Right constituency. And increasingly in the late 1970s Helms sought to make evangelicals a reliable part of the conservative coalition. "We've had preachers in politics for 50 years, to my knowledge," he told one group of fundamentalists in Florence, South Carolina, in June 1980, "but they've always been on the other side."[51] "By golly, ladies and gentlemen, we have all got to react together," Jesse declared in another speech in Washington a month later to 1,500 people at the American Family Forum. His language here and elsewhere suggested that Christian evangelicals should make common cause with the conservative movement. Liberals did not want "men of God" to stand forth and say, "Stop making a god of government." Government—and forces of secular humanism—had been harassing pri-vate enterprise and public education, while endangering individual free-dom. Now, he warned, government was turning its attention to the Christian family by imposing new, humanist values. "If they want to call us reac-tionaries," he said, "let them do it."[52]

Joining with the Christian Right, Helms was opposed to the same cluster of values they found outrageous. In early 1977, when Dade County, Florida, which included Miami, enacted a local ordinance prohibiting discrimination based on sexual orientation, a popular movement began. Former Miss America Anita Bryant formed a grassroots organization, Save Our Children, Inc., in a successful effort to repeal the law in June 1977. Bryant's campaign became the first manifestation of an anti-gay movement attracting support from around the country. Helms endorsed Bryant's campaign in March 1977 and described her as a "fine and decent lady, a dedicated Christian, who had dared to speak out."[53] In June 1977, when Bryant's movement succeeded in repealing the ordinance by a two-to-one margin, Helms wanted to expand nationally Bryant's anti–gay rights movement. Meeting with Bryant in Washington, Helms helped to discuss a national strategy to defeat other local anti-discrimination ordinances. He also suggested that he might seek an anti–homosexual rights bill in Congress. Consistently opposed to gay rights in all forms, Helms established an unequivocal record about homosexuality in the 1970s.[54]

Opposition to feminism became another issue binding the Religious Right to the conservative cause. "We must reverse the trend," Jesse declared, "that says that women must be liberated from the dignity of motherhood and from femininity of her natural development."[55] In 1972, Congress approved the Equal Rights Amendment, and the measure was submitted to the states. But after twenty-two states quickly ratified, an anti-ERA movement emerged, and in 1977 Indiana became the thirty-fifth—and last—state to ratify. An opponent of manifestations of feminism, not surprisingly Helms opposed the ERA and became allied with Phyllis Schlafly, perhaps the best-known anti-feminist of the 1970s. Both opposed Title IX of the Educational Amendments of 1972, which equalized gender differences in intercollegiate athletics, and in 1975, Helms introduced the Equal Educational Opportunity Amendments Bill of 1975, which proposed to reverse Title IX.[56] Anti-ERA activists feared that the amendment would transform the family and women's role in it; 1970s feminism aroused widespread anxieties. In 1977, the International Women's Year (IWY) provided Helms with an opportunity to exploit the issue. Two years earlier, in 1975, after the United Nations sponsored an International Women's Conference in Mexico City, Congress provided $5 million to sponsor state-level conventions and a national-level meeting about women. Supervised by the National Commission on the Observance of IWY, state conventions elected delegates to the National Women's Conference, which would be held in Houston in November 1977. The Houston conference was supposed to make resolutions that would form the basis for congressional legislation representing the feeling and thinking of a majority of American women. From the outset, pro-ERA feminists dominated these proceedings, and during the spring and summer of 1977, the state-level IWY conventions advanced a strongly feminist agenda to the Houston meeting. Objecting, anti-feminists resisted by organizing opposition in the state-level conventions and making their cause known nationally.[57]

Helms opposed the IWY process from the outset. The IWY state conventions, claimed Helms staffer Sarah Sims in July 1977, lacked a truly representative cross-section of women. "We've got complaints from every state in the union," she said. "There hasn't been a cross-section [of women] anywhere." Anti-feminists charged that the meetings were inadequately advertised deliberately, in order to provide feminists the opportunity to endorse their own resolutions and to elect their own delegates.[58] Helms, in a Senate speech on July 1, 1977, condemned the IWY state meetings as dominated by "militant feminists" using "steamroller tactics." Pointing out that of the forty-two members of the national IWY commission, only one opposed the ERA, he asserted that groups such as STOP ERA, Eagle Forum, and National Right to Life were unrepresented. At the state conventions, whenever groups advocating traditional values attempted to speak up, they were squelched. Because feminists dominated these meetings, Helms argued, the IWY process was an improper expenditure of public funds. He inserted in the *Congressional Record* copies of written instructions from the National Women's Political Caucus providing advice about how to forestall a "takeover" by anti-ERA and anti-abortion forces at the state conferences. For Helms, this amounted to an effort to suppress groups such as STOP ERA and National Right to Life from participating, and he announced that his staff would initiate an investigation.[59]

Helms's attack on the IWY publicized his opposition to feminism while it made the case that feminists were operating undemocratically. In another Senate speech three weeks later, Helms claimed that letters from women across the country described "their frustrations" with the IWY state conventions. Preparing a seventy-page report, his staff had found a "widespread pattern and practice of discrimination by IWY [participants] against those women who do not agree with the narrow and negative ideology and partisan biases of the IWY organizers." The state conventions involved "rigged sessions, hand-picked committees, stacked registration, and little or no publicity to women at large." The Houston conference, he believed, promised to be nothing more than a "rubberstamp, unrepresentative debacle." On this basis, he demanded a congressional investigation into the IWY process. The $5 million in congressional funds had been illegally used, the report charged, for lobbying. President Jimmy Carter had appointed the wrong people to the IWY leaders, Helms's staff maintained, while those "representing women with traditional beliefs and values were left off the national organizing committee." This was discrimination, and because Carter appointed the committee, "the blame rests at his door." Helms had received complaints about the North Carolina IWY meeting, which oc-curred on June 17–19 in Winston-Salem, because the meeting was sched-uled on Father's Day, when many traditionally minded women were likely to be at home.

IWY organizers responded that they had made every effort to be rep-resentative: in North Carolina, for example, Elizabeth Koontz, who chaired the state committee, described how sixty-six meetings in the state solicited opinion. Organizations such as STOP ERA and anti-abortion organizations received adequate notification, Koontz said. Other IWY leaders made the same claim.[60] Helms, undaunted by the reality that he possessed little hope of persuading the Democratic congressional leadership to permit an official congressional investigation, organized his own hearings. By so doing, he es-calated the conflict into a full-blown—and well-publicized—conflict with the IWY leadership. On September 7, he announced that he would hold these ad hoc hearings on September 14–15 in the caucus room of the Old Senate Office Building. In a prepared statement, Helms reported violations of the law in the IWY's meetings, which had been taken over, he said, by a "determined, narrow minority of extremists." His goal, Jesse said, was to block the national IWY conference in Houston. "From what I've been told so far," he declared, "I question whether a national IWY conference should even be held at taxpayers' expense."[61]

Helms's ad hoc hearings became a publicity-seeking event that in-tended to discredit the IWY process. A parade of witnesses during two days' testimony claimed that ERA supporters, gay rights campaigners, and abortion rights activists had sabotaged the state meetings. "If feminists want to lobby for legislation in which they are interested, fine," said Anne Bag-nall of Winston-Salem, but "let them do it at their own expense, just as we do." The IWY state convention represented only "one small but vocal group—the radical wing of the so-called Women's Liberation Movement." Before an audience of several hundred women at Helms's hearings, others claimed that the IWY state conventions were rigged. The testimony was highly sensational. A woman from Minnesota claimed that "hundreds of purple-banded lesbians" dominated sessions in the state convention, dis-tributing "militant Marxist literature" and written instructions on "oral sodomy." In the California convention, a woman testified that she saw displays of female genitalia, along with T-shirts that read "Jesus Was a Lesbian." In the Virginia convention, still another described a workshop on "Women and Spirituality" that was "run by witches." According to further testimony, half of the women at delegate selection meetings were lesbians; and at the meetings dances demonstrated lesbian techniques in order to "shock the church people into leaving before the voting." According to one witness, Inez Franko, anti-ERA and anti-abortion speakers at New Jersey's state convention were "booed, hissed... physically abused by members of the audience." Feminists at the IWY meeting, she said, "screamed for equal rights but denied us ours." A "widespread pattern of practice and discrimination" existed against conservative women, Helms concluded, and he suggested that the IWY meetings had violated federal law requiring all advisory commissions to be balanced by diverse viewpoints.[62]

Helms's hearings became a stage show devised for the benefit of the media, to attract attention to his anti-feminist agenda. Testimony came from sixty-one people from forty-one states, none of whom supported feminist goals. Jesse claimed that the IWY leadership had been invited but none were willing to attend. "I don't think they want to answer any questions... all they have is epithets," he said. "They don't want to present facts." He had tried repeatedly to obtain IWY people willing to testify, he said, but he never received an answer. He doubted whether IWY representatives were willing to testify because "they know I'm going to sock it to 'em." Although he told reporters that he would keep an open mind, there was no doubt that his mind was already made up, and he urged that Congress cut off the funds for the Houston conference. The IWY response was terse. "Well, how should we put this politely?" said Linda Dorian, general counsel for IWY, in response to Helms's suggestion that IWY organizers had avoided testifying. "That's a deliberate untruth." Helms was abusing his office, she charged, and using "McCarthyesque" tactics. She explained that IWY leaders chose not to participate because Helms had bypassed normal Senate processes and was holding rogue meetings in which he was able to have "hand-selected the witnesses." These hearings, she said, were a "farce" and a "snakepit," and the national organizers had avoided participation. North Carolina IWY leaders, however, made a deliberate, though unsuccessful, effort to testify. Jean LeFrancois, executive director of the state conference, reported that, although she made contact with Helms's office a day before the hearings, her telephone calls were not returned. She and Elizabeth Koontz, the state IWY chair, traveled to Washington. Once inside Helms's hearing room, a Helms staffer informed them that they could testify by presenting a statement, but the two women did not feel that they had adequate time to do this.[63] Later, Koontz convened a press conference in North Carolina to denounce Helms's hearings as a travesty. Because his staff had made it difficult to present the IWY point of view, the hearings were a "waste of time, energy, tax dollars and resources to use the public forum to present only one side of an issue and call it a hearing." She emphatically rejected Helms's central contention—that the IWY meetings were stacked against anti-feminists and that the national IWY organization was dominated by radical feminists and lesbians. "No scare tactics, no smear tactics, no belittling, no casting of aspersions, no kangaroo-court tactics, no inquisition-like tactics, no intimidation by innuendo, no accusations or efforts to imply guilt by association," Koontz announced, would "stop this movement called a women's movement, for it is a movement not only for women's rights but also for human rights."[64]

Although Helms's IWY proceedings had no official standing, he used Senate resources because, as a White House official put it, "none of the other Congressional people will speak out against the hearing because it violates accepted protocol."[65] But Congress took no action to cut off funds, and the Houston national conference proceeded. Editorial reaction to Helms in the mainstream media was generally negative. The *Raleigh News and Observer* condemned Jesse for his hearings, which, it predicted, would be "disturbingly Salemite."[66] Helms's hearings had sought to investigate charges that the IWY meetings "were stacked and rigged to exclude conservative points of view," said a *Winston-Salem Sentinel* editorial, but actually Jesse had "stacked and rigged his own hearings to exclude the views of IWY conference organizers, suggesting that he is guilty of the same narrow-mindedness he deplores."[67] Polly Paddock, a columnist for *The Charlotte Observer*, characterized Helms's depiction of the IWY meetings as "ridiculous." After Congress funded IWY, Helms had gone into "high gear." "He hasn't stopped since." In general, Helms had little interest in debate, only in "silencing the opposition." If anti-feminists attending the Houston meeting wanted to "use beepers and rally their supporters, that's fine," but if they wanted to "disrupt for the sake of disruption, that's unfair to women who are genuinely interested in debate." Paddock believed that Helms's "emotional rantings" had not helped, though "his staying out of it might." Nonetheless, Jesse had achieved his main objective: reminding his constituency of anti-feminists that he would steadfastly support them and pursue their cause.[68]

OVER TIME, HELMS'S conservative message became increasingly tied to foreign policy issues. Staunchly anti-Communist, on his WRAL *Viewpoints* he had urged an unwavering and unequivocal support for waging the Cold War. A tireless opponent of the Soviet Union, he supported authoritarian regimes abroad because they opposed Communism. Jesse was especially interested in the developing world, in both Latin America and Africa: in both, he saw potential for subversive inroads and the necessity to protect the free enterprise system. In Latin America, Helms remained opposed to Castro's Cuba, while he supported right-wing regimes in Latin American countries such as Argentina and Chile that were waging "dirty wars" against their left-wing opponents and imprisoned, tortured, and killed thousands of their own citizens. In April 1975, Helms spoke to the World Anti-Communist League meeting in Rio de Janeiro, in Brazil, where he praised the military regime there for having "reversed an almost-certain decline into Communist dictatorship." Praising the rightist coup in Chile, he declared that the "people themselves, when faced directly with Communism, as a life-or-death threat," had the "power of rousing themselves, to save their nation." Helms contrasted this with the western world's unwillingness to face up to the threat of subversion.[69] In 1976, Jesse visited Argentina and urged Americans to support military efforts to suppress the left-wing insurgency that was, he said in a Senate speech, "radicalizing the social structure and undermining the economy." As a right-wing regime took power in Argentina in March 1976 that began a dirty war against left-wing opponents that lasted for the next seven years, Helms urged U.S. support in order that Argentinians "be spared the destruction of their society." Americans, in viewing the coup, should "have forbearance, and attempt to understand the extreme situation in which Argentines find themselves today." The military takeover "should be applauded," he said.[70]

As anti-Communist authoritarian regimes took power in the mid-1970s, Helms became their advocate in Congress. In July 1976, Jesse visited Argentina, Chile, and Uruguay, and returned home reporting to his constituents favorably about their authoritarian regimes. His visit to Argentina occurred shortly before the military junta staged a coup, and Helms met with a number of members of the military.[71] Helms also interacted sympathetically with the Chilean junta. There, he noted approvingly that the "communist regime" (it was actually the elected Socialist government of Salvador Allende Gossens) was overthrown by popular demand; those demanding its overthrow, he claimed, were housewives and mothers suffering from 1,000 percent inflation. He cited a Gallup poll claiming that a full three-quarters of the population supported the military dictatorship of

Augusto Pinochet. In contrast to what the mainstream American media described, reports that Chile was a "nation of oppression" were "simply not true." Ordinary Chileans, Helms claimed, wondered why critics of the Pinochet regime favored the Communists. The liberal media and liberal congressmen, who had never opposed Cuba's Fidel Castro, were "constantly attacking Chile with questionable charges that reliable citizens of Chile have told me personally simply are not true." "Why do we hear no criticism of communist dictators?" Helms asked. Why did liberal political leaders and media only criticize non-Communist countries? Rather than thugs and gangsters, the Pinochet regime, maintained Helms, was composed of leaders of "impressive ability, motivated by high religious and philosophical principles and concern for their people."

Helms claimed to have no great love for Latin American dictators, and his defenders argued that his policies reflected an attempt to resist the expansion of Cuban-style revolutionary nationalism. But Helms's defense of Latin American military regimes led him to support repressive violence. On September 21, 1976, Orlando Letelier, Chilean ambassador to the United States during the Allende government, was killed by a car bomb that exploded in Washington, killing Letelier and his American assistant Ronni Moffitt. Chilean intelligence services had masterminded the bombing, and their involvement likely extended to the highest reaches of the government. The Letelier assassination was part of Operation Condor, a campaign of assassination directed at opponents of right-wing regimes of Chile, Argentina, Bolivia, and Uruguay. Three days after Letelier's assassination, Helms delivered a Senate speech defending the Pinochet regime. The future of the free world lay with authoritarian, anti-Communist governments, he said. In Chile, the Pinochet dictatorship replaced a chaotic, Communist government, and Letelier supported this overthrown regime. As a Chilean exile, Helms argued, Letelier was employed by the "far-left" Institute for Policy Studies and thus abused American hospitality by embracing concepts that were "alien to our social and political heritage." It was possible that the Chilean government at "some level of government" was involved in the killing, but authorizing such an act of terror would have been an act of "national self-destruction" on the part of the Chileans. More likely, Helms believed, was that Letelier was the victim of left-wing Chileans seeking to make him into a martyr.[72]

As part of Jesse's intense interest in Latin America, he opposed efforts to abandon American control of the Panama Canal, which he saw as aiding the spread of Communism. Castro was exporting revolution and terror throughout Latin America, Helms said, and he was a "ring-leader behind the demands that the United States surrender its rights in the Panama Canal." Negotiating a transfer of the canal's sovereignty meant turning control of this strategic asset to "a dictator who is getting closer and closer to Castro every day."[73] Helms had long opposed transferring sovereignty of the canal to Panama. In July 1973, he described the construction of the canal as a "historic American achievement," and he opposed any surrender of U.S. control. Emerging as a political issue during the 1976 Republican primary campaign, the Panama Canal issue resonated with voters, and the Ford administration suspended negotiations because of conservative political pressure. When Jimmy Carter's administration renewed talks with Panama in 1977, Helms led the opposition. In February 1977, Helms charged, apparently without foundation, that Sol Linowitz, the chief American negotiator, had business interests in Panama that created a conflict of interest; Helms described Linowitz as "a banker who is in bed with [Panamanian leader Omar] Torrijos." Helms also joined four other Republican senators in bringing suit in federal court to block the administration from negotiating a canal treaty without explicit congressional consent. After the courts dismissed the case, Helms initiated another lawsuit claiming that the treaty needed the approval of both houses of Congress, and not just the Senate, because it involved the disposal of government property.[74]

During the summer of 1977, when it appeared that the Carter administration would successfully negotiate a new treaty, Helms rallied opposition. According to one report, after Carter courted Reagan's support, Helms telephoned Reagan warning that his conservative base would regard any compromise as a betrayal, a "second Schweiker." Reagan remained opposed to canal negotiations.[75] At a meeting of the Florida Conservative Union in Clearwater in July 1977, Jesse described Senate minority leader Howard Baker as "squirming like a worm over a hot brick" about the issue, while another report—which he denied—quoted him as describing moderate Senate Republicans (and negotiation supporters) Jacob Javits of New York, Mark Hatfield of Oregon, and Clifford Case of New Jersey as "pseudo-Republicans."[76] As Carter was preparing to announce the treaty, Helms told reporters that public opinion polls revealed that while 78 percent of Americans favored retention of the canal, only 8 percent favored turning it over to Panama. The stage was set for a major political showdown with Carter over the canal treaties that promised to rally the conservative base on an important, though largely symbolic, foreign policy issue, and to establish further Helms's reputation as a leader of a national conservative movement.[77]

On August 10, 1977, Carter announced that a treaty agreement had

been reached with Panama, and Jesse began one of the most important political battles of his life. According to one poll, when Carter announced the
treaty, thirty-seven senators were inclined to support it, twenty-five were
opposed, and the remaining thirty-eight were undecided.[78] Helms announced his strong opposition in a two-page statement released to the
press. The treaty was a "grave error" on the part of Carter, and it constituted a threat to regional peace and stability because it meant the immediate surrender of the canal. "If the Canal falls into the hands of Torrijos'
Communist friends," he warned, "what would be the value of any so-called
rights of defense in President Carter's treaties?" The president had ex-
ceeded his constitutional powers, Helms announced, and he had forced a
constitutional crisis.[79]

In the days immediately following the treaties' announcement, Helms
continued the attack. He had concluded, he told one reporter in a telephone interview, that transferring the canal to Panamanian control would
place a vital security asset in Communist hands. Panamanian president
Omar Torrijos and Carter were, he claimed, "bosom buddies." Most U.S.
"friends" in Latin America—by that he meant right-wing authoritarian
regimes—favored continued American control, and we should maintain
their support.[80] In a speech in North Carolina, Helms urged an alternative
to a canal giveaway, including the infusion of funds to modernize the canal;
this would, he said, both benefit Panama and maintain American sovereignty. On August 21, Helms and Senator Strom Thurmond appeared on
NBC's *Meet the Press* and warned that they would employ all methods, including filibuster, to defeat the treaty.[81] Helms personally attacked Carter,
who, he claimed, had negotiated in bad faith. The president's advisers, he
claimed, persuaded him to wait until Congress' adjournment before announcing the canal treaty. Carter had provided senators only "perfunctory
briefings" that lacked much substance.[82] In late September, Helms, in a sensational and unsubstantiated assertion, informed the press that U.S. intelligence agents had tapped Panamanian phones, but that, after they were
discovered about a year before the treaty was signed, the Panamanians
blackmailed the Americans into acceding to a weak treaty.[83]

Helms tapped into these feelings of many Americans, who felt stung by
the Vietnam and saw relinquishing the canal as a matter of national pride.
"The United States cannot afford to be a second-rate power," Helms
warned in May 1976, "but, unfortunately, that seems to be what we are becoming."[84] The anti-canal campaign became a popular crusade that coa-
lesced conservative groups in an offensive that included mailings, lobbying,
and a planned march on Washington. The crusade challenged Republican

leadership in Congress, as anti-canal activists sought to leverage more con-servative control of the party. Richard Viguerie took up the campaign, and his direct mail machine helped get the word out.[85] Howard Phillips, an-other anti–Canal Treaty activist and a former Young Americans for Free-dom member whom Nixon recruited to disband the Great Society's Office of Economic Opportunity, was founder and chairman of the Conservative Caucus.[86]

Between the summer of 1977 and the Senate's consideration of the treaties in February 1978, treaty opponents waged an intense campaign. The American Conservative Union launched a national letter-writing effort and newspaper ads critical of the treaties. "There is no Panama Canal," read one newspaper ad appearing in August 1977 in Jackson, Missis-sippi. "There is an American canal. Don't let President Carter give it away." In late October, the ACU ran television ads on twenty-nine stations in Texas, Louisiana, and Florida. Designed to pressure senators and to raise funds for the anti-treaty campaign, the ad featured appearances by Helms, Paul Laxalt, and Utah senator Jake Garn.[87] In January, Helms and Laxalt toured seven major cities in order to rally local government and business leaders against the canal treaties, and the tour attracted local media.[88] Helms relied on other appeals. From Monroe, Frank Poindexter, a salesman for Time Steel in Charlotte and part-time musician, put out a bluegrass record, "Please Don't Give Away Our Canal," that featured military drums in the background and a banjo strumming to the tune of the "Battle Hymn of the Republic." Jesse purchased three hundred copies, and the song was sent to 330 radio stations.[89]

When the pro-treaty forces proposed, with the support of the admin-istration, accepting an amendment guaranteeing an American right to de-fend the canal, Helms dismissed it as window dressing and denounced "any treaty that surrenders our sovereign rights." He raised other objec-tions. The treaty stipulated that the United States would pay off the Pananamian debt, but since this went to banks in New York City, it amounted to another bailout of that city. Jesse also publicized a Library of Congress study that concluded that assembling a fleet in the event of So-viet invasion of Europe would take forty days with the Canal and fifty days without it. In anticipation of Senate debate, Helms threatened to tie up Senate business: when a revision of the federal criminal code was pro-posed, he produced two hundred amendments, and this was interpreted as a maneuver seeking to delay a treaty vote to the off-year congressional elections of 1978. Delay, he admitted, might "serve some purpose from our strategic standpoint."[90]

Once they came up for Senate consideration in late February and March 1978, Helms led opposition to the canal treaties, using all of his parliamentary skill against them. But he entered the debate knowing that key senators, such as Majority Leader Robert Byrd and Minority Leader Howard Baker, had lined up behind the president and that other senators were joining them.[91] Short on votes, treaty opponents sought delay until the November congressional elections, hoping to increase political pressure.[92] But the pro-canal forces, holding on by a small but solid margin of votes, won a series of test votes. Treaty supporters sequenced the votes so that a measure guaranteeing an American right to intervene to defend the canal came first. Subsequent attempts by treaty opponents to introduce a series of killer amendments—which would add treaty provisions unacceptable to the Pananamians—were defeated. When Helms suggested in a Senate speech on February 20 that Pananamians were involved with drug dealers in "an organized system in which Panama served as the vital link," the Senate Intelligence Committee issued a statement declaring that there was no evidence of such involvement.[93]

Despite delaying efforts by opponents, the votes on the treaties proceeded during March and April 1978.[94] Despite these tactics, treaty supporters moved forward toward ratification, and, on March 16, the Senate approved the treaty guaranteeing the canal's neutrality by a 68–32 vote—one more than the necessary two-thirds majority. Helms described this as "like a two-game series with the first game not counting if you win the second," and he doubted whether Carter would have "a lot to barter the second time around."[95] About a month later, despite attempts at delay, the second canal treaty, which transferred control to Panama in the year 2000, came up for vote on April 18, and was ratified by a 68–32 margin. The treaty was ratified, Helms said, because supporters had "lots of things to trade and we had nothing to trade. This is why I never forecast once that we would win."[96]

For the next few years, Helms unsuccessfully battled implementation of the canal treaties. But though he lost the battle, he may have won the war. Like many of his past fights, the struggle over the canal forced his opponents to commit to a politically unpopular position: most Americans had serious reservations about the treaties, and opposition struck an emotional chord. As a result of the treaty fight, Helms's staffers John Carbaugh and Jim Lucier both became better known and more powerful; the battle also solidified Jesse's conservative following. The canal became, as Tom Ellis put it, a "springboard" for heightened national visibility, and Helms and the Congressional Club now had plenty of material to work with in future political campaigns. The example of fellow North Carolina senator Robert Morgan was instructive. Morgan, a conservative Democrat facing reelection in 1980, agonized over the canal treaties. He told one interviewer that he was haunted by the image of Frederick Muhlenberg, the first speaker of the House of Representatives, who voted in favor of the unpopular Jay's Treaty in 1795 and then ended his political career as a result of his unpopular stance. Morgan, like Muhlenberg, became convinced that supporting ratification was the right decision. Based on intelligence briefings and his legal background as a former state attorney general, he believed that the treaties were in America's national interest.[97]

Morgan's decision to support the treaties was not, however, popular among his constituents. Receiving adverse mail, in March 1978 he complained that the treaty fight had become "ugly, personal, and threatening."[98] According to columnist Carl Rowan, Morgan was one of those senators who, because of his support for ratification, had "earned badges of courage even if they didn't make headlines." After the canal vote, Helms and the club realized that Morgan was politically vulnerable: as soon as he cast his vote, they began contemplating a reelection challenge in 1980. "People are prone to forget issues mighty quickly," Tom Ellis said soon after the final canal treaty vote. But if it would help politically, he said, the Congressional Club would remind voters how Jesse and Morgan disagreed about the canal. Interestingly, Morgan and Helms had been allies and friends for much of their political careers: both had been strong supporters of I. Beverly Lake's 1960 gubernatorial campaign (Morgan was his campaign manager) and both supported East Carolina's drive for a medical school. But, with the canal treaty fight, the two men had broken politically, and Morgan would pay a political price for his vote.[99]

ONLY WEEKS AFTER the 1976 presidential election Ellis committed to a wholesale effort, using direct mail, to create a national fund-raising base. Direct mail involved two steps: in the first, prospecting pieces were sent to a large list, while, in a second step, subsequent mailings went to recipients who had responded. The second step was, according to one direct mailer, crucial because it identified the donor as part of a constituency. Persuading a person to donate meant composing a letter that identified and emphasized specific conservative issues; also essential was that the letter come from a nationally known conservative such as Helms. The end point of this process was the creation of an ongoing house list consisting of reliable givers.[100] Meeting in Chicago in late 1976, Viguerie, Ellis, and Helms agreed to a two-year exclusive contract, according to the terms of which Viguerie's company ran fund-raising for Helms's 1978 Senate reelection campaign. Possessing the best existing list of conservatives, Viguerie maintained a large database. Sending millions of pieces of mail at huge expense, he kept a substantial portion of the receipts, as much as 90 percent, from prospecting letters. But he was also a committed ideologue who realized the value of working with Helms's operation because of the senator's national appeal to conservatives and his fund-raising power.

Viguerie was the true believer's true believer. Described as a "political guru and financial wizard," he was a "lean, intense 43-year-old, who keeps a Bible on his desk and an electric golf putting game in a corner of his office." The mid-1970s were "dark, dark days," he recalled, and movement conservatives were frustrated.[101] Originally a Louisiana Cajun, Viguerie ran his operation from offices outside Washington, in suburban Falls Church, Virginia. By 1977, he had become not only one of the most savvy fund-raisers in the country, but someone who was connected to movement conservatives around the country. Participating in the Reagan campaign, he also was a leading figure in discussions in 1975–76 to organize an independent conservative third party.

From Viguerie's office, other New Right organizations were connected, including Howard Phillips's Conservative Caucus, Paul Weyrich's Committee for the Survival of a Free Congress, Terry Dolan's National Conservative Political Action Committee (Nickpac), and Phyllis Schlafly's fifty-thousand-member, anti-ERA organization, the Eagle Forum. By the mid-1970s, these movement conservatives wanted to control the Republican Party and, ultimately, the national government in Washington. Every Wednesday morning, in a sort of conservative brain trust, Phillips, Dolan, Weyrich, the Heritage Foundation's Ed Feulmer, and conservative activist Morton Blackwell would meet around Viguerie's kitchen table at his home in McLean, Virginia. By the late 1970s, they would sometimes reconvene Wednesday evenings and work with "insider" conservatives in Congress, such as Georgia congressman Newt Gingrich. A key element of their strategy was what Weyrich called "reverse engineering the left"—to study techniques that had worked for their liberal opponents and then to replicate them. Movement conservatives began to construct an infrastructure: the left had relied on foundations, political action committees, single-issue groups, and strong fund-raising. By the late 1970s, the New Right possessed all of these components.[102] Viguerie provided direct mail for conservative groups, but they had all taken on a life of their own. Each worked in concert toward an objective of conservative ascendancy, each came into existence in the mid-1970s, and they relied on an interconnected national conservative constituency. The Conservative Caucus, like Viguerie, had a large, national contributor base. These groups looked to Helms for leadership. He was "extraordinarily important to the development of conservative politics in the Senate," said Weyrich, because he was steadfast in his views despite political pressure from moderate Republicans in Congress and the White House.[103]

By early 1977, money from Viguerie's operation began to flow into the club's coffers. Paul Reynolds, who worked with the club in the late 1970s, remembered going to the post office on Raleigh's New Bern Avenue, where he saw thirty or forty trays that were full of mail containing checks.[104] Between January and July 1977, nearly $1.4 million was raised. The Congressional Club's direct mail fund-raising had two important qualities: first, nearly all of the contributors gave less than $100; the average contributor donated between $12 and $15. Second, the money came with no strings, no obligations to contributors; it was, Wrenn later said, the "purest money in politics."[105] As part of the lead-up to the 1978 election, the money continued to pour in, and by the time of the election Helms had raised more than $7 million, about $3 per North Carolina voter, with most of the money coming from 100,000 out-of-state contributors, many of them senior citizens. A large portion went to Viguerie in the earliest phases of the fund-raising, but as the club began to refine its donor list, it received a higher percentage of receipts.[106] After 1977, Mike Dunne joined the club as a fund-raising consultant, and he began to expand support among North Carolina donors. Learning direct mail from Viguerie, almost immediately he began to develop his own in-house operation by focusing on developing a donor list in North Carolina. By 1978, meanwhile, Alex Castellanos was running a highly successful in-state direct mail effort.[107]

The infusion of money transformed the club. With hundreds of employees and millions of dollars coming in, recalled Ellis, club headquarters, in North Raleigh, was "like General Motors." Smart, highly analytical, unflappable, Wrenn commanded the operation. The club's expansion marked an important change in Helms's power base, and its success catapulted him toward greater power—but also greater distance from the club's operations. Like most politicians, Helms possessed an intense desire for adulation, and Wrenn noticed that he had become "sort of like a rock star," with a complex policy operation in Washington that set him apart from the club's rough-and-tumble political world. Driven by ideology and winning elections, Ellis and Wrenn increasingly began to find Helms unpredictable and difficult to manage. Helms insisted on rewriting all the fund-raising letters that went out under his name—something, Wrenn recalled, that "used to drive me out of my mind." Helms wanted the political power and influence that the club brought, but he also wanted to be insulated from negative political repercussions. Helms had a strong self-preservation instinct, and an important condition of the Helms-Ellis relationship was, according to Wrenn, that "Ellis take the heat" and at times even "fall on his sword." With Ellis more ideological and ruthless than Helms, and with the senator insistent that he be insulated from the club's ruthless tactics, there was a natural tension between Helms and his political operatives.[108]

As was true in all of Helms's Senate campaigns, in 1978 he at first appeared vulnerable. One poll, taken in November 1977, found 75 percent undecided and only 14 percent favoring Helms, a result that the *Greensboro Record* called a "miserable landslide."[109] Some national newspaper reports identified Jesse as a Democratic target and North Carolina as an electoral battleground, while other commentators wondered whether Republican infighting might weaken Helms's cause. Jesse was moving to the political center, according to *Raleigh News and Observer* editor Claude Sitton, as an indication of "an awareness that he will face stiff opposition in the general election under circumstances quite different from those under which he was first elected in 1972." In early 1977, Helms added Hamilton Horton, a former North Carolina state senator, to his Senate staff; the move was intended to shore up Helms's operation administratively and politically. Described as "an adviser distinguished by his personal civility, by his understanding of North Carolina attitudes and issues and by a fairly wide political acceptance within the GOP," Horton's arrival seemed to represent a softening of Jesse's image and a greater North Carolina presence in his office. In early 1977, Jesse supported Carter's food stamp bill and his human rights position, appeared at Governor Jim Hunt's inauguration "smiling broadly," and described Raleigh liberal Baptist minister William W. Finlator as a "longtime friend of mine." Helms also favored filibuster rules changes and aligned with the University of North Carolina on the desegregation fight. All this, to Sitton, indicated that Helms might be moderating his conservatism.

In fact, there was little evidence that Helms had changed his political positions. As Helms himself made clear in an interview with a reporter, "I am what I am."[110] In June 1977, in a speech in Winston-Salem, he denounced Carter's recent pardon of Vietnam-era draft resisters; he would never endorse pardon, he said, "for those who cut and ran when their country needed them." National security, Helms claimed, was "never in greater peril than now."[111] Jesse described Carter's U.N. ambassador, former civil rights leader Andrew Young, as a "one-man wrecking crew," and Helms made Young, as former aide to Martin Luther King and a leading African American in politics, into a favorite target of ridicule. Helms used Young in often thinly veiled racial messages; race, said one reporter, "was always part of Helms' political toolbox." He told a joke on the campaign trail frequently that had racial overtones. "Andy Young sent me a get-well card," said Helms. "He said some of his friends in Africa wanted to have me for dinner."[112] Rob Christensen, who covered Helms for many years for the *N&O,* recalled that Helms presented the subject of Andrew Young derisively. He would refer to "Am-bass-a-dor Andrew Young," with each syllable drawn out in "mock reverence." The implied message, Christensen realized, was: "Can you believe that there's this black man at the United Nations?" Christensen had little doubt that audiences in eastern North Carolina recognized this as a racial appeal.[113]

In 1978, the Democratic field seemed to favor Luther Hodges, Jr., a prominent banker and son of the former governor, who had the largest number of endorsements and the biggest campaign war chest. Certainly, Helms's staff expected him to win the nomination. But Hodges's campaign never took hold, as he failed to establish much connection with voters, and in the May 1978 primary, state insurance commissioner and primary underdog John Ingram, who had made his reputation as a populist opponent of corporations, won the nomination in a surprise upset. Ingram, however, practiced a maverick style of politics that was ill-suited to a Senate campaign. One reporter recalled that when he met Ingram as a freshman member of the North Carolina statehouse, he wore a "suit the color of red wine and red, white and blue patent leather shoes." Ingram had changed little since, except that he had put on some weight. His campaign, according to one account, was "an organizational nightmare," but Ingram maintained absolute control.[114] Though a vigorous campaigner, his approach in 1978 puzzled political observers. Ingram's campaign was woefully underfunded—he spent around $150,000 in the campaign—and suffered from poor organization. With little money and few paid staffers, Ingram seldom planned ahead.[115] When he won the runoff primary, noted one Democratic leader, it was like "having your daughter come up pregnant. You don't like it, but you try to make the best of the situation."[116]

In contrast to Ingram, the Helms campaign enjoyed superb organization, fund-raising, and planning, and in the 1978 contest Tom Ellis, who led Helms's campaign, was prepared to overwhelm any potential opponent. In the 1970s, North Carolina was still majority-Democratic in registration, by a margin of three to one, and Jesse relied on a loyal non-Republican

following.[117] Ellis oversaw the campaign from his law office in the old Sir
Walter Hotel building that was filled with mementos, including a photograph of Helms with evangelist Billy Graham and a portrait of Robert E.
Lee, along with woodcut representations of Civil War battles on the wall.[118]
Ellis relied on a large campaign staff located in Raleigh on two floors of an
office building and in twenty other sites across the state; by the end of the
campaign, the staff included one hundred full-time workers, fifty part-
timers, four hundred headquarters volunteers, and as many as three thousand volunteers statewide. Secretive and suspicious of the press—visiting
reporters were carefully screened, photographs were limited, and electronic detection devices were part of an elaborate security system—the
Helms operation was dominated by young staffers in their twenties. Operating almost entirely outside of the Republican Party apparatus, the campaign was tightly organized and highly centralized. It included some
familiar faces such as Alex Castellanos and Arthur Finkelstein, who worked
on political strategy, as well as younger newcomers such as Paul Reynolds,
who handled finances, and Doug Davidson, who managed the campaign's
organization. In addition to the official campaign, the Congressional Club
had grown into a much larger operation. With Wrenn in charge, the club
had identified 100,000 Helms voters who were listed on cards that were
used by telephone and door-to-door volunteers.[119]

The sudden emergence of the Congressional Club as a powerful force
reflected sea changes in American politics. The infusion of money changed
campaigning, and in the summer of 1978 Jesse's campaign announced that
they would refuse public financing in order to avoid spending limits.[120] The
availability of money made it possible to run a longer campaign: the Helms
campaign had organized by early 1977 and began in earnest later that year,
twelve months before the election.[121] But the most important change was
the realization that traditional, county-level organization was less important than the use of the media. In 1977 and 1978, Ellis spent nearly $3 mil-
lion to construct an elaborate organization; using Helms on weekends,
Wrenn organized dinners across the state designed to recruit volunteers for
a statewide organization. Despite these labor-intensive efforts, by the spring
of 1978, Helms had only moved up a few points in polling. In May 1978,
Finkelstein urged Ellis and Wrenn to put Helms on the air during the
Democratic primary. After spending $250,000 on media, Helms's poll
numbers improved, in the space of only a few weeks, by about ten points. It
had become "clear as a dadgum bell," said Wrenn, that television had replaced old forms of political organization and "had really changed the
whole world." Arthur Finkelstein had long argued that television was

transforming the way in which voters received information. The experience in 1978 confirmed the truth of this transformation to Ellis and Wrenn, and the Helms operation moved to a new "budget paradigm" in which nearly four-fifths of their funds would go toward television advertising and in which they largely abandoned traditional political organizing. Moving headlong into television, Helms's political operatives mastered the method of media production. It began with ideas that came from Finkelstein and his polls, but it also involved a production team headed by Earl Ashe, who joined the Helms team full-time in what Wrenn called a "marriage made in heaven." From 1977 to 1990, Ashe produced all of Helms's TV ads. Ashe had a background in news production rather than advertising, but he had an uncanny ability to sense how to reach average people and to communicate the message in a clear, understandable way. Ashe's motto in creating political spots was: "Don't get any bigger than what you can put on a bumper sticker." The final stage in the production of political ads came in ad placement and in buying TV time, a task completed by Ruth Jones and later Robert Holding. Having made a fortune in selling products on television, Holding was a tough negotiator and a genius at maximizing ad dollars through a placement strategy. By the late 1970s, the production side had evolved into a completely in-house operation.[122]

Once Ingram captured the Democratic nomination in May 1978, Helms's media campaign intensified. In June, the campaign launched a $40,000 ad campaign attacking Ingram in three-fourths-page ads in forty daily newspapers, along with radio ads. One ad asserted that Ingram wanted to "turn North Carolina education over to another new Washington bureaucracy—A Department of Education." Another claimed that Ingram, if elected, would have given away the canal, cut military spending, ineffectively protected tobacco farmers, and opposed tuition tax credits for private schools. After Democrats claimed that these attacks were based on "half-truths," some North Carolina editorialists joined in condemnations. The *Lenoir News Topic*, saying that the media campaign exhibited Helms's "well-known penchant for misrepresentation," declared that the "senator has no shame." Although the *Fayetteville Observer* acknowledged that it was a "minor masterpiece," Helms's media campaign was based on "innuendo, distortion, half-truths, and fragments of quotes wrenched out of context."[123] The ad campaign accelerated during the autumn, while Ingram's limited budget meant that he aired no media until late October.[124]

The money-intensive media campaign—Ingram would claim that Jesse was the "5 million dollar man"—meant that, for Helms, retail politics—the personal, face-to-face business of traditional campaigning—became less important. Because of heavy advertising, it seemed to make little difference in September 1978, in the middle of the campaign, when Jesse suspended personal appearances after undergoing back surgery for a ruptured lumbar disc. Helms had suffered back pain since 1964; this was his first surgery, and, although it sidelined him, it seemed to have little impact on the election. With Helms incapacitated for six weeks, Ellis unleashed a massive television campaign that widened his lead in the polls. Jesse returned to campaigning in mid-October, and at a press conference attacked Ingram, asserting that there was "not one scintilla of difference between the way John Ingram would have voted and the way [Senator] George McGovern voted." During October, Helms's lead in the polls grew from seven to eighteen points, and he cruised to an easy victory. When Ellis told Helms about his lead in the polls, Helms responded: "Looks like my coming back did some good." "You could have knocked Mr. Ellis over with a feather at that point," Wrenn recalled, but this exemplified how little Helms seemed to understand about campaigning. The key to winning, Ellis and Wrenn realized and Helms did not, was television, and the election, though never competitive, became a learning experience.[125]

On November 7, election night, the networks called the election in Helms's favor at 7:44 P.M., only fourteen minutes after the polls had closed. Helms was well prepared for his victory: his campaign had long concluded that the election was over. But he wanted to wait to declare victory, in order to maximize media exposure to a national audience by ensuring that his speech would be carried on national television. Jesse thus waited until nearly 10:30 before he spoke to his supporters. The *Raleigh News and Observer* had dubbed Helms "Senator No," because of his penchant for obstructionism, and he happily embraced the nickname. On election night, his enthusiastic supporters began chanting: "Senator No is on the go! Senator No is on the go!," and two of them waved "Jesse for President" signs. The crowd then broke into a refrain of "Hello, Jesse, Well Hello, Jesse," and the band switched to "Hey, Look Us Over, Lend Us an Ear, We're All for Jesse, Everyone Who's Here." "This was not a personal victory," Helms told the crowd, but was rather a "victory for the conservative and the free enterprise cause throughout America." This was a "bipartisan victory for people everywhere" who were "tired of turning to Washington with their problems." Rather than the solution, he said, "Washington is the problem." "I'm Senator No and I'm glad to be here!" he shouted to the crowd. Indicative of his indifference to regular party organization, he mentioned nothing about the Republican Party in his speech.[126]

The combination of Ingram's disastrous campaigning and Helms's

superb organization had led to Jesse's electoral triumph. Ingram communicated no alternative to Helms, and he ran on an incoherent populist platform. "His severe shortcomings as an orator," observed one reporter, "left
many people wondering if he had either the temperament or the intelligence to be a competent senator," while other Democrats saw him as "shal-
low, eccentric and perhaps not very bright." "You can rationalize it all you
want to," said one Democrat, "but the bottom line is that there are a whole
lot of people who just don't like John Ingram."[127] Governor Jim Hunt lent
the assistance of his formidable political organization, but he made it clear
that he was unenthusiastic.[128] The usually Democratic-leaning press found
Ingram decidedly unattractive. Calling Ingram's campaign a "farce," *Raleigh
News and Observer* editor Claude Sitton described Ingram's campaign as
"one of the most poorly financed and uncoordinated efforts ever made here
by a Democratic senatorial nominee."[129] the *Charlotte Observer* was so disgusted with the campaign that it refused to endorse anyone in the Senate
contest. In the end, remembered reporter Howard Covington, no one was
excited about the campaign "except John Ingram."[130]

What was perhaps the most surprising outcome of the 1978 campaign
was the small margin of Helms's victory. Despite a huge advantage in
money, organization, and media—and a campaign in which he outspent his
opponent by thirty-two to one—Helms attracted only about 53 percent of
the vote. Although his own polling was predicting a landslide, Ingram was
able to attract over 40 percent of the voters. Ellis noted a few days after the
election that it "just shocked the hell out of me that we didn't get a wider
margin"; he was convinced that the Helms campaign would "get in the real
high 50s or 60 percent of the vote." Helms told a reporter that he "thought
we'd do better" and that his polls "showed we would," while Democrats observed that it was "amazing" that Ingram attracted as many votes as he did.
Although commentators concluded that this reflected straight-ticket
voting—a "dead dog," said one Democrat, "would have come close to 40
percent just being listed in the polls"—it also suggested the extent to which
Helms polarized the electorate. In none of his five Senate elections did
Jesse ever attract more than 54 percent of the vote.[131] Helms, observed veteran *Wall Street Journal* reporter Vermont Royster, aroused "visceral reac-
tions, pro and con": while he had enthusiastic supporters, he also had "foes
to whom he is anathema." With "no soft edges," Helms was no intellectual;
he reached decisions on issues without recognizing that there were "things
to be said on the other side as deserving attention and respect." The result
was a rare thing for a politician: a person "to whom you can put a question
on any issue and get an unequivocal reply."[132]

WITH HIS SENATE victory in 1978, Helms solidified his position as a national conservative leader. During the campaign, he hinted that his second term might be his last, but he soon repudiated that notion and sought ways to strengthen his power base.[133] After the election, the Congressional Club, which sought to run its own direct mail operation, declared its independence from Viguerie. In 1978, the club became the subject of an inconclusive inquiry from the Federal Election Commission about whether it was violating election law by exceeding the maximum contribution limits, but the upshot was the formation of Jefferson Marketing, Inc. (JMI). Wrenn called Stanton Evans, editor of *Human Events* and head of the American Conservative Union, and he recommended that he consult about election law with John Bolton, who later was George W. Bush's controversial choice for U.S. ambassador to the United Nations. Bolton, fresh out of Yale Law School and working with the Washington law firm of Covington & Burling, had been involved in the *Buckley v. Valeo* case (1976), in which the Supreme Court ruled that the Federal Election Campaign Act of 1971 could not limit the activities of independent political action committees. Bolton urged Ellis and Wrenn to make sure that the club was affiliated with the Helms campaign but that it remained independent. After subsequent legal advice, Ellis decided to create a new corporate structure in which Jefferson Marketing served as a for-profit entity that would conduct fund-raising and political advertising, and would pay the salaries of most of the club's employees. Incorporated in January 1978, JMI assumed control of the club's operations, and it received most of its money as payment for its services.[134] With the contract with Viguerie expired, JMI continued to contract with different direct mail operations; the biggest included Viguerie and Bruce Eberle, and they continued to use them for continued prospecting: mailing lists had to be constantly updated and expanded, and prospecting was a large operation. But Ellis and Wrenn were free to harvest the names of 200,000 donors, and they created a list of a rock-solid group of conservatives—"The List"—who supported Helms's cause. Including eighty thousand names from North Carolina, most of The List came from around the country, including ten thousand from California, ten thousand from Texas, and some six thousand from the Northeast. Although Helms ended his 1978 campaign nearly $200,000 in debt, the money flow would erase the deficit, and The List provided a source of power for the next decade and a half.[135]

Chapter 6

ARCHANGEL OF THE RIGHT

The Reagan Revolution

Jimmy Carter's presidency, which was marked by economic problems of inflation and stagnant growth, fed a growing popular impatience with liberalism and the New Deal order that had spawned it. Abroad, the United States suffered a humiliation with the seizing of American hostages in Tehran, Iran, in November 1979, and the hostage crisis seemed to exemplify the nation's weakness in the post-Vietnam era. In the late 1970s, the Soviet empire seemed to be testing American resolve, and the policies of détente seemed no longer tenable. Although most of his first term in the Senate had been occupied with domestic issues, Jesse saw an interrelationship between foreign affairs and conservatism at home, and beginning in the late 1970s he began to press his agenda. Beset by domestic and international problems, Carter became one of the most unpopular presidents of the twentieth century, and his unpopularity fed gains among Republicans. Helms remained a consistent critic of Carter and of Democratic liberalism, and he was one of the most avid promoters of a conservative revolution that would rethink both domestic and foreign policies. If Helms set the stage for the Reagan Revolution, in the early 1980s he became its most powerful protector.

Ronald Reagan's triumph in the presidential election of 1980 rewarded years of organizing and networking by a far-flung, grassroots conservative movement. Reagan rode a wave of frustration about Carter's economic and foreign policy failures that emphasized liberalism's bankruptcy. Reagan promised tax cuts and reduced regulation, an assertive posture toward the Soviet Union, and attention to a cluster of so-called social issues. Jesse Helms stood at the center of the Reagan Revolution: he had nurtured the modern conservative movement, becoming in the 1970s its best-known national spokesman. "No conservative, save Reagan," according to conservative pundit Fred Barnes, "comes close to matching Helms' influence on American politics and policy since he won a Senate seat in North Carolina." No person in Congress, wrote Elizabeth Drew in *The New Yorker,* had "ever put together a political apparatus of the scale and nature that Helms has." He was "not just another senator," he was "a force" that represented a "new political phenomenon." Liberal activist Ralph Neas would describe Jesse as the "father of the modern Republican right-wing movement," with younger protégés eventually running Congress and influencing the George W. Bush administration.[1] Its most ardent advocate in the 1970s, Helms became modern conservatism's most determined protector in the following decade. During Reagan's first administration, Helms fought hard to preserve conservatism's purity, but this often put him at odds with the White House and Republican leaders. Although part of a Senate majority, Helms reluctantly relinquished what one observer called an "opposition impulse."[2]

FOLLOWING THE 1978 Senate elections, Helms lobbied successfully for a seat on the Senate Foreign Relations Committee. He became the fourth-ranking member on this crucial committee, behind Senators Howard Baker, Jacob Javits, and Charles Percy of Illinois. Despite efforts by chairman Democrat Frank Church and Javits to persuade other, more liberal Republicans to take Helms's place, he was named to the panel.[3] Helms was joined by other conservative Republicans, such as Indiana senator Richard Lugar and newly elected California senator S. I. Hayakawa. The shifting balance of power on the Foreign Relations Committee suggested that the bipartisan consensus that had characterized foreign policy since the advent of the Cold War was cracking.[4]

On the Foreign Relations Committee, perhaps the Senate's most important committee, Helms discovered a major forum. His closest advisers, John Carbaugh and Jim Lucier, formed Helms's foreign policy cabinet. Lucier, who served as chief legislative assistant, was a native of Detroit with a Ph.D. in English from the University of Michigan who had written editorials for the *Richmond News Leader* and worked for conservative columnist James J. Kilpatrick. Lucier, who was forty-five years old in 1979, had known Helms since the mid-1960s, when they corresponded and exchanged conservative editorials, and Jesse described him as a "deep thinker whose sense of history is nothing short of remarkable." Lucier wrote speeches, conducted research, and conceived legislative strategy for the senator.[5]

In the 1960s, Lucier had been a regular contributor to the John Birch Society's journal, *American Opinion;* though never a member of the society, between 1963 and 1966, he published fourteen articles in that journal. Newly independent African nations were becoming socialist, he warned in 1963, because it was "easy to convince cannibals and savages that socialism will supply abundance without necessitating the earning of it." Black African leaders, Lucier wrote, had "learned to grasp only the concept that one eats one's enemies." In a September 1964 issue of the *News Leader,* he described South Africa as containing three and a half million men who were "outnumbered by nine million aboriginal invaders and two million other citizens of color." Lucier expressed other controversial views: fellow journalists remember that he created a controversy when he criticized John F. Kennedy in the *News Leader* shortly after his assassination.[6]

John Carbaugh, another key staffer, worked directly with Helms on the Foreign Relations Committee. Unlike Lucier, he was an exuberant personality and an extrovert. One reporter described him as a "self-confessed political 'junkie'" who kept his two-hundred-pound body and five-foot-nine frame in perpetual motion, while another called him "amiable but thoroughly mischievous." Originally from Greenville, South Carolina, Carbaugh worked for the Nixon White House and as a staffer for Senator Strom Thurmond. Although, like Lucier, Carbaugh had academic training—he had a law degree and a master's in history from the University of South Carolina—he did not consider himself an intellectual. Affable and garrulous, Carbaugh constructed a network of contacts. Jesse described him as working on "nine parts adrenaline, one part blood"; because he sometimes operated hyperactively, the senator sometimes felt compelled to "rein him in." Carbaugh cultivated national reporters; not infrequently, he was seen having a champagne lunch or a drink with the *Washington Post*'s Robert Novak or the *Los Angeles Times*'s Jack Nelson, and reporters regarded him as the Helms staffer who best represented the senator's views. Troubled by Helms's image among the press as "some kind of simplistic Neanderthal," Carbaugh was determined to show reporters that Jesse was a "reasonable, honest man." Carbaugh was also known as an "intrepid leaker and planter of news items."[7]

By the late 1970s, Helms's foreign policy staff had created a network of institutes and think tanks that sought to compete with liberal organizations such as the Brookings Institution. One such organization was the Institute of American Relations (IAR), which Helms helped to establish. First active during the canal treaties debate of 1977–79, the IAR eventually supplied, according to one estimate, three-quarters of the literature printed during the treaty fight. Relying on direct mail fund-raising, the IAR funded foreign travel by Carbaugh and Lucier; in 1979, for example, it spent nearly a million dollars financing Helms's foreign policy operation. When Helms traveled to Latin America in 1978 and, a year later, to meet with British prime minister Margaret Thatcher, the IAR paid his travel bills. Similarly, it sent Utah senator Orrin G. Hatch and two of his aides to four NATO countries, while it paid for visits by Helms staffers to Latin America and Africa. During 1977–78 alone, the IAR reimbursed Carbaugh and Lucier $33,000 for travel. Along with the IAR, parallel institutes—the Institute of Money and Inflation, the American Family Institute, the American Education Legal Defense Fund, and the Center for a Free Society—functioned as nominally independent organizations that served as part of Helms's larger operation. These organizations were permitted under Senate and IRS rules as long as Helms had nothing to do with their operation. Operating outside Helms's direct control under Carbaugh and Lucier—in the same way that the Congressional Club operated autonomously—these think tanks served as holding companies for Helms's foreign policy machine.[8]

Helms's most important foreign policy position was his advocacy of unilateral American power and his unrelenting opposition to the Soviet Union. Rejecting détente along with the human rights approach of Jimmy Carter, Helms favored an aggressively nationalist policy in which the United States advanced its own interests, rejected arms controls, and largely abandoned the collective security and multilateralism of the United Nations. As he told a meeting of the Conservative Political Action Conference in February 1980, he favored withdrawing from any international agreements limiting the United States's freedom of action. Helms rejected the "death-grip of interdependence" in foreign policy.[9] He also emphasized the global nature of the Soviet threat. In October 1979, Helms created a brief flurry of excitement when he charged that a Soviet "combat brigade" was stationed in Cuba and that the Soviets had concluded that the United States had withdrawn from "its regions of influence, even from its defense perimeter." In a replay of the Cuban Missile Crisis of 1962, the "combat brigade" incident suggested the weakness of Jimmy Carter's approach to the Soviets.[10] Helms led the charge in demanding a confrontation.[11] Jesse also remained a staunch opponent of the Strategic Arms Limitation Talks

(SALT) agreement of 1972 and SALT II agreements, which Carter negotiated with the Soviets in 1979. In response to the Soviet invasion of Afghanistan in late 1979, moreover, Jesse demanded the end of further support of the Soviet regime, including ending grain sales, technology deals, or, as he put it, "anything that will be useful to the Soviet Union in any way."[12]

During the 1970s, Helms strongly supported the white minority regimes in Rhodesia (now Zimbabwe) and South Africa. In contact with white Africans since the 1960s, he connected their cause with the cause of white Southerners. After Ian Smith, the head of Rhodesia's minority government, declared independence on November 11, 1965, the new regime attracted international condemnation and U.N. economic sanctions. The United States observed an international embargo until 1971, when an amendment sponsored by Senator Harry F. Byrd, Jr., permitted the importation of Rhodesian chrome. In December 1973, the Senate repealed the Byrd Amendment, but the measure failed in the House. Calling American policy toward Rhodesia a "contradiction wrapped in an absurdity and cloaked in a confusion," in December 1973 Jesse claimed that the United States might now be forced to buy this strategic material from the "world's wickedest regime," the Soviet Union.[13] By the 1970s, a black nationalist guerrilla war had begun in Rhodesia that intensified after Mozambique won independence from Portugal in 1975, and the Smith regime came under increased pressure. On March 3, 1978, Smith negotiated a peace at Governors Lodge, Salisbury, with black leaders (both of whom were not guerrillas) Abel Muzorewa and Ndabaningi Sithole. The Governors Lodge Agreement provided for elections, but it guaranteed whites a minority of seats in the parliament and a quarter of positions in the cabinet.

The Rhodesian peace talks were accompanied by efforts in Congress to lift sanctions. In March 1977, in a resolution sponsored by Majority Leader Robert Byrd, the Senate authorized the president to suspend the enforcement of Rhodesian sanctions, if it would encourage a transfer of power to a black majority government. After the Governors Lodge Agreement, Helms pressed hard to end sanctions, based on the argument that a majority-rule government would take power. Helms remained sympathetic to the Smith government; Tom Wicker of the *New York Times* called Smith Helms's "kindred soul."[14] The Carter administration opposed Helms's efforts; it believed that a premature lifting of sanctions would undermine American credibility as negotiators. In June 1978, Helms offered an amendment to the foreign relations authorization bill that would lift sanctions until the end of 1979. When this met a narrow defeat, Helms urged Smith to send Muzorewa to visit Washington, and Jesse ushered him around Capitol Hill. In late July, Helms modified his amendment by proposing to suspend sanctions for a trial period. His amendment attracted anti-administration sentiment, and it only narrowly failed after New Jersey senator Clifford Case brokered a compromise in which the Senate instructed Carter to lift sanctions once free elections had occurred. Helms described Case's amendment as a victory. "It's not as much as I wanted," he said, "but boy we moved them way over."[15] Helms thereafter continued to campaign for the removal of the Rhodesian sanctions, even while British efforts tried to broker multiparty talks. In October 1978, he sponsored a visit to Washington from Smith and the black members of his government. In the spring of 1979, following the election of a government headed by Muzorewa, Helms introduced legislation, in what became known as the Helms-Byrd Amendment, requiring the removal of all sanctions. In June, the Senate voted by a margin of 52–41 to revoke the sanctions, though the proposal did not make its way any further in Congress.[16]

When the all-parties Rhodesian peace talks convened in London in September 1979, Helms sent Carbaugh and Lucier as observers; the trip was paid for by the Institute of American Relations. A newspaper report was published claiming that Carbaugh had privately urged Smith to "hang on" during negotiations, in the expectation that Congress might remove sanctions. On September 19, 1979, the State Department reportedly received a "very serious" complaint from British foreign minister Lord Carrington that Carbaugh and Lucier had intervened, and Secretary of State Cyrus Vance telephoned Frank Church, chairman of the Senate Foreign Relations Committee, and Jacob Javits, ranking Republican member. Both met with Helms in the Senate cloakroom, where he vehemently denied any inappropriate action, telling them, according to his account, that "if they had any idea they could intimidate me, to forget it." Helms described the charges as a "perfect absurdity." Carbaugh and Lucier went to the London talks because Helms mistrusted the State Department, but Ian Smith did not need any urging about a hard line. Although his aides might have given Smith a status report on sanctions, according to Helms, "at no time did they lobby anybody." Smith was a man who stood up against the world for fourteen years, Lucier said, and it was "ridiculous to think a man like me could go over there and change his mind about anything." Carbaugh, meanwhile, described the matter as a "tempest in a teapot." Meanwhile, the *Raleigh News and Observer* criticized Helms for sending "two of his ideological bird-dogs" to London to tamper with the peace talks. This was Jesse's "unilateral foreign-policy operation" and "reckless senatorial activity by any standard" that amounted to obstructionism taken to an international level.[17]

Rather than disturbed by the State Department report, Helms enjoyed the publicity: his enemies had "thrown the senator in the briar patch." The State Department, he claimed, was leaking this information in order to undermine the Helms-Byrd Amendment. In a Senate speech on September 20, Jesse claimed that he had spoken with British undersecretary of state for foreign affairs Richard Luce, who denied the existence of any British complaint about Helms's interference. Luce's statement was, according to Helms, confirmed by Foreign Minister Lord Carrington's private secretary. When a State Department official explained that the British had complained informally about Helms, he denied the assertion. "Vance obviously misspoke himself, to use a word from the Nixon administration," Helms declared. "Whether he misspoke it of his own volition or whether some of his underlings misled him is something I can't say." There was "something a bit too preposterous about the original story," editorialized the *Wall Street Journal*. How could Ian Smith have been influenced by "a couple of Senate aides"? It believed that the leaks were designed to influence not only the London talks but the House-Senate conference dealing with the Helms-Byrd Amendment. Soon after the *Wall Street Journal* editorial appeared, Helms accused the State Department of getting "caught in the act" of "trying to pull a dirty trick." Their true intent, he said, was to undermine the Helms-Byrd Amendment. Helms might have been correct in this assessment, as the amendment failed to make it past conference. Senate Minority Leader Howard Baker on September 27 suggested that Vance should apologize to Helms in what appeared to have been a "fabricated . . . leak," and he became, in effect, a "party to an untruth."[18] Meanwhile, the parties to the Rhodesian conflict signed a general treaty, known as the Lancaster House Agreement, which provided for multiparty elections under British supervision. In April 1980, power was transferred to a new, majority-black government. In the wake of these developments, Helms's anti-sanctions campaign effectively died.[19]

IN 1980, IN the presidential campaign of Ronald Reagan, Helms recognized the opportunity to move from his status outside the political mainstream, a position that he had occupied since his election to the Senate in 1972. In the 1980 campaign for the Republican presidential nomination, Reagan battled George H. W. Bush, and Ellis feared that party moderates would rally against Reagan in a Bush candidacy. In a brainstorming session, Ellis proposed that Helms campaign for vice president as insurance against a Bush nomination and as a way to promote the conservative cause. Helms liked the idea—and took it even more seriously than Ellis had intended. In

July 1979, Helms announced his interest in the office: as vice president, he would run the Senate, and "stop whatever I wanted to" and "would get this country straightened out." The *Los Angeles Times* concluded that Helms saw the vice presidency as a "powerful, independent way to stamp his own right-wing ideology on the Senate and legislation that comes before it." Although the North Carolina Republican Party pushed Jesse's vice presidential campaign and organized a television advertising campaign in late 1979 and early 1980, the Republican presidential candidates ignored him. "Any Republican presidential hopeful who invites Helms to join his ticket with that kind of game plan," noted the *Raleigh News and Observer,* "will be in the same league with the woman who invited Jack the Ripper into her apartment to give her a neck massage."[20]

Ellis discovered that New Hampshire, alone among primary states, had a separate ballot for vice presidential candidates. He immediately saw the public relations possibilities. Wrenn traveled to New Hampshire with a group of workers, and in December 1979 they collected the necessary 1,100 signatures and paid the $500 filing fee to put Helms on the February 26 New Hampshire primary ballot; he was the only candidate for the vice presidential nomination. With Tom Ellis and North Carolina Republican state chair Jack Lee orchestrating, Helms did no campaigning, though in encounters with the press he urged that Americans should have a better way to select vice presidential candidates.[21] But Helms's campaign made no progress, in New Hampshire or elsewhere; the "only one taking it seriously," Wrenn later said, "was Helms."[22] By April 1980, after Reagan swept through the primaries, Jesse accomplished little in his own campaign. Despite eight months' work and the expenditure of $100,000 in his vice presidential campaign, he had no convention delegates for the July 1980 Republican National Convention in Detroit.[23]

When Republicans assembled at the convention, however, Helms and Republican conservatives were clearly in charge. A residue of the bad feelings from the 1976 campaign remained between the Helms and Reagan camps, and only after Reagan fired John Sears in the spring of 1980 did Jesse unequivocally endorse his candidacy.[24] In Detroit, Helms complained that Reagan managers were excluding him and his conservative allies; on his arrival, he discovered that his room reservation had been canceled by someone from the Republican National Committee. In a letter to conservative delegates, Helms warned that liberals were preparing to take over the convention.[25] Despite the rhetoric, at Detroit Jesse had become a Republican leader, and he attracted even more attention than he had four years earlier. "He can't go two feet," said one reporter, "without being mobbed" by "middle-aged groupies with STOP ERA buttons" who wanted autographs and Polaroid snapshots.[26] Aided by a team that included five staffers, Ellis, Wrenn, and North Carolina state GOP chairman Jack Lee, Helms became a media star at Detroit, much in demand by television interviewers. On July 15, he began his day when ABC sent a limo at 6:20 for a television interview on *Good Morning America;* at 7:20, he moved over to an interview with CBS, followed by conversations with Associated Press radio, an interview with a Virginia newspaper, and an hour-long conversation with a *New York Times* reporter. Jesse was interviewed so many times that his staffers lost track of him.[27]

Most of Helms's programs and policies were incorporated into the 1980 Republican platform, including conservative positions on legalized abortion, the Equal Rights Amendment, a demand for military "superiority" (language that Helms inserted) over the Soviets, and the appointment of judges who observed "traditional family values and the sanctity of innocent human life." With Tom Ellis and Helms ally Phyllis Schlafly working behind the scenes, conservatives dominated the subcommittees writing the platform. Ellis coordinated activities with Helms's Senate staffers, each of whom was assigned to a different subcommittee.[28] With the upper hand, Helms beat back attempts to moderate the platform's language.[29] But Helms's uncompromising conservatism made Reagan, as the *Baltimore Sun*'s Jules Witcover observed, "come off rather miraculously as a voice of moderation." Whether a deliberate strategy or not, Helms staked out the right flank, thus enabling Reagan to portray himself as reasonable; thanks to Helms, Reagan would be nominated "not as a hard-nosed dictator of the platform, but as a benign recipient of a platform worked out by others— that just happens to suit him fine."[30]

Four years earlier, Jesse had belatedly denounced Reagan's selection of Richard Schweiker as a betrayal of the conservative cause, and the true intention of his quixotic 1980 vice presidential campaign was to keep Reagan to the right—and to forestall the nomination of a moderate or liberal Republican.[31] His fears seemed to be realized by Reagan's choice of George Bush for vice president.[32] Bush was considered too moderate, and when Reagan announced his selection, on July 16, Helms learned what he told reporters was the "bad news" while he was interviewed by CBS anchor Walter Cronkite. While Cronkite had Jesse on television, correspondent Lesley Stahl appeared, trying to get the anchor's attention. Helms read her lips: "Walter! Walter! It's Bush." Helms remembered that he was astonished because Reagan aides had assured him Gerald Ford would be the choice. Helms met at his motel in Warren, Michigan, with conservative allies

Howard Phillips, Phyllis Schlafly, and Congressman Robert Bauman of Maryland. Conservatives were described as bitterly disappointed in the decision; Jesse, according to Ellis, was in "utter shock." At a meeting of the North Carolina delegation held soon after Reagan announced the decision, reporter Ferrel Guillory recalled seeing Ellis standing on a table, "spitting with anger." But Helms quietly accepted the nomination once the Reagan people assured him that Bush enthusiastically supported the GOP platform. Sensing victory in the fall presidential election, Helms made a calculated decision not to oppose the Bush nomination.

There remained the matter of Helms's vice presidential campaign. Ellis obtained a promise of prime-time exposure for the senator if he withdrew. But Jesse, who had become entranced with the idea of the vice presidency, resisted. Only after Ellis promised to explain things to Dot and his daughters did the senator agree to this arrangement, and, on the evening of the 17th, Helms withdrew. He lined up behind the Reagan ticket, although in the end he attracted fifty-four delegates (including thirty-five North Carolina delegates). In a ten-minute speech to the convention, he described a "new majority in America" that was interested primarily "only in what is right and what is wrong."[33] The conservative *Greensboro Record,* which called Helms's 1980 vice presidential run "sheer nonsense," recognized that it was a "bold but ridiculous man[e]uver for power" that sought to make Reagan "dance to his tune."[34]

With Ronald Reagan's sweep to victory, the 1980 election marked a high point in Helms's conservatism. During the primary campaign, Ellis used the Congressional Club's mailing list after he organized Americans for Reagan as an independent fund-raising committee. The club not only enthusiastically supported Reagan's campaign, it expanded its activities to other campaigns around the country, spending a total of $7.6 million in 1980. Nicpac was the only national organization to spend more. The club also managed the North Carolina candidacies of I. Beverly Lake, Jr. (running for governor), Bill Cobey (running for lieutenant governor), and John East, who challenged Robert Morgan for his Senate seat. In September 1979, a year before the election, the club ran negative ads against North Carolina governor Jim Hunt, claiming a "political payoff" in a $1 million state contract that the state government awarded to North Carolina AFL-CIO head Wilbur Hobby. The ad opened by showing a stack of $100 bills and the hands of a person placing the bills into another set of hands. The scene switched to a shot of a newspaper story outlining the details of the contract: "What does the state do with our money?" the narrator asked, then posing the question: "Was this a political payoff?" "You shouldn't have to share your money with a union boss. You'll never spend it. Wilbur Hobby will." The ad was considered so negative that most of the TV stations in North Carolina refused to run it. But Lake had little chance against Jim Hunt, an incumbent governor with the best political organization in the state, and the negative advertising did little good.[35]

East's campaign was also a long shot, but Morgan was considered vulnerable. East had run unsuccessfully for Congress in 1966 and North Carolina secretary of state in 1968, and he served in 1976 as a Helms delegate to the Kansas City Republican convention. Well regarded in the Helms camp for his nimble intelligence and ability to speak extemporaneously, Ellis recruited East because he knew him from the 1976 campaign and because he wanted a candidate who could attract eastern North Carolina votes.[36] East's 1980 run marked the first time that the club had engaged in all-out, negative attacks on television—according to Wrenn, a "huge turning point." Because the club had raised millions of dollars in the 1978 Senate race but lacked an effective opponent, it was able to experiment freely. This was "grad school" in "nuts-and-bolts politics," said Wrenn, and "we could try anything that we wanted to try." Helms's managers came out of the 1978 campaign far ahead of perhaps anyone else in the country about the use of media and money.[37] The conventional wisdom had always been that negative advertising on television would backfire, and candidates confined attacks to radio and newpapers. In planning for the campaign, Finkelstein, who did East's polling, argued that the campaign should target Morgan and go negative. Now was the time, said Finkelstein, to transform the role of television in politics.

But going negative had risks. Morgan had been Helms's political ally in the 1960s; during Helms's reelection campaign in 1978, he remained neutral and even, at one point, defended Jesse against Ingram's attacks as "a good man, a man of integrity." Morgan and Helms had clashed frequently in the Senate, however, and the club perceived him as an enemy of the cause, a "get-along, go along" collaborationist with the liberal establishment. Helms personally had reservations about using negative media against Morgan, and the 1980 East campaign exposed tensions between the Senator and the club. Ellis was determined to elect conservative candidates to the Senate, at whatever cost, while Helms was more reluctant to make East and other Senate colleagues into enemies. According to Wrenn, Helms endorsed East, but was intent on avoiding the "crosshairs" of the East-Morgan battle. Despite Wrenn's effort to involve him, Helms was unhelpful. When presented with anti-Morgan fund-raising letters, Helms insisted on removing negative references. "He didn't put much red meat on that thing," remembered Wrenn. At one point, Wrenn developed an ad asserting that East opposed the Panama Canal treaties, without mentioning Morgan by name. When Earl Ashe took the ad to Helms, he rejected it, saying that the message was an attack on Morgan. Instead, he rewrote the script and, in the new ad, read a statement endorsing East and describing him as a "fine Christian." But Jesse's effort to avoid the fray blew up in his face when Morgan became offended by the implication that he was not a "fine Christian."[38]

The bruising nature of the East-Morgan campaign meant that Helms, despite his best efforts, could not avoid entangling himself: in a sense, Jesse's strategy of noninvolvement only made things worse. In September 1980, Morgan's staff had cautioned him about Helms, but when Jesse sent out fund-raising letters on East's behalf, Morgan considered this no more than party loyalty. When his staff warned him that Helms was trying to block his judicial nominee, Charles Winberry of Rocky Mount, Morgan did not believe them. "He was the only one in the office for a long time that wouldn't believe it," said one aide. "He's naive in some respects." But, by September 1980, when the club unleashed a new round of negative ads, Morgan changed his mind.[39] Part of the club's attack strategy focused on the incumbent senator's vote in favor of the canal treaties. When Morgan, after agonizing about it, voted in favor of ratification, Tom Ellis had predicted a political price and had promised retaliation. The club's polling showed that most voters opposed the Panama Canal treaties but did not realize that Morgan had voted in favor of them. Other ads also focused on defense and foreign policy issues, including Morgan's supposed opposition to the B-1 bomber and his support for organized labor: in both instances, the club's ad greatly distorted Morgan's record, which was resolutely pro-military and anti-labor.

Unlike East, Morgan's campaign followed a more traditional political paradigm, which called for using money to build a grassroots organization rather than to saturate the airwaves with a political message. East was, in contrast, what Wrenn called North Carolina's "first pure media candidate." He paid for the television barrage with highly successful fund-raising— East had raised $1.2 million by mid-October—and he outspent Morgan, especially in the campaign's late stages. The negative media marked the first time that the club used television in a systematic way, and Morgan denounced the ads as "gross distortions" and "outright fabrications." As would subsequently become the case, the club's researchers reviewed Morgan's voting record and then made claims about his positions based on it. In the campaign's last days, on the advice of Arthur Finkelstein, the club transitioned from foreign policy to economic issues, in thirty-second attack ads that charged that Morgan was a weak protector of tobacco and textiles. The ads pointed out that the Carter administration threatened the tobacco program with its anti-smoking campaigns and textiles with its intention of granting China most favored nation trade status. Eventually, the East campaign gained traction. Although Morgan had a large, two-to-one lead in the polls only a week before the election, the Reagan landslide in North Carolina carried East to a narrow upset victory.[40]

The Congressional Club's media blitz was critical. When the campaign was over, East had spent $665,000 compared with Morgan's expenditure of $177,000 to buy TV time. Tom Ellis believed that East, lacking a strong statewide identity and suffering from the opposition of all the major newspapers, needed the television exposure in order to communicate his message to voters.[41] Morgan took the defeat hard, and blamed Helms's intervention. In his last weeks in office, between the election and the convening of a new Congress, Morgan opposed Helms anti-busing maneuvering in the Senate. Preparing to leave his Senate offices in December 1980, he ran into Jesse on the elevator. "Well, well," said Morgan, "if it isn't the fine Christian gentleman Jesse Helms." Helms was reported as "startled" by the encounter, "not only by having one of his favorite descriptions thrown back at him but also by the open hostility with which it was done." Flustered and embarrassed, he fumbled for an answer, finally saying: "Well, if it isn't my fine Christian friend Robert Morgan" and then walking away. While Morgan never forgave Helms, for his part, Jesse remained shocked by Morgan's bitterness. In September 1981, he told the *Raleigh News and Observer* that he had hoped to resume his friendship and was "taken aback" by Morgan's hard feelings, commenting that he was "out of his mind." He claimed that in the campaign he had urged Tom Ellis and the club to tone down their attacks.[42]

As PREPARATIONS WENT forward for Reagan's inauguration on January 20, 1981, Helms ranked high on most lists of Washington's powerful people. During inaugural week, he appeared on *Meet the Press* and attended Reagan's first state dinner, one of seven members of Congress invited. In the early months of 1981, Helms met with Reagan four or five times. Jesse was known—as he was always known—for his workaholic habits and a personal life that focused on his four grandchildren, early rising, eating scrambled eggs and thick-sliced bacon, and snacking on ice cream and vanilla milk shakes. A teetotaler, Helms chain-smoked Lucky Strikes—apparently

his only vice. Both homebodies, Jesse and Dot shunned the Washington social circuit. His favorite television shows were *Little House on the Prairie* and
Trapper John, M.D., his favorite movies *The Sound of Music* and *Gone with the
Wind*, and his favorite actress Julie Andrews. Jesse's preferred reading, he
told a reporter, was the Bible. That there was little controversial or particularly interesting about his life outside of his work created a paradox, according to a *Wall Street Journal* account. Although strait-laced, Helms
surrounded himself with a staff "that churns and bubbles with bizarre
ideas, clashing egos—and sometimes with plain good spirits."[43] Helms attracted attention from the national media as a conservative leader. During
the first half of 1981, the *New York Times, Washington Post, Los Angeles Times,*
and *Wall Street Journal* all published major feature stories on him. National
attention peaked in September 1981, when *Time* placed Helms on its
cover. Described by *Time* as a "saint to his fans" and "a dangerous buffoon
to his foes," Helms was characterized as the "New Right's righteous warrior."[44]

In 1981, Helms's power base was substantially expanded, with Republicans in control of the Senate for the first time since 1952. One reporter, in
July 1981, called him the "second most powerful conservative in the country" and "one of the shrewdest and toughest political operators in American
politics, even to the point of downright meanness, especially on racial matters."[45] Another reporter, writing for the *Los Angeles Times*, described him as
the "godfather of New Right politics across the country, an ideological
larva transformed into a butterfly." He was the right's most effective fund-
raiser, a "guru" to a network of groups, organizations, and tax-exempt foundations that pursued conservatism in domestic and foreign policy. Helms,
the reporter asserted, was the "de facto chairman of a political conglomer-
ate," what another commentator called "the spiritual leader of the new bloc
of ultraconservatives in Congress who are convinced that their day is only
beginning to dawn."[46]

Helms, despite Reagan's victory and Republican control of the Senate,
had little interest in governing or cooperating with those that did. Since
Reagan's election, he admitted in early 1981, he had observed that it was a
"decidedly different feeling to be catching the hand grenades instead of
throwing them."[47] The conservative movement that Helms was leading followed a deliberate strategy. "Conservatives used to believe their job was to
lose as slowly as possible," Howard Phillips told a reporter. According to
Phillips, since the mid-1970s conservatives had hoped to take over at least
one house of Congress. But "we don't have the White House yet": Reagan,
he said, was not "conservative enough."[48]

Nonetheless, Helms's relationship with Reagan remained strong; philosophically, he told an interviewer in February 1981, his approach to the new administration remained unchanged. The president would never doubt his loyalty; they had an enduring friendship. Helms chaired the Senate Steering Committee, a group of about seventeen Republican senators who allied themselves together as a conservative bloc and met over lunch every Wednesday in the Senate Dining Room. Conservative activist Paul Weyrich had helped to organize the group, and he relentlessly promoted a conservative agenda and coordinated plans with congressional conservatives. The Steering Committee had grown since Jesse entered the Senate in 1972. Along with James McClure of Idaho, also elected in 1972, it included Paul Laxalt of Nevada and Jake Garn of Utah, both elected in 1974, Malcolm Wallop of Wyoming and Harrison Schmitt of New Mexico, elected in 1976. The Steering Committee expanded in importance, and during the summer of 1980 Helms had invited George H. W. Bush to one of its meetings, during which he urged him to adhere to conservative principles, if he was going to join Reagan's ticket as the Republican vice presidential candidate.[49]

The Congressional Club by 1978 had become the most successful political organization in the country because of its ability to raise money through direct mail and to develop highly targeted political advertising. The club's model soon spread. Under the leadership of former Helms's staffer Charlie Black and conservative activist Terry Dolan, Nicpac contributed to the election in 1978 of Orrin Hatch of Utah, William Armstrong of Colorado, Roger Jepsen of Iowa, and Gordon Humphrey of New Hampshire. In 1980, sixteen new Republican senators entered Congress as part of the Reagan sweep, and five of them were hard-core conservatives elected by New Right political organizations. John East, who was elected in 1980 in a campaign run entirely by the club,[50] became known as "Helms on Wheels" (because his disability confined him to a wheelchair) and "Senator No-No" (because of his loyalty to Helms). Visitors to his Senate office noticed that prominently displayed on his wall was a large photograph of Jesse. Along with East, other hard-core conservatives included Jeremiah Denton of Alabama, founder of an anti-pornography organization; Steve Symms, who defeated incumbent Senator Frank Church of Idaho on the abortion issue; Charles Grassley, who upset incumbent Iowa senator John Culver, with Nicpac's assistance; and Don Nickles, elected from Oklahoma with the support of the Moral Majority. Many Republicans participated in a "candidates' school" run by another conservative organization, Paul Weyrich's Committee for the Survival of a Free Congress.[51] With an active national conservative constituency regularly contributing to the Congressional Club,

Helms received two thousand letters per day. He was a "guru of an amorphous but apparently large coalition of right-wing conservatives," according to a *Washington Post* reporter, and they considered themselves the "foot soldiers of a political, even spiritual, revolution." Described by PBS commentator Bill Moyers as a "counter-cultural revolutionary," Jesse wanted to reverse the cultural changes of the 1960s. Although quick to say that he was no revolutionary—his positions, Helms said, had for the past twenty or thirty years remained "precisely" the same—the country had come full circle on the issues. The time was ripe, Helms believed, to bring on a conservative revolution.[52]

Helms's relations with the Reagan presidency were complicated by a struggle within the White House between the ideologues and pragmatists. Jesse had already battled with Reagan pragmatists in the 1976 campaign. Soon after Reagan's election in November 1980, Helms met with the president-elect, and he declared his satisfaction to reporters that Reagan's heart remained "still in the right place philosophically."[53] But Helms's main goal was to preserve the conservative revolution.[54] Suspicious of Reagan's advisers, Helms and his staffers wanted to root out moderates. Backed by an energized national conservative constituency, said one reporter, Helms served as the point person for efforts to prevent a lapse into the "normal Washington pattern of compromise, consensus-building and expediency" and a move toward a "netherworld of the political center." Helms acted as an "Archangel of the Right" who would swoop down, hurling thunderbolts on enemies like an "avenging angel of old-time religion." Some in the Reagan White House had been "singed already." During the early months of the Reagan Revolution, Jesse's determination to maintain its conservative purity caused considerable anxiety among White House pragmatists.[55]

In the case of North Carolina's tobacco program, however, Jesse chose pragmatism over ideology. The system of federal controls and subsidies that made up the tobacco program was a "good ol' piece of the New Deal," wrote Roy Parker, Jr., in the *Fayetteville Times,* that could "even make a pragmatist out of Bro' Helms, who otherwise fancies himself the protector of the Republic against any attempt by the Debbil Government to dabble in our private affairs."[56] Helms, who had in the 1950s and 1960s opposed federal farm supports, had become a protector of tobacco. Soon after his election in 1972, Ellis advised him of the importance of service on the Agriculture Committee. Jesse, said Ellis, would need to "eat a stalk of tobacco every morning for breakfast."[57]

Helms followed that advice religiously by serving on the Agriculture Committee after he joined the Senate in 1973, and, with Republicans taking charge in the Reagan sweep of 1980, Helms became chair. From this seat of power, Helms's main purpose was to protect the tobacco program, a system of federal regulations that, since the 1930s, had maintained the prosperity of eastern North Carolina farmers. Under the helm of Louisiana's Russell Long and Georgia's Herman Talmadge, the Agriculture Committee had been a quiet and dull Senate sinecure. Over many years, federal agricultural programs remained unchanged, buttressed by a rock-solid political coalition of southern and midwestern supporters. But Helms's ascent to the chairmanship coincided with changes in federal agricultural programs, and, during the early 1980s, he faced the challenge of accommodating budget cuts with a political need to protect the status quo.

Among eastern North Carolinians, the tobacco program had long been an article of faith. In North Carolina, as Helms once explained, "tobacco isn't a commodity, it's a religion."[58] The system provided for allotments, or a license authorizing tobacco growing; nonallotment production was taxed. Tobacco allotments could be passed, inherited, or leased to a third party, and allotment holders agreed to cooperate on production levels in order to maintain prices at a minimum level; if prices fell below that level, the Flue-Cured Tobacco Cooperative Stabilization Corporation—which tobacco growers owned and operated—bought the surplus with federal loans. Although it required a massive intervention in the marketplace, for nearly fifty years the tobacco program had sustained prosperity among North Carolina producers. By the 1980s, however, the future of the tobacco program was cloudy. Joe Califano's attack on tobacco, though unpopular in North Carolina, inaugurated a federal public health campaign against smoking, and smoking came under increased scrutiny. Under the pressure of budget cuts, moreover, the agricultural coalition backing the federal farm programs threatened to collapse.

Other forces besieged North Carolina tobacco producers. The subsidy system spawned inefficiencies by encouraging growers to produce lower-grade tobacco, and the common practice of leasing allotments imposed additional costs on tobacco producers. In the 1960s, cigarette manufacturers looked abroad, primarily in South America and southern Africa, for cheaper leaf. In the 1970s, tobacco imports doubled, while the foreign-grown portion of American-manufactured cigarettes increased from 11 to 30 percent. Under a loophole of the law, moreover, manufacturers imported large quantities of "scrap" tobacco, which, under customs regulations that dated from 1909, included any machine-threshed leaf. Subject to a much lower tariff, scrap tobacco competed with American-grown leaf. In some respects, tobacco had already become politicized because of Helms's willingness to use it against the Carter administration, and, with Helms chair of Agriculture, North Carolina Democrats eagerly turned the tables by demanding import restrictions and stronger protective measures. Soon after the inauguration of the Reagan administration, Helms pressed the White House to drop the effort to limit scrap tobacco.[59] As the *Raleigh News and Observer* noted, Jesse insisted "on a political evenhandedness for the Republican administration that he did not grant to a Democratic administration." Helms believed that tobacco should not "become a political football" after "he had already finished playing the game."[60]

Helms, in effect, worked simultaneously toward achieving conflicting goals: to preserve North Carolina's tobacco program, institute cuts in agricultural programs, and maintain the congressional farm coalition. For the first time since he entered the Senate, as Agriculture Committee chair, he was required to engage in consensus building. This was a new side of Jesse that the Senate had not yet seen. Tom Boney, who was recruited to work for the committee by new staff director George Dunlop, recalled that Helms was "extremely fair" in handling the committee, and he usually worked by consensus. He worked well with people, once a relationship of trust had been established. On the other hand, he never forgot dishonesty. "If they lie to you once," he once told Boney, "they'll lie to you twice." He remembered observing how Jesse could read the body language of Agriculture Committee members and determine when a consensus had been reached—and when to move for compromise at the most opportune moments. Despite his reputation as a bomb thrower, as a committee chair Helms would "watch and read" other senators in order to move things forward. He often turned to Majority Leader Robert Dole, who served on the committee, to articulate a compromise position that would unite the committee.[61]

Early into the new Reagan administration, Helms mounted a political offensive. Soon after David Stockman became Reagan's budget director on January 27, 1981, Helms met with him about the tobacco program, and he had conducted a similar lobbying campaign with John R. Block, the new secretary of agriculture, who visited North Carolina in December 1980. In negotiations with the White House in late February 1981, the tobacco program emerged untouched, but it was threatened as the administration subsequently returned in search of budget reductions.[62] Stockman proposed eliminating the free tobacco inspection service, and there were those in the adminstration who favored doing away with the loan/price support system entirely. Helms accepted the elimination of the federal inspection service for leaf, but his Democratic opponents criticized him. The effective date of the end of the free inspection service, July 1, would hurt North Carolina's bright leaf producers, whose crop was harvested and cured in the late summer.

Helms fought hard to preserve tobacco's price support program. North Carolina producers were willing to do their share to reduce the deficit, Helms said on *Meet the Press* on March 2, 1981, but he defended the tobacco program. There was "no such thing as a tobacco subsidy," he announced; North Carolina farmers were not "asking for a free ride, and they've never got one." Cigarette smoking was "neither as good or as bad as some people say."[63] Throughout the following weeks, Helms expressed the same point: though North Carolina farmers should share in budget cuts, he insisted that there was no tobacco subsidy program. Despite borrowing $172 million during fiscal year 1980, federal loan authorities were usually fully repaid; in each of the previous two decades, the program broke even or made money. Since the 1930s, the tobacco program had cost federal authorities a total of $57 million, compared with $2.3 billion for the cotton program during the same period. As Jesse told the annual gathering of the Tobacco Associates, a tobacco grower export sales group: "I didn't go to Washington to preside over the demise of the tobacco program."[64]

Inevitably, Jesse crossed swords with the White House over farm programs. As a longtime opponent of the "rathole" of foreign aid, Helms doubtless saw this as a delicious irony.[65] Jesse was more supportive of other reductions. For example, in March 1981, serving as Reagan's legislative spokesman in the Senate, he successfully blocked a $146 million increase in milk price supports.[66] Presiding over month-long Agriculture Committee hearings about the budget, Helms endorsed an agricultural policy that supported but did not "dominate the farmer." He favored a market-oriented agriculture that emphasized the private sector, and he did not disagree with Stockman's recommendations to eliminate crop subsidies, reduce milk price supports, and cut food stamps. But most of Jesse's colleagues on the Agriculture Committee wanted to preserve these popular federal programs.[67] In early April 1981, Helms presented an agriculture bill to the committee that differed significantly from the administration's version and, as it turned out, enjoyed little support. While the White House wanted reduced price supports for peanuts, Helms's bill retained the status quo, proposing a support price of $650 per ton rather than the administration's $450 per ton. Helms's bill further required Block to reduce milk subsidies, then costing $1.5 billion annually, more slowly than the White House.[68] After the committee consideration in April, numerous amendments only made things worse: by the end of the month, Senator Dole described the bill as a "monster" that was running nearly $6 billion higher than the administration version.[69]

Jesse was more of a free market enthusiast when it came to the food stamp assistance program, which served 22 million Americans in 1981. Expected to cost as much as $12.8 billion annually, it consumed nearly half of the federal agriculture budget. The cost of food stamps had risen steadily throughout the 1970s, with Congress typically appropriating extra funds to cover increases on an ad hoc basis. For fiscal year 1981, for example, Congress authorized $6.19 billion; by June it needed another $2.56 billion.[70] For 1982, at current rates the program was expected to continue rising. Along with other Senate conservatives, Helms had long sought ways to reduce the food stamp program. Two days after the November 1980 elections, he told the *Raleigh News and Observer* that he supported major cuts. Favoring limiting food stamps to the "truly needy," Helms wanted to eliminate "freeloaders" from the system. "We have a monster on our hands," he said, declaring that waste and extravagance accounted for as much as 40 percent of its costs. Although various officials contested this figure, in late November 1980 Helms released a philosophy statement that recommended providing food stamps on a need-only basis, extending aid based on nutrition rather than income, rooting out fraud, requiring many recipients to work, instituting a base fee, and shifting responsibility from the federal government to the states.[71] Embracing a middle ground, the Reagan administration favored a 25 percent cut in the program that, spread over two years, would achieve savings by counting free school lunches against food stamp allowances and tightening eligibility requirements.[72]

Although the White House eventually proposed a more moderate cut of $2.6 billion, the attack on food stamps aroused the opposition of church and civil rights groups, labor unions, women's organizations, grocery workers, and hunger advocates. Helms, described by one food stamp advocate as having a "long history of contempt and lack of understanding of the food stamp program," attracted their fire.[73] Food stamp cuts alarmed other constituencies. Urban congressmen, who represented recipients, were opposed. In November 1980, Frederick W. Richmond (D-NY), chairman of the House Agriculture subcommittee that oversaw food stamps, told the *News and Observer* that he opposed any significant changes. Helms's portrayal of widespread waste was exaggerated; according to his estimates, the fraud rate was no more than 8 percent, while the rate for business was usually around 5 percent. If Helms tried to gut the program, Richmond promised retaliation. Declaring that Jesse should retreat from his "irresponsible comments," Richmond announced his "personal guarantee" that "serious risks" would result from major cuts in food stamps. Behind Richmond's threat lay a political reality: federal agricultural programs, including the tobacco program, depended on a political coalition composed of urban and rural congressmen. Rural constituencies benefited from federal farm programs, urban constituencies from welfare measures such as food stamps and free school lunches. The votes of both groups sustained political support for these programs, and it was a relationship of mutual dependency. "Without a food stamp program as part of the package," Richmond warned, there was "no way" a general farm bill—including the tobacco program—would pass.[74] Although Helms claimed that the *News and Observer* had inaccurately reported his positions and that Richmond had assured him that he would not retaliate against the tobacco program, Jesse's anti–food stamp campaign carried a high political price.[75]

Still another critical political constituency in the food stamp debate were farmers, especially farmers from the midwestern food belt. Senator Dole, who opposed drastic cuts and represented the big farm states of the Midwest, brokered a compromise in mid-February 1981 that provided for a significantly lower cut of about 15 percent (or $1.8 billion in the food stamp program). Jesse did not give up easily, however. In March, he announced that he was seeking an additional $500 million cut beyond the Dole-Reagan reductions. There was a "demonstrable fact" of waste, he said in March 1981. Helms pointed out other abuses: instances of food stamps used in speciality stores, bakeries, Maine lobster houses, and Maryland crabhouses. Recipients reported their stamps as stolen or lost and then illegally received replacements. Americans, Helms said, resented food stamp abuses and wanted them corrected. That meant deeper cuts, and his hearings would provide material that Helms could use on the hustings.[76]

Helms's conservative base loudly cheered his anti–food stamp stance. He had achieved a status "approaching political sainthood" among conservative activists around the country, according to one account. Increasingly, this conservative base included an ever-loyal group of evangelicals, whose politicization grew markedly during the 1980s. At a meeting of the National Religious Broadcasters and the National Association of Evangelicals, host David Hofer asked the crowd to hold their applause for the one hundred senators and congressmen present. The crowd remained silent until Hofer reached Jesse's name, and the announcement triggered "an ovation that rolled across the huge hall as the spectacled senator smiled down from his perch on the four-tiered dais." Helms might have been frustrated in the Senate, but he was highly effective at identifying and publicizing issues that excited the Religious Right. He could easily generate telephone calls, telegrams,

and letters to congressmen on various issues.[77] Food stamps had already become such an issue.[78]

But in the Senate, Helms anti–food stamp campaign enjoyed little support, especially among his colleagues on the Senate Agriculture Committee.[79] Buckling under White House pressure, on May 7 the committee
repudiated Jesse's food stamp cuts and instead adopted a more modest $1.9
billion cut advocated by Dole, an alternative that had the backing of ranking Democrat Patrick J. Leahy of Vermont. The Dole-Leahy bill reduced
income eligibility levels, required recipients to work at public service jobs,
and eliminated inflation indexing. The panel rejected Helms's and the administration's proposal to end food stamps for free school lunch recipients,
count low-income energy assistance as income in determining food stamp
assistance, and require that recipients pay off stamp benefits by working for
local governments without salary.[80] Helms remained unfazed. His strategy
all along, he explained, was to make the administration's proposal look
more acceptable by presenting more stringent reductions.[81]

By the late summer of 1981, the agriculture bill, and the tobacco program, faced accelerating attacks. The farm coalition was in danger of split-
ting, as cuts seemed to be falling more severely on dairy and grain farmers
than on Helms's constituents, peanut and tobacco growers. Tobacco opponents became emboldened: when Ohio senator Howard M. Metzenbaum
proposed eliminating the tobacco program on May 12, 1981, he attracted
the votes of forty-two senators. An "anti-Jesse mood" existed among Senate Democrats. California senator Alan Cranston, a prominent opponent,
said that Helms was a "a kind of time bomb for Reagan, I think, the way
McCarthy was for Eisenhower," while another adversary, Massachusetts
Democratic senator Paul E. Tsongas, said that Helms had made the Senate
less genteel and more "Darwinian."[82] Other senators openly sought retribution against Jesse. Democratic senator Edward Zorinsky of Nebraska had
clashed with Jesse about Central America, and, with Zorinsky up for reelection, Republican political operatives had used the issue in negative political
ads that had Helms's "fingerprints." When Helms asked him for his support
on the tobacco program, Zorinsky told him to go to hell.[83] Described by Rob
Christensen of the *News and Observer* as a "highly controversial and divisive
figure in Congress," Helms had created a backlash. He had been "so vicious
and unbending toward social programs," and he had so antagonized Congress, said Congressman Frederick Richmond, that they wanted to "get back
at Helms through the tobacco program." He believed that Helms was the
"worst liability you have in the state of North Carolina."[84]

Helms responded to this criticism by claiming that the "backlash" was a creation of his media critics and his congressional opponents. Rather than an anti-Helms phenomenon, this represented an attempt to force him to change his positions. Newspapers such as the *N&O* were suggesting that he should "close my eyes to such waste of the taxpayers' money in order to appease liberal members of Congress who built their careers on giving away the taxpayers' money." This was a "contrived political thing at the *News and Observer*." Its editors woke up every morning, he said, and asked "What can I get on Jess today?"[85] In late August, during the Labor Day break, Helms barnstormed through eastern North Carolina, reassuring tobacco growers that the tobacco program would be preserved. With his head count of congressmen showing a majority in favor, he told farmers: "Don't lose any sleep over it."[86] Rather than moderating his tone, Helms went further by attacking Richmond, and on August 9, in a television interview, he announced that he would not "yield to any blackmail from some loudmouth congressman from Brooklyn" with what he called a "curious lifestyle."[87] Richmond had been arrested in the summer of 1978 for soliciting a young man for sex acts, though the charges were dropped after he pled not guilty and agreed to participate in a first-offender program. Richmond's case attracted little attention, and he was easily reelected in 1980. In a press conference on September 1, John East provided reporters with more specific details of the charges against Richmond. East also launched an attack against Senator Thomas Eagleton of Missouri, who was briefly George McGovern's vice presidential nominee in 1972 before it was disclosed that he had been treated for depression with electroshock therapy. Eagleton was considered an enemy because he sponsored an amendment to the agriculture bill that would provide assistance only to farmers who grew tobacco and not to leaseholders. East reminded reporters of what he called Eagleton's "mental problems."[88]

Helms's and East's personal attacks won them few friends. "Neither North Carolina nor King Tobacco can afford poisonous rhetoric," declared the *Asheville Citizen*. "When in Doubt, Smear," said the *News and Observer*. Helms, said editorialist Claude Sitton, had loaded his "smear gun" at Richmond, while East "launched from his smear gun." Although "partisan jousting" about the tobacco program was typical politics, Helms and East had "descended into a political gutter where North Carolinians need not wallow."[89] "To suggest that one moral aberration or a bout with mental illness" was a "permanent liability" revealed a "lack of fact and feeling," said *The Durham Sun,* and this put Helms on a "lonesome and vulnerable pedestal of perfection." Even in the bruising environment of political combat, this kind of personal attack was repugnant. For Helms, the danger was that it might evoke a "painful backlash" that might provide ammunition for the enemies of the tobacco program.[90] Weathering blistering criticism, Helms and East backed down: while Jesse offered a tepid apology, East wrote Eagleton a two-page "letter of explanation" in which he refused to apologize but tried to moderate his language.[91] But neither Helms nor East offered any admission of guilt. East extended Richmond no apology, said one of his staffers, because he believed that he "intended no personal criticism." (A Richmond staffer sarcastically wondered what East did "when he gets personal.")[92] Eagleton refused to accept East's explanation. When Senator James Exon of Nebraska approached Eagleton and asked him, "Which one are you, Tom, the homo or the nut?," Eagleton turned to East and said: "Which one am I, John, the homo or the nut?" East had no response.[93]

Although Helms might have scored political points with his conservative constituency, he was less successful at governing. For him, the Reagan Revolution had changed his role in the Senate but little, and in 1981 he continued to reject defiantly any attempt to be a part of a ruling majority. Sustaining his fight against liberal enemies, he also opposed the Reagan administration on a number of fronts. In his own immediate area of responsibility, his attempts to impose severe cuts on the food stamp program and to maintain large subsidies for farm programs had been rejected by the fellow members of his own Agriculture Committee. Now his character attacks on Richmond and Eagleton further eroded his credibility just as the Senate would consider the farm bill.

Jesse's first year as agriculture chairman was thus not an easy one. When the agriculture bill was presented to the Senate, Helms turned over much of its management to Dole. What followed was a chaotic four days, between September 16 and 19, 1981, of debate and maneuvering. On September 16, the Senate reduced federal support for peanuts, an important commodity grown in North Carolina, by abolishing acreage allotments.[94] During the next three days, Helms's opponents then focused on doing the same thing to tobacco. Only after intense lobbying by Helms and East did an anti-tobacco measure fail by a vote of 41–40, after Pennsylvania senator Arlen Specter switched votes at the last minute. A day later, a "killer amendment" by Eagleton that would have empowered the agriculture secretary to lower price supports by 25 percent for tobacco was defeated 48–45. On the same day, a measure by Mark Hatfield of Oregon to end the tobacco program entirely was defeated 53–42. In a last-gasp attempt by anti-tobacco forces, Eagleton reintroduced his amendment, and although Helms later admitted that he was "scared silly," it failed by one vote.[95]

The bill subsequently passed review by the House—which changed it only by raising its costs—and the tobacco program was saved, but this was the closest call since its creation in the 1930s. Helms told reporters that he "never pretended the tobacco program does not have political problems." He further suggested that tobacco's problems reflected the willingness of North Carolina Democrats to politicize agriculture. But the experience suggested Helms's inability to see legislation through from start to finish.[96] In 1981, facing a politically difficult agriculture bill in which he was caught between budget reductions and his obligation to represent his constituency at home, he made no effort to mediate compromises and construct alliances that would navigate agriculture through these dangerous waters. His committee was seriously divided; during the bill's final consideration, according to the *Washington Post,* members turned "against each other and their chairman." His fellow senators noted that Jesse's predecessor, Herman Talmadge—known as "Old Hummin"—would never have permitted this deterioration. Talmadge was, according to one reporter, a "master at putting together coalitions and keeping logs of accommodation rolling at a furious but felicitous pace," but he never faced the challenges of the early 1980s. Unchanged from an adversarial role, Helms lacked the inclination, experience, or interest in behaving politically. He needed to be knowledgeable about agricultural programs and have the ability to take a "broad view," said another senator. Jesse did neither. Instead, he communicated to the committee that "all he really cared about was peanuts and tobacco and if he was not satisfied with those two he was willing to see the whole bill go down." In the end, though the tobacco program survived intact and the peanut program partially so, the southern tobacco legislators' unyielding defense antagonized other senators and threatened the farm coalition.[97]

SPEAKING TO THE graduating class at the conservative Christian Grove City College in Pennsylvania on May 15, 1982, Helms warned his audience of the possible "destruction or repudiation of the moral and ethical patrimony that has sustained the West for thousands of years." During the past three decades, "liberal elites" in the courts and the media had launched a "ferocious assault on the fundamental institution of the family," which was "targeted for revolutionary change by leftists and liberals." A popular groundswell was doing battle against liberal elites, Helms said, and it was this groundswell that had swept Reagan to power in 1980. High taxes were oppressing ordinary people, but so was forced busing, as elitist judges and bureaucrats were imposing social engineering on children. Busing, Helms said, was "racist to the core," and it revealed the "fundamental contempt that left-wing ideologues have for ordinary people." So also was the case with school prayer and abortion, matters of policy that had been forced on common folk by the court system.[98]

Soon after Reagan took office, Helms insisted that social issues should remain at the top of the Republican legislative agenda. When Majority Leader Howard Baker announced in late March 1981 that the Senate's consideration of social issues would await the passage of Reagan's budget, Jesse quickly responded that conservatives would not wait, and Baker backed off.[99] Long opposed to "forced" busing, Jesse wanted to cripple the structure of southern desegregation efforts that had been in existence since the early 1970s. Republican control of the Senate appeared to provide him with an opportunity to do so. In June 1981, in his weekly newsletter, Helms quoted Sam Ervin by calling busing the "worst form of tyranny now being practiced upon the people of this country." School desegregation had been in the hands of bureaucrats who were "obsessed with requiring school boards to impose forced busing."[100] In April 1981, Helms aide Samuel T. Currin predicted Senate passage of an anti-busing bill, and in a Senate speech Jesse declared his support for legislation permitting school officials to fashion freedom-of-choice attendance zones.[101] Jesse's strategy was to offer an amendment, or rider, to a major appropriations bill, and he thus introduced an amendment to the annual $2.46 billion authorization for the Justice Department that banned the department from mounting any legal action to "require directly or indirectly" school busing beyond nearby neighborhood schools for the purposes of integration. Subsequently, Louisiana Democratic senator Bennett Johnston would amend Helms's language with a provision that limited the courts' power to require busing for distances longer than more than five miles or fifteen minutes' driving time beyond their homes. Johnston's measure more seriously threatened civil rights groups: it would prevent not only the Justice Department but third parties, such as the NAACP, from filing suits to require integration. At Helms's instigation, Congress had earlier banned the Justice Department from initiating litigation that would lead to a cutoff of federal funds, and this new rider would complete the defanging of federal intervention in school desegregation. Similar legislation had been approved by Congress in 1980, but it was stopped by Carter's veto. This time, however, Helms faced another obstacle: a filibuster by Connecticut senator Lowell P. Weicker, Jr., who, in a long speech on September 16, promised that he would fight Helms's "anti–civil rights, anti-Constitution" amendment strenuously, "every inch of the way."[102]

Weicker, one of a dwindling number of northeastern liberal Republicans that Helms had long despised, waged a lonely, one-man filibuster battle.[103] In early July 1981, Weicker was joined in the filibuster by eleven senators, including liberal-to-moderate Republican senators Charles Percy of Illinois, Mark Hatfield of Oregon, Charles McC. Mathias of Maryland, John H. Chafee of Rhode Island, and Arlen Specter of Pennsylvania.[104] This coalition successfully blocked a vote on the Helms-Johnston amendment, defeating efforts to end the filibuster by a cloture motion four times in July, August, and September. On the fifth attempt, on September 16, cloture was adopted and the rider passed, but Weicker was able to delay full consideration of the entire bill by demanding roll call votes, a tactic that Helms frequently used to obstruct legislation. By December 1981, Baker removed the anti-busing measure from consideration, after a six-month struggle with Weicker. "It would look to be a good year's project," Weicker predicted, "before this lemon becomes lemonade." Then, although the Senate overcame Weicker's opposition and passed both amendments in February 1982, the measure became bottled up because of the opposition of House Speaker Thomas P. "Tip" O'Neill.[105]

Following this protracted struggle, Helms essentially abandoned further attempts to impose congressional restrictions on school busing. The issue had, in a sense, been rendered moot by the Reagan administration's announced reluctance to pursue school desegregation cases. There was, meanwhile, a reluctance on the part of the Reagan White House to support Helms's efforts, which it considered counterproductive.[106] While the Supreme Court had already signaled its unwillingness to require busing as the primary method of ending school segregation, in much of the South a decade of experience with busing had made it a familiar and less threatening phenomenon. The wind had gone out of the sail of busing as a political issue, a fact that was reflected in declining congressional interest. Thus, in October 1983, when the Senate adopted what amounted to Helms's original amendment, there was little interest in the measure. Helms, having obtained Senate approval, immediately withdrew the measure and announced that he wanted "Justice Department bureaucrats to know again that this Senate has voted against busing" and to put "everybody on the record."[107]

Among the most important of the New Right's social issues was opposition to the legalization of abortion. Four days after Reagan's inauguration, on the eighth anniversary of the *Roe v. Wade* decision, fifty thousand anti-abortion supporters gathered at the Ellipse, below the White House. Helms was unequivocally opposed to abortion. One of the Ten Commandments clearly spelled out the "awesome implications of destroying innocent human life," he declared, and if it ever became acceptable national policy to kill unborn children, then the killing of elderly or sick people might become conceivable "simply because it may be inconvenient to have them around." Helms refused to condone the "deliberate termination of innocent human life, whether it be an unborn child or an elderly person, or anyone in between." In January 1981, Helms waffled between continuing to support a constitutional amendment, or to support a different approach in a Human Life statute. In contrast to the Human Life amendment, which sought to define life at conception and hence to ban all abortions, Helms believed that legislation—because it required only a majority in Congress and no ratification by states—would be more easily accomplished. With the co-sponsorship of Representative Henry Hyde of Illinois, the bill had Reagan's support. But, as events would show, the bill tested the power of the anti-abortion coalition.[108]

In late April and early May 1981, John East conducted hearings on a Human Life bill, but Democratic members of his subcommittee complained that he had violated Senate rules by preventing minority counsel from including their witnesses or even from questioning testimony. Held in one of Capitol Hill's largest hearing rooms, East's proceedings were packed with supporters and opponents, and they included testimony from eight distinguished scientists who testified that life began at conception. Three members of the Women's Liberation Zap Action Brigade who jumped on their chairs were removed and arrested for displaying banners and exclaiming: "A woman's life is a human life. Stop the hearings!" But East made little effort to disguise his intentions. According to the *Charlotte Observer*, those present were startled by his conduct, including his "use of power of his chairmanship and his apparent lack of familiarity with both the rules and traditions that govern hearings."[109] The *Raleigh News and Observer* described East's hearings as a "misguided attempt," and his performance "neither established a reputation for personal fairness nor helped relations with his fellow committee members." Although the protesting women's disruption was "regrettable," East's inability to provide "any semblance of balance helped turn stern opposition into sheer anger."[110]

Others opposed Helms's approach because they believed that it undermined the Supreme Court's ability to interpret the law. According to the *Washington Post*, Helms was seeking an "end-run around the constitutional amendment process and is trying to make policy by gimmick on a delicate issue about which citizens on both sides have strong feelings."[111] Back in North Carolina, the *Wilson Daily Times* described the statutory approach as an "an all-out attack on constitutionalism."[112] One of the Senate's strongest opponents of abortion, Orrin Hatch, of Utah, favored limiting abortion by constitutional amendment, and while East's subcommittee deliberated, Hatch's Judiciary Subcommittee on Constitutional Amendments took a different route. When East reported a bill from subcommittee in July 1981 by a split 3–2 vote, Hatch's constitutional amendment, which stated that a right to an abortion was not "secured by this Constitution" and that Congress and the states possessed a "concurrent power to restrict and prohibit abortions," emerged from subcommittee in December 1981. According to Hatch's constitutional amendment, state law had precedence if it was more restrictive than federal legislation. The divergence of strategy marked a significant difference in the anti-abortion movement, but the Helms-Hatch conflict meant that neither approach could go forward in early 1982.[113]

The divisions between the Hatch and Helms approaches threatened to create a major dispute within the anti-abortion movement. The Human Life bill had originated with Stephen H. Galebach, an attorney with the Washington law firm Covington & Burling who later joined the Reagan White House. The Hatch amendment would address the chief criticisms of Helms's bill by providing both the states and Congress power to limit abortion and to eliminate the possibility of any constitutional protection. The Helms-Hatch dispute revealed a wider conflict among those opposing abortion, with advocates of each approach convinced that the opposite side was guilty of selling out. Critics of the Hatch amendment suggested that it was a cynical political ploy that had little chance of success. Paul Brown, executive director of the Life Amendment Political Action Committee, wrote to senators that support for a constitutional amendment constituted a "total anti-life vote." Conservatives were eager to heal the breach,[114] and they sought a compromise that would cut off federal funding for abortions, except when a woman's life was endangered by the pregnancy. Helms endorsed this approach, which had the support of Hatch and of moderate Republican senator Mark Hatfield of Oregon, and, bypassing committee consideration, he brought it directly to the Senate floor in March 1982.[115] But Helms's measure to cut off federal funding included portions of his 1981 bill along with a statement that the Supreme Court had erred in its *Roe* decision legalizing abortion. Helms had originally intended to include language that defined life as beginning at conception, but he realized by the summer of 1982 that he lacked the votes, and he attached an amendment to federal legislation raising the debt ceiling.

Five previous Congresses had enacted bans on federal support for abortions: what was different about Helms's measure was that it would make the ban permanent, with language containing constitutional implications. Although when Helms introduced his rider on August 16, 1982, it had

the support of the "three Hs"—Helms, Hatch, and Hatfield—the measure
was stymied by a successful filibuster in September 1982 conducted by
Robert Packwood, Republican of Oregon.[116] The difficulty of obtaining
significant federal restrictions on abortion illustrated a reality: most Americans favored retaining some form of choice, a preference public opinion
polls confirmed. Pro-choice groups had also become more fully mobilized,
and the debate of 1982 demonstrated their ability to marshal their forces
and to use hardball tactics such as filibuster to greater effect. Much of the
pro-choice sentiment focused on Helms. During the August–September
filibuster, for example, one lobbyist displayed a button with a picture of a
coat hanger surrounding the phrase "Abort Jesse."[117] Helms continued to
appeal to an anti-abortion constituency, which regarded him as their leading advocate. On the tenth anniversary of the *Roe* decision, in January 1983,
Helms, in a speech to the March for Life Education and Defense Fund dinner in Washington, described the *Roe* decision as a "a day that will live in
infamy." The Supreme Court had set the nation on a "steady downward
slide since 1973," and he declared that the media was concerned "only in
the rights of atheists and agnostics," scorning efforts to save innocent human life. "They wear 'Save the Whales' on their lapels," he said, but "they
say it's okay to kill the babies."[118] Still, the fact that public opinion now opposed an outright abolition of abortion became clear in the fate of Hatch's
constitutional amendment. When it came before the Senate on June 28,
1983, it was defeated 50–49, some eighteen votes short of the two-thirds
that were required for passage. Helms, who had clashed with Hatch on
strategy, voted "present," essentially abstaining in the matter. Regarding
abortion, the social issues agenda appeared to have reached a dead end.[119]

HELMS ALSO MADE little progress regarding school prayer, which became entangled with the August–September 1982 debate about abortion.
On September 15, 1982, Helms attached an amendment to the debt-
ceiling bill that would eliminate the jurisdiction of federal courts in school
prayer. Like Helms's abortion measure, his school prayer measure would
circumvent the lengthy and politically difficult process of a constitutional
amendment, but it also raised issues about the courts' independence.
Helms's approach, warned the *New York Times,* sought to "overturn by sub-
terfuge the Supreme Court's rulings against organized prayer in public
schools and buildings, prayer that would inevitably acquire the aura of government sponsorship." At stake was the "fundamental role of the Federal
courts as guardians of the Constitution." In the spring of 1982, Reagan

endorsed a voluntary prayer constitutional amendment, and when Helms's rider came before the Senate, Reagan sent mixed signals: while he lobbied for the measure and used it as a campaign issue in the congressional elections of that fall, he also announced that he was officially neutral. Attorney General William French Smith also expressed public doubts about the measure's constitutionality.[120]

Liberal opponents mounted a filibuster soon after Helms introduced the school prayer rider, and, led by Weicker in a filibuster, supporters fended off attempts at cloture. Some of them, such as Daniel Moynihan, denounced the Helms school prayer rider as a "court-stripping bill" that amounted to "legislative tyranny."[121] The issue was "all political," said Senator Dale Bumpers, an Arkansas Democrat. Helms's presses were running, he said, and his letters were going out to his direct mail constituency. What possible advantage was there in putting "people on the record 10 times instead of nine?" Even Howard Baker lamented the "legislative gridlock" that had resulted from Helms's tactics.[122] But Helms had reached the end of the line with the school prayer rider, and on September 23, after he lost a fourth and final vote on cloture 53–45 Baker announced that he would support tabling Helms's measure. "I've had my shot at it," said Helms, and he had "done the best I could." He blamed the defeat on a lack of good, conservative "horses" in the Senate, which he described as "Conservative it ain't, Republican it is." "I've never said I had the votes to pass anything," he told interviewers. Jesse further criticized the White House's halfhearted support: there was not a "single vote," he said, "that the White House obtained for us." He predicted that during the coming elections Americans would be able to "examine the voting record of all of us, myself included."[123] Max Baucus of Montana described the battle as evidence that the "New Right cannot end-run the Constitution" and that there would "always be people willing to stand up and fight for the Constitution." Helms remained sanguine. "You win some, you lose some and some days you're rained out," he told reporters. "It will be fair weather another day." Helms seemed pleased to take the school prayer debate back to his constituents.[124] Senate liberals had "done us a service," he told an interviewer a day later, because his "troops all across the country" had become "very attentive to what has been going on in the Senate." The abortion and school prayer fights had "raised the adrenaline level" of his supporters. "You ain't seen nothing yet," he told a school prayer rally on the Capitol grounds on September 25.[125]

Although remaining a hot-button issue, legislation designed to overturn the Supreme Court's ruling on school prayer would never come closer to enactment. Reagan continued to support a constitutional amendment, but when the Senate finally considered the measure, it failed adoption by a two-thirds majority by eleven votes. Helms vowed to continue the fight, telling supporters after the vote that there was "more than one way to skin a cat." This was only "Round 1," said Helms, promising "many more rounds to come" and that he and his supporters had "just begun to fight." This was yet another instance of Helms's inflated rhetoric: it marked the end of his efforts on school prayer during Reagan's first term. Yet this was also an issue that served to motivate Christian evangelicals even further into political mobilization. "Like those of ancient Israel who cried out to their oppressors, 'Let my people go,'" declared evangelist Pat Robertson, host of *The 700 Club,* a popular television ministry, "those of us who are oppressed by our political leadership today are also crying to them to let us go," he said. "Let us go—or we plan to let them go in November."[126]

Chapter 7

A PURE GOSPEL
OF CONSERVATISM

Protecting the Revolution

With Reagan's election in 1980, Jesse Helms became the Senate's most aggressive protector of the conservative revolution. Insisting on purity, he oversaw the White House's domestic agenda, and, during the early 1980s, he pushed for enactment of social issues legislation. The struggle with Reagan was subtle: Helms, like other conservatives, revered Reagan, seeing him as a genuine leader of conservatism. But he believed that Reagan's advisers were unreliable moderates who wanted to move the president to the center. Generally, Helms believed that if he could go directly to Reagan and break through the pragmatists' protective cordon, the president would see the truth of the conservative position. Much of this conflict played out in appointments. Helms and conservatives were convinced that holdovers from the Nixon-Ford years were eager for office, but that their presence would doom the success of the Reagan Revolution. Helms was equally determined about foreign policy appointments, and he became an active obstructionist, insisting that all of Reagan appointees have no history of association with Kissinger's détente or with Carter's foreign policies. Early on, Helms battled not only White House pragmatists but also Reagan's California cronies, who, in a group known as the "Sweet Sixteen," dominated the appointment process.[1]

EVEN BEFORE REAGAN'S inauguration, movement conservatives worried about how moderates had taken over the White House. Soon activists were complaining about their exclusion. "We've all been had," said one congressional conservative aide in January 1981. "We boys on the right have gotten snookered." Reagan's domestic policy nominees included moderates Donald T. Regan as treasury secretary and Terrel H. Bell as secretary of education, while the Reagan White House was dominated by "people who simply do not share the same vision of America" as Ronald Reagan, said Nicpac's Terry Dolan. People without any strong conservative commitments had displaced activists. Richard Viguerie believed that something was "very wrong"; Howard Phillips complained that "true conservatism" might not be attempted during the Reagan presidency. On February 1, 1981, Reagan aide Lyn Nofziger met with representatives of twenty-eight conservative groups, including Terry Dolan, director of Nicpac; Robert Heckman, who headed Young Americans for Freedom; and Tom Winter, editor of *Human Events*.[2]

The right's protests about appointments in early 1981 had an effect: Reagan was surprised to learn about conservatives' unhappiness. Much of the resentment was directed at Pendleton James, head of the White House personnel office, who was tied to Reagan's California cronies. The White House responded by making a concerted effort to appoint conservative purists, and they filled offices in midlevel or secondary positions. James A. Baker III, the White House chief of staff, admitted to a reporter in March 1981 that the administration was justifiably criticized, and he was determined to ensure that "we didn't forget the people who got us where we are." According to Pendleton James, the criteria for appointments had not changed, but "vocal criticism" demonstrated that "we had a communications problem." According to one estimate, in the first fourteen months of the Reagan administration, Helms helped to place some thirty associates and allies in various levels of the foreign policy system. The appointment of Helms supporters—often coming from Helms's office and related institutes—became an important building block in the conservative revolution.[3]

As part of the struggle over Reagan's appointments, Helms became involved, somewhat unwittingly, in a struggle to name a new head of the National Endowment for the Humanities (NEH). Conservatives considered the NEH an important agency because it funded scholarly research, much of which, they claimed, was left-leaning and secularist. Conservatives rallied behind the candidacy of Melvin E. Bradford, a William Faulkner scholar at the University of Dallas who had supported George Wallace's 1972 presidential campaign. A prominent Texas Republican, Bradford had helped to organize Scholars for Reagan. He was also known for unconventional ideas, such as those expressed in one essay in which he criticized Abraham Lincoln for his Civil War leadership, his "misinterpretation" of the Constitution, and his "hypocritical" moral stand about slavery. A contributor to William F. Buckley's *National Review,* Bradford was also well known in conservative intellectual circles and enjoyed the support of figures such as Russell Kirk, Jeffrey Hart, Gerhart Niemeyer, M. Stanton Evans, Andrew Lytle, and Harry Jaffa. In October 1981, sixteen Republican senators sent Reagan a letter supporting Bradford and describing his credentials as "impeccable." The chief organizer of the pro-Bradford forces in the Senate was John East, who knew Bradford professionally and who enthusiastically embraced his cause.[4]

Bradford's leading opponent became William Bennett, then serving as the director of the National Humanities Center in Research Triangle, North Carolina. With a Harvard Law degree and a Ph.D. in philosophy, Bennett joined the faculty of Boston University and became a protégé of its president, John Silber. In 1976, Bennett joined the newly created National Humanities Center as its associate director and became its director in 1980. He was well known among "neoconservatives"—former Democrats and liberals who had renounced the foreign and domestic policies of the New Deal and espoused an aggressive conservatism. Bennett co-wrote a book criticizing affirmative action, and he served on a number of conservative boards. In late 1980, Helms wrote a letter of endorsement supporting him as NEH director after meeting with him. Bradford's entry into the game complicated things by provoking a fight between New Right conservatives who supported him and neoconservatives favoring Bennett. Although Bennett, as a North Carolina resident, could normally expect Helms's support, Bradford had the strong backing of John East. He and Bradford served together on the board of *Modern Age,* a conservative journal founded by conservative intellectual Russell Kirk in 1957, and there was immediate chemistry between the two men. Both embraced a conservatism that exalted, much like the Nashville Agrarians had done in the 1930s, a lost southern agrarian lifestyle. The two men, according to an East aide, valued rural and family values, "gentlemanly manners" that involved men opening doors and tipping their hats to women. Both were ardent defenders of what they described as southern white cultural values, and both felt excluded by northeastern, left-wing intellectual elites, who dominated the most attractive jobs and had access to the best grants. Both proudly displayed Confederate flags. According to columnist George Will, Bradford was part of the "Confederate remnant in the Conservative movement."[5]

Although East had proposed Bradford as early as February 1981, the

White House had delayed action on the nomination until a presidential task force on the arts and humanities had completed its work. The task force director, William Schaefer, executive vice chancellor of UCLA and operating director of the Modern Language Association, reviewed twenty possible candidates. But a conservative backlash brewed. In an editorial entitled "Halt! Stop This Appointment!," *National Review* described Schaefer as "caving in before all demands from the cultural Left." While serving at the Modern Language Association, he had done "nothing to check its progress toward becoming an ideological zoo."[6] But, on September 20, 1981, when *The New York Times* published a report describing Bradford as a leading candidate to head the NEH, neoconservative intellectuals such as Irving Kristol rallied behind the Bennett candidacy. Bradford actively campaigned for the job, sporting a three-piece suit and cowboy hat and visiting congressional offices. He was also sharply critical of the NEH and promised to purge the left-wingers from the agency.[7]

Meanwhile, there was a brewing movement against Bennett. Conservative columnist Pat Buchanan suggested that Bennett's nomination meant that Reagan would "ditch scholars whose pens have defended him since *Death Valley Days*—to mollify new, nervous, uncertain allies."[8] Critics on East's staff and Helms aide Jim Lucier feared that Bennett's nomination would mean a surrender to academic liberalism, and they argued their case forcefully to Helms. Bennett's critics charged that the scholars who had visited the National Humanities Center were "liberals, many are radical leftists, and a couple are actually Marxists or Communists." Historian John Hope Franklin was described as a "hard core leftist historian." According to East aide Jim McClellan, the National Humanities Center was a "powerful subversive influence in N.C." because, he claimed, it had excluded conservative scholars.[9]

In late November 1981, expressing doubts about Bennett's ability to change the NEH and suggesting that the majority of the National Humanities Center's grants had gone to liberal scholars, Helms reversed himself. Writing to Reagan aide Max Friedersdorf on November 23 in a letter that was released to the public, Helms announced that he felt "betrayed" about the Bennett nomination. Had the White House staff conducted a thorough enough check of Bennett's background? Although he had attempted to be cooperative on the nomination, Helms found himself "in the uncomfortable position of having gone along in good faith, when apparently no check was made into the qualifications of the proposed nominee."[10] As Jim Lucier explained, Helms had come to believe that the NEH during the Carter administration had become "a highly politicized instrument supporting radical social and political change" by supporting scholarly projects with a leftist agenda. The NEH should be "restored," said Lucier, to supporting programs "undergirding our traditional moral and cultural values."[11] Helms's reversal on the Bennett nomination prompted widespread criticism. Jesse's comments revealed a "dangerous lack of understanding of the function of the Endowment and of the academic enterprise in general," according to the *Raleigh News and Observer*. Although academia had "its own brand of politics" that was "as nasty as a National Congressional Club campaign," Bennett's record indicated that he placed "scholarship above electoral politics."[12] Bennett, never a person to mince words, then responded. Telling the press that he did not know what the "fuss" was about, Bennett declared that the National Humanities Center did not have "quotas" and did not seek scholars "on the basis of race, sex or political coloration."[13] In private correspondence with White House personnel staff, Bennett defended his conservative credentials and his history of "public confrontation" with left-wingers to such an extent that he had excited their "dislike and calumny." To describe John Hope Franklin as a "known Marxist" revealed "only ignorance." Bennett did not believe, in any event, that scholarly standards should be subjected to political litmus tests—from the right or the left. Despite Helms's efforts, Bennett took office on December 21, 1981, in a recess appointment, which installed him in the office until the Senate could consider him. But this seemed to quiet Bradford's supporters, and Bennett was confirmed in February 1982.[14]

HELMS'S BATTLE OVER appointments was perhaps most pronounced in foreign policy positions. In 1980–81, John Carbaugh served on a fifteen-member transition team for the State Department; the sight of Carbaugh moving through State Department corridors, according to a *Washington Post* reporter, was a "phenomenon comparable to a Vandal running loose inside the walls of Rome."[15] Early in his tenure, Secretary of State Alexander Haig fired Robert White, U.S. ambassador to El Salvador, who had often clashed with Helms and had complained during the transition about Carbaugh.[16] But Haig proved less cooperative about appointments. A Kissinger protégé and a veteran insider, Haig had no intention of overseeing a radical restructuring of the State Department. Soon after receiving the report from the transition team, Haig abruptly dismissed it and brushed aside Carbaugh's influence. In the week before the inauguration, Helms wrote to Haig indicating the Republican right's unhappiness.[17]

Haig's sub-cabinet appointments—the undersecretaries and assistant secretaries of state who ran State's vast bureaucracy—would be mainly moderates with connections to past Republican administrations. Leading a group of about sixteen conservative senators, Helms opposed many of these nominations. Early in Reagan's presidency, he tried to block the nomination of Caspar W. Weinberger as defense secretary and Frank Carlucci as his deputy. Both had long résumés: Weinberger, who worked as Reagan's finance director when he was governor of California, served as HEW secretary under Nixon and Ford. Carlucci, who roomed with Weinberger and Donald Rumsfeld at Princeton in the early 1950s, served as deputy director of the CIA during the Carter administration. Although a loyal Republican, his association with the Carter White House was damning, in Helms's eyes. Only four hours after Reagan's inauguration, on January 20, 1981, Helms opposed Weinberger's nomination on the Senate floor. He opposed Weinberger, he said in a forty-minute speech, because Weinberger had been unable to make a "clean break with the very policies of the past" that had resulted in America's decline. Carlucci, he said, could only reinforce Weinberger's "weaknesses and obviate his strengths." America faced a crisis of "sheer survival," Helms asserted, and Weinberger's "dedication to efficiency, frugality and sound management" were "simply ... not enough." Naive about arms control, Weinberger lacked either "resolution" or "vision" in the struggle with the Soviets, Helms claimed. With only Helms and East voting negatively, the Senate overwhelmingly confirmed Weinberger. Jesse told his constituents in his newsletter that this was "one of the most difficult votes I've cast as a Senator," but he wanted to send a message about his "grave concerns about our deteroriating national defense." This was, according to one observer, an "Inauguration Day signal that he would oppose the new President he had helped elect on any deviation from the pure gospel of conservatism."[18]

Helms used senatorial privilege to his advantage. The use of the senatorial hold dated to the First Congress in 1789, when two Georgia senators successfully opposed George Washington's choice for a Savannah customs inspector. The senatorial right to block appointments through holds thereafter became established. A hold on a nomination meant, in theory, that the senator would be informed prior to any floor action; in practice, it meant that any nomination could be blocked until the Senate leadership was willing to overturn the hold. Defeated on Weinberger, Helms continued the fight against Carlucci by placing a hold on his nomination. The White House regarded Helms's opposition seriously enough to arrange for a brief meeting for about a half hour between Reagan and him on the afternoon of January 26. Laying out his position in a letter to the president on January 22, Helms noted that, when the Senate Steering Committee had met the day before, what should have been a "euphoric mood" was "tinged with forboding" about appointments. Reagan's advisers, Helms warned, were managing things in a way that was "completely out of control" because in many cases jobs were given to people who were "only nominal Republicans and nominal Reagan supporters as well." He had been deputized by the Steering Committee to urge Reagan to push for more conservative appointments.

The Reagan White House took Helms's warning seriously. The president's staff urged him to make the Steering Committee's "inventiveness and coordination...assets, rather than problems," and they recognized Helms's following as a "hero" among the right. In the ten-minute meeting, Reagan stressed their long association, how Jesse had supported him when he ran for president and how he now needed his support in the new Congress. He appreciated Helms's leadership in the Steering Committee; he looked to him for leadership in the Senate. Jesse immediately responded to Reagan's personal appeal, and, following this meeting, declared himself "nearly satisfied" with the appointments.[19] Although he dropped the hold on Carlucci's nomination and visited with the nominee—and apparently received Weinberger's promise that conservative Fred Iklé would receive a high-ranking position in the Department of Defense—he delivered a scathing speech against his nomination when the Senate considered it on February 3. Carlucci, Helms declared, was a "faceless bureacrat who has posed as an apolitical technocrat to promote left-wing ideology." Despite Helms's efforts, the confirmation went through on February 3 by a 91–6 vote.[20]

Defeat on these nominations did not faze Jesse, and he continued to battle away. For much of the spring of 1981, he threatened actions against objectionable appointees at the State Department, and the administration, fearing a fight, delayed nominations until several months into the Reagan presidency.[21] In February 1981, an unnamed source reported that Helms had the State Department "tied in knots" in his attempt to prevent what he saw as "career elitists" from taking office. But neither the White House nor fellow senators were willing to take Jesse on. Fearing Helms, the White House was unwilling to challenge him for fear of a further "broadside against their appointments." Charles Percy, the chair of the Senate Foreign Relations Committee, lacked the will to confront him. Helms complained about State Department leaks, denying that he was sabotaging appointments. "I've never practiced obstructionism," he told reporters, "even with nominees with whom I have differed very strongly." His main concern,

Helms said, was protecting the purity of Reagan's foreign policy. Reagan was elected in opposition to Kissinger's policies, Helms told his constituents, but he had numerous appointments and depended on advisers to screen appointees. The conservative voters who elected Reagan did not want a return to Kissinger's policies. His image as an obstructionist was a product of the liberal media, he said, and Helms was simply exercising his constitutional obligation of advise-and-consent.[22]

Helms's real objective was to gain leverage over Reagan's foreign policy.[23] During the Carter presidency, relying on Carbaugh and Lucier, Helms had created a shadow diplomacy that, he hoped, would set the standards for the new administration. When he added Carbaugh and Lucier to his staff in the mid-1970s, he told a reporter, he hoped to "provide a counterbalance to the foreign policy that I consider to be a disaster." Helms's staff created what he called "our own State Department" because he was suspicious of most information coming from the diplomatic bureaucracy. By the late 1970s, Carbaugh and Lucier had obtained a good degree of exposure, having traveled to England, Germany, South Africa, Rhodesia, Chile, Uruguay, Brazil, Nicaragua, El Salvador, and Guatemala—trips that Helms's network of semi-independent think tanks and institutes had financed. Helms's staff made early contacts with Britain's Margaret Thatcher, who was courted by Carbaugh prior to her election as prime minister in 1979, and she and Helms established close ties that remained for many years. Carbaugh, freewheeling and flamboyant, sometimes irritated the senator, who complained to him about his drinking champagne in the middle of the day and being away from his wife and children too long. Even Helms admitted that there were a "number of people in Washington who would buy John a one-way ticket to anywhere." A thorn in the side of anyone in the State Department who did not share his "conservative Helmsian view of the world," Carbaugh was regarded suspiciously by Reagan insiders. In April 1981, Haig offered Carbaugh that one-way ticket—an ambassadorship to Paraguay—but Carbaugh leaked the offer to the press and then rejected it. Subsequently, his flamboyant style caught up with him. His nebulous relationship with the organizations that he had helped to found—the Institute of American Relations and the Institute of American Relations Foreign Affairs Council—were found to be in violation of Senate rules, and in June 1982 Carbaugh became one of the only two Senate staffers that the senator ever fired.[24]

With the nominations in limbo, on April 25 Helms wrote a ten-page letter to Percy explaining his rationale. He had maintained holds on the State Department nominations, he said, because he remained unsure that the nominees agreed with Reagan's views, and he believed that it was his duty to alert Haig and Reagan about his concerns. Helms sought to "do whatever I can to try to assure that the policy-makers nominated in the name of the president actually reflect, to the fullest extent possible, the president's views." Helms was not responsible for the delayed nominations, he asserted: a better reason was the White House foot-dragging. He was constitutionally obliged, at any rate, "to offer such advice as each senator deems proper and later to give or withhold consent."[25] After Reagan, in late April, telephoned Helms once again to inform him that he supported the nominations, Jesse dropped this line of attack, but his holds further delayed their consideration.[26] But the White House avoided a confrontation, and following a mid-May meeting in which Helms listed his objections and proposed lower-level appointments, Haig did little to promote the nominations and instead let each nominee deal directly with Helms.[27] In 1981, Helms's efforts to shape Reagan's foreign policy by pressuring nominations appeared to have yielded little. In none of the nomination fights did Jesse prevail, either in a committee or floor vote—or even come close. After six months of struggle that required all of his senatorial skills, Helms, said one commentator, had "won little that is visible on the surface." For the most part, pragmatists won this battle, though Helms would continue the war.[28]

POSSESSING NUMEROUS CONTACTS across the Western Hemisphere, Helms and his staff were interested primarily in promoting alternatives to Cuban-style revolutionary nationalism in Latin America. His ultimate goal was to construct an anti-Communist alliance. The "bottom line," Helms explained to a reporter in 1982, was to "maintain the possibility of a coalition of countries that have one common purpose at heart—that is to keep communism out of this hemisphere." The survival of the United States depended on preserving this coalition with authoritarian regimes that could withstand Soviet-Cuban attempts to infiltrate the region. "You don't have perfect choices in trying to prevent a communist takeover of this world," he told one reporter.

Focusing most of his attention on Latin America during the Reagan years, Helms remained the most loyal supporter in the Senate of anti-Communist right-wing authoritarian regimes in Chile, Bolivia, Guatemala, Brazil, Argentina, and Uruguay. In November 1980, when Bolivian interior minister Colonel Luis Arce Gómez visited Washington, he was shunned by the Carter administration, which had cut off aid and withdrawn its ambassador, condemning the regime as guilty of "widespread, even savage violations of human rights." Under President Luis García Meza, the Bolivian junta was known not only for human rights abuses but also for protecting narcotics traffickers and death squads. Reported by congressional investigators as in league with cocaine traffickers and as responsible for the torture of political opponents, Gómez was forbidden from laying a wreath at Arlington National Cemetery. Helms greeted Gómez warmly on his visit, and even took him to lunch in the Senate Dining Room, and later promised that he would promote Bolivia's cause in Congress. "I am impressed with the progress Bolivia has made in recent months in providing security for its citizens, which is among the most fundamental of human rights," Helms wrote in a letter to Gómez in December 1980, "despite the misguided policies of our Government." Helms promised to seek a "re-examination of our policies toward Latin America."[29] He favored lifting the ban on the sale of military equipment to Argentina and Chile that Congress had imposed because of the gross human rights violations during the dirty wars against the political left in both countries. Helms promoted these regimes—serving as what one critic called a "sort of public relations office for some of these more reprehensible governments"—despite their egregious activities. He thus sponsored a visit from Argentinian president Roberto Viola in March 1981. At Helms's urging, Viola also met Reagan, only his fourth foreign visitor, and, in December 1981 Jesse succeeded in persuading Congress to lift the arms embargo on Argentina that had existed since 1978.

Helms's alliance with the junta was sorely tested by Argentina's invasion of the British-held Falkland Islands on April 2, 1982. Urging negotiations, Helms argued that the Argentinians had invaded with justification.[30] The British, he believed, had "bit off more than they could chew" and had violated the Monroe Doctrine by occupying the islands (even though they had been a British possession for several centuries). Argentina had a legitimate claim on sovereignty, he thought, but he urged that both sides "cool off" and negotiate.[31] Because of his close ties with the junta, some hoped that Helms might broker negotiations, and Secretary of State Haig consulted with Helms and even carried a letter from Jesse to Argentine president Leopoldo Galtieri when he visited Buenos Aires. According to some reports, Haig authorized Helms to make a statement suggesting that a settlement might be based on a compromise involving the preservation of British traditions and institutions on the Falklands but a recognition of Argentine sovereignty. Modeled on the Channel Islands government, Jesse called this the Channel Islands Solution, which he formally proposed in a Senate speech on April 21, 1982.[32]

Willis Smith addresses crowd on his front lawn in Raleigh, June 6, 1950.

Helms as TV editorialist, sometime in the 1960s.

Helms and Nixon during presidential visit to Greensboro, North Carolina,
November 1972.

Helms and Aleksandr Solzhenitsyn in front of the White House, June 1975.
JESSE HELMS CENTER ARCHIVES

The North Carolina Congressional Club, November 12, 1979 (Tom Ellis and Carter Wrenn in foreground, Bob Harris in background).
COURTESY OF THE NORTH CAROLINA STATE ARCHIVES

Helms and Ronald Reagan in the Oval Office, January 26, 1981.

From left to right: Jerry Falwell, Helms, and Lamar Mooneyham, 1983.

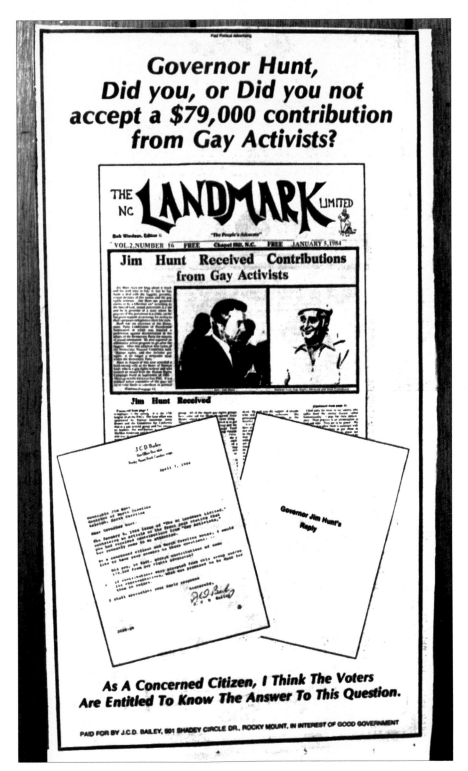

Anti-Hunt ad, June 1984.

Helms-Hunt debate, July 29, 1984.

Helms and Secretary of State Madeleine Albright, late 1990s.
JESSE HELMS CENTER ARCHIVES

Helms and Bono, September 20, 2000.
JESSE HELMS CENTER ARCHIVES

Jesse Helms, c. 1975.   JESSE HELMS CENTER ARCHIVES

Helms's support of Argentina isolated him from nearly all of his Senate colleagues. On April 29, when Joseph Biden of Delaware proposed a resolution declaring that the United States "cannot stand neutral" and should seek "to achieve full withdrawal of Argentine forces" from the Falklands, Helms offered the only dissenting vote.[33] He maintained this position, despite overwhelming support of American public opinion for the British cause. Helms criticized the Reagan administration's decision in early May to abandon impartiality and support the British military effort, a decision he believed had "driven a wedge" between America's European and Latin American allies.[34] Even after the British achieved a decisive victory over Argentine forces in early June 1982—a victory that would eventually bring down the Argentine junta—Jesse remained convinced that American policy was wrong. The United States should never have taken sides, he told reporters even while Britain was celebrating its victory, and the American government had "contributed to the encouragement of the violence down there." If the United States had remained neutral, violence might have been averted. This "terrible price" in lost lives was unnecessary.[35]

Helms also strongly opposed revolution to Central America, and in Nicaragua and El Salvador he favored policies that supported right-wing regimes. Late in Jimmy Carter's presidency, in July 1979, the Sandinista Liberation Front, in Nicaragua, overthrew the dictatorship of Anastasio Somoza Debayle. The Sandinistas, who received support from the Cubans, installed a new government, and the Carter administration attempted to engage them, providing $75 million in aid. In March 1981, Helms told questioners on *Meet the Press* that the aid had been suspended, something the State Department confirmed. Subsequently, in April 1981, the Reagan administration, under pressure from Helms, eventually ended what was left of American aid to Nicaragua, claiming that the Sandinistas were permitting arms shipments to guerrillas in El Salvador.[36]

In El Salvador in the early 1980s, a left-wing insurgency, the Farabundo Martí National Liberation Front (FMLN), fought an oligarchic regime. Under Carter and Reagan, U.S. policy sought to encourage democratization through free elections and land reform. Where Carter's policy emphasized economic aid, Reagan's policy stressed military support and, in the spring of 1981, the administration dispatched American advisers to help combat the insurgency. Helms had no patience with Carter's policy and very little with Reagan's. As elsewhere in Latin America, he preferred authoritarian regimes willing to fight Communist or left-wing rebels without reservation. In September 1981, Helms opposed a Senate measure that tied military and economic aid to El Salvador to progress in improving human rights, ending "indiscriminate torture and murder," holding free elections, and working toward a negotiated peace. This measure passed over the opposition of the Reagan administration, and Jesse also rejected efforts at land reform, which he considered socialist.[37] In July 1982, he opposed a Senate resolution demanding that the Salvadoran government show evidence that it had made progress in solving the murders of six Americans in 1980 and 1981 (the evidence indicated that Salvadoran military forces were involved). The resolution, he said, did not "mention the atrocities of the guerrillas; it does not mention the thousands of deaths which are directly attributable to the terrorists' avowed aim of destruction and intimidation." In the end, however, what one reporter called Jesse's "lonely battle" had little support, and in late July the Senate adopted the resolution by a 95–2 vote.[38]

Helms opposed Reagan's support of Salvadoran moderate José Napoleon Duarte, leader of the Christian Democrats, whom he considered left-wing. In a speech to the Conservative Political Action Conference in Washington in February 1982 that was attended by Vice President George H. W. Bush and nine cabinet members, he described Duarte as "far to the left of George McGovern" and his government as "left-wing socialist." Land reform, which Jesse called a "vast failure," was nothing but unnecessary American meddling. With elections scheduled in late March 1982 to organize a Salvadoran Constituent Assembly, Helms believed that matters should take their course, which, to him, meant withdrawing support for Duarte and permitting the "natural political life of El Salvador" to take over. There were many "honest and attractive politicians in El Salvador," Helms said, "men who are for the free enterprise system, who are absolutely faithful to the United States, who are for human dignity, who are for traditional values." Helms favored Duarte's opponent in the elections, former military intelligence officer and Salvadoran rightist Roberto D'Aubuisson, and he would continue to see him as the hope for the country's future.[39]

D'Aubuisson fit Helms's prototypical Latin American authoritarian. Robert White, who served as American ambassador to El Salvador and was fired by Secretary of State Haig because of his conflict with Helms, described D'Aubuisson as a "psychopathic killer" who was deeply involved with the death squads and widespread civilian killings that were occurring in the Salvadoran civil war. In April 1981, moreover, White testified at a Foreign Relations Committee hearing that there was "compelling, if not 100 percent conclusive" evidence that D'Aubuisson was responsible for the March 24, 1980, killing of Salvadoran Archbishop Óscar Arnulfo Romero y Galdámez. In 1993, a U.N. Truth Commission investigating the El Salvador Civil War of 1980–92 concluded that D'Aubussion ordered the assassination and provided specific instructions about the killing to members of his security service.[40] Helms promoted D'Aubuisson as his solution for the problem of El Salvador. Calling him a man "who openly espoused the principles of the Republican Party in the United States," Helms would later describe him as a "courageous anticommunist." Jesse was convinced that D'Aubuisson was a genuine patriot, and despite determined efforts by his information network, he could find no evidence of his associations with death squads.[41]

Aides Deborah DeMoss and Chris Manion (Clarence Manion's son) made frequent visits and had frequent contacts with all sides in El Salvador, including D'Aubuisson's Republican Nationalist Alliance Party (ARENA); one reporter said that DeMoss was the Salvadoran military's "favorite gringa." According to a January 1984 account by the *Albuquerque Journal*'s Craig Pyes, DeMoss and Manion established close ties with D'Aubuisson and his supporters during the early 1980s, and they maintained telephone contacts with wealthy Salvadorans living in the Miami area who supported D'Aubuisson. According to Pyes's account, Manion urged the Salvadoran right to enter the democratic process by organizing ARENA, and he assisted its leaders in drafting a platform that borrowed from portions of the 1980 Republican presidential platform and merged it with "principles from authoritarian nationalist parties such as the German Nazis to form the ARENA creed." ARENA had been very successful: attracting 25 percent of the vote in Constituent Assembly elections in March 1982, it was poised to elect D'Aubuisson as president two years later.

Helms called the *Albuquerque Journal*'s report "garbage"; Manion claimed that he spent more time with Duarte's Christian Democrats than with ARENA leaders. According to Deborah DeMoss, who served as Helms's Latin American adviser, reports of Helms's connections with ARENA were "all blown out of proportion...but we do know these people." DeMoss later asserted that Pyes never spoke with anyone on Helms's staff. But there is little question that his office's connections with D'Aubuisson were close; Helms either understated his staff's involvement, as the *N&O* put it, or "his aides run around in Central America out of his control." Either way, there was a "strong circumstantial link" to ARENA, and this constituted an "ad hoc foreign policy separate from the Reagan administration and its State Department." The Reagan administration denied a visa to D'Aubuisson as late as March 1984, but Helms arranged and hosted the visit of five ARENA leaders who arrived in the United States in February. Helms maintained that he would have nothing to do with those leaders tied to death squads. "If I had found even one credible link between D'Aubuisson and the so-called 'death squads,'" he insisted, Helms would have "repudiated him instantly." At one point, sometime in 1984, Jesse even met with CIA director William J. Casey to investigate the charges against D'Aubuisson, and demanded evidence of any such connections. Casey could not produce evidence, and he was unable to verify any links between the ARENA leader and the Romero assassination.[42]

Helms became even more involved after neither Duarte nor D'Aubuisson could obtain a majority in the presidential elections on March 25, 1984, and a runoff election was scheduled for May 1. Helms claimed that American diplomats were working, overtly and covertly, to tilt the elections against D'Aubuisson. The senator's aides reported evidence that Agency for International Development (AID) funds were being used in support of pro-Duarte labor unions, which, in turn, provided political support. In a letter to Reagan on May 1 that was released in El Salvador a few days later, Helms claimed that by interfering in the Salvadoran elections, American ambassador Thomas R. Pickering had "used the cloak of diplomacy to strangle freedom in the night." Helms demanded Pickering's immediate recall.[43]

Helms had opposed Pickering's nomination in July 1983, and a confrontation had been avoided only after National Security Adviser William Clark made an appeal to the senator.[44] Now, less than a year later, Helms claimed that Pickering was trying to influence the elections and intimidate leaders and voters. In a Senate speech a week later, Helms described a two-year program of covert aid in which the CIA "bought the election for Duarte," and Pickering was "merely the purchasing agent." The El Salvador elections marked the first in a series of covert operations that the CIA ran in Central America—including a much more extensive intervention in Nicaragua. Helms opposed the CIA's intervention on two grounds: first, he opposed further pollution of the democratic process, and, as he would make clearer later in the 1980s, he supported a move toward democracy across the region. Second, Helms was outraged that the CIA had operated without appropriate oversight by Congress. When he discovered the CIA's involvement in Salvadoran elections, he went to Senate Intelligence Committee member David Boren, of Oklahoma, and Boren told him that he knew nothing about it. Boren, similarly outraged, encouraged Helms to go public in his Senate speech.[45]

Far from promoting democracy, Helms charged, the CIA's covert program was a misuse of the democratic process. American interference overstepped Reagan's original presidential order, which authorized CIA funding to promote democracy, but not to influence an election. D'Aubuisson, he said, had been unfairly maligned with unsubstantiated charges and "malicious accusations." The result of this meddling, according to Helms, was that the United States had lined up behind Duarte, whom he characterized as a socialist. "If Duarte is a centrist," he said, "then our former colleague, George McGovern, is an extreme right winger."[46] When Duarte won the runoff, Helms's campaign escalated. On May 8, 1984, in a Senate speech Helms charged that the CIA had "bought the election" through a program of covert money funneled into Duarte's campaign over the past two years that involved funds for local political organization, paid media, and computer voter registration. This was confirmed when the House and Senate intelligence committees were informed that over $2 million of covert funds had been spent in El Salvador, including $960,000 on Duarte's behalf. Helms was accused of having leaked intelligence materials available to all senators; on May 15, the chairman of the Senate Intelligence Committee, Barry Goldwater, along with vice chairman Daniel Patrick Moynihan, sent a letter to Helms that rebuked him for violating Senate rules by disclosing this information. Denouncing the accusation, Helms said that his information came from El Salvador, and, though he refused to disclose details, the information came from DeMoss's network. Helms's staff hadn't looked at classified materials in order to avoid any charges of leaking; the senator also refused to look at classified documents or to attend classified briefings. DeMoss, who had learned of the CIA intervention from numerous sources, believed that most classified materials were little more than information commonly available. In her experience, Senate intelligence had "absolutely nothing" of value that "you couldn't get out of the newspaper."[47]

The White House subsequently disavowed Jesse's charges: in a press release in early May, it announced that the president affirmed his "support for the process of genuine electoral democracy" and his "continued confidence" in Pickering. One of Reagan's aides wrote Jesse that the president had "utmost confidence" in Pickering, who, he said, had "done a superb job in promoting democracy and safeguarding U.S. interests in El Salvador." Surprisingly, Helms's disclosures did not damage his influence with the White House. After writing to Reagan urging Pickering's dismissal, Helms met with the president, and the two agreed that he would attend Duarte's inauguration on June 1, 1984. In addition, although Reagan had signed a presidential finding authorizing the CIA program in 1982, he denied knowledge of its activities, while Goldwater tried to persuade reporters that he had not, in fact, rebuked Jesse for disclosing classified materials.

Helms's disclosure about the CIA covert operation in El Salvador created an uproar. D'Aubuisson and ARENA supporters were enraged at American interference, and they blamed Pickering for overseeing what D'Aubuisson called two years of "support and organized plans to suborn the sovereign will of the Salvadoran people."[48] Helms wrote to D'Aubuisson and informed him of the CIA program, singling out Pickering for using "his diplomatic capacity to strangle liberty during the night."[49] Soon after the election, there were charges that ARENA supporters had plotted to kill Pickering to avenge the election loss. Sometime in early May, White House chief of staff James Baker called Helms and asked him to tell DeMoss to telephone D'Aubuisson to head off the plot. Helms called DeMoss late at night, something he rarely did. DeMoss was shocked. D'Aubuisson, she believed, had little incentive to assassinate Pickering; she thought that the charges were ridiculous. She found it awkward to call D'Aubuisson and ask him "not [to] kill the American ambassador," and she did so only reluctantly. When DeMoss reached D'Aubuisson, she conveyed this news from the "highest levels of government." He was "just floored" and called the charges "absolutely outrageous." The next day, he promised, he would make an announcement denying the existence of any plot and denouncing anyone contemplating it. When the story went public, reports indicated that a plot was still afoot, and retired General Vernon Walters was dispatched to meet with D'Aubuisson on May 18. According to these reports, D'Aubuisson had been tipped off about the nature of Walters's mission by someone on Helms's staff—according to a subsequent cable from the U.S. embassy, DeMoss. She later described these charges as fantastic, since the original request to contact D'Aubuisson had come directly from the White House. DeMoss later suspected that the matter reflected an attempt to circulate rumors, probably from the CIA, that would further discredit D'Aubuisson.[50]

The upshot of the discredited plot against Pickering was to lend greater respectability to D'Aubuisson and to Helms's Central American policy: later in 1984, the State Department granted D'Aubuisson a visa. At Duarte's inauguration, Helms met with D'Aubuisson, informing him of the approval of his visa and urging him to work within the constitutional system. Along with drawing ARENA into the democratic process, the White House also sought to entice Helms into political dialogue. Yet D'Aubuisson's visit to the United States did not dispel the cloud of suspicion over him, and he encountered a cool reception on Capitol Hill. The ranking Senate Democrat on the Foreign Relations Committee, Rhode Island's Claiborne Pell, refused to meet with D'Aubuisson, saying that he had "no desire to talk with a man who I really believe is responsible for so many deaths." Citing his connections with death squads, Senate minority leader Robert Byrd also refused. Of the one hundred senators invited to participate in a reception for D'Aubuisson, only fifteen or sixteen showed up. Even Helms distanced himself somewhat from the visit: Ted Stevens, not Helms, took responsibility for showing the visiting Salvadoran around Capitol Hill.[51]

THE FIRST TWO years of the Reagan presidency were, for Helms, frustrating. His stewardship of the tobacco program only narrowly avoided disaster; his advocacy of the social issues agenda achieved little. Regarding even his most core belief—the reduction in the role of the federal government through reduced taxation—Helms's legislative experience was an unhappy one. Under intense pressure from Reagan, Helms, along with John East, voted for a $99 billion deficit reduction package that included an 8 cent increase in the federal cigarette tax. Although Helms had originally voted against the measure, after a phone call from Reagan from aboard Air Force One on July 22, he and John East switched their votes, providing the margin of victory. Helms had promised Bob Dole that he and East would only vote in favor of the measure if they provided the margin of victory. Helms continued to support Reagan's tax increase, after another presidential phone call on August 12.[52] In voting for a tax increase, Jesse later admitted that he had been "forced to walk the plank" politically. Ellis was enraged about the negative political consequences: according to Wrenn, the two men did not speak to each other for months afterward. By betraying the tobacco interest by voting for an increased cigarette tax, the senator had violated a political taboo in the state. Ellis was especially aggravated that East had been dragged into this duplicity: if Helms wanted to "cut his own throat," that was one thing, but he hated for him to "cut John's throat." Although Helms obtained the important concession that the cigarette tax increase would expire after three years, his political enemies in North Carolina were delighted. Democrats ran newspaper ads describing Helms and East as the "tobacco tax twins." "With friends like this," the ad read, "tobacco doesn't need any more enemies." Helms rushed to a tobacco warehouse to try to explain his decision; he urged that leaders avoid "partisan politics" about tobacco.[53]

Jesse's political frustrations bore fruit in the congressional elections of November 1982. Although Republicans maintained control of the Senate, Democrats solidified their House majority. All five of the Congressional

Club–backed candidates for Congress lost in North Carolina, despite heavy advertising, while Democrats that were targeted at a national level survived. This was a "wipeout," remembered Wrenn, his first experience with the "tsunami going the wrong way"; the only thing to do, he recalled, was to "get to the top of the palm tree and hold on." Meanwhile, Governor Jim Hunt, in command of a large grassroots organization that he had built up since his election as lieutenant governor in 1972, was credited with successfully mobilizing an anti-Helms coalition. Hunt's organization was based on the strategic use of patronage and state contracts; in both areas, the governor possessed great power. Each county had a "county key" who headed the governor's political operation, dispensed state patronage, and, according to reporter Chuck Alston, "got to call all the shots about the county." It was only a mild exaggeration, said Alston, to say that even road scrapers got their jobs only after Hunt's political lieutenants signed off on the appointment. Hunt had also constructed a formidable public relations operation, and all this amounted to a powerful political machine. "If there was a ribbon to cut" in the state, recalled Congressional Club operative Mark Stephens, "the governor was there to cut it." Charlie Black, who joined the Helms campaign as a consultant, described the governor as "certainly the best politician of his generation in North Carolina, except for Helms." The elections of 1982, said Democratic National Committee chair Charles T. Manatt, had destroyed "the myth of invincibility of Jesse Helms." It was "written in the wind," he declared, that "the prince of darkness will be retired in 1984 by a leading Democrat in North Carolina." He rated Helms as the "most vulnerable" of the nineteen Senate Republicans up for reelection.[54]

Immediately after the elections, with Reagan's backing congressional leaders sought a $5 billion roads bill, financed by a 5 cent increase in the gas tax, that would have helped to employ workers in public service jobs. Although the bill enjoyed overwhelming support, Helms sought redemption among conservatives for his previous apostasy on the cigarette tax. He objected to the gas tax, he told his constituents in his newsletter, because it was a tax increase and because the revenue would go from North Carolinians to "big cities for their mass transit systems." This legislation was rushed through the legislative process; in their haste to return home for the Christmas recess, most senators had not even read the bill. Along with John East, Gordon Humphrey of New Hampshire, and Don Nickles of Oklahoma, Jesse conducted a filibuster that tied up most Senate business during a lame-duck session of the 97th Congress held just before Christmas 1982. With Jesse and allies maintaining the filibuster—Helms slept in cots at his Senate hideaway office—Reagan telephoned him on December 14, at Baker's request, urging him to back down. Although Helms told Reagan that he would "go into a corner & give this prayerful consideration," he continued the fight. Jesse was also under pressure from North Carolina supporters. On Saturday, December 17, his old friend Carl Monroe, who owned a Greensboro construction company, flew up to Washington, and Jesse and aide Scott Wilson met him at National Airport. But when Monroe suggested that the filibuster might hurt Helms politically, that struck a nerve: Jesse took pride in never making a decision because of political pressure. That was "the worst thing you can tell him," said Wilson, and it was like throwing "Br'er Rabbit in the briar patch." "If it costs me my seat," Helms told Monroe, "I'll just go home. I'm not going to give up my principles just to stay up here."[55]

By December 21, even Jesse's Republican colleagues were seething. "Seldom have I seen a more obdurate and obnoxious performance," said Wyoming Republican senator Alan K. Simpson. Senate rules were not created to "protect a minority within a minority within a minority," and Simpson predicted retribution against the tobacco program. Privately, Simpson confronted Helms, calling him a "son of a bitch" for prolonging the legislative session. Asked to characterize the Senate mood, Bob Dole said: "Angry." Back home, the Raleigh News and Observer dubbed Helms and East "Senator No" and "Senator No-No." The gas tax filibuster, wrote Sitton, was an "encore of Dixie demagoguery" with a "new note of meanness toward other senators." Helms's performance reminded him of Joe McCarthy and his "red-hunting rampage." Helms remained unfazed, however. "This senator did not come to Washington to gain popularity with his colleagues," he declared. "He came here to do what he believes is right."

Oklahoma senator Don Nickles, who had been elected in the Reagan sweep of 1980, joined Helms in the filibuster, but he realized that the hostility of other Republicans was making the effort counterproductive. He and Helms spent time together praying about the matter; they even spoke to evangelist Billy Graham about it over the phone. Nickles urged Jesse to give up the fight, and on December 22 Helms agreed to a cloture vote that ended debate.[56] Senators facing a cloture vote were entitled to ask for twenty-four hours' delay, but Jesse's colleagues requested an earlier vote in order to recess for the holidays. Helms refused. At 1:00 A.M. on December 22, Jesse strode over to Simpson and offered his hand, saying "Let's be friends." Simpson refused to get up from his seat and just stared at Helms, who eventually turned away. Helms was also alienated from the White House: although he had long maintained that any differences he had with Reagan reflected policy disagreements with his advisers, he admitted that this time he clashed with the president, who supported increasing the gas tax in order to provide public service jobs. Reagan lobbied Jesse during the filibuster, but he refused to change his position. When the president asked Jesse to permit a vote, Helms reminded him that Reagan had once said that only a "palace coup" would force him to support increased taxes. "Mr. President," Jesse said, "when did the palace coup occur?" He then listed the provisions in the bill and asked Reagan if he agreed with them. Reagan agreed that he did not.[57]

Based on this steady number of legislative defeats, many commentators in the early 1980s were prepared to write Helms's political obituary.[58] As early as May 1981, a *Charlotte Observer* reporter wrote that Helms, once a "towering figure to be feared and courted since the Republicans took over in January," had unsuccessfully translated "his popular backing into real power in the Senate."[59] During the next few years, that Helms had become an ineffective and perhaps irrelevant ideologue became a prevalent story line. In September 1982, an assessment from the *Washington Post* concluded that Helms, once "one of the most powerful members of the Senate, possessor of one of the sharpest swords in town," had watched his Senate standing fall "markedly." The "qualities that serve him as outsider have not translated well, have not also made him an effective insider and committee chairman in the Republican-controlled body." An ineffective leader of the Agriculture Committee, he was accused of "high-handed tactics" in tying up the Senate, and his credibility had eroded among fellow senators. "For all his huffing and puffing," said William Hamilton, a lobbyist for the Planned Parenthood Federation of America, "the emperor doesn't have any clothes." According to a southern senator, Helms had "worn about as thin as tissue paper with most members." Helms and his conservative supporters had overreached themselves, according to this narrative, and their power from the start had been exaggerated by the press.[60]

But these assessments missed the mark with Jesse. The reports of his demise, said the *Greensboro News and Record* in September 1982, were "greatly exaggerated."[61] Helms had provided a show in the gas tax filibuster of late 1982; the conventional wisdom was that he had become a pariah. Yet his constituents, inside and outside North Carolina, saw things differently. After the gas tax struggle, which he described as "one of the most tiring experiences of my life," Jesse drove south on Interstate 85. Weary and dispirited from the long battle, he started to run off the road, and he decided to pull into Hardee's, a fast food restaurant, in South Hill, Virginia, about an hour from the North Carolina border, to order black coffee and a hamburger. Entering the door, a truck driver recognized him and said: "Hey, there's

Jesse Helms." Within seconds, eight or ten truckers—whose income was imperiled by higher gas taxes—stood up and applauded.[62]

For Helms, a legislative victory was less important than preparing for the future. While enraging his liberal opponents, he solidified his standing with his conservative base. His unpopular stands on a variety of issues fed this incongruity: while he appeared ineffective, even hapless, he became a courageous, appealing spokesman to his supporters. Helms's support translated into a continued flow of dollars; reporter Elizabeth Drew called him the "most effective single political fundraiser in America—with the exception, perhaps, of Ronald Reagan." Helms's Congressional Club continued to draw on a highly organized constituency—according to Richard Viguerie, "an organized army"—providing him a large war chest for future political campaigns. He was "still the generalissimo of our movement," an anti-abortion activist said, who had obtained "what we wanted: recorded votes." Helms's guerrilla tactics won him few friends on the Senate floor, but they succeeded in pressuring the Reagan administration on a variety of domestic and foreign policy issues.[63]

During 1983, Helms underwent a political transformation that radically altered his status: from a candidate who was perceived as a likely loser, he reemerged as a potent candidate. The remaking of Helms's image was assisted in September 1983, in one of the last major crises of the Cold War, when Soviet aircraft shot down Korean Airlines flight number 007, which originated in New York and had inadvertently strayed into Soviet airspace, killing 269 passengers. Aboard the flight were a number of Americans traveling to Seoul, South Korea, for a three-day conference commemorating the thirtieth anniversary of that country's mutual defense treaty with the United States. The most prominent victim was Representative Lawrence McDonald, a five-term Republican congressman from Georgia who had been recently elected national chairman of the John Birch Society. Other members of the congressional delegation who attended but took other KAL flights were Senators Steve Symms of Idaho, Orrin Hatch, Edward Zorinsky, and Representative Carroll Hubbard, Jr. (D-KY). Helms, who was originally scheduled to be aboard KAL 007, had been in Houston and was delayed because of a Dallas fund-raiser, and so he took KAL 105 out of Los Angeles, with Symms and Hubbard also traveling with him. The two flights both refueled in Anchorage, and the passengers mingled with one another before KAL 007 left on its ill-fated journey. Helms suggested to Symms that they take the earlier KAL flight and arrive in Seoul twenty minutes earlier, but Symms declined, saying that they would still have to wait for their bags. "That's the last time I'll take a tip from Jesse," Symms later said.[64]

For Helms, the KAL 007 shoot-down provided an opportunity to reaffirm the constancy of his anti-Soviet position.[65] In September, Helms led a fight for punitive reprisals. In a Senate resolution condemning the shoot-down, Helms demanded sanctions that called for recalling the U.S. ambassador to Moscow, reducing the number of Soviet diplomats in the United States, and engaging in a "comprehensive reappraisal" of trade and arms control.[66] But the Reagan administration opposed severe penalties, asserting that they would be counterproductive. When the KAL 007 resolution came to the Senate, Helms led the conservative charge, and he called for "real action" penalizing a "criminal, brutal, premeditated, cowardly act by the Soviet Union." Kissinger's flawed policy of détente, amounting to appeasement, was devoid of moral content and indifferent to the "preservation of a way of life basic to our civilization." Détente had failed in restraining Soviet behavior. Only a hard line would work, and the KAL shoot-down marked a turning point in Soviet-American relations. After eight hours of debate, the Senate overwhelmingly rejected a seven-part Helms amendment to a general resolution and instead condemned, by a unanimous 95–0 vote, the Soviets' "criminal destruction" of the Korean airliner. Helms remained undaunted. "We created a dialogue to keep this slaughter in the public consciousness," he told reporters, and "millions of Americans will be looking to see how their senators voted."[67]

Whether Jesse prevailed made little difference politically, for his role in the KAL 007 affair energized his standing among conservatives nationwide and reinforced his political status in his home state. After the vote, Helms took off on a twin-engine plane to Winston-Salem, and following the defeat of his resolutions he was described as "effusive." He didn't "expect to win," he said, but he "sure would hate to go home and explain that I voted against a proposal to send communist spies back home."[68] The KAL shoot-down became a rallying cause in speeches that Helms would give in the coming months. Helms was armed with a new "talking point" in his reelection arsenal; and his fight against godless Communism, his belief in western, Christian values, and his unwillingness to compromise became a part of his standard stump speech. Previously, Helms had been "off balance and defensive." Now he could use the opportunity of the KAL 007 shoot-down to "speak with emotion, to go on the offensive, to try to define his candidacy more in his own terms."

Helms subsequently told audiences the story of his fateful stopover in Anchorage, where he played with two little girls, ages five and three, who were on KAL 007 and who were returning to Korea after visiting grandparents in Greece, New York. Those children, he tearfully told reporters in phrasing that he frequently repeated, reminded him of his own daughters when they were young. His last recollection as they boarded the plane was of the girls blowing him kisses. Over time, the story subsequently grew to include Helms observing how the girls' mother read Bible stories to them; he used this as an example of how all children should be exposed to school prayer. He also used the KAL 007 in fund-raising. In a letter that went out October 4, 1983, he retold the story of the little girls, how he played a game with them of an imaginary house at the end of each finger, with each hand a neighborhood. At one speech in Henderson, he told his audience of three hundred the story of the children, saying he could not talk about it "without almost weeping."

However hard the subject of the tragedy of KAL 007 was to discuss, noted veteran journalist Ferrel Guillory, Helms managed to bring up the subject frequently, on the Senate floor and in political speeches. Was this "an appropriate story in a campaign context?" he was asked. Helms responded that it emphasized "the way I have felt all along about communism." Another reporter noted that Helms spoke about the KAL 007 shoot-down to campaign audiences "at almost every stop," and his recounting was "eloquent, laced with the same kind of raw emotion that made him a successful television commentator and helped him win two Senate elections." The meeting with the two girls became the centerpiece of the story, and he told how, his "voice choking with emotion," "the little girl kissed me on the cheek" as she boarded KAL 007 in Anchorage. "I may be paranoid. I may be obsessed," he said, "but I think if there was ever a time to nail the communist hide to the wall, it is now," he said. "They are not folks just like us. They are cruel barbarians. They will do anything to destroy freedom."[69]

NOT LONG AFTER the KAL 007 shoot-down, Helms captured the headlines—and solidified his political standing—with another stand on principle. During the 1960s, Helms's reputation as a television broadcaster had rested on his *Viewpoints* message of opposition to racial change. In July 1973, conservative newspaper editor William Loeb urged Jesse to meet William Shockley of Stanford University, a Nobel Prize winner in physics who maintained controversial views about inherent differences in intelligence between whites and blacks. Shockley could help, Jesse wrote, to restore "sanity in this racial business." "You can bet your boots that I'll be delighted to see your friend," Helms said.[70]

Now, in the 1980s, Helms's racial views remained fundamentally unchanged. Unlike leading segregationists such as George Wallace or Strom

Thurmond, Jesse never underwent a public renunciation of his past views about white supremacy, civil rights, and race. To the contrary, Helms insisted that he had been right and civil rights activists wrong about segregation. When asked by reporters, he always answered that the Civil Rights Act of 1964 had been a mistake. He admired Rosa Parks for her courage by refusing to give her seat to a white passenger in Montgomery, Alabama, in December 1955. But, some forty-five years later, Jesse asked: "What is so important about a seat in the bus?" Helms remained equally unapologetic about his political alienation from black voters. He regarded black political mobilization as unnecessary, and he always declared that he was the good friend of the service workers and custodians that he knew on Capitol Hill. As late as February 2000, he told an interviewer that he did not "know how to appeal to black people."[71] As was so true of his position on most things, Jesse displayed a remarkable consistency—and unwillingness to change. Jack Betts, who wrote for the *Greensboro Daily News* and the *Charlotte Observer,* later said that Jesse's racial views were much like the "older folks in my family": they had grown up with black people under segregation, believed that they understood them, and were puzzled by the changes of the civil rights era. This was a widely held set of attitudes among white Southerners of Helms's generation.[72] Jesse was also capable of what one reporter called "startling anachronism." In June 1981, during Senate debate, he was quoted as saying: "On the floor we fight hard; we're free, white and 21, as we say in North Carolina." A year later, when a Durham African American asked that Helms meet with him about the Voting Rights Act, Jesse responded: "I's ready when you's ready."[73] Jesse's racial attitudes were of another era, and these had little changed over the years. In 1984, when *Charlotte Observer* reporter Bill Arthur interviewed Helms in his Raleigh home, the senator went over to the wall and took down a framed picture of a grinning, toothless black man on a porch, with a drink in his hand. "This is what me and Martin Luther King had in mind," the caption read. "That'll get me in trouble," Helms said.[74] Years later, in 1998, after Democrat John Edwards had won election to the Senate, Helms invited his wife and him over for dinner. In conversation, Jesse mentioned that he could not understand why "colored people didn't like me."[75]

Since the 1950s, Helms had been offended by any suggestions that he was racist, and he often pointed to his record of employing African Americans while he was at WRAL, which he once described as "perhaps one of the most integrated television stations in the country." According to Helms, in the 1940s he hired North Carolina's first black radio announcer, and WRAL hired African Americans in skilled and supervisory positions. During the 1960s, the station's janitors were white. Jesse also liked to point out that he was one of the best-liked senators among the mostly black custodial staff on Capitol Hill.[76] In the summer of 1983, when it was pointed out that none of his Senate staff was black, he hired Claude Allen, a recent black graduate of UNC, as his press secretary. Only twenty-two when he joined Helms's staff, Allen had worked as press secretary for Chapel Hill Republican William Cobey's unsuccessful campaign in 1982 for the 4th District seat. A born-again Christian, Allen's strong evangelical and libertarian views attracted him to Helms. Despite the rough-and-tumble of racial politics in the mid-1980s, Allen remained a Helms loyalist.[77]

But the hiring of Allen, and Helms's generally cordial relations with the African Americans that he knew personally, did not change a reality: that Helms was willing to exploit race for advantage more than any politician of the 1980s. When increased press scrutiny followed his national fame in the early 1980s, profiles of Jesse invariably considered the matter of race, and these profiles were usually unflattering. Helms was stung by these depictions. His memoir, published in 2005, makes the case that racial motives had little to do with his attitudes toward the civil rights revolution. Nonetheless, his account also makes clear that he remained opposed to the freedom struggle, which he called "a long campaign of ridicule and distortion... aimed at the Southern way of life." If "people of goodwill" had sought to resolve differences without the intervention of government, Helms contended, the "stirring of hatred, the encouragement of violence, the suspicion and distrust" that came with the civil rights movement could have been avoided.[78]

In the Voting Rights Act and Martin Luther King, Jr., Helms found two powerful symbols of the civil rights legacy that he despised. The Voting Rights Act, which was enacted in 1965 and revised in 1970 and 1975, had been truly revolutionary, ending disenfranchisement and expanding black political power. It had placed a burden on southern states with a history of voter discrimination, requiring federalization of voting. Helms opposed the original act, and he opposed all of its subsequent revisions. With Republican control of the Senate, he intended to oppose the Voting Rights Act even more vigorously when it came up for amendment in 1982. In October 1981, the House enacted legislation by the overwhelming margin of 389–24, and the bill came to the Senate in 1982. The measure strengthened the Voting Rights Act's provision by making two important changes. First, in the permanent section of the law, it empowered the Justice Department to nullify state measures if it could demonstrate a discriminatory effect. This change was significant: in 1980, the Supreme Court, in *Mobile v. Bolden,*

required that federal voting rights officials had to demonstrate discriminatory intent in order to enforce the act. Second, the law would extend the
"preclearance" provisions of the law—which compelled any state with a
history of discriminatory voting practices to submit all electoral changes in
advance for review—for another twenty-five years.

Helms vigorously opposed both of these new provisions. In April 1982,
declaring that he was "just carrying out the fight that Sam Ervin began,"
Jesse announced his opposition, demanding a liberalized "bailout" provision
that would enable the forty counties of North Carolina under the Voting
Rights Act's supervision to be removed from federal supervision. Joined by
John East, Helms succeeded in delaying consideration of the act in the
spring of 1982.[79] Helms enjoyed no support from the Reagan administration,
which favored modifying the law by easing regulation of the states and retaining the provision that required proof of intentional discrimination. Bob
Dole became the administration's main advocate in seeking a compromise
that would move the bill forward. Strom Thurmond, who was unenthusiastic about the bill, objected to Helms's methods, especially his willingness to
obstruct the Senate Judiciary Committee, which he chaired. Eventually, he
would endorse the legislation—an indication, perhaps, of how he had
changed his positions about civil rights, while Jesse had not.[80]

Helms was, in fact, intent on provoking a VRA confrontation. On May
5, 1982, the Judiciary Committee, by a vote of 17–1—with John East the
lone dissenter—sent a compromise bill to the Senate that extended the law
for twenty-five years, provided for some conditions for bailout from the
preclearance requirements of the law, and required congressional review in
fifteen years. The bill had the support of the Reagan administration.[81] But it
did not have Jesse's support. East and Helms attempted to delay by amendment; both also suggested strongly the possibility of a filibuster.[82] Three
weeks later, Helms promised that unless major changes were made he
would be "obliged to oppose it to the maximum possible extent." In another
speech on June 9, Helms promised to filibuster "until the cows come home"
if North Carolinians were made "second-class citizens" because of the intervention of "Big Brother" in Washington. Why should every change in
local election laws, he asked, have to be brought to federal authorities?
"Senator No" was "again engaging in obstructionism," said a *Raleigh News
and Observer* editorial, and he was not "trying to eliminate discrimination
but rather to promote it." How could "this old segregationist" make this
claim?[83] But Senator No fought on, and in mid-June he insisted on two
changes: a bailout provision that was "fair and equitable" and the application of the Voting Rights Act equally to all states, north and south.[84]

Helms enjoyed little support for his position, aside from East and Orrin Hatch, who warned that the law would bring "racial gerrymandering and racial bloc voting."[85] After several senators accused Helms of conducting a "verbal sit-in," Helms slammed down a committee report on his desk and said, "You are saying, 'You are un-American,' in effect. I reject it, and I resent it." A sharp exchange occurred between Helms and Edward Kennedy, who declared that Helms's speeches sounded like a "broken record," while Helms claimed that the bill's supporters were "arrogant and sarcastic." Howard Baker promised to keep the Senate in session until the bill was enacted, and, as Dole put it, there were a "a lot of rather restless Republicans" who had lost patience.[86] With about eighty senators promising to vote for extension, Helms attempted a filibuster, but a cloture vote was easily reached on June 15. Helms then sought further delay and amendment, but four amendments from East were easily defeated. By June 17, after six days of filibuster, Jesse conceded defeat. "We've done as much as we can do," he told reporters, "in terms of making senators aware of the implications of this bill." A day later, after thirty hours of debate, the Voting Rights Act passed the Senate by an 85–8 margin—with Strom Thurmond voting in the affirmative—as Jesse ended his delaying tactics after Baker promised to help with his legislation on abortion and school prayer. To Helms, this indicated that his fellow senators failed to understand the measure and had surrendered to civil rights lobbyists, who were "running the Senate from the anteroom."[87]

HELMS OPPOSED THE civil rights heritage on another front—by attempting to prevent the establishment of a federal holiday honoring Martin Luther King, Jr.'s, birthday. Four days after King's assassination in April 1968, legislation was introduced in Congress to create a holiday in his honor, and during the next fifteen years, a campaign to honor the slain leader ensued. In 1970, petitions endorsing a holiday including six million names were delivered to Congress. Three years later, Illinois became the first state to enact a King holiday, and by 1983 eighteen other states had followed suit. The holiday became a flash point about the historical memory of the civil rights revolution, and, for African Americans, honoring King in this way became a part of the legitimization of the civil rights heritage. In August 1983, the House passed a bill, by a 338–90 margin, creating a tenth federal holiday on the third Monday in January in King's honor. The bill had been rushed through without hearings, and when the Senate proposed equally quick consideration, Helms announced his opposition, citing its high cost.

Helms and his allies—which included conservative activist Howard Phillips—assembled a critique that included an assault on King and the heritage he exemplified.[88] On October 2, 1983, Jesse announced that he would mount a full-fledged effort to block the bill, including a filibuster. "I'm going to do everything I can to resist this proposal," he said, "realizing the cards are stacked against me." Most senators, he thought, were "thoroughly intimidated by political pressure" that was applied by "just a handful of activists led by Martin Luther King, Jr.'s, widow Coretta Scott King." "I'm not going to sell my soul to stay in the Senate," he declared.[89]

Helms launched his attack on the King holiday with a long Senate speech the next day, October 3. Beginning his speech with an estimate that the proposed holiday could cost as much as $12 billion per year in lost productivity, Jesse moved on to attack King's legacy. Federal holidays should be reserved for those who expressed "shared values," but King's past remained a "source of tension, a deeply troubling symbol of divided society." King had exploited nonviolence as a "provocative act to disturb the peace of the state and to trigger, in many cases, overreaction by authorities." His legacy was "division, not love." King expressed a "religious imagery with which he cloaked his political concepts," and there was a tension between the religious and the political that was "matched by the tension in his methods." Although the divisive anger of the civil rights era had dissipated, mistrust remained. King's views were "those of a radical political minority that had little to do with racial minorities." Most would agree that any movement whose participation and direction involved Marxists was suspect, he said: this was, he asserted, true of the civil rights movement and King's part in it. King had exhibited a "pattern of associations and activities" indicating that, at the least, he did not object to Communism, but he also "welcomed collaboration with Communists." Although warned about associating with subversives, he took few measures to dissociate himself from the "most extreme political elements in the United States." He and his Southern Christian Leadership Conference were "subject to influence and manipulation by Communists": Helms cited King's opposition to the Vietnam War, which was based on his sympathy for the North Vietnamese and on "an essentially Marxist and anti-American ideological view of U.S. foreign policy." Some might argue that King's views were "merely Marxist in its orientation," but the problem was that Marxism-Leninism, Communism's "official philosophy," was an "action-oriented revolutionary doctrine." King exhibited an "action-oriented Marxism" that was "not compatible with the concepts of this country." Helms demanded the legislation be sent to the Judiciary Committee for hearing and a fuller consideration.[90]

Helms's attack on King restated themes about Communism and civil rights that he had expressed for many years on WRAL. They also repeated charges of subversion that southern segregationists, and the FBI director, J. Edgar Hoover, had asserted about King. But no thoroughgoing examination of King has ever demonstrated any evidence of a sympathy with Marxism-Leninism or Communism. He was deeply influenced by Christian socialism, although at least two of most important advisers, Stanley Levinson and Bayard Rustin, were Communist Party members at some point in their lives. But none of his biographers has given the charges any credence, and an exhaustive study of the 200,000 pages of King's FBI files done by a Justice Department task force in 1976 found no evidence that he ever belonged to the Communist Party or sympathized with its objectives.[91]

The mainstream press in North Carolina objected vigorously to Helms's filibuster. The real issue, said John Alexander of the *Greensboro Daily News,* was that a King holiday would recognize race as "the single most determining force in American history," something that had its origins in slavery and the Civil War and culminated in the civil rights movement. Despite its significance, African Americans had "very little to point to today that can legitimate and sanctify their struggle."[92] Helms's attack characterizing King as a Marxist was "an old red herring that thousands of racists used in the 'Fifties and 'Sixties as a means of trying to discredit the civil rights movement," said the *Fayetteville Observer.* Helms's description of King as Communist was "mindless"; his struggle was for "real citizenship" and an "end to real mistreatment of blacks." Despite J. Edgar Hoover's efforts to "paint him several shades of red ... the evidence just wasn't there."[93] Helms had "engaged in a smear," maintained the *Raleigh News and Observer,* that intended to "tarnish King and the civil rights movement anew by hanging on them the 'Marxist' label." This was a "replay of the segregationist nonsense" that Helms had used against the freedom struggle during the 1960s. It was "poison enough" when Helms smeared it over the airwaves: now he had "injected his poison into the deliberations of the U.S. Senate." North Carolinians had left behind segregation and learned to live with the changes coming with the civil rights revolution, and it was sad to see Helms engage in "smear tactics that invited ridicule and contempt."[94]

Helms's old adversary Ed Yoder, now writing for the *Washington Post,* described the entire matter as "vintage Helms." He admitted to a "sense of déjà vu." Although there were legitimate questions about whether another federal holiday should be added, Yoder noted, "depend on Jesse Helms ... to contaminate a serious argument with debating points from the gutter." Helms was a "stopped clock if ever American politics had one," and he was

repeating the "coarse irrelevancies with which many bewildered Southerners consoled themselves" decades ago when Jim Crow was disintegrating.
For southern whites to believe that the civil rights struggle "sprang from
real grievances, and drew upon authentic American values, was to confess
that their sense of justice had slept for a century." For whites of the 1960s,
as for Helms of the 1980s, this was "too bitter a pill to swallow." Yoder believed that it was "mere stupidity" to associate the movement with Communism: King's struggle so obviously blended "basic American values,
Biblical prophecy and Gandhi." Helms had once again gone off on a rant,
though Yoder suspected he intended to rally his "misguided followers by
posing as the nation's savior from a King holiday."[95]

On the same day that Helms began his filibuster, Reagan announced
that he would sign the bill, and Howard Baker prepared to speed it through
the Senate. Strom Thurmond, who broke with Jesse about the Voting
Rights Act, announced his support for the holiday. Republican senators
such as Dole, Arlen Specter of Pennsylvania, and Pete V. Domenici of New
Mexico all lined up behind the bill. As one of Domenici's aides put it, Republicans wanted "something to do for black recognition, and this is a relatively easy one."[96] Jesse's October 3 speech, moreover, provoked general
outrage. "I will not dignify Helms's comments with a reply," said Ted
Kennedy, pointing out that the Judiciary Committee had already held two
days of hearings on a similar bill in 1979. Saying that Helms's comments
did not "reflect credit on this body," he declared that the attack on King
should be "shunned by the American people, including the citizens of his
own state." While he was alive, "archsegregationists" had tarred him with
Communist insinuations; now these "unfounded" allegations, nothing but
"Red smear" tactics, had been resurrected. Other Republican senators
agreed. Specter called King a "Herculean figure on the American scene,"
while Dole advised those worrying about the holiday's cost to use "pocket
calculators and estimate the cost of three hundred years of slavery, followed
by a century or more of economic, political and social exclusion and discrimination." Brushing aside Kennedy's attack, Helms dismissed Kennedy's
comments as "baloney." Anyone who disagreed with Kennedy, he said, was
labeled a "racist and right-winger." Helms told reporters that he doubted
whether there was "any question" about whether King was a Marxist-
Leninist; the "whole movement" was composed of "Communists at the
highest possible levels." "If it has webbed feet, if it has feathers and it
quacks," he said, "it's a you-know-what."[97]

That Helms faced overwhelming opposition in the press and the Senate did not faze him: if anything, it encouraged him in the rightness of his

stand. Despite attacks from the media, he told constituents, "I will not retreat." King did not deserve the honor of a holiday, which would celebrate
a person who "expressed contempt for America."[98] Nonetheless, Howard
Baker filed a cloture motion on the same day that Jesse delivered his attack
on King. Abruptly, Helms abandoned the filibuster and permitted a vote,
following the Columbus Day holiday, on October 19, in the hope that senators would hear from their constituents in the intervening two weeks.
Baker was eager to dispose of the King holiday bill because West German
president Karl Carstens was scheduled to visit the Senate, and Baker
wanted to ensure that there were no disruptions. Baker thus agreed to
schedule early consideration of the tobacco and dairy bills, Jesse claimed,
in exchange for his cooperation. "I got everything I desired," he claimed.[99]

But Helms was far from finished. Another line of attack had to do with
the civil rights leader's sexual indiscretions, which involved numerous ex-
tramarital affairs. Jesse's objection to King, he would later tell an interviewer, involved "the kind of moral man he was not." As an adulterer, King
did not possess the "morality that he ought to have had," he said. Jesse believed that King's message, given his behavior, was a "message of pretense."[100] In early October 1983, one reporter described Helms's insinuations
about King's sex life as threatening to "burst to life like a long-dormant
virus." Still, Helms trod carefully. In late September, Helms's ally Howard
Phillips and his Conservative Caucus convened a press conference demanding the release of the FBI's voluminous King surveillance tapes during the period 1963–68, which had been sealed for fifty years by court order
in January 1977.[101] After abandoning the filibuster, Helms entered into a
lawsuit seeking to unseal these documents, and he claimed that he was unable to reach an "informed" judgment about the King holiday without
them. In an affidavit that Jesse filed with the case, he stated that there had
been "tremendous speculation over the years as to the contents of the records generated by the FBI with regard to the surveillance of Dr. King," and
it was now "imperative" that questions about King be resolved before the
Senate reached a decision. That "imperative" trumped any right to privacy
that King's family might enjoy. Within days the Reagan administration
went to court to oppose Helms's efforts, while conservative activists such as
Richard Viguerie and Paul Weyrich rallied to his cause. Although Helms
and Phillips denied it, many suspected that they wanted the documents released in order to tarnish King. As Claude Sitton caustically put it, rather
than revealing "King's arm around the neck of some Soviet spook," Helms
hoped that the tapes would provide "evidence not of high treason but of
low lechery, a peek through the keyhole, a sweaty, panting encounter with

the panderer's art." Sitton was told in the 1960s that reporters who saw these files described them as having a "pretty low calorie count, not the kind of thing you'd expect to hear from a minister but nothing that would raise more than an eyebrow in the local bar."[102]

On October 18, Judge John Lewis Smith dismissed Helms's suit, refusing to interfere in congressional affairs. The Senate then brushed aside, by a vote of 71–12, Jesse's efforts to delay the bill's passage by referring it to committee. In a speech that day, Jesse again opposed the King holiday. Why, he asked, should Congress not instead establish a holiday for Thomas Jefferson, whose birthday was not honored? Helms then described King as a representative of the "elements of the far left and the Communist Party U.S.A." The Senate should not go forward with this legislation until questions about King's loyalty were resolved; the public's right to know and the Senate's "responsibility to know" were paramount. New York senator Daniel Patrick Moynihan denounced Jesse's attack as "filth" and "obscenities," but the most heated reply came from Kennedy, who rose to King's defense and denounced the "smear campaign" against him and the "completely inaccurate and false" accusations that accompanied it. Helms responded testily. Kennedy, he said, had violated Senate rules by accusing him of "conduct or motive unworthy or unbecoming a senator," and this came close to forcing a vote on whether Kennedy could continue speaking. Further, Kennedy's argument was not with Helms, he said, but with "his dead brother, who was president and his dead brother who was attorney-general," who had approved the King wiretaps and warned the civil rights leader about his Communist associations. "Flushed with emotion," Kennedy said that he was "appalled" at the "attempt of some to misappropriate the memory of my brother Robert Kennedy and misuse it as part of a smear campaign." "Those who never cared for him," he said, "in life now invoke his name when he can no longer speak for himself." Admitting that the Kennedy brothers had authorized a wiretap, he asserted that they had warned King for the good of the movement. If Robert Kennedy were alive today, he said, "he would be the first person to say that J. Edgar Hoover's reckless campaign against Martin Luther King was a shame and a blot on American history." The Senate then brushed aside Helms's amendments by a vote of 90–3.[103]

As a last-ditch effort, while East introduced a substitute establishing a national civil rights day on James Madison's birthday, Helms offered bills establishing a holiday for Thomas Jefferson, issuing a presidential pardon for Marcus Garvey, and creating a holiday for Hispanic Americans. Helms and East, said New Jersey senator Bill Bradley, were not "etching another

American profile in courage in this debate." Rather, they were "running their old campaign, as old as the interaction of race and politics in America," in which they played up to "'old Jim Crow,' and all of us know it." Helms's attempts at delay failed, however, and the Senate then, as Coretta Scott King watched from the gallery, overwhelmingly approved it by a vote of 78–12. Helms's conservative network produced mail and phone calls against the bill, and some senators reported hostile reaction among their constituencies. "If the voting was based on mail and phone calls," said Dole, who was the bill's floor manager, "I'm not sure there would be any votes for it." Reagan, after the bill's passage, reaffirmed that he would sign it, though he refrained from enthusiastic support. If it had been up to him, he told reporters, his preference would have been for states to determine whether to have the holiday. But since civil rights activists seemed "bent on making it a national holiday," he said, "I believe the symbolism of that day is important enough that I'll sign that legislation when it reaches my desk." Regarding Helms's fight, Reagan did not question his sincerity in seeking to "know everything we should know about an individual." Asked whether he supported Helms's assertions, Reagan responded cryptically: "We'll know in about 35 years, won't we?" Although Reagan subsequently apologized for this statement, he sympathized with Jesse's critique. He signed the bill into law on November 2, 1983.[104]

Helms's reaction, despite the adoption of the King holiday bill, remained defiant. The law was passed in an "atmosphere of intimidation, political harassment...screaming and yelling and threats," he said. Moynihan described the information about King as "filth," but, Helms said, "maybe they were filth" because it "accurately portrayed part of King's career." He was not acting from racist motives, he said emphatically. "I'm not a racist, I'm not a bigot," he told reporters. "You ask any black who knows me." He denied any political motives, though he admitted that he might use his fight in fund-raising. "I'm not going to say it's not going to be mentioned," he said. "You do the best you can with what you have."[105]

Helms's position on the King holiday provides yet another example of the disjuncture between what the mainstream press thought about him and how his constituencies regarded him. When he began his filibuster in early October, contemporaries debated whether it was "political brilliance or political blunder." Former Helms aide Charlie Black observed that the King issue itself would not be a major political factor, but he believed that Helms's reputation for consistency and his willingness to assume unpopular stands would resonate with conservative white voters, who connected Marxism and the civil rights movement. Still another observer, liberal Will

D. Campbell, found the episode "both heartening and discouraging." Although honoring King in this way would have been unthinkable a decade earlier, the rhetoric in the debate recalled "the most turbulent days" of the civil rights era. Helms's "fulminations" did not, he hoped, represent the national mood of 1983, but the senator probably spoke for a "sizeable number of people."[106]

Years later, Helms remained adamantly opposed to the King holiday. When King's statue was placed in the Capitol Rotunda, he complained to Ray House, his old high school mentor, that virtues were assigned to King "which he never possessed when he was alive." It was commonly known, Helms said, that King "engaged in fornication and adultery constantly while traveling around the country," and he "didn't even attempt to be discreet about it." This might make him a racist, but Jesse's resentment about honoring King "would be the same if he had been white and had the same character weakness."[107] Nothing had been "more twisted and misunderstood," he wrote in 2005, than his stand on the holiday, a position that was "based on the fact, not on personality and certainly not on race." Although King was not a Communist, he associated with people who were, despite warnings from his friends. He opposed intervention in Vietnam and slandered American motives in that conflict. What a shame, he wrote, that holiday supporters "were not willing to submit to a full examination of all the facts about Dr. King, so that the worthiness of this honor could have been examined without pressure or prejudice." This was, Helms wrote in his memoirs, a holiday honoring a man who "emphasized discontent."[108]

In retrospect, Helms's battle about KAL 007 and the King holiday were turning points in his political standing. "I don't know of anything he has done in the last two years," one conservative Democrat not attached politically to Helms commented in late October 1983, that had "channeled more positive support in his direction than the Korean Air Lines incident and the Martin Luther King holiday."[109] Hunt's advisers, meanwhile, saw polls that suggested the issue was helping Helms and that, if the upcoming election polarized on the basis of the King holiday, Hunt might well lose the election.[110] About six months later, a comprehensive survey taken by the UNC School of Journalism's Carolina Poll indicated that Helms's position in the polls changed in large part because of the race issue. In April 1983, this poll reported a Hunt lead of 22 percentage points (54 to 32 percent). Prior to October 1983, according to this polling, Helms ran behind in a critical category—whites in counties with fewer blacks. While Helms led by an 18 percent margin among whites in counties with a large black population, Hunt maintained a lead of 30 percent in counties with less than 10 percent black population. Hunt identified with rural whites; he was one of their own. By the spring of 1984, however, these figures had changed radically: Helms had surged ahead by ten percentage points in the largely white counties—a turnaround of forty-two points in six months. According to the same polling, North Carolina whites overwhelmingly opposed the King holiday, no matter where they came from—by a margin of 83 to 17 percent—and Helms maintained a 38 percent lead among these whites. Those North Carolina whites who supported the holiday supported Hunt by thirty-eight points, while those indifferent about the issue were divided equally. Helms "turned that thing around," said UNC political scientist Thad Beyle, "at the point he raised the racial issue."[111]

Helms's Martin Luther King holiday filibuster provided a way to inject race into the upcoming political campaign. By raising the issue, said Guillory, the senator "sent signals that this was the genuine Helms."[112] His political organization realized the value of the King holiday fight. In February 1984, club operative David Tyson, in a memo to Ellis and Wrenn, noted that the polls were showing a movement of white voters into the Helms camp. "We have used the King holiday," along with civil rights activist Jesse Jackson's efforts to register black voters, "to spur this shift," he wrote, and he suggested that adding another issue, such as Hunt's support for District of Columbia statehood, "could open the flood gates." Because everyone knew that the District was "totally black," Helms could effectively use this issue. He suggested ads that included images of "high ID" blacks who might represent Washington in Congress.[113] Twenty-three years after the fact, Helms's political adviser Carter Wrenn admitted that Helms's noisy position on the King holiday was a matter of him "playing the race card" in order to reestablish his political stature with North Carolina voters. Polling had shown that nearly three-quarters of his electorate was opposed to the holiday, and his position was a "big political plus." His criticism of the holiday's high cost was, Wrenn thought, simply "window dressing" that made the issue more palatable to white voters. The King holiday issue made "the whole wagon shake—it didn't break it, but it made it shake." Many of the rural white voters who liked both Helms and Hunt moved into the senator's camp because of the issue. Although they did not change their minds immediately, the King holiday now made them undecided for Hunt and, subsequently, in favor of Helms.[114]

Chapter 8

A LIONHEARTED LEADER OF A GREAT AND GROWING ARMY

The Election of 1984

Because of Jesse Helms, Ronald Reagan told a Washington gathering in the senator's honor in June 1983, "our grassroots movement is alive, well, and getting stronger every month as America strides forward on the road to greatness again." With the advent of a widespread conservative revolution, Helms had become a "lionhearted leader of a great and growing army."[1] The early 1980s marked the most serious crisis in Helms's political career. His battles over the Reagan Revolution during the early 1980s required most of his skills as a political fighter, media manipulator, and parliamentarian. Oddly, although his party controlled the White House and the Senate, Helms functioned as an outsider, and his bomb throwing did not end with the Reagan presidency. Over time, the stakes grew higher: he was determined to sustain the conservative revolution beyond the confines of the Reagan presidency. Serving as a conscience of the right, Helms insistently advocated conservative causes, even when his advocacy headed nowhere. Seemingly losing credibility, in Jim Hunt he faced the most significant challenge of his political career, and the fight to keep his Senate seat would be a massive battle that tested his political abilities and the skill and potency of his political organization. The Helms-Hunt senatorial race in 1984, as one Congressional Club worker put it, was a "war."[2]

SOON AFTER HELMS'S return from Washington in December 1982, club operative Tom Fetzer remembered seeing the senator enter the club offices having "limped back" to North Carolina after his unsuccessful filibuster of the gas tax. Jesse arrived sporting a V-neck sweater and a tie and an old tweed hat, and carrying an old leather briefcase. Club operatives had bad news for him.[3] Arthur Finkelstein presented Helms with what Wrenn remembered was a "terrible poll" that suggested overwhelming Hunt support among North Carolina voters. Winning reelection, his advisers warned, would be a long, uphill struggle. Out of a combination of indifference and a sense of self-preservation, Helms awarded Ellis wide discretion in managing political affairs: the only exceptions were Jesse's insistence on reviewing fund-raising letters and in reviewing political ads. Only rarely did Ellis and Wrenn permit Helms to see polls. Early in the senatorial campaign of 1972, Finkelstein had shown Helms a poll that suggested that his name recognition was low in North Carolina and that he trailed his opponent, Nick Galifianakis, by twenty points. Jesse refused to believe the polls, insisting that Finkelstein tell him whom he had polled. Helms thereafter went into a deep funk about the poll results.

Now, in late 1982, Helms would hear the bad news. The chief problem, according to Finkelstein, was Helms's astoundingly high unfavorables (well into the high 30 percent range) and low favorables (somewhere close to 40 percent), combined with Hunt's rating of nearly 70 percent favorable and 20 percent unfavorable.[4] With Helms running nearly 25 points behind Hunt, Finkelstein told Helms that he would not easily bring down his own unfavorables: he had been senator for twelve years, and the people who disliked him would continue to oppose him no matter what. Ellis, meanwhile, argued that Helms should continue to represent the conservative cause. Helms responded that it was unlikely that he would run again; he had promised Dot, he said, that they would return to North Carolina. Finkelstein then asked a telling question. What if he could wave a magic wand and return to the Senate for six more years? Would he then want to run again? "Well, sure I would," responded Jesse. "I love serving in the Senate."

With Helms's approval, Ellis and Wrenn agreed to mount a massive, media-driven campaign to resurrect Jesse as a candidate. While Helms established a political image of strength and character to white voters in North Carolina through his congressional obstructionism, his political machine sought to define Hunt as a vascillating, weak personality. The campaign against Hunt, Jesse's political managers concluded, depended on which candidate voters disliked less. The Helms campaign would pursue a relentless character attack on Jim Hunt that would seek to raise his unfavorable rating to something close to Helms's high levels—and thus even the playing field. The campaign, recalled Mark Stephens, required "transforming Hunt into a liberal and liar." The Helms campaign group decided to adopt this strategy by late 1982. "Moving Hunt's unfavorables," said Wrenn, "was really all that election was about."[5]

For their part, the Hunt forces saw the goal of banishing Jesse to political oblivion as a sort of crusade. Democratic pollster and political consultant R. Harrison Hickman recalled attending the National Governors Association meeting in August 1981 in Atlantic City, where he ran into Hunt adviser Gary Pearce on the boardwalk. Pearce asked Hickman whether he thought that Hunt should challenge Helms in 1984. Considering the question, Hickman responded that he believed that Hunt would do better, if he had any ambition about eventually running for president, to defer a Senate campaign until 1986, when he could run against John East, who Hickman thought was a weaker and more vulnerable candidate. What did Pearce think? "Some things," Pearce told Hickman, "are more important," and he believed that Hunt should conduct a crusade to remove Helms from the Senate. Hunt himself was convinced that the "paramount" consideration was removing Jesse Helms from the Senate.[6]

But Hunt had little idea of what lay before him. Beginning in the spring of 1983, fully eighteen months before the election, Helms's political operatives began a massive political advertising campaign that filled printed media and the airwaves, and the governor would experience more negative ads run against him than any other candidate in American history. Although there were sporadic ads put out by both sides as early as 1981, the Helms forces began in earnest in April 1983, when they ran ads in 150 small-town newspapers and aired spots on seventy-two radio stations in small- and medium-sized towns. The radio ads, broadcast three times a day, saturated North Carolina media markets outside the urban areas; according to one estimate, between April and June 1983, Helms's message went out fourteen thousand times. The intensive media campaign cost about $20,000 per week, and by the fall that would increase to as much as $50,000 a week. The Helms campaign attacked Hunt for relying on out-of-state fund-raising, using state aircraft for political events, and associating with liberals such as Edward Kennedy and former Minnesota senator Walter F. Mondale.

The ads struck hard on issues of race, asserting a close connection between Hunt and the civil rights establishment. Jesse Jackson, who was running a campaign for the Democratic nomination for president in 1984 that registered and mobilized thousands of black voters, became an especially potent symbol. One Hunt adviser later said, referring to a notorious television ad run by George H. W. Bush's presidential campaign, in 1988, that the Helms campaign transformed Jackson into a menacing racial symbol, the "Willie Horton of '84." In their ads, the Helms campaign found the "darkest, most threatening pictures" of Jackson in order to demonize him politically.[7] Hunt, the ads suggested, was leading a massive drive on the part of African Americans to seek political power. In a radio ad, civil rights leader Julian Bond was described as the head of a fictitious "Black Pac" and a Hunt supporter. A widely run newspaper ad featured a photograph of Hunt sitting with Jesse Jackson in a March 1983 meeting in the governor's mansion. "Gov. James B. Hunt, Jr., wants the State Board of Elections to boost minority voter registration in North Carolina," read the ad. "Ask yourself: Is this a proper use of taxpayer funds?" Another newspaper ad showed six teachers, all black, holding "On Strike!" signs, with a caption that read "Jim Hunt's Union Payroll Checkoff."[8]

Helms's newspaper and radio attacks continued through the summer of 1983, by which time his campaign had spent $697,000 on the advertising campaign, which included 3,937 ads in 167 newspapers, 353 commercials on fifteen TV stations, and 25,542 commercials on one hundred radio stations. Helms's media campaign of the spring and summer of 1983 reached an estimated cumulative audience of 25 million people.[9] In the summer of 1983, the Helms campaign began using television. The first spots were, in contrast to the newspaper and radio media, softer. They sought to restore Jesse's reputation among Republicans, which Finkelstein's polling showed had weakened; in thirty-second ads, President Reagan praised Jesse's courage, compassion, and effectiveness.[10] In other spots, Republicans such as Bob Dole and Howard Baker testified to Helms's integrity. The ads also emphasized Helms's common touch: in one, Reagan declared that the major tax cut adopted by Congress in 1981 was for "working Americans," who paid "this nation's bills and need higher taxes like they need a plague of locusts." Concluding with a picture of Jesse in the background, the narrator announced: "Jesse Helms: working for all of us."

Helms's massive media campaign depended on the Congressial Club's continued success in raising large amounts of money through direct mail. Because of the club, Helms was better positioned than any other senatorial campaign in the country during 1984, and, in the first half of the year, the club raised $1.73 million, while it spent $1.54 million. As the candidates entered 1984, it was estimated that Helms would have nearly $14 million at his disposal as a war chest. This was far ahead of any other senatorial candidate: the next highest-spending senatorial candidate, Rudy Boschwitz of Minnesota, spent $282,442 during the same period. But the Helms campaign spent nearly everything they raised on constant barrages of advertising, and frequently ran ahead of the revenue flow.[11]

In these early months of the campaign, the Hunt campaign refused to respond to Helms's media barrage. Hunt strategists worried about running out of money: can you imagine anything worse, they told each other, than, a month before the election, having no funds on hand? In one of the ironies of this campaign, Hunt's more conservative spending strategy resulted in a surplus at the end of the campaign of nearly $800,000. Late in the contest, Hunt's fund-raisers tapped a strong anti-Helms sentiment nationally, but as funds rolled in the campaign was simply unable to spend the money. In contrast, the Helms team lived dangerously: they spent everything they raised, and they lived month to month, usually in debt. Helms himself had little understanding of these intricacies. Ellis recalled that the only time that Helms visited the campaign headquarters in Raleigh was a few days before the election, when he and Dot sat down with Wrenn. While Jesse was "tight," said Ellis, Dot was "tighter." Both of the Helmses wanted assurances that there would be no campaign debt remaining once the election was over. With Wrenn managing the money flow, he and Ellis played it like riverboat gamblers. "Their strategic decision about money," said one Hunt adviser years later, "was right, and ours was wrong." Underfunded and hampered by conservative financing, they were always attempting to catch up.[12]

HELMS FACED A twenty-point deficit for much of 1982–83, but, by November 1983, in an October poll by North Carolina Opinion Research, the margin had now narrowed to six points.[13] Only at this point, after eight months of Helms's unchallenged ad campaign, did Hunt make a counterattack by buying $50,000 in radio spots that attacked Helms for inadequately protecting Social Security, weakly defending the tobacco program, and for voting for tax relief for oil companies while seeking to end subsidized school lunches.[14] Hunt's radio ads of November 1983 provided an opening for a major theme in the Helms campaign. Taking out a full-page ad in the *Raleigh News and Observer,* Jesse announced that he was "disappointed" in Hunt's radio ads; he also pointed out that Hunt had repeatedly ducked invitations to debate. Now, he was told, Hunt had hired a New York advertising firm to create radio commercials that intentionally distorted his record. Helms had never tried to disguise his positions, he claimed, and he suggested that Hunt was a typical, unprincipled politician. "Not everyone agreed with my opposition to the Martin Luther King national holiday," Jesse wrote, "but they knew where I stood. Where did you stand, Jim?"

Helms then went into a "where did you stand, Jim?" litany on issues of the gas tax increase, Reagan's Grenada invasion, busing, school prayer. The list could go on, he wrote, but he asked Hunt to address issues "on which you have been silent."[15]

Helms's "Where Do You Stand, Jim?" letter led into a series of ten-second TV ads that began airing in early December 1983. The shift in Helms's political message reflected a conscious decision by the Helms managers. Originally, they had intended to pull back from the media campaign and spend about $1 million on media in January 1984, as both candidates prepared to make formal announcements. But Hunt's radio attacks changed matters. Wrenn favored radio ads, while Ellis preferred television. With their coffers nearly empty, they had little to spend on a television campaign. Why not run ten-second ads? asked Finkelstein. They then told Bob Harris, who in September 1985 became the subject of a feature story on CBS's *60 Minutes* and was bedridden because of muscular dystrophy, to produce some scripts. While still a student at N.C. State, in the summer of 1977 Harris had started working with the club as a volunteer opening mail. Noticing Harris, Wrenn wanted to find something that Harris was physically better able to do. Ellis suggested that he read the clips that were coming in from a newspaper service; he marked these up and sent them to Ellis. After Harris graduated in 1978, Ellis hired him full-time, and Harris wrote most of the organization's fund-raising letters. In the John East campaign of 1980, Harris pulled together materials for many of the negative ads against Morgan, and he was so effective that, after 1981—though completely confined to his bed—Harris became the club's chief researcher. When Wrenn went to Washington, for part of 1981 to set up East's Senate office, Harris ran things in Raleigh along wth James P. Cain, another operative. For the 1984 campaign, Harris, said to have a photographic memory, scoured Hunt's legislative and political record, amassing a huge file and working closely with strategists and ad production people. All ads began with research: the campaign team would let Harris know about an idea, and he produced bullet points and a draft script for an ad. Harris's material was then dispatched to Alex Castellanos and Earl Ashe. The club also began to videotape Hunt's public appearances, and to keep files of tape for later use.

Another club operative, Mark Stephens, ran Helms's 1984 campaign on a day-to-day basis. The son of a retired military man who had lived around the country, Stephens moved to North Carolina in the 1970s, worked as a banker in the eastern North Carolina town of Clinton, and then became drawn into conservative politics. In 1979, he read a newspaper article about

Tom Ellis, and he wrote to him expressing interest. Soon he received a phone call inviting him to join the club as a paid staffer. Although he had a wife and three children—and although the position paid very little—Stephens joined the cause. Working in the East and Lake campaigns in 1980 and North Carolina congressional races in 1982, Stephens became an important part of the club's operation. He remembered the organization as an assemblage of "cause-oriented…twenty-five-year old kids," with one of them, Wrenn, in charge, and with Ellis, a "real genius" presiding over things from afar.[16]

Also providing important advice was Charlie Black, who periodically visited North Carolina from his Washington office.[17] Black, who in 1984 served as a campaign strategist for Reagan's presidential campaign and Phil Gramm's race for a Texas Senate seat, had become a Washington insider who operated a high-priced lobbying and political consulting business. Lee Atwater, who served as Reagan's deputy campaign manager and would later mastermind George H. W. Bush's 1988 presidential victory, joined Black's firm in 1985. Black and Atwater usually sought to drive up opponents' negatives—precisely the same strategy that the Helms campaign was using. Atwater later recalled that candidates whose negatives were higher than thirty or forty percentage points "just inevitably lost." "One of the conclusions I've reached," Atwater said, was that "in a two-man race, if one of the candidates can't win, and the other one is yours, you are going to come out all right."[18]

With Black advising on general strategy, the media came through Wrenn, Harris, and Ashe. Although the club hierarchy usually heavily edited Harris's scripts, the "Where Do You Stand, Jim?" ads remained intact. After speaking with Wrenn, Harris faxed eight of them—all emphasizing the "Where Do You Stand, Jim" theme—and the campaign agreed to run them. Finkelstein, according to Wrenn, "just fell in love with them," and without changing a word, they were dispatched to the production facility. The "Where Do You Stand, Jim?" ads marked a thematic turn in the Helms campaign: while earlier their ads had attempted to polarize ideologically, the new ads stressed character and Hunt's integrity. As a sitting governor, Hunt remained at a disadvantage: he had a track record of brokering compromise, but compromise could be portrayed as weakness, vacillation, and a lack of character. In contrast, as part of this re-created mosaic, Helms's obstructionism became transformed into unflinching, unwavering character. The Helms message focused on values, strength, and trust, while Hunt emphasized the issues. The "Where Do You Stand, Jim?" theme resonated with voters. The ads had a "viral" impact that shaped voters' attitudes,

Hickman remembered, and the slogan became a part of the political lingo, with a "powerful impact."[19]

The Helms campaign continued to emphasize Hunt's flip-flopping. Wrenn remembered that voters perceived the important issues as not left/right ideology but character. The entire focus of the election, he recalled, shifted after December 1983: the Helms campaign had discovered Hunt's Achilles heel. The attack strategy "just stuck," Harris recalled. Helms stressed his consistency and Hunt's inconsistency on issues such as Reagan's tax cuts, the King holiday, aid to Nicaragua, the gas tax, the Social Security system, school prayer, and the Grenada invasion.[20] After both candidates had formally announced in early 1984, the TV war heated up even further. An ad endorsed by "Teachers for Helms"—which reporters quickly described as a bogus organization that contained five members, two of whom were not teachers—suggested that Hunt's reputation as an education governor was an exaggeration. "Our SAT scores are near the bottom nationally," the narrator declared, and Hunt's education board chief said that "our schools are failing." "Our children are not to blame," said another ad produced about the same time, and they were the true victims. Jim Hunt bore responsibility for a poor school system. In other spots, Helms continued attacks on Hunt's reputation as an educational reformer. Ads appearing in late March and early April 1984, displaying statistics illustrating North Carolina's educational backwardness, concluded that Hunt's program did "more for his political image than for education." "After eight years as the self-proclaimed 'Education Governor,'" said another ad, "Jim Hunt appointed a commission to study education, and study education, and study education. Isn't that just like a politician in an election year?"[21]

The Helms campaign became adept at rapid production of ads: the creative team of Harris, Wrenn, Finkelstein, and Ashe arranged with studios to have access to their facilities whenever they needed them. On occasion, local TV producers would tip off Robert Holding and the media-buying team about an upcoming Hunt ad, and this provided additional time to mount a response. The Helms managers became effective at reacting swiftly to any Hunt attacks—usually they responded within twenty-four hours—and their organization and media production provided a significant advantage. The Helms campaign also succeeded in running these ads over a long period of time without losing the voters' attention or expending their patience. There was a "drip, drip, drip" effect that chipped away at Hunt's political integrity, *Raleigh News and Observer* reporter Rob Christensen later noted, and in the "easy, single strategy" of bringing Hunt down, the Helms people were clever, inventive, and often used humor to diffuse a possible backlash. Jesse's political advertising eventually reached North Carolina's swing voters, especially less-educated white voters, and, combined with Helms's noisy stand on the Martin Luther King holiday, left an indelible political image in the public mind. The Helms attacks remained unanswered; the governor's pollster, Peter Hart, did not poll between the spring of 1983 and Christmas of that year, and when he did poll he discovered that Hunt's double-digit lead had disappeared.

The Hunt campaign only began television advertising in earnest in February 1984.[22] While one set of television ads criticized Helms for his support of a tax on cigarettes in 1982, in radio spots Hunt blasted the senator for his support of Reagan's tax cuts and his indifference toward education. Hunt also claimed that Helms had ineffectively represented North Carolina: "the job of the senator from North Carolina," said Hunt in a radio ad, was not to be the "senator from New York or California somewhere," but the "senator from North Carolina." "We need people who can get things done," he said on another occasion, "not crusaders and lone rangers."[23] Helms continued to hit Hunt hard, from a variety of angles. In one series of ads, he attacked the governor for supporting the Panama Canal treaties, which, the ad claimed, "opened the door" for Central American Communism.[24] In February 1984, Hunt attended the National Governors Association meeting and endorsed a proposed $217 billion deficit-reduction package that included a combination of tax increases and spending cuts, but he also said that he opposed a general tax increase. The Helms campaign then ran ads accusing him of favoring tax increases. Further advertising on the tax issue suggested that Hunt was straddling the fence.[25]

On March 5, the Helms campaign unleashed a TV ad that took on Hunt's assertions about out-of-state fund-raising: at campaign appearances and in radio ads, Hunt had asserted that Jesse should be the senator from North Carolina, not from Massachusetts, or New Jersey, or California. At the end of February 1984, Hunt raised $130,000 at two New York City benefits, and Bob Harris sent the information over to Earl Ashe, whose "eyes just lit up," and he rushed into Wrenn's office.[26] Ashe then produced radio and television ads juxtaposing Hunt's criticisms of Helms's out-of-state fund-raising with the name and address of the pro-Hunt New York fund-raising committee. "Where do you stand, Jim?" the narrator declared. The ads, remembered Wrenn, "hit Hunt in the character solar plexus." The "only consistent fiber in Jim Hunt," said Claude Allen, was that "he's inconsistent." The real issue, he said on another occasion, was "Jim Hunt's credibility."[27] When Hunt responded at a press conference on March 14 by explaining that young, recent UNC graduates had organized the New York event, the Helms campaign quickly produced another round of ads. After displaying video of Hunt's press conference, the narrator asked incredulously: "Young people from North Carolina?" and then listed honorary co-chairs who included New York governor Mario Cuomo. Saying that "there is something wrong here," the narrator urged viewers to write to the New York Committee to Elect Jim Hunt to get a complete list of those involved.[28]

By early 1984, North Carolina media markets were saturated with political advertising. According to one report, by August 1984, before the official Labor Day beginning of the campaign, commercials for either Hunt or Helms had appeared at least fifteen thousand times, consuming 125 hours of viewing time, with eleven thousand spots for Helms, four thousand for Hunt.[29] "His pounding for 14 months when we couldn't answer on television obviously took its toll," Hunt told a reporter in June 1984. "He got away with an awful lot, and it has hurt, without question."[30] The Helms campaign possessed overwhelming resources, having raised during 1983 about three times as much money as their opponents ($4.4 million versus $1.4 million) and spent about six and a half times as much ($4.2 millon versus $645,000). During 1984, the money would continue to flow, and when the campaign had ended it would be, by far, the most expensive senatorial race in history, with Helms spending significantly more than Hunt, about $13 million versus $8 million. About $10 per registered voter, this amount was estimated to be enough to pay the salaries of all one hundred senators for three years.[31]

Meanwhile, the Helms political machine had grown into a huge operation. As it became more skilled at fund-raising, the Congressional Club—which had become the National Congressional Club—had spun off its media production to Jefferson Marketing, but the line dividing the two entities was unclear. Following the 1982 elections, North Carolina Democrats, led by U.S. representative Charles Rose, filed suit with the Federal Election Commission, claiming that Jefferson Marketing had provided its production services at below-market rates, thus constituting an illegal campaign contribution. Although the lawsuit's results were not made public until after the election, it eventually exposed how the existence of the club and Jefferson Marketing only thinly disguised a unified political operation. Thirty-two of the Jefferson Marketing employees previously worked for the club; the two entities shared office space; and Jefferson Marketing never reported a profit. Jefferson Marketing was a wholly owned subsidiary of the

Educational Support Foundation, with Tom Ellis, Wrenn, and Ellis's son-in-law, Eden attorney Terrence Boyle, as trustees. Helms remained entirely insulated from these relationships, in what political reporter Ferrel Guillory called the "many pieces of the Helms empire."[32]

AS HUNT CONTINUED to criticize Helms for his positions on tobacco, tax cuts, and the economy, he also began to attack Helms for his foreign policy positions. On May 11, Hunt accused Helms of conducting an independent foreign policy in El Salvador through his support for right-wing politicians such as Roberto D'Aubuisson and, implicitly, death squads.[33] In May and June, in speeches and interviews, Hunt continued to criticize Helms's involvement with the Salvadoran right and charged that he had been "sabotaging" American foreign policy. Helms had offended "everyone from President Reagan to Barry Goldwater and his Senate colleagues," and this demonstrated that he could not "effectively and constructively represent the people of this state."[34] Tensions over Helms's Central American policy, and his relations with the Salvadoran right, flared up in June 1984 at the state Republican convention in Raleigh. The Helms campaign was enraged by the media's coverage of the senator's involvement in the Salvadoran presidential elections and the foiled plot against U.S. ambassador Thomas Pickering. In the heat of the campaign, there was also a cumulative resentment against the press: big-city reporters were seen as the enemy— as working hand-in-hand with the Hunt campaign.

The *N&O* especially attracted the hostility of Helms supporters, who viewed it as an arm of the Democratic Party. The newspaper was sensitive to this criticism: although its editorial pages were openly critical of the senator, the news side made an effort to remain impartial. In 1984, the *N&O* cut ties with an in-state pollster and contracted with the Gallup poll to provide a more "legitimate, thorough" source of polling data.[35] But all this meant little to Helms supporters, and during the 1984 campaign there was a marked change in attitude toward the press, with unusually restrictive limitations over access to the senator. The press secretary, Claude Allen, operated under strict control, and rarely had any information. Because Helms's positions were so absolute, the press secretary had little work to do. As one reporter remembered, "my five-and-a-half-year-old daughter could be his press secretary."[36]

Much of their anger against the *Raleigh News and Observer* was directed at its lead political reporter, Rob Christensen. His relationship with the

Helms forces had been deteriorating. In the early 1980s, when he wrote stories suggesting that Helms's social conservatism was endangering the to-bacco program, Helms and John East delivered speeches denouncing him by name, while Helms attacked him in the weekly columns that he distrib-uted to small-town newspapers. Christensen recalled that while he worked as the *N&O* correspondent in Washington he once took a cab driven, he discovered, by a North Carolina native. When the cabbie learned his name, he told Christensen that he still received a subscription to his hometown newspaper. "Wait a minute," he told him, "you're the one who's not fair to Jesse Helms." By 1984, relations were so poor with Helms that he had cut off Christensen and refused to speak with him.[37]

Not long before, the *N&O* quoted a report claiming that Reagan had called Helms into the Oval Office and reprimanded him. Helms's support-ers claimed that the report ignored a statement from Howard Baker deny-ing the existence of any reprimand. On June 23, at the Republican state convention, with Christensen and another *N&O* reporter, Dan Hoover, in attendance, John East attacked the "liberal" media in a speech. Club worker David Tyson then offered a resolution—with Wrenn's approval—charging the *N&O* with "distortions and attempts to cover up the truth," describing the newspaper as the "Jim Hunt hit squad," and calling for the eviction of all *N&O* reporters. Before the convention could even debate Tyson's mo-tion, the crowd rose to its feet, and convention chairman Barry McCarty, a fundamentalist minister from Elizabeth City, called for the two reporters to leave the building. The crowd, many of whom were cursing while standing in their chairs, cheered as the two reporters were escorted from the build-ing. "The cancer," exclaimed McCarty, "has been removed." After they left, cooler heads prevailed, and gubernatorial nominee Jim Martin and Greensboro Republican Eugene Johnston persuaded the convention to readmit the reporters. Later, Christensen approached McCarty. "Barry," he said, "I've got some news for you. The cancer is back." Not long afterward, Helms called Christensen to say he had nothing to do with his eviction from the convention.[38]

HUNT'S SHARP ATTACKS on El Salvador culminated in a thirty-second TV ad, first appearing on June 27—while D'Aubuisson was visiting the United States under Helms's sponsorship. The ad opened with black-and-white still photographs of dead Salvadorans, with the sound of machine guns firing in the background. "This is what they do—death squads in El Sal-vador," said the narrator. "Men, women and children—murdered in cold blood." The ad flashed a picture of D'Aubuisson, identifying him as the "man accused of directing those death squads," and introduced Helms as "the man whose aides helped D'Aubuisson set up a political party in El Salvador," as his "best friend in Washington, maybe his only friend." As the picture of D'Aubuisson disappeared, Helms's image grew larger. "Now Jesse Helms might be a crusader," said the narrator in the closer, "but that's not what our senator should be crusading for."[39] The ad—soon known as the "dead bodies ad"—reflected a desperate desire on the part of the Hunt campaign to gain the momentum and to arrest the slippage in the polls by piercing Helms's image of integrity and morality.

Hunt campaign advisers remained divided about the dead bodies ad. To a certain extent, there was a generational divide, as young advisers advocated attack ads that hit Helms hard, while others—including the governor himself—remained squeamish. Hunt's poll numbers had stagnated, and it appeared to many that "we had to do something to shake up the race."[40] The Helms camp responded immediately. The senator continued to deny that he was associated with D'Aubuisson, and his only interest was in ensuring that fair elections occurred in El Salvador. As for the ads, Helms took the high road, declaring that he had "thought better of the governor than that." He added that Hunt knew "as much about foreign policy as a pig does about roller-skating."[41] More important, perhaps, the Helms campaign immediately responded on the airwaves. In an ad that appeared within days of the Hunt attack about El Salvador, the Helms campaign produced a spot that opened with a clip from Hunt in which he said he opposed attack ads. The spot then showed the Hunt commercial. "Jim, you've gone too far," said the narrator, "you've crossed the line of decency and fair play, just to gain political office." Another ad made the same point. "What kind of man," it said, "would attempt to tie his opponent to murders just to gain political office? Jim Hunt's political ads tell you more about Jim Hunt than Jesse Helms."[42]

It is difficult to assess whether Hunt's attack ads backfired, although some have come to that conclusion. For the time being, those in the Hunt campaign favoring a softer campaign prevailed, while others continued to disagree. "If we were going to take the shit," remembered Gary Pearce, then "we may as well get the benefit." He believed that the El Salvador ad was a "pretty good ad" and "very powerful."[43] Because Hunt almost immediately dropped the spots, they appeared to have had little overall effect, and if anything they suggested the continuing defensive position that the governor occupied. Mark Stephens later observed that the dead bodies ad was flawed chiefly because it was not believable and thus held little appeal to swing voters looking for a reason to vote for Hunt. In focus groups, Harrison Hickman found that participants were most concerned about the ad's emphasis on foreign affairs rather than on matters of importance to North Carolinians. Why was Hunt so concerned about what's going on in Central America, people in the focus group wondered.[44]

In response to Hunt's aggressiveness, the Helms campaign moved on the offensive. The issue of race had already figured into the campaign, as Helms used his positions on the King holiday and Hunt's associations with North Carolina black leaders to emphasize racial differences. Race had already become a marker in the campaign that was reemphasized periodically in the campaign. The methods of communicating the race issue were subtle. On February 8, for example, Helms sent out a fund-raising letter that urged contributions in order to counteract Jesse Jackson. The letter, mentioning Jackson twenty-four times, warned of his efforts to register black voters. The demonization of Jesse Jackson was working. While he inspired a large number of black voters to register, he also became a negative symbol, according to a Democrat, "with a vengeance." He was exploited as symbol that could "stir up the old conflicts and the old hatreds." One Helms flyer displayed pictures of Helms and Reagan on one side, and Hunt and Jackson on the other. "Where Do You Stand," it read, "Helms-Reagan [or] Hunt-Jackson?" Helms himself admitted that Hunt needed an "enormous black vote" in order to win but that if "enough of our people go to the polls it will be OK."[45]

The use of race continued to figure significantly in Helms's strategy late in the campaign. White audiences immediately recognized his racialized political rhetoric, though very often proxies communicated the message. In early August 1984, for example, GOP state chairman David Flaherty sent out a fund-raising letter to 45,000 people in North Carolina urging whites to the polls, and he warned of some "important and frightening" new black voter registration that could prove "disastrous." Jesse Jackson, the letter said, was registering millions of minorities in a "new and frightening racist campaign." Flaherty would later tell an oral history interviewer that "we used race...because we knew we couldn't beat Jim Hunt on issues."[46] Late in the campaign, moreover, Helms operatives sent out bogus postcards to registered voters in predominantly black districts asking that the post office return undeliverable items. Reporters speculated that this was a way to identify registrants with incorrect or inaccurate addresses so that they could be challenged at the polls.[47]

There was, however, a gap between how Helms campaigned and his self-image: he considered charges of racism to be outrageous. Anyone who knew him, he often declared, would regard him as anything but racist. African Americans who knew Helms were, however, almost always in a subordinate position; he was especially friends with Senate custodial workers and security officers, who were overwhelmingly black.[48] Nonetheless, in response to charges that he was using the race issue politically, for the first time Helms began to incorporate African Americans into his inner circle during the 1984 campaign. In an effort assisted by Reagan aide Bill Keyes, more African Americans appeared in prominent positions. Claude Allen, his black press secretary, played a visible campaign role, and Helms allied himself with former NFL football player Roosevelt Grier, a conservative evangelical. In January, Helms announced that he would try to improve "one-on-one" communications with blacks, and he stumped with Grier in Greensboro.[49]

The disjuncture between Helms's overtly political use of race and his self-perception became apparent during October, when he visited the all-black Livingstone College, in Salisbury, at its weekly campus assembly. No doubt, there was a political motive—a desire to tone down the heated rhetoric and to reassure moderate whites—and Helms had been urged by Finkelstein to seek the votes of those undecided whites who "might choke Jesse down if they don't think he's a racist." Provide these voters with some evidence that indicated that the senator was not a racist, Finkelstein told Helms. The Livingstone visit was "purely calculated politically," according to Wrenn. "The sorry truth of this whole tale," he said, was that "it was all calculated, it was all racial politics, and that what we were after were some moderate whites. . . . If we could just get the smell off the skunk, they might vote for Jesse."[50]

Helms nonetheless encountered a hostile reception at Livingstone. Students organized a boycott of his appearance, and about 150 of them stood locked arm-in-arm in a silent vigil outside of the college's Varick Auditorium. In an exchange with the protesting group, a student refused to shake Helms's hand, and the senator responded: "Just the same, I love you." With faculty and about two dozen students inside the auditorium, Helms told the group that he would not "engage in any pretense about this election." He realized "how you're going to vote"; he knew this "when I came in here." Yet he believed that Livingstone students protesting outside the auditorium were "shooting themselves in the foot" by not coming inside. "One thing's for certain," he said. "They will not learn anything about where I stand by standing out there." African Americans had been taken for granted, he said, and they should "wake up and smell the coffee and realize that the Democratic Party has been jerking you around for 35 years." If students wanted to boycott, he respected that, but "at least I came here to tell you where I stand." He was seeking, he said, a dialogue with blacks after the election that would be rooted in a "common denominator" of "faith in the Lord." If Jesse hoped to portray himself as open-minded, it cannot be said that the Livingstone visit was a success. A confrontational question-and-answer period followed. When asked about the heritage of slavery, Helms asserted that the "people that brought the slaves over here were the blacks themselves" and that "I never owned a slave, I wouldn't own a slave, [and] doubt my family ever owned a slave." Federal programs should not, he believed, identify an individual "because his grandparents or great-grandparents were mistreated." The free enterprise system was open to everyone, he claimed.[51]

But the disjuncture between Helms's self-perception and his political impact on race remained. Immediately after the visit, Helms called Wrenn, pleased about the confrontation and certain that he had scored political points: the black student's refusal to shake his hand had violated North Carolina's etiquette of civility. "He played that like a fiddle," said Wrenn.[52] Helms's conceptions of race and the way he perceived interactions with blacks as individuals clashed with his raw use of race and racial attitudes. "The overriding impression" of observing Helms in such a setting, noted veteran North Carolina political reporter Jack Betts, was that the senator was "not only uncomfortable before a black audience, but that he does not know how to handle himself, does not understand the people he is facing and does not know what to do." His comments about slavery suggested that, in his worldview, "blacks themselves were responsible for slavery, while whites had nothing to do with it." Unlike other politicians who had adapted their political styles to the new, post–Voting Rights Act political system, Helms had not changed. Even in making "obvious overtures to blacks," Helms remained less than "comfortable with the idea."[53] Roy Parker, writing in the *Fayetteville Times,* noted that Helms considered himself the "great and faithful friend of black North Carolina." The truth was that the achievement of civil rights had occurred "over the unrelenting opposition of the man who is now North Carolina's senior senator." During the 1950s and 1960s, Helms opposed integration "with a vengeance—every march, every boycott, every act of Congress." Jesse believed that the problem was less a matter of racist policies and laws and more the fault of the people "who paraded down the streets in protest against those policies."[54]

HELMS'S USE OF race during the campaign of 1984 was far more overt and confrontational than it had been either in 1972 or 1978. So also was his use of a new set of cultural issues that had bubbled to the surface in the late 1970s and early 1980s. Helms's incorporation of these issues—and the constituencies behind them—foresaw a major late-twentieth-century political development: the emergence of the Christian Right. In the 1970s, Helms had carefully cultivated fundamentalists as a political constituency. During the 1978 Senate campaign, Arthur Finkelstein had conducted a poll, at Ellis's request, asking voters if they would be more likely to vote for Jesse if they knew that he was a "dedicated Christian." The response was overwhelmingly positive, and Ellis began using "Jesse Helms, a Dedicated Christian" as part of the tagline accompanying his political ads.[55]

In 1984, the Helms campaign realized that they needed an evangelical mobilization in order to win the election. They simply needed additional votes, and those votes, they knew, would not come from black voters and would come only in insufficient numbers from most white voters. The most important cluster group would be white evangelicals, a group that was historically nonpolitical. Only through a massive mobilization would that vote help Helms win the election.[56] Helms often told fundamentalist audiences how he relied on prayer in the Senate, and he spoke of God's role in the campaign. Christians were "confronted daily by direct attacks," he told a group in February 1984. Children were no longer permitted to pray in schools, abortion and pornography had become legally protected rights, and homosexuality was "just another 'lifestyle.'" Christianity was "our birthright," but there was "encircling gloom" seeking to overwhelm it.[57] He had "never once run into trouble," he said to one group in April 1984, "when I first prayed for guidance."[58] Secular humanism was a "false religion, but a religion nonetheless," he wrote to an evangelical supporter in July 1982.[59] Though sometimes "subtle," secular humanists sought to "confuse and deceive" Christians through a "cacophony of voices—political, news media, television, movies—mocking the very moral and spiritual base from which America grew to greatness." The time had passed to permit a distinction between public life and morality. Those that favored freedom of religion, he claimed, really meant "freedom *from* religion," and "in doing so they are running full tilt against the very meaning of America."[60]

Promoting an agenda of "profamily, promoral" laws, school prayer, opposition to abortion, and a strong national defense, Helms appealed to evangelical voters. In February 1983, the Moral Majority decided to commit to an effort to register new voters. In July, Helms joined Falwell in a statewide tour that sought to increase white registration, using evangelical

churches as voter registration centers and ministers and church leaders as
workers. Falwell described efforts to register "the kind of people who make
a difference," and an objective of enlisting some 200,000 new voters in
North Carolina.[61] Efforts to build a grassroots evangelical network in North
Carolina included the Reverend Lamar Mooneyham, who headed the
Moral Majority's state chapter, and Coy Privette, who headed the Christian Action League, which came into existence during the late 1970s as part
of efforts to defeat liquor-by-the-drink referenda. Leading the Moral Majority's voter mobilization efforts was Ron Godwin. In 1977, he had begun
work with Falwell at Liberty College, but by 1979 he was managing the
Moral Majority headquarters in Washington. In the morning, five days
a week, he flew on a Cessna 214 twin-engine plane from Lynchburg to
Washington's National Airport; in the evenings, he flew back and spent the
night with his family. Godwin coordinated with national conservatives, and
in the early 1980s participated in the morning strategy sessions taking place
around Richard Viguerie's kitchen table, where he made plans with other
movement conservatives. He and Viguerie struck up an alliance; Viguerie
would later call Godwin his "best friend." During the late 1970s, Godwin
hurriedly assembled Moral Majority chapters in all fifty states, and the
business of constructing a political organization was all-consuming. In addition, on a national level, he also mounted an effort to register white evangelicals. Godwin went to Lee Atwater, then on Reagan's 1984 reelection
campaign, and persuaded him to provide seed money for voter registration.
Working with the American Coalition for Traditional Values and backed
by a large budget and the support of major religious leaders such as Falwell,
Jim Bakker, Jimmy Swaggart, James Robison, and Kenneth Copeland,
Godwin sought to politicize the large white evangelical vote.[62]

The North Carolina Moral Majority was closely associated with the
Congressional Club; Godwin described his organization as its "appendage."
The club concurrently ran its own aggressive effort to register white evangelicals, as campaign manager Mark Stephens hired seven or eight "kids,"
many of whom were from the conservative evangelical Bob Jones University, and they worked with churches in voter registration. Stephens recalled
this as a "slow, laborious effort" that eventually brought results. The efforts
of the club and Moral Majority were intertwined, and they involved circulating flyers in church lobbies and setting up voter registration tables to recruit new voters after church, as well as running phone banks, door-to-door
canvassing, and direct mail appeals. The Moral Majority/American Coalition for Traditional Values campaign depended especially on evangelical

churches, whose congregations served as local-level organizations to spur registration and turnout. Especially important were the new megachurches, with large numbers of members, though much of the effort was also focused on identifying unregistered voters in the many, scattered evangelical churches across the state. Although ministers could not legally (because of IRS regulations about the churches' nonprofit status) overtly campaign for Helms, they often urged congregants to support candidates opposed to abortion, gay rights, and other moral issues—which, in the Senate race, meant Jesse. The line distinguishing the secular from the political was, in reality, nonexistent. In August 1984, Privette used a mailing list of the 18,825 Southern Baptist preachers and Sunday school superintendents to send a letter urging Helms's reelection because he believed in "traditional family values and morality." In what one newspaper said "might almost be called laundered," Privette purchased the list for the Christian Action League for $450 and sold it to the Helms people for the same amount. Despite a controversy that flared up about the violation of the traditional Baptist separation of church and state, the great majority of Southern Baptists in North Carolina were strong Helms supporters.[63]

There was some trepidation among some in the Helms camp about the evangelicals' embrace. Tom Ellis had promoted an alliance with the Religious Right, but Wrenn and Finkelstein worried that too close an association on moral issues might alienate moderate voters. Wrenn believed that Jesse was on "thin ice" about abortion, where his polling showed a sharply divided electorate. In addition, he and Finkelstein worried about Jesse's own character problem: the perception, particularly among moderate voters, that he was mean and preachy, what Finkelstein called the "Elmer Gantry factor." In one poll, they discovered that voters, by a margin of two to one, said that they prefer candidates who had not received money from gay organizations. But when the Helms campaign experimented with ads that pointed out Hunt's association with gay groups, polling showed that the issue tended to hurt Helms. Wrenn and Finkelstein believed that the issue of morality was tricky because meanness sometimes overshadowed everything else, and the issue became one of Jesse's character. Not everyone in the Helms camp agreed with this analysis, however, and some favored making the election into a moral crusade.[64]

By late 1984, the evangelical mobilization was bearing fruit, in direct competition with efforts at black registration. Overall, the percentage of all eligible voters registered in North Carolina grew from 58 to 77 percent between 1982 and 1984. In effect, the racial polarization was accompanied by a cultural polarization: an army of new white registrants pressed a new, evangelical political agenda. In the end, white registrants would dominate. Between October 1982 and May 1984, some 113,575 new black voters registered in the state, a stunning increase that reflected Jesse Jackson's presidential campaign in 1984. Some 77,020 of these registered in the first four months of 1984. But more striking was the surge in white registrations: during early 1984 alone, 142,348 whites registered, and at least half of these, according to some estimates, were white evangelicals. By November 1984, according to one estimate, the Republicans had registered some 150,000 white evangelicals. White registration surged after the May 1984 primary, and, overall, Republicans were the beneficiaries, with a 24 percent increase in registration. Before mid-1984, said state Democratic chair David Price, Democrats did well, but thereafter there was a "good deal of evidence that the other side has done considerably better."[65]

For evangelicals, the most important emerging cultural issue was homosexuality. In the late 1970s, when the issue of gay rights burst onto the scene, Helms's Senate office began receiving information from anti-gay groups around the country. Jesse had become a leading opponent of gay rights, and his positions on homosexuality became a major talking point with evangelical audiences. In September 1981, Helms and East joined forces with the Moral Majority to oppose a District of Columbia law, enacted by the City Council in July 1981, that removed criminal penalties for homosexual acts. Helms and East favored overriding the law in Congress.[66] The issue appeared more prominently in August 1983, when Helms sent out a five-page fund-raising letter declaring that homosexuals had "drawn a bead on my campaign" and were bankrolling the Hunt campaign.[67]

Although the sexuality issue became more fully developed after 1984, it had already become another part of the effort to cement the senator's evangelical support. Helms introduced the issue less subtly than he had the race issue. On March 1, 1984, he told the Conservative Political Action Conference, based on the positions of aspirants for the Democratic presidential nomination, their party was composed of "homosexuals, pacifists, feminists, and those who want to share the wealth—that is to say, YOUR wealth."[68] About a month later, he told the Baptist Fundamentalism Conference in Washington that the same people who were after Reagan were after him—the "atheists, the homosexuals, the militant women's groups, the union bosses, the bloc voters, and so on."[69] In his weekly newsletter, Helms wrote that at "almost every stop" in North Carolina he was met by a "shouting, jeering picket line of women protesters" representing the National Organization of Women who opposed him as senator because of his refusal to support gay rights. "I will never support legislation of that kind, regardless of the political consequences," he wrote. "If that's the price of remaining in the Senate, I refuse to pay it."[70]

For the most part, the attack on sexuality came through proxies, either authorized spokesmen in the Helms campaign or an unauthorized third party. In June 1984, for example, Republican chair David Flaherty charged that Hunt's campaign had received contributions from gay rights activists and that the governor had "waffled" on the question of support from homosexuals. Flaherty claimed that gays had purchased a bloc of tickets to the New York City fund-raiser, and he also pointed out that Massachusetts senator Paul Tsongas—identified as a co-sponsor of legislation to ban workplace discrimination based on sexual orientation—had hosted a fund-raising dinner in Boston.[71] The gay issue eventually burst into the open. the *Landmark,* a right-wing tabloid published in Chapel Hill since 1983, began attacking Hunt in early 1984, suggesting that Democrats had become dependent on fund-raising by gay rights groups. Hunt had made a deal, the *Landmark* claimed, with the "faggots, perverts, sexual deviates of this nation."[72] In June, the use of the issue became nastier when Jack C. D. Bailey, a Republican who owned a Hardee's franchise in Rocky Mount, ran a full-page ad that reprinted the *Landmark* article in the *N&O:* "Governor Hunt," the editorial asked, "did you, or did you not accept a $79,000 contribution from Gay Activists?"[73]

Bailey's *N&O* ad was mild, however, compared with an attack that was published in the *Landmark* on July 5, 1984. In an article written by editor Bob Windsor entitled "Jim Hunt Is Sissy, Prissy, Girlish and Effeminate," the publication made the outrageous claim that Hunt, while a student at N.C. State, had a "pretty young boy" as a lover. The article also charged that Hunt had a long-standing relationship with a "former high-priced call girl used by the banks and big companies in Winston-Salem to entertain their guests." Windsor claimed that Hunt's wife, Carolyn, had ended the affair when she caught wind of it. The Hunt campaign immediately denounced the story and, while calling for an investigation about connections between the *Landmark* article and the Helms campaign, threatened Windsor with a libel suit unless he issued a retraction within five days. Windsor, a real estate developer in Chapel Hill who started *The Landmark* in 1981 and operated it as free weekly tabloid, claimed a circulation of thirty thousand. An erratic, unpredictable figure, Windsor had merely "printed rumors," he said, and he admitted that he could not verify whether the charges that Hunt was gay were the "truth or factual in any way." Windsor compared the story to Hunt's unsubstantiated assertions about El Salvador that had labeled Jesse Helms "a murderer by proxy." "I never accused Hunt of being a fag," he said.[74]

The *Landmark* did not even exist until the 1984 campaign; most of its pages were devoted to attacks on Hunt. With no paid circulation, the *Landmark* depended on advertising, much of it from the Helms campaign. Windsor had been promoting the anti-gay theme as a political issue against Hunt since early 1984, when he charged that the governor was receiving contributions from gay activists. Windsor noted, in one article, that the governor, while chairman of the Democratic Party commission on presidential nomination, had helped to pass an anti-discrimination rule regarding sexual orientation—what Windsor called "an affirmative action program to go after the faggots."[75] In March 1984, Windsor told readers that Hunt had visited with a "limp wrist set and its sympathizers as well as the arty set" at the fund-raiser in New York.[76] In June 1984, Windsor claimed that Hunt had accepted "dirty money" from gay groups, and if "good Christians, right thinking people of North Carolina know the truth they will send him back to Wilson County [Hunt's home county]."[77]

Windsor had featured pro-Helms materials in the *Landmark,* including advertising, and when Wrenn called Windsor to pull the Helms ads, Windsor "threatened" him. Wrenn should check with his campaign, Windsor suggested, and he implied that some of Helms's supporters wanted an all-out assault using the gay issue.[78] There were, to be sure, suspicious connections between the Helms campaign and Windsor; one reporter covering the campaign said that he was "confident" that such ties existed, though he could never prove it. But the precise relationship remains unclear. His tabloid had functioned, according to Christensen, as a "propaganda arm of the campaign," with lots of links to the Helms campaign. The same issue of *The Landmark* attacking Hunt in July 1984 included a photograph of Helms with his arm around Windsor, seven other images of the senator, and a page and a half of ads from his campaign. Jesse responded to the *Landmark* piece with a statement announcing his belief that Hunt was a "moral family man" and that any other suggestion was "regugnant and unfair" and "destructive and demeaning to the political process." But beyond this statement, his response was more qualified. In Helms's campaign records, the *Landmark* story and Jesse's statement about it went into a file entitled "Hunt Homo File." In addition, in his statement Jesse suggested that the governor had it coming for his low blow about Roberto D'Aubuisson. He had a "deep and abiding sympathy for the governor and his family," Helms said, because he knew how it felt to "endure bizarre suggestions, widely circulated, that I am somehow linked to the murder of men, women and children when in fact there is not one shred of evidence." Both sides should "lower our voices and encourage an examination of the real issues." Helms's disavowal of Windsor was halfhearted, at best, as he made clear in comments to reporters a day later. Denying any connection with the story, he declared that the "next thing the governor is going to blame me for is the bubonic plague, and I didn't have anything to do with that either." There was not a "soul in North Carolina, especially Jesse Helms," who believed the rumors about Hunt. He criticized the press for making too much of the story and declared that he would not disavow Windsor's support. "I would welcome the support of anybody," he said. Helms had "disavowed only the deed, not the doer and his methods," said the *Raleigh News and Observer,* and this was "hardly the tough indictment of campaign scurrility that voters should expect."[79]

On July 7, two days after the article appeared, Windsor printed a retraction announcing that he had been "dead wrong" to publish the story.[80] But the story was part of a larger campaign thrust. Flaherty bought thousands of copies of the *Landmark*—though it was free—and provided mailing labels to distribute the attacks on Hunt across the state.[81] The "whole purpose" of Flaherty's efforts, he later admitted, was "just to turn the race on issues that would play strong and get people's adrenaline going—one of them was the black-white, the other was the gay rights, and that was our focus." A Helms operative told Flaherty that "every damn time you hit those homos" Jesse's poll numbers increased substantially.[82] The *Raleigh News and Observer* condemned the entire affair, saying that it would "rank forever as one of the lowest political blows ever struck against a public official in North Carolina." Windsor's article, it believed, was "especially suspect as a part of a continuing campaign by Hunt's opponents to picture him as a champion of gay rights and somewhat less a man than his opponent, Sen. Jesse Helms."[83] Claude Sitton was even more pointed. The Windsor attack was comparable to the Smith-Graham campaign of 1950, with one important difference. While Smith partisans "mugged" Frank Porter Graham by using "demagogic appeals to fears of blacks and communists," in this campaign gays had "supplanted communists, a substitution made elsewhere in the South and nation by the Republicans."[84]

Into the summer, Windsor was still mailing copies of the *Landmark* articles.[85] As the campaign wound down, Claude Allen, in an interview with Chuck Alston of the *Greensboro News and Record,* told of Hunt's connections with "the homosexuals, the labor union connection, the radical feminist connection, the socialist connection." Allen also suggested that a connection existed between the governor and "queers." Alston was convinced that

Allen made the comment inadvertently because he later telephoned and tried for a half hour to persuade him not to use the quotation. Commenting that Allen's comment was "good for ten points for you guys Down East," Alston ran the story anyway. Although Allen told reporters that his comments were an "indiscretion," he stood by the statement in what the *Salisbury Post* called an effort by the Helms campaign to "to sideswipe Hunt with the vehicle of homosexuality." Years later, when George W. Bush nominated Allen to become a federal appeals court judge, Alston, who was then working for the Democratic Leadership Council, sent a copy of his 1984 article to the Senate Judiciary Committee, and the "queer" comments became one of several issues that sank the nomination.[86]

In October 1984, the homosexual issue continued to appear in the campaign. A letter signed by anonymous "Southern Christians for Helms" was sent to eight prominent educators and librarians in the Raleigh–Durham–Chapel Hill area. The letter called for libraries to remove books by "known" homosexuals such as Homer, Plato, Socrates, Shakespeare, Jean-Paul Sartre, and Eleanor Roosevelt. It denounced homosexuality as a "filthy sin devouring the minds and bodies of young people," and urged North Carolinians to vote for "moral" politicians. A second letter from "Southern Christians for Helms" was sent to UNC president Bill Friday. It charged that homosexuality and Communism existed in "epidemic proportions" at the university. Accusing Friday of creating a supportive environment for homosexuality, the letter demanded that all UNC employees take a lie detector test, threatened to expose thirty gays teaching at the university, and identified Helms as a "devout Christian" who had "launched a campaign against this Godless filth." "As Christian taxpayers," the letter read, "we demand that this...degradation, which festers like a cancer on the forehead of North Carolina education, be excoriated from our presence." Denouncing the letter as a "scurrilous piece of hate mail," Friday referred it to the State Bureau of Investigation for investigation. After the bureau judged it bogus, Friday called the letter a "vile" attempt to "induce fear and harass people" and to drag UNC into the Senate campaign. Although Allen denounced the letters as "despicable," many suspected that both of the "Southern Christians for Helms" letters came from the Helms campaign.[87]

Although the gay issue was not fully formed in the 1984 campaign, it played a significant role. Late in the campaign, Chuck Alston appeared on *Face the Nation* with Texas journalist Molly Ivins, as part of a panel reporting on major Senate elections. In 1984, Republican Phil Gramm charged that Democrat Lloyd Doggett had accepted money from gays, and

Ivins pointed out that the homosexual issue had emerged as an important campaign issue in Texas. When asked about North Carolina, Alston responded that the gay issue had similarly arisen in North Carolina, except that the Helms campaign "calls them queers." The comment slipped out, and Alston was grateful that it was soon forgotten, but it was indicative of the way in which the issue had entered the dialogue.[88]

IN THE SUMMER and fall of 1984, the campaign's focus shifted toward the debates. After avoiding them for more than a year, once the race tightened Hunt agreed to debates in May 1984, proposing as many as ten of them.[89] In the first debate, which was held July 29, Hunt went on the offensive about tobacco, arms control, Social Security, and Central America, and his performance was designed to show that he was not the vascillating weakling that Helms's ads had created. Hunt came well prepared. Thoroughly briefed on the issues, he had engaged in mock debates with pollster Harrison Hickman playing Helms as the "meanest sonabitch you've ever seen." Hickman grew up in old Wake Forest, east of Raleigh, and as a boy he and his Democratic parents—both of them precinct workers for Terry Sanford's gubernatorial race in 1960—listened to Helms's *Viewpoint* editorials on WRAL. Like most progressive Democrats, they were often angered by what they heard; Hickman recalled that, as a boy, he once even wrote Helms a protest letter. But Hickman realized that Helms represented the small towns of the South, where they both came from; Hickman believed that he had "a pretty good appreciation of what people liked about him." Hunt's first mock debate was held in Chapel Hill, and Hickman had prepared by rereading old *Viewpoint* editorials. He presented two versions of Jesse, the first an opponent who would aggressively attack the governor, the other a more avuncular, passive debater. At one point, he baited Hunt by suggesting that liberals were nothing more than Communist sympathizers. "You know, Senator," Hunt responded in the mock debate, "you refer to just about anybody you don't like as being a Communist or socialist. You know, some of these people that you refer to are just about as anticommunist as you are." Hickman, without losing a step, asked Hunt to name one of them. The governor remained there with a "blank look," and just then, with a thunderstorm hitting Chapel Hill, the power went out in the building, and the governor was spared the need to answer a difficult question. Hunt later sent Hickman a photograph with the inscription that he was "the only Senator that beat me in a debate."[90]

The governor responded to Hickman's verbal beating by preparing even more intensively. Hunt was tough and resilient. While a college student at N.C. State, Hunt used to hitchhike from North Carolina to Iowa, and in order to protect himself he would take a switchblade.[91] Helms, who had not prepared himself seriously and remained overconfident, came to the debate unfocused and unprepared. Ellis and Wrenn had sent him material, but he ignored it. Not long before the debate was to occur, Ellis rented a room in a Raleigh office building and had campaign worker David Tyson participate in a mock debate in which Tyson stood in as Hunt. Ellis urged Tyson to take his job seriously and to "beat up on Ol' Jesse." Tyson aggressively challenged the senator's record, and, as one club operative remembered, "David ate him alive." Red-faced, Helms announced that the mock debate was over, and he stomped out of the room. After an angry phone call to Wrenn, the campaign canceled future mock debates. Helms's claim at the first debate that the only preparation he had made for the debate was a haircut was, according to Wrenn, the "Lord's truth." Jesse, said Tom Fetzer, "went into a gunfight without even a knife."[92]

In later years, Helms observed that challenging Hunt to debate was a mistake. After the debate was over, according to one account, Hunt seemed "ebullient," Helms "subdued." Ellis was embarrassed by Helms's showing, and he was so angry that he nearly came to blows with a reporter after the debate. Rob Christensen sat behind Ellis and Wrenn during the debate, and he remembered that Ellis's neck turned red as it became apparent that Helms was getting clobbered. After the debate ended, Wade Hargrove, attorney for the North Carolina Broadcasters Association, which sponsored the event, came up to Ellis to inquire about future arrangements. "What are you," Ellis exclaimed, "a fucking debate broker?" Most observers agreed that Hunt had gotten the better of Helms. The governor, a UNC political scientist told a reporter, had "really whipped" Helms. Privately, the Helms campaign agreed. Wrenn remembered concluding that Hunt had "killed" Helms in the first debate; Harris believed that the governor had "cleaned his clock"; and Stephens said that Hunt "creamed us, just creamed us." Polling soon confirmed these conclusions. Fortunately for the Helms campaign, Ellis had insisted on a rule that none of the debate footage could be used in campaign ads—a matter, he recalled, of simple luck. The Helms campaign tried to limit some of the damage by buying $200,000 worth of new TV ads. Ellis then "wiggled out" of a second debate scheduled for late August.[93]

Ellis feared future debates might be as bad or worse, and he called Jesse's childhood friend from Monroe, James "Bud" Nance, who persuaded Jesse to participate in prep sessions. At the Republican National Convention at Dallas, Ellis and Nance closeted themselves in a hotel room with Helms; Ellis had rented a truck to haul debate materials to Texas, and the club sent additional workers to help with the preparation. But after only twenty or thirty minutes of debate prep, Jesse walked out of the meeting, and the session "got nowhere." Helms wanted to do something to improve, and Ellis decided to prepare scripts, which were organized into file folders by topic. Ellis delivered these files to Helms and laid them out on the pool table in the basement of Jesse's Raleigh home. Beyond this, Ellis, completely exasperated after the first debate, told the senator that he was on his own. On September 9, at the second debate in Wilmington, Helms came prepared with a large file of scripts.

Wrenn remembered that when they arrived they found a podium and a small table; Jesse insisted on a large enough table to hold his files. Ellis had earlier negotiated terms for the debate that required that the camera would be on the candidate only as he was speaking. "Why I put that rule in there, I'll never know. The Lord must have done it," Ellis recalled. When Hunt went on the attack about issues, Jesse pulled his files out and found an appropriate script that he could read. Jesse, with years of experience reading *Viewpoints,* "could read a statement like you and I could talk," Wrenn recalled. In the ensuing debate, Helms returned to issues of race, reminding voters that he had opposed both the Voting Rights Act extension and the King holiday. Hunt responded by suggesting that North Carolina had made "a lot of progress" on race, though perhaps Jesse did not know "what's been going on here." When Jesse appeared rattled and slightly nervous, Hunt told him to "calm down," but Helms rallied for the rest of the debate. In what would become a major issue in the last week of the campaign, Helms described his opponent as a "Mondale liberal." Helms lost the second debate, but his performance had clearly improved. In part, he had discovered, as one aide put it, that it "didn't matter what people asked you" in these debates, that candidates needed to make their points, even if they ignored the questions. The scripts, according to Ellis, were "the only thing saving ol' Helms."[94]

By August, Mondale was hurting Hunt. Hunt aide Gary Pearce remembered attending the Democratic National Convention in San Francisco in July 1984, where he heard Mondale make his acceptance speech. Looking at the large budget deficits facing the country, Mondale urged a "new realism." "Mr. Reagan will raise taxes, and so will I," Mondale said. "He won't tell you. I just did." This bold gambit—in which Mondale informed Americans that he would raise their taxes in order to reduce the budget deficit—sent Pearce into a deep gloom, and he realized that Hunt faced a long road ahead.[95] In the last two debates, held September 23 and October 13, Helms continued to draw connections between Hunt and Mondale, while telling voters that "the President and I need your support." Ellis, at the October 13 debate, arranged for Republican senators Howard Baker and Bob Dole to attend and to sit in the front row, in an attempt to rattle Hunt. Helms knew his scripts better, and his performance improved.

By the October 13 debate, the Hunt people realized what Jesse was doing with the scripts, and they instructed the governor to ask ten-second questions—not enough time for Helms to locate the script. "But by then," said Wrenn, "he had sort of memorized all that stuff anyway," and this was his best performance. At the same time, the debates remained bitter. In the debate of September 23, after Hunt criticized Helms for describing veterans' benefits as "welfare," Helms reponded: "And which war did you fight in, Jim?" Hunt, who had not served, testily rejoined: "I don't like you questioning my patriotism." Earlier, the head of the North Carolina Veterans of Foreign Wars had endorsed Hunt, and Helms saw this as a "terrible blow," and he fretted. One of the Helms researchers, David Tyson, urged the senator to hit Hunt for his lack of military service, but his advisers regarded it as a "stupid idea" and a "cheap shot" that would backfire. Helms decided that he was going to bring the issue up anyway. As Hunt was "white-hot" in his response, Helms, off camera, played an air violin, the shadow of which could be seen behind Hunt. "He came out of the debates all right," recalled Ellis, "but he had no business coming out of them all right."[96]

Both sides imported celebrities to make their case. While Hunt enjoyed the support of former New York Yankees pitcher Jim "Catfish" Hunter (who had supported Helms in 1978) and TV star Andy Griffith, film actor and conservative activist Charlton Heston filmed a TV spot urging Helms's reelection.[97] With a Reagan landslide likely, Helms continued to draw connections between himself and the president late in the campaign, and his managers realized that drawing on the popular president's support was, as Wrenn put it, "the whole key really." They constantly polled the Reagan vote, estimating that they would need 85 percent of it in order to win the Senate election. Through intensive TV ads, Helms told voters that Hunt favored tax increases; to the extent that he distanced himself from Mondale, Hunt was guilty of inconsistency and flip-flopping.[98] In a thirty-second ad, released on October 18, that displayed scenes of abandoned buildings and unemployment lines, the Helms campaign drew a further link between Hunt and Mondale on economic issues. If Mondale and Hunt raised taxes, the narrator warned, the Reagan recovery would come to an end. Still another ad showed a person playing a slot machine, with images of Hunt, Mondale, and Jesse Jackson "with the biggest Afro you've seen in your life" appear. A voiceover by Helms then intoned: "I'm for the reelection of Ronald Reagan. Where do you stand, Jim?"[99] Hunt responded with strong attack ads, striking hard on the Social Security issue by claiming that Helms had "one of the worst records of any U.S. senator" on protecting senior citizens. By the end of the campaign, Hunt had produced some eight different ads about Social Security. At the same time, Hunt claimed that Helms had done little for North Carolina's embattled textile industry.[100]

Chuck Babington, who during the early 1980s wrote for the *Greensboro Daily News* and then the *Dallas Morning News,* joined the *Raleigh News and Observer* with only a few weeks left in the Helms-Hunt campaign. The *N&O* and *Charlotte Observer* had thrown all their resources at the campaign, which they regarded as the "race of the century." Because the *N&O* "needed all the help they could get," Babington was called in to cover both candidates. He recalled that Hunt, near the close of the contest, made an appearance at the state fair in Raleigh; he followed a country rock band. When Hunt appeared the "boos rained down," and, although Babington doubted whether any political candidate would have been well received, he wondered about Hunt's fate. He remembered feeling "in my bones" that Hunt would lose.[101] In the waning moments of the campaign, with a large portion of the electorate decided, the election came down to swing voters, and both sides fought for votes. Especially important were female voters. The Helms campaign ran an ad in which a young female voter told viewers that she would be unable to buy a car if the Reagan tax cuts were repealed. The Hunt campaign meanwhile targeted elderly voters about the Social Security issue and young females about the abortion issue. In October 1984, political consultant David Sawyer, who was advising the Hunt campaign, arranged for Dick Morris, a political consultant who later worked for both Helms and Bill Clinton and whom Sawyer described as "kind of strange, but brilliant," to conduct a poll and make recommendations. The Hunt people convened at the executive mansion in Raleigh, in the main dining room, to hear Morris's report. Along with the governor, the room was full, with about twenty people attending. Morris informed Hunt that his polling showed that the governor was "wishy-washy" and a "flip-flopper." In order to reverse that perception, Morris urged them to make the campaign on abortion: he found in his polls that when people discovered that Helms opposed legal abortion, even in cases of rape and incest, "they go crazy, especially women."

But the Hunt campaign remained divided. The governor, whom

Pearce described as a "teetotaling, Freewill Baptist from rural North Carolina," was uncomfortable in making the election about this issue. According to one reporter, his wife, Carolyn, held pro-life beliefs. As a result,
according to Pearce, "we did it half-assed" and, six days before the election,
ran a radio commercial rather than a television ad. The ad told listeners
that Jesse Helms opposed abortion, even in cases of rape and incest, while
he also opposed most forms of birth control. Helms's Human Life bill, the
commercial claimed, would "outlaw many of the birth-control devices that
millions of American women use today—like the IUD and many forms of
the Pill." Wrenn, who heard the ad on his car radio, refused to believe that
the ads were credible, but his tracking polls showed that they were having
a significant impact on females. Alarmed, Ellis and Wrenn swung into action. Helms issued a statement calling Hunt a "consummate liar." The
Helms campaign contacted the White House, drafting a letter stating that
Reagan had, along with Helms, supported abortion legislation that would
have permitted contraception. The White House, after some discussion,
refused to send the letter. The Helms campaign immediately ran response
ads, the only case in the election in which they responded to Hunt—which
indicated the seriousness with which they took the issue. Fetzer was instructed to locate Jesse with a quickly written script refuting the radio ad;
they wanted Dot to appear in the ad defending her husband. Later that
night, they produced an ad with Dot saying that Helms did not oppose
birth control, while avoiding the abortion issue, and describing Hunt's attack as "disgusting and dishonest." Hunt had accused "my husband of sponsoring legislation outlawing a woman's right to use contraceptive devices
including the birth control pill," Dot declared in the ad, and she described
this as an "outright falsehood....I'd have never believed that Jim Hunt
would stoop this low." At this point, Hunt "blinked," according to Wrenn,
and pulled the ads. To this day, Wrenn believes that Hunt gave up using an
effective issue. For Hickman, this was a case of the truism that "blind hogs
will sometimes find acorns," but in this case they abandoned their riches.[102]

IN THE LAST weeks of the campaign, Helms returned to themes that excited his Christian evangelical base. "There's nothing wrong with this
country that good leadership and high moral standards won't cure," he told
an audience of 150 at a Siler City restaurant in late October 1984. Secular
humanists claimed that "you must not let religion or Christianity show its
head in the political process." "To heck with that," Helms said, for America
was "founded on those principles." The country's problems began "when

we decided to make a god of government instead of realizing that this is a government created with and by God's guidance." The crowd responded enthusiastically.[103] Three days before the election, he expanded on these themes in a speech to a meeting of the North Carolina Christian Educators Association. His enemies had characterized him as the "Prince of Darkness" because he favored school prayer and opposed abortion. He promised, nonetheless, not to "back off even if it costs me the election" because some things were "more important than the election." Congress was permeated with secular humanism, but he intended to reverse that. As far as Jesse was concerned, it was the "meaning of America." The group, composed of four hundred people, cheered wildly, and at the end of the meeting the group's president thanked God for Jesse's willingness to "stand up without wavering or compromising."[104]

The bitter tone continued during the last days of campaigning. Behind in the polls by about two or three points—a lead that Helms had sustained since mid-September—Hunt launched attacks on the incumbent senator in a series of press conferences. Helms was involved in a "Watergate-like cover-up" of a Federal Election Commission investigation of the Congressional Club, and he was "trying to buy reelection with tainted money." An FBI crackdown on voter fraud, prompted in part by former Helms aide Sam Currin, he claimed, was actually an effort to intimidate Democratic voters.[105] North Carolinians were not well represented by a person who placed his "first priority on Jerry Falwell and the Moral Majority" and Latin American dictators, Hunt said a day before the election. His campaign meanwhile broadcast a thirty-minute television film, airing the Sunday and Monday evenings before election day. Hosted by TV actor Hal Linden, it described Helms as a "right-wing extremist" in charge of a "tight, ideological, right-wing political network" that was connected to New Right figures around the country as well as "right-wing political and military dictators around the world." Helms also pulled few punches. Many of Hunt's supporters were "the homosexuals, the labor union bosses and the crooks," and he warned, in a not-so-subtle racial reference, of a large "bloc vote." The governor, Jesse said, was a person "not to be trusted." "I hope," Helms declared, that he never "has another day in public office."[106]

When all was said and done, the two-year campaign cost more than $25.4 million—the most expensive in the history of the Senate—with Helms spending $16.5 million and Hunt more than $10 million. Significantly, the great bulk of Jesse's funds came from small contributors, and only 5 percent from independent political action committees. Between 1983 and 1985, the Helms campaign sent twelve million fund-raising letters, which yielded $19.7 million from 178,837 contributors. While 98 percent of the contributions were less than $100, the average donation was about $30. North Carolina's airwaves were inundated, more than during any other previous campaign in history: within the campaign's final five weeks, Helms broadcast 5,259 television ads, while Hunt ads were aired 2,536 times.

In the end, Helms narrowly carried the day, with about 52 percent of the vote and a winning margin of nearly 87,000 votes. According to exit polls, Hunt received about 99 percent of the black vote, and in thirty-five precincts with the highest concentration of black voters, Helms attracted less than one percent of the vote. Although African American voter registration rose significantly, by about 37 percent after early 1983, from 451,000 to 619,000, there were not enough black votes to carry the day for Hunt, and black turnout actually declined between 1980 and 1984, from 63 to 61 percent. Helms won 63 percent of the white vote, and his margin of victory came from small towns across the state, especially white males and older voters. Women voted for Hunt by a substantial margin, 57 to 43 percent, and a narrow majority of voters under the age of fifty voted for him. While born-again Christians went for Helms by a margin of 60 to 40 percent, those describing themselves as conservatives voted for him by a three-to-one margin. Reagan's strong victory in North Carolina—he carried 62 percent of the vote—had coattails that helped Jesse back into office; Helms carried only counties that voted at least 60 percent for Reagan.

Helms victory was a testament to the power of the hard-hitting, well-focused, and well-financed politics of conservatism that he espoused. In the end, concluded Mark Stephens, "Helms stunk less than Hunt did." In his victory speech, delivered to a crowd of supporters in Raleigh who chanted, "Jesse, Jesse, Jesse," Helms declared that the "cruel hoax of liberal politics has run its course for the last time." To a cheering throng, he flashed the October 23, 1983, issue of the *Washington Post*, with the headline, "Jesse Helms Has a Problem; He Is Destined to Lose in '84." North Carolina, he said, had delivered a message to the world that it was a "conservative, God-fearing state . . . a state where people believe in school prayer and they want to restore it," where people believed "in the sanctity of human life," and where people believed that a "bloated federal government is a threat to freedom." With Claude Allen at his side, Helms made a plea for racial reconciliation, in the wake of a campaign that had polarized the electorate racially.[107]

In the final analysis, the 1984 campaign, involving a clash between two political traditions in North Carolina, reflected superior command-and-control and strategy by the Helms managers. Overconfident, the Hunt forces relied on an older, and ultimately outmoded, model that placed more emphasis on field organization than on media exposure. The Hunt campaign, according to Rob Christensen, was the "last of the big Democratic machines," with a large, grassroots organization that included a "mass of consultants," but the Democratic organiztion was "committee driven" and susceptible to slow, sometimes paralyzed decision-making. Harrison Hickman recalled that the Hunt campaign essentially reflected his gubernatorial administration: it reached decisions under a big tent, through a consensus that reconciled competing views. In contrast, he said, the Helms operation was "basically a bunch of white guys about the same age, and a very small number of them" operating in a "command model." Hunt's campaign strategy, remembered press secretary Gary Pearce, had a "foot in the past" and remained "way behind" the Helms team's sophisticated understanding of how television could shape a political message. "We didn't know what we were getting into," he later said.[108]

Helms's injection of the race issue into the campaign through his King holiday filibuster was crucial: a post-election poll by Harrison Hickman determined that the holiday was the most consistent predictor of support, as nearly all Helms's supporters opposed the holiday and nearly all of Hunt's voters favored it. The King holiday issue helped to make the election less about concrete issues and more about values, something that worked to Helms's advantage. Jesse knew "all along what would appeal to his voters," observed Jack Betts, and what would "turn them out at the polls." In September 1984, Ken Eudy drove the length of North Carolina on U.S. Highway 64, which wove eastward through the small towns of the state. He found consistently that the small-town world of North Carolina, by the fall of 1984, had rallied behind Helms. The King holiday appeared to have been crucial, at least in its cumulative effect, and Eudy did not recall meeting any white males who said that they would vote for Hunt.

But the election also came down to strategy. Hunt's people remained uneasy about how to respond to attack ads and how to mount their own, and they were more conservative about raising and spending money. As the campaign wound to a close, a flood of money came into Hunt's coffers, much of it coming from a national anti-Helms constituency. So much money was pouring in, said Ken Eudy, that the governor's managers were simply unable to spend it; they "couldn't spend it fast enough" and "didn't know how to."[109] When it turned to attack ads, the Hunt campaign did so ineffectively and hesitantly, and they often backed off—even when, as in the case of birth control, they had actually stumbled onto a winning issue. While Hunt's team was hesitant about attacking, the Helms people, observed Ferrel Guillory, simply "didn't get queasy" and "went beyond the norm." Without hesitation Helms's supporters used issues of race and, to a certain extent, sexuality to polarize the electorate. Even more important, the Helms campaign waged a new sort of campaign—an assault on their opponent's character. The strategy worked, and national political consultants "went to school" on the 1984 campaign. In the end, however, the decisive factor was Reagan, and his landslide tilted the election in Helms's direction. Although Hunt ran well ahead of any other Democratic statewide candidates—141,000 votes ahead of Mondale and 56,000 votes ahead of Democratic gubernatorial candidate Rufus Edmisten—the pull of Reagan's coattails was decisive.[110]

AFTER THE ELECTION, Hunt commissioned Hickman to conduct a poll to try to understand the election's results. Hickman's polling group yielded the same result as the election—Helms ahead by a few points—but the poll scrutinized voters' attitudes. The election was overwhelmingly about the character issue: voters were concerned about Hunt's character, and they saw Helms as a more nonpolitical candidate. One of the questions that Hickman asked voters was whom they would have voted for if Hunt had run against Helms for governor, and the poll respondents, by a double-digit margin, chose Hunt. Voters liked having an ideologue for senator and an effective manager as governor. Jesse and Hunt appealed to the same rural, down-home voter. Jack Betts recalled traveling with Helms during his 1978 senatorial campaign, and during one stop in southeastern North Carolina many of his supporters at a rally were wearing Jim Hunt buttons. To Betts, this indicated the strong appeal that both men had for the rural heartland. Nonetheless, he reflected that, after covering Hunt, Betts eventually found him "tiresome": he was "always on message," rarely kicking back to be a regular person. In contrast, Helms often lit up one of his Lucky Strikes and made his companions "feel as if you were speaking to a human being." Helms had an ability to communicate with and connect with voters. Hunt was a "button-down sort of guy," remembered Ken Eudy; even in political ads showing the governor appearing in a denim shirt, its creases suggested that it had just been broken out of the box. Though he was aware that there was a difference between the "courtly" and "firebrand" Helms, Eudy admitted that he found Jesse to be more "fun and interesting" than Hunt.

The Helms-Hunt contest inspired a similar ambivalence among voters. Voters liked Hunt as a governor, but they were more comfortable with Jesse as an adversarial senator. If voters thought about going out on a date with either Hunt or Helms—a question that Hickman posed in focus group settings—the women respondents tended to see Hunt as stern, Helms as a more carefree and fun dinner companion. Hickman's post-election survey also revealed another sharp distinction on religious attitudes, as he found that "moderate, mainstream" Protestants gravitated to Hunt; these were people who used Christianity "to do good for other people." In contrast, "true believers" were overwhelmingly Helms voters.[111] Years later, Hunt himself would admit that it was a mistake to permit Helms to become the evangelical Christian candidate: the governor committed a strategic error, he believed, in avoiding any discussion of religion in public life.[112]

Chapter 9

I AM BEYOND YOUR REACH

New Directions

By the late 1980s, Jesse charted out a new future for himself—and new issues for American conservatives. Gradually abandoning the social issues agenda of the 1970s and early 1980s—issues such as abortion and school prayer had reached a kind of dead end in Congress—Helms explored new directions. Reviving his long-standing hostility to the liberal media, he mounted an attempt to take over CBS that, although almost entirely rhetorical, succeeded in focusing attention on the problem of the "liberal" media. He continued as chair of the Senate Agriculture Committee, fulfilling a 1984 campaign pledge and once again extending the life of the tobacco program. But increasingly his real interest lay in foreign affairs, and here he began to express a noisy presence. Expressing traditional themes of anti-Communism and support for authoritarian regimes in the developing world, Helms discovered new enemies to fight in the State Department and CIA. By 1987, when he took over as ranking member of the Senate Foreign Relations Committee, he began to assemble an impressive record on an array of foreign policy questions.

FOLLOWING THE 1984 campaign, when Democrat Paul Simon defeated Illinois Republican senator Charles Percy, Helms became eligible to head the Senate Foreign Relations Committee. Despite pleas from fellow conservatives, however, Helms announced that he was honoring a promise that he had made to North Carolina voters that he would remain as chair of the Agriculture Committee.[1] Chairing Agriculture meant, of course, protecting the besieged North Carolina tobacco growers. Tobacco's problems paralleled those of agriculture generally. The 1982 revision of the tobacco program did little to alter its general decline, and in 1985 it was on the verge of collapse. Expanding imports, a severe drought in 1983, the expensive American dollar, and the inefficiencies of federal subsidies created a surplus pool of 800 million pounds of flue-cured tobacco and 590 million pounds of burley tobacco. Cigarette manufacturers turned to cheaper imported tobacco, which by 1985 composed about half of the leaf used in American cigarettes. The reforms in the tobacco program that Helms in 1982 had helped to push through Congress were financed by fees imposed on growers, and the expenses of carrying a large surplus meant that, between 1982 and 1985, fees had risen from 5 cents to 25 cents per pound. In June 1985 Helms and nine tobacco-state legislators endorsed a plan by which farmers and cigarette manufacturers would share in the costs of the program, and he introduced it as legislation on July 10. In exchange for selling the existing surplus to the manufacturers at a 90 percent discount, they would pay half of the costs of the program. Growers, in exchange for these concessions, would accept lower price supports, while manufacturers would participate in determining the size of the domestic bright leaf crop.

With divergent interests represented on the Agriculture Committee, Jesse occupied a difficult position, as his fellow committee members wondered why the tobacco program should receive special treatment. In late July 1985, committee members were almost in open revolt over the proposed reductions in price supports. With the Senate adjourning for its Labor Day recess, the Agriculture Committee entered September 1985 without any bill to report.[2] With the Agriculture Committee in chaos, Helms moved to protect tobacco. When the Senate returned from its recess, on September 18, he made a deal with Bob Dole in which he agreed to the permanent extension of the 8 cent per-pack cigarette tax of 1982 in exchange for the inclusion of his tobacco rescue plan in the Senate Finance Committee's deficit-reduction package. But the Dole-Helms proposal encountered sharp resistance, and the Finance Committee narrowly defeated a measure that would have doubled the cigarette tax to 32 cents a pack.[3] Although farm-state members complained about tobacco's special treatment, by the conclusion of the budget process in late 1985 Helms had prevailed. His adversary in the House, Charlie Rose, in December 1985 described Helms's plan as "Black Friday the 13th" because of its effect on small tobacco producers, but most legislators saw this as the only way to protect tobacco.

Nonetheless, with the close of the 99th Congress, Helms succeeded in pushing through the revision in the tobacco program via the back door, even while the farm bill remained stalled in the Senate until late 1985.[4]

ABOUT A WEEK after the election, on November 13, 1984, Tom Ellis, Carter Wrenn, and Raleigh attorney Jim Cain organized Fairness in Media (FIM). Staffed and led by the Congressional Club, Fairness in Media occupied the same offices and had the same staff as workers in Jefferson Marketing and the club, and, for all practical purposes, was indistinguishable from other elements of the Helms-Ellis political empire. The idea of creating Fairness in Media coincided with the club's heady victory in 1984. Ellis believed that he was taking the fight to the enemy, while Helms was delighted to gain the publicity. In the aftermath of an election, moreover, this would also sustain interest in the Helms agenda.[5] Under Helms's signature, Fairness in Media sent a letter to a million conservatives; the mailing cost $500,000 and was financed by an advance from Jefferson Marketing. The decision to send a mailing to a million conservatives, which included JMI's 250,000-person mailing list and additional names purchased from outside vendors, was a reckless act. Ordinarily, JMI sent a test mailing of perhaps five thousand names; the response from the test mailing provided a basis for a larger mailing. In this instance, the club gambled that it could send a single, general mailing of a million pieces. "Pride," said Wrenn, "really got the better of us." Although thousands of recipients of the letter responded by buying stock, very few made contributions to Fairness in Media. The result was the Helms organization lost hundreds of thousands of dollars, and it found itself in a "deep hole financially."[6]

Fairness in Media's letter proposed to launch a conservative attack on the liberal media. "For years," the letter read, "good Americans like you have asked President Reagan and me what can be done to combat the flagrant bias in the liberal news media." Now there was a way to fight back by buying CBS stock and mounting a takeover of the network. The group's objective, the letter announced, was to "urge conservatives to buy CBS stock, lead CBS stockholders, and, if necessary, conduct a fight to elect Directors who will end CBS's unfair news coverage." Tipped off by an anonymous source, *N&O* reporter Chuck Babington obtained two copies of the direct mail letter and broke a story that soon attracted widespread national attention.[7] Helms immediately embraced Ellis's FIM campaign. The effort "hit a nerve," Helms told reporters soon after FIM's efforts became public. On January 18, at a victory dinner in Washington celebrating the 1984 win over Jim Hunt, Helms announced that "momentum was building" toward a CBS takeover.[8] On March 1, 1985, Jesse expanded his attack on CBS in a pointed speech to the Conservative Political Action Conference in Washington. His audience was with him: when he rose to speak, a person from the crowd shouted: "CBS has its camera on you, Jesse." "You're the big boss." Repeating themes that had been a part of the Helms repertoire, Helms denounced the "elite media" as "profoundly out of sympathy with the ideals and goals of the American people." Media leaders were, he claimed, people who, "if they do not hate America first, they certainly have a smug contempt for American ideals and principles." If there was a threat to freedom of speech and the American constitutional system, it was "on our TV screens every evening and on the front pages of our newspapers every day." The accounts that appeared on the pages of the *Washington Post* or on the airwaves differed substantially from what he "personally witnessed early that day or the day before." Very often, Jesse said, he went home and told his wife that there must have been two meetings of the Senate Foreign Relations Committee: "the one I attended and the one I read about in the *Washington Post*."

Ironically, given his take-no-prisoners political style, Helms accused his media opponents as engaging in character attacks. Public figures, he said, were open to character assassination because of the protections that the Supreme Court had provided in the *New York Times v. Sullivan* decision in 1964, which narrowed the definition of libel in cases regarding public figures to those in which reporting involved malice. But this had created an "impossible standard of justice for victims of libel" and fostered a kind of media arrogance. Public figures were now "fair game, free game. Take a potshot. Run them down. Kill him. Assassinate his character." Matters had come to the point, perhaps, in which the "elite media" was no longer a defender of democracy but had become "a threat to democracy." All Fairness in Media wanted, Helms said, was an "even bite at the apple" in the forms of added protections for media objectivity. There was nothing personal in the FIM campaign, Helms said. Addressing the reporters in the room, he assured them that he did not "want to offend any of you fellows back there." "Good luck to you," he said, "and I hope your dog comes out and wags its tail when you come home tonight." After the address, Helms even gave two reporters a ride to their offices.[9]

The Fairness in Media campaign functioned much like Helms's political campaigns: he had delegated considerable power to Tom Ellis and Carter Wrenn. Nonetheless, he enjoyed the steady stream of publicity that the CBS takeover attempt produced. He had nothing to do formally with

FIM, he told reporters; they were "my friends, though." The media masters at CBS, he said at the American Pork Congress on March 6, were "now living on a diet of fingernails." He believed that the campaign had already forced CBS to reevaluate its editorial policies.[10] FIM produced good material for his followers. "I say this to CBS or anybody else who wants to get tough," he told a victory dinner organized by his supporters in Raleigh in late March. If the liberal media thought it could "intimidate us, they better think again." "I say again, let 'em try. Let 'em make my day."[11]

Nonetheless, the Fairness in Media campaign met a determined response. A day after the *N&O* disclosed Helms's letter, on January 11, CBS announced that it would resist any effort by this organization to influence the network; on February 5, CBS chairman Thomas H. Wyman, in a speech at Duke University, denounced FIM's activities. Filing suit in United States District Court in Manhattan, CBS lawyers named as defendants the leaders of Jefferson Marketing and the National Congressional Club.[12] FIM, meanwhile, sought outside financial resources in support of their campaign. Wrenn was dispatched to meet with possible backers, including T. Boone Pickens and Bunker Hunt. He also met with CNN owner Ted Turner, who told Wrenn that he would be delighted to run CBS. Turner wanted to expand his media empire through takeover, and two years earlier, he had made an unsuccessful approach to CBS. But, like the other potential backers, Turner would not risk the financial resources necessary for a takeover attempt. Eventually, Wrenn's negotiations with Ted Turner about an alliance appeared in press reports. Turner was even subpoenaed by CBS lawyers, and he confirmed his discussions with FIM.[13] Helms told reporters on March 1 that he and Turner had communicated; Turner told him that his plan to pressure CBS was a "great idea" and that he had "put my folks in touch" with Jesse about cooperating.[14] The prospects for a Turner-Helms alliance attracted a good deal of attention, but it was an alliance of convenience, with little chance for permanence. After his conversations with FIM, which occurred sometime in January 1985, Turner and Helms's political organization had no further communications.[15]

Lacking any financial muscle, the FIM effort remained a publicity event that sought to rally Helms's national conservative base against media enemies.[16] Despite Helms's bellicosity, the campaign fizzled by April 1985. But the CBS takeover attempt coincided with a period of volatility in media companies, as conglomerations were reshaping the news and entertainment business. The Fairness in Media campaign called attention to the relatively low stock price of media companies and spurred intense interest

among Wall Street investors.[17] While Helms was attracting attention about
CBS, for example, Capital Cities Broadcasting, Inc., announced a friendly
$3.5 billion takeover of ABC.[18] The price of CBS stock rose rapidly in ad-
vance of a possible takeover: between January 10 and the end of March, it
increased more than $37 per share.[19] Wall Street raider Ivan F. Boesky qui-
etly purchased 8.7 percent of the company for $250 million, and more ru-
mors swirled, including possible alliances between Turner and various
financiers.[20] In April 1985, Turner announced a takeover bid for control of
CBS, while Fairness in Media continued its campaign among stockholders.
In June 1985, FIM announced a new campaign to urge conservatives to buy
CBS stock in ads appearing in the *Washington Post* and other newspapers.
FIM aired ads on cable television, including Turner's WTBS superstation.
Although the Congressional Club and Jefferson Marketing ended up nearly
a million dollars in debt as a result of mailing costs and legal fees, the
quixotic effort to take over CBS served as another Ellis effort at bomb throw-
ing and mischief making.[21]

EVEN BEFORE REAGAN'S second inaugural in January 1985, Helms returned to hit-and-run attacks against the foreign policy establishment. His
love-hate relationship with the Reagan White House became most pronounced in international affairs, and his basic strategy was to make numerous demands in order to obtain concessions.[22] Soon after the election,
Secretary of State George Shultz reshuffled diplomatic appointments,
alarming Helms and his supporters. In December 1984, reports appeared of
an imminent purge of conservatives in the State Department; Shultz,
Helms feared, preferred career professionals to ideologues.[23] In response,
Helms and Senate conservatives waged what one critic called a "dirty little
war" against Reagan's diplomatic nominations.[24] On June 12, twenty-three
conservative senators met for over an hour with Reagan, charging that an
"ideological purge" was under way in the State Department. Reagan spent
most of the meeting listening. He remained committed to the conservative
cause, Reagan declared, but he observed that conservatives sometimes
"preferred to go off the cliff with all flags flying."[25] About a week after meeting with Reagan, Helms, with the support of other Senate conservatives,
wrote to Shultz, demanding a meeting and threatening holds on twenty-
nine nominations.[26]

　　Helms had long suspected the State Department of being filled with
compromisers and careerists and lacking enough dedicated conservatives.
Jesse was convinced that Shultz, as Jim Lucier put it, had been "completely

captured" by the Foreign Service and had become "its mouthpiece." The paranoia of Helms's attitudes toward State dominated his posture, but Lucier, who was even more suspicious of liberals' influence, encouraged and reinforced these attitudes and pushed for further confrontation. In memos to Helms in the summer of 1985, Lucier argued that the foreign service establishment, filled with careerists and Kissinger and Carter holdovers, was dominating the State Department.[27] Shultz was generally unwilling to compromise with his conservative critics, though he did make some concessions by providing positions for Helmsites in the State Department.[28] On June 25, Foreign Relations chair Richard Lugar hosted a meeting in his office between Shultz and Helms and other conservative senators, but bad feeling remained. The White House continued to press its case on June 26, when Reagan again met with conservative senators to urge quick confirmation. According to news reports, White House chief of staff Don Regan promised positions for conservative diplomats in the reorganized State Department.[29] But the Helms-Shultz deadlock continued past the July 4th recess, and the press generally blamed Helms.[30] The delay in confirmations, said the *Atlanta Constitution,* was the fault of Helms. His chief motivation was opposition to Shultz's "professionalizing the ambassadorial corps," which he and his Senate allies construed as a purge.[31] The *Los Angeles Times* criticized "Helms' wrecking crew" for "ideological blackmail" in delaying the nominations. "Somehow we doubt," it wrote, "that Reagan or his secretary of state has been taken over by dangerous liberals."[32] Eventually, however, the logjam broke. On July 8, Helms reached an agreement that cleared the way, lifting the holds in exchange for positions for the six conservative diplomats. Helms declared himself as "elated" by the outcome, and he voted against most of the nominations after he permitted them to reach the Senate floor.[33]

For much of the 1980s, Helms continued to battle the State Department by slowing the nomination process, and there were hard feelings.[34] "I have endured doubletalk, delays, and obviously deliberate confusion," he complained to Dole on July 11, 1985, "from the Secretary of State and the underlings who run that department." Shultz was equally bitter: the *Wall Street Journal* reported that he was "visibly angry" about Helms's stalling tactics.[35] At a Washington holiday cocktail party in December 1985, the secretary of state reportedly called Helms a "constitutional ignoramus"; Jesse responded by saying that Shultz "may not have had all four wheels on the ground" at the party.[36] Helms and his staff remained unsatisfied that the State Department bureaucracy had changed its ways. The professional diplomatic corps was an elite group, liberal and even socialist in its sympathies,

Jim Lucier told a reporter. Helms wanted a "good, yeasty leaven of [Reaganites] in there so they can have an influence."[37]

BY CONTESTING OTHER nominations, Helms exacted additional foreign policy concessions. When Winston Lord was proposed as ambassador to China in July 1985, Helms stalled the nomination for months, in part because of Lord's past associations with Kissinger's foreign policies. But figuring even more importantly than Helms's dislike of the State Department establishment was his opposition to U.S. overseas abortion policies. For several years, Jesse had been engaged in a battle with the Agency for International Development (AID) and its administrator, M. Peter McPherson, over U.S. support for international family planning. Claiming the existence of an "abortion network" at the agency, in May 1983 Helms staffers had met with McPherson about AID's history as "an agent for pro-abortion and anti-family policies."[38] On January 30, 1985, Helms wrote to McPherson objecting to continued support for United Nations birth control policies, which, he claimed, supported coercive abortions in China. McPherson responded by promising a comprehensive review, and on March 30 he announced that he would release $36 million to the United Nations Fund for Population Activities (UNFPA) but would withhold $10 million that supported its activities in China. Conservative Republicans were outraged. They believed that an amendment by New York congressman Jack Kemp—which in August 1985 had banned any support for family planning programs employing coercive abortions—already required a complete cutoff of UNFPA funds. In addition, the $10 million could only be permanently withheld with legislative changes in the foreign assistance law (which Congress enacted in August 1985). McPherson, over the weekend, made this decision irreversible by initiating an electronic transfer of the $10 million in funds. On April 2, Helms complained in a letter to Reagan that AID officials were not enforcing the existing law. In meetings with Republican congressmen on April 4, 1985, McPherson maintained that the law did not permit him to cut off all funds to UNFPA, only that portion going to China. Conservative Republican Congressman Jack Kemp of New York, believing that the will of Congress had been flouted, was incensed. Rather than a congressional recision of the $10 million, they insisted that the United States withhold all UNFPA funds until policies in China were changed. Later, McPherson met with the Stanton Group, representing about forty conservative organizations, to allay their fears, but they left the meeting angry at AID policies that seemed to support coercive abortion policies—along with other policies that, they charged, provided assistance to Marxist governments in Mozambique and Ethiopia. Denouncing McPherson as a "disgrace" and "unfit to hold office," conservative activist Paul Weyrich demanded his resignation. Helms, meanwhile, requested that the AID inspector general conduct an investigation to determine whether McPherson had enforced congressional intent.[39]

When Lord testified before the Senate Foreign Relations Committee on September 30, 1985, Helms questioned him closely. Although Lord supported the withholding of $10 million from the the U.N. population planning program, Helms remained unsatisfied. What was Lord's position on Chinese massacres when they invaded Tibet in 1950, he asked, and why had Lord not condemned it? When Lord responded that it was not his job "to sit here and engage in a litany of insults" against other countries, Helms said that he had "kind of disappoint[ed] me." After the Foreign Relations Committee approved Lord's nomination by a 16–1 vote—what one commentator called "sixteen to Helms"—Jesse wrote to Reagan in early October 1985 declaring that his opposition to Lord was based on the family planning issue. The State Department, meanwhile, sought to avert a wider diplomatic breach. China objected voiciferously to the congressional debate; Chinese president Li Xiannian described accounts of forced abortions as a "total fabrication and distortion."[40] When rumors surfaced that AID might release the $10 million to satisfy the Chinese, Helms and three other senators wrote to White House chief of staff Donald Regan, warning that such a decision would "greatly distress" President Reagan's conservative supporters. China was using coercive abortions in population planning, Helms insisted, and the United States was effectively condoning such practices, contrary to law. Although Reagan wrote to Jesse on October 6 and assured him that U.N. programs in China would be monitored—Reagan's letter was followed by a similar letter by McPherson on November 4— Helms wanted firmer guarantees. Lord's nomination would be approved as soon as Helms received a letter from the White House "to the effect that we will not support in any way coerced abortion and sterilization," Lucier told reporters.

Helms's fight over the Lord nomination was really directed at the diplomatic bureaucracy. Speaking with Reagan on November 4, Helms declared that the Lord nomination concerned the fundamental issue of whether AID and the State Department would obey the law. He wanted an "unfettered assurance, without loopholes" that the administration would follow congressional intent by requiring that UNFPA withdraw from China unless it changed its policies. He had personally assured Reagan, he told the Senate, that he had no intention of unduly delaying nominations. Rather, the fight was against the "foreign policy establishment," Helms maintained, which included State Department lawyers and AID bureaucrats. "If they think they are going to wear me down, let them try," he said. "If they want to continue to play games, they are going to have games." He had a message for both Lord and for his liberal supporters: "I am beyond your reach."[41] Reagan's personal intervention—which came in a phone call—ended the impasse, though Helms had already made his point to the public.[42] The Reagan administration promised to end American funding for China's population control practices. For the future, moreover, the door remained open for further pressure on other forms of family planning, including forms of birth control and abortion. Helms, the *New York Times* concluded, had "cowed the State Department into an embarrassing and counterproductive stand." During much of the rest of Reagan's second term, Helms would continue to fight AID over its family planning policies.[43]

HELMS'S SUSPICIONS OF the State Department extended into the area of Soviet-American relations. He strongly favored supporting anti-Communist "freedom fighters" in Central America, Afghanistan, Angola, and Ethiopia because they opposed Marxist-Leninist regimes that were, he believed, threats to western civilization.[44] Helms also remained suspicious of arms control negotiations with the Soviets. Shultz was unenthusiastic about Reagan's "Star Wars" program, the Strategic Defense Initiative (SDI), which sought to provide a space-based missile defense against nuclear attack, because he believed that it would undermine the upcoming summit talks between Reagan and Soviet head Mikhail Gorbachev at Geneva. In October 1985, in a Senate speech, Helms declared that Shultz was trying to "undermine and destroy the president's policy" and that his opposition to SDI constituted "appeasement" and "bargaining away SDI" on the eve of the Geneva summit "With one stroke," he said, Shultz had "cast into doubt the credibility of arms control and the utility of the forthcoming summit."[45] Helms was so concerned about Shultz's influence that he threatened to travel to Geneva with his foreign policy team to keep an eye on things, the prospect of which apparently sent "shivers through the administration high command."[46]

Helms was able to demonstrate his hostility to Soviet totalitarianism on October 24, 1985, when a twenty-five-year-old Ukrainian electrician, Miroslav Medvid, jumped into the Mississippi River at Belle Chasse, Louisiana, from a massive 120,000-ton grain freighter, the *Marshal Konev,* as it was nearing New Orleans to pick up 1.5 million bushels of yellow corn. Swimming to shore, Medvid asked bystanders to take him to a local police station so that he could defect. Interviewing him with a translator, immigration authorities, in a decision that all later agreed was mistaken, returned him to the ship. As he returned aboard a small launch, he again jumped into the river. Medvid was tackled and subdued with handcuffs and taken kicking and screaming back to the *Marshal Konev*. Four days later, on October 28, federal officials took Medvid off the ship, but he repeatedly declared his desire to return to the Soviet Union. On November 6, a federal judge refused to prevent the freighter from leaving port.

The senator then used his authority as chair of the Agriculture Committee to subpoena Medvid to testify. Helms's staffers visited Medvid's ship captain and delivered a carton of cigarettes—with a subpoena inside.[47] But, on November 9, New Orleans customs authorities, operating on instructions from the State Department, permitted the *Marshal Konev* to leave New Orleans in defiance of Helms's subpoena. As the freighter left port, members of the Ukrainian American Justice Committee exclaimed: "Stop that ship now! Stop that ship now!" For Jesse, the Medvid case provided additional evidence of the duplicity of the State Department.

After customs authorities ignored his subpoena, Helms conducted hearings anyway on November 12. Helms heard testimony from Dr. William E. O'Malley, a Waterford, Virginia, neuropsychiatrist who reviewed the State Department transcripts of the October 28 interview with Medvid. The government doctors examining the Ukrainian sailor, said O'Malley, exhibited "criminal negligence" in the case because they failed to take blood and urine samples that would have established if he was drugged. He concluded that the Soviets had tortured and drugged Medvid in order to prevent his defection.[48] "Why was the U.S. government so protective of the Soviets at this time?" Helms asked at the hearings. The Soviets behaved as if the ship enjoyed a kind of diplomatic immunity, and the State Department seemed to concur. The administration might have reached a secret agreement with the Soviets to send defectors back, he suggested, and the State Department might have thought that it was more important to appease the Soviet Union than to permit Medvid's freedom. The senator and his aides subsequently raised other possibilities, including a story that the Soviets had substituted an impostor for Medvid who had forged the statement renouncing his intention to defect.[49]

Years later, on February 6, 2001, Medvid, who had become a Roman Catholic priest in Ukraine, visited Jesse in his Senate office for about an hour. He told his story. After American immigration officials first returned him to his Soviet ship, he said, he came under heavy pressure from KGB agents. His mother had suffered Siberian imprisonment for eleven years for "bourgeois nationalism," and Medvid had been plotting his escape for a long time. He had joined the merchant marine in order to flee the Soviet Union, and he attempted to leave the freighter at its first port of call, New Orleans. Returned to the freighter, he had twice unsuccessfully attempted suicide by using a smashed light bulb to slash his wrists. When he was returned to the Soviet Union, authorities ruled that he was criminally insane, kept him shackled to his bed, and he underwent electroshock treatment and medication. A nurse sympathizing with his plight secretly injected his mattress, and Medvid was eventually returned home. Despite continued KGB surveillance, he studied to become a priest and left the seminary about the time the Soviet Union collapsed, in 1990. The Soviets had failed to extinguish his hope for freedom, said Medvid in 2001, because of Jesse Helms.[50]

SINCE HIS ARRIVAL in the Senate, Jesse had not always been an unequivocal supporter of Israel. In 1973, he proposed a resolution calling on Israel to return the West Bank to Jordan; two years later, he told the Senate that there would be no peace until the Palestinians achieved a "just settlement of their grievances." Later, he supported efforts by the Carter and Reagan administrations to supply arms to Arab allies, despite the opposition of Israel, while in the 1980s he favored cutting economic aid to Israel unless it stopped building settlements in the West Bank. In 1982, following the Israeli invasion of Lebanon, Helms supported breaking relations with Israel unless Israeli prime minister Menachem Begin agreed to a cease-fire.

These views began to change after August 1984, when Helms took a trip to Israel that he described as "easily the most meaningful week of my life."[51] Jesse's transformation into an avid Israel supporter in part reflected the involvement of staffer Darryl Nirenberg, who joined the senator's Agriculture Committee staff in 1984.[52] There was, however, a political motive in Helms's increasingly pro-Israel positions. After Jim Hunt accused him, during the 1984 Senate campaign, of having the the worst "anti-Israel record of any member of the U.S. Senate," Helms shifted his views. In addition, the Likud faction, a conservative/right coalition that governed Israel under Prime Minister Begin, cultivated contacts with the American Religious Right. In August 1985, Helms visited Israel with the freshman senator from Nevada, Chic Hecht, a Jewish Republican. In Jerusalem, Helms held a press conference in which he described Israel as "the only reliable ally we have in this area which is anti-communist, with impeccable moral principles."[53] Israel was "vital to the survival of western civilization," he told a group of Jewish and conservative leaders in January 1986.[54]

Helms's primary interest in foreign policy remained in the developing world, especially Africa and Latin America. In both regions, seeking to prevent Soviet influence, he supported authoritarian regimes. As he had been for nearly thirty years, Helms remained the Senate's strongest supporter of the South African apartheid regime. But the political dynamics were changing in black Africa. As Congress questioned continued economic relations with the white-minority regime, support for the Reagan administration's policy of constructive engagement with South Africa disappeared. Rising black resistance, followed by brutal South African repression, outraged American public opinion. In early April 1985, House Democrats voted in favor of economic sanctions against the "evil and unacceptable apartheid system," while the Senate voted 89–4 to condemn that country's racial practices (with Helms voting against the resolution).[55] By the summer of 1985, public opinion had swung against the apartheid regime, and South Africa was facing nearly complete isolation.[56]

In June 1985, the Senate Foreign Relations Committee, with only Helms dissenting, approved legislation to ban bank loans and military computer sales to South Africa, and required American companies employing more than twenty-five people to provide equal employment and housing without regard to race. Meanwhile, the House enacted even more stringent anti-apartheid measures.[57] Leading opposition to the sanctions legislation in the Senate, Helms mounted a filibuster, and his Democratic adversary Alan Cranston criticized Jesse for the "dirty undercurrent of racism" and "anti-communist blindness" that was "rising to the surface in the tolerance of apartheid and the apparent lack of concern over the suffering of 23 million blacks." Helms's filibuster, on July 10, 1985, met a quick defeat with a cloture vote, a stinging rebuke for Helms's pro–South Africa approach and for Reagan's constructive engagement policy[58] The White House temporarily ended the congressional revolt in September 1985 by imposing some sanctions by executive order and thus avoiding passage of the bill.[59]

But with the uprising occurring in South Africa and the white government responding with more repression, anti-apartheid sentiment did not subside. In June 1986, the House adopted a divestment bill, which included a trade embargo and the withdrawal of most American assets from the country. In August, the Senate Foreign Relations Committee approved new and tougher sanctions that ended landing rights of South Africa's national airline in the United States, froze nondiplomatic bank holdings of the South African government, banned coal, steel, uranium, and cement imports from

South Africa, and prohibited new American investments in and loans to South Africa. These Senate sanctions would remain until South Africa freed imprisoned African National Congress leader Nelson Mandela, legalized black political parties, and suspended its state of emergency. Helms, along with South Dakota senator Larry Pressler, was alone in opposing these measures, though his opposition was futile.[60] Although Reagan vetoed the sanctions legislation, Congress overrode his veto on October 2, 1986, by a 78–21 vote. Not surprisingly, Helms led the effort to sustain the veto.[61]

In Latin America, of particular concern to Helms was Mexico, which he feared might engulf the United States with a flood of immigrants as a result of a social and political disintegration. Helms first became interested in Mexico during a series of hearings that he held in North Carolina and elsewhere in 1984 dealing with drug smuggling, as many of his witnesses from the Drug Enforcement Administration and customs officials reported that Mexico had become a major source of the drugs pouring into the United States. Mexico was unquestionably facing a crisis. The 1970s oil boom gave way, in the 1980s, to a slumping oil economy and rising debt and international pressure on the peso. In 1982, Mexico ran out of money to pay its international debt, and budget austerity and a deep recession followed. The collapse of oil prices in 1985–86 placed its economy under additional stress, with the peso in crisis. Mexicans considered suspending debt payments, but as a result of falling oil prices government revenues declined by a fourth in the first half of 1986. Mexicans sought additional loans from the International Monetary Fund and a renegotiation of its existing $97 billion foreign debt, with as much as $7 billion in new loans. Treasury officials, in talks, sought further budget cuts.[62]

In mid-May 1986, Jesse convened hearings, as chair of the Foreign Relations subcommittee on Latin American affairs, on the Mexican debt focusing on corruption, and U.S. commissioner of customs William von Raab and assistant secretary Elliott Abrams both testified. Beforehand, the Mexican embassy, Helms told reporters, called him three or four times with a warning that critical testimony would "fracture relations." During the first day of hearings, on May 12, testimony occurred behind closed doors; the next day, the same two witnesses testified publicly. Both men sharply criticized the problem of corruption and drug trafficking. Von Raab, who had seen a flood of drugs coming across the southern border during his watch, warned of a larger crisis in the ruling Institutional Revolutionary Party (PRI). An "ingrained corruption" existed in the Mexican law enforcement community, said von Raab, that was "massive... all the way up and down the ladder." When it came to Mexico, von Raab said, customs officials assumed that most Mexican politicians were corrupt. Abrams confirmed von Raab's assertions about official corruption and drug smuggling.[63]

Von Raab's and Abrams's testimony caused an uproar. The Mexican government recalled its ambassador to the United States, and an anti-American demonstration of about sixty thousand people occurred in Mexico City. American officials in Mexico apologized in response to the protests, while administration officials distanced themselves from the testimony. Secretary of the Treasury James Baker offered the ambiguous comment to reporters that Meese said that von Raab's statements did not "represent administration policy, even though they may be true."[64] According to the *Washington Post,* the testimony suggested that Treasury was not behind Helms's "inflammatory and inaccurate attacks," and that Jim Baker had "decided not to assist Sen. Helms in his vendetta against Mexico."[65] But Helms refused to back down, asserting that the publicity from his hearings had blocked a disastrous U.S. bailout. His message, he said, had "gotten through loud and clear."[66] Americans needed to know "what kind of neighbors we have, because that's a way to persuade them to clean up their act," he told the *Charlotte Observer.* Latin Americans, he further observed, were a "volatile people," and he was thus "not surprised at the volatile reaction."[67] Although Helms claimed that he had been misquoted in these comments,[68] he was widely condemned. Hispanic leaders sent a letter to Senate majority leader Bob Dole, denouncing Jesse for his "callous, irresponsible and insensitive remarks" and calling on the Senate to censure him for his "erratic, offensive and unstatesmanlike behavior."[69] The *Washington Post* described Helms's characterization of Latin Americans as containing "extraordinarily false, condescending and harmful words." This was an "undeniable embarrassment to American foreign policy." How could it be explained to Latin Americans that the "practice of ethnic insult" was "still a live political commodity in the United States?" Mexican-American relations, which had "never have been so central and so delicate," hung in the balance.[70]

Helms's motivation in pressing the May and June 1986 hearings about Mexico is uncertain. No doubt Helms, as always, was interested in gaining additional leverage in the conduct of Latin American policy. But there were likely wider motives. Helms disliked the Mexican government, said Arizona governor Bruce Babbitt, and he believed that Helms's hearing could "impeach its legitimacy" and somehow destabilize it.[71] Others speculated that Helms was working with elements in the Reagan administration who were displeased with the government of Miguel de la Madrid, and the appearance of Abrams—who headed the Latin American desk at the State Department—seemed to confirm this. An important consideration, in addition, was Helms's anger toward Mexico for doing little to oppose the Nicaraguan Sandinistas. Certainly Helms subscribed to this view. "Mexico ought to be out there helping keep communism out of Central America instead of doing the opposite," Jesse said. Mexican diplomats, expanding on Helms's comments, informed reporters that the senator's campaign against their country reflected the work of a "small group of ultraconservatives."[72]

Not yet finished with the Mexicans, Helms held further subcommittee hearings on June 17, 1986. There he charged that the PRI ruling party had maintained its power through fraud and that the $9 billion that the United States had provided in 1982 had ended up in Swiss bank accounts.[73] Helms also asserted that de la Madrid was elected in a bogus election in 1982 and that the legislative elections of 1985 were tainted. The PRI maintained two sets of election results, he claimed, one public, the other private. PRI candidates always won according to the public results, but the true results were another matter. Claiming access to a report written by de la Madrid's military chief of staff's office, Helms maintained that de la Madrid should have received 39.8 percent of the vote in 1982, rather than the official tally of 71.3 percent. A true tally of the 1985 legislative elections, Helms charged, showed that PRI candidates received 48 percent of the vote, rather than the official count of 71.1 percent. Voter fraud undermined the PRI's legitimacy, he said, and supported a pervasive system of graft and political corruption. Despite the uproar against him, Helms's critique of the Mexican political system was fundamentally accurate. Rampant corruption in Mexico had grown worse with the impact of drug smuggling to the United States. Jesse pulled few punches, and he tied Mexican corruption to his old hatred of socialism. The PRI was rotten to the core, he charged, sustained by "socialist methods of economic control to direct graft and corruption to the ruling circles." "If the situation in Mexico continues to be one of fraud, corruption and the strangling of democracy," Helms declared, "then vast infusions of U.S. taxpayers' cash will only open up more opportunities for corruption and fraud." American aid should be tied to political reform, Helms insisted.

On June 28, Helms continued his campaign against Mexico with a third set of hearings. Repeating allegations that had recently surfaced in the news media, he claimed that de la Madrid's cousin, Edmundo de la Madrid Ochoa, and the head of the Mexican Judicial Police, Florentino Ventura, were both involved in cocaine trafficking.[74] The Mexican government immediately denounced Helms's charges of political corruption and drug smuggling as "groundless and most probably ... intended to confuse public opinion." De la Madrid's military chief of staff, it said, had nothing to do with voting and that the results were tallied in a public process. State Department officials declared that they had "no reason to believe such charges" and had "never seen any evidence to support them." Jesse's Mexican sources came from his own intelligence network that his aides had carefully cultivated throughout Latin America, and in this instance—as in others—he had information that was not generally available. Helms's network confirmed his assertions that the PRI was riddled with corruption, and it had maintained a one-party state through electoral malfeasance. In contrast to past attitudes toward Latin American governments, moreover, Helms had now become a champion of democracy and human rights. But in raising the issue—and continuing to raise it—Helms threatened to create an international incident.[75]

Helms remained opposed to any American bailout on the Mexican debt crisis. Appearing on *Meet the Press* on June 22, he said that the $9 billion bailout in 1982 had been a mistake. "Look what's happened since 1982," he said. "They're on a slippery slope because it's a socialized country, because it has a one-party government." The United States should "look several times," he said, "before we further supplement and support a socialized government that is driving the people down, driving the people out."[76] When de la Madrid visited the United States in August 1986, Helms made a point of sponsoring additional hearings to gather testimony of Mexican dissidents about fraud and political corruption.[77] Helms continued to press on the Mexican issue over the next three years. The Anti-Drug Act of 1986 included provisions that required the State Department to certify that countries receiving foreign aid were not involved in drug smuggling, and Helms challenged Mexico's certification. Helms assembled a bipartisan coalition of senators, including Dennis DeConcini, a Democrat from Arizona, John Kerry of Massachusetts, and Alfonse D'Amato of New York. In March 1987, Helms and Kerry unsuccessfully challenged the Reagan administration's efforts to certify that Mexico was cooperating against drug trafficking.[78] A year later, in April 1988, Helms's anti-drug coalition had grown larger, and the Senate voted, by a margin of 63–27, to cut off aid to Mexico.[79]

HELMS'S CRITIQUE OF Latin American political corruption and drug infestation also included Panama. Never fully accepting the 1978 Panama Canal treaties, after 1985 Helms became an unyielding critic of the regime of General Manuel Antonio Noriega, who had, two years earlier, effectively assumed power. In September 1985, Hugo Spadafora, a physician and critic of the regime, was brutally murdered, apparently by Panamanian forces under Noriega's direction. The Panamanian middle class was outraged at the murder—eighty thousand people appeared at his funeral—and President Nicolás Ardito Barletta was forced to resign. But American officials did little to pressure Noriega, whom they saw as a reliable ally in the American-supported war by anti-Sandinista contras in Nicaragua with close connections to American intelligence (for many years, in fact, he was on the CIA payroll). In December 1985, Spadafora's brother, Winston Spadafora, lobbied fruitlessly in a visit to Washington, but Helms, at Deborah DeMoss's urging, agreed to meet with him on January 23, 1986. Showing Jesse the graphic photographs of his brother's body, the senator became intensely interested. Looking at the photographs for a long time, he put them down and shook his head. "I'm going to promise you something," Helms declared. "I'm going to promise to work my hardest to get justice for your brother and to raise the issue to the level of President Reagan's agenda."[80]

From early 1986 until December 1989, Helms worked relentlessly against the Noriega regime. Until then, Jesse had shown less interest in protecting human rights and democracy: that changed in Panama. In part, this reflected his long-standing opposition to the canal treaties, but Panama became, for Helms, a just cause, and he became a crusader, coalition builder, and coordinator. Soon after his meeting with Winston Spadafora, Helms introduced an amendment to the foreign aid bill imposing economic sanctions on Panama until Hugo Spadafora's killers were brought to justice. Although the amendment attracted only one vote in committee and two others in the full Senate, Jesse pressed on. In March and April 1986, Helms held hearings as chair of the Latin American affairs subcommittee of the Foreign Relations Committee, despite the opposition of the White House, which increased military aid from $8.4 million in 1986 to $14.6 million in 1987. When Helms summoned Elliott Abrams, assistant secretary of state for Latin American affairs, Abrams defended Panama as an ally having "a civilian government with military interference in areas of interest to the military." In contrast, another witness, former National Security Council staffer Norman Bailey, testified about how drug trafficking was "endemic" in the Panamanian military.[81]

Gradually, Helms's refrain about Panama began to attract the interest of others. In a major story that appeared on June 12–13, Seymour Hersh of the *New York Times* described widespread political corruption and killings of dissidents in Panama; a week later, Hersh charged that Noriega had rigged the 1984 Panamanian presidential election. Hersh further suggested that Noriega had long been on the CIA payroll. On June 22, Helms, appearing on *Meet the Press,* repeated charges that Noriega was responsible for the Spadafora assassination, money laundering, and protecting drug smugglers in "the biggest drug-trafficking operation in the Western Hemisphere." The senator further suggested that Noriega may have been complicit in the death of his predecessor, General Omar Torrijos, who was killed in a plane crash in 1981. If Noriega were innocent of these charges, Helms said, he should "call for an immediate, full independent investigation and say 'Look at everything I've done.'" But, he added, "I wouldn't hold your breath until he does that."[82]

Helms worked assiduously, through his staffers, to construct bipartisan support for an anti-Noriega policy. In late September 1986, he introduced an amendment to the intelligence bill requiring the CIA director to report on the Panamanian military's involvement in smuggling of drugs and arms, human rights violations, money laundering, and the Spadafora killing. CIA director William Casey argued hard against the amendment, and he telephoned Helms. Casey, insisting that the amendment be pulled, became so angry that he hung up on the senator. Despite Casey's opposition, Helms's amendment passed on September 24, by a vote of 53–46, with significant Democratic support.[83] By February 1988, John Kerry had joined with Helms in sponsoring Senate hearings on connections between Noriega and drugs. At those hearings, witnesses testified to Panamanian drug connections. For the most part, Helms remained in the public background: the Panamanian drug hearings were run by other senators. But by early 1988, he had assembled a coalition of senators that included Kerry, Ted Kennedy, Al D'Amato, and David R. Durenberger of Minnesota. In November 1987, the lead Latin American staffers for the five senators traveled to Panama. DeMoss, who represented Helms, was already well known in Panama. It later became known that the CIA had provided a report on DeMoss to Noriega, and during earlier visits, the Panamanian strongman arranged for coverage in the pro-government Panamanian press that sought to discredit her. DeMoss suffered from the flu, and she checked into a hospital when she arrived in Panama. While there, doctors and nurses greeted her as a hero, urging her to continue the fight against Noriega. After she recovered, Noriega subsequently ordered her arrest at her hotel, which she averted only after a hotel staffer tipped her off and she escaped to the American embassy through a rear entrance.[84]

Helms continued to pressure the Reagan and Bush administrations to oust Noriega. In July 1987, Reagan suspended economic and military aid to Panama; in late 1987, Congress extended the cutoff. In 1987 and 1988, federal law enforcement officials pursued Noriega, and a Miami federal grand jury indicted him in February 1988. But, as opposition to Noriega grew in Panama, Helms favored stronger measures. Sometime in 1989, Helms and Kerry arranged a meeting with Colin Powell, who was national security adviser under Reagan and became chairman of the joint chiefs of staff under Bush. The senators had consulted with the U.S. Marshals Service, and, with a detailed plan in hand, told Powell that it would be possible to assemble a strike force to capture Noriega and transport him to an American courtroom. Unless drastic measures were taken by the adminstration, the situation would inevitably deteriorate; Noriega was unpredictable, even crazy. Eventually, they argued, a full-scale American invasion would become necessary. Powell, who was well known for his reluctance to commit American forces to combat, would have none of it. "Panama," he said, was "not worth losing one American life over."[85]

But events soon proved otherwise. On October 3, 1989, members of the Panamanian Defense Force, led by Major Moisés Giroldi, mounted a coup against Noriega. They had informed the White House two days in advance, but the administration proceeded indecisively, refusing any involvement of American forces against the Panamanian military. The coup proceeded at 7:00 A.M. on October 3, and when the conspirators received no support from the United States Southern Command, they called Helms's office at about 9:30, saying that they had Noriega in custody in his general headquarters, the *Comandancia,* and that they wanted to turn him over to the Americans. DeMoss had already learned about the coup from her sources in Panama. The coup leaders also wanted the American military to block access by pro-Noriega forces to the *Comandancia,* where the strongman was being held. Helms's office remained on the line for the duration of the crisis—about four hours, until pro-Noriega forces flew into Tocumen Airport and proceeded unhindered to liberate Noriega. The loyalist troops eventually stormed the *Comandancia* where he was being held, and the phone went dead.

At one point in the crisis, Noriega was brought to the phone, and DeMoss was convinced that it was he. When she asked him if Noriega and his supporters were being held, he made a "cutting remark," saying, "Yes, they are, but they won't be for long." DeMoss spread out a map of Panama in Helms's Senate offices, and during the crisis monitored troop movements. DeMoss's information was "exact, accurate, and virtually up to the minute," according to a later assessment, and it even identified Noriega's exact location in the *Comandancia.*[86] According to DeMoss, Helms repeatedly tried to communicate this information to administration officials, but they refused to take his call. The Bush White House remained paralyzed by inaction and confusion; by now, Colin Powell had authorized a covert team to seize Noriega, but the operation could proceed only if direct conflict could be avoided. According to some accounts, the American military was willing to take Noriega, but only if the rebels delivered him. The rebels wanted Noriega to resign and, fearing the presence of pro-Noriega forces, they insisted that Americans send a helicopter. Lacking any significant American support, the Giroldi coup collapsed, and its ringleaders were executed.[87]

The White House's inaction reflected a reluctance to intervene militarily in Panama, a hesitation to put American troops at risk, and suspicions about Giroldi. General Maxwell Thurman, who had just taken over military command, was convinced that the coup was a trap set by Noriega himself; according to one account, Thurman was simply "dead wrong" in his assessment of the situation, and his refusal to intervene shaped the White House's response.[88] But administration policy exposed a general policy paralysis. On the day of the failed coup, in a Senate speech, Helms criticized the White House, saying that it had no plan "other than to do nothing" in Panama. The administration was nothing more than a bunch of "Keystone Kops" who had shown a "total lack of planning." No further coups could be expected from the Panamanian Defense Force given the absence of American support. Two days later, on October 5, Helms, in another Senate speech, provided a detailed narrative of the Giroldi coup that, in precise detail, documented White House incompetence. Jesse then proposed a message that would authorize the president to use military force against Noriega and bring him to trial in the United States, but this was defeated by a vote of 74–25. The Bush White House strongly contradicted Helms's version of events, in what one historian has called a "post-coup cover-up" of the true events.[89]

Much of what the administration claimed to be the case proved to be outright falsehood. Defense Secretary Dick Cheney told reporters in a television interview that the American military forces "would have been happy" to take custody of Noriega but the coup rebels refused to permit it. Giroldi had been a crucial figure in suppressing a 1988 coup attempt against Noriega, and Cheney claimed that American officials were concerned that this "might well have been a setup." Bush had made a "very sound decision," Cheney asserted. He further claimed that the administration was never certain that Noriega was in custody, and their information was that he was "in

another place, another location." Cheney, on October 6, continued the public relations campaign by asserting that Congress's strict rules against covert
operations had hampered the administration's ability to act.[90]

In a *New York Times* report, an unidentifed White House official attacked Helms's staff, saying that he was "badly misserved" by his advisers.
"Any charge that we were somehow offered Noriega and didn't take him is
hogwash," said White House spokesman Marlin Fitzwater. Helms's account was "full of it" and "not true." In a bald-faced lie, Fitzwater told reporters that the White House had no knowledge of the coup plot, nor had it
had any "direct discussions" with the rebels.[91] Privately, White House chief
of staff John Sununu telephoned Helms after his speech, demanding a
meeting. Helms demurred, sending DeMoss and Lucier, while Sununu was
joined by National Security Adviser Brent Scowcroft and his deputy,
Robert Gates. Sununu was outraged, saying that nothing had happened and
the coup plotters never had possession of Noriega. Both he and Scowcroft
were enraged—at one point, Sununu threw a book in disgust—and they
demanded to know Helms's sources. DeMoss's version of events was a lie,
they charged. "You say it's a lie, we say it's true," DeMoss responded. "We
have good sources. You don't." DeMoss and Lucier refused to provide their
sources, however, saying that they had promised confidentiality because
their informants feared for their lives. During the coup, Helms had tried repeatedly to communicate with the White House; he had not gone to the
press; he had not grandstanded. The meeting at the White House, which
lasted about a half hour, ended acrimoniously. On the way out, Gates, who
had remained silent during the meeting, privately confirmed that their account of Helms's role was accurate.[92]

About two months after the failed Giraldi coup, the situation in Panama
deteriorated even further, and, in Operation Just Cause, United States
forces invaded Panama, arrested Noriega, transported him to a Miami
prison, and made provisions for elections.[93] In the end, Helms appeared
vindicated, though the conclusion was yet another American invasion of a
Latin American country. Still, his actions in Panama largely belied the reputation that he had earned in foreign policy in the 1970s and 1980s. Helms
pressed his case relentlessly with the Reagan and Bush administrations,
though both regarded him as an irrelevant irritant. He had constructed a bipartisan coalition opposed to a dictatorial and corrupt regime. Insisting on
his case, often behind the scenes, he became what *Human Events* called an
"unsung hero" in the effort to intervene in Panama.[94]

HELMS ALSO FOCUSED attention on U.S. policy toward Chile, although, unlike either Mexico or Panama, his chief goal was to support the authoritarian regime in power. Under the iron grip of Augusto Pinochet's junta since September 1973, Chile was undergoing change by the mid-1980s. Beginning in 1983, the urban poor protested the regime from their shantytowns, and anti-Pinochet demonstrations were met with brutal repression. In central Santiago, Chile's capital, the demonstrators' barricades only sometimes prevented marauding troops from assaulting protesters. In May 1986, nineteen-year-old Rodrigo Rojas de Negri, who lived in Washington and recently graduated from high school there, flew to Peru and took a bus across the border to Chile. Rojas's mother, a former Communist Party activist who was beaten and raped at prisons in Valparaiso and Santiago, had gone into exile in 1977. Young Rojas arrived in Santiago and spent several months visiting with his cousins and taking photographs, and he found a job working on computers at a Santiago medical school. Rodrigo was swept up in the anti-Pinochet protests, and, as he photographed their eruption in the Santiago shantytowns, he became more deeply involved in the revolt.

On July 2–3, a general strike against the Pinochet regime gripped Chile. In the early morning of July 2, Rojas and Canadian student (another young returning Chilean exile) Carmen Gloria Quintana, joined a protest in Nogales, a northern Santiago working-class suburb. Caught by an army patrol, they were beaten with rifle butts, doused with gasoline, and set afire. Presuming them dead, the soldiers wrapped Rojas and Quintana in blankets, threw them in the back of a truck, and dumped them in a ditch. Though badly injured and burned, somehow they crawled out and obtained help. After Rojas died from severe burns four days later, his case generated international pressure on Pinochet. The State Department sent Robert S. Gelbard, a deputy assistant secretary for inter-American affairs, to investigate, and an American spokesman called on the government to conduct a "complete and thorough investigation into this tragic incident." The American ambassador, Harry Barnes, announced that he would attend Rojas's funeral on July 9. But during the ceremony, which was attended by thousands of mourners (many of them from the Chilean left), riot police attacked the crowd with water cannon and tear gas, and Barnes, along with other diplomats present, was gassed and forced to flee the scene. The pro-Pinochet press blamed the American ambassador for the violence.

The incident that became known as *Los Quemados*—"The Burned Ones"—coincided with a visit to Chile by Helms and aides Deborah DeMoss, James Lucier, and Clifford Kiracofe, Jr. Helms had last visited Chile in July 1976, when he had urged international recognition for the Pinochet junta.

His visit a decade later, which was sponsored by Chile's National Agricultural Society, was also designed to bolster the Chilean regime. But almost immediately Helms's visit became consumed by the Rojas case. Meeting with the ministers of Interior and Foreign Affairs, as well as the president of the Supreme Court, Helms discussed the case with Pinochet. Helms's staff also was in regular contact with investigating authorities, and Helms accepted the official version, criticized the State Department's response, and urged the U.S. government to accept Pinochet's explanation. Five days after the incident, on July 11, Pinochet asserted, in a televised address, that Rojas and Quintana had set themselves on fire while trying to attack the soldiers. Few observers gave much credence to this explanation. Within days, under American pressure, Pinochet would admit that the military was involved, and twenty-five soldiers were arrested but then released. An army lieutenant was brought to trial before a military court for failing to get Rojas and Quintana to a hospital quickly enough. Subsequently, Quintana was awarded $600,000 in compensation; Rojas's mother received a $300 per month pension. In 1988, the Organization of American States's Commission on Human Rights, ruling that the Chilean government was guilty of violating Rodrigo's and Carmen's right to life, declared that the Nogales patrol had deliberately set the two young people on fire.[95]

Helms's defense of the Chilean regime was based on his belief that it was a reliable partner, stable politically and free of drug influence, and well positioned to combat world Communism.[96] Meeting privately with Pinochet for two hours on July 11, Helms attacked press coverage of events, which he called "totally misrepresentative." He had never seen "a socialistic government that the *New York Times* or the *Washington Post* did not like." The United States, he said, should "understand that Chile is one of two countries in the entire Latin American area that resists communism." Chile's development, Helms said, remained on "an orderly course." But Helms went further. In angry exchanges, he sharply criticized the State Department, which responded to the Rojas case by increasing pressure on Pinochet to accelerate a return to democratic rule. Helms especially criticized Ambassador Barnes: by attending Rojas's funeral, Barnes was guilty of "planting the American flag in the midst of communist activity." If Reagan were president, Helms said, "he would send this ambassador home."[97]

Helms and his staffers regularly ran afoul of American embassies. Typically, Jesse's operation worked outside regular channels; Helms staffers, when visiting countries, usually arranged their schedules without the ambassador's help. Barnes, who had embraced the Rojas cause, had already lost patience with Helms, while the senator was convinced that Barnes was conducting an anti-Pinochet policy that went beyond even what the State Department endorsed. On July 12, Helms complained directly to Barnes in a stormy twenty-five-minute meeting at the American embassy. Jesse told the ambassador that he and "the people in Washington" had "screwed it up." Not only should Barnes have refused to attend Rojas's funeral, Helms declared, but the State Department should back off from its insistence on an independent investigation. Based on information from Pinochet, Helms claimed that Rojas's burns were self-inflicted, the result of an accidental explosion of his own incendiary device. The "boy's mother was a communist," Helms further suggested, and that Quintana belonged to a "communist group." Barnes was not impressed, and like most observers, then and since, he had already concluded that Pinochet's explanation was ludicrous. What DeMoss remembered as a "very unpleasant meeting" ended badly, as Barnes angrily left the room.[98]

Helms's visit to Chile attracted hostile reaction from his newspaper critics back home. Most agreed with the assessment of the *Raleigh Times,* a conservative evening newspaper, which facetiously suggested that some organization should start a campaign to buy new glasses and hearing aid for the senator. What he really needed, it editorialized, was "an open mind and compassion, but those qualities can't be purchased." During his Chile tour, Jesse had "doggedly ignored that country's atrocious human rights record" and blamed the American media because they covered the Pinochet regime's terrorizing of its citizens. He had swallowed the ridiculous position of the Chilean government about Rojas "without qualms" despite its track record of murder and terror. Jesse's "paranoia over Communism" had "anesthetized" him to the truth, rendering him "deaf, blind and dumb to official policies of corruption and torture."[99]

In Washington, the State Department responded to Helms by unequivocally supporting Barnes. Describing Helms's involvement as indefensible, Elliott Abrams said that those Americans who favored "an indefinite extension of military rule in Chile" were "playing into the hands of the communists" by encouraging further revolt. One advantage of the publicity surrounding Helms's visit to Santiago, Abrams believed, was that it had permitted "us to clarify our commitment to a return to democracy in Chile." "Before that, we were locked into a position of reacting to events in Chile," he told a reporter. Because of Helms, American diplomats could "make our position clear to the American public and to the Chilean government" that Helms's views were "completely isolated" and that there was a "broad consensus among American conservatives about the need for a transition to democracy."[100] Helms responded to Abrams's criticisms with a phone call on July 14. According to Abrams's account, Helms noted the criticism, but asserted that Barnes "had no business going to a funeral of someone who was not an American and whose mother is very anti-American." Although he urged the State Department to patch up relations with Pinochet, he found an unresponsive audience in Abrams.[101]

In an interview with the *Raleigh News and Observer* on his return to Washington, Helms continued to argue his case. Chile under Pinochet, Jesse believed, possessed the "elements of a democracy." Helms continued to conceive of Chile in primarily Cold War terms—the threat of Communism, he believed, justified the repression, even though Communists posed no real danger to the country. During his visit, he discovered little evidence of governmental repression, while, in contrast, the outbreak of violence was "500 to 1" the work of Communists.[102] On July 20, Helms appeared with Chilean writer and Duke University professor Ariel Dorfman on *This Week with David Brinkley*. Dorfman told the television audience that the Pinochet government was so fundamentally dishonest that its account could not be believed. "There are just so many lies piled on top of another I think at times the lies are more vicious than the violence." Calling Dorfman "one of the prime disinformation agents of the radical Chilean Left," Helms asserted that the chief cause of the violence in Chile was "the communist minority." There was a "war on down there, between communism and anticommunism, and the sooner we understand that, the better off we are going to be." In early August 1986, Helms continued the attack. In a speech, he declared that Rojas's mother was partly responsible. "While we can all sympathize with a mother's grief," he said, according to his information she had once been a "militant member of the Communist Party of Chile, skilled in psychological warfare."[103]

Helms's battle over Chile continued when he was accused of disclosing classified intelligence information. On July 18, the Senate Intelligence Committee requested that the FBI investigate alleged leaks of information by Helms or his staff; the leaks were supposedly of American eavesdropping on Chilean armed forces, which had provided details about Rojas's death and the army's culpability in it. The leaked intelligence also supplied some details about opposition to Pinochet within the Chilean military. According to Senate rules, the Senate Intelligence Committee was required to request an FBI investigation in the event of leaks. CIA director William Casey was reportedly angered by the alleged Chile leak; Secretary of State Shultz was described as "furious."[104]

Helms vehemently denied any leaking, asserting that the FBI inquiry was political. "The State Department and the Central Intelligence Agency are constantly trying to discredit me," he told a reporter, "and they're not going to be able to do it." The "real need" instead was for the "State Department and the C.I.A. to clean up their acts." Further, he said, if these agencies wanted a "game of intimidation, of harassment and of leaks, we'll meet them right in the middle of the field." "What I say about the C.I.A. and the State Department," he declared, "I say publicly, while they dodge around in dark corners and leak to the *New York Times*," he told reporters.[105] The State Department and CIA were "lying through their teeth," he told the *Raleigh News and Observer;* the allegations were "dirty pool" that would "come to nothing."[106] In a press conference a day after the *Times* story appeared, Helms continued his vigorous denial. These "trumped up" charges were, he said, part of "a smear campaign" engineered by his State Department enemies. "They don't like the fact that I am opposed to their little agenda down there, which is to sell out the friends of the United States and cozy up to the adversaries of the United States," Helms claimed.[107]

Helms continued to dispute the leak story, which he insisted was itself a leak designed to discredit him. Calling the entire affair a hoax, Jesse demanded that the State Department supply documentation about his office's involvement. "You have the makings of a nice little conspiracy down there in the State Department against a senator who has dared to call their hand about the private agenda of the bureaucracy," he said. The "yo-yos" at the State Department and CIA were settling scores, he added in a speech in Greenville, North Carolina, on August 6, because he had exposed them in El Salvador in 1984.[108] Jesse went further in his attack against the CIA, when he charged that intelligence services had spied on him during his July visit to Chile. On August 8, Helms asked Attorney General Edwin Meese to investigate whether the CIA had violated the law by mounting either "electronic or physical surveillance" against him. He also intimated that he might strike back by delaying Senate action on CIA funding.[109]

Helms's feud with the CIA and the State Department extended into the waging of the contra war. Edén Pastora, a Nicaraguan contra who had switched from the Sandinista side and who was known for his erratic behavior, was known as "Commander Zero" for his daring tactics. But Pastora ran afoul of his CIA handlers, and the agency cut off aid in 1984. Appealing to Helms, Pastora's advisers made contact with the senator's staff sometime in 1985. In a secret trip to Nicaragua in March 1986, retired U.S. Army general John K. Singlaub attempted to broker an agreement by which Pastora would join in a united front with other contras in exchange for the restoration of American aid. Although according to a subsequently released cable from the American ambassador to Costa Rica, Lewis Tambs, Singlaub met with Pastora as "the envoy of Sen. Helms," his office denied that Singlaub came in any such capacity.

Since the late 1970s, Deborah DeMoss worked as a translator and adviser on Latin American affairs and ran an extensive network of contacts in Latin America; she was known as responsible for operating a "shadow State Department" that possessed its own information-gathering network that often rivaled the real State Department for its accuracy. The State Department, she recalled, had a "fear" of Helms and his staff that was sometimes unreasonable. Years later, when she married and moved to Honduras, she used to attend American embassy functions, and embassy personnel would react strangely when she introduced herself. "Oh, *you* are Deborah DeMoss," they would say. She often responded by asking them if they kept a dartboard with Jesse Helms's face on it. DeMoss met with Secretary of State Shultz—and under the first George Bush, Secretary of State Jim Baker—and often urged them to seek conciliation with Helms, rather than conflict. The senator was a "puppy," she said, and "all you need to do is to talk to him."[110]

In March 1985, DeMoss told the press that she had met with Singlaub both before and after his trip. She had also met with Pastora in January 1985, and Helms briefly met with the contra leader. Helms also delivered speeches praising Pastora and sponsored a meeting between Shultz and him. "A lot of people in the administration didn't like him," she recalled, and "we couldn't figure out why." Still, DeMoss denied that her conversations with Singlaub amounted to a direct relationship. She met with him, DeMoss said, "but I certainly did not tell him to go to Nicaragua or ask him to go to Nicaragua." The involvement of Helms's staff suggested a continuing suspicion about the activities of the CIA in Nicaragua, and the furor that accompanied the Iran-contra scandal—which involved illegal arms sale and support for the contras—suggested the divide between the Helms people and White House officials such as Oliver North. Helms remained loyal to the Reagan administration as the Iran-contra scandal unfolded, but he denounced the CIA as responsible for a "massive intelligence failure" leading to bad decision-making by North and the National Security Council. Despite the "myth" that the CIA was a "right-wing extremist organization," it was actually "the operating wing of the State Department." When all was said and done about Central America, he asserted the CIA "did more to undermine the contras in Nicaragua than the left-wing Democrats in Congress."[111]

Helms thus turned the leaking flap into a more general critique of American policy in Chile. In a Senate speech on August 7, he claimed that a combination of intelligence agencies, the media, and the State Department was mounting a "massive campaign of disinformation" designed to undermine Pinochet, with "no lie too improbable, no distortion too great, no smear campaign too dirty for the State Department and the media to embrace." Ambassador Barnes wanted to disrupt the transition to democracy, and his presence at the Rojas funeral sanctioned "a Communist takeover by the totalitarian left." Barnes was subverting Reagan's larger objectives in Chile; he had made "common cause with the enemies of the United States" by spreading the "myth" of human rights abuse in Chile. Rather than freedom fighters seeking to improve human rights, Pinochet's opponents were nothing more than "terrorist revolutionaries seeking to destroy freedom." The media had accepted left-wing disinformation perpetrated by Chileans in the United States such as Ariel Dorfman, "a self-appointed spokesman for Chile." In Dorfman's left-wing version, Rojas and Quintana were "merely idealistic young reformers," but the reality, said Helms, is that they belonged to a "group of terrorists carrying gasoline, molotov cocktails, and rubber tires for erecting burning barricades." Helms recited the now discredited account that the two young Chileans burned themselves. Rojas and Quintana refused to go to the hospital, he added, and an "inexperienced soldier" had made a "fatal misjudgment by allowing them to go free"—an interesting version of the true story, which was they were left for dead in a ditch. Helms preferred his version to what he called the "Communist version of the story." The left-wing version, he said, contained four consistent themes: that Chile was stalling in its transition to democracy; that the democratic left offered the best protection against Communism; that military forces tortured and killed Rojas and prevented the two from obtaining medical attention; and that Rojas was "an idealistic young man, struck down in the flower of his youth." Helms argued that these contentions were all part of disinformation campaign: the democratic left represented the same forces that, under Allende, had taken Chile down the road to totalitarian Communism; Rojas and Quintana belonged to families of "Communist activists" seeking to impose a totalitarian system "upon a hapless Chile."[112]

Surviving an assassination attempt on September 7, 1986, Pinochet responded by arresting twenty-three people and imposing martial law. Helms remained an unqualified supporter of the regime. Americans, in the same situation and facing a Communist threat, might have done the same thing, Helms said. In a curious constitutional interpretation, he told reporters: "A lot of people don't understand or are not aware of what our constitution provides. It provides martial law, with all of the implications of that, suspension of habeas corpus." In fact, of course, the Constitution includes no provision for its suspension and the imposition of martial law—though it does provide, in Article I, Section 9, for the suspension of habeas corpus in cases of "rebellion or invasion"—but this did not deter Jesse from proceeding further. "I fear that the same sort of terrorism will come to this country on a large scale and maybe in the not too distant future," he declared, "in which case you will see martial law and whatever is necessary to quell that sort of thing." Helms had justified, incredibly, the suspension of civil liberties in the United States, if necessary, at some point in the future. "If that's an extreme statement, then so be it."[113]

In late September 1986, Helms then struck back against the CIA by attaching two amendments to annual authorization legislation for the CIA. Describing the agency as a "loose cannon," Helms asserted that Congress had never "really given the C.I.A. any direction as to what it expected." He insisted on an outside review, conducted by a panel of fifteen experts, to evaluate the success of the CIA's intelligence efforts. Helms identified a long list of questions that focused on alleged violations of arms control agreements that, conservatives charged, the CIA had in the past failed to identify. In addition, Helms's amendment sought to make the Pentagon's Defense Intelligence Agency—generally perceived as hard-line anti-Soviet—independent of CIA control and the main authority for intelligence on military matters. The legislation composed part of the "black budget," normally outside public purview, but the press learned that Helms's amendments, offered on the Senate floor, had held up the law's enactment. Their acceptance, it appeared, was the price for passage.

Helms's amendments should be seen in the context of his disagreement with the CIA and the State Department over Latin America—and his desire to curb the power of both. His perception that the CIA was part of a larger effort to undermine anti-Communist regimes in the region contributed to his stance, and, although he denied it, there was a whiff in the air of retaliation. CIA director Casey, at first, did not recognize the threat. In the course of the legislative maneuvering, on September 23 Helms spoke with Casey by phone, and the CIA director agreed to the amendments. Once Casey understood the limitations that Helms was seeking, however, he began to lobby against them. That night, Helms learned about Casey's opposition at a White House dinner, where he also heard that Casey had urged Senator Paul Laxalt to oppose the bill. When Casey and Helms spoke again on the next day, September 24, an angry Casey told Helms that his legislation would result in the "micromanagement" of the CIA. Removing the amendment, Helms responded, was "asking me to unscramble an egg." "I just couldn't change it," Helms told him, and "I didn't want to." The phone conversation abruptly ended, according to Helms, with Casey hanging up on him. The CIA director got nowhere with other senators; Majority Leader Dole would not even take his call. Despite Casey's objections, Helms's amendment went through, something that Casey attributed to Senate Intelligence Committee chair David Durenberger's decision to wait until the end of the session to seek reauthorization. "There was pressure and Durenberger figured this was the quickest way to get an authorization bill," Casey explained to a reporter. "Then they made that deal with Helms. I didn't have anything to do with it."[114]

BACK HOME IN North Carolina, after John East's decision not to run for reelection to the Senate in September 1985, a wild scramble ensued to replace him. Suffering from hyperthyroidism and depression, East committed suicide in his Greenville home on June 29, 1986. Helms learned the news when aide Clint Fuller telephoned just as he and Dot were preparing to leave for church. "Hold on to your hat," Fuller told him. "I've got some bad news for you." Helms then telephoned East's unlisted number in Greenville, but a police detective answered. He then located East's wife, Priscilla, who was spending the weekend in Hilton Head, South Carolina, and delivered the news to her. "I don't know if you have ever had to do something like that, but it is not easy," he told reporters at a Raleigh press conference, as he fought back tears. "It's just a blow," and he would never "get over it." Jesse was described as "devastated," and he called East's suicide a "tragedy of monumental proportions."[115] Various candidates vied for East's seat. On the Republican side, David Funderburk, a former Campbell University political scientist and conservative ideologue, had served as American ambassador to Romania in the early 1980s. He enjoyed the National Congressional Club's endorsement. Opposing him was Congressman James Broyhill, a leading moderate Republican. The Funderburk-Broyhill competition was heated. Broyhill, Wrenn believes, went to Helms in an effort to secure his support, and the senator essentially "gave him the green light." But Helms, despite these private assertions, remained neutral in the Republican primary. This was an instance, according to Wrenn, in which "Jesse did what's best for Jesse politically," in which practical survival superseded ideology. Although Funderburk was more ideologically pure, Helms realized that his "best move" was to stay uninvolved and avoid angering either

side. But the club did not take things that way, and they resented Helms.
The club went after Broyhill full throttle during the May 1986 primary.
Funderburk ads attacked Broyhill for possessing liberal positions on defense. Attack ads further asserted that Broyhill had voted in favor of tax-
funded abortions and that he was the sole North Carolina Republican who
favored the "Tip O'Neill budget" in the previous year. In the end, Helms
also angered Broyhill, who believed that he had been double-crossed by
the senator.[116] Although Broyhill received the nomination in a divisive
primary in May 1986, sixty-nine-year-old Democratic candidate and former governor Terry Sanford, in a political comeback, was elected in November 1986.[117]

Sanford's election contributed to the Democrats' recapture of the Senate in 1986. A few days after the election, asked by a reporter how he would
be affected by the Republicans' minority status, Helms reponded that it
"might not be so bad" because it was "a lot easier to throw a grenade than it
is to catch one." As part of the reshuffling of Senate leadership, Helms immediately let it be known that he intended to assert his position as ranking
minority member of the Senate Foreign Relations Committee. Although he
had fulfilled a campaign promise two years earlier by chairing the Agriculture Committee, in the two years since then foreign policy had become a
consuming obsession for Helms. Asserting his seniority, however, meant
that Helms would run squarely against the ambitions of Indiana senator
Richard Lugar, the Foreign Relations chair for the previous two years. On
November 5, 1986, a day after the election, Lugar telephoned Jesse to feel
him out. Although Helms remained coy, two days later he wrote to Lugar
announcing his intentions. His 1984 promise to North Carolina voters, he
claimed, did not apply now that Democrats controlled the Senate. Since
coming to the Senate in 1973, he "greatly desired" the Foreign Relations
post, and this might be his last opportunity while a senator. In an interview
with the *Charlotte Observer*, Helms explained that he planned to turn to foreign affairs now that the tobacco program was "fixed." About a week later,
Lugar responded that he intended to fight for his chairmanship in the Republican caucus.[118]

The Helms-Lugar struggle reflected ideological and dispositional divisions. Lugar had run the committee as a consensus builder; he had worked
cooperatively rather than confrontationally with Democrats, the State Department, and the White House. On policy questions related to areas such
as South Africa and Latin America, Lugar and Jesse opposed each other.
Lugar disagreed with Helms's obstructionist tactics, while Helms saw Lugar as excessively friendly with the State Department bureaucracy. The

diplomatic bureaucracy was "putting on a full-court press," Helms told a
Raleigh News and Observer interviewer in mid-November 1986. "They've got
a red alert down there," and they were "making calls to senators."

Jesse faced this struggle with Lugar armed with two tactical advantages. One was that Bob Dole remained neutral, indifferent to Lugar's fate
in part because of his competition in the past for party leadership; in 1984,
Dole defeated Lugar in the party caucus vote for majority leader. Jesse's
second advantage was that the seniority system, which was honored by Republicans especially, worked in his favor. If the seniority system was ignored, Jim Lucier told reporters, chairmanships would "become a personality
battle" that could "badly split Republican ranks at a time when we're in the
minority." Although he entered the Senate four years after Helms, Lugar
said, both joined the Foreign Relations Committee in the same year, in
1979. Lugar had performed his job as committee chair well; he deserved to
be able to keep the post. Equally important, Lugar contended, was the substance of the matter: he represented effective leadership rather than ideological grandstanding. The Senate should have action, Lugar declared, "not
confrontation or fireworks." In a letter sent to his colleagues in January 1987,
Lugar stressed his "record of constructive service" as a committee chairman
along with the White House's need for "skillful and winsome leadership in
foreign policy issues."[119]

In early January 1987, the Republican members of the Foreign Relations Committee voted unanimously in favor of Lugar retaining the chairmanship. News accounts suggested that the battle was over; Lugar applauded
the vote as a "vote of confidence." Helms failed to show up for the vote, declaring its results meaningless. Following party rules, he appealed the decision to the full forty-five-member caucus. Lugar had actively campaigned
for the position, and he had made numerous phone calls to Republican senators in order to lobby. In contrast, Helms said that he had not "made one
single call" or asked any senator to vote him. "I'm simply saying it's put-up
or shut-up time about the seniority system," Jesse maintained. "If they want
to destroy the seniority system, fine, I can live with that." Helms's claim of
noncampaigning reflected a larger strategy of turning the caucus vote into
a referendum on the Senate's seniority system. Jesse did not, however, prevent his supporters from making his case, and both the National Congressional Club and the Conservative Caucus conducted a mail campaign
promoting a Helms chairmanship.[120]

The seniority argument carried real appeal to Helms's Republican colleagues. Lowell Weicker, who opposed the senator on most issues, supported Helms. In December, Weicker explained his position to Jesse. "You

better get yourself some smelling salts, Jesse," he told him. Helms was correct in his stance, Weicker decided, and in a letter sent on December 8 that he co-signed with Idaho senator Steve Symms—a pro-Helms conservative—Weicker defended the seniority principle. Lugar's challenge was a "precedent-setting change of the Senate's traditional seniority system," Weicker wrote. As a liberal senator without seniority, Weicker had little opportunity for leadership positions. If the Senate awarded committee chairmanships on the basis of ideology, what would prevent the leadership from using this rationale to exclude minorities within the party? Seniority made possible an "equality of senatorial representation which transcends policy, philosophy, geography and personality." If eliminated, the "effectiveness of today's Republicans in the Senate and tomorrow's minorities in our party would be severely undermined."[121]

The competition with Lugar ended on January 20, 1987, when the Republican caucus voted by a margin of 24–17 in favor of Helms, with Weicker speaking forcefully on his behalf. The caucus also endorsed a resolution that Helms should be elected "in order to preserve the vital principles of party unity and Senate seniority." Along with Strom Thurmond, Weicker spoke in defense of seniority. Helms's victory was a surprise, as Lugar and his supporters had been confidently predicting victory. Lugar, who took over the Agriculture Committee chairmanship, was described by one reporter as appearing "stunned" by the result; he explained how he had "underestimated how strongly our members would head for the seniority issue," which became "delicate and uncomfortable" for many senators. Lugar left the meeting "clearly surprised." The vote also reflected Jesse's support among conservative senators. Helms, emerging from the meeting, needled reporters on his way out. "I'm sorry to disappoint you folks," he told them. His message for the media editorialists: "I hate to ruin your day, but you lost." Helms also suggested that his adversaries in the State Department were behind Lugar and that they made telephone calls on his behalf. For many years, Lugar remained hurt by the decision, and friction remained between his office and Helms's.[122]

Helms's ascension to ranking member of the Foreign Relations Committee represented what one staffer called a "defining moment" in the direction of American foreign policy. Although he was not finished with his domestic political agenda by any means and although he would not become Foreign Relations chair until 1995, increasingly the rest of his time in the Senate would become absorbed with international affairs.[123] The January 1987 vote installing Jesse in this position of power had reverberations. Sometime after 1980, he told the Conservative Political Action Conference in February 1987, Reagan's foreign policy vision had fallen by the wayside, and the "so-called professional diplomats took over, the foreign policy establishment moved in like a tidal wave, and the power was seized by the multilateral business enterprises and the international economic czars who used New York as a mail drop." This establishment foreign policy insisted on "consensus," but that meant a surrender of America's "deepest values," and it was run by an elite out of touch with traditional values. Articulating his principles, Helms favored unqualified anti-Communism and opposition to Soviet influence, a foreign-aid policy that broke up corrupt government domination, and support for free market American allies even if they had not "solved all of their problems yet." Helms also favored unrestricted American power. There was "no international commitment or interest," he declared, that was "more important than American sovereignty."[124]

Helms's break with past foreign policy traditions was alarming. The foreign policy establishment in the White House and State Department "reacted with dismay," according to the *New York Times,* and an unnamed White House official declared that the senator's ascension to ranking member on the Foreign Relations Committee was "definitely not seen as a plus." Another official was blunter. "There are an awful lot of people walking around in shock and horror," he said. Bruised feelings with the State Department continued, with the animosity between Helms and Shultz having acquired a personal tone. Following Helms's election, the secretary of state made a brief phone call to the senator. Apparently, the weekly luncheons that had occurred with Lugar were not mentioned, and, according to one reporter, "the peace pipe was certainly not burning."

Chris Manion, one of Helms's staffers, offered a reassuring spin to reporters. The media, he said, was producing a "caricature" of Jesse that the "liberal foreign policy establishment has lovingly cherished over the years." His critics, he said, would be surprised by Jesse Helms.[125] Most other commentators noted that Jesse's ascent to a leadership position in the Foreign Relations Committee meant a new phase for the American right. In this new turn, more attention would be paid to foreign affairs, and, with Helms acquiring power, a new globalist agenda that sought to transform America's relations with the world could be advanced. The radical right now had a "platform from which to trumpet its peculiar view of the world and America's role in it," said Claude Sitton. With a weak incoming chairman in Senator Claiborne Pell of Rhode Island and with an "outspoken dislike of the State Department and his master of the parliamentary cheap shot," Helms would likely prove a "feared adversary."[126]

Chapter 10

JESSE'S SPIDERWEB

The Politics of Sexuality

Speaking to a Congressional Club dinner in February 1989, Jesse Helms described a "variety of wars" that righteous Americans were then battling. In a struggle against godlessness, at home and abroad, not only was the nation combating Communism abroad, it was also fighting the spread of drugs and moral decay. Americans had to decide "whether we will participate in those battles, or whether we will choose to sit them out."[1] Helms occupied a lead position in the late-twentieth-century conservative culture wars, and these emerged as the older social issues of the 1970s—school prayer, busing, and abortion—had run their course. The Religious Right had been energized by "family" issues—by the apparent erosion of moral values and threats to the traditional, heterosexual family structure. "Family issues" became a code phrase for fears about sexuality, and Helms had long warned about the consequences of the 1960s sexual revolution; he became the Senate's most aggressive moral crusader. In Helms's view, loosening standards of censorship led to an explosion of pornography; changing roles were equally threatening, but most threatening of all was homosexuality. Leading a campaign about the AIDS epidemic that made him among the greatest villains of the gay community, he also took on the public-supported arts community. Jesse's war on culture led into a Senate campaign in 1990 in which both culture and race would play a major role.

Helms's shift into issues of culture and sexuality was related to the seismic shift occurring on the world scene with the end of the Cold War. In the

1980s, Helms continued to regard any arms control negotiations with the Soviets as fraudulent. Perceiving glasnost and perestroika as smoke screens for Soviet deception, he opposed the Intermediate Nuclear Force negotiations and the treaty that sought to remove nuclear missiles from Europe.[2] With the fall of the Berlin Wall in 1989 and the collapse of the Soviet empire two years later, however, old issues of anti-Communism were receding. Older domestic social issues such as school busing, school prayer, and abortion had achieved a sort of dormancy, and, for various reasons, they failed to mobilize the national conservative base. The future lay with new-generation social issues that related to the deteriorating structure of the family, morality, and, above all, homosexuality. In the post–Cold War political environment, the "bogeyman of Marxism," wrote one observer, had become replaced by "the horrors of homosexuality, AIDS, and 'perverted art.'" An "opening salvo," as one of Helms's staffers later put, had begun in a larger culture war.[3]

IN JUNE 1989, the featured speaker at Raleigh's first Gay Pride parade was Armistead Maupin, San Francisco writer and author of *Tales of the City*, which first appeared in the *San Francisco Chronicle* and then, in 1976, was published as a best-selling fictional account of gay life in the Bay Area. For Maupin, who had grown up in Raleigh's exclusive Budleigh neighborhood as a member of one of the city's most powerful families, his return to Raleigh was a homecoming. As the featured speaker at the Gay Pride parade, he walked past the Confederate monument that his great-great-grandmother helped to erect, past the block where his Confederate general grandfather had grown up, up to the capitol steps. Publicly declaring his sexual orientation, said Maupin, "felt rather satisfying for me." His father, Armistead Maupin, Sr., was Tom Ellis's law partner, and the younger Maupin had known Jesse Helms since childhood. Although Maupin had realized, from his teenage years, that he was a homosexual, he recalled that he compensated for his sexuality by becoming an active conservative—in part, to please his ultraconservative father. Maupin, as a student at UNC from 1962 to 1966, became a leading conservative voice. While at UNC, he wrote what he called *The View from the Hill*, a regular satirical column that appeared in the *Daily Tar Heel*. Maupin's column, he said, combined the humor of Art Buchwald and the political commentary of William F. Buckley, but it drew its inspiration from Helms's *Viewpoint* editorials. An avid watcher of Helms's WRAL broadcasts, Maupin later described Jesse as not "an easy guy to look at it, even when he was my hero." As a sort of "token conservative" at UNC, Maupin "took a lot of shit" from fellow students for supporting Helms, an archenemy of the university. Attending UNC Law School immediately after graduation, Maupin grew disenchanted with the career that his father had planned for him. After one year of law school, he walked out of his exams and never returned.[4]

In what became a central irony of his life, Maupin's career change was brokered by Jesse Helms. After his son dropped out of law school, Maupin Sr. asked for Ellis's help. Having read Maupin's *Daily Tar Heel* pieces, Ellis was certain that young Armistead could become the "next James J. Kilpatrick." At Ellis's urging, Jesse agreed to take Maupin Jr. on for a summer working at WRAL in 1966. Later, after a few years in the Navy and in Vietnam, Maupin worked as a journalist for the *Charleston News and Courier*—Helms's old friend Tom Waring hired him—and in 1971, he secretly collaborated with the Nixon White House in attempting to discredit John Kerry's Vietnam Veterans Against the War. Maupin organized a tour in 1971 by ten Vietnam vets who traveled the country promoting the accomplishments of the war for the Vietnamese people. The group also earned him a trip to the White House and a thirty-minute visit with President Nixon. With the president having little to say to the young vets, the meeting was very awkward, Maupin later remembered, and he "had to carry the ball" in the conversation by feeding him "conservative stuff" to talk about. Most of the vets were "creeped out" because Nixon, sweating profusely, was "very weird," was uncomfortable and did not "know how to talk to young men." In 1972, based on Maupin's efforts with the Vietnam vets, Helms successfully nominated Maupin for a Freedom Leadership Award from the Freedoms Foundation in Valley Forge, Pennsylvania. Maupin's exposure with the pro-Vietnam campaign led to a job with the AP and work in San Francisco.

Maupin remembered one especially vivid moment during the summer of 1966, when he covered a Klan rally for WRAL outside Raleigh. Interviewing a Klan leader, he asked him what he thought of the news that Secretary of State Dean Rusk's daughter had married a black man. "You know that Dean Rusk is a liberal," the Klansman responded, but "besides, what else would you expect from a man who is a practicing homosexual." Maupin eagerly brought the footage back to Helms. But when he showed him the interview, "all the blood drained" out of Jesse's face, Maupin recalled. Describing someone as homosexual, Jesse exclaimed, was "the worst thing you can say about anybody." Homosexuality, Helms said, was a subject that "was not even to be mentioned." "That was the first time I realized," Maupin later reflected, that "libel laws were one more way of keeping homosexuals as second-class citizens." Maupin, after he came out in the early 1970s, had nothing further to do with Helms, though the senator remained a symbol of his own complex past. The unwritten code in Raleigh society, a code that Helms subscribed to, was that homosexuality would be tolerated if it did not become public. Yet the premise of the gay rights movement was that homosexual behavior needed to emerge from the closet in order to achieve a public respectability and tolerance.[5]

Years later, Maupin wondered why Helms had become such a vitriolic opponent of gay rights. Jesse had been, for Maupin, a kind of father figure: during the summer of 1966, he was "very generous" with him, and he often invited Maupin into his office to discuss politics. Maupin saw a side of Jesse "that is hard to remember now": there was a "gentleness" to him, and he was a "lot nicer than a lot of the other conservatives that I knew." Helms took on a parental role in advising Maupin and in encouraging him to be a writer, telling him that he had talent and could do something with it. Helms was "very, very meticulous" about language, an "extremely smart man" whose mind worked with remarkable efficiency. Still, Maupin's estrangement from Helms was wrapped up in his estrangement from the conservative values that he had left behind in North Carolina. Like Helms, his father's attitude toward homosexuality had always been "Keep your mouth shut about it."[6]

Helms's campaign against homosexuals, Maupin noted, took on an increasingly bitter edge. He wondered sometimes if "something awful happened to him when he was a kid" to turn him against homosexuals. "I feel like it's something personal—that's as close to it as I can get," he declared. Maupin never saw Helms again after 1971. His closest encounter came in 2005, when his father died, and Helms arrived a half hour after Maupin had left. His father had kept up with Jesse: "One of the last thrills of my father's life," Maupin declared, was when, disabled by a terminal disease and riding in a wheelchair, he was placed next to Jesse's—by then, also in a wheelchair—and they talked at an installation ceremony of a local judge. Maupin often wondered what would happen if he sat down and talked with Jesse, but he realized what "I would get": "a lot of graciousness," the assurance of fond memories, but a disapproval of his lifestyle. Musing about this meeting that never occurred, Maupin concluded: "I'm sure that's what it would have been."[7]

FOR THE LAST half of his career in Congress, Jesse became a determined opponent of homosexual rights.[8] Outspoken in his views, he energized anti-gay political sentiment, while he became the most hated political symbol to gay political organizers. In some respects, Helms's positions on gay rights resembled his views on civil rights for blacks: in both instances, he condemned special treatment for a political minority. But in other respects his treatment of gay people went well beyond his posture toward African Americans. He "instinctively" recoiled at the very notion of civil rights for gay people, he told an interviewer in February 2000, and he objected primarily to any efforts to legitimize homosexual lifestyles. Like many people of his generation, he did not object to closeted gay people; he had "no problem" with their private behavior, but he objected to homosexuals "parading around" and demanding that they be regarded as "normal." Why, he asked, did gays "feel compelled to announce that they are gay?"

Since the 1970s, homosexuals had been seeking civil rights protections, but the advent of the AIDS epidemic, which disproportionately afflicted homosexuals in the early stages of its outbreak, changed the movement's focus. In the 1980s, gay activists not only pushed for increased federal funding for AIDS research, but also for other programs that aroused the ire of opponents of homosexual rights. Gay rights supporters, for example, favored expanded civil rights protections and confidentiality for AIDS sufferers; their opponents maintained that the public health emergency demanded mandatory testing and stronger restrictions. Gay rights advocates argued for heightened public awareness through education campaigns that promoted safe sex practices among gay people; their opponents claimed that this amounted to the federal government legitimizing their lifestyle.

Jesse opposed any special legal or civil rights status for homosexuals, and in the debate over AIDS he became the Senate's most vocal enemy of the gay rights movement. He depended on a young, aggressive staff. His lead staff person on the AIDS issue, Mary Potter, was a young attorney recently graduated from Campbell University Law School. His first female legislative assistant, hard-nosed and ideologically motivated, Potter joined a staff that was deeply committed to conservative causes. Unlike other senators, Helms hired staffers with the "same mindset" as he held, "rock solid conservatives" who truly believed in the cause. Potter possessed solid conservative credentials: her father was conservative federal judge Robert Potter, who had presided over the 1989 trial of PTL founder Jim Bakker, and who was known as "Maximum Bob" because of his strict approach to sentencing. Mary Potter, who came to the office as a strong opponent of abortion, believed in Helms's moral agenda, and she headed up staff work on the AIDS crisis; Jesse called her "AIDS Mary." Potter believed that the senator should argue that AIDS was primarily a health issue rather than a civil rights issue. Gay rights groups had, she believed, imposed a "lockdown on information" and were controlling the public discussion. The opportunity existed, Potter realized, for limiting the further legitimization of homosexuals.[9]

On May 27, 1986, the District of Columbia City Council enacted an ordinance prohibiting insurance carriers from denying coverage to clients testing positive for the AIDS virus. On June 19, 1986, Helms co-sponsored a joint congressional resolution, with Representative William Dannemeyer (R-CA), overturning the law. According to 1974 legislation that provided for District of Columbia home rule, Congress could veto city laws by joint resolution; in twelve years, it had exercised this power only twice. With support from the Moral Majority and evangelical groups, Helms and Dannemeyer viewed this as a chance to make a strong statement against gay rights. The "homosexual rights crowd" had "managed to twist the AIDS issue into one of civil rights," Helms told the Senate. The D.C. ordinance provided "special treatment to AIDS-exposed homosexuals over others who are exposed to other serious health risks." The ordinance, Jesse believed, was "reeking with the odor of special interests," and it established a bad precedent.[10]

In the fight over the D.C. ordinance during the next year and a half, Helms attracted growing support. The issue aroused evangelical Christians: beginning in June 1986, Religious Right groups campaigned to put a referendum on the District ballot overturning the law. Insurance carriers also opposed the law; they stopped writing new health and life insurance policies in the District and brought suit against the ordinance. Even the *Washington Post* regarded the law as unwise and sloppily written, though its editorial pages objected to Helms's interference. Eventually, Congress agreed with Helms, and twice, in August and October 1986, the Senate voted to repeal the law, though the measure failed in a House-Senate conference.[11] Jesse finally prevailed in October 1988, when Congress overturned the AIDS insurance law and, for good measure, also repealed a portion of Washington's anti-gay discrimination law.[12] Throughout the late 1980s Helms continued the fight against gay rights activists and the AIDS issue. As he had in resisting the D.C. insurance ordinance, he insisted that AIDS should be treated as a public health crisis without regard to gay civil rights, and he favored coercive measures against the disease.[13]

Helms also opposed AIDS education that would legitimize homosexuality or homosexual practices. AIDS infection, he suggested, was primarily a disease of homosexuals, whose behavior had hastened the disease, and providing special treatment for gay people, as one aide put it, was "fundamentally unfair." Public health measures focusing on safe sex were less effective than attempts to limit or eliminate homosexual behavior. The truth, he declared, was that "sodomy, adultery, and fornication are not now, nor have they ever been, safe." Current AIDS education efforts, which focused on safe sex, revealed that public health officials had "their heads in the sand." AIDS threatened the majority of the heterosexual population; strict public health measures should isolate the homosexual minority and protect the heterosexual population. Despite public discussion of the disease, Helms said in a Senate speech in June 1987, there had been few steps to "protect from this dreaded disease those who do not now have it"; the "real discrimination" was that the law left the uninfected unprotected. AIDS had become the first "politically protected" disease in history, and "powerful homosexual rights groups" had silenced the opposition. Gay rights groups protested "any public initiatives to protect the general public beyond research and education" because they believed that public welfare was less important "to their civil rights to engage in unnatural and immoral sexual behavior."[14]

Helms sought to publicize the AIDS issue by exposing what he contended was the improper use of government funds to promote a homosexual agenda. On October 14, 1987, Jesse charged, in a Senate speech, that a New York City group, the Gay Men's Health Crisis (GMHC), used funds from the Centers for Disease Control to produce comic books that sought to instruct readers about AIDS prevention through safe sex practices. The group had received $680,000 in federal grants for AIDS education; these efforts had resulted in a comic entitled *Safer Sex Comix*. The GMHC comics, Helms said, promoted "sodomy and the homosexual life style" by recounting, in graphic detail, sexual encounters between two gay men. He had circulated copies of the comics to fifteen or twenty senators—in an anonymous brown envelope marked "personal and confidential"—and they were, Jesse said in his Senate speech, universally "revolted." Helms also showed the comics to President Reagan, who, according to Jesse's account, "looked at a couple of pages, closed it up and shook his head, and hit his desk with his fist." Rather than encouraging changes in what he called "perverted sexual behavior," the GMHC promoted "sodomy and the homosexual life style as an acceptable alternative in America." "We have got to call a spade a spade," Helms declared, "and a perverted human being a perverted human being." If most Americans saw these materials, they would be "on the verge of revolt." An aggressive minority had promoted its agenda at the expense of majority values, but even worse, Jesse asserted, this had occurred with the support of public funds. Although a subsequent investigation by the Department of Health and Human Services concluded that the comic books were not produced with federal funds, in November 1987 Helms sponsored an amendment prohibiting funding for anti-AIDS efforts that "promote or encourage, directly or indirectly, homosexual activities." The measure also required that federally supported educational efforts emphasize sexual abstinence. Although denounced by Helms's adversary, Edward Kennedy, as "toothless" and a "foolish exercise," the bill overwhelmingly passed the Senate. Once again, Jesse had made his point.[15]

Helms's stridency about the AIDS issue—and especially his attempts to connect the health crisis with a "perverted" lifestyle—drew criticism. The restrictions placed on AIDS education, said one gay leader, seemed "to be saying let's protect the general population and let the gay community die of AIDS."[16] In an op-ed piece in the *New York Times* on November 7, 1987, New York City mayor Edward I. Koch noted that only a few congressmen had had the "common decency to resist homophobic hysteria" by voting against Helms's amendment. Although Jesse might not like gay people, Koch wrote, he should remember that they and other AIDS sufferers were the "sons and daughters of families who love them." Helms reponded to Koch's op-ed piece on November 23. Describing Koch as "mean-spirited," Helms defended his amendment. There was no such thing as "safe sodomy," he said. The use of condoms did not guarantee AIDS prevention; the only safe measure was abstinence. "To admit that abstinence from homosexual activity—not sodomy with condoms—is the most effective way to avoid AIDS," he wrote, "would force Mr. Koch to admit also that casual sex is a perilous vice." In fact, said Helms, it was the sexual revolution of the 1960s that had "ravaged this nation for the last quarter of a century." The choice for Americans was clear: "Reject sodomy and practice morality." If they were unwilling to make the right choice, "they should understand the consequences."[17] In debate, Helms condemned homosexuality and connected AIDS with gay men. "Let me tell you something about this AIDS epidemic," he said. There was "not one single case of AIDS reported in this country that cannot be traced in origin to sodomy." The AIDS issue had become a way for homosexuals "to promote and legitimize their life style in American society."[18]

Helms continued to call for compulsory, coercive measures to isolate AIDS sufferers from the rest of society. The most important of these included mandatory testing. In June 1987, Helms had successfully sponsored legislation requiring mandatory AIDS testing for immigrants, who could be excluded if they were HIV-positive.[19] Jesse's AIDS legislation included compulsory testing for those applying for marriage licenses, federal prisoners, patients at Veterans Administration hospitals, and applicants for military service, and it threatened those states refusing to participate in these limitations with a loss in federal funding. The legislation also made it a felony to donate HIV-positive blood, body fluids, or organs, while it required the closing of bathhouses where homosexual activities occurred. By preventing the further spread of AIDS, Helms contended that his prime objective was "to protect the people who are innocent"—meaning heterosexuals.[20]

The 1988 AIDS appropriation bill, the first comprehensive federal law dealing with the disease, attracted Helms's opposition. Although versions of the bill were approved by both houses of Congress in October 1988, Jesse obstructed and stalled. Yet the law achieved passage nonetheless.[21] Two years later, Helms opposed the Ryan White Comprehensive AIDS Resources Emergency Act of 1990, which provided $2.9 billion to fight the disease. Named for an Indiana teenager who contracted AIDS from a blood transfusion and died of the disease at the age of nineteen after combating discrimination, the law provided the largest federal expenditure ever for AIDS, authorizing it over five years for health services in hospitals and clinics. Claiming that the bill reflected a "hysteria" that verged on "terror," Helms charged that Ryan White "was portrayed as a typical victim, not the exception that he was." Were it not for the "perverted" behavior of those who were "demanding respectability," Ryan White would not have died of AIDS. Federal funding should be no greater for AIDS than for other diseases such as Alzheimer's, cancer, and diabetes, Helms argued, and these diseases had been "cast aside" because of the gay community's political pressure. The Ryan White bill had become "another legislative flagship for the homosexual segment of the AIDS lobby and its apologists in and out of Congress, and in and out of the major news media." What had started as a response to a public health crisis, Jesse warned, had evolved into a "weapon, frankly, for the deterioration of America's Judeo-Christian value system."

Clearly, Jesse was no friend of the gay community; indeed, he was now the most visible symbol of homophobia to gay communities across the country. Jesse claimed that he was threatened by gay people and required protection from the Capitol police. The AIDS debate, he said, now "borders on terror."[22] In July 1990, the activist group ACT UP occupied Helms's Senate office, conducting a same-sex "kiss-in" in which they distributed flyers and condoms and then sat down in the middle of the office until removed by police. Six protesters—four women and two men—were arrested in what one organizer called a demonstration against "everything Jesse Helms has done and has not done over the years."[23] Helms's confrontational relationship with the gay community was also manifested in his position toward federal hate crimes legislation, which Congress considered in February 1990. In a Senate debate on February 8, Jesse claimed that "militant homosexuals" had exaggerated the extent of anti-gay violence. The bill represented a "cave-in to the homosexual-gay rights movement" and was another example of how gay rights advocates wanted a "fundamental right to commit sodomy." "If you don't know what sodomy is," he added, "look it up." Restating his views of the AIDS crisis, Helms asserted that the disease "cannot and will not be controlled until the homosexuals change their promiscuous lifestyles." At the last minute, Helms offered an amendment stating that "the homosexual movement threatens the strength and survival of the American family as a basic unit of society" and requiring enforcement of state sodomy laws. His amendment was defeated only after the bill's supporters added language to the hate crimes bill asserting that the American family was the "foundation of American society" and stipulating that no federal funds could be spent to "promote or encourage homosexuality." Despite Helms's continued opposition, in February 1990 hate crimes legislation passed the Senate by the overwhelming vote of 92–4 and was signed by President George Bush.[24]

As the hate crimes debate suggested, by 1990 Jesse's attempts to link AIDS with a discussion about homosexuality had become increasingly unsuccessful. There were significant differences among Senate conservatives: Orrin Hatch, for example, chided Jesse for focusing excessively on gays. "We may disagree with that life style," he said, "but they are human beings and should not be brutalized." "They're citizens of this country," he added, and "they ought to be treated like citizens of this country." The hate crimes bill enjoyed broad support: its principal sponsors were the conservative Hatch and liberal Senator Paul Simon of Illinois, and by the time the bill reached the floor there were sixty total sponsors. Diverse organizations such as the Anti-Defamation League of B'nai B'rith, the National Association for the Advancement of Colored People, the People for the American Way, and the Fraternal Order of Police were supporters. So were mainstream Protestant churches, Jewish groups, Mexican Americans, and civil rights groups.[25]

In Jesse's AIDS rhetoric, there were few restraints in the generally derisive way that he characterized gay people. There was little of the coded language that he employed in explaining his positions on race, little attempt to disguise his contempt. In many instances Helms expressed himself in openly abusive language. Consider his speech in the Senate on June 23, 1989. On June 24–25, 1989, several New York City post offices were issuing a special postmark honoring Gay and Lesbian Pride Week, on the twentieth anniversary of the famous Stonewall Riot of New York City, an event that possessed almost legendary status as sparking the modern gay rights movement. On June 19, Jesse wrote a letter of protest to Postmaster General Anthony M. Frank in which he warned that the government should not be "in the business of dignifying perversion." In his Senate speech, Helms declared he was appalled at the willingness of the U.S. Postal Service to permit the use of "political propaganda" in order to "pander to the whims of the militant homosexual minority." Gay people, said Helms, were "in a battle against American values" in which their objective was to force Americans to "accept the proposition that their perverted 'lifestyle' is as worthy of protection as race, creed, and religion." "I do not buy that," said Helms, and "a pox upon whomever in the Postal Service made this completely misguided decision." As thousands died from the AIDS epidemic, "homosexuals proclaim the virtues of their perverse practices."[26]

ON MAY 18, 1989, New York Republican senator Alfonse D'Amato rose to speak in protest. Over the past several weeks, he said, he had received an avalanche of letters and phone calls from constituents expressing "shock, outrage, and anger" about a juried exhibition of work by the artist Andres Serrano. The National Endowment for the Arts provided $15,000 in support for an exhibit sponsored in 1988 by the Southeastern Center for Contemporary Art (SECCA) in Winston-Salem, North Carolina, and it appeared in ten cities around the country. At issue was Serrano's *Piss Christ,* a sixty-by-forty-inch print of a crucifix that was immersed in urine. This "trash," said D'Amato, was "shocking, abhorrent and completely undeserving." In April 1989, four months after Serrano's show opened, the Reverend Donald E. Wildmon, a Methodist minister and executive director of the American Family Association in Tupelo, Mississippi, launched a national letter-writing campaign in which he claimed that *Piss Christ* was "anti-Christian bigotry." Wildmon, who had earlier led an effort in 1988 to suppress Martin Scorsese's *The Last Temptation of Christ,* a film that depicted Jesus as having a love affair with Mary Magdalene, criticized the NEA for supporting the Serrano show with public funds.[27]

Sometime before D'Amato's Senate speech, John Mashburn, one of Helms's legislative assistants, noticed the controversy that Serrano's work was generating. Like Helms's other legislative assistants, Mashburn oversaw incoming mail and supervised responses. Managing incoming mail was a critical function of Helms's operation: not only was it part of his highly efficient system of constituent services, incoming mail served as an important source of information about issues concerning ordinary Americans. Having heard from Wildmon, Mashburn learned more about the Serrano exihibit after someone sent him a copy of the SECCA catalogue. "Now they've gone too far," he told himself after having examined the catalogue, and he took the matter directly to Senator Helms.

Helms's conservative message had always had a populist, anti-elitist flavor: in the 1960s, he warned his television audience that a liberal minority, at the expense of most Americans, was undermining their values. Jesse's unqualified disdain for homosexuality was consistent with these views, but his campaign against the National Endowment for the Arts combined his long-standing opposition to unwarranted interference of a federal bureaucracy, his hostility toward cultural elites, his disgust at homosexuality, and his suspicion of the arts community. Although Jesse's campaign against the NEA earned him the lasting enmity of artists, his efforts reflected a keen appreciation of public opinion, and, as events would prove, were consistent with popular attitudes about the arts that prevailed among many people outside Washington.[28]

After 1989, Mashburn became the point person for the struggle over the NEA. Originally from Lexington, North Carolina, he became involved in the right-to-life movement in North Carolina and attended UNC Law School. His wife, then his girlfriend, was an artist, and she took him to art shows in the state. They once went to SECCA in Winston-Salem, not far from his hometown, and in one exhibition he noticed a piece of art, *Joseph Awaits the Immaculate Conception.* The piece three-dimensionally depicted a couple copulating in a bedroom while another person watched television. Noticing that the show was subsidized by the NEA, he wondered why public funds could be used to support what, he thought, seemed to be anti-religious art. He approached a docent at the show. Was this not a violation of separation of church and state? Were public funds not supporting something that undermined religious belief? The response of the docent, which Mashburn remembered as "flippant," made a lasting impression. This was the way things were, was the response, and there was nothing that could be done about it.

Now Mashburn had the chance to do something about it. With the SECCA catalogue in hand, he began to prepare this as an issue that Helms might take up in the Senate. Like the other legislative assistants, Mashburn realized that frequently his work went unrewarded. He might spend many hours preparing issues, but he estimated that 80 or 90 percent of his work never got past the senator's desk. In the meantime, D'Amato had become interested in *Piss Christ* primarily because it offended his Roman Catholic constituents. One of D'Amato's aides visited Mashburn and borrowed his catalogue. "The next thing I know," recalled Mashburn, the aide and D'Amato had gone to the Senate floor with the catalogue.[29] Denouncing this "so-called piece of art" as a "deplorable, despicable display of vulgarity," D'Amato criticized the use of public funds. To add insult to injury, the NEA had financed a published catalogue that made *Piss Christ* even more widely available. If artists wanted to be "perverse," D'Amato said, "so be it, but not with my money, not with the taxpayers' dollars, and certainly not under the mantle of this great Nation." In a dramatic flourish, D'Amato took his copy of the catalogue, ripped it in half, and threw it on the floor. He also sent a letter to acting NEA chairman Hugh Southern, co-signed by twenty-two senators, expressing their outrage about *Piss Christ*.[30]

D'Amato would eventually abandon the NEA issue because of pressure from his New York constituents, who received more federal arts support than artists in any other state. The New York senator wanted, Mashburn wrote to Jesse, "out of the spotlight (all glory, no guts)," and he was prepared to "declare victory" with the Southern letter. Yet the letter was "not victory," Mashburn argued, and the issue should not die. Helms eagerly agreed, assuming leadership of the anti-NEA forces.[31] When Mashburn took the SECCA catalogue to him, Jesse was "profoundly offended," he remembered, "both on a policy level and on a personal level." Mashburn had alerted him about D'Amato's upcoming speech, and he had prepared Jesse with a binder full of talking points. He did not have his catalogue; his copy was the one that D'Amato ripped in half.[32] Immediately following D'Amato, Jesse took the floor. He denounced the "blasphemy of the so-called artwork." Serrano, he said, was not an artist but a "jerk" who was taunting most Americans, and the senator resented the NEA for spending public funds to support Serrano's work "If we have sunk so low in this country as to tolerate and condone this sort of thing," Jesse added, "then we become a part of it." Serrano was honored with an NEA grant by displaying "blasphemy and insensitivity toward the religious community," and this suggested "something about the state of this Government and the way it spends the money taken from the taxpayer." In overwhelming numbers, Helms said, callers to his office were angry. Although the Constitution might protect "this Serrano fellow's—laughably, I will describe it—'artistic expression,'" it did not require taxpayers to "fund, promote, honor, approve, or condone" his work. Helms went further: he insisted that the endowment was "badly flawed" in the way that it administered its programs. Such abuses should never happen again.[33]

Piss Christ thereafter attracted the full fire of the Religious Right: on June 9, the broadcaster and Republican presidential candidate Pat Robertson attacked the NEA and Serrano on his Christian Broadcasting Network, describing it as "blasphemy paid for by Government." Robertson demanded that Congress eliminate public funding for the NEA unless the agency could provide concrete assurances that such "patently blasphemous" art or "pornography" would no longer be supported with public money. Three days later, on June 12, Texas conservative Republican congressman Dick Armey also attacked public support for the Serrano show. The artist could display "bad taste and bad manners," Armey said, but he should not receive taxpayers' money. The attack on Serrano blended with an assault on the work of photographer Robert Mapplethorpe, an exhibit of whose work was organized by the Philadelphia Institute of Contemporary Arts with a $30,000 NEA grant. A traveling show of Mapplethorpe's photographs appeared in Philadelphia and Chicago in the spring of 1989 and was scheduled to show in Washington. When the show later exhibited at the Cincinnati Contemporary Arts Center, its director, Dennis Barrie, was charged with violating a local obscenity ordinance. Although Barrie was eventually acquitted, controversy followed Mapplethorpe.[34]

Mapplethorpe, who died of AIDS in March 1989 shortly before his traveling exhibit opened, was a celebrated photographer whose work had homoerotic themes. His work was often vividly graphic in its depictions of homosexuality and sadomasochism, and he included photographs of nude children. Under mounting pressure, Washington's Corcoran Gallery, on June 12, 1989, decided to cancel the Mapplethorpe show that was scheduled to open on July 1. The museum's general budget included nearly $300,000 in federal funding, and its director, Christina Orr-Cahall, was a former NEA chair. Criticism by Helms and other congressmen prompted the decision. Meanwhile, the arts community rallied against what was perceived as censorship, and the value of Serrano's and Mapplethorpe's work in art markets skyrocketed. On June 16, arts activists picketed the Corcoran, and slides were projected onto the museum's outer wall in the evening. Protesting artists boycotted the Corcoran, prompting the cancellation of two shows, while Lowell Nesbitt, a painter, withdrew a $1.5 million gift. Six of the museum's professional staff resigned, including chief curator Jane Livingston. In December 1989, under pressure from the museum board, Orr-Cahall resigned. Meanwhile, the Mapplethorpe show exhibited at the Washington Project for the Arts during July and August to large crowds. In

New York, on August 1, the arts advocate group Art Positive—affiliated with ACT UP, the AIDS activist group—drew about one thousand people to protest Jesse's amendment outside the Metropolitan Museum of Art. Art Positive, the group declared, was organized against "homophobia and censorship in the arts."[35]

Mashburn had been alerted about the Mapplethorpe show after someone sent Helms's office a catalogue. He soon realized the Mapplethorpe materials were even more explosive than *Piss Christ*. The issue, for Mashburn, did not simply concern obscenity. Rather, he questioned whether a cultural elite should impose their values on the majority. The "weird stuff" being produced by the artistic community—and the fact especially that it was publicly supported—was galling. The artistic community was certain that it could "rub the rest of the country's face in what they were doing."[36] Convinced that most Americans were on his side, Helms exploited the furor. When an arts advocate wrote to the *Washington Post* on June 18, the senator brought the letter to the Senate floor. This was nothing but "specious mouthings" of a person who objected to American taxpayers' resentment that their money was "being wasted on crude, blasphemous, and childish 'works of art' by people to whom nothing is sacred." Jesse then gave a graphic description. "Pictures of male genitals placed on a table is not art," he declared, "except perhaps to homosexuals who are trying to force their way into undeserved respectability." Although NEA supporters might regard Helms as "reactionary" and "small-minded," he had a message to deliver: "good, decent taxpaying citizens" were prepared to put this cultural elite in its place.[37]

In response to Serrano and Mapplethrope, the Senate prohibited NEA funding to organizations sponsoring the Serrano and Mapplethorpe shows, while the House cut $45,000 from the NEA budget—the exact amount of the grants to both exhibits. Meanwhile, Mashburn worked with North Carolina legislators in attempting to cut state funding for SECCA. Helms wanted to go further, and attorneys on his staff advised that using obscenity restrictions would be a legal and constitutional way to limit arts funding. Mashburn urged the senator to take up the NEA issue by proposing amendments that would publicize the arts funding issue.[38] On the evening of July 26, in a nearly deserted Senate chamber containing only eleven senators, Jesse introduced an amendment to a $10.9 billion Interior Department appropriation bill. The amendment prohibited the NEA from supporting "obscene or indecent" art depicting sadomasochism, homoeroticism, the exploitation of children, or individuals engaged in sex. Helms's amendment also prohibited any art that "denigrates, debases or reviles a person, group or class of citizens on the basis of race, creed, sex, handicap, age or national origin," while it banned NEA funding of work that was offensive to "the objects or beliefs of the adherents of a particular religion or non-religion." His amendment, he told the Senate, sought to prevent NEA support of "such immoral trash" as the Serrano and Mapplethorpe exhibits. Efforts by his fellow senators to regulate NEA funding did not go far enough, he said, because they "will not prevent such blasphemous or immoral behavior by other institutions or artists with Government funds."[39]

Helms's amendment of July 1989 marked the outbreak of all-out hostilities in the war between cultural conservatives and their opponents in the gay and arts communities. Jesse dared anyone to oppose him. If his fellow senators wanted the federal government to support "pornography, sadomasochism, or art for pedophiles," Helms said, then "they should vote against my amendment." If they believed that most voters opposed such things, they should vote in favor of it. While on the Senate floor, Helms displayed a copy of the exhibit catalogue from the Mapplethorpe show to other senators, and Majority Leader Robert Byrd was so shocked by Mapplethorpe's photographs that he agreed to rush Helms's amendment through by voice vote. Byrd remained appalled by what he saw, and he became a Helms ally on this issue. Arts advocates then turned to the legislative conference in hopes of defeating Helms's amendment.[40]

Jesse had left his Senate opponents flat-footed. Helms had made fools of them, said *Washington Post* columnist Jonathan Yardley. As "wily and contemptible a character as one could hope to meet in public life," Helms had entered the political scene "with just the kind of legislation that politicians dread: a bill they can scarcely afford to vote against, yet one that makes them look foolish, and even philistine, for supporting it." Few senators could oppose legislation seeking to suppress obscenity, indecency, and child nudity. "Like a quarterback deploying his receivers in every area of the secondary," Yardley noted, Jesse had "all his ground covered." Even Helms's liberal adversary, Ohio senator Howard Metzenbaum, refused to oppose the Helms amendment "because it's hard to oppose an amendment of this kind because it sounds so right." "Another fly," Yardley observed, was thus "caught in Jesse's spider web."

Although Yardley opposed Jesse's cultural war, he realized that he possessed an advantage in the arrogant and naive attitude of the arts community. People in the arts possessed a "sense of entitlement," and they resisted accountability to the public. Defense contractors were subject to scrutiny over the expenditure of public funds: why should the publicly funded arts not experience the same supervision? Museum directors and artists expected "taxpayers to nod approvingly while tax dollars go to projects approved by no one except artists and their janizaries." Peer review, Yardley believed, did not represent the broad public interest; most people realized that the most serious obstacle to the "responsible allocation of grants" was the peer review process. Rather than the public interest, reviews represented "artistic and scholarly cliques," and they awarded money to "allies and proteges, feather their own nests and keep it all in the family." Congress could "huff and puff as much as it likes" about obscenity in the work of Mapplethorpe and Serrano, but the process was "firmly in place to produce more such controversies in the future." The arts community greeted "any and every suggestion" of reform arrogantly. It had "been slopping at the trough long enough to have developed a habit, and it's not about to let anyone else tell it what, or how much, it should eat."[41]

Helms was personally appalled at the ways in which the art world had tested sexual convention, but he seemed to enjoy an almost pornographic interest in Mapplethorpe's photographs, which he often showed off privately as well as in public gatherings. He was often the person opening and closing the Mapplethorpe book. At home he even showed it to Dot, who peeked at it, he said, and slammed it shut. "Lord have mercy, Jesse," she told him, "I'm not believing this." He told one reporter how offended he was by a Mapplethorpe photograph of a small girl holding up her dress. "I'm embarrassed to even talk to you about this," he said. "I'm embarrassed to talk to my wife." In early August 1989, for shock effect he sent four Mapplethorpe photographs to twenty-six congressmen. In one photograph a prepubscent girl partially exposed herself; in another, a man in a polyester suit was shown with open zipper and exposed penis; while still others showed a naked boy and a penis lying on a pedestal. In an accompanying letter, Jesse advised the congressmen to inspect the photographs and consider whether "the taxpayer's money should be used to fund this sort of thing." Helms staffers suggested that these were not the worst Mapplethorpe photographs: "on a scale of 1 to 10 on what's in the show," said one, "these are about a 5."[42]

In the arts community, the reaction against Helms's anti-NEA amendment was profoundly hostile.[43] In September 1989, the arts community lobbied hard against Helms's amendment. Serrano achieved celebrity as a result of the NEA fight; years later, he wrote to Helms, thanking him for making him famous.[44] New York's Whitney Museum took out $50,000 in full-page ads in the *New York Times* and *Washington Post* that asked readers: "Are you going to let politics kill Art?" On September 20, about one hundred students from the Corcoran protested against arts censorship; a large majority of teachers and students were appalled by the decision to cancel the Mapplethorpe show. "If the Helms censorship amendment passes, artists of the future will not be able to express how they experience the world," the students declared. As Congress returned from the Labor Day recess, it was greeted by thousands of letters and faxes in a well-orchestrated campaign. Even the Corcoran Gallery, which canceled the Mapplethorpe show in June 1989, reversed itself and joined the fight by sending out letters to ten thousand of its supporters urging them to oppose Jesse's amendment. In Phoenix, an artist produced a photograph with an image of Helms floating in an amber liquid: appropriately, it was entitled *Piss Helms*.[45] In April 1990, New York artist Hans Haacke produced *Helmsboro Country,* a large sculpture reproduction of a flip-top cigarette box with Jesse's image on it, while singer Loudon Wainright produced a single entitled "Jesse Don't Like It" that ridiculed Jesse's anti-obscenity campaign. "If Jesse thinks it's dirty it don't get any funds," went one line, and "They use that taxpayers' money on tobacco and guns."[46]

During most of September, Helms's July 1989 amendment, which had passed both houses, was deadlocked in a House-Senate legislative conference. Only after a compromise emerged from the conference that reduced the sweeping language of Helms's amendment but which banned the NEA from supporting any "obscene" art in the future did the deadlock end.[47] The new law, Helms told reporters, represented a significant victory. "The American people expect Congress to take a stand on this," he said. The NEA heard "a message," and "I don't believe you're going to see any more of this garbage being funded by the taxpayers." Although his opponents might claim victory, Jesse said, "I hope I get defeated like that all the time from now on."[48] Nonetheless, Jesse promised to continue the fight. "Old Helms has been beaten before," Helms declared, "but Old Helms doesn't quit." Rather than ending matters, the NEA battle would continue, and Jesse predicted that he would continue adding amendments "to bill after bill after bill, month after month."[49]

Helms's NEA fight symbolized a brewing cultural war. To his opponents, he represented a backward, anti-artistic and anti-intellectual sensibility that seemed to be sweeping the nation. He was, according to *New York Times* columnist and native North Carolinian Tom Wicker, "the Senate's most persistent yahoo." Senator No, he wrote, had become, Senator Know-Nothing.[50] Helms's concept of art, wrote syndicated columnist Clarence Page, made sense only "if your idea of art is black velvet Elvis portraits." He thought that Americans had "received whatever moral message Sen. Helms intended to send," and it was now "time for him and his fellow philistines to back off."[51] Ed Yoder, declaring that "repression is Helms' middle name," called him "one of the prissiest politicians who ever drew breath."[52] Helms was now eligible for the "Yahoo Hall of Fame," commented still another columnist.[53] The "forces of reaction," said novelist Larry McMurtry, controlled the arts funding debate, and "in their hands the narrative is a stunted thing, a story with only one character, that old Puritan fellow-traveler (and proven vote-getter) Fear-of-Sex." Helms and his allies sought to end public funding for anything with sex in it, in "rigidly chaste" fashion. Jesse and "his debating partners" were "simply vacant" on the subject of art, "unlike many millions of Americans who do respond to it, do love it and do need it." Millions of Americans who loved art, he said, should "take back the narrative and turn it on those who would remove art from the budget." Without public support, art would be "starved practically out of existence in many regions of this country." The "Fear-of-Sex Follies" in Congress should be "hooted off the stage by an audience of grown-up Americans who might enjoy a mature art." Even Helms might still be "dumbstruck and in awe before Raphael or some other masterwork."[54]

After 1989, Helms maintained his pressure on the NEA. Beginning in the fall of 1989, he routinely requested copies of numerous NEA grant applications in order to oversee its funding; this yielded numerous examples of homoerotic art.[55] Helms, meanwhile, sought further restrictions: in March 1990, he asked the General Accounting Office to investigate whether the NEA had violated the law by funding obscene art, or whether "other possible irregularities" existed in the execution of congressional intent. In April, he asked the GAO to determine whether the NEA had engaged in illegal lobbying activities. The "other possible irregularities" included NEA support for performance art by Annie Sprinkle, a self-proclaimed porn star, the San Francisco Gay and Lesbian Film Festival, and a "Degenerate with a Capital D" exhibition in New York City. In May 1990, the GAO concluded that the NEA had complied with the regulations, while it ruled that the arts agency was involved in no illegal lobbying.[56] That spring, other proposals appeared in Congress, ranging from Representative Philip Crane's bill to abolish the NEA to Representative E. Thomas Coleman's proposal that 60 percent of NEA funds be given to states (previously, the proportion had been 20 percent).[57]

In October 1990, a year after congressional restrictions on NEA funding passed Congress, the issue arose again in the endowment's reauthorization bill (the 1989 legislation had been reauthorized for only one year). The NEA and its supporters pushed hard to remove the anti-obscenity requirement, and in August 1990 the National Council on the Arts, which advised

the NEA, voted to seek an end to the anti-obscenity pledge that grant recipients were required to sign.[58] On October 11, the House voted overwhelmingly to reauthorize the agency. While the legislation asserted that
obscenity should be determined by the courts, it instructed the NEA chairman to award grants by "taking into consideration general standards of decency and respect for the diverse beliefs and values of the American
public."[59]

In advance of the 1990 debate about NEA, Helms's staffers had prepared various amendments, including imposing a ban of NEA support for
child pornography, requiring that all NEA review panels be open to the
public, limiting funding to institutions rather than artists, and instituting a
tax checkoff that would enable voters to refuse to fund the NEA.[60] On October 24, 1990, Helms offered an amendment that would prohibit federal
funding for work that depicted "in a patently offensive way, sexual or excretory activities or organs," but it was rejected by a vote of 70–29. The
Senate also rejected another Helms amendment that would have restricted
NEA grants to artists making less than 1,500 percent of the poverty level,
which at 1990 standards was $94,665 for individuals and $190,125 for families. Not only was the panel process flawed, Helms suggested, but grant
money was going to "professionally accomplished and economically successful artists" able to sell their work at a considerable profit. Emphasizing
an anti-elitist message, Helms declared that many of these artists were
"much wealthier than the average American worker, to say the least"; many
of them nonetheless succeeded in getting "handouts from the National
Endowment for the Arts." Helms reminded the Senate about how NEA-
supported art had offended the "moral and religious sensibilites of the majority of the American people." While one performer had drenched his
nude body in chocolate, another performance artist, he said, had urinated
on stage while telling her audience to engage in a "gynecological" exam.
No newspaper, he reminded his fellow senators, was willing to publish the
Mapplethorpe photograph of "a naked man with a bullwhip protruding
from his posterior." Helms, in fact, had sent Mapplethorpe photographs to
newspapers; he used Federal Express rather than the Postal Service so that
he would not violate federal obscenity laws. If newspapers were unwilling
to publish the photographs, did that not make the photograph obscene, he
asked his fellow senators? At stake in the NEA debate, he said, was whether
Americans would permit "this nation to sink slowly into an abyss of slime"
and permit the ascendancy of people who wanted "to destroy the Judeo-
Christian foundation of this republic."[61]

Over Helms's opposition, on October 24 the Senate acquiesced in the removal of the 1989 anti-obscenity requirement.[62] Despite the outcome in 1990, the Serrano-Mapplethorpe controversy provided Helms with fodder for future campaigns. In correspondence, he would often list the most outrageous photographs: the one that depicted a nude man with a bullwhip in his rectum, or another showing a man with his arm up another man's rectum. Helms kept a thick notebook of the Mapplethorpe photographs that he displayed at campaign appearances and to reporters, and eagerly—sometimes too eagerly—showed off to visitors. "See the guy urinating in another guy's mouth?" Helms asked a *U.S. News & World Report* journalist with mock disgust. "How do you like them apples?" he said while flipping through his black Mapplethorpe notebook. He produced the notebook on his own. "No one has asked North Carolina's senior U.S. senator to show the photos," said the reporter, but that did not "stop him from volunteering." When he reached an especially vivid Mapplethorpe photograph, Helms closed the book emphatically and said: "Oh, I don't even want to see them. You've seen enough."[63] A *New York Times* reporter received the same treatment when he was invited to the senator's office to view Helms's "small stash" of Mapplethorpe homoerotic photographs. According to this reporter, Jesse often made viewing the photographs a "condition for news interviews."[64]

Helms's anti-obscenity campaign against the NEA rallied his national constituency and spurred on his direct mail base to continue the money flow. There was enthusiastic support for Helms's campaign among an energized national conservative constituency. Both the American Family Association and Pat Robertson's 700 Club—key organizations of the Religious Right—mounted a media campaign against indecency. In April 1990, Alan Wildmon (Donald Wildmon's brother) sent out an anti-NEA flyer to 178,000 pastors and to every member of Congress. At home, the issue again served to reinforce his image as a man of principle and a dedicated conservative. According to the *Durham Morning Herald*, Helms's campaign against obscenity, art, and the NEA meant that "North Carolina's number one fuddy-duddy might have sunk his teeth into a re-election issue." Although arts supporters were attacking Jesse, the senator loved a fight, and he realized that it drew attention to his cause. A larger problem for Helms bashers, the *Herald* asserted, was that the "guy is right": the federal government should not support the "despicable" work of Serrano and Mapplethorpe. Helms's approach, though "overkill," addressed the "right of the people in a democracy to decide how they will spend their money."[65]

HELMS'S CAMPAIGN AGAINST the NEA fed into his reelection battle in 1990, an election that, like the one six years earlier, was characterized by a bare-knuckled use of television advertising. As had been true for all of Jesse's previous campaigns, the Congressional Club would run Jesse's campaign, with essentially the same team. A conspicuous exception was polling and political wizard Arthur Finkelstein. Increasingly, he found Helms's emphasis on Religious Right issues unattractive: Finkelstein was a libertarian, and Helms's anti-government positions had attracted him to his campaigns. Finkelstein's departure from the club was probably due to his homosexuality—although neither Ellis nor Wrenn then knew it—and his realization that Helms would be making anti-gay rhetoric an important part of his political message.[66] By the time Finkelstein parted ways with Helms, however, the club had refined the techniques of political communication and management to a degree unprecedented in American history. The club became a sort of laboratory that tested and developed new political techniques, especially in the use of polling, advertising, and manipulation of the media. In the 1970s and 1980s, the club mastered the fine art of direct mail fund-raising, creating a huge money machine. Not only did the club refine the development of a donor list, they also polled the list, and from the polling learned about the demographics and giving habits of their donors. They discovered, to their surprise, that donors came in different categories: some gave frequently, others only once a year, and the club learned whom to ask and when to ask them.

The Congressional Club learned how to use political advertising with maximum efficiency. Neither Finkelstein nor anyone at the club placed much faith in the vogue of focus groups. The only thing that came close to focus groups were instances when the club's creative team used its own employees—especially women employees—for an impressionistic view of how an audience might react. Finkelstein and Wrenn both believed in the accuracy of polling, and they employed massive amounts of it. At the same time, part of the genius of the club's use of polling and media was to discover the most effective means to place political advertising. The club thus polled TV watchers, but, unlike Nielsen pollsters, they sought to determine the political makeup of the television-watching electorate. Armed with a highly sophisticated knowledge of the television political constituency, they then knew how to reach specific groups through advertising. The club worked with one of the best time buyers—the people who bought ad time—in Robert Holding, and working with him, they were able to maximize the impact of their money on television. An experienced television person and what Wrenn called the "best damn horse trader I ever saw,"

Holding exacted discount rates from television stations in massive buys. In the campaigns of the 1980s and 1990s, the club could obtain efficiencies that provided them with more ad times at a lower cost than their competitors. In all of these innovative methods of polling, media, and political advertising, the Congressional Club became what Wrenn called a "college for politics."[67]

These methods were in place by 1984 and perfected by 1990. Finkelstein's successor as pollster, John McLaughlin of New York, was a person whose conservatism was rooted in a Roman Catholic moralism. Ellis and Wrenn operated a tightly focused, well-managed effort that depended on a steady money flow from a national conservative constituency. The campaign, Wrenn would recall, was "a lot like '84," except perhaps that Helms's message was even "stiffer and harder." The club organized an effort that relied even more on televised ads and even less on grassroots organizing. The Helms managers, who began organizing the campaign in January 1989, realized that the 1990 campaign, like 1984, would involve an electorate with fixed and largely negative views about the incumbent senator; their strategy would revolve around driving up the negatives of their opponent, whoever that might be. From February 1989, when Jesse decided to run, to June 1990, the Helms campaign focused on fund-raising and determining their opponent.[68] The club's media campaign again depended on hard-hitting attack ads that flooded the airwaves and sought to define their opponent in order to drive up negative perceptions about him. As was true in 1984, the main issue in the campaign was Jesse, and his track record in his two-year campaign about AIDS, indecency, and NEA obscenity was transparent. Just as he had through his career, Helms pushed the envelope and, more than any other campaigner in late-twentieth-century America, used issues of sexuality and culture to distinguish himself from his opponent. But the 1990 campaign was also a campaign about race. Helms's opponent, Harvey Gantt, who won the Democratic senatorial nomination in June 1990, was the first African American in North Carolina history to mount a serious statewide campaign for political office. While in 1984 the Helms campaign ran a campaign that was coded in terms of race, in 1990, Helms was opposed by a black candidate, and the race issue rarely left the minds of the electorate.

As late as the spring of 1990, however, it remained uncertain who would oppose Helms for his fourth term. In August 1989, Jim Hunt decided against running; three years later, he would be elected to the first of another two terms as governor, and he had little stomach for another bruising struggle with Jesse.[69] With Hunt out of the race, former Charlotte mayor Harvey

Gantt won the Democratic nomination after primary and runoff elections in May and June 1990. A successful architect, Gantt grew up in poverty in Charleston, South Carolina, attended Iowa State in 1961, and then attempted to apply to transfer to Clemson University, which had never before enrolled black students. After a federal lawsuit, Gantt was admitted in 1963, a few months after James Meredith became the first African American student enrolled at the University of Mississippi. Subsequently, Gantt was elected as Charlotte's mayor, the first time that an African American had won that office in a large North Carolina city. In 1987, Republican Sue Myrick defeated Gantt in his attempt for a third term by campaigning on traffic jams and governmental mismanagement and by charging that Gantt had used his status as mayor to obtain a share of a local television station that he later sold at a profit.

The Helms managers considered Gantt the weakest candidate in the field. "We wanted Gantt," recalled Wrenn, "and we got Gantt."[70] Gantt's nomination was historic: he was not only the first black to run with a major party nomination for statewide office in North Carolina, he was the first African American in the nation to run as a Democrat for Senate. Matched against a black candidate, Helms did not need to inject race into the campaign, but he had to approach things differently. Running against Gantt, said Mandy Grunwald, who managed his campaign, might throw the Helms forces "off their usual game," something like a boxer facing a left-handed opponent. Race would not enter the campaign, Helms promised soon after Gantt won the nomination, and he had warned his campaign that "some heads will be cracked if anything is done that even appears to be racist."[71]

Gantt's primary campaign was "forthrightly liberal," as the *Raleigh News and Observer* described it. With strong positions on abortion, health care, environmental protection, improved education, military spending, and the role of government, Gantt offered an alternative. The race immediately attracted national attention, most of it focusing on the race issue: *Newsweek* dubbed it "the most colorful, expensive and nasty Senate contest in the country," and the "New South" versus "Old South" narrative became a common part of national news coverage. This was a "test of just how much North Carolina has moved away from its segregationist past," wrote a *Baltimore Sun* reporter, while *U.S. News & World Report* declared that "Gantt cannot escape his role as the symbol of the next stage of Southern progress."[72] The Helms-Gantt contest also attracted national attention because nationally organized arts, pro-choice, and gay rights groups were dedicated to Jesse's defeat. In June 1990, the AIDS activist organization

Cure AIDS Now announced a boycott on North Carolina tourism and of companies that had contributed to the Jesse Helms Center, which was under construction at Wingate College and scheduled to open in 1992.[73]

The intensity of anti-Helms groups played well into the senator's campaign strategy. Probably most voters sided with Jesse in his disgust about the NEA: Charlie Black, who worked episodically as a political consultant for Helms in the 1990 campaign, described it as a "centerpiece social issue" in the campaign in a state in which a majority held conservative values. As long as voters understood the difference, they would choose the conservative candidate.[74] The Helms forces eagerly embraced distinguishing their candidates on the basis of ideology. "What you have opposing Helms is a coalition of homosexuals and artists and pacifists and every other left-wing group," said Carter Wrenn shortly after Gantt's primary win in June 1990, and he suggested that the campaign might be even more expensive than the 1984 contest. During the campaign, predicted Democratic political consultant Harrison Hickman, Harvey Gantt would turn on the television and radio and "hear Jesse Helms slowly peeling the skin off of his back." It would be difficult, agreed the *Winston-Salem Journal,* for the high road to prevail, given Helms's "jugular style."[75]

Gantt sought support from liberal groups outside the state; in July 1990, for example, he was a featured speaker at the National Organization for Women annual meeting in San Francisco.[76] Later in the campaign, in September 1990, he raised $250,000 in a day and a half of fund-raisers during a visit to Washington. Gantt appealed to the arts community not only because of Helms's anti-NEA positions but because, as one Washington art dealer said, he was "part of the art world," favored choice, opposed censorship, and "really appeals to people."[77] But gay rights groups especially mobilized against Helms, raising funds and organizing, though their effect may have been at best uncertain among the North Carolina electorate. Members of the local chapters of ACT UP protested a Helms $1,000-a-plate dinner in Washington in June 1990, and they demonstrated by honking air horns, shouting and whistling as attendees entered the Republican Party's Ronald Reagan Center. Helms slipped into the dinner by a side door, and, unconcerned about the protest, left in his brown Oldsmobile. Strom Thurmond, who attended the dinner, walked out the front door and ignored the protesters. Munching on grapes and a brownie, he responded to a reporter who asked about the impact of the protest: he thought that the protesters would increase Helms's lead ten points by being there.[78] In June 1990, when the Fifth Annual North Carolina Lesbian and Gay Pride March occurred in Chapel Hill featuring a theme of the "Gay

'90s," its organizers described the gathering as the "first big display of people out in the streets against Jesse Helms." On July 27, gay bars in San Francisco and three other cities held events in which they dumped Miller beer—manufactured in North Carolina—in protest of Helms. Democratic congressman Charlie Rose, describing the event as "absolutely counterproductive," noted that publicity about these events simply aroused the average North Carolinian's "great fear of gays."[79]

Among the many similarities with the 1984 campaign was the hostility of the Helms team toward the press, which they regarded as pro-Gantt. By September, Helms's campaign press secretary, Beth Burrus, announced that she would answer reporters' questions only if they were faxed in advance. Jim Morrill, who covered the campaign for the *Charlotte Observer,* recalled that Burrus rarely provided anything beyond a "canned" response unless she first checked with Carter Wrenn. Burrus—whose previous job was managing a yogurt shop—seemed to have little information of any importance. Helms was generally shielded from contact with journalists; Morrill remembered him as "pretty inaccessible." Along with other major newspapers in 1996, the *Observer* ran a series entitled "Your Voice, Your Vote," which polled voters to determine important issues and then interviewed candidates about their positions. Helms categorically refused to participate. When Morrill went up to the senator at a Boone rally in order to get some information for the series, he referred to his notes when he interviewed Helms. Later that evening, Jesse singled Morrill out as a reporter who "couldn't even look me in the eye" when he spoke to him. Reporters, as in previous campaigns, became a "comfortable foil."[80]

In contrast to the 1984 race, the 1990 campaign did not involve intense election activity until late in the campaign cycle. In part this was so because the Gantt campaign, which was run by Charlotte associates such as former state senator (and future congressman) Melvin L. Watt, operated outside the Democratic Party apparatus, and it took some time before they established a fund-raising and organizational apparatus.[81] Early polls, taken in the aftermath of Gantt's primary win, gave the challenger a slight lead, but the race remained competitive into the fall.[82] Gantt challenged Helms to renounce the large expenditures and heavy media of past campaigns and to agree to a series of face-to-face debates. He also suggested that Jesse, in his obsession with foreign policy and ideological crusades, had grown out of touch with voters. Jesse was "more interested in what's going on in Mozambique and El Salvador" than he was in the welfare of tobacco farmers and textile workers, Gantt told the Democratic state convention in June 1990.[83] Helms and his managers, recalling the nearly disastrous experiences with

Hunt in 1984, refused to debate; Helms would never again engage in televised campaign debates. Even more than in previous elections, Helms left
the running of the campaign to his subordinates, and he remained in Washington for most of the contest. By the middle of August, Jesse had made
only ten campaign appearances in North Carolina, with only one of them
between June 20 and August 25—a shockingly low number. Early Helms
television commercials were soft, emphasizing Jesse's personal qualities
and featuring endorsements from various people, including President
Bush.[84]

In August, the campaign heated up with attack ads from both sides.
Gantt supporters struck first. In 1984, Helms had been perceived as vulnerable on the abortion issue, but Hunt had pressed the issue only hesistantly.
Gantt was less restrained about the issue, and he enjoyed the support of the
National Abortion Rights Action League (NARAL), which hired Democratic political consultant Harrison Hickman, to run anti-Helms ads. Hickman argued that the ads should take an aggressive posture on the abortion
issue, which in North Carolina had a different and distinctive history.
North Carolina was one of only a few southern states that had legalized
abortion before *Roe,* and it provided state support for abortions for indigent
women long after the federal government had cut off such assistance. Hickman argued that NARAL should run an ad that stated that "Jesse Helms
thinks your daughter ought to have Willie Horton's baby." Hickman referred to one of the most famous political ads in American history, George
H. W. Bush's attack ads against Michael Dukakis in the 1988 campaign,
which accused him, while governor of Massachusetts, of having furloughed
convicted black rapist Willie Horton. Hickman believed that an aggressive
ad on abortion that also exposed the hypocrisy of Helms's position would
make Jesse's core supporters "stark raving mad." What better way to explore the "nexus of fundamentalism and racial attitudes" and examine the
abortion issue in the context of race? But Hickman's suggestion was "suffi-
ciently controversial," even for NARAL, that they decided on a less aggressive approach. On August 12, thirty-second ads appeared in eastern North
Carolina television markets informing viewers with the message that
Helms had ten times proposed constitutional amendments to ban abortion
even for victims of rape and incest. Helms, the ad's narrator said, wanted
the "government and politicians to make this personal decision for you."[85]

The NARAL ads provided a boost to Gantt's campaign. According to
Wrenn, Helms's polling revealed a surge in support for the challenger that
was fueled by the abortion issue. Jesse had always been vulnerable on this
issue; the Helms campaign avoided the issue, and never ran an ad on it in

any campaign. Helms's polling confirmed the Achilles heel: roughly nine out of ten voters favored legal abortions in cases of rape and incest, but few knew about Helms's views. The injection of this issue in August 1990, according to Wrenn, "put Gantt in the race," and the margin between the two candidates narrowed.[86] Jesse's political managers made him acutely aware of the unpopularity of his abortion views. In September, he commented on the Senate floor that abortion rights activists were "invading my state" and that he was "running some risk" in his views.[87]

Helms's managers responded with an even more intense media campaign. In mid-August they unleashed hard-hitting radio ads in eastern North Carolina that claimed that Gantt favored five different tax increases while Charlotte mayor. Other ads attacked Gantt for opposing the death penalty. Gantt had said no to the death penalty for drug kingpins, rapists, and police killers, declared a TV ad. The incumbent and challenger possessed different values, the ad claimed, with Gantt representing "extreme liberal values" and Helms "North Carolina values." In other radio ads, the Helms campaign suggested that "gay and lesbian political groups, the Civil Liberties Union, all the extreme liberal special interests" had come from New York, Washington, and San Francisco to defeat Helms. Gay activists were supporting Gantt, and the ad told listeners to send a message to these "extreme special interests": "Go home. We don't want your values, your ads or your advice on how we should vote in North Carolina." Gantt opposed Jesse's efforts to limit "taxpayers' money going to pornographers," and he "got the gay and lesbian alliance on board" in this fight. The Gantt campaign responded with its own radio ad. "You knew it was coming," said the narrator. "Now he's at it again. This time Jesse Helms is out to tear down Harvey Gantt."[88]

The Helms campaign then sought to defuse the abortion issue. In ads appearing in early September, a middle-aged white woman in a red dress—a Helms volunteer from Charlotte—claimed that Gantt favored permitting late-term abortion for sex selection. That, the woman declared, was "too liberal" a position about abortion. Gantt denied the charges, criticizing the "whiny woman" who sought to deflect the discussion from the "real issue." The ad was a "lie" about his position on abortion. But the Helms campaign had laid a trap. Weeks earlier, Earl Ashe had sent out a camera crew to film all of Gantt's press conferences: today, this is a common practice, but in 1990 it was unusual. In a press conference in Wilmington in August, Gantt was asked about abortion; he responded that he unequivocally supported choice. What about abortion for sex selection? Gantt responded by reiterating his support for unqualified choice for women. "I don't want to get involved in why a woman may be motivated to have an abortion," he said. "That is really left to the woman, I mean her reasons, her motivation are her decision . . . whether it's sex selection or whatever reason." With Gantt's press conference comments contradicting his unqualified denial that he supported unrestricted abortion, Ashe took the film of the Gantt press conference and transformed it into an attack ad that appeared on the airwaves on September 18. The ad, as was typical of Ashe's work, was cleverly produced. With a full image of Gantt before them, a narrator told the audience that Gantt had denied endorsing abortion for sex selection. But "Harvey Gantt told the press that he would allow abortions," the narrator said, using the press conference footage, "whether for sex selection or for whatever reason." The ad then rewound Gantt's image, and the narrator said: "Did he say even for sex selection?" The screen then twice rewound Gantt uttering the phrase "whether for sex selection or whatever reason"; the second time, the time was rewound in slow motion, and a voiceover said "Read his lips." In what became a familiar sign-off, a voice proclaimed: "Harvey Gantt, extremely liberal with the facts." The ad had the effect of neutralizing the abortion issue; Walter D. DeVries, a political consultant, called the ad "devastating," hitting Gantt's credibility "right between the eyes." According to Wrenn, the ad "worked like a charm" by pushing Gantt "as far to the left as Helms was to the right."[89]

The race issue also crept into Helms's ads. In September 1989, Helms hired James Meredith as a special assistant, his first black Senate aide. Meredith, after the celebrity of the Ole Miss desegregation fight in 1962, had become an increasingly erratic figure, at odds with mainstream civil rights leaders. NAACP head Benjamin Hooks described him as having a "difficult time keeping in touch with reality."[90] Beginning in 1988, Meredith sent a letter to all members of Congress, criticizing black civil rights leaders as corrupt and involved in drugs. On December 9, 1988, Meredith and Jesse both spoke in Miami at a foreign affairs forum. After Jesse heard Meredith speak about race and his support for the Republican Party, the two men met for the first time and spoke over a cup of coffee. They then struck up a correspondence in late 1988 and early 1989 in which Meredith wrote of a "sense of divine guidance" that was guiding him as a black leader. Meredith told Jesse that he wanted to come to Capitol Hill, and he offered to work for free. Helms eventually offered him a job, urging him to promote his agenda through the senator's office, and Meredith immediately accepted.

Named as Helms's special assistant, his duties remained unclear, even to his co-workers; he was reportedly receiving the lowest pay of any regular staffer. Others in the Helms office viewed Meredith as quirky, mystical, and even incoherent. He seemed to pursue his own agenda; he did not fit into the office structure. Clint Fuller remembered that he "never understood" why Meredith had been hired, and, although chief of staff, never knew what his responsibilities were. At one point, when Meredith came to Fuller asking what he should do, Fuller responded: "James, I guess just keep on doing what you've been doing." In late October 1989, nearly two months after coming to Washington, Meredith told a reporter that he had seen Helms only once since he had joined his staff. Helms evidently hired him for political purposes, to counterbalance his civil rights critics. Soon after Meredith joined the staff, Helms made a point of introducing him to his liberal adversary Edward Kennedy. "Have you met my new staffer, James Meredith," he asked. On the floor of the Senate, Helms in February 1990 told of Meredith's critique of the liberal welfare state and the threat it posed to the American family.

In March 1990, Meredith told an audience at Chapel Hill that affirmative action was part of a plan by white liberals that sought to make the "black race incapable of competing." White liberals, he said, "created the concept in order to provide a system of payoff and control of the black elite they needed as leverage to control the black masses." Speaking at Suffolk University in Boston a few days later, Meredith declared that slavery was "no big deal" and that the movement seeking divestiture of American investments in South Africa represented an attempt by the liberal elite to control the black vote. In July 1990, Meredith declared that over 60 percent of the three thousand delegates to the NAACP meeting were "involved in the drug culture" and that more than 80 percent engaged in "criminal or immoral activities." Helms refused to disavow the statement, telling reporters that Meredith was "entitled to his judgments, and his judgments are good on many, many things." In an essay that appeared in a publication of the Heritage Foundation, Helms said that Meredith was "absolutely right" in his analysis that too many civil rights leaders had "no desire whatsoever to achieve equality for all blacks." Meredith's attack caused a stir, with many North Carolina black leaders believing that this represented an attempt to discredit black leaders and Gantt specifically. Other observers agreed. "You can't say it was planned," UNC political scientist Thad Beyle told *Newsweek* in an interview, "but you can't say it wasn't part of the campaign strategy." "One of the things Helms always does is send a signal to the boys at the gas pumps, the good ole boys."[91]

Racial themes also appeared in Helms's fund-raising. On August 10, 1990, Jesse's campaign sent out a letter featuring a photo of Democratic

National Committee chairman Ron Brown—Brown was black—and pointing out that Gantt was the "first black man elected mayor of Charlotte."
Critics perceived racial undertones. According to Charlotte political scientist Ted Arrington, the Helms campaign was trying to "connect the idea in
people's minds that Harvey [Gantt] and the Democratic Party in general
are controlled by blacks." In a subsequent fund-raising letter a week later,
Helms linked Gantt with black activist Benjamin F. Chavis, Jr., and his
campaign warned, apparently without basis, that Chavis was leading a
voter registration drive. Although Gantt described these fund-raising letters as "clearly racist," the Helms campaign issued a statement asserting
that the challenger was trying to "hide his record by calling people 'racist.' "
"If you can't answer a question," Helms said a few days later, "you shout
bias, bias, racial bias."[92]

For the remainder of the campaign, Gantt campaigned tirelessly, emphasizing issues of health care, the environment, and education, while
Helms stayed in Washington and relied on the club's management of the
election and its media attacks. Jesse was a "remote controller," charged the
N&O, of the "nation's most lethal campaign mudmobile."[93] This had long
been Helms's style of campaigning, and he typically refused to leave the
Senate before it adjourned. But during this election he remained even further removed from day-to-day electioneering, in what Jack Betts later
called "essentially a broadcast campaign." The onset of the Persian Gulf
crisis, brought on by Iraqi dictator Saddam Hussein's invasion of neighbor-
ing Kuwait, provided Helms with added reason to remain in Washington.
In early September, he visited American troops in Saudi Arabia, along with
a large congressional delegation. According to an account by *New Republic*
editor Sidney Blumenthal, Helms dosed off while Saudi King Fahd was
giving a speech—something that Helms vehemently denied.[94] Gantt, who
had logged more than forty thousand miles of travel across the state by the
end of October, complained that Helms had refused to debate and that he
was running a candidacy that relied entirely on paid media, while a *New
York Times* reporter called the Helms campaign "perhaps the most controlled in history." Even Helms's Republican supporters worried that his
low profile might endanger the party's other candidates.[95]

By late October, perhaps reflecting Helms's lifeless campaigning, the
race had tightened, and predictions were rife that Helms's eighteen-year
Senate tenure was nearing an end. While Jesse was "aging and tired," said
his old adversary, Ed Yoder, his opponent offered a "new and attractive
face." Hit hard by the nationwide recession and the exodus of textile jobs,
Yoder speculated, perhaps North Carolinians had grown weary of Helms.[96]

Gantt's coffers were filled with about $100,000 a day in contributions—during the first half of October he raised $1.7 million, compared to $1.2 million for Helms—and his ads filled the airwaves. During the last weeks of the campaign, Gantt was actually outspending Helms on media buys. The Gantt ads stressed Helms's poor record on the environment, health care, and education. On October 20, a poll by the *Charlotte Observer* reported that Gantt led by eight points, 49 to 41 percent. Election officials also reported rising black voter registration. Political observers described a "Wilder Factor" in which white voters told pollsters one thing and did another when they voted. It was so named for Douglas Wilder, a black Democrat who won the 1989 gubernatorial race in Virginia, but by a much narrower margin than polls had predicted. In Gantt's 1987 mayoral race in Charlotte, polls had him ahead of his Republican opponents by nine points, but he lost by 995 votes. The Wilder Factor, according to some experts, meant that if Gantt led by eight points, the race was essentially even. Helms's internal polls showed a similar skew.[97]

The Helms campaign, responding to the tight race, ramped up their attacks. In ads and in Jesse's speeches, they stressed ideological differences: Helms was conservative, Gantt was liberal. "If ever there was a clear-cut choice—between a certified liberal and an unabashed believer in America's free enterprise system," Helms told a Rocky Mount audience in late September, "this is it." If Gantt was elected, Ted Kennedy would "welcome him with open arms."[98] Television commercials meanwhile emphasized sexuality and race. In campaign stops, Helms liked to remind voters about the NEA fight. In one of his infrequent appearances in August, Helms spoke to a group in Burlington and brought with him two notebook binders that contained Mapplethorpe's homoerotic photographs. When he finished speaking, he invited the men in the audience to look them over: "I say to the ladies," he added, "don't look at it." "If you think I'm shooting bull," he told the audience, "you men step up here and take one look at the pictures here." "You'll be sick." He reminded his audience that a coalition of liberal media and arts advocates were mounting a defense of "filthy so-called art" and locking "arms with the homosexuals and the lesbians in a crusade to defeat Jesse Helms."[99]

By late October, Helms launched a new attack on Gantt's homosexual supporters. His supporters were collecting money from Washington, New York, and San Francisco gay bars, Helms told an audience in Fayetteville on October 22; "radical groups," he said, were donating millions. Gantt, Helms told another audience, was nothing but a "two-bit politician." Television, radio, and newspaper commercials, emphasizing Gantt's gay support, hit the airwaves, meanwhile, on October 23.[100] The TV ad began with images of newspaper articles about Gantt's trips to raise funds outside North Carolina, along with clippings from gay publications and a picture of a Washington gay bar. Gantt, the narrator said, was running a secret campaign with "fundraising ads in gay newspapers," and he had raised "thousands of dollars" in gay bars across the country. Gantt, the ad charged, supported "mandatory gay-rights laws." The radio ad was even sharper. "Militant gays," it said, wanted a "liberal, pro-gay senator" like Ted Kennedy, and Gantt, the ad charged, was running ads on "all-black radio stations" with promises that he would raise "more welfare spending and more quotas for minorities." Why were "homosexuals buying this election for Harvey Gantt?" read a newspaper ad. "Because Harvey Gantt will support their demands for mandatory gay rights!" These homosexual rights might include having gays teach in the public schools, it warned, adding that this "may be O.K. in San Francisco or New York—but not North Carolina!" "Think about it," Helms said in another campaign appearance in late October. "Homosexuals and lesbians, disgusting people marching in our streets demanding all sorts of things, including the right to marry each other. How do you like them apples?"[101]

The sexuality issue—brought out in Helms's anti-gay proclamations—served to galvanize already strong support among Christian evangelical groups. During the 1980s, the Christian Right had become a core group of supporters. The "greatest threat" to America, he told the American Association of Christian Schools in February 1989, came not from invasion from abroad but from within, those who were "dead-set on making our nation a God-less one, rather than one nation under God." Secular forces were winning the battle. The Ten Commandments, to secular humanists, had become the "ten suggestions." Churches had receded in influence as government and welfare programs grew. As a nation, America had changed from "God-centered" into a "self-centered abyss." As evidence of this "self-centered abyss," Helms cited sexual promiscuity, divorce, teen pregnancy, and abortion, but also drugs, poverty, increasing crime, and homelessness. The key to moral regeneration lay in combating the "anti-God, elite establishment" that was dominating public life. Jesse identified organizations such as Planned Parenthood and the Children's Defense Fund as "determined to destroy the morale of America." The "arrogant homosexual lobby" must be fought "for the sake of our families." The AIDS epidemic posed a threat to society, but it also involved an "underlying drive to make homosexuality simply an 'alternative lifestyle' rather than the deviant, immoral, perverted behavior that it really is." Challenging that establishment required courage and resistance to "surrender, tyranny and oppression." He compared politically aroused Christians battling the secular threat as like David and Goliath: evangelicals were the "Davids of our time," Goliath "all around us."[102]

Helms's political managers worked with evangelical churches to facilitate voter registration, and the Republican Party hired operatives with contacts in fundamentalist churches who targeted unregistered evangelical voters. Republican Party officials, working with the Helms organization, communicated with fundamentalists to identify a young church member willing to do this field work. Especially when Democrats engaged in well-publicized black voter registration drives, the Republican effort brought thousands of new evangelical voters into the electorate.[103] The Moral Majority, which had provided key support in 1984, had dissolved in 1989, but the Christian Coalition, headed by TV evangelist Pat Robertson, mobilized evangelicals in support of Republican candidates. Late in the campaign, according to one account, Helms called Robertson and explained that he was down in their internal polling. The Christian Coalition swung into action by providing approximately 750,000 "scorecards," voter guides urging evangelical voters to support Helms over Gantt. The scorecards, which were inserted into church bulletins and distributed as leaflets, emphasized the differences between the two candidates on social issues. According to Christian Coalition director Ralph Reed, the group also made thirty thousand phone calls on Helms's behalf. Jesse's political managers later suggested that the Christian Coalition, in claiming a decisive influence, exaggerated its impact. "I'm not saying what they did hurt," remembered Mark Stephens, but "I can tell you what they did wasn't decisive." Subsequently, the Federal Election Commission asserted that these efforts were illegal because they involved financial support from an independent political group.[104]

THE RACE ISSUE, meanwhile, grew more important during the waning days of the campaign. President Bush vetoed a civil rights bill and, on October 24, the Senate upheld the veto. While its supporters described the bill as intending to make it more difficult to discriminate against minorities and women in employment, its opponents characterized it as a "quota" bill. After Gantt criticized Helms's vote in support of the Bush veto, he also criticized his use of race in his radio ads. Denouncing the Helms campaign contention that Gantt was heavily advertising on black radio stations as "just garbage," he described Helms as race-baiting.[105] After Helms returned to the state for full-time campaigning, on October 28, his campaign began broadcasting the first of two controversial TV ads containing strong racial overtones. Reviving the criticism of Gantt's 1985 deal regarding WJZY, a television station in Belmont, near Charlotte, in which he bought and sold part ownership at a profit, the ad claimed that Gantt benefited from the sale because he was black. "Why was Harvey Gantt defeated as mayor?" the narrator asked in the thirty-second ad that contained only text. Gantt had invested $679 in a "minority preference to get a TV station license to help minorities" and then sold it for $450,000. Even black leaders, said the ad, believed that Gantt had sacrificed "principle for profit." A day later this same ad ran with one significant change: it said that Gantt had "become a millionaire" by using his "minority status."[106]

On the stump, Helms denied any race-baiting. At campaign stops in eastern North Carolina, which he reached via a motor home, Helms played a Gantt radio ad that featured a conversation between a man and woman in which the man told of dreaming that he had forgotten to vote. In the dream, Helms won the election by one vote. The man concluded that Gantt was the candidate who was good for "us" on the most important issues. Gantt, Helms claimed, had injected race into the campaign by "saying one thing to the black citizens of the state" while "saying another to the rest of the citizens." "I wonder if you want a senator in Washington who doesn't know how to tell the truth," Helms said at a campaign stop.

Helms also pounded away on the television station issue. Gantt was guilty of "betraying" Charlotte blacks by personally enriching himself through a minority preference; he had a swimming pool and tennis court at his house. "He broke a covenant with the black citizens of Charlotte," he would tell an eastern North Carolina audience, "and they threw him out of office." Later, Helms also asserted that Gantt tried to obtain an interest in a Morehead City TV station in 1986–87, again by using minority preferences. Jesse also reminded eastern North Carolina voters that he had voted to sustain Bush's veto of the civil rights legislation. "If you want quotas to dominate or dictate whether you get a job or a promotion," he said, "you vote for Mr. Gantt." At another rally that same day at a tobacco warehouse in Dunn, Jesse told listeners that the civil rights bill—which Helms called the "quota bill"—meant that "race comes before qualifications in job selection or promotions." Responding, Gantt claimed that Helms was spreading "lies and distortions" while waging a "politics of fear." As he had in previous campaigns, Jesse maintained that the press had distorted his record about race and portrayed him unfairly. Sticking his finger in the face of a *Greensboro News and Record* reporter during a campaign swing through Greenville,

Helms asked him "how much money" did the Gantt campaign "pay you"? He found his audiences receptive, with one attendee commenting that if Gantt were elected he would give taxpayers' money "away to the hippies, the Jews, the niggers."[107] "People will say this reason or that one," commented another North Carolina voter, "but a lot of them aren't going to vote for a black man."[108]

Although Helms claimed that he was not using race as a political issue, it played a central role in a campaign strategy that was designed to compete for swing voters, virtually all of whom were white. By running against a black candidate, the race issue was thrust before the electorate: would white voters choose a black candidate? As political scientist Merle Black observed, Helms was a "master" of racial politics, more so than any other politician since "George Wallace got out of the business."[109] As the campaign entered its home stretch, the Helms campaign pressed the issue by promoting thinly coded language; he frequently emphasized the quota issue to audiences. The best-known political ad of the 1990 campaign, without question, was the "white hands" spot, which began running during the last week of the campaign. Showing a pair of white hands opening and then crumpling a letter, the narrator declared: "You needed that job, and you were the best qualified. But they had to give it to a minority because of a racial quota." The ad concluded with Gantt's image next to that of Senator Edward Kennedy, with the narrator concluding that Gantt supported "Ted Kennedy's racial quota law that makes the color of your skin more important than your qualifications." The ad seriously distorted the truth. The 1990 civil rights bill—which President Bush vetoed in October 1990—did not impose quotas, which the Supreme Court, since the *Bakke* case of 1978, had held unconstitutional. The quota issue was, in fact, a false one that was intended to inflame white fears. Helms was not the only Republican to exploit the quota issue, but he used it more avidly than any other candidate in the country.[110]

The "white hands" ad would be remembered as a critical piece of political advertising. Because the Helms campaign could not obtain studio time in North Carolina, it turned to Alex Castellanos; Ellis, Wrenn, and Ashe flew to meet with Castellanos in Washington and brainstormed scripts. The hands in the ad came from a cameraman, with Castellanos operating the camera in an Alexandria hotel, and when they had finished, Ellis packed up the videotapes and headed to the airport, where he checked his bags, which contained the tape dubs. When his flight was canceled, Ellis insisted that airport officials retrieve his luggage. He then rented a limousine and drove through the night to rush the commercials back to North

Carolina. Ellis arrived back in Raleigh "in a bad mood" during the predawn hours, and campaign manager Mark Stephens had about fifteen couriers ready to drive the dubs out to television stations around the state in time for their noon deadlines.[111]

Wrenn did not dispute the importance of the quota issue and how the Helms campaign had exploited race. "I can't tell you we planned it or polled it or calculated it," Wrenn told a *New Republic* reporter about a month after the election. "We responded to what happened." But subsequently Wrenn would change these views: he later admitted that the Helms campaign's approach on race came directly out of polling and research. Bush's veto of the 1990 civil rights bill and the unsuccessful attempt to override his veto provided an unforeseen opportunity. Wrenn later admitted that the use of the quota issue was an instance of the Helms campaign's "aggressive playing of the race card." Still, Wrenn claimed that the impact of the "white hands" ad was greatly exaggerated. According to polling by the Helms organization, the ad "flopped" and did not resonate well with voters, and it was pulled after several days' airing. The "white hands" ad, Wrenn claimed, was less effective than the ad attacking Gantt on the TV station deal, which, according to Wrenn, "worked like dynamite" because it combined questions about affirmative action with questions about Gantt's character, and the character attacks always worked well in Helms campaigns.

Although the "white hands" ad might not have had a direct impact, it served the purpose, as *Charlotte Observer* reporter Jim Morrill later said, of "warming up the audience" to the issue of affirmative action.[112] Both the "white hands" and TV station ads used themes of race to distinguish between Helms and Gantt, and this proved effective in driving white swing voters into Helms's column. From the outset of the campaign, the Helms team had hoped that they would face Gantt because he was black. They realized that the race issue, pitting a white incumbent against a black challenger, would define the 1990 campaign, for there were too many white voters in rural North Carolina who simply would never vote for a black candidate. It was a "tribute to Gantt" that he did as well as he did, Wrenn later said; of the three Helms campaigns that he ran, Wrenn believed that Gantt mounted the best campaign of any opponent. But in the end, race trumped everything else. "Don't let anybody kid you," said Wrenn, "the definitive issue of that campaign was race, from start to finish."[113]

THE RACE ISSUE played out on another front in the campaign's late stages. Sometime in late October, Republican Party officials sent 125,000 postcards out to voters in predominantly African American precincts in twenty-nine counties advising voters that, in order to vote legally, they were required to have lived at their address for at least thirty days before the election. The postcards further informed voters that supplying incorrect addresses violated election law because it provided false information to registration officials. Voters who had moved but not changed their address, the postcards claimed, were committing a "federal crime, punishable by up to five years in jail"; those appearing at the polls would be asked how long they had lived at their residence. In fact, these were false claims: voters who moved but had not changed their addresses could still vote, and this was an obvious attempt to discourage black turnout. As early as the summer of 1990, according to Justice Department officials later investigating the case, the Helms campaign and Republican Party officials had been discussing implementing a ballot-security program, but the plan did not come into effect until it appeared that the black vote might become significant. The Helms campaign and Republican leaders discovered that black voter registration had increased by 10.6 percent, versus a 5.3 percent white increase, between April and October 1990. The Helms campaign also worried about polls in mid-October that showed Jesse behind Gantt by eight points.

During the late 1980s, party officials had worked laboriously to construct a system by which they could identify voters so as to maximize turnout, but they noticed significant numbers of registered voters with invalid addresses. Republican state chairman Jack Hawke and Wrenn decided to attempt to root out these voters, nearly all of them black, as a fail-safe in case of a close election. In mid-October, about the same time that news of increased black voter registration and of Gantt's lead in the polls became public, the Helms campaign contracted with Charlotte political consultant Edward Locke to run a ballot-security program, and he was provided with an office and staff support. Between October 26 and 29, Locke, with an office and some staff provided by the Helms campaign, mailed 81,000 postcards to voters in eighty-six mainly African American precincts, with addresses that Jefferson Marketing supplied; in the targeted precincts, blacks were 94 percent of all voters. On October 29, a second mailing went out to another 44,000 voters who were selected from a master list of 260,000 voters whose residences had changed and whose addresses were different from those identified in their registration. The target voters were entirely African Americans. According to the Justice Department's investigation, the ballot-security program was run by the Helms campaign, and, more specifically, by JMI. Although Helms later claimed to have known nothing about the program and although his campaign would never admit to these charges, this was an operation that came out of his political organization.[114]

In response to the postcards, in the days before the election local boards of election received numerous phone calls, nearly all of them from black callers who were worried about whether they should vote. Democrats claimed that this was part of a deliberate strategy to intimidate black voters and suppress turnout: the chairman of the state party claimed that this was "blatant intimidation." Democrats also produced a Helms fund-raising letter in which he requested money to support ballot-security activities designed to lower black turnout. The Justice Department subsequently dispatched a team to investigate the charges, while the Democratic National Committee argued that the mailings violated a consent degree in which the Republican National Committee agreed that it would not conduct ballot-security activities in precincts where racial or ethnic considerations figured importantly. Although the judge agreed that these tactics resembled those banned by the consent decree, it did not govern the activities of state political parties. More than a year later, in February 1992, the Congressional Club—even while denying wrongdoing—agreed to an out-of-court settlement. "The so-called civil rights bureaucrats left us no choice but to accept this agreement," Wrenn told reporters, saying that Helms's political organization did not want to pay for legal fees to fight the case. Gantt, reflecting about the ballot-security measures, later described them as "voter intimidation, pure and simple."[115]

Nearly sixteen years later, Carter Wrenn would claim that the ballot-security program of 1990 was a "screw-up from start to finish." The campaign, he said, anticipated that the election would be close, and in the event that Helms lost, they intended to challenge Gantt's votes. Wrenn had authorized Locke's mass mailing of postcards in order to track the returned incorrect addresses and thus to create the basis for asserting the existence of invalid ballots. He had authorized the program, but when the copy for the postcard passed his desk, he had "twelve other things" in front of him, and he simply overlooked it. So, apparently, did Hawke. Had he been more careful, Hawke later said, he would have reviewed the language in the postcards in order to determine its legality. Surveying voter registration to determine legitimate voters was legal, Hawke later realized, but using language that would intimidate or suppress the vote was not. The same explanation came from Mark Stephens, by then head of JMI. He also called the program a "big screw-up" in which, "if we were guilty of something, it was not having as watchful eye as we should have had." If this had been a planned political move, Stephens recalled, "it would have been pure stupidity." As it was, the exposure of the program, Stephens maintained, probably cost Helms more votes than it gained.[116]

Whether this explanation is credible is another matter. According to Hawke, he reviewed the postcard's copy and sent it to Bob Hunter, who was then chairman of the state elections board and was also a Republican attorney from Greensboro. Although Hunter approved the copy—as did GOP official Alex Brock—the 1990 ballot-security program was clearly racial; both Hawke and Wrenn should have realized that the postcards would eliminate black votes with incorrect addresses. Although this was legal, it targeted African Americans and was designed to invalidate questionable ballots. In addition, on October 31 and November 1, 1990, after the press had exposed the existence of the ballot-security program, JMI operatives sent out another mailing of postcards to voters in Mecklenburg County whose addresses had been misreported because of computer error. Where Wrenn, Stephens, and Hawke believed that matters had gone beyond their control was in those postcards that went to voters with legitimate addresses; the postcards' language sought to discourage and intimidate voters, and it formed part of a larger and more overt effort to drive a racial wedge in the electorate to a greater extent than in any of Helms's other senatorial campaigns. Would it be possible for a person so closely attuned to detail as Wrenn to permit a mailing such as this—a mailing that came in two phases—without knowing about it? In a close election, an election in which the club was playing the race card, it was surely tempting to use other methods to minimize black turnout.[117]

WITH HELMS'S SHARP-EDGED attacks providing last-minute momentum, the election headed toward a conclusion as Jesse comfortably won re-election, by a margin of 53 to 47 percent. Helms proclaimed a victory over his liberal enemies. "If the liberal politicians think I've been a thorn in their side in the past," he declared in his victory statement in Raleigh, "they haven't seen anything yet." Watching the "grim face" of CBS news anchor Dan Rather as his victory became clear, Helms realized that there was "no joy in Mudville tonight" as the "mighty ultra-liberal establishment" had struck out. Although Gantt attracted a majority of voters under age thirty, Helms received 60 percent of those over sixty years old. Most important, Gantt was unable to attract enough white votes; he received about 37 percent of the white vote. Helms's use of the race issue, and his drumbeat about gays, stimulated a last-minute white turnout. Overall, voter turnout increased by a half million voters over 1986 (when Democrat Terry Sanford captured John East's seat), and, according to Helms's polling data, the people most likely to sit out a nonpresidential contest were white conservatives. The turn to race during the last week of the campaign brought them out to the polls. The pollsters' predictions of a Wilder Factor, it appeared, came true, as what most pre-election polls had predicted to be a close race turned into an easy Helms win. The last-minute round of ads attacking Gantt on issues of race and sexuality worked with white voters; appeals that linked race with the quota issue were especially effective. The racially tinged ads drew a sharp distinction between the two candidates, and a large, last-minute white turnout went in Jesse's direction. According to one poll, of those deciding late in the campaign, 61 percent went for Helms. The senator also succeeded in painting Gantt into an ideological corner by convincing voters that his opponent represented political positions that were alien to traditional North Carolina values. Unlike Hunt, Gantt ran on a liberal platform that directly challenged Jesse on the issues.[118]

The 1990 campaign resembled Helms's race against Hunt six years earlier in yet another respect: in the large amount of money raised and spent by both candidates. All told, Helms and Gantt spent $24.7 million, only slightly less than the $26 million spent in 1984. While Jesse spent $17 million, about $15.60 for each vote, Gantt spent $7.7 million, or about $7.84 per vote. Because of the expensive operational costs of Helms's direct mail fund-raising, the amount that was left to spend on the campaign, especially in the last month or so, was much less than the overall two-to-one ratio would suggest. From July onward, the two candidates spent roughly the same amount on their campaigns. Gantt was more successful in raising money from liberal political action committees, most of them out of state, and he had abundant cash during October and November. When the campaign concluded, moreover, the Helms organization had about a $1 million campaign debt. The usually overwhelming advantage in money and television, in other words, had quickly disappeared, and to a certain extent Helms was a highly vulnerable candidate in 1990. This made the use of wedge issues of sexuality and race all the more important.[119]

Chapter 11

THE CONSERVATIVE LION
IN HIS WINTER

Transitions

As he entered his fourth term in the Senate and began his seventh decade of life, the early 1990s were a period of profound change for Helms. Personally, Helms began to experience health problems that seriously hampered his ability to maintain his previous pace. To some extent, at the height of these health problems, he partially withdrew from public life, maintaining a very limited schedule. In the operation of his office and the structure of his political organization, there were other changes. In 1992, he swept aside his longtime staff of foreign policy advisers, most of whom had provided ideological intensity and ammunition for battles over Latin America, South Africa, and the Soviet Union. He also cut ties with the National Congressional Club and his longtime political managers, Tom Ellis and Carter Wrenn. In the aftermath of these changes, Helms's most important advisers were less hard-edged: though still committed conservatives, they were less combative, more consensual, and more willing to strive toward the political center.

IN 1991, DOT experienced two blows, the first occurring when her brother died in May, the second when she experienced a recurrence of cancer in August in an encapsulated tumor in one of her kidneys. Surgeons at Raleigh's Rex Hospital successfully removed the tumor, and Dot subsequently received twenty-eight radiation treatments and six rounds of chemotherapy.[1] Although Dot went on to make a full recovery, Jesse's health problems, as he neared his seventieth birthday in October 1991, manifested themselves. In May, doctors informed him that he was afflicted with Paget's disease, which resulted in bone loss and affected his hips, causing a limp. Although the press reported the diagnosis, the disease would have little effect on Helms's subsequent health. During a routine blood test in June, the attending physician for Congress, Dr. Robert Krasner, diagnosed Helms with prostate cancer, and he underwent radiation five times a week—in what would be a total of thirty-eight treatments. Jesse insisted to reporters that his health was not affecting his work habits. "Anybody who wants to start picking a successor," he said with remarkable accuracy, "better wait about 11 years." His work as a senator had "not been inhibited in the slightest," Helms said in a statement, claiming no side effects from the radiation.[2] By November, the doctors had given him a clean bill of health. "I've got the thing licked," he told one reporter.[3]

Helms developed more serious health problems some months later. One morning, in May 1992, he woke up and had difficulty breathing, and George Dunlop, who lived next door to Helms in Arlington, rushed him to Bethesda Hospital. Dr. Bert Coffer, an anesthesiologist and personal friend, then persuaded him to be examined by doctors at Rex Hospital, though he worried about taking on this responsibility. "Jesus," he remembered wondering, "if anything happens to this guy, I'm in trouble."[4] The Raleigh doctors found that Helms was suffering from congestive heart failure caused by a bad mitral valve, plus a blockage in three arteries.[5] Helms and his staff kept the status of his health from the public: a reporter for the *Charlotte Observer* heard a rumor of health problems and went to see the senator, but he and his staff denied any problems. In Raleigh, before the operation, Helms had told reporters that the surgery was so common that it amounted to "little more than an appendectomy did just a few years ago," and he predicted that he would return to work in six weeks. Coffer, when interviewed, said that Helms was "looking ahead" and had not decided to leave the Senate when his term expired in 1996. But the media remained skeptical: the "feisty politician," read one account, "may be losing his vim," and Helms appeared "a bit out of place" and "less forceful than usual." His doctor refused to operate on him if he continued to smoke. When Helms responded that he had quit smoking, the doctor asked when this had occurred. "Twelve minutes ago," Jesse said. But having smoked unfiltered Lucky Strike cigarettes for nearly forty years, he adhered to the profile of the typical heart patient.[6]

Surgery came quickly after the public announcement. At the last minute,

Coffer learned that he was in charge of security and press relations; all information, he was told by Helms's chief of staff Darryl Nirenberg, would be filtered through him. Coffer remembered seeing the scores of broadcasting trucks outside Rex Hospital that "scared the crap out of me."[7] On June 3, Raleigh surgeon Dr. W. Charles Helton completed a quadruple coronary bypass and replaced one of his heart valves with a pig's valve. Reporters were informed that the senator's work continued: his staff was working with fellow senators in an unsuccessful attempt to cut off funding for the Corporation for Public Broadcasting because of alleged "liberal bias" and for sponsoring programs that, as Jesse had expressed it, "blatantly promoted homosexuality as an acceptable lifestyle."[8] Helms suffered from complications soon after the surgery. With a poorly functioning vascular system, he was kept on the heart-lung machine longer than usual, while he went on the ventilator twice—in large part because of the mucus buildup in his lungs that resulted from smoking. He was at times delirious and suffered from confusion. Three days after the surgery, at 5:00 A.M. on June 7, while still in cardiac intensive care, Helms suffered from a respiratory arrest later attributed to his lung secretions. He stopped breathing for two minutes, and he was placed on a respirator. Although Coffer assured the press that this was not unusual, he later recalled that he "thought it was all over."[9] While still on the respirator, Jesse communicated with his wife by sign language, which they had learned several years before in a church group.[10]

Helms continued thereafter to recover steadily. On June 17, two weeks after he entered Rex Hospital, he was able to return to Caswell Street to convalesce. While in the hospital, he had received over ten thousand get-well cards, a fax from President George H. W. Bush while en route aboard Air Force One to Brazil, and a telephone call from Bob Dole.[11] Still, there was speculation that Helms's health problems would force him to resign his seat. In July, while recuperating, he tried to quash those rumors. In an interview with the news anchor of Raleigh's WRAL-TV, Charlie Gaddy—his first with the media since his operation—Jesse declared that he would not resign before his term expired. Saying that he felt "great," Helms told Gaddy that he was now driving and had transported himself to the barbershop. He refused to say when he would resume full-time work, explaining that his physicians preferred that he not hurry back to the Senate. The experience with heart surgery made him confront his mortality, but he was not afraid, he said. "If the Lord took me five minutes from now," Helms said, "He's still given me more than I deserve."[12] When driving by pork barbecue restaurants, Jesse would often ask companions—referring to the pig's valve connected to his heart—whether "any of his relatives were on the menu."[13]

IN THE AFTERMATH of the heated senatorial contest against Gantt, there were the usual tensions with the Congressional Club, which in 1994 renamed itself the National Conservative Club.[14] In the 1990 campaign, it had continued to run as a well-oiled machine, which, in two decades of its relationship with Helms, had raised nearly $100 million. In the three years before the 1990 campaign alone, the organization put out some 13 million fund-raising letters, paying the Postal Service $2.7 million and using vendors across the country. Working with the club, Helms, according to one expert, was "the single most successful political fund-raiser of anybody other than a presidential candidate." The club maintained a close relationship with an interlocking set of organizations that included Jefferson Marketing, Campaign Management, Inc., and Computer Operations and Mailing Professionals. Most of the money flowed from a national conservative constituency, nearly 70 percent of whom lived out of state. Many of them were small donors: some 211 contributors gave more than twenty-five times each, while one donor donated eighty-four times. As part of the money machine, the club incurred high operating costs: as much as 30 percent of what they took in went toward expenses.[15]

For twenty years, Ellis and Wrenn had enjoyed freedom in running the senator's campaigns, and over time he became increasingly distanced from, and to a certain degree less interested in, day-to-day management. Removing himself from politics and focusing on policy "liberated" him from mundane concerns, said Scott Wilson, who served as political liaison on his Senate staff during the early 1980s. He was a reluctant candidate who hated asking for money and political support. The club was usually unable to persuade him to make phone calls asking for money, and he avoided money matters, remembered Mark Stephens, because he was primarily a "policy wonk." One reason that the club embraced direct mail fund-raising so enthusiastically was that Helms wanted nothing to do with fund-raising. This "wasn't by design, it was by desperation," said Stephens. Over the years, Helms was both "removed and not removed," as Wrenn remembered it, from the club's operations. In the public face to the relationship, it was the "intentional policy" of Ellis and Wrenn to protect Helms by maintaining a "plausible deniability" in which Helms would be able to distance himself, if necessary, from their activities. Some of the details, such as polling, were kept from the senator, and Helms was shielded, for his own good. In other respects, he was closely involved. The senator continued to carefully scrutinize all fund-raising letters that went out under his name, usually applying a heavy editorial pen to the text, to Wrenn's annoyance. Helms later claimed that he had little detailed knowledge of the club's political advertising, but Wrenn would later assert that the senator was directly involved in suggesting ideas. In any ads in which Helms appeared, he read scripts in advance (again, he often rewrote the copy), and he usually saw videotapes before ads were aired. Wrenn, during campaigns, spoke with the senator more than once daily in order to keep him informed of strategy and developments.[16]

The alliance between Ellis and Wrenn and Helms had been a marriage of expedience. Each needed the other: "Without him signing those letters," observed Mark Stephens, "we were nothing." "We didn't always get along with each other perfectly," Wrenn said, and their relationship was "sort of like Simon and Garfunkel": Helms and Wrenn "fought, but they made good music." There was tension in the relationship, remembered Wilson, who often served as an intermediary between the senator and the club, and the fights with Ellis and Wrenn almost always concerned direct mail fundraising. *Charlotte Observer* reporter Jim Morrill recalled receiving a phone call from the senator after he had written a story about how the club had targeted vulnerable elderly voters and appealed to them for donations based on Helms's poor health. This was a sore subject with Helms, who told Morrill that he was fit and energetic enough to campaign. Further, he said, he had not written the letter, which was the responsibility of Wrenn and his organization. When Morrill then wrote a story saying that Helms did not write his own direct mail, the senator was even more infuriated about what he thought was a "cheap shot."[17]

There was, to be sure, plenty of mutual misunderstanding in Jesse's relationship with the club. Helms did not fully appreciate Ellis's "genius," observed Wilson, and how much the club's fund-raising machine had boosted Jesse's esteem and reputation. Ellis and Wrenn, for their part, handled Helms roughly, hauling him around the campaign trail. They "should have treated him better," Wilson recalled. After years of this contentious relationship, Wrenn later observed, "we were just tired of putting up with each other," and the "bloom was off the lily." The relationship was simply "wore out." Over the years, according to another account, while Helms had regarded Wrenn as "too sarcastic and verbally abusive," Wrenn viewed Helms as "too disinterested in campaigning and political pit fighting." There were ideological tensions; Ellis suspected that Helms sacrificed principle for political expediency, while Helms wondered whether the club had grown too hungry for power and money. Usually these tensions between the senator and the club grew after the election cycle, when they needed each other least.

Some of these tensions revolved around the club's entrepreneurial and risk-taking methods. It operated by cash flow and by estimates of how much money would be raised, rather than how much cash they had in hand. Ellis and Wrenn wanted to run as high a post-election debt as possible: the club hired CPAs to estimate how much they could safely borrow. This became yet another way of maximizing its money advantage over its opponents. Helms was never comfortable with this risk taking; fiscally conservative—some would say tight-fisted—he feared that the debt would follow him personally. Yet he also tolerated these methods. Wrenn re-called, a few weeks before the 1984 election, discussing a prospective debt with Ellis and Helms in Ellis's car. Although Helms objected to the debt, as he always did, he did not prohibit it. "I'll leave it up to you all," he told El-lis and Wrenn. That, said Wrenn, was all Ellis needed in order to proceed. Following the 1990 election, Helms was appalled at the $1 million debt that the campaign had incurred. Almost ritualistically, Helms had insisted at the outset that his campaigns should not incur any debt, but this ran counter to the club's more adventurous philosophy. It was typical, in fact, for cam-paigns that depended on direct mail fund-raising, as did Helms's cam-paigns, to realize a large portion of their donations at the end of the election cycle and immediately thereafter. Helms never completely understood these intricacies, and he would bitterly complain that the club had abused his good name, which had become a "cow to be milked." The club's need for money meant that letters constantly went out under Jesse's name; and the letters depended on pumping hot-button conservative issues to a largely el-derly population. Jesse later complained that supporters would ask whether he was really in the dire financial condition that his fund-raising letters sug-gested. "Jesse never saw any money," Helms said, and "I didn't need any money."[18]

Ellis and Wrenn had constructed an elaborate network of organizations to funnel money into conservative campaigns, and this money machine rankled Jesse. These organizations included the Coalition for Freedom, which Ellis and Wrenn established in 1979 and which was later charged with illegally supplying, as a tax-exempt organization, money to political campaigns. In 1986, the Federal Election Commission ruled that the rela-tionship that had existed between Jefferson Marketing and the club—in which JMI functioned as a for-profit entity that financed the club's activities—was illegal, and Wrenn had reorganized yet again. In 1986, in response to the FEC ruling, JMI was spun off into a privately held, for-profit company that Mark Stephens operated. Wrenn organized PEM Management, a company under his personal control, along with Hanover

Communications, which handled mail, political ads, research, and data processing, and Continental Direct, which did mailings. PEM Management became Wrenn's political consulting business, and between 1990 and 1994 the Helms organization paid it $1.2 million. This elaborate structure, which was designed in response to evolving electoral law, was perceived by Helms as a political organization that was veering out of control. These were "file cabinet corporations," Jesse would later claim.[19]

Not long after the 1990 election, antagonisms between Helms and Wrenn burst into the open. According to Wrenn, Helms wrote a formal letter to Ellis disassociating himself from the 1990 campaign debt; Wrenn recalled this as a "snooty letter" that was "clearly written" so that Jesse would have no remaining legal liability. He found Helms's letter "offensive" and a "venal thing to do," and he ignored it. Ellis, however, wrote Jesse back and promised that the club would assume campaign responsibility, without using Helms's name in fund-raising. Still, the matter was the source of considerable "acrimony."[20]

Helms generally had little to do with the club's operation, with one exception: he insisted that he review, and edit, any letter that went out under his name. Sometime in 1991, Wrenn had sent out a fund-raising letter that, a year earlier, according to Wrenn's account, Helms had approved, opposing statehood for the District of Columbia. After he received a phone call from a reporter about the letter, Jesse claimed that he had not approved the letter; Wrenn believed that he had forgotten. Furious, but also sick, Helms placed an angry call to Wrenn. He first reached Wrenn's assistant, Paula Kay, and "reamed her out." Next he spoke to Bob Rosser, who worked with Wrenn, and spoke angrily with him. Rosser was certain that Helms had approved the letter, but the approval had been misfiled, and was not found for nearly another year. Wrenn was out of the office, en route by train from North Carolina to Washington, and when he heard from his office, he was outraged that Helms had abused the sixty-four-year-old Kay. That was, he believed, "really a pretty shitty thing to do." Wrenn reached the senator, and the two men had words. Wrenn objected to the abuse of his staff; Helms objected to the implication that he had done anything untoward.

Club workers remained convinced that Helms had signed the letter but that, as was common practice in direct mail, it was reused later on: Jesse had simply forgotten that he had approved the letter.[21] But the details mattered little: as Wrenn recalled, it was simply a "rack you hang your coat on." Wrenn had had enough; for years, he had put up with Helms's outbursts, and if he waited them out, Helms would eventually be "sweet as a lamb." Helms, for his part, was sick of his association with the sordid world of fund-raising. He had always loved being a senator; he resented having to be undignified in letter solicitations. But, as Wrenn recalled, "he liked the money," which he realized was the key to his power and his "single biggest political strength."[22] There had been, over the years, constant squabbling about the content of the direct-mail letters that went out under Helms's name: always the careful editor, he insisted on scrutinizing the language. Frequently, recipients of the letters—and of solicitation phone calls—sent complaints to Helms's Washington office, and Clint Fuller insisted that these went directly to Jesse. Fuller, remembered Scott Wilson, might have even "got a kick out" of seeing Helms's reaction and the inevitably angry phone call to Wrenn. According to Tom Fetzer, Fuller saw club operatives "as a nuisance, more than anything else." Jesse felt similarly. He liked to say to congressional aides that the inscription on his gravestone would be: "Thankfully, the beggar dies."[23]

From that point forward Wrenn and Helms refused to speak to each other, and they conducted business in a "very oriental relationship." Helms would call Wrenn but only deal with him through Kay; Wrenn refused to speak directly with Jesse. The split with Wrenn became widely known: in November 1993, Helms told a reporter that they had not spoken in "two or three years." "I do not know how they spend the money that they take in or who gets it," he said. "I just have no information about the club and don't want any." In March 1994, the Helms-Wrenn relationship continued to be strained when George Dunlop, serving as the interim director of the new Jesse Helms Center at Wingate College, wanted the Congressional Club's mailing list. In August 1994, Sam Currin, former Helms aide, was dispatched to obtain the list of more than 500,000 names. Wrenn had no hesitation about supplying the list, but the club had used a complicated database Helms's computer people had difficulty deciphering. Dunlop, recalled Wrenn, thought "we'd hoodooed him." This was, Wrenn recalled, another example of the ongoing "messy divorce" between Helms and the Club.[24]

These tensions were aggravated by the Duncan McLauchlin "Lauch" Faircloth campaign of 1992. Almost immediately after the Senate election of 1990, Ellis sought out Faircloth, who had served as commerce secretary under Hunt in the 1970s but backed Helms in 1990 and switched affiliation to the Republican Party in February 1991. Ellis wanted to recruit him to run against incumbent Democrat Terry Sanford, who, they believed, was vulnerable, and Ellis knew Faircloth well, having represented him in a recent divorce case. Ellis had always preferred candidates who, like Faircloth, were eastern North Carolina conservative Democrats who could appeal to the crossover vote. Faircloth and Sanford were old friends and allies. Both worked for Frank Graham in the 1950 senatorial campaign—Faircloth had worked as Graham's driver and handler during the campaign—and on Kerr Scott's 1954 run for the Senate. While campaigning, Faircloth and Sanford once even shared a bed at a friend's house. Between 1969 and 1972, Faircloth served as chair of the State Highway Commission under Governor Bob Scott, and he was secretary of commerce under Jim Hunt between 1977 and 1983. In 1984, Sanford supported Faircloth's unsuccessful campaign for the Democratic gubernatorial nomination. But after Sanford's abrupt decision to run for senator in 1986, which Faircloth regarded as a betrayal that denied him the nomination, the old friends stopped speaking. Faircloth would run for Sanford's Senate seat, said one observer, "out of spite."[25]

Relations had continued to deteroriate between Faircloth and Sanford, who was quoted as saying that Faircloth would lose should he challenge him. That "just irritated the shit out of me," Faircloth recalled. Ellis dispatched Wrenn to visit Faircloth at his farm in Clinton, and, when he arrived, Faircloth told him that he was interested in challenging Sanford for his seat, but he wanted to know how much it would cost. Wrenn estimated that he would need $6 million to win a Senate seat; he promised that the club could provide $5 million. Faircloth's evident willingness to put up $1 million sold Wrenn on Faircloth's candidacy, which was announced in April 1991. In 1980, in contrast, when the club had recruited John East to run for the Senate, there was no discussion of money, and, for Wrenn, his willingness to take on a candidate for money reasons indicated "how far we'd fallen" from pure ideology to a combination of ideology and power.[26]

Neither Wrenn nor Ellis had, in fact, considered whether Faircloth was a true conservative. About two weeks before Faircloth was scheduled to announce his candidacy, Ellis remarked to Wrenn: "You know, we've never asked where this sonabitch stands on an issue." They then arranged a dinner with him to discuss his positions on key conservative issues. When Ellis asked him what his position was on the issues, Faircloth's face went "completely blank." "You write the music," he told them, "and I'll sing it however you say." Soon after he announced his candidacy, it became obvious that Faircloth held ambiguous political positions. At the news conference announcing his campaign in April 1991, he was asked about the abortion issue; in his 1984 campaign for governor, he had supported tax-paid abortions for poor women. When he told reporters that he maintained the same position on the issue, Wrenn, who was present at the news conference, unsuccessfully attempted to end reporters' questions. Wrenn would later describe Faircloth as perhaps the "most disappointing candidate" that he had ever worked with. Both he and Ellis should have realized that ideology meant nothing to Faircloth, Wrenn later observed, and "we should have run for our lives." But the true attraction to Faircloth lay at least partly in his willingness to put up $1 million of his own money for a campaign, and that and the desire to defeat Sanford, rather than ideological purity, persuaded them to manage his race.[27]

In May 1991, the club launched Faircloth's campaign with a fund-raising letter, followed by ads that were aired in August.[28] By the spring of 1992, Faircloth's most serious opponent had become Charlotte mayor Sue Myrick.[29] Although Helms refused to endorse either candidate, Myrick was convinced that Jesse was working behind the scenes against her. Helms was "not happy," and in December 1991 he wrote to Myrick, confirming his neutrality. "When the people at the Congressional Club choose to support a candidate," Helms wrote, they are "not speaking for me." Myrick then released the letter.[30] Ellis and Wrenn meanwhile resented Helms's neutrality. The election of Faircloth, who won the Republican nomination without a runoff and then upset Sanford in the November 1992 election in part because Sanford, who was seventy-five years old, was hospitalized a month before the election with heart valve replacement surgery, did not ease tensions.

Faircloth and the club soon parted ways, as the new senator wanted more complete control. Only a few months into his term, in March 1993, he told the *Raleigh News and Observer* that Wrenn and the club were hired to "run the campaign, not to run a Senate office." Faircloth was especially resentful of Wrenn and his "constant demands for fundraising" and the seeming absence of accountability of the funds.[31] Eventually, Faircloth went to Helms, complaining about how the club had run up a debt in his campaign and was continuing its fund-raising operation. "Is this normal?" Faircloth asked Helms. Subsequently, as the Faircloth-club split would become complete, Ellis became convinced that Helms had "poisoned the well" by changing the new senator's attitude toward the club. In fact, the senator was already reevaluating his attitude toward his longtime political managers; he dispatched a political lieutenant to investigate after he learned that Wrenn was involved in an attempt to buy WPTF, a Durham radio station, and that he lived in a big house in Raleigh. How did Wrenn get that kind of money? Helms's aide reported back that Wrenn was profiting from the club's operation—all of it legally—but that layer after layer of the complex operations had made him a wealthy man.[32]

The crowning blow would occur over the firing of Helms's daughter,

Jane Helms Knox, from St. Timothy's Day School, a private Episcopal school in Raleigh. After serving as the rector of St. Timothy's church for three decades, in the spring of 1993 George B. S. Hale retired after thirty years at the church. A conflict then developed over the new rector, J. C. James. Hale, who had founded the school in 1958, faced mandatory retirement; under Episcopal canon law, rectors were required to leave the ministry by age seventy-two. Canon law also stipulated that Hale should leave St. Timothy's and join another church, but he remained as chairman of the school's board. In the fall of 1993, however, James dissolved the school's board, removed Hale, and placed his own supporters on the boards. Jane, who was principal of St. Timothy's School, became entangled in this conflict, in what Wrenn called a "three-way fight" between Knox, Hale, and James, and they "were all fighting like cats and dogs." In the spring of 1994, a former board member accused Knox of permitting the teaching of the Bible in class, a violation of the principle of the separation of church and state that had governed the school since its founding. Several weeks later, the board severed the school's connections with Hale, who had taught philosophy and overseen religious functions. If Jane Knox had "done nothing," believed Wrenn, she would have survived, but instead she appealed to parents to take sides in the conflict, and the battle became even more charged and personal, with two armed camps. In the end, with parents deeply divided, both Jane and Hale were placed on a paid leave and eventually left the school.[33]

Both Wrenn and Ellis served in leadership positions at St. Timothy's. While Wrenn served on the church's governing board, the vestry, Ellis had served as senior warden of the church, had helped to found the school, and had served as a member and chairman of its board. According to his account, he and the board were rubber stamps: only when the accreditors visited did the group ever meet. Ellis had long supported Jane: some years earlier, at Jesse's request, he had recommended her for a teaching job, and, in 1989, he also successfully pushed her candidacy to become principal. Now, through little action of his own, he moved into the middle of the brewing conflict. While he was in South Carolina participating in a judicial golf outing, the senator called him. "What are you going to do about Jane?" Helms asked Ellis. "Jesse," he responded, "there ain't nothing I can do right now." "Thanks a bunch," Ellis recalled Helms saying angrily, slamming the phone down and hanging up on his old friend. For some time after, Helms and Ellis did not speak to each other.[34]

The fight over St. Timothy's School was, according to Wrenn, an extension of the "messy divorce" between Helms and the club, in which the estranged parties were fighting over furniture and pots and pans.[35] Some months after the Helms-Ellis fissure, in August 1994, the senator announced the end to his relationship with the club. Helms appointed a new treasurer of the Helms for Senate (HFS) organization, Jack Bailey of Rocky Mount, who had long been associated with Jesse and had been active in promoting anti-gay political ads against Hunt in the 1984 campaign. Helms's embrace of Bailey, who in 1993 had feuded with Ellis and Wrenn over a failed deal to buy the Durham radio station WPTF, offered additional evidence of the break, as the Helms campaign had split into Wrenn and Bailey partisans.

The precipitating factor in Helms's 1994 split with Ellis and Wrenn was the Federal Election Commission suit against the Helms for Senate organization, which, it charged, had illegally worked with the Christian Coalition in mobilizing evangelical voters during the 1990 campaign. In April 1994, the FEC issued a subpoena demanding records about contacts and collaboration between Helms's organization and the Christian Coalition, and, as it appeared that Wrenn's interest and those of the senator might diverge, both sought separate counsel. In early August, Helms moved to purge the HFS organization in order to mount a more effective defense of the lawsuit, and the HFS moved out of the North Raleigh quarters that it had shared with the Ellis-Wrenn operation.[36] Helms and Wrenn became even more bitterly estranged, as Helms charged that Wrenn benefited financially from his role in the Helms money machine. Wrenn, in response, released a financial statement in October 1994 that disclosed a net worth of only $152,532. "If you compare my financial statement with Sen. Helms' over the last 22 years," he told reporters, "I think it will verify that I have not profited unduly."[37] Wrenn insisted, at the same time, that a difference existed between the pre- and post-split HFS, and he refused to turn over records until the FEC ordered him to do so in April 1995.[38] Meanwhile, the club began work on supporting a conservative candidate for president in 1996 to run against Bill Clinton—that candidate would eventually become Steve Forbes, and Wrenn would run his campaign—and Bailey explained that this involvement "in other campaigns besides that of Senator Helms" meant that a split should occur. Jesse now preferred to return to "an organization of private citizens and supporters," Bailey said in a statement, "the way it was initially intended."[39]

The end of the working relationship between Helms and the Congressional Club marked a major turning point. The reasons behind its demise went beyond minor disputes and personality conflict and got to the core of a transition, a sort of final chapter, in Jesse's career. Rob Christensen, who covered Helms for the *Raleigh News and Observer* for thirty years, believed that Helms, in breaking with Ellis and Wrenn, was "getting rid of the rusty knife." Over the years, the club had done Jesse's dirty work by running campaigns and winning by whatever necessary methods. The club had done "rough things over the years," and Helms had permitted these things with a "wink and a nod." Now, however, Helms was more concerned with his "long-term image," and it simply did not fit into his plans.[40] Wrenn had done Helms' "dirty work" for him over the years, wrote *Charlotte Observer* columnist Jerry Shinn, including managing the money machine and helping to create attack ads that freed the senator from campaigning. Helms was feeling "a bit tarnished by what Wrenn did so well."[41] Club loyalists offered another perspective. The alliance between Helms and the Congressional Club empire had lasted two decades, said Stephens, and "in the world of politics, that's a long time." He thought the club's demise meant "an end of an era." After the 1984 election, the Helms political organization lost some of its steam and energy, and, with direct mail revenues on the decline, it had already reached its peak of power and effectiveness. With the end of the Cold War and the irrelevancy of anti-Communism as a political force, the glue that had held together conservatism was dissipating. The club had been mostly "a bunch of kids in their twenties, with a whole lot of money to spend in elections" who were trying to "make a difference." These "kids" had made precious little money, but took part in an exciting ride, and they "had a blast."[42]

HELMS DISCARDED ANOTHER "rusty knife" by breaking with one of his most ideological and his longest-serving policy adviser, James Lucier, who had worked as the senator's chief legislative aide since 1973 and then, after 1987, headed up the minority staff of the Foreign Relations Committee. Helms had always encouraged his Senate staff to be entrepreneurial. Helms gave his staff, remembered journalist Fred Barnes, "an incredibly long leash."[43] This approach offered opportunities for motivated, energetic, intelligent staff, but it also provided a great deal of latitude. In charge of the Foreign Relations Committee's minority staff, Lucier developed issues and agenda for all the Republicans on the committee. But, by the late 1980s, he had become more and more autonomous. Long after the shoot-down of KAL 007 in September 1983, Lucier insisted that its survivors were being held against their will in the Soviet Union and, according to one report, sent out a message insisting that the Russian leadership should disclose their location. Lucier also pushed the POW issue, asserting that Vietnam-era

American soldiers remained imprisoned in Southeast Asia. In late October 1990, Lucier prepared a report that claimed not only a "probability" that POWs were being held—it claimed to have evidence of 1,400 live sightings—but that the Bush administration was complicit in a cover-up. The report further claimed that the Defense Department in 1973 told the public that no POWs were being held but then discovered in the next year that several hundred remained. Moreover, the report contended, American POWs had been held in the Soviet Union since World War II, and more may have been transferred there during the Korean and Vietnam wars. American officials sought to undermine claims of live sightings, the report asserted, and in two instances caskets supposedly containing remains were in fact empty. The U.S. Army's forensic laboratory, the report claimed, was involved in deceiving American families. The "deeper story," Helms told an interviewer, was that there might have been a "deliberate effort by certain people in the government to disregard all information or reports about living MIA-POWs." "I just want the truth," he said, "and I don't think certain people in the government have been interested in pursuing it." Based on what his staff told him, Helms predicted that there would be concrete evidence of a live POW in Southeast Asia, yet none was produced.[44]

As it turns out, the report contained errors and unsubstantiated rumors and innuendo, and it embarrassed Helms, who subsequently had little to say about the POW/MIA issue. The appearance of the report also angered Republican members of the committee. Later, a special Senate committee on POWs and MIAs, on which Helms served, concluded in January 1993 that there was "no compelling evidence" that missing or captured American servicemen were still alive.[45] But after Helms backed off from the issue, he incurred the wrath of POW/MIA advocates, many of whom were in close contact with Lucier. Some even threatened to oppose Jesse's reelection effort in 1996.[46] Lucier's 1990 report was issued from the Foreign Relations minority staff, but few of the other Republicans had known about it in advance.

Lucier was a doctrinaire conservative, remembered Tom Boney, who "would occasionally take Helms to the brink" and liked to "take it right to the edge." Although both Helms and Lucier were deeply ideological, in terms of personal style they were very different: Lucier was professorial and could be absentminded, Helms was systematic and organized. Sometimes Lucier went too far, even for Helms, and the senator was becoming impatient with the instances in which he lost votes by large margins on the Senate floor. The Lucier staff had a "predetermined ideological bent," remembered Steven Berry, who was chief of staff of the House Foreign Affairs

Committee in the late 1980s and later joined Helms's staff. He eventually believed that Lucier was providing a "great disservice" to the senator. Lucier and his staff filtered out materials for the senator, but sometimes their filtering prevented his being fully informed. Berry found them uncooperative and uninterested in achieving results. Helms's views were colored by this highly ideological but also somewhat freewheeling Foreign Relations staff. Helms's most important foreign policy advisers possessed a "skewed view of reality in the world," Berry believed, and to a large extent Helms was a captive of their views.[47]

Also undermining Lucier was the troubling case of Quentin Crommelin, a member of a distinguished Alabama family, decorated Vietnam veteran, and Senate staffer for Senators Jim Allen, Strom Thurmond, and John East. In 1987, Crommelin joined the Foreign Relations staff as minority chief counsel. There were rumors about Crommelin's drinking and sexual improprieties, however.

Staff complaints about Crommelin soon reached Lucier, and then Helms. Eventually, Helms confronted Crommelin with these charges, and, when he denied them, the senator did nothing. Charges such as these were grotesque to Helms, who found it difficult to believe that Crommelin was capable of abusing women. He considered him a fine conservative, a dedicated Christian who was incapable of committing what were, for the prim and proper Helms, inconceivable improprieties.

Within a year after Crommelin's arrival, four young females quit the Foreign Relations staff because of inappropriate remarks. "He was just awful, really crude," one employee anonymously told the *Washington Post*, and he would "make comments about legs and all." Helms remained reluctant to get involved, and Crommelin blamed his woes on "liberal" opponents around Capitol Hill. The problems with Crommelin became even more serious after it became apparent that reporters were on the scent. Although the official explanation was that he left because he was eager to return to the private sector, Crommelin was fired in June 1988. After he left Helms's office, Crommelin was charged with abducting and sexually assaulting a young woman who worked on Helms's staff. Subsequently, in July 1989, he pled guilty to aggravated sexual battery in an Arlington court and received a ten-year suspended sentence, five years' probation, and mandatory therapy for psychosexual disorders.[48]

The Crommelin case brought Lucier's estrangement out in the open. Lucier had long been one of Helms's brightest and clearest thinking speechwriters. Now his colleagues found he had become dysfunctional, unable to produce work for the Senate, and obsessed with his own agenda. After the departure of Darryl Nirenberg—who had succeeded Tom Boney as deputy staff director—Lucier tried to install the twenty-four-year-old Sean Moran, and there was a "major falling out" because of objections among some staff. Both Nirenberg and Boney had served in that position as a liaison between Helms and the staff, interpreting and screening the senator from the staff. After what one observer described as a "staff revolt," Lucier became convinced that the rest of the office was out to get him for "alleged slights or missteps," and he isolated himself. Lucier insisted on working on his own staff and even instructed his assistant to say that he was out of the office when Helms called. Staffers that produced materials for Helms sometimes discovered that their work went no farther than Lucier's office. When Helms instructed foreign policy staff to go around Lucier and to send materials directly to him, Lucier became angry and demanded exclusive access to the senator. In defiance and denial, Lucier seemed convinced that Helms would not fire him because of his long tenure. Paranoid about his position in the office, he was suspected of checking Helms's typewriter tape and even the computers of other staff to see if anything had been said about him.

Things came to a head in August 1991. After Deborah DeMoss confronted Lucier about the staff problems, he responded by trying to fire DeMoss and four other committee staffers present. But DeMoss went to Helms and detailed Lucier's problems, telling the senator that his legacy was imperiled. It was hard for Helms to realize that Lucier had gone wrong. Tom Boney served as a deputy staff director of the Foreign Relations Committee under Lucier, placed there by Helms in order to shield the senator from ever-insistent committee staffers and in order to interpret staff work to him. Boney realized that there were tensions when he left in the fall of 1990 to return to North Carolina to run his family newspaper in Graham, North Carolina. Sometime in 1991, he received a puzzling phone call from the senator. If Boney had to decide between the truthfulness of Lucier and DeMoss, Helms asked, which one should he trust? He found the phone call "really puzzling," and he had no immediate answer to the senator's question. But he realized that the DeMoss-Lucier breach had gone far, and that trouble was brewing.

Helms was also receiving complaints from Republican senators on the Foreign Relations Committee during the spring of 1991 about Lucier's performance. Many of them were already alarmed about the strange POW/MIA report, but they were also aware that he had, more generally, done little to serve their needs and interests. Under the chairmanship of Claiborne Pell, Democrat of Rhode Island, the committee's seven subcommittee chairs had gained expanded authority with increased staff and the power to mark up legislation. There were also divisions among Republicans who wanted consensus and those, like Lucier, who went for ideological conflict. "We were squabbling among ourselves more often than with the Democrats," said one Republican. Helms was forced to act. He asked staff to document everything regarding Lucier. Because staff relations had become so bitter, Jesse called in, as an honest broker, James "Bud" Nance, ex-Navy test pilot and retired rear admiral, former skipper of the amphibious USS *Raleigh* and the aircraft carrier USS *Forrestal,* a retired Navy admiral, and Helms's school chum from Monroe whom he had known since the first grade. Nance, who was born within two months of Helms and grew up two doors away, enjoyed Jesse's full confidence. Helms liked to joke that, of these two men from Monroe, at least one had "amounted to something."[49] In mid-November 1991, Helms appointed Nance as the committee's deputy minority staff director, and the senator asked him to remedy the staff turmoil.[50]

Helms's decision to bring in Nance was a brilliant move. Helms told Nance to interview staff, determine where the problems existed, and to clean up the situation. Nance immediately went to work, occupying a small corner office, in which he met all day long with Helms's entire staff, one by one, to determine what they were doing and how effectively they were performing their jobs. He also spoke to people inside and outside the Senate; by the time he had finished his work he had spoken with more than one hundred people. In mid-December 1992, Nance went to Helms and informed him that the situation with Lucier had only scratched the surface, and it was far worse than the senator realized. He had found a "zoo" in the Foreign Relations staff, Nance later said, "without a zoo keeper." "When I came up here, the staff was in absolute turmoil," he recalled. Matters were "out of control," with a staff that was in "great disarray." In conversations with other congressional staff people, he was told, Lucier's operation was "the worst staff on the Hill." Lucier had to go immediately, Nance told Helms; effectiveness needed to be reestablished in the Foreign Relations Committee.

Helms agreed, but he delegated the task to Nance. Assembling his staff while he was in North Carolina, Helms spoke to them by speakerphone. He had appointed Nance as his staff director, and there would be changes; Nance had full authority to implement them. Nance then called in staff people individually and delivered the news. On January 6, 1992, he fired Lucier and a total of eleven staff people from Foreign Relations—out of a total of twenty-one. Nance came out of retirement to take Lucier's place in charge of the minority Foreign Relations staff. Accepting an annual salary of less than $1,600—Senate rules required that he receive a salary—he told a reporter that he was not out "to get another job" and that he was not "building myself up for another job." "I'm sure not here for the money," he added, noting in 1992 that with taxes and other deductions he took home about $77 a month.

The reasons for Helms's Foreign Relations staff purge reflected both the disarray of the later Lucier regime years and a desire to change Helms's approach on foreign affairs. Jesse, according to one unnamed aide, "got the vibes and finally acted on it." "We had too many doing administration and not enough doing the action the staff is supposed to be doing," Nance told the press, and it was "difficult for me to see exactly who was doing what." "He was attempting to impose "some order in the chaos," he said. The Foreign Relations staff needed to "get reoriented and refocus" on important foreign relations issues. Nance, who had served as deputy national security adviser under Reagan, wanted to restructure Helms's staff according to the White House's national security structure. The world had changed, Nance said. Under Nance's leadership, the staff would become less ideological. Contemporaries described Nance as conservative and ideological, but more genial in his style. He was, according to reporter John Monk, "like the uncle you'd want at Thanksgiving dinner." Other senators and their staff on the committee welcomed the change. "There was little communication or effort to cooperate," according to one Republican. "They had gotten Helms isolated." Saying that Nance was "absolutely right" in his decision, Helms told a reporter that "if you don't do your job, you just ought to get out." "I just hope the word goes out," he said, "that we're not going to have people who don't do their jobs."[51]

Lucier never saw the purge coming. He had done nothing, he said, "without the senator's full knowledge, full consent, full participation, and full urging." The last meeting that he had ever had with Jesse occurred a week after his firing. Lasting only five minutes, Helms, Lucier recalled, rambled incoherently. One staffer accurately described Lucier as "Helms' alter ego." Although initially refusing newspaper interviews, Lucier told *Congressional Quarterly* that the staff purge indicated that Helms was "no longer interested in political battle." Noting that Helms had become less aggressive in committee debate, he attributed his changed attitude to his bout with prostate cancer, which "obviously sapped his energy." During the last six months of 1991, Lucier told the *Raleigh News and Observer* in 1993, Helms was "under tremendous physical and psychological stress" because of his and his wife's cancer, and he was "physically depleted" and "out of the office half the time" and would "come in a few hours in the afternoon."

That meant that their conversations—and communication—were limited to only "the most essential things." Under pressure, Helms turned matters over to Nance, and he "betrayed him." Under Nance's control, Lucier charged, Helms had effectively "turned the committee over to the rest of the Republicans while remaining the nominal head." Nance, Lucier charged, hired staff people who were not ideological conservatives but instead were "mostly social Democrats or people with no outlook at all." He was appalled at the people under consideration for staff positions, he told the *Charlotte Observer*. These people, mostly "academic think-tank types," had "very little connection with the Jesse Helms that I know."

Although Lucier greatly exaggerated the changes that occurred in Helms's foreign policy views, there was some truth in his assertions. With Lucier as the committee's minority staff director, Helms had pursued a style that was combative, isolated, and sought to score points with a conservative constituency. With Lucier's firing, Helms, as Rob Christensen observed, had discarded yet another "rusty knife": the use of foreign policy as a part of a raw warfare against liberalism. Just as he would make a change in his political organization, Helms would also lay the basis for his emergence as a statesman. Beyond the strained interpersonal dynamics of Lucier's minority Foreign Relations staff, the fact that Helms was moving into a different, post–Cold War world made Lucier's hard-hitting polemics less relevant. Helms, concluded *U.S. News & World Report,* "may be mellowing." Rather than loading the committee with "hard-line conservatives" who "pursued an independent agenda that reflected the views of neither the White House nor most Senate Republicans," he was moving more toward a consensus style.[52]

Helms's purge of his foreign policy staff reflected a larger transition in his Senate office. In 1991, Clint Fuller, who had served as his administrative assistant and top adviser since he took office in 1973, developed cancer in 1991, retired, and then died two years later. Because the more inexperienced Nirenberg replaced Fuller, a less steady hand was exerted over office affairs. Interviewed in November 1991, Fuller described "morale problems" that existed in part because of Nirenberg's lack of control. Nirenberg, Fuller said, was "extremely difficult to get through to," and he would often communicate through subordinates. The staff chaos, in part, seemed to have reflected a lack of control. Fuller would have preferred if Helms had chosen old hands Andy Hartsfield or Mark Fleming to run the Senate office. Nirenberg remained in place until 1995, when Jimmy Broughton, grandson of Governor Broughton, succeeded him. Broughton, personable and open in his dealings, followed Fuller's style of management.

Fuller had joined Jesse in the summer of 1972; along with Lucier, he was a last link to the past. Fuller was responsible for running the senator's office, and he ran it, Helms liked to say, like a good manager of a small business—"efficiently and with a smile." The senator genuinely mourned his passing. He had known Fuller since his WRAL days, and he joined the Senate staff even though he remained a registered Democrat. "To old Jesse Helms," the senator told the press on his death, "he was one of nature's noblemen. I regarded him as a brother." Across North Carolina, he said, Fuller was "known and loved by literally thousands of North Carolinians because he was never too busy to extend a helping hand."[53]

MOST OF THE people closest to Helms would later admit that the health crises of the early 1990s slowed him down considerably. His long convalescence led to a slower pace; he was simply unable to keep up the demanding schedule of the 1970s and 1980s. Helms's usually impeccable voting record slipped. In 1991, with Dot's cancer and his own radiation treatments, only two senators had a worse attendance record than he. Jesse missed twenty-two votes because, he said, Dot needed him. "I don't apologize for being with my best friend and roommate of 49 years," he told a reporter. In 1992, he continued to miss votes at an unusually high rate. At Dr. Bert Coffer's insistence, meanwhile, he gave up driving himself back and forth between Washington and North Carolina. Close aides doubted that he would run for reelection in 1996.[54]

Nevertheless, Helms emerged from his health problems of the early 1990s reinvigorated: later described by Dr. Coffer as "totally recovered," he was once again ready to do battle.[55] Darryl Nirenberg believed that Helms had the same experience as other heart bypass patients: he returned with renewed energy. Rob Christensen covered Helms for the *Raleigh News and Observer* for nearly three decades, and in November 1993 he visited him in Washington. Jesse, Christensen wrote, was "the conservative lion in his winter," but he had now returned "in full form, with all his claws." Seventy-two years old, with restored health, he appeared to be "more like the Helms of old," with "color in his cheek, more of a spring in his step and plenty of the old bite (vitriol, his foes would say) in his remarks on the Senate floor." "I feel good," the senator told Christensen. "Frankly, I thank the Lord for letting me feel so good." His only problem lasting from his heart operation was weak legs; the quadruple bypass required that some of his veins in his legs were removed, and he followed a program of daily exercise and regular physical exams. Lauch Faircloth described him as looking "100 percent better" than he did two or three years earlier. If you asked around the Senate, Helms told Christensen, his colleagues would say "'What the hell happened to this guy?'" "Did he get some sort of injection for a race horse?" Although he refused to comment about running in 1996, he declared: "I have to answer with a double negative. I am not inclined not to run." With Bill Clinton in the White House in 1993, commented another veteran reporter, "Jesse Helms has been rejuvenated," and there was a "definite gleam in his eye."[56]

The Conservative Lion continued to wage battles in the Senate. In 1991, he served on the Senate Ethics Committee, which investigated charges against the "Keating Five." Among the multibillion-dollar collapse of the savings and loan industry, no culprit became better known than Charles H. Keating, Jr., and his Lincoln Savings and Loan of Irvine, California. In late June 1991, the committee's special counsel, Robert S. Bennett, wrote a report recommending the full Senate adopt a censure of Senator Alan Cranston of California, but the report was buried.[57] Helms then sent what one reporter called the "political equivalent of a Scud missile." Working with Bennett, who was frustrated with the inconclusive end to his work, Helms's staff, especially chief aide Darryl Nirenberg, crafted a 247-page report that appeared under Helms's signature. The report concluded that Cranston's conduct was "clearly and unequivocally unethical" and "reprehensible," and he recommended censure. Further, Helms called for the adoption of more stringent guidelines by the Senate in order to establish standards for "those who need written guidance to discern wrong from right." When Ethics Committee co-chairs Terry Sanford and Warren Rudman suggested that this was a leak, Jesse denied this vehemently, since this was his own report, based on public information. The committee had worked for two years, at a cost of $2 million—and "brought forth a mouse." Nonetheless, the prosecution of Cranston proceeded at a slow pace. On November 20, 1991, the Ethics Committee recommended that Cranston be reprimanded, and he retired at the end of the congressional session.[58]

ON JULY 22, 1993, Helms and Senator Carol Moseley Braun of Illinois, elected the previous November as the only female African American member elected to the Senate and only the second black senator of the twentieth century, clashed over the North Carolina senator's attempts to obtain an extension of the United Daughters of the Confederacy's (UDC) design patent on the organization's insignia. The design included the original Confederate flag (not the Stars and Bars, the crossed flag that most people

today assume was the emblem of the Confederacy) that was encircled by a
wreath with "1861" and "UDC" underneath it. Although Congress had authorized the design patent since 1898 and although the Senate had approved a fourteen-year extension in 1992, the House adjourned before
considering the measure. Moseley Braun opposed the repatenting because
it provided official sanction of the flag, the symbol of the slaveholder republic. The UDC did not need such sanction, she said, and the UDC insignia was protected by other existing copyright and patent law. At her
insistence, renewal of the design patent was defeated in the Judiciary Committee on May 6, 1993. Helms then joined forces with South Carolina's
Strom Thurmond to revive the measure by attaching it as an amendment
to a national service bill that passed by a vote of 52–48. Alerted by an aide
to Helms's legislative maneuver, Moseley Braun rushed to the floor, saying
that this public approval of the Confederate flag was an "outrage" and an
"insult" that was "absolutely unacceptable to me and to millions of Americans, black or white."

This flag, she said, was the "real flag of the Confederacy" that fought a
war whose main issue was chattel slavery, "whether or not my ancestors
could be held as property, as chattel, as objects of trade and commerce in
this country." The Confederate flag, which symbolized slavery, should not
be "underwritten, underscored, adopted, approved by this United States
Senate."[59] Moseley Braun's speech, which the *New York Times* called "majestic," swayed her fellow senators, who now reversed themselves and defeated Helms's amendment. Denouncing the introduction of the race issue
into the discussion as a "political ploy," Helms claimed that the senators
who switched their votes were nothing less than "gutless wonders." Jesse
described the design patent as a symbol of the UDC, a group of "elderly"
people, "all of them gentle souls who meet together and work together as
unpaid volunteers at veterans hospitals." Moseley Braun disagreed, saying
that this was not a case of "little old ladies walking around doing good
deeds" but a larger question of a racist past. But the majority of the Senate
saw things as did Moseley Braun, who, according to the *New York Times,*
"woke up a sleepy Senate to the unthinking way the white majority can offend minority Americans."[60]

An outraged Moseley Braun, in response, challenged Helms and Thurmond. Placing the "imprimatur of the United States Senate on a symbol of
this kind of idea," she said in Senate debate, recalled memories of black
servitude and white supremacy. Those whose ancestors possessed "human
chattel under the Confederate flag," she declared, were "duty bound to
honor our ancestors as well by asking whether such recognition by the U.S.

Senate is appropriate." The Confederate flag symbolized opposition to black freedom; in the year 1993, "when we see the Confederate symbols hauled out, everybody knows what that means." "This vote is about race," she said, "racial symbols, the racial past, and the single most painful episode in American history." With Moseley Braun promising opposition "until this room freezes over" and she was able to "put a stake through the heart of this Dracula," her objections motivated a number of senators to oppose the Helms-Thurmond amendment. Despite Helms's claim that this was an "inflammatory political gambit" with the UDC's "fine, gentle ladies" as its victims, the Senate defeated the repatenting of the UDC design by a margin of 75–25, with ten Democrats and seventeen Republicans changing their votes. Many of Helms's deserting senators were from the South. Senator Howell Heflin of Alabama, whose own family, he said, was "rooted in the Confederacy" and whose ancestors would be "spinning in their graves," made an about-face and supported Moseley Braun against the flag, saying "we live today in a different world." Americans should "get racism behind us" and "move forward," he told the Senate.[61]

Moseley Braun had gotten the better of Jesse, something he did not easily forget. Sometime after the vote, on August 3, 1993, the Illinois senator stepped into the Senate elevator in the Capitol, and Utah's Orrin Hatch and Helms joined her en route. Helms began singing "I wish I was in the land of cotton." Helms turned to Hatch and said: "I'm going to make her cry. I'm going to sing 'Dixie' until she cries." "Senator Helms," Moseley Braun remembered responding, "your singing would make me cry if you sang 'Rock of Ages.'" Helms and Hatch remember this as a friendly encounter, and they were both surprised when Moseley Braun a few days later related the story to a National Urban League convention. More than two years after the incident, Helms told a reporter that she had "really fixed my wagon by coming up with such a retort—because I had such a bad voice." At the time, even Moseley Braun would describe the exchange as lighthearted.[62]

But media accounts focused on Helms's racial insensitivity, and over time he came to blame her. There were few senators with whom Helms was not courteous: Edward Kennedy was one such senator. Because of Kennedy's supposed moral transgressions—and the strident way in which he often took on Helms in public—Helms was openly contemptuous. Earlier in 1993, for example, Jesse joked in a Senate speech that he was unable to match Kennedy in "decibels or Jezebels, or anything else, apparently." Matters also became personal with Moseley Braun. Nearly three weeks after her remarks to the National Urban League, Helms, in a WRAL television interview, said that her behavior was "not the way a senator acts," while he challenged her sincerity. Moseley Braun, he said, was from "Trinidad or Jamaica or somewhere" and did not have an American slave ancestor. The incident in the elevator was in good fun: "the devil makes me do things," Jesse said. Moseley Braun, he claimed, was engaging in "phony-baloney theatrics," with phony tears about the Confederacy and slavery. Helms went further, questioning her integrity by reviving a charge made about her during the 1992 Senate campaign that her mother, Edna Moseley, failed to report income from inheritance to the state Medicaid system. This was a case in which Moseley was "caught with her hand in the cookie jar."[63] Subsequently, Helms would reveal his penchant for settling old scores, as he did several years later when he unsuccessfully tried to block Senate confirmation of Moseley Braun's nomination as ambassador to New Zealand.[64]

Helms, reelected to the Senate in 1990 on racial themes, did not leave the subject, and to many he seemed like a throwback to a long-past South. He continued to oppose new versions of the civil rights bill that Bush had vetoed in the fall of 1990, and beginning in late June 1991 he introduced an amendment to the crime bill that prohibited employers from personnel policies that provided any preference based on race, color, religion, national origin, or sex. Changing racial attitudes to some extent passed Helms by: many of his own constituents in North Carolina, especially suburban Republicans, were growing uncomfortable with his racial message, and the national party no longer wanted to be perceived as obstructionist. For this reason, a compromise civil rights bill passed the Senate by a 93–5 vote in October 1991, despite Helms's opposition.[65] He continued to work against affirmative action, and he occasionally joined the national debate that occupied much of the 1990s. In March 1995, he introduced a bill in the Senate that he entitled "An Act to End Unfair Federal Preferential Treatment." It would have ended the 160 federal affirmative action programs that pushed minority hiring by companies holding federal contracts. This was not about race, Helms said in a statement, but rather involved "putting an end to reverse discrimination at the hands of ruthless bureaucrats." Three decades after the onset of affirmative action, he said in a Senate speech, the country had become "more racially and ethnically divided as a society than ever before," and, if anything, social cohesiveness was "slipping away." Affirmative action, he said, had "outlived its usefulness," and it was now time for the federal government "to scrap these programs and restore the principles upon which this country was built: personal responsibility, self-reliance and hard work."[66]

Just as Jesse had fought against the Martin Luther King holiday in

1983, a decade later he opposed the establishment of a National African American Museum as part of the Smithsonian Institution in Washington. Representative John Lewis of Georgia, a former civil rights worker, first introduced legislation for the museum in 1988, and after the House passed it in 1993, Jesse bottled up the bill in the Senate by delaying the Rules Committee consideration, claiming that the cost would be excessive. Helms would continue to oppose it, and not until 2003, the year after Jesse left the Senate, was it passed.[67]

Helms's position on the National African American Museum represented what one reporter called a continuing "blind spot" about race. Although he opposed it on budget grounds, the museum carried a powerful symbolism for African Americans, and his opposition rekindled old feelings about Jesse's views on race.[68] Throughout the 1990s, he struggled with his public image as "Old South" on racial issues, though he remained mystified by why. In November 1994, when Helms was interviewed by Durham television co-anchors Larry Stogner and Miriam Thomas, an African American, and referred to his interviewers as "Larry, you and your little lady friend," many callers from the region were outraged. "At least he didn't call her Fred," was the response of one *N&O* columnist, referring to the report of one journalist in 1984 that Helms often referred to black people as "Fred."[69] Jesse sent signals that sometimes offended or even astounded audiences. In September 1995, he made an appearance on CNN's *Larry King Live,* with conservative columnist Robert Novak substituting for King, and the senator took a call from someone in Alabama, evidently an admirer. Helms should receive a Nobel Peace Prize, the caller opined, "for everything you've done to help keep down the niggers." "Whoops, well, thank you, I think," a startled Helms uttered. "Oh, dear," Novak added, informing the caller that he had said a "bad word" and something "politically incorrect." Novak and Helms agreed that they could not "condone" such language; Helms repeated his often told tale about how "one of the worst spankings" he ever received was when he used the N-word, "and I don't think I've used it since." Helms's aides, never sure what Helms would say in an interview, winced at what they believed was his naïveté and lack of political skill and what others regarded as racial insensitivity.[70]

In January 1991, the strange alliance of Helms and James Meredith ended, and the two men parted ways. It remained unclear whether the former civil rights icon left of his own accord or was fired: probably, his departure was a combination of both. Some months before, sometime in 1990, Helms told legislative assistant Andy Hartsfield to inform Meredith gently that he should look for another job. Helms circumvented Fuller, who was always given the task of hiring and firing staff, but Hartsfield avoided communicating with Meredith for months. Finally, Fuller gave him the news: he could take a few months' leave, but he should expect to leave the office. One day, Fuller recalled, Meredith simply left the office without informing anyone.[71] Before he left, in January 1991, Meredith informed Chuck Babington of the *News and Observer* that his time on Helms's staff constituted a "last stage" of his work among blacks; he was a "prophet" and a "savior for the black race." He had also presented Helms with an eight-page memo outlining an agenda, the culmination of seventeen months' research, which called for the elimination of food stamps, subsidies for school lunches, and minimum wage legislation. He also favored inculcating values that taught blacks how to become successful capitalists, and Meredith urged ending the use of the word "minority." When reporters faxed a copy of Meredith's memo to Helms's office, however, they were told that he had left the office. Although he remained "very fond" of Meredith, Helms said that Meredith had decided to leave because his work on Capitol Hill was over and because he needed to care for an ill son. In an interview in 2002, Helms described Meredith as a "nice guy" but "not a heavyweight." When he spoke to him about his agenda, Meredith "would draw a blank." "He wasn't any help to us," he recalled. Subsequently, in October 1991, Meredith was reported as recording commercials on behalf of David Duke, the former Klansman who was running for the Senate from Louisiana.[72]

IN SEPTEMBER 1991, Helms continued to war against the National Endowment for the Arts by offering two amendments to the $12.7 billion Interior Department funding bill that provided $176 million for the NEA. While the first prohibited the endowment grantees from promoting, disseminating, or producing "materials that depict or describe, in a patently offensive way, sexual or excretory activities or organs," the second required that half of NEA funding go through state organizations rather than through what he called "those elitist experts" at the Washington headquarters. In using the term "patently offensive," Helms cleverly proposed a standard of indecency that the FCC had already used to regulate content on the airwaves. The "so-called 'art'" was "so rotten, so crude, so disgusting, so filthy," Helms declared, that it would turn "the stomach of any normal person." "Self-proclaimed perverted artists" offended basic values and used public funds to "promote rotten, disgusting material." Why was it necessary, he asked, to "promote and subsidize obscenity and vulgarity" by a "decadent 'artistic elite' at the expense of the deeply held beliefs of the vast majority of Americans?" The Senate passed Helms's amendment by a vote of 68–28.[73]

But Helms's anti-indecency effort died in the House-Senate legislative conference. In the House, Helms's measure met the determined resistance of House Democrat Sidney Yates, a congressman from Chicago and NEA advocate. Yates struck a deal with Robert Byrd of West Virginia: in exchange for dropping substantially increased grazing fees on western federal lands, Helms's amendment was killed. Immediately dubbed a "corn for porn" deal, the legislative maneuver outraged Helms. In a final flurry of activity, Helms displayed a magazine, *Performance Journal Three,* put out by a New York City organization that promoted performance art, Movement Research, which was the recipient of a $4,400 NEA grant. Flourishing a copy of the magazine, which contained sexually explicit material, Helms told fellow senators to examine the "filth and rottenness" that appeared with NEA support.[74] Although Helms lost this vote, as the *New York Times* editorialized, he remained "as mischievous as Puck, and Congress has given pointers to the theater of the absurd."[75]

Helms, on other fronts, continued to wage a culture war. In April 1992, he offered a successful amendment cutting funding for the National Institutes of Health because it provided $18 million to UNC to study the sexual behavior of 24,000 teenagers. The survey investigators, he charged, were primarily interested in buttressing "their political and social pretense" that homosexuality was not deviant behavior. "And of course," he declared, "it is deviant behavior."[76] Gay activists, meanwhile, regarded Helms as their leading enemy in Congress. In September 1991, Treatment Action Guerrillas, affiliated with the AIDS activist group ACT UP, sponsored a protest at Helms's house in Arlington by putting a fifteen-foot condom—a nylon balloon—on the roof of his house for twenty minutes that was inflated by two hot-air blowers. This was a "condom to stop unsafe politics," read their banner; Helms was "deadlier than a virus." The demonstration continued until neighbors called the police. Neither of the Helmses was at home. Jesse was apparently tending to Dot, who was receiving a cancer treatment, and police dispersed the protesters, and removed the balloon, without incident.[77]

Jesse moved against other manifestations of gay rights. In September 1992 he introduced an unsuccessful amendment that would cut federal funds to any organizations that forced the Boy Scouts to accept homosexuals or atheists as members. The Boy Scouts had adopted regulations excluding "avowed homosexuals" from participating in the organization. The Scouts supported "traditional family values" and believed that gays did not "provide a role model consistent with these family values." Several donor organizations, including the United Way, had sanctioned the Scouts. Helms took up the cause of the Scouts. "The Scout Oath and the Scout Law are not up for sale," said Jesse. The "so-called homosexual lifestyle," Jesse said, was focused on "instant gratification" and promiscuous sexual behavior; the average homosexual male, he reported in his speech, had between twenty and 106 different sex partners annually. This "reckless sexual behavior," he said, violated Scout regulations about remaining "morally straight" and "physically clean." Scouts should stand firm: "Hooray for the Boy Scouts and their strong stand for what is right in the face of costly and venomous attacks by militant liberals."[78]

In August 1993, when he voted against Bill Clinton's nomination of Ruth Bader Ginsburg to the Supreme Court, Helms explained this as a vote not only against the unrestricted right to abortion but also in opposition to the "homosexual agenda."[79] Jesse battled against gay rights on other fronts. In July 1994, he introduced an amendment to the agricultural appropriations bill prohibiting the U.S. Department of Agriculture from condoning homosexuality as a legitimate lifestyle; his amendment, which passed overwhelmingly, also banned funding for educational programs seeking to recruit gay employees. The amendment arose from the case of a USDA employee, Karl Mertz, who objected to sensitivity programs about gay workers. "We need to be moving toward Camelot, not Sodom and Gomorrah," Mertz told a Mississippi television station, "and I'm afraid that's where our leadership is trying to take us." After Mertz was disciplined for his comments, Helms took up his cause and introduced a successful amendment protecting the right of any USDA employee to free speech about department policy about gays and requiring that Mertz be restored to his job. Senator Dale Bumpers subsequently muted Helms's amendment by substituting a broader amendment protecting free speech among employees generally, but Jesse had made his point.[80] Meanwhile, Helms placed holds on all legislation affecting the USDA and all its nominations until Mertz was reinstated to his previous position. The USDA, Helms told the Senate after Mertz was reinstated, was "overrun by homosexuals, and they have been running the store to a great extent."[81]

About two weeks later, in early August 1993, Jesse co-sponsored another amendment, which passed overwhelmingly, to the $12.5 billion Elementary and Secondary School Act banning the use of federal funds for schools that promoted homosexuality "as a positive life style alternative" or referred students "to an organization that affirms a homosexual life style." Helms displayed a copy of a set of publications—including one entitled *Heather Has Two Mommies,* about a gay couple, along with AIDS education literature that included graphic sexual descriptions—that he called "disgusting, obscene material that's laid out before school children in this country every day."[82] In January 1994, Helms took his anti-gay campaign to the United Nations. His staff discovered that the United Nations's Economic and Social Council had granted consultative status to the International Lesbian and Gay Association, a group that had as one of its members the North American Man Boy Love Association (NAMBLA), which was dedicated to promoting sex between men and boys. Describing NAMBLA as an organization "catering to the twisted desires of pedophiles," Helms introduced an amendment to the State Department authorization bill requiring that the United States cut $119 million in U.N. funding until the president certified that the United Nations had no connections with groups promoting pedophilia. The Clinton administration, Jesse said, had been "fast asleep at the switch" in watching over the United Nations. The amendment passed unanimously.[83]

Into the 1990s, Helms continued to resist any concessions on gay rights. Soon after his election in November 1992, Clinton announced that he would end, by executive order, the ban against homosexuals in the military. Helms strongly opposed the measure. He had "no respect for homosexuals—for perverts," he told the *Charlotte Observer,* adding that if that statement was considered shocking, it remained "exactly the way I feel about it."[84] In 1994 and 1995, moreover, he sponsored amendments barring the use of federal funds to hire gays or to sponsor gay employee associations in the federal workplace. He sought to save public funds, he said in January 1995, and he opposed the Clinton administration's "concerted effort to give homosexuals rights, privileges and protections throughout the Federal agencies—to extend to the homosexuals special rights in the Federal workplace, rights not accorded to most other groups or individuals."[85] Helms also saw direct political benefits in his anti-gay campaign. As in other Senate maneuvers, he forced fellow senators to vote on controversial measures, and their votes could be used against them later in attack ads. Few senators, at least during the early 1990s, were willing to vote against measures limiting gay rights. Pressing the homosexuality issue, at least for the time being, involved "little risk for Helms," according to the *Raleigh News and Observer.* While portraying himself as a "great defender of traditional values," he depicted his opponents as "supporters of depravity."[86]

Helms also opposed Clinton's energetic efforts to appoint gay people to federal offices. All told, the president selected some two dozen gays to various posts. In February 1993, the president nominated San Francisco city supervisor Roberta Achtenberg, a lesbian, as assistant secretary at

HUD for Fair Housing and Equal Opportunity. Because she was the first homosexual nominated to high federal office, the nomination attracted fire. Helms opposed Achtenberg's appointment, he told the *Washington Post*, because "she's a damn lesbian," and "if you want to call me a bigot, fine." "I am not going to put a lesbian into a position like that." Jesse and other conservative Republicans mounted a large campaign against the appointment. In September 1992, serving as consultant for the Forestry Department, Achtenberg wrote a report, *Sexual Orientation: An Issue of Workplace Diversity,* which provided a guide for equality for gay people in the federal workplace. Equally alarming to cultural conservatives was that Achtenberg had led a campaign against the Boy Scouts because of its policy of excluding gays. While serving on the board of the Bay Area United Way, she had helped to cut funding for the Boy Scouts in 1991. A year later, while serving as a San Francisco supervisor, Achtenberg introduced a nonbinding resolution recommending the withdrawal of $6 million from Bank of America because it continued to donate to the Boy Scouts. In an interview, Jesse described Achtenberg as a "militantly activist lesbian" whose entire career was dedicated to promoting a gay agenda and who "tried to bully the Boy Scouts of America."

Helms's anti-gay rhetoric went further. Achtenberg was "not your garden-variety lesbian," he declared. A threshold had been crossed: for the first time in American history, "a lesbian has been nominated by a President of the United States for a top job in the U.S. Government."[87] In Senate debate on May 18–19, 1993, Helms played a videotape for fellow Republican senators that, he claimed, included images of Achtenberg kissing her partner "fervently" while they rode together in a float at San Francisco's annual Gay Pride Parade in San Francisco in June 1992. "Call it gay-bashing if you want to," he said in a Senate speech. "I don't call it that. I call it standing up for America's traditional family values." Responding to assertions that sexual orientation was a matter of privacy, Helms maintained that Achtenberg "sure wasn't private when she was hugging and kissing in that homosexual parade in San Francisco." When asked during debate by Senator Donald W. Reigle if he had actually used the term "damned lesbian" to describe Achtenberg, Helms admitted that this was "largely correct," though he was "not sure about the damn." Despite Helms's noisy opposition, on May 24, Achtenberg was confirmed as the first openly gay appointee to high federal office in American history.[88]

As it had in the past, much of Helms's battle on sexuality focused on funding for AIDS programs and research. In July 1991, he proposed two amendments that were adopted by the Senate: the first established long prison terms for HIV-infected health care workers performing invasive procedures who failed to report their disease to patients, the second permitted surgeons to test patients for HIV without their permission.[89] But Helms's most significant fight focused on the reauthorization of the Ryan White Comprehensive AIDS Resources Emergency (CARE) Act of August 1990. Under terms of the act, Congress provided major funding for treatment and education; it accounted for $633 million for AIDS/HIV care and treatment in 1994 alone. The Ryan White law was authorized for five years, and when it came up for reauthorization, Jesse stalled the measure in early 1995, and in April 1995, he put a hold on the bill and planned a series of amendments.[90] In an interview with the *New York Times,* Helms explained why he favored drastically reducing AIDS funding. The disease, he claimed, was the result of the "deliberate, disgusting, revolting conduct" of homosexuals. AIDS, Helms claimed, was a less deadly disease than other afflictions, and he favored more "equity" in federal funding for other lethal diseases. But Helms's main justification for his opposition to AIDS funding was that he identified it as a gay disease and opposed any special treatment for gay people. "We've got to have some common sense," he said, "about a disease transmitted by people deliberately engaging in unnatural acts."[91]

Helms was unqualified in this position: he condemned homosexuality, and for this reason opposed special treatment for AIDS. Jesse was correct—AIDS was receiving special treatment—but it was also true that it represented an unprecedented health emergency. But his opposition to reauthorization of the Ryan White Act employed hateful language, which came out without restraint. In July 1995, asked if he was misquoted in his description of homosexuality as "disgusting," Helms told a *Charlotte Observer* reporter: "I meant it. It is disgusting." The gay rights lobby was after him, he said, because he opposed providing gay people with "special rights." "I would not have to say these things if they would keep their mouths shut and their bedrooms closed. No, they parade naked. They commit sodomy right there in the streets of San Francisco . . . and they expect us to accept their lifestyle."[92] Nonetheless, Helms's strong anti-gay language rallied his base. Immediately before he made his controversial *New York Times* comments, his Senate campaign sent out a fund-raising letter declaring that Jesse had become "the man they hate most" to the "militant homosexuals who parade through the streets of America."[93] Gary Bauer, president of the Family Research Council, praised him for his "great work" in late July for his stand. The Ryan White Act, Bauer claimed, provided federal funding to "normalize and promote the homosexual lifestyle." Among other Republicans, the stridency of Helms's language evoked a strong reaction. Haley Barbour, Republican National Committee chair, told reporters that he opposed a language of "discrimination or intolerance." President Clinton, in a speech at Georgetown University on July 6, declared that the assumption that all AIDS sufferers contracted the disease through homosexual activity or drug use was "just wrong." "The gay people who have AIDS are still our sons, our brothers, our cousins, our citizens," Clinton said. "They're Americans, too.... They're entitled to be treated like everybody else."[94]

Jesse's noisy stand against the reauthorization of the Ryan White Act, aside from providing an opportunity for homophobic venom, had little real effect: on July 27, 1995, the Senate reauthorized funding by a vote of 97–3.[95] During the days that preceded the vote, Helms again connected AIDS with homosexuals, whose behavior he called "incredibly offensive and revolting." The program in the CARE Act was part of "thinly veiled attempts to restructure values of American families in favor of the homosexual lifestyle." White's death, he asserted on July 26, was the result of the spread of blood that was tainted "by homosexual conduct somewhere generations back." AIDS was "a chronic disease of sexually promiscuous people," Helms said, citing "reliable surveys" that claimed that many gays averaged sixteen sexual partners a month and 182 a year. Rather than urging abstinence from the homosexual behavior that Jesse believed was the main source of AIDS, gay organizations were demanding expanding federal funding. Helms continued to wage the fight against the Ryan White bill into July by attempting disabling amendments, even though he admitted that Congress would rush the bill through and President Clinton would "sprain his ankle grabbing a pen to sign it." In a speech on July 21, Jesse again called homosexuality a "filthy, disgusting practice." "I said it, and I meant it," he declared, "and I repeat it today." He preferred not using the word "gay," he said in another speech on July 26, "in connection with sodomy." There was "nothing gay about these people," and "gay" was once a "beautiful word, but it has been corrupted by these people." Nonetheless, Helms said that he did not hate homosexuals: "I don't even know any homosexuals." But he opposed having Congress "bow and scrape to homosexual pressure and give them rights and privileges that other Americans are denied."[96] Nonetheless, Helms's last-ditch strategy of offering amendments yielded little success.[97]

Helms's statements about AIDS and gays went far beyond anything said by Republican leaders in Congress, though there were reports that many in the party favored reducing AIDS support. To Representative Barney Frank (D-MA), the only openly gay member of Congress, Helms was a "bigoted fool." Clinton himself responded, saying that the Ryan White CARE Act was a "model of compassionate caring for people in need," and at a time when AIDS had become the leading killer of young people, "we cannot let re-authorization of the Care Act be held up by divisive arguments about how people contracted HIV." The notion that HIV/AIDS was receiving a larger share of federal support was "false": in total federal spending, spending for the disease represented one-third of that spent for cancer and less than one-sixth that for heart disease. Helms was seeking to "blame people with AIDS for being sick," added Ryan White's mother, Jeanne White-Ginder. Did he feel "the same about Americans dying of cancer because they smoke?"[98]

Helms's homophobic rants hit a nerve with Raleigh resident Patsy Clarke. She had been married to a conservative Republican, Harry Clarke, who in March 1987 died in a plane crash. Helms was a friend, and he inserted a tribute to Harry, after his death, in the *Congressional Record.* Patsy suffered an additional tragedy when her son, Mark, a thirty-one-year-old law student, died of AIDS in March 1994, about the time that Jesse made his most strident comments regarding the "disgusting" behavior of gay males suffering from the disease. Reading an account in the *Raleigh News and Observer* that quoted Helms as describing homosexuality as a "filthy, disgusting practice," Clarke decided to send the senator a letter. Writing on June 5, 1995, she explained that she had recently lost her gay son from AIDS, and that the disease was "not a disgrace, it is a TRAGEDY." Homosexuality, she wrote, was also not a disgrace: "we so-called normal people make it a tragedy because of our own lack of understanding," and gay people deserved not judgment but compassion. Rather than asking for more money for AIDS care or research or even to stop condemning gay people, she wrote, she wanted Helms "to share his memory with me in compassion." About two weeks later, Clarke heard back from the senator, who denounced the "militant homosexuals" who had "climbed onto the roof of Dot's and my home and hoisted a giant canvas condom." "As for homosexuality," he wrote, "The Bible judges it, I do not." "As for Mark, I wish he had not played Russian roulette in his sexual activity." Clarke burst into tears when she read Jesse's letter. Then, she later wrote, "I got mad." Clarke went on to help found Mothers Against Jesse in Congress (MAJIC), which campaigned against Helms's 1996 reelection.[99]

Despite major changes in his professional and personal life, Helms gained new momentum in the 1990s by championing conservative causes. He had abandoned the "rusty knife" and had moved away from a heritage as an uncompromising conservative ideologue. By cutting ties with the

Congressional Club, he no longer depended on political organizations run by Tom Ellis and Carter Wrenn to raise money and promote a sharply edged political message. Helms, by the 1990s, was so well established in Washington that he could promote himself as a national conservative. At the same time, he abandoned his position as an ideologue in foreign policy, and completed a move toward a foreign policy that was more geared toward results than scoring rhetorical points. All this did not mean that Jesse was any less ardent a conservative: in his campaign against homosexuals, which took on bitter and often even hateful language, Jesse embraced his final moral crusade. With the election of Bill Clinton in 1992, Helms again strapped on his rhetorical armor, and initiated a final battle to sustain the conservative cause in Washington.

Chapter 12

A BIG ROCK IN A RIVER

Resisting Clinton

In the mid-1990s, Jesse Helms used the Senate to preserve the conservative revolution that he had helped to construct but that was threatened by the election of Bill Clinton in 1992. Like other conservative Republicans, he conducted a war against the Clinton White House at many levels, including resistance of domestic policy and obstruction of foreign policy. The anti-Clinton war gained steam in 1994, when Republicans took control of Congress. Helms continued to use senatorial privilege to influence policy, but he spent less time on domestic issues than in any of his three decades in Washington. His final years in the Senate were spent instead on foreign policy. After the Republican landslide in 1994, Helms took command of the Foreign Relations Committee, and from this position he sought to articulate an alternative foreign policy. To a greater degree than any time while in the Senate as Foreign Relations Committee chairman, Helms became a shaper of policy rather than a conservative guerrilla fighter.

THE ELECTION OF Democrat Bill Clinton to the White House in 1992 seemed to provide a new purpose for Jesse, who promised to lead parliamentary opposition to the Democratic agenda.[1] The arrival of Clinton "energized" Helms, said *Charlotte Observer* columnist Jack Betts in early 1993, and, with his health problems apparently behind him, he was seen donning new ties, flashier shirts, and "spiffy wire-framed glasses." According to the *News and Observer,* his "color was good, and his gait spry"—a description that Betts said was the "nicest thing the paper has said about Jesse Helms since the crust of the Earth began cooling." Jesse felt so good that he strongly hinted to reporters that he would likely run for a fifth term in 1996. By June 1993, Helms had notified the Federal Election Commission that he was exploring a reelection bid.[2]

In early 1993, Lauch Faircloth, who defeated incumbent Democrat Terry Sanford, became a strong Republican partisan. Indeed, Faircloth was known as so conservative that Bob Dole liked to call him "Senator Gridlock," while he described Helms as the "liberal senator from North Carolina."[3] In August 1993, Faircloth joined Helms in trying to block the nomination of Walter E. Dellinger III, a Duke University law professor, who was nominated as deputy attorney general and was mentioned as a possible nominee to the Supreme Court. Although the Dellinger nomination went through, Helms was sending the message that Dellinger could never make it to the Supreme Court.[4] Helms attempted to block other Clinton nominations as a way of opposing the Democratic administration. In September 1993, he attacked Joycelyn Elders, nominated as the first African American surgeon general, because, Helms claimed, she supported sex education for kindergarteners, federal support for abortions, and the distribution of birth control implants for prostitutes. While she "preached condom usage to teenagers," said Jesse, she remained "silent in seven languages about abstinence," and she had not uttered "one syllable on behalf of chastity or personal responsibility or restraint." The Senate confirmed Elders anyway.[5] Helms's attack on Elders resembled his posture toward Health and Human Services Secretary Donna Shalala, who, like Elders, favored increased educational programs encouraging the use of condoms to prevent AIDS. In a Senate speech, Helms even called Shalala "Madam Condom."[6]

Like other Republicans, Helms opposed the centerpiece of Clinton's domestic agenda, health care reform, and when the outlines of the president's plan of managed care became public in June 1993, he denounced it as a "first step down the dangerous socialist path traveled by Sweden and Canada." In May 1994, at Jerry Falwell's Liberty University, he said in a commencement address that the Clinton health care plan was a product of "those children of the sixties who are now in charge." He had few anxieties about the possibility that Clinton's legislation would pass; he told aides that it would almost certainly meet defeat in the Senate. When the plan came to Congress, on August 10, 1994, he introduced a "sense of the Senate" resolution that declared that health care reform was "too important to enact in a rushed fashion." The resolution further called on Congress to "take whatever time is necessary to do it right by deferring action until next year." Helms's motion narrowly lost, and the slim margin indicated that a Republican filibuster against the bill would succeed. Not long after, Clinton health care reform was buried.[7]

In the Whitewater scandal, one of several controversies that troubled the Clinton presidency, Helms also played a role. Before he was elected president, Clinton had invested in a land deal in Whitewater, Arkansas, that involved a failed savings and loan institution, and an independent counsel, former Republican judge Robert B. Fiske, Jr., conducted an investigation. By 1994, the investigation had widened to include the suicide of White House counsel Vince Foster. In July 1994, Congress reauthorized the law providing for an independent counsel investigation, but Fiske, who was moving toward exonerating Clinton, was criticized by Republican critics of Clinton as pursuing a lackluster investigation. The independent counsel law provided for a panel of three judges who were responsible for the appointment of the counsel, and the panel was headed by David B. Sentelle, a former Helms supporter from North Carolina whose appointment to the D.C. Court of Appeals in February 1987 Helms had sponsored. Faircloth had been one of Clinton's leading tormentors in the Senate, and he wrote to Attorney General Janet Reno on July 1, 1994, urging that Fiske be replaced. On July 13, a group of ten Republican congressmen then wrote to Sentelle with the same request. The next day, July 14, Faircloth and Sentelle had lunch in the Senate Dining Room; frequently interrupted by votes, Helms joined them from the Senate floor. After the lunch, Faircloth was seen riding the Senate subway engaged in energetic, animated conversation with Sentelle. Three weeks later, on August 5, Sentelle announced a two-to-one decision by the panel to replace Fiske with Kenneth Starr, and Starr would lead a much more aggressive and expanded investigation of the Clinton White House that would continue for the next six years, until the end of the Clinton presidency. Considerable press attention was paid to the Sentelle-Helms-Faircloth gathering, but there was never any evidence that the Whitewater investigation was discussed. Yet Faircloth, in subsequently recalling the conversation, would say that the three discussed the investigation and how Fiske was "not aggressive enough" and needed to be replaced.[8]

HELMS'S PRIMARY INTEREST was in exerting pressure on Clinton's foreign policy, and, as always, he exploited his ability to obstruct appointments.[9]

Helms's moves in foreign policy involved more than obstruction, however, and in the mid-1990s the outlines of his foreign policy vision were beginning to emerge. In the post–Cold War world, Helms favored a staunchly nationalist approach that rejected multilateralism, peacekeeping, and nation building. He preferred a strong military and aggressive defense. Jesse opposed the American intervention in Somalia, which was designed to provide food relief in a country that was wracked by famine and civil war. Although the American relief effort began under George Bush, in early October 1993, eighteen Army Rangers were killed and eighty-four were wounded in an attempt to apprehend Somalia warlord General Mohamed Farrah Aidid. The Clinton administration possessed "no constitutional authority to sacrifice U.S. soldiers," Helms said in a Senate speech on October 7, 1993. Backing an effort by Robert Byrd to cut funding for the Somali mission, Jesse declared that "the time to get out is now." To describe this as a humanitarian mission was a "tragic mischaracterization.'"[10]

Similarly, Helms also opposed Clinton's intervention in Haiti in October 1993. In 1991, Haiti's generals exiled Jean-Bertrand Aristide, who was overwhelmingly elected a year previously. After the United Nations mediated Aristide's return to power, Haitian paramilitaries forced American troops attempting to land to turn back on October 12, 1993. The Senate was in an uproar. In debate, Helms proposed legislation that would prohibit Clinton from deploying American troops without congressional authorization. Helms regarded Aristide as another left-wing populist who, like Fidel Castro, would undermine American interests. Describing Aristide as "one of the most brutal people to hold office in this hemisphere in my lifetime," Helms called him a "killer" and "psychopath" and compared him to Hitler. Jesse also unveiled a picture that Aristide allegedly had on display on the wall of the presidential palace of tires, flammable gasoline, and matches. These were the ingredients of the infamous "necklacing" of political opponents—murders that involved filling a tire with gasoline, putting it around a victim, and then setting it afire.

In making the case against Aristide, Helms arranged for an intelligence briefing of some Republican senators and staffers by CIA official Brian Latell. Deborah DeMoss, who had visited Haiti on a missionary trip and from her contacts there was alarmed by Aristide, urged the senator to use Latell. There was no "sinister connection" between Latell and DeMoss. As a student in a Georgetown graduate course in Latin American studies, DeMoss knew Latell, and she also realized that his detailed knowledge about Aristide would help Helms on Capitol Hill. His briefing reinforced Jesse's opposition to sending American troops in Haiti. Latell told the senators in the briefing that Aristide was mentally unstable, had spent time in a Canadian mental hospital (a charge later proven false), and had plotted violence against his opponents, including assassination. About ninety-five senators attended, and DeMoss remembered that they were "riveted' by Latell's "extremely convincing" presentation; she recalled that he was a "much better briefer than professor in grad school." Latell's presentation reinforced Helms's opposition to sending American troops in support of Aristide. This was a place, Jesse declared, where the United States "does not have a dog in this fight." "I do not think," he said, that "we have any business whatsoever... risking the life of one soldier or one sailor or other American to put Aristide back into office." On October 21, a Helms resolution barring Clinton from deploying American troops failed by a vote of 81–19, but the senator had made his point.[11]

While opposing intervention on Aristide's behalf in Haiti, Helms kept a close eye on developments in Central America. In Nicaragua, the Sandinistas yielded power in elections in February 1990 to a government headed by President Violeta Barrios de Chamorro. Helms nonetheless denounced the election because, he argued in a Senate speech, Chamarro was elected not by the "choice of a free opposition," but as "an alternative supported by the U.S. Government in a blatant attempt to stage a fake election to legitimize the present Communist regime in Managua." In a betrayal of the "true freedom fighters of Nicaragua," Congress had sanctioned a "moral tragedy of immense dimensions."[12] The senator continued to press for the elimination of Sandinista influence in the Chamorro government. After nearly a decade of war against the contras, the country was ravaged, and its economy suffered under severe hyperinflation. The government depended on international aid, and especially American sponsorship, for survival. After $1 billion in American aid and loans went to Nicaragua, Helms demanded that the Bush administration exert more pressure.

Helms remained unsatisfied that his long-term objective—eradicating the Sandinistas—had been accomplished. In 1992, he pressed the Bush administration to withhold $116 million in aid unless the Sandinistas relinquished power over Nicaragua's military forces and police forces and made restitution of American property seized by the Sandinista regime. Jesse continued the fight after Clinton became president. Helms's approach seemed particularly hard-hearted after an earthquake and tsunami killed 116 people and left more than 16,000 homeless.[13] But after a generation of resisting leftist regimes in Latin America, Helms was determined to prevent the Sandinistas from returning to power. On August 31, 1992, Helms's Foreign Relations staff released a report, written by DeMoss, that charged that Chamorro was nothing more than a figurehead and that "all real power" remained with her son-in-law and chief minister Antonio Lacayo. The Sandinista leadership, the report concluded, maintained the reins of power. Although Nicaraguan officials denounced DeMoss's report as "plagued by inaccuracies . . . even lies," the State Department did not challenge the assertions, and many Bush advisers were sympathetic. The report further asserted that the Chamorro government was corrupt and nepotistic, appointing dozens of relatives to government positions. The regime still contained violent elements; widespread political murder was common, according to DeMoss's report, and some 217 former contras had been killed. In addition, in a chapter entitled "Who Stole What," the report described how the Sandinistas had stolen ninety-eight properties; 450 Americans, mostly Nicaraguans who were naturalized Americans, were seeking compensation of two thousand properties. Foreign Relations Committee staff director Bud Nance denounced the Nicaraguan government as "overwhelmingly controlled by terrorists, thugs, thieves and murderers at the highest levels." There would be no solution to this "corrupt mess," said Helms, until the Sandinistas were purged. In an arrangement negotiated by Secretary of State James Baker in August 1992, Chamorro sought to appease Helms by firing the Sandinista national police chief, Rene Vivas, and replacing a third of Sandinistas in the police force. In exchange, Baker promised to release $50 million in aid to the Nicaraguans. Chamorro urged Helms to relent; she told one North Carolina reporter that she prayed that he would recover from his heart ailments "so he could understand what Nicaragua is all about" by visiting the country. But DeMoss and Nance visited one thousand cheering Nicaraguans and played a tape from Helms in which he told them that he would "not back down" and called Chamorro that "defiant lady in Managua." Speaking in Spanish, DeMoss told her audience: "Let us ask God to guide us in this struggle for a truly free Nicaragua."[14]

Helms's staff continued to insist that Chamorro's reforms were insufficient. In September 1992, the State Deparment dispatched a delegation to Nicaragua, and Baker sent signals indicating that he agreed with Helms's analysis that the changes should be more far-reaching. Although Bush was defeated in the presidential election of November 1992, in December he released $54 million to Nicaragua over Jesse's objections, and left the disposal of the remaining portion of $50 million in aid to the incoming Clinton administration. In April 1993, when Clinton decided to release the aid, Helms denounced any American aid to the Chamorro government as "an outrageous waste of the American taxpayers' money and an insult to them as well."[15] In July 1993, Helms scored a major victory when the Senate adopted an amendment cutting off Nicaraguan aid unless the Chamorro government demonstrated that it had no ties to international terrorism. Helms's amendment came in response to reports linking the Sandinistas to the World Trade Center attack in New York City of 1993. Later, in September 1993, the Senate overwhelmingly passed legislation prohibiting aid to Nicaraguan until Americans whose property had been confiscated were properly compensated. Although the Sandinista leadership denounced Chamorro for a decision that sought to satisfy Helms, her government removed the Sandinistas, and Helms, in the end, had scored a major victory.[16]

ON NOVEMBER 8, 1994, Republicans, capitalizing on a wave of popular reaction against the president and Democratic Congress, were swept to control of both houses of Congress for the first time since 1952. Days after Clinton's election, in November 1992, staffers Robert Wilkie and John Mashburn visited with the senator to lament the Republicans' loss. But they found Helms in "jovial" mood. Why was he so happy, they asked Helms. "You don't understand," he said. "You're looking at the next chairman of the Senate Foreign Relations Committee." Helms had been around a long time, he said, and "we've never elected a character" like Bill Clinton. "He'll give us the Congress."[17]

As early as August 1993, Jesse was publicly predicting that Republicans would win the Senate in the midterms elections. About a month before the 1994 elections, he told reporters that he intended to lead the Foreign Relations Committee, should Republicans win control of the Senate.[18] With the advent of the 104th Congress in January 1995, as ranking member Helms became the first person from North Carolina to chair this committee for 170 years. The day after the elections, a reporter noted that Helms seemed "downright gleeful" and "jubilant." Helms, who was in Raleigh, held a press conference. One reporter remembered that the senator, with a "Cheshire Cat's grin on his face," held a large plate of chocolate chip cookies that he individually served to each reporter. "Playful" and "almost a bit giddy," Helms, to this reporter, was basking in his moment of triumph. Meanwhile, the White House was profoundly alarmed at the prospect of Jesse leading the Foreign Relations Committee. According to Marc Thiessen, who joined the Helms Foreign Relations Committee staff in late 1994, the Clinton administration was in "panic mode" and "didn't know what to make of us." The State Department, according to Steven Berry, was "stunned" and "beside themselves" about the prospect of working with Helms.[19]

Helms had first met Secretary of State Warren Christopher when he worked in the State Department under Jimmy Carter, and, although they were often described as having good personal relations, the two men had clashed in the past. During Christopher's confirmation hearings on January 13, 1993, a testy exchange ensued after Helms told the nominee that he would be submitting questions in writing and Christopher responded that he hoped that they would be "relevant." "We got a right to ask questions in any number we want to," Jesse declared, clearly annoyed. "We were elected. You have not been elected." Helms and Christopher continued to spar over Nicaragua and Cuba. When Democrats attempted to limit his questioning, Helms claimed that there would be no "love-in" with Christopher, and the committee majority would not "ride roughshod over me." "I'm not going to be bullied by anybody," he announced.[20] On November 4, 1993, Helms sharply criticized Clinton's Haiti policy and engaged in a sharp exchange with Christopher. After Christopher claimed that the administration's policy sought to restore democracy, Helms responded heatedly. "When in the hell, Mr. Secretary," Jesse declared rhetorically, "did democracy prevail in Haiti?" Christopher said that Aristide had won a free election. "So did Hitler," Jesse interjected. Asking the secretary of state about Aristide's poor human rights record, Christopher refused to comment. "A few people," he said, had "sometimes misunderstood my courtesy for a lack of resolve," Christopher added. "But I think they've been sorry when they've made that mistake."[21]

Speaking with reporters not long after the elections, Jesse said that he would pursue different objectives than Clinton regarding peacekeeping in Bosnia, the United Nations, and foreign aid. Helms promised that American troops employed in U.N. missions should come under foreign control only when the nation's vital interests were served. Jesse had for years suspected the United Nations, which he described as the "longtime nemesis of millions of Americans." Clinton's plans to double support for population planning would be reduced, and Helms favored cutting American funding for U.N. peacekeeping from 32 to 25 percent of the total. Helms's harshest words were reserved for the management of the United States's foreign aid programs. After the expenditure of $2 trillion, "much of it going down foreign rat-holes, to countries that constantly oppose us in the United Nations, and many which rejected concepts of freedom," he promised a different approach. Americans were tired of Congress spending their money "like drunk sailors." One aide predicted "deep, slashing cuts" in foreign aid, along with major cuts in funds for the World Bank and other international organizations such as the United Nations Development Program and the Fund for

Population Activities, and the World Food Program—and wholesale reductions in refugee relief in Somalia, Rwanda, and Sudan. Especially important would be a reduction in the size of the Agency for International Development.[22]

Soon after the elections, Helms clashed directly with Clinton. On November 14, Helms wrote to the president regarding the recently signed General Agreement on Tariffs and Trade (GATT), which Clinton hoped to push through the lame duck Democratic Congress. The treaty established a 123-member World Trade Organization (WTO) as a new body overseeing trade regulations that would possess the power to sanction signatory countries that violated its regulations. But Senate conservatives feared that GATT relinquished too much American sovereignty by providing an equal vote to member countries. "I'm for world trade," said new House Speaker Newt Gingrich, "but I'm against world government." Clinton had placed the treaty on a "fast track" status, which permitted no amendments and required a vote after twenty hours of debate. Helms wrote to Clinton, asking that GATT be considered by the Republican 104th Congress, but, because GATT enjoyed the support of the Republican leadership, however, it was approved by the lame duck Congress, despite Helms's opposition.[23]

Helms had little regard for the president, whom he described to an interviewer as a "joke." Chiefly Jesse objected to Clinton's well-established record for sexual immorality. In an oral history interview, Helms later characterized Clinton as "sexually maniacal" and as a person who "tried to put the make on women all the time."[24] On November 18, 1994, a little more than a week after the elections, in an appearance on *Evans and Novak*, he was asked whether the president was "up to the job" as commander in chief. "Well, you know, you ask an honest question; I'll give you an honest answer," Jesse responded. "No, I do not. And neither do the people in the armed forces." Although Helms went on to say that he considered Warren Christopher to be a "decent man" that he could work with, this conciliary comment was largely lost in the press coverage. Helms feared Clinton's "corrosive effect" on the military, as one staffer recalled, and he was convinced that those in the Clinton White House were "children of the 1960s" and were "contemptuous" of the military. On November 22, Helms tried to explain himself in a telephone interview with *Raleigh News and Observer* reporter Jim Rosen. Asked an unexpected question, Jesse said, he had "either had to dodge it or lie or tell the truth, and I always opt to tell the truth." "Every schoolboy knows that the elected President is Commander in Chief." There was "nothing novel about that," but should that make Clinton "immune from criticism"? Nonetheless, he admitted that he "should have said it better." The most memorable statement in the *N&O* interview was buried in the fourteenth paragraph of Rosen's story. Military personnel had written to him, confirming their belief that Clinton was an unfit commander; he remained highly unpopular on North Carolina's military bases because of military cuts and because of his support for gays in the military. "Mr. Clinton better watch out if he comes down here," Helms declared on the thirty-first anniversary of the assassination of John F. Kennedy. "He'd better have a bodyguard."[25]

News of the "bodyguard" comments quickly raced through the media. Describing Jesse's comments as "unwise and inappropriate," Clinton said that the choice of the Foreign Relations chair was up to the Republicans: "That's a decision for them to make, not me." The Secret Service investigated whether there was a real threat to Clinton. With phones at Helms's office in Washington ringing off the hook, a media frenzy occurred; between November 22 and 28, one hundred stories about Helms's "bodyguard" comments appeared in newspapers and weekly magazines around the country.[26] the *Charlotte Observer* characterized Jesse's statements about Clinton as "threatening, inappropriate, and downright idiotic." The *Raleigh News and Observer* called Helms's comments "partisan abuse from someone who knows the low road like the back of his hand." It mattered little whether Helms had made these comments casually or jokingly; "reckless statements about the president's safety are to be taken seriously whether they come from garden-variety lunatics or a United States senator." "How dare he be so careless—and how dare he cast such a heinous reflection on this state's people?" The *New York Times* editorialist went further: Helms, it said, should step aside as Foreign Relations chair.[27] Jesse was "behaving like an out-of-control cruise missile these days," Michael Ruby wrote in *U.S. News & World Report*.[28] By questioning Clinton's fitness, said the *New Republic,* Helms was "acting like a right-wing politician in one of the Latin American dictatorships for which he has always had an affinity."[29]

Much of the media frenzy reflected uncertainty about Helms's foreign policy views. Many commentators saw him as an isolationist. Jesse seemed to follow an "antiquated set of experiences and assumptions," wrote Steven Roberts and Gloria Borger in *U.S. News & World Report.* They quoted an unnamed "GOP consultant" as describing him as an "old-fashioned, America-first, somewhat isolationist, hawkish Republican." His health problems, they believed, had reduced his political capacity, as had the split with the Congressional Club. On the other hand, he remained a "formidable opponent." Roberts and Berger predicted that the Democrats and Clinton would seek to isolate Helms and cultivate relationships with moderate Republicans such as Indiana's Richard Lugar and Nancy Kassebaum of Kansas. Helms was a "big rock in a river" that had to be avoided, said one anonymous Republican. But "even a diminished Jesse Helms remains a formidable opponent," they reported, and Clinton would need to be "very careful in navigating the treacherous rapids around Point Helms."[30]

Within twenty-four hours, Helms offered an apology, of sorts. "I made a mistake last evening which I shall not repeat," he declared in a statement. He had made the comments, he said, during an informal telephone interview with a North Carolina reporter. In an "offhand remark," he wanted to stress "how strongly the American people feel about the nation's declining defense capability and other issues." He had not meant the comments to be taken literally, and he "far too casually" made some unfortunate comments. Helms added that Clinton would "of course be welcomed by me and other citizens of North Carolina and other states anytime he chooses to visit us." But beyond this explanation Helms would offer no apology for his caustic remarks. The *N&O* reporter had "asked my opinon," he said in his statement, and "I tried to be candid in my response." Clinton, after all, had "personal problems with his record of draft avoidance, with his stand on homosexuals in the military, and with the declining defense capability of America's armed forces."[31]

The "bodyguard" incident revealed Helms as, to a certain extent, a victim of a media feeding frenzy. Jim Rosen, who interviewed Helms for the story, and Frank Daniels, publisher of the *Raleigh News and Observer*, both agreed that the national media had distorted the story. According to Helms aide Jimmy Broughton, Rosen developed a close relationship with Helms, but it was perhaps "too comfortable," and Helms started joking without realizing what he was saying. Rosen appeared to agree with this view of things. "It never occurred to me for a moment that anyone would take Sen. Helms literally," Rosen told an interviewer in December 1994. Because the "bodyguard" statement seemed insignificant, Rosen made no attempt to qualify or contextualize the remark. Rosen believed that some in the media "intentionally misconstrued" Helms's comment, and he considered much of the coverage was "ridiculous." Daniels concluded that Helms's comments attracted such intense attention because of the elections and because Democrats were "like wounded animals in a corner." The *Washington Post* had stated that the *N&O* buried the lead: Daniels believed "quite the opposite; we played it right." "In this case," he said, "somebody said something a little stupid and others took advantage of it."[32]

Twelve years later, Rosen confirmed that the bodyguard story had been distorted, but he added an important qualification. Certainly, Rosen said, the senator was not intending to communicate any threat to Clinton, and if he could have rewritten the story he would have used the word "quip" to describe Jesse's comment. But this was a "Helmsian quip" in the classic sense: it was an attempt to make a point by making a joke, and he often said "his meanest, nastiest things about his political opponents...in a joking fashion." The bodyguard comment served as a kind of "rhetorical bridge" to a larger point: that Clinton was unfit to serve as commander in chief. For Helms and his aides to suggest that his comments were taken out of context, Rosen later declared, was "disingenuous." When a political leader of Jesse's "political smarts and experience says something like that, even in joking, about a president," it was obvious that humor was not his larger intention: "Helms knew what he was saying." Not only was this a "nasty dig" at Clinton, Helms's comments were designed to undermine public confidence in the office of the presidency.[33] Certainly, to his core constituencies, Helms's statements about Clinton seemed to ring true. Among North Carolina residents, a *News and Observer* poll taken after the bodyguard comment found that 45 percent approved of Helms's job performance, while 52 percent agreed that Clinton was unfit to be president. In another poll conducted by the newspaper in early December 1994, Helms's approval rating among North Carolina voters had decreased by six points, from 51 to 45 percent, while 52 percent agreed with Helms's assessment that Clinton was unfit to serve as commander in chief. In contrast, Helms's approval rating nationally ranged between 13 percent in a CBS poll and 29 percent in a *Times-Mirror* survey.[34]

Blaming the "bodyguard" comments about Clinton on press distortions, Helms was angry toward the media. In a speech to the North Carolina Farm Bureau in Winston-Salem on December 6, 1994, he denounced the liberal media for its "intellectual dishonesty"; "liberal elitists," he said, had "shot themselves in the foot," and most Americans did not trust them. The liberal press, he said, was having "nightmares about Jesse Helms being in charge of their committee," and he jeeringly called the *New York Times* the "New York office of the Clinton State Department." The bodyguard flap was, he said, a "non-story" and a product of media distortion. "It was never a threat and everybody knew that," he declared angrily. Why had reporters not followed up his contention that the comment was made in "lighthearted conversation"? Helms then explained that the bodyguard comment came in a story that he told Rosen during the course of the interview. A North Carolina sheriff who lost an election badly, according to the story, had a large person with him, and when asked who he was said that "anybody who can't get more votes than that had better have a bodyguard." In his interview with Rosen, Helms was suggesting that Clinton, also rejected by the voters, needed a bodyguard as much as the sheriff did.[35]

In late November 1994, Helms announced that all future exchanges with the media would only occur in formal settings and that he would no longer provide off-the-cuff remarks. The press pursued him nonetheless, and the pattern of their encounters with the senator did not seem to have changed. Following an early December press conference, Rosen described a "gaggle of reporters" following him down a Russell Office Building hallway. Helms refused questions. "I don't have a tape recorder," he told them. "I'm not going to be interviewed without my own tape recorder." As he entered an elevator, three reporters from North Carolina newspapers ran down the stairs after him, catching up at the Dirksen Senate Office Building. Helms then entered a senators-only elevator. "Now I'm getting rid of you," he told them as the elevator doors closed. Another reporter, John Monk of the *Charlotte Observer*, called him "media-spooked."[36] Helms's hostility to the media persisted into early 1995. When a reporter from the *Washington Post*, Serge Kovaleski, asked for an interview, Helms refused but agreed to answer questions submitted in writing. After the senator answered the questions and the *Post* never published the interview, Helms's office released a full transcript on their own. "Since you elected to confine yourself to loaded and insulting questions," Helms wrote to Kovaleski, "I cannot avoid the conclusion that you are not interested in a balanced and objective discourse between you and me."[37]

BY JANUARY 1995, when Helms convened his first session of the Foreign Relations Committee as its chair, the "bodyguard" fiasco was forgotten. Jesse, for his part, had abandoned his hostile attitude toward the media. "Our friends in the news media," he declared, had been "busily speculating" since the elections regarding the "dark and dangerous things they are so sure are about to happen." That, he announced, was "wishful thinking" on their part.[38] Although much was made of a gentler Jesse, this was, according to Bud Nance, the "same old Jesse, the same guy I've known for 70 years." The difference, he thought, was that reporters were on a "Jesse-hunt," hoping that he would "say something meaningless, and then they'll jump all over it and have it on the night TV."[39] Although he told reporters that his move to the Foreign Relations chairmanship had not diminished his zeal for social issues, the remainder of Helms's Senate career would be completely absorbed with foreign affairs. Beginning in 1995, he hired Marc

Thiessen to serve as press secretary—since he came to the Senate in 1973, Jesse had always prided himself as not having such a staff position, mainly because he wanted to deal directly with the press himself. Now, with Helms's advancing age and the increasing complexity of his Foreign Relations chairmanship, he needed a filter.[40]

In February 1995, Helms began an effort to restructure the foreign policy establishment that he had long opposed. Helms described the diplomatic bureaucracy as "a mess," and he had been convinced for many years that foreign aid was wasteful and often hostile to free enterprise. Years earlier, in *When Free Men Shall Stand,* Jesse described foreign aid as "the greatest racket of all time" and a "rip-off of the American taxpayers." Just as he opposed a welfare state at home, Helms also opposed creating a "welfare world abroad," and he believed that aid policies worked to encourage socialism.[41] In a letter to President Reagan in September 1985, he urged that foreign assistance programs be overhauled. He believed that the Agency for International Development (AID), in particular, had failed in its mission of economic development. Although disbursing billions, most of it went through governments and encouraged bloated bureaucracies and corruption. Helms advocated a wholesale reorientation of foreign aid that bypassed governmental involvement and encouraged private foundations and faith-based aid.[42] For the first two years of the Clinton presidency, Helms pressed for restructuring. Sometime in 1993, Helms staffer Steve Berry visited the State Department's undersecretary for management, Richard M. Moose, and they discussed possible reforms. Moose reported to Berry that internal discussions were already under way in the Clinton administration, but that AID administrator Brian Atwood was firmly opposed to any move to reduce his agency's independence. Atwood instead favored transforming AID into a cabinet-level position.[43]

Helms outlined his ideas in a *Washington Post* piece that appeared on February 14, 1995, entitled "Christopher Is Right." Vice president Al Gore had headed up the Clinton administration's downsizing efforts, and Secretary of State Christopher proposed a restructuring plan that would combine and fold three agencies—the Agency for International Development, the Arms Control and Disarmament Agency, and the United States Information Agency—into the State Department. After nearly three weeks of discussion, Gore, bending to aggressive lobbying by AID administrator Brian Atwood, rejected the restructuring plan. Calling Christopher's proposal "bold and innovative," in the *Post* piece Helms claimed that it had fallen victim to the "frenzied lobbying" of the "bureaucratic hierarchy." He believed that this "significant proposal" should not be "sacrificed on the altar of bureaucratic self-preservation." Rather, this proposal—the "most thoughtful reorganization of U.S. foreign affairs institutions since World War II"—would streamline and reinvigorate the "existing creaky, inefficient and outrageously costly foreign policy apparatus." In his version of this reorganization, Helms proposed to create a single foreign affairs department, but the emphasis would be on reducing bureaucracy, and, especially in aid, to privatize development assistance. The reorganization would yield significant savings, Jesse claimed, and he was simply following Christopher's recommendation.[44]

In proposing the foreign policy reorganization, according to the *Washington Post*, Helms had "ambushed" the Clinton White House.[45] Testifying before the Foreign Relations Committee on February 14, Christopher refused to take Helms's bait. "The vice president has concluded that each of the agencies should remain independent," Christopher said, "and I fully accept that conclusion." Yet he added that he was "always grateful for your support wherever I receive it, in whatever newspaper." Gore's program in "reinventing government," Helms charged, remained "mostly talk," and the current foreign policy bureaucracy was a "mess," with "no one person in charge." Why, if the Cold War had ended and most experts were urging restructuring, were "the same old bureaucracies spending the same amount of money on the same worn-out programs?" "I am disappointed that there is no real reform," he added, "notwithstanding your efforts, Mr. Secretary."

Helms's reorganization plan, presented to the press in mid-March and then fully unveiled in legislation in May 1995, was based on the premise that the foreign policy apparatus had "spun off into a constellation of money-absorbing, incoherent satellites," he said, "each with its own entrenched, growing bureaucracies and its own bureaucratic interests." As a result, the system had become an "incoherent mishmash, which no one policymaker can control."[46] Helms's proposals contained not simply restructuring but also significant cuts in the $21.2 billion international affairs budget. Helms's plans called for the closing of all AID overseas missions, a reduction in its staff by half, and budget cuts of 25 percent at USIA and 14 percent at State. Overall, under his plan, foreign assistance would be reduced by a total of $3.6 billion. He promised not to preserve the same level of assistance to Israel and Egypt, though he was considering cutting $1.2 billion in nonmilitary aid in exchange for forgiving Israel's debt to the United States.[47]

Helms's reorganization plan amounted to a far-reaching overhaul of foreign aid. Under his plan, a privatized system would operate under a new International Development Foundation, which would function as part of the State Department but would be managed by nongovernment organizations (NGOs). AID field offices would close down around the world and nine thousand AID workers would be eliminated, replaced by a privatized system that eliminated the inefficient American foreign aid bureaucracy and sometimes that of corrupt foreign governments. Jesse's restructuring plans sought to "revolutionize the way we deal with foreign aid," he wrote on April 26, 1995. "If the whole concept of foreign aid seems foreign to many Americans, it should because it doesn't make any sense," Helms told the Senate Foreign Relations Committee. Helms sought, according to one of his aides, to get "rid of the middle man and give the NGOs block grants." Since aid would almost certainly be cut, "Helms or no Helms," said one of Jesse's aides, the real issue was whether it went into the "pockets of bureaucrats" or was invested in "local projects where it can do the most good." "If anyone but Helms had proposed this," he added, "they'd be calling it innovative and brilliant."[48]

Helms's proposals, perhaps predictably, were very unpopular with the foreign policy establishment. AID director Brian Atwood denounced them as "mischievous," declaring that they demonstrated that the senator was an "isolationist."[49] The restructuring proposals encountered the united opposition of the USIA, AID, and ACDA, along with the Clinton White House, which in May 1995 indicated that it would veto legislation. In May 1995, Jesse's staff issued a press release entitled "Captured Enemy Documents" that contained internal AID memoranda documenting the agency's efforts against the reorganization proposals. These materials had been anonymously leaked to Helms in blank envelopes, and the senator's staff took full advantage with blast faxes designed to embarrass AID. Press releases from Helms's office publicized examples of AID waste and boondoggles.[50]

Despite opposition from the bureaucracy, Helms sought out White House support. In August 1995, in a meeting with Clinton in his private quarters on the second floor of the White House, Helms and his aides presented his reorganization plan. Veteran committee staffer Steven Berry, vacationing at Rehoboth Beach in Delaware, got a call from Bud Nance summoning him back to Washington. Berry remembered that Clinton, at the meeting, was intensely interested and asked many questions. Turning to Gore, he said: "Al, that sounds good." But the Clinton meeting appeared to have had little effect in resolving the deadlock, which continued into the fall because of opposition from Gore and Atwood. According to Jesse's account, Clinton had said: "Who can be against this? Jesse, I'll get back you." The president, Helms reported in September, "hasn't gotten back to me."[51] When the foreign operations bill reauthorization came before the

Senate, on September 20, 1995, Helms attached an amendment containing his reorganization plan. But the deadlock persisted, part of a larger stalemate, in late 1995, between a Republican Congress and a Democratic president. Although Helms permitted State Department reauthorization without his reorganization amendment, he raised the pressure by suspending all business meetings of the Foreign Relations Committee, freezing four hundred promotions at the State Department, and blocking treaties on chemical weapons, arms reduction, an international convention on women and the environment, and a dozen other bilateral trade treaties. He also blocked funding for the Middle East Peace Facilitation Act, which enabled the Palestine Liberation Organization to participate in the peace process.[52]

Helms's struggle with the Clinton White House persisted for four months, with a resulting paralysis of the Foreign Relations Committee, until December 1995. After intense negotiations, Massachusetts's John Kerry and Helms reached a compromise. Rather than eliminating any of the three agencies, the White House agreed to a plan by which Clinton would devise his own consolidation plan and save at least $1.7 billion. If the president failed to take action within six months, the law provided that all three agencies would be abolished. "After a long deadlock," the *Washington Post* announced, "Sen. Jesse Helms has freed his captives." Jesse saw things differently. "We're not saving enough in my judgment," Helms said to reporters, but he wanted "get started on this business of saving taxpayers' money." "I've had to console myself with the fact that saving taxpayers $1.7 billion is better than saving taxpayers nothing." Helms dismissed critics of the bill, describing their complaints as "mewling and puking" about "how we are tromping on the foreign service." The "mewling and puking" was a Shakespeare reference from *As You Like It,* in which the first of seven stages of human life is described as "At first the infant, mewling and puking in the nurse's arms."[53]

DESPITE THE USUAL press speculation, there was little doubt that the seventy-four-year-old Jesse would run for a fifth Senate term. Unlike his previous four Senate campaigns, he did so without the support of the Congressional Club. He was intent, as he wrote Bruce Eberle, that he would rely on a "new and different" campaign organization.[54] Jesse assembled a small circle of close advisers, family, and friends, including Rocky Mount businessman Jack C. D. Bailey, Raleigh physician Bert Coffer, and Barbara Goodmon, the wife of A. J. Fletcher's grandson, Jim Goodmon. In late January 1996, Helms officially filed as a candidate, saying in a statement that he welcomed the chance to run once more in order to communicate the "clear distinction" that existed between conservative and liberal political philosophies. Harvey Gantt once again emerged as the Democratic front-runner, despite a well-financed primary challenge by former Glaxo Corporation chairman Charles Sanders. Jesse hired familiar political operatives, but without the Congressional Club he had limited options. Alex Castellanos, a club alumnus and now an independent political consultant, participated in the early stages of the campaign, as did Charlie Black, who worked for the national Republican senatorial campaign and had managed Phil Gramm's unsuccessful 1996 presidential run. Terry Edmondson, who had worked for Bailey in his Rocky Mount fast food business and later become involved in Republican politics and fund-raising, served as money person and campaign manager. David Tyson, longtime club operative who had broken with Wrenn in the mid-1980s and then worked for Eberle as a political consultant, became chief strategist. Described as a "gut fighter," Tyson was combative and ideological; Edmondson later described him as "like a Tom Ellis in his younger days," with a "volcanic personality" and creative but "always sort of on the edge." Tyson and Edmondson became the key campaign operatives, though they brought Neil Newhouse, from Washington, for polling and Scott Howell, from Dallas, to produce TV ads. Howell was a relative unknown, having worked in political campaigns in South Carolina and then as an operative for Lee Atwater at the Republican National Committee in the 1980s. The chairman of the state GOP, Sam Currin, was a former Helms aide and loyalist. With the star power of a well-known incumbent, Helms had little trouble raising money: by January 1996, he had raised $2.2 million, and by the end of the campaign in November, he had spent $14.6 million. The senator rejected a heavy reliance on direct mail fund-raising; though this might be a "fatal mistake," he told an interviewer, "I am not going to permit my friends to be badgered for contribution after contribution after contribution." Instead, Jesse's fund-raisers focused on high-dollar fund-raising, from special interest groups, political action committees, and, for the first time in his career, fund-raising dinners. In 1995–96 alone, Helms participated in over seventy fund-raising events across the country, and these were set up and managed by Edmondson. Not ordinarily a glad-hander, Helms nonetheless reached the point where he enjoyed these events.[55]

Overall, the Helms Senate campaign in 1996 differed from previous contests. Edmondson involved Helms more directly, showing him polls periodically and ensuring that he became aware of the campaign strategy. According to Edmondson, Helms responded by enjoying himself more than he had in any other campaign except perhaps for his first, in 1972. According to Edmondson, Helms wanted to prove that he could win without the club, and the election of 1996 "got the club off his back" and "showed he could win." Smaller than the massive operations of earlier years, the campaign operation was composed of Edmondson and Tyson, plus a few office workers, with a total operation employing around thirty people. The campaign followed a "different philosophy," according to Edmondson. Helms's involvement sometimes made things more difficult, mainly because he had been so long shielded from the realities of elections. When Newhouse presented a poll to the senator in Washington, his reaction was to question the need for such extensive surveys. "Who in the hell are you?" he exclaimed. "Why did we hire you? Why do we need a pollster?" Helms had always objected to having a campaign debt, and Ellis and Wrenn had nonetheless ended their 1984 and 1990 campaigns with a debt of more than $1 million. Helms was determined not to have this reoccur, but Edmondson faced the same political calculus: should the campaign borrow money in order to maximize media exposure, knowing that, if they won, the money would eventually be raised? In what Edmondson called a "calculated decision" about a month before election day, he decided to go into debt. Helms was unhappy, but eventually came to peace with the decision.[56]

As was the case in 1990, the Helms campaign sought to influence the outcome of the Democratic primary. Castellanos, often credited for producing the notorious "white hands" ad of 1990, produced ads that accused Gantt of supporting racial quotas and Glaxo's Sanders of favoring health benefits for homosexual partners (which had occurred at the pharmaceutical firm under his leadership). But Castellanos had left the campaign by April 1996. The press suggested that his hard-hitting ads smacked too much of Congressional Club tactics, but Edmondson subsequently had another explanation. According to him, Castellanos and Black wanted too much control over the campaign's direction, and Edmondson was determined to preserve control by North Carolinians.[57] In a campaign plan drawn up by pollster Neil Newhouse in late 1995, the Helms campaign expected to run against Sanders, who they thought would easily win the primary and whom they considered the more dangerous candidate. Despite spending $3.1 million, including $1.7 million of his own money, Sanders lost to Gantt in the May 7 primary by a margin of 53 to 41 percent. The stage was set for a Helms-Gantt rematch. "Six years older, wiser, grayer and tougher," Gantt declared himself ready for battle.[58]

Helms remained vulnerable: burdened by unfavorable ratings and a shrinking core of supporters, his advisers feared that the 600,000 new voters of the 1990s might form a potentially anti-Helms electorate. Although the number of registered Republicans had increased, the most rapidly increasing group were unaffiliated voters, who had increased by 69 percent since 1990. Helms was also older, with more health problems; one reporter described him as "visibly aged." Never one of his favorite activities, electioneering held even less appeal to him than in his previous four campaigns. As the electorate aged, Helms's strongest supporters—middle-aged and elderly white males, especially those without college degrees—were diminishing. None of his campaigns was easy, and his controversial positions had exposed him, during each election cycle, to a large portion of the electorate that disliked him. Jesse's cultural politics, confrontational and adversarial, possessed little appeal to the suburban migrants arriving from the North during the 1990s, and younger voters would perhaps find his message on sexuality unappealing. North Carolina was "changing out from under him," observed Castellanos in an interview, with "a generation growing up inside the state that doesn't know him."[59]

But Helms also possessed advantages in 1996. The growing number of white immigrants to the suburbs coincided with the emergence of the Republican Party in the South, and, especially after the GOP landslide in the midterm elections of 1994, the party had evolved into a powerful magnet for new voters. The South became a Republican base, though this trend was less true in North Carolina, where Democrats maintained a foothold in state elections and maintained control over the governorship. But in elections focused on national issues, Republican candidates, including Helms, possessed a natural edge. New residents of North Carolina were registering Republican in the 1990s by a margin of three to one, and between 1990 and 1996 Republicans registered 328,000 voters, as compared to 110,000 new Democrats. Three-fifths of these new voters lived in the urban crescent that followed Interstate 85 between Raleigh and Charlotte.[60] Helms avoided directly engaging Gantt; as he had since 1984, he refused to debate his opponent, and his appearances remained infrequent until late in the campaign, usually only among his most loyal supporters. Gantt, in addition, lacked the crusading quality that his campaign possessed in 1990, and the novelty of his candidacy, as one reporter remembered, had worn off. Focusing on bread-and-butter issues of jobs, education, and health care, Gantt articulated centrist, traditionally Democratic positions that would appeal to middle-class and working-class white voters. "Let's put aside the foolishness, the stuff that's thrown at you on television, this bashing of one group or another," he told voters in Greenville late in the campaign. "Let's get down to the business of how we educate our children, how we access health care, how we protect the environment, how we get job security." Although Jesse claimed to represent ordinary people, Gantt told another group in Goldsboro, he was "carrying the water for some big corporations and for some foreign governments." Gantt successfully attracted money, much of it from out-of-state Jesse haters, along with union, gay rights, women's, and environmental groups. In total, some 84,000 contributors donated an average of $55 to his campaign. By November, the flow of money into the Gantt campaign even exceeded Helms's fund-raising, and the senator was outmatched by his opponent. But, relying on his war chest for a media blitz, Gantt did not attempt to construct a field operation; he depended on the state Democratic Party organization for field work and used TV ads to communicate his message. Political observers saw this as a gamble—"risky, even suicidal," according to one assessment—given that Gantt was challenging an entrenched incumbent. Helms maintained a comfortable six- to ten-point margin throughout the campaign.[61]

In order to attract new voters to his ranks, Helms's managers tried to moderate the senator's polarizing image. In a campaign plan drawn up in November 1995, Helms's political advisers stressed running soft media in the early parts of the campaign. At the same time, however, they also realized that they could not "reinvent" Helms, who, said one adviser, was a "known and polarized figure" to most voters.[62] In the summer of 1996, the Helms campaign, following Newhouse's recommendation, ran soft media, emphasizing the senator's family connections and long service in the Senate in what the sharply critical *Independent* called the "gauzy commercial narrations of his granddaughters."[63] But Helms was not, in many respects, a changed candidate. At a campaign appearance in Cumberland County, near Fayetteville, he warned that the "homosexuals and the lesbians" were "rolling into this state just as they did in 1990 in their effort to defeat me, along with the labor unions and the militant women." Asked by a reporter in September if he had mellowed, Jesse said that he was "the same guy I've always been" and that he was "no kinder or less kinder or whatever." "I haven't changed one bit," he said. Race continued to be an important part of Jesse's campaign. He remained unashamed of the "white hands" ad in 1990, which, he said, expressed "God's truth." He had nothing against blacks, but he noted that they were not prepared to "become assimilated into the election process as far as I know; they would rather vote as a bloc."[64]

By early September, Helms began airing attack ads—suggesting, some observers concluded, a tightening of the race—that exploited Gantt's courting of liberal constituencies after 1990. The ads sought to define Gantt as a liberal and to fend off his attempt to move to the center. In a spot that began airing on September 9, a narrator claimed that Gantt was promoting the same "liberal agenda" that North Carolina voters had rejected in 1990. The ad asserted that the ACLU had honored Gantt in 1991, while in 1992 he favored a gay rights proposal in Charlotte. Gantt opposed the death penalty, the ad continued. "Harvey Gantt says the liberal label fits just fine," the narrator concluded. "But does Harvey Gantt fit North Carolina?" At the same time, the Helms campaign rotated softer ads that ran regionally in the Charlotte, Greensboro/High Point/Winston-Salem, and Raleigh-Durham markets that stressed Helms's contributions as senator to these areas. Another ad claimed that Gantt supported gay marriage, a national gay bill of rights, and the rights of gay teachers to be in the classroom. What was the difference between Bill Clinton and Harvey Gantt, a narrator asked viewers in another ad appearing in October. Clinton supported the death penalty; Gantt opposed it. Clinton opposed gay marriage; Gantt did not oppose it. Gantt, said the ad, was "more liberal than Bill Clinton, too liberal for North Carolina." The attack ads ran for most of the next month, with apparent effectiveness.[65] Responding, Gantt described these charges as false. "I believe," he said, "in the traditional form of marriage that I believe most of you believe." He had never indicated otherwise, though the ad suggested that he did. Helms's ad had a "familiar and depressing" theme, editorialized the *Greensboro News & Record,* and the campaign was "beginning to sound like the unsavory contest of 1990." Rather than debating the issues in an open forum, it claimed, the incumbent senator was hiding "behind a phalanx of media consultants and their misleading TV ads."[66] Helms was unashamed of the ad, telling reporters that he wanted to remind voters that Gantt had "a flaw in his character." Gantt subsequently also launched his own attack ads that charged that Helms had favored cuts in Medicare, but the Helms campaign responded swiftly, and their internal polls showed that an overwhelming majority of viewers believed the senator.[67]

Helms benefited from the arrival of Hurricane Fran, which wreaked destruction throughout much of eastern and central North Carolina on September 6, 1996. For much of the next month, Fran and its aftermath consumed newspaper headlines, and, according to one commentator, compressed the campaign into the month of October.[68] With a few weeks left before election day, Jesse once again boarded his RV and toured the state; his Winnebago trip, said the *N&O*'s Rob Christensen, meant that political theater was "now becoming a road show" that soon might be "coming to a theater near you." On campaign stops, Jesse attacked Gantt and another familiar target—the media. At a speech to an audience of about three hundred in a Goldsboro Moose Lodge—his first announced appearance in

North Carolina since August—he made familiar jabs. Pointing to national media from NBC, CBS, and CNN, he suggested that they were doing "their best to be helpful—to the other side." They were "praying I'll be defeated." When the major media worried about his campaigns, Helms said, "I am delighted."[69]

The Goldsboro speech was a rare occasion in which the Helms campaign informed the media in advance about his campaign schedule. He continued to remain isolated from reporters, and he refused to engage in campaign debates.[70] In Goldsboro, reporters had a rare opportunity to see Helms, and a media frenzy ensued as reporters and camera crews jockeyed to get near him. CBS chief Washington correspondent Bob Schieffer requested an interview but was rejected, and Helms aides refused all of his requests for information. One staffer, Schieffer claimed, even tried to provoke a fistfight. He told the *N&O* that the Helms staffers were the "rudest group of people I've ever run into in my life."[71]

The Helms campaign remained confident about winning—the polls continued to show a solid lead over Gantt—but they were concerned about two issues: Helms's age and his attitudes toward African Americans. Helms's managers were armed with response ads if Gantt had gone on the attack on these issues, but the ads remained on the shelf.[72] On October 21, after the polls suggested that the race had tightened slightly (according to a Mason-Dixon poll, Helms's lead had decreased from ten to seven points, while a CBS survey had Gantt in the lead by two points), the Helms campaign released attack ads reiterating the charges of the 1990 campaign—that Gantt had unduly profited from a minority preference enabling him to buy a Charlotte TV station. Gantt "used his minority status to purchase interest in a TV station under false pretenses," said a narrator of the ad, and then weeks later he sold the station to a white-owned company and made millions. The ads also contended that Gantt in 1994, as an architect, had obtained preferential treatment on school contracts in Charlotte. In mid-October, the North Carolina Republican Party distributed about 500,000 flyers that printed pictures of Gantt and black congressmen such as Mel Watt of Charlotte and Eva Clayton of Warrenton. "Do you want Senator Harvey Gantt to join Congressman Mel Watt in Washington?" asked one flyer. Critics charged that this constituted a racial appeal.[73]

During the closing weeks of the campaign, newspaper reports appeared regarding Helms's ethics. On October 9, the *Raleigh News and Observer* ran a story stating that Helms had underreported rental income from Dot's homes in the Raleigh area that she had inherited from her father; he neglected to list six properties with the Senate Ethics Committee and had undervalued their worth by about half. Later reports suggested that some of the homes were unheated and in disrepair, and Democrats, calling Jesse a "millionaire slumlord," demanded a Senate investigation and filed an ethics complaint. Helms responded by saying that the charges were "making a mountain out of a molehill."[74] On October 26, the *Washington Post* reported that the Jesse Helms Center had received donations from foreign governments, including $100,000 from Kuwait in 1991 and $225,000 from Taiwan two years later. The *Post* also focused attention on large corporate donations. Donations to the center were not limited by campaign finance laws, but John Dodd, who became director in 1994, stopped accepting gifts from foreign governments. Helms produced a letter from the Senate Ethics Committee declaring that the Kuwait contributions had not violated Senate rules. "As long as it's lawful, what's wrong with it?" Helms told an eastern North Carolina audience. This was "typical right-before-the-election" tactics. A few days before the election, in early November, Helms aired ads that described Gantt's attack as a "desperate smear campaign." Although Gantt tried to make this into a campaign issue, the matter had little impact on voters.[75]

In the November 1996 elections, Helms won a fifth term with 53 percent of the vote—the same percentage that he had received six years earlier. In a victory speech on election eve, Jesse declared—using the same line that he had employed in previous campaigns—that he could hear the "gnashing of teeth in the editorial department of the *Charlotte Observer,* the *News and Observer,* the *Greensboro Daily News,* the *Winston-Salem Journal.*" Dan Rather, he said, was "trying to avoid announcing who is the winner." He promised "six more years of torment for Ted Kennedy and all those other liberals." Exit polls revealed that Helms's coalition remained intact: religious conservatives, white males, and rural and small-town voters all remained loyal. He attracted few black voters, while Gantt increased his share of the white vote from 35 percent in 1990 to 38 percent in 1996. The new voters that had arrived in North Carolina since 1990 preferred Gantt by a margin of 59 to 41 percent. Jesse's 1996 campaign incurred a $1 million debt, something that annoyed Jesse but was a reality of modern campaigning.[76]

Nine months after his reelection in 1996, Helms reflected on his relationship with Bill Clinton. Although he steadfastly opposed Clinton's domestic and foreign policies and would later support his conviction during the president's Senate trial, Jesse admitted a grudging admiration. In March 1997, on a visit to North Carolina, Clinton noted that his relationship with Helms had lost some of its enmity. In a reference to North Carolina–born Erskine Bowles, that "ever since I got a chief of staff that does not speak with an accent, we've been getting along better, Senator Helms and I." The arrival of Bowles as White House chief of staff undoubtedly made a difference; Helms, long a friend of the Bowles family, "thought the world of him," according to Broughton.[77] Clinton subsequently made an impression on the Helms family—a key to Jesse's heart. After Hurricane Fran hit North Carolina in September 1996, the president called Helms's daughter Jane, offering assistance in rebuilding her damaged school. When Helms took his granddaughter, Jennifer Knox, to a White House dinner, she was "all eyes." When a Secret Service agent told the senator that the president wanted him and his guest to come to his table for a picture, Jennifer was "up like a rocket." Clinton, said Helms, "could charm a bird out of a tree." "I get a kick out of him," he told the *Charlotte Observer*. "He's a very personable fellow." According to one staffer, Helms alternated between periods of "grudging respect" and hostility about Clinton.[78]

But the honeymoon period in Helms's relationship with the Clinton White House did not last long. The disclosure of the president's sexual relationship with intern Monica Lewinsky that became public in January 1998 was, for Helms, damning; he had little tolerance for sexual transgressions. "Anybody who believes that Clinton's alleged infidelities should be excused," he said, had "already announced their total lack of character."[79] Could the "fragile survival of freedom in the world," he asked the Conservative Political Action Conference meeting in January 1998, "be entrusted to leadership making the kind of strange judgments leading to personal irresponsibility that has made this country the laughingstock of the world?"[80] The Lewinsky scandal made him feel a "deep sense of sadness for our country," he told an audience in February 1998, and he felt "particularly . . . sad" for Clinton's daughter, Chelsea. This was a "bad chapter, and a bad time, and I hope we can move by it," though he was bothered by those who said that Clinton's sexual relationship with Lewinsky did not matter.[81]

Helms proceeded carefully on the impeachment issue: he was not one of the Senate's leaders seeking conviction, and he refrained from announcing his vote until immediately before Clinton's Senate trial in January 1999. But he believed Clinton should be removed from office. He had brought "this nation of ours to the point of being ridiculed all around the world," he told a reporter. "I think that's a high crime, and I think it's abuse of office, and I think the details speak for themselves."[82] Although the Senate acquitted Clinton on February 12, 1999, the day before, Helms had delivered a stinging speech in favor of conviction. The news media, he said, had trivialized "what should be respected as our solemn duty." The scandal surrounding the Clinton presidency had become a national disgrace: American schoolchildren were learning that it was "OK to lie, because the president does it." "Our citizens tune out in droves, preferring the daily distractions of everyday life to an honest appraisal of the depths to which the presidency of the United States has sunk." He believed that senators should "simply summon our courage and yell, 'Stop tampering with the soul of America.' "[83]

SOON AFTER HIS reelection, on December 5, 1996, President Bill Clinton nominated as his new secretary of state Madeleine Albright, who for the past three years had served as ambassador to the United Nations. In advance of Clinton's announcement, the White House extended feelers to Helms, who indicated his support. The first woman to serve in this position, her nomination was popular in Congress, and Helms praised her as a "tough and courageous lady" and foresaw few problems in her confirmation.[84] Appearing before the Foreign Relations Committee on January 8, 1997, Albright encountered what the *Washington Post* described as an "atmosphere of bipartisan warmth," with "little dissent and mostly admiration." Helms, Albright later reflected, was "at his most courtly."[85] Helms addressed her as "secretary-to-be," though he noted that they disagreed about issues such as State Department reorganization and United Nations reform. "I know the things you've said are sincere," Helms told the nominee. "I just believe you're sincerely wrong." "Instead of Bully Helms," noted *The Economist*, "there was a kindly old southern gentleman," something that the British observer regarded as "especially strange since senator and nominee have often disagreed sharply." While Albright endorsed Clinton's humanitarian interventionism in Somalia, Haiti, and Bosnia and his multilateralism, Helms was described as "the closest thing to an isolationist that the Senate offers these days." Personal relationships were all-important to Jesse, and they seem to have figured importantly in his dealings with Albright. She recalled that at her confirmation hearings in 1993, Helms was introduced to Albright's three grown daughters, and he displayed his "southern courtliness, especially toward women." In her memoirs, Albright recalled that Helms seemed especially taken with her youngest daughter, twenty-six-year-old Katie. Helms and Albright had bonded further when she spoke at St. Mary's College during a visit to Raleigh in 1996.[86]

For the past two years, Helms had had difficult relations with the State Department. Warren Christopher incorrectly assumed that Helms would not negotiate, and, according to Thiessen, he was like a turtle "backed into a shell" who "just wouldn't deal with us." The only communication seemed to be between Thiessen and the State Department spokesman, Nick Burns; no one else would take Foreign Relations Committee calls, and Christopher's office seemed to believe in the caricature of Jesse. Helms remained puzzled by the secretary's unwillingness to deal with him; there was a deadlock of noncommunication that dominated relations with the White House.[87] Albright's arrival indicated a new page in this relationship: she was the White House's "designated charmer," and Helms was charmed. In 1948, she had escaped Communist rule in Czechoslovakia with her family, and her tough approach to foreign policy was appealing to the senator. For her part, Albright came to believe that Helms possessed "important redeeming qualities," including patriotism, honor, faith, and commitment to family. Over time, Albright and Helms became so close that they greeted each other with kisses; they danced with each other at her sixtieth birthday party. In 1997, during a visit to North Carolina she presented him with a T-shirt adorned with the words "Someone in the State Department Loves Me."[88] Helms, during her confirmation hearings in January 1997, called her a "joy" to work with as U.N. ambassador. Because of Clinton's mismanagement of American foreign policy, the nation's adversaries doubted "our resolve at this moment." Many Americans hoped that Albright would bring "some coherence, direction and fresh ideas to America's foreign policy." Though Helms realized that it was inevitable that he and the new secretary of state would disagree—and though he knew that she was "sincerely wrong" in some of her positions—he believed that they could work cooperatively.[89]

Although Albright was recommended by the Foreign Relations Committee and quickly confirmed by the Senate, Jesse took the occasion to restate his opposition to Clinton's policies. In a Senate speech on January 22 made immediately before Albright's confirmation, Helms warned that his support "should in no way be misconstrued as an endorsement of President Clinton's conduct of foreign policy." Clinton's policies had been "vacillating and insecure," Helms claimed; he had responded to events abroad rather than attempting to shape them. He then provided specifics. In Haiti, half of an island of little strategic interest to the United States Clinton had replaced "one group of thugs with another"—at the cost of over $2 billion. American weakness and indecision had led to the deaths of American soldiers in Somalia. In Bosnia, Iran had provided arms while the American government had refused to do so, while in Iraq, dictator Saddam Hussein was "now politically stronger than before." American weakness toward China encouraged that country to bully Taiwan. As Foreign Relations chairman, Helms would be watching Albright "closely" in order to ensure that Clinton had "learned from the disasters of the first term." Helms then announced his own foreign policy agenda. He planned to press for the reform of the State Department, and he hoped to trim its bloated foreign policy bureaucracy. He further hoped that Albright would work with him toward restructuring "our foreign-affairs institutions to meet the new challenges we will face in the next century."[90]

Under Bud Nance, the Foreign Relations Committee attracted young, aggressive staffers who fit into the group's chemistry temperamentally and ideologically. They joined the staff, said one, "because we believed in certain ideas."[91] They included Marc Thiessen; Steve Biegun, who worked on the issue of Bosnia and later became, after Nance's death in 1999, his successor as staff director; and Marshall Billingslea, who served as the committee expert on arms control. Nance also hired Danielle Pletka, who joined the staff in 1992, and she helped to chart policy related to the Middle East. Nance was the "patriarch" among these strong personalities, as Steve Biegun remembered, often joining them for lunch and creating an esprit de corps. Like Helms, Nance was very conservative in terms of finance: it pained him to pay high salaries, and he believed in keeping the budget low. Enjoying the unqualified confidence of Helms, he was one of only a few people who spoke with complete candor. Nance created a "strong glue" between the young, enthusiastic staffers and the senator.[92]

As was always true, Jesse used the nomination process to oppose presidential policies. For example, he blocked the nomination of Brian Atwood, head of AID during the Clinton administration, as ambassador to Brazil; Atwood then instead led the American relief effort in Kosovo.[93] A more extended battle occurred over the nomination of William Weld to be ambassador to Mexico. In April 1997, at the White House Correspondents Dinner, Massachusetts governor Weld told the press of Clinton's plans to nominate him. When the news drifted back to Helms, he told reporters that the only way Weld would go to Mexico would be "as a tourist." Later, Helms told an interviewer on Fox News that Weld was not "ambassador quality." Weld was "a little loose with his lips sometimes," he said, and, although he had "nothing against him ... I don't think he ought to be Ambassador to Mexico." He promised to block the nomination.

Helms's reasons for opposing the Weld nomination ran deep. During Weld's unsuccessful Senate campaign against John Kerry in 1996, Weld had refused to say whether he would vote to keep Helms on as Foreign Relations chair. The *Boston Globe* later reported that the governor's wife, Susan Roosevelt Weld, had contributed $199 to the 1996 Gantt campaign. According to the *Charlotte Observer*, the senator felt "dissed," while others noted that his family was deeply offended by Weld's slight. Jesse also questioned Weld's conservative purity on issues such as the medical use of marijuana, abortion, and gay rights. Weld had antagonized the Republican right with his views on these issues, and in 1988 he had infuriated them when he resigned as head of the criminal division of the Reagan administration's Justice Department to protest the policies of Attorney General Edwin Meese. Weld was the "most adamant, militant, pro-homosexual Governor in the country," said Howard Phillips of the Conservative Caucus. As a Republican moderate sympathetic to the Clinton administration and a blue-blood New Englander, he represented a shrinking wing of the party that Jesse despised. Helms opposed sending a "soft-on-drugs Deadhead to Mexico," said one anonymous Helms ally. Prepared to use his powers as committee chairman to quash the nomination, as a *Boston Globe* columnist put it, Helms rendered Weld "both a lame duck and a dead duck."[94]

The struggle grew more bitter when Weld held a news conference on July 15 and, without the White House's permission, attacked the senator. Claiming that Helms had resorted to "ideological extortion" by blocking his nomination, Weld refused to accept another position with the administration. "I intend to stand and fight for the Mexico ambassadorship," he said, and he expected the president to "join me in a fight worth fighting." Helms's charges about Weld's weakness on the drug issue were "complete phony baloney," masking a conservative-moderate power struggle among Republicans. "In plain language," Weld said, "I am not Senator Helms' kind of Republican. I do not pass his litmus test on social policy. Nor do I want to." Although Clinton advisers privately admitted that the Weld nomination had little chance of success, the governor's press conference meant that the White House could not appear to give in to Helms. Clinton submitted the nomination to the Senate on July 23, 1997. Although Weld resigned about a week later as Massachusetts governor in order to devote full time to the confirmation battle, his attack on Helms sealed his fate. "If the governor wants a fight," Thiessen told reporters, "I guess he is prepared to lose."[95] Senate majority leader Trent Lott declared that Weld's "biggest problem" was that he had "shot his foot off," and although there had been some chance for accommodation, by attacking Helms "unfairly" and with "political rhetoric that was just uncalled for," his prospects were slim. There had never been an ambassadorial nominee who began the confirmation process by attacking a Senate committee chairman, Thiessen later added, "and I don't expect there'll be one soon." With an uneasy White House unwilling to challenge Helms, concluded *the Washington Post,* rarely had a nomination been in "worse shape." This was a "hopeless mission," concluded one administration official. Many speculated that Weld was less interested in the appointment than in positioning himself as the leader of Republican moderates.[96]

In early August, Weld visited Washington, met with Clinton at the White House, and lobbied senators. Advised to tone things down during his visit, Weld was restrained, telling reporters that he had made "a little progress." But Weld had thoroughly alienated Helms. Since the Republicans had taken control of Congress, the senator had occupied a different role as less of a bomb thrower and more of a manager. Now the Weld fight brought out what one staffer called the "old passion" in Helms. This was "personal for him."[97] On August 3, Richard Lugar appeared on *This Week*, criticizing Helms as "dictatorial" and "unilaterally difficult." A possible "civil war" might erupt among Republicans; he thought that the committee should vote on Weld's nomination. Lugar later hinted that he might delay the Senate Agriculture Committee's business—which included consideration of an impending $368 billion settlement of litigation against tobacco companies—as retaliation against Helms. He was tired of Helms's methods, Lugar said. The North Carolinian often won because he was the "most adamant and the most constant," even if he inconvenienced other senators. Lugar was "objecting in the most direct public manner that I can." But Helms refused an open fight. "I'm not calling Weld a skunk," he told the *Raleigh News* and *Observer*. "I'm not going to pick up his challenge." As for Lugar, Jesse realized that his chairmanship provided him with extraordinary power. Spending much of August in North Carolina, Jesse refused to lobby. "I'm staying out of it," Helms explained in an interview with Fred Barnes, even though the media wanted a "feud." When a Boston reporter asked him about Weld, Jesse broke his silence. *"Res ipsa loquitur,"* he said, which translates as "The thing speaks for itself."[98]

The Weld fight was highly personalized: Weld and Helms disliked each other, and Lugar's resentment over losing the Foreign Relations chairmanship to Jesse in 1987 bubbled to the surface. Jesse had taken Senate foreign policy leadership in a starkly different direction, and Lugar admitted that the old feud played a role. "I don't plead totally guilty," he said, "but partially guilty." There were also stark substantive differences between Lugar and Helms. A *Washington Post* reporter called Lugar's struggle against Helms "what may develop into the finest moment in a distinguished career on Capitol Hill," part of a larger effort to "defend an embattled internationalist agenda within his party and the U.S. Senate."[99] On September 5, Lugar joined the Democratic minority in demanding hearings on Weld's nomination. Reported by the press as taking intensive Spanish lessons, Weld meanwhile appeared on September 7 on *This Week,* apparently with the White House's blessing. Although he avoided directly criticizing Helms, he said that his suppression of a hearing was "not the American way." The main issue, he said, was whether the Senate would fulfill "not only its responsibility but its duty to hold a hearing." In a speech at American University on September 9, Clinton urged hearings. But the pro-Weld campaign bore little fruit. Lott, supporting Helms, declared the nomination "dead" and urged the White House to withdraw it.[100]

Helms agreed to a committee meeting on September 12, but he insisted that it was not a hearing about Weld's nomination. He relented to committee members' insistence on a committee meeting, Thiessen remembered, but their move was a "terrible blunder" because it played to Helms's strength: his ability to manipulate parliamentary procedure. Staffers set up the meeting so that the witness table, normally in front of the senators, was moved to the back of the room, and they had interns occupying the front row seats. Sitting with his wife in the spectators' section, Weld encountered Helms in the corridor; Helms asked him sarcastically if he had his visa to Mexico. Maintaining a firm grip on the proceedings, Helms permitted only a brief statement from Joe Biden, the ranking Democrat on the committee, and he prevented other senators—including Lugar, who was described as smiling "wanly" throughout the meeting—from speaking. Lugar was challenging his authority as chair and, by implication, was challenging "the authority of all other committee chairmen, now and in the future." When Paul Wellstone interrupted, insisting that others should have the chance to speak, Jesse gaveled him down. The meeting's "sole purpose," he said, was to discuss past nominations that had failed because of committee chairs who had denied hearings; Jesse's staff produced 154 such instances in the previous decade, which were displayed on large posters, including instances of both Biden and Lugar exercising their power as committee chairs. In opposing the Weld nomination, Helms had "a lot of company." Monopolizing almost all of the half-hour meeting, Helms charged that Weld had made a "plethora of self-serving declarations to the news media"; his statements over the past two months suggested that he did not have the "foggiest notion of what he was talking about." Looking in Weld's direction, Helms declared: "I do not yield, Mr. Weld, to ideological extortion." To the possibility of Weld waging a war within the Republican Party, Jesse responded: "Let him try!"

Helms had consulted with Majority Leader Trent Lott ahead of time, and they discovered a Senate rule under which no committee could meet two hours after the full Senate went into session. Lott agreed to call the Senate in session; it was further arranged that another senator would object to the Foreign Relations Committee meeting, and Jesse had practiced a statement that he read to the committe, timing it to make sure that it used up precisely half an hour. Once he had finished speaking, Helms then declared the meeting over promptly at noon, and he ended the proceedings. Democrat Dianne Feinstein complained that this was the "first time I have felt ashamed" to be in the Senate; John Kerry characterized the meeting as a "triumph of rules over reason and of confrontation over common sense." Afterward, Biden, Lugar, and Weld met with reporters. Denouncing the spectacle, Weld claimed that Helms was "set on a course" to "prove that the United States Senate" was a "despotic institution." But in the end, according to Thiessen, this was another example in which Helms had "masterfully used the Senate rules and his prerogatives as chairman." Thiessen remembered that after the meeting one of the committee's junior members wrote Helms a note. "Awed" by what he had done as chair, he thanked him for teaching him a lesson about running a committee.[101]

Following the committee meeting, President Clinton announced that the battle was "not over yet," while Michael McCurry, the White House spokesman, announced that the president "absolutely will not send another nominee." Appearing on *Meet the Press* on September 14, Weld promised to fight on. The committee meeting a few days earlier had made him feel "a little bit ashamed to be an American citizen." The struggle over his nomination demonstrated that Helms was dominating Republican affairs, though he hoped that public outrage might force things. Lott, appearing the same day on *Face the Nation,* declared that Weld had acted "really outrageously" toward Helms and Senate traditions, having pursued the nomination in "absolutely the wrong way." The majority leader urged Clinton to abandon the nomination.[102] The Weld nomination was thus effectively dead, despite his defiant rhetoric. On the same night as Weld's *Meet the Press* appearance, Clinton told deputy chief of staff John Podesta that he was considering withdrawal. By the morning of the 15th, Weld, realizing the hopelessness of his nomination, met with the president in the Oval Office and withdrew from consideration in a White House news conference.[103]

Nearly a decade later, Thiessen described the fight over Weld's nomination as a "pivotal" moment. Helms had opposed the nomination primarily because he regarded Weld as weak on drugs, and representing the United States in a country such as Mexico sent the wrong message, he believed. But the policy issues were less important than Helms's authority as Foreign

Relations chair. Once the fight had begun, Thiessen later observed, "if you win your power grows exponentially, and if you lose your power dissipates." The Weld nomination had evolved into a larger struggle with the Clinton administration and with Helms's rivals on the committee, Biden and Lugar. This was a test about his ability to exercise his power, and he had passed the test. If he had lost, the chairmanship would have been "hobbled," but, because he won, his power grew and affected everything else subsequently. The Weld nomination, according to Thiessen, was an "epic power struggle" with much more at stake than an ambassadorial nomination.[104]

HELMS CONTINUED TO oppose Clinton on other fronts. Remaining a persistent gadfly, he prevented the president from appointing a judge to the 4th U.S. Circuit Court of Appeals. Due primarily to appointments by Reagan in the 1980s, the 4th Circuit had a reputation as the most conservative appeals court in the country. In 1990, Congress had added a seat to the court, but Jesse's choice for the new seat in 1991, North Carolina conservative (and Tom Ellis's son-in-law) Terrence Boyle, faced Democratic stalling that killed the nomination. Clinton chose a series of African Americans— Charles Becton in 1993, James Beaty, Jr., in 1996, and James A. Wynn, Jr., in 1999—but Helms blocked the nominations, and in 1995 he killed the nomination of white attorney Rich Leonard. The seat, along with that of retiring circuit court judge Dixon Phillips, Jr., thus remained unfilled through the 1990s, and the 4th Circuit had no North Carolina member. Jesse was retaliating for Boyle's failed nomination. Boyle "never even got the courtesy of a hearing," Helms complained, and he wanted "some redress for the mistreatment of our nominee by the Democrats." Further, based on a study by Iowa senator Charles Grassley and the testimony in 1997 of 4th Circuit chief judge J. Harvie Wilkinson to a Senate subcommittee, Helms maintained that additional 4th Circuit seats were unnecessary, and he introduced legislation to have them eliminated. Back-channel negotiations with the Clinton administration occurred and, though they came close to a settlement, an impasse remained. In July 2000, when Clinton nominated another African American, Virginia lawyer Roger L. Gregory—in effect, giving up on providing a seat to a North Carolinian—Jesse continued in opposition. At the NAACP's annual meeting, Clinton sharply criticized Helms, calling the situation "outrageous" and suggesting that racial motives were guiding him. Gregory's appointment occurred only after Clinton made it as a recess appointment, while shortly before leaving office he resubmitted the Wynn nomination (although Jesse continued to block it). Still, Helms's obstruction had a long-term impact in preserving the 4th Circuit as one of the most conservative appeals courts in the country.[105]

Helms exercised leverage over other nominations. In October 1999, after Clinton nominated former senator Carol Moseley Braun as ambassador to New Zealand, newspaper reports revived accounts of their clash over the Confederate flag in the summer of 1993. Telling a reporter that she should apologize for the problems she caused "a wonderful group of little old ladies," Helms quipped that she "better look for another line of work." But the thrust of his criticism concerned Moseley Braun's ethics. Her Republican opponent in her 1998 reelection campaign, Peter Fitzgerald, raised questions about financial irregularities and about a controversial trip that she took in 1996 to meet Nigerian dictator General Sani Abacha, and Moseley Braun lost the election.[106] The nomination, Helms said, thus came with an "ethical cloud." Illinois voters had already decided that she was unfit to be senator. Before committing any further, he asked that the Clinton administration forward "essential papers" about her. If charges against her were false, Helms told a reporter, "she'll get a hearing and we'll let her be voted on." There was "nothing racial about this thing, never has been," he insisted.[107]

Soon, the *Washington Post* was describing Moseley Braun's nomination as "pretty much dead." Helms, meanwhile, experienced heightened press scrutiny. In one encounter, a *Chicago Tribune* reporter, Michael Dorning, caught Helms in the Capitol and asked him if he still insisted on an apology from Moseley Braun for the 1993 Confederate flag debate. Jim Rosen, from the *Raleigh News and Observer*, then asked him about charges that his opposition to Moseley Braun was racially motivated. "I don't like her," Helms responded. "I didn't admire her as a senator, but I would not have liked her if she was lily-white. Race has nothing to do with it." Helms became more visibly angry. "Is that all you can ask about?" he said. "If the world comes crumbling down, is that all you can ask about? You're not worth a damn as a journalist." Jesse, by then riding in a scooter because of knee surgery, abruptly gunned his cart, running over Rosen's foot.[108]

In the end, the White House and Helms met halfway. On October 26, Jesse indicated that the nomination could go forward if the White House supplied some documents from the Justice Department and IRS regarding their looks at the ethics charges against Moseley Braun. Helms backed off of his earlier bellicose statements, reflecting his isolation in the Senate. Jesse's opposition to the nomination could hurt the Republican Party, and Helms was forced to permit hearings to occur on November 5. He refused to attend the hearings, however, and when the nomination came to the Senate floor on November 9, he was one of two senators voting against it.

There had been, he charged, a "successful coverup of serious ethical wrongdoing." He had watched the November 5 committee hearings on C-SPAN, and it was a "sight to behold," a "political rally lacking only a band and the distribution of free hot dogs, soda pop and balloons."[109]

THE END OF 1995 thus brought a new role for Helms into sharp relief. In another battle of his senatorial career, he had taken on the Clinton White House and the Democratic minority with a radical proposal to restructure the foreign policy bureaucracy. Much of Helms's war was against the foreign aid bureaucracy, and he used the power of his chairmanship to advance his objectives. Using the senatorial privilege of a hold, which could be placed on AID overseas projects, Jesse delayed projects in the former Soviet Union, Africa, and South America, prevented funding for presidential elections in Haiti, and blocked projects in Nicaragua and India. All told, in 1995 Helms imposed some eighty-four such holds—a much larger number than in the past. Meanwhile, Helms's staff requested all AID publications and asked for frequent staff briefings. AID officials complained that these demands seemed like a deliberate effort to undermine the work of the agency by requiring a large amount of staff time and communicating the message that Helms would exert close scrutiny over AID projects. But Helms's intense activity as Foreign Relations chair meant that he had very little time left to spend on social issues, and after 1995 he moved into an exclusive focus on foreign policy. With his last reelection campaign over, his previous emphasis on social issues, and especially gays and AIDS, now gave way to a heightened focus on America's role in the post–Cold War world.[110]

Chapter 13

TIME TAKES A TERRIFIC TOLL

Elder Statesman

H elms advocated a vision that was sharply at odds with Clinton's internationalism, in many ways anticipating the foreign policy of George W. Bush. Although some would describe his vision as isolationist, in reality he favored an assertive American global presence. His foreign policy, vigorously nationalist, sought to complete the American victory in the Cold War by spreading liberal democratic institutions through unquestioned military power. Rejecting the humanitarian expeditions of the Clinton presidency, Helms embraced a new entrepreneurialism to foreign aid policies, and he would continue to seek fundamental reforms in the State Department's structure and in the United Nations.

IN THE POST–COLD War world, Helms championed American unilateralism. He strongly opposed a treaty, written in Rome in 1998 and signed by more than ninety-five countries, establishing the International Criminal Court, empowered to try war criminals. Previously, only the United Nations Security Council could authorize war crimes prosecutions, and this provided the United States with the security of its veto. Helms wanted this protection preserved. "I'm not going to put our servicemen in the posture of being hauled into court by some people who don't care a thing in the world about them," Helms told a reporter in July 2000.[1] Although President Clinton shared some of Helms's reservations, he favored the treaty but realized that it had no chance with Jesse as Foreign Relations Committee chair. Not long before he left the White House, in December 2000, Clinton signed the treaty in an attempt to bind incoming President Bush. By then, some 136 countries had signed the treaty, with twenty-five of the necessary sixty ratifying. Helms described Clinton's decision as "indignant and inexplicable," and he promised that it "will not stand." One of George W. Bush's first actions was to withdraw the treaty.[2]

Beginning in Clinton's first term, Jesse favored the further isolation of Fidel Castro's Cuba. In February 1995, newly installed as Foreign Relations chair, he proposed penalizing foreign firms doing business with Cuba; the legislation would also require the Clinton administration to oppose Cuban membership in the International Monetary Fund and to seek U.N. support for a global trade embargo. Helms's bill severely penalized foreign corporations that owned or traded with American property during the Cuban revolution. While the bill would also cut off aid to countries that violated the American embargo against Cuba, it also limited the flow of money from Cuban Americans to relatives in Cuba. "Whether Castro leaves Cuba in a vertical or horizontal position is up to him and the Cuban people," Helms declared in a news conference. Co-sponsored by Representative Dan R. Burton, Republican of Indiana, the Helms-Burton bill—also known as the Libertad bill—represented a major congressional intervention in foreign policy—and an attempt to prevent any liberalization of U.S.-Cuban relations. It would also formalize the U.S. trade embargo on Cuba, which up to now had been the result of executive order.[3] Although Helms-Burton languished because of White House opposition and a threatened veto, it gained new momentum after February 24, 1996, when the Cuban government shot down two private planes and killed four anti-Castro Cuban Americans. On March 12, 1996, Clinton signed the measure into law after it overwhelmingly passed both houses of Congress. At the signing, Clinton gave Helms one of the seventeen pens used to sign the bill, and Jesse gave his pen to Cuban American supporter Elena Amos. "You deserve this and I don't," he told her.[4]

For Helms, the next step in the fight over Cuba involved pressuring the White House to enforce the new law. Within months of its enactment, Clinton, fearing an uproar among American trading partners in Europe and Canada, suspended enforcement of the trade provisions; the law provided him with that power. Clinton, complained Helms in June 1996, had "once again taken a firm stand on both sides of an important issue." Helms then retaliated by holding Clinton's nomination for the assistant secretary of state for Latin American affairs.[5] Six months later, facing a furor from abroad, Clinton made the suspension permanent. Denouncing Clinton's actions as a "terrible mistake," Helms cited Mexico and Canada as two countries that possessed "shameful" trade policies toward Cuba. "I cannot understand why," he said, "just as we are beginning to make progress, the President has decided to give up the very leverage that brought such progress about."[6] Subsequently, Helms maintained pressure. In July 1997, he wrote to Clinton asserting that it was apparent that the law would be unenforced; only two companies had suffered American sanctions. He was discouraged by the president's unwillingness to enforce the law, he wrote, though he acknowledged that Clinton possessed that authority. But he accused Clinton of ignoring Title IV of the law—which contained no waiver authority and which required that visas be lifted for executives of foreign companies doing business with Cuba. Clinton, he charged, had unilaterally ignored that mandatory part of the law. Subsequently, Helms demanded that the White House provide all documents related to the enforcement of the law.[7]

Suspicious of the diplomatic bureaucracy, Jesse had long wanted structural changes in the State Department and United Nations. Frustrated in his attempts to eliminate AID, ACDA, and USIA and to merge them with the State Department in 1995–96—Clinton vetoed a compromise bill in 1996—Helms persisted. Budget cuts reduced the size of AID's work force from 11,500 employees in 1993 to less than eight thousand by 1998; its programs operated in seventy countries, down from 120 in 1993.[8] But Helms succeeded in leveraging further concessions by linking Senate consideration of the Chemical Weapons Convention to State Department reorganization. In September 1996, Jesse blocked the treaty, which had been negotiated by the Bush administration and submitted to the Senate by Clinton in November 1993. Fearing inadequate verification and ineffective controls over outlaw countries such as Iraq and Libya, Helms, despite Clinton's strong support, continued to stall consideration of the treaty, which 161 countries had signed and more than seventy had already ratified. The Chemical Weapons Convention, he wrote in *USA Today* in September 1996, would only "improve rogue nations' access to chemical agents" while imposing restrictions on the United States. But he offered a deal to the White House. On January 29, 1997, writing to Majority Leader Lott, Helms insisted on further delay unless Clinton produced concessions on State Department reform. No progress on this treaty, he announced, would be possible until the "enactment of legislation fundamentally restructuring the antiquated foreign policy agencies of the U.S."

Clinton was eager to make concessions in order to obtain Helms's support, and he agreed to twenty-nine amendments to the Chemical Weapons Convention. In addition, in February, *U.S. News & World Report* described

an "intense, behind-the-scenes lobbying effort" to persuade Helms to compromise, and National Security Adviser Sandy Berger went to the Senate
to lobby. In late March 1997, Vice President Al Gore called Helms. Gore
told reporters that the White House was planning to review State Department reorganization and make a recommendation in the next month. "I appreciate the signal," Helms responded in an interview. "I shall signal right
back—let's work together." On March 25, Madeleine Albright visited the
Helms Center in Wingate, where she and the senator discussed the Chemical Weapons Convention and State Department reorganization. The
Helms-Albright friendship was at its height, and Jesse was quoted as saying
that "if both sides will sit down and be realistic about it, there is a very real
chance of approving the treaty." In a speech at Wingate, Albright urged the
adoption of the chemical weapons treaty, which, she said, was part of an effort to control weapons of mass destruction—those weapons that could
"kill horribly, massively." Although Helms's argument that the treaty could
not be verified was "sincerely made," she declared, "to me it is not convincing." "We cannot let the bad guys write the rules." Subsequently, Helms
aides stressed that the negotiations were continuing; according to Jesse,
"reports of my capitulation have been greatly exaggerated." Helms experienced some pressure to resist compromise, as the Republican right opposed
the chemical weapons ban. On the other hand, Lott favored compromise.
Facing strong opposition from conservatives, Lott pushed forward, and dispatched his aide Randy Scheunemann to determine from the Senate parliamentarian whether he could free the treaty from Helms's grasp. After Bob
Dole announced support for ratification, a breach emerged among Republicans between what one observer called "go-it-alone nationalists led by
Jesse Helms and try-it-together internationalists led by the party's past and
present majority leaders."[9]

The impasse ended in mid-April 1997, when Helms permitted the
treaty to come to a vote with the understanding that the Clinton White
House would agree to Jesse's State Department reorganization plan. The
treaty was adopted on April 24 by a vote of 74–26; twenty-nine Republicans
joined forty-five Democrats supporting ratification. After Clinton promised
that the United States would abrogate the treaty if American security was
threatened, or if it proved unable to limit chemical weapons, Lott announced his support. Realizing that opposition to the treaty was crumbling,
Helms approached Lott on the Senate floor. The two senators clasped
shoulders. "Good statement, you can't win 'em all," Helms told Lott, who
responded: "I hope you understand. Maybe you were a victim of your suc-
cesses." Helms offered additional amendments to the treaty after it passed,

but they lost by wide margins. The adoption of the Chemical Weapons Convention became, according to the *Washington Post*, the "biggest legislative win" of Clinton's second term. But, according to Thiessen, this was not a defeat but a "sort of neutering" of the convention. More important for Helms was the victory he achieved in State Department reorganization, in which two independent agencies, AID and USIA, were eliminated and folded into the diplomatic bureaucracy. Although Secretary of State Albright made no drastic changes in foreign aid, the basis was laid for extensive change during the Bush administration.[10]

Clinton agreed, as part of the arrangement permitting a vote on the chemical weapons treaty, to support Helms's 1995–96 State Department reorganization, a major victory for the senator. On April 17, 1997, as a prelude to the chemical weapons vote, the White House announced a reorganization plan in which the State Department would absorb the Arms Control and Disarmament Agency; its head would become an undersecretary; the United States Information Agency would be eliminated and merged into State's public affairs bureau; and the Agency for International Development, though remaining autonomous, would become incorporated into the diplomatic bureaucracy and would no longer separately report to the president. Helms would later say that if he had had his way, AID would have been abolished, but the reorganization, by folding both AID and USIA into the State Department, would end AID's "often arrogant independence." He foresaw this as only one step in a "perhaps lengthy process of reinventing the foreign affairs apparatus of our government."[11]

THE CHEMICAL WEAPONS fight was part of a larger debate between Clinton and the Republican Senate over arms control. Clinton had negotiated agreements about anti-ballistic missiles (ABM) with Russia, the Kyoto Protocol to limit global warming, and an agreement on conventional forces in Europe. The Clinton administration argued that these agreements were not treaties and thus did not require Senate ratification, but Helms insisted on Senate ratification and announced to the president in January 1998 that he would not consider the Comprehensive Test Ban Treaty (CTBT) unless these agreements were submitted to the Senate. Clinton wanted to expand ABM controls to all of the nations of the former Soviet Union, but Jesse had no faith in arms control agreements and in particular in the ABM treaty, which he saw as a "dangerous arms control pact." Once Clinton agreed—at Jesse's insistence—that these agreements had to obtain Senate ratification, Helms pledged his opposition, promising to turn the debate into a "confidence vote on the entire ABM treaty along with its perverse strategic rationale, which insists that defending the American people from ballistic missile attack is somehow destabilizing." He favored an aggressive missile defense program, even if it meant abrogating the 1972 ABM treaty.

Clinton's attempt to renegotiate ABM thus faced a firewall of opposition, and Russian leader Vladimir Putin refused to negotiate because of the hopelessness of the situation. Since the CTBT would be impossible to verify, Helms's staff believed that it would place the United States, whose security depended on its nuclear arsenal, at a major disadvantage. As Foreign Relations staff director Steve Biegun later reflected, the chemical weapons treaty, though "useless," was less important because the United States had already renounced the use of these weapons. In contrast, the CTBT was simply a "bad treaty" because it was "classic superficial arms control." In February 1996, Helms introduced legislation requiring that the United States withdraw from the ABM treaty. Although Jesse's bill had little chance of success, Clinton later negotiated modifications to the treaty that clarified the use of short-range missile defense systems.[12]

In 1996, Clinton signed the CTBT, making the United States the first of 151 countries agreeing to ban all nuclear tests. When Clinton submitted the test ban treaty in September 1997, Helms delayed hearings for nearly two years, insisting that the United States–Russia ABM negotiations should come before the Senate for consideration. When India resumed nuclear testing in 1998, moreover, Helms said that this had shown that the treaty would be "scarcely more than a sham." On January 21, 1997, Helms informed Clinton that there would be no hearings about the test ban treaty unless the Senate could consider the ABM issue. The president had "unwisely and unnecessarily engaged in delay," he wrote, "in submitting these treaties to the Senate for its advice and consent."[13] In July 1999, the *Washington Post* complained that Helms had the CTBT in a "parliamentary grip," held hostage to his "personal agenda." "In hijacking the test ban," it asserted, the senator was "unswayed by the argument that in fairness the Senate deserves an opportunity to debate and judge the treaty on its merits."[14]

In early October 1999, Jesse abruptly shifted tactics by agreeing to an immediate vote on the treaty, without hearings. The treaty's supporters had been pressing for a vote; "they attacked," recalled Foreign Relations staff director Steve Biegun, "and they weren't ready."[15] Realizing that treaty supporters lacked the votes, Helms saw an opportunity to inflict a major defeat on the Clinton administration. When Democrats objected to rushing the treaty forward without committee hearings, Helms responded that the treaty had been discussed on fourteen occasions during the past nineteen months. Although no formal hearings had actually occurred, he listed the occasions in the *Congressional Record* and accused the media of not reporting the story. The same people "clamoring for action," he said, now went "running for the hills. If it were not so pitiful, this behavior would be amusing. I am not going to let senators have it both ways."[16]

Working with anti-treaty allies such as Arizona senator John Kyl, Helms had laid a trap. In April, Kyl, whom Biegun described as "more instrumental" in the anti-treaty efforts "than Helms in the end," learned that Clinton was planning an international conference in September 1999 to rally support for the treaty.[17] Fearing that this would serve as a springboard to a ratification effort, Kyl mobilized Republican opposition, lining up votes, preparing briefing books, and lobbying intensively. By late September 1999, an anti-CTBT group that included Helms, Lott, Georgia senator Paul Coverdell, and Kyl, counted forty-four solid votes against the treaty—well beyond the necessary thirty-four votes—and they agreed to move the treaty out of committee. In what the *National Review* called a tactical mistake by the Democrats of "major proportions," Minority Leader Tom Daschle agreed to schedule a vote after twenty-two hours of debate. Because treaty opponents already had a solid bloc of supporters behind them, the agreement spelled the treaty's doom. In early October, Clinton mounted a determined effort to persuade undecided Republicans; at a White House dinner, the president, angry and frustrated, reportedly hit the table and told the group that Lott had him "by the short hairs." On October 8, Helms held one-day hearings, where opponents described the treaty's weaknesses. Even Lugar, who had often supported the administration, turned against the White House.

At the last minute, CTBT supporters tried to save the treaty. Helms and Majority Leader Lott permitted the White House a way out: just as Jimmy Carter had done with SALT II in 1979, treaty supporters could withdraw the CTBT from consideration, but only on the condition that they not bring it back up during the current congressional term. The White House refused, and on October 8, Clinton, in Canada to meet with Prime Minister Jean Chrétien, urged delay but would not provide an ironclad guarantee that the treaty would be removed from consideration. Rejecting the treaty, Clinton said a day later, would be a "dangerous U-turn" from American leadership in arms control. Helms's approach was to "negotiate up": as it became obvious that the treaty lacked the votes, the senator renewed his offer to permit the treaty to be withdrawn, but he insisted that the president put his withdrawal in writing.[18] As the vote approached, there was a move toward compromise. On October 12, the day before the scheduled vote, sixty-two senators supported a compromise in order to avoid the international embarrassment of a rejected treaty. Under this compromise, the White House agreed to delay consideration until after the 2000 election. But, for Helms and his supporters, the time for compromise was over, and the White House, as Biegun recalled, "never understood how bad their situation was."[19] Late on the afternoon of October 12, Helms, in his trademark motorized scooter, headed from the Senate cloakroom to Lott's spacious office and informed him that any compromise was unacceptable and would lead to "an internal Republican bloodbath."

The Republican majority leader thus did not repeat his betrayal in the Chemical Weapons Convention of two years earlier. Clinton and his supporters were outfoxed, overconfident, and perhaps a little indifferent. Calling the CTBT "the most egregious arms control treaty ever presented to this body for its advice and consent," Helms denounced it in a Senate speech. Because the treaty was unverifiable, its defeat would aid the future security of the United States. Clinton was now a lame duck, and future presidents should be "unencumbered by the failed policies of the current, outgoing administration." There should be a "clean break" for a future administration, and credibility should rest not on "scraps of paper, but on clear American resolve." The treaty's defeat would also send an important message to Clinton and future presidents. "This administration, and future administrations," he said, "will henceforth think twice before signing more bad treaties which cannot pass muster in the United States Senate." A last-minute, desperate effort by Albright to reach Helms on the senate floor was unsuccessful: matters had now gone too far, and the senator refused to take her call. Turning to an aide, Helms asked why Albright was insistent. Because she thought that she was your friend, the aide responded. Albright, Helms replied, "was about to learn the limits of our friendship."

In the end, the CTBT fight resulted in the most significant foreign policy defeat of the Clinton presidency: by a vote of 51–48, the Senate rejected the treaty, in what *Newsweek* called "the most dramatic repudiation of an international treaty since the Senate failed to endorse the creation of the League of Nations in 1920." Bitter feelings prevailed after the defeat of the treaty, which marked a turning point in the arms control history of the United States. Clinton denounced Helms and the anti-arms-control forces that he represented. "Imagine the world we will live in if they prevail," he told reporters. "I think it will be a bleak, poor, less-secure world. And I don't want my children or my grandchildren or your children and your grandchildren to live in it." He predicted the triumph of opponents of arms control would lead to a buildup of nuclear weapons and of the military generally. "This same crowd," he predicted, "would be coming in and saying... 'We

need you to increase the budget for all this, to the labs and Pentagon, by another 30, 40, 50 billion dollars a year. So I'm sorry, we'll just have to get out
of the business of funding education. We can't afford to invest any more in
health care." In a speech to the Council on Foreign Relations in New York,
Clinton's national security adviser, Sandy Berger, criticized Congress' isolationist right, which held, he believed, a "distinctly defeatist" approach to foreign relations that favored a "survivalist foreign policy—build a fortified
fence around America, retreat behind it." The Senate's rejection of the
treaty, said the *Washington Post,* was a "product of short-term domestic political calculation" that would have a chilling effect on arms control. This reflected the Republicans' "recklessness" and their "determination to push
ahead now for partisan advantage." The criticism left Helms unfazed. The
Senate had rejected the CTBT because it was a "dangerous and unverifiable
treaty that would have endangered the safety and reliability of the U.S. nuclear arsenal and undermined U.S. security and the security of our allies," he
wrote in the *Wall Street Journal.* He did not "give a doodle" what supporters
of the treaty thought of him, and this was "just liberals singing their song."
Those people who claimed that an overwhelming proportion of Americans
favored the treaty relied on the same pollsters who "can't understand why
I've been elected five times to the Senate." Helms blamed Clinton for the
treaty's failure. He had provided a written promise that he would send the
ABM and global warming agreements to the Senate for consideration, but
he reneged. "His word is no good," he claimed.[20]

HELMS HAD, SINCE the 1950s, disliked the United Nations and its
mulilateralism. In the 1990s, he led Congress' refusal to pay about $1.3 bil-
lion in U.S. dues to the U.N., citing corruption and inefficiency under the
administration of U.N. secretary general Boutros Boutros-Ghali. Helms
also feared that the U.N. would assert its power at the expense of American
sovereignty. A large portion of the U.S. arrears resulted from U.N. peacekeeping missions that were failures, and the Clinton administration had
avoided seeking congressional appropriations to pay for them. In Bosnia,
U.N. peacekeeping had been "absolutely feckless," remembered Steve
Biegun, and its involvement had done nothing to prevent the massacre of
Bosnian Muslims. Clinton's policy had been to avoid intervention in the
former Yugoslav republics; Helms's staff had demanded action. Avoiding
congressional financial support for peacekeeping—and then permitting
American support to go into arrears—became a "backdoor way" of obtaining congressional authorization. Helms and his staffers considered support

for ineffective U.N. peacekeeping in Bosnia to be "blood money," and the result was a deadlock over U.S. support for the U.N.[21]

Nonpayment of U.S. dues could have crippled the organization, as the United States was responsible for a quarter of the U.N.'s budget. In the fall 1996 issue of *Foreign Affairs,* Helms laid out a program of reform. The United Nations, he claimed, had become bloated, bureaucratic, and anti-American. Boutros-Ghali wanted a "standing U.N. army and the power to collect direct U.N. taxes." Helms proposed budget cuts that would reduce the U.N. bureaucracy by half and the secretariat's budget by 75 percent, and he also proposed that member nations be permitted to pay only for those measures that they supported. Helms opposed a second five-year term for Boutros Boutros-Ghali—even though he secretly had dinner with him in New York—because he was an aggressive globalist. Because they regarded him as symbol of U.N. ineffectiveness, the Clinton administration also opposed Boutros-Ghali, and, in 1997, Kofi Annan of Ghana would succeed him. Helms believed that the U.N.'s peacekeeping missions had grown out of control, and the U.N.'s role in the world remained ill-defined. Reform, wrote Helms, was a "gargantuan and perhaps impossible task," but if it could not be accomplished, the organization was "not worth saving." In that event, "I, for one, will be leading the charge for U.S. withdrawal."[22]

In early 1997, Helms recommended legislative benchmarks for reform: if the United Nations agreed to specific Helms proposals, the U.N. would receive American funding in installments. After Annan became secretary general in January 1997, one of his first actions was to visit Washington, at Helms's invitation, to confer with Clinton and the senator. During his visit on January 23, Helms "blindsided" Annan with a surprise announcement about his benchmark/installment repayment plan, and the secretary general, off guard, responded by reassuring Jesse of his "firm commitment" to U.N. reform. Helms announced before the meeting that these discussions suggested "the beginning of an on-going dialogue between us, that we can work together to bring real reform to the United Nations." Among Helms's most important proposals was the reduction of Annan's staff by 25 percent, and there remained significant differences for much of the spring of 1997. When Annan proposed cutting one thousand jobs and $123 million from the budget, Helms spokesman Marc Thiessen called this a "shell game" containing "repackaged ideas from old, discredited reform proposals."[23] A wide gap remained between the U.N. and Helms, whose positions, editorialized the *Washington Post,* remained solidified in an "antique isolationist fashion" that signified "sheer destruction."[24]

In the end, Helms's U.N. proposals prevailed. With the support of

Democratic senators and the White House, Helms introduced legislation providing for the repayment of $819 million in back dues; Congress would also forgive $106 million that the U.N. supposedly owed the United States. Helms's legislation provided for a phased repayment linked to Helms's benchmarks, and it also required that the United States pay a reduced percentage of the total U.N. budget (from 25 to 20 percent over three years). This was a "pretty good deal, the whole ball of wax," Joe Biden, the ranking minority member on the Foreign Relations Committee, declared. He supported the proposals, which became known as the Helms-Biden bill. Although Annan was unenthusiastic, he appeared to have little choice but to accept.[25] But the Helms-Biden U.N. compromise became stalled after New Jersey Republican Christopher Smith attached a rider to the bill stipulating that no U.S. funds could be used in support of international abortion programs. During the 1980s, Reagan had banned the use of aid funds to support abortion; Clinton reversed this when he took office. After Clinton threatened a veto of Smith's rider, Helms-Biden stalled for another two years but finally passed Congress and was signed by the president in December 1999. It contained the basic parameters of Helms's U.N. reform legislation: the United States would repay $926 million, but the money was contingent on U.N. reforms. Subsequently, intensive lobbying by the Clinton administration led to a deal with U.N. member nations a year later, on December 23, 2000. Under its terms, U.S. regular dues decreased from 25 to 22 percent of the total budget, while its share of peacekeeping costs was cut from 31 to 26 percent.[26]

Helms's U.N. campaign culminated with an invitation, engineered by United States ambassador to the United Nations Richard Holbrooke (who was serving as rotating chair of this body), to address the Security Council on January 20, 2000. During his confirmation, Holbrooke had urged Helms to visit the U.N.; in December 1999, he renewed the invitation. Also instrumental in persuading Helms was Charlotte civic leader Irvin Belk, who served as an honorary U.N. alternate. Holbrooke, who had brokered the peace accords in 1995 ending the long and bloody war in Bosnia, had developed an effective working relationship with the senator. When Holbrooke came up for confirmation, Helms's staff prepared a detailed series of questions focusing on his financial dealings; Helms announced that the Foreign Relations Committee would hold five days of hearings. Albright's State Department was "leaking like a sieve," according to Biegun, and there was little love lost between Holbrooke and the secretary of state. But Holbrooke won the senator over by offering testimony that directly accepted responsibility for his financial activities. Holbrooke and Helms then developed what Holbrooke described as a "very productive collaboration." Jesse "told you where he stood," Holbrooke said, and "he stuck to it." Helms, for his part, genuinely liked and respected Holbrooke.[27]

The first American congressman ever to speak before the United Nations Security Council, Helms was invited as part of a group to discuss U.S.-U.N. relations. Holbrooke wanted him to come to the U.N. to solidify congressional support, but he decided against a General Assembly speech because too many of Helms's old adversaries—such as Cuba and Mexico—would attend. The Security Council offered a more controlled environment.[28] Accompanied by the members of the Foreign Relations Committee (he would hold a "field hearing" about U.N. reform), Jesse brought along Dot and daughter Jane Knox, and they met privately with Kofi Annan. "Welcome to the house of peace," Annan reportedly told Helms. Jesse took the occasion to make an address laying out general principles.[29] He worked on the speech with his chief speechwriter, Marc Thiessen, and he rewrote the draft on his manual typewriter. New York City had just had an ice storm before their arrival, and Thiessen slipped and broke his arm. But Thiessen was determined not to miss the event, and he watched the speech with his arm in a sling. Holbrooke was "having kittens" in anticipation of the speech, according to Steve Biegun, who heard that the White House was worried that Helms might use the speech to attack Al Gore, who was running for president. The night before the speech, Holbrooke visited Helms and his party at the Waldorf-Astoria hotel in New York, hoping to see an advance copy. When Helms's staff provided him a copy, Holbrooke was "greatly relieved" to discover nothing about the vice president in the speech.[30]

Helms had instructed Thiessen to draft a speech that had an "iron fist" contained in a "velvet glove." He intended to provide a warning to the United Nations that it should not reject Helms-Biden; such an opportunity would not happen again. Jesse began his speech by joking that he hoped that there was a translator available "who can speak Southern" and announcing his ignorance of the "elegant and rarefied language of the diplomatic trade." Helms came representing what he said was widespread resentment among Americans about the U.N.; its prevalent anti-Americanism had made them grow "increasingly frustrated with what they feel is a lack of gratitude." To the charge that the United States had been a "deadbeat" member, Helms pointed out that American military support of U.N. operations in 1999 cost nearly $9 billion. Americans expected the U.N. not only to respect American sovereignty, but to operate more effectively and more efficiently. Helms urged the U.N. to accept the recently enacted Helms-Biden compromise. The alternative, he said, was a further erosion of U.S.-U.N. relations and a breach that "would have served the interests of no one." Reminding his audience of Woodrow Wilson's failure to persuade the Senate to accept the League of Nations, he told them that Clinton's acceptance of this compromise had saved American participation. The United Nations was not an end unto itself: Helms asserted a strong belief in uncompromised American power, and the U.N. was only "one part of America's diplomatic arsenal." Only to the extent that the U.N. was effective would Americans support it; if the U.N. became ineffective, "the American people will cast it aside." The U.N.'s chief purpose, Helms said, was to coordinate "coalitions of the willing" and provide a forum for communication during crises, while it should also provide peacekeeping and humanitarian relief. These were "core tasks" beyond which the U.N. should not venture. Helms further admonished the organization not to become a "central authority of a new international order of global laws and global governance." He concluded with these strong words: "A United Nations that seeks to impose its presumed authority on the American people without their consent begs for confrontation and, I want to be candid, eventual U.S. withdrawal."[31]

Jesse's blunt talk did not fall on receptive ears. Following his speech, some ambassadors pointed out that the United States had not paid its U.N. dues; the U.N. "expected the United States to keep its word," said Russian ambassador Sergey Lavrov. Nor had the United States always observed the sovereignty of other countries; Namibian ambassador Martin Andjaba reminded Helms that he had supported white regimes in southern Africa. After Helms said in his speech that "Fidel Castro claims that it is his sovereign right to oppress his people," the Cuban ambassador, Bruno Rodríguez Parrilla, rushed to the front and attempted, unsuccessfully, to speak.[32] Helms's address was more pointed than either Annan or Albright had anticipated. Albright, whose relations with Holbrooke were often testy, was not informed when Holbrooke authorized television cameras to broadcast the speech. According to one story, Albright was in her office, and when she turned on her television she was shocked to see Jesse. This was a "bold move" by Holbrooke, and Albright "hit the roof." Albright was thus determined to reassert some leadership by smoothing over hurt feelings about Jesse's speech. Most Americans saw "our role in the world and our relationship to this organization quite differently than does Senator Helms," she told the Security Council a day later, while Biden and Holbrooke both tried to assure U.N. officials that Helms's visit marked a positive step forward. Helms was a "man of conviction, and a strong advocate of a distinct point of view about the United Nations and America's relationship to it," Albright declared, but only the president "can speak for the United States."[33]

Helms' visit to the United Nations provided evidence of a new "Helmsmanship"—and an attempt to impart a foreign policy legacy. There were other examples of Jesse's late-career statesmanship. The first was his changed attitude toward Mexico, a country that he had often criticized as corrupt, drug-infested, and a source of illegal immigrants. As recently as 1995, Helms had opposed the Clinton administration's efforts to bail out the collapsing peso. In Mexico, Helms was known as a leading opponent and critic; one reporter called him "the most recognized person in the U.S. government besides the president." A Mexican expert described Jesse as the "icon of Mexico bashing" in that country. His decision to visit Mexico early in the George W. Bush administration was thus highly significant. The election of Vicente Fox in 2000 as president and the end of the seventy-one-year rule of the Institutional Revolutionary Party (PRI) suggested that the country's political system might be undergoing change. In February 2001, Jesse wrote a piece for *Reforma,* a Mexican newspaper, in which he warned Fox to avoid the "militantly defensive posture of the old PRI authoritarians" that had run Mexico but urged Bush and Fox to work "to facilitate lawful immigration that benefits both countries." Helms denounced the "absurd suggestion that the United States somehow owes Mexico an apology for policing our own border." Fox's foreign minister, Jorge Castañeda, visited Washington, and during a meeting, Helms proposed that he visit Mexico. The success of his U.N. visit encouraged him to try another trip; four Foreign Relations Committee members, all Republicans, would join him on the trip, which occurred on April 16–18, 2001. Helms and his staffers were aware of the comparisons with the U.N. visit. The U.N. similarly had new leadership in Kofi Annan, leadership that was seeking change that Helms sought to encourage; both Mexico and the U.N. were also frequent targets. Helms's visit to Mexico would mark the first time that a congressional committee would hold a joint meeting with a committee of another country's parliament on foreign soil. Helms called the meeting a "historic first," and he saw it as a way to solidify the friendship between Bush and Fox. Traveling aboard Vice President Dick Cheney's Air Force Two, Helms faced hard questions in Mexico. Fox sought support for major changes in U.S. immigration policy that would legalize the status of millions of undocumented Mexicans in the United States and permit more to immigrate legally. In the end, Jesse's visit to Mexico, despite the hopes accompanying it, pointed up significant differences between Helms and the new government, especially on the issues of drug smuggling and Mexico's longtime friendship with Cuba.[34]

Helms's visit to Mexico occasioned some speculation that he had undergone a transformation into a "kinder, gentler" Jesse. This was a time of transition. His old friend and chief foreign policy adviser Bud Nance died, after a bout with leukemia, in May 1999; the old hands that had been with him as advisers were now gone. In combination with his visit to the U.N. Security Council, observers noted that Jesse was looking toward his legacy. Helms was seeking a "more positive record to be remembered by, not just as a curmudgeonly, ideologically hostile" Foreign Relations Committee chairman, said veteran Washington observer Thomas Mann. Jesse worked closely with Joe Biden in managing the committee; the alliance with Biden seemed to soften partisan lines. Helms wanted "to make the committee relevant," Biden said, and Jesse believed that "he will be judged more by what he does than by what he doesn't do." Much of the assessment of a "kinder, gentler" Helms was, of course, an exaggeration, and he continued to oppose Clinton's policies and to serve as a leading spokesman for conservative causes. Helms's change should more properly be understood as a shift in strategy: no longer in opposition, he chaired the most powerful committee in the Senate. During his tenure as chair, he thus moved into a different role: rather than a guerrilla fighter, he became a shaper of policy.[35]

Jesse's friendship with the Irish rock singer Paul Hewson—better known as U2's Bono—provided another example of Helmsmanship. On September 20, 2000, Bono visited Helms in his office to lobby for relief for Third World countries suffering under an enormous debt owed to western countries. In many instances, rapacious governments no longer in power had incurred large debts, and crushing interest payments were preventing the current governments from providing basic services. In the late 1990s, industrialized countries sought to reduce the $216 billion debt owed by the HIPC (Heavily Indebted Poor Countries). Earlier that year, the Clinton White House proposed that $435 million in debt be forgiven; while the Senate responded by appropriating $75 million, the House increased this to $125 million. Bono, who made debt relief a personal cause, met with Helms in his office, and he was escorted by Representative John Kasich, an Ohio Republican, who had befriended Bono because of their shared religious faith. Bono did not describe himself as a Christian, though he had once belonged to a Christian commune. But he was spiritual and thoroughly familiar with biblical imagery, and he searched for a common ground with the Republican right. Long interested in Africa, Bono had participated in Live Aid, an effort by rock musicians in 1984 to provide assistance to famine victims in Ethiopia. Along with his wife, in 1984 he traveled to Africa and spent weeks working in an orphanage. In 1999, he joined forces with a European evangelical group, Jubilee 2000, which was campaigning for African debt relief. By 2000, Bono took his campaign to Washington and the Republican Congress. "The great thing about hanging out with Republicans," Bono later said, was that it was "very, very unhip for both of us." "We have to take 'good guys' and 'bad guys' out of this and just have a dialogue," he said on another occasion. "I couldn't disagree more with Senator Helms on some issues," Bono declared, but he realized that he needed the senator's help. Bono's lobbying efforts were part of what the British newspaper the *Guardian* would describe as "an assiduous effort to court Washington's Republican elite" and to construct an alliance of Christian evangelicals, Bush supporters, AIDS activists, and supporters of foreign aid. U2 guitarist The Edge was skeptical: he told Bono "not to hang out with the conservatives." "I'd have lunch with Satan if there was so much at stake," Bono responded.

Bono spoke with Anne Chitwood, Helms's scheduler, and, a fan of U2, she immediately agreed to a meeting. She and Jimmy Broughton then went to Jesse to try to convince him. "I don't want to see any rock star," he said. "Why does he want to see me?" "Go home tonight and call your grandkids," Broughton responded, "and ask them if you should meet with Bono." Arriving the next morning, Helms declared: "What time is he coming in?" Arriving at Helms's office with his entourage at about 5:30 P.M., Bono was scheduled for a twenty-minute courtesy call that turned into a much longer meeting. Helms had met with celebrities before: earlier he had seen John Travolta, who was lobbying for protections for Scientology in Germany. Bono, according to Broughton, understood the issues, and he had a thorough command of the facts. He described the privation and misery that most African children faced, while he described their plight in biblical terms. According to Bono's account, he sought conservative Republicans such as Helms because of their common connection through Christianity. Helms had been "very tough" about foreign aid and "very bleak" about AIDS. "He's a religious man," recalled Bono, "so I told him that 2,103 verses of scripture pertain to the poor and Jesus speaks of judgment only once—and it's not about being gay or sexual morality, but about poverty." Bono quoted Matthew 25:36: "I was naked and you clothed me." Bono also discussed the Jubilee Year, and the notion, appearing in Leviticus, that slaves should be free and people liberated from their debts every forty-nine years.

Bono and Helms were an unlikely pair: the unshaven rocker appeared in the senator's office in a dark green suit, with his shirttails out. After Bono's presentation, the senator was described as "really moved," and he told a reporter that he was "deeply impressed" at Bono's "depth." Bono had been "led by the Lord to do something about the starving people in Africa." Jesse told him, with tears streaming down his face, "You can have your four

hundred and thirty-five million dollars. You can have more." Kasich recalled that the meeting "may have been the most amazing meeting I was
ever in." "If I ever thought I could contribute to helping save lives like you
do, Mr. Bono," Helms reportedly said, "I would leave the Senate and I
would go and do what you do." Although Helms's staffers described the
meeting differently—the senator did not cry, according to their account,
nor did he mention leaving the Senate—they agreed that the meeting had
affected Jesse, and, with his support, Clinton signed legislation on November 6, 2000, that provided the full $435 million.

Bono and Helms made a connection at that meeting. Although he
thought Helms "was going to spit on me," Bono recalled that "we bonded."
He had met "many moral men" in Washington, Bono wrote, but "none as
forthright in their despair about the state of the third world as yourself." He
noted that he had watched Jesse's eyes "redden with the same despair" that
Bono had about the unwillingness to help Africa. God, Bono wrote, was
"angrier and sadder than you or I." About Bono, Helms would later say:
"You can see the halo over his head." His meeting with Bono, Jesse wrote in
November 2000, "left me with an enormous respect for you and for your
genuine concern for the African people and...especially those precious
children." The Helms-Bono relationship was mutually beneficial: while it
provided a new aura of statesmanship for Helms, it provided cover among
conservatives for Bono.[36]

Although much would be made of Helms's conversion and Bono's role
in it, the senator's approach to foreign aid had already changed. A loyal
supporter of white minority governments in Rhodesia and South Africa
and a critic of black Africa, he now advocated humanitarian assistance to
the continent. There was some consistency in Jesse's approach: when he
criticized the "foreign rat-holes" of foreign aid, he was attacking the inefficiency of Washington bureaucracy, which funneled money toward corrupt
foreign governments, not aid recipients. Helms favored instead a new system of foreign aid that went directly to recipients through networks of private, mostly church-affiliated groups. Helms was especially swayed by the
efforts of Franklin Graham, son of Billy Graham, who had been involved in
African aid through his organization, Samaritan's Purse. Conversations
with Graham, Helms told a reporter, "had a very large impact on me in
terms of the possibility of really accomplishing something in Africa." In
July 2000, Helms had sponsored hearings by the Foreign Relations Committee about African problems, and he invited Graham to testify.[37]

The Helms-Bono alliance continued into the George W. Bush administration, when the senator called Vice President Cheney to urge the White

House to support expanded aid to poor countries. Bono orchestrated a campaign in which U2 fans sent some twenty thousand e-mail messages urging White House action. Bono's campaign for Africa embraced not just increased aid, but an expanded attempt to limit the spread of AIDS, a disease that was ravaging black Africa.[38] In March 2002, in a press conference with Bono present wearing his trademark blue sunglasses, Bush supported a three-year, $5 billion increase in aid that would be targeted to assist poor countries—the first significant increase in aid in a decade. "I'm traveling in some pretty good company today—Bono," Bush told reporters, and he described the rock star as "willing to lead to achieve what his heart tells him, and that is nobody—nobody—should be living in poverty and hopelessness in the world."[39]

The Helms-Bono friendship attracted widespread media attention. On June 14, 2001, Jesse attended a U2 concert in Washington with his grandchildren; the night before, he and Bono had dinner together. Helms visited with the band backstage prior to the concert, which he watched from a skybox. Although he told a reporter that he was "fascinated" with the concert, he described it as the "loudest thing I ever heard." "I turned my hearing aids all the way down," he said, "and kept my hands over my ears much of the time." The music was so loud, he thought, that "I couldn't really understand what he was saying." Helms noted that the concert venue was "filled to the gills," with the audience "moving back and forth like corn in the breeze." Bono, he said, "had that crowd going wild." Helms was especially struck by Bono's athleticism. "I don't see how he lasts physically. He runs and skips and just goes and goes." After the concert, Bono wrote to Helms. "Hope you had fun at the concert," he said. "We are really confusing the cynics with our friendship and our action in Africa. You are blessed [as] I am to know you. Love, Bono."[40]

In 2002, in his last significant act as senator, Jesse announced a different posture toward AIDS. At a Washington conference sponsored by Franklin Graham that was entitled "Prescription for Hope," Helms declared on February 20, 2002, that he had "been too lax too long in doing something really significant about AIDS." Whether in Africa or the United States, the seriousness of AIDS was unavoidable, he said. The "treachery" was "in ignoring it." He was, he said, "so ashamed that I've done little." If he could speak to God, Jesse said, He might say: "You are late, but thank you for joining the crowd." Helms's seeming conversion about AIDS—which was connected to his friendship with Bono—attracted widespread attention. Bono wrote to Jesse the next day and praised him for his "honest outburst, as un-political as it was humble." Even Helms's old adversary, the *Raleigh News and Ob-*

server, described his remarks as a "helpful and compassionate step."[41] But Jesse had not altered his views about homosexuality and AIDS. When asked in early March 2002 if he had changed his views about gays, he told a reporter that he would "make myself sick if I did such a thing, because I don't have any idea of changing my views on that kind of activity." He still believed that it was wrong to move "so much money away" from other health problems in favor of AIDS research. Homosexuals, he maintained, remained the "primary cause" of the spread of the disease in the United States. His comments in February 2002 were about AIDS in Africa, he declared; if they were extended to homosexuals, "I would have said so." He remained a strong opponent of gays and gay rights. "I think 95 percent of the American people feel that way right now" because homosexuals were "so flagrant in what they do."[42]

Nonetheless, Helms moved forward in expanding federal support to combat AIDS in Africa. On March 13, 2002, he met again with Bono and black actor Chris Tucker in his Senate office; invited also were Republican senators Mike DeWine of Ohio, Rick Santorum of Pennsylvania, and Bill Frist of Tennessee. Bono was stopped at a metal detector when he entered the Dirksen Building; his blue-tinted sunglasses set off the alarm. Helms let Bono drive his scooter around the Senate, while tourists gathered for a glimpse of the rock star. "We really got started," Helms told chief of staff Jimmy Broughton after the group left. "Bono knows what he's doing."[43] Then, in the March 24 edition of the *Washington Post,* Helms announced that he would co-sponsor, with Frist, an amendment to Bush's request for funds to fight the war in Afghanistan. The amendment would provide $500 million—contingent on raising an equal amount in the private sector—for the Agency for International Development to support anti-AIDS/HIV efforts in Africa that would provide treatment for pregnant mothers who were HIV-positive. The stakes, he wrote, "could not be higher." Already an entire generation was affected; some two million pregnant women in sub-Saharan Africa were infected, and, of these, perhaps a third could pass the disease to their babies. Helms sought to work with private groups such as Samaritan's Purse, which he called the "finest humanitarian organization I know of." Despite the inconsistency between his views about homosexual AIDS and the ravages of the disease in Africa, Helms wrote, "like the Samaritan traveling from Jerusalem to Jericho, we cannot turn away when we see our fellow man in need." His conscience was now "answerable to God," and, in his eighty-first year, he was now perhaps "too mindful of soon meeting Him."[44]

Helms's support of efforts to eradicate AIDS in Africa carried a powerful

symbolic message, and it marked his last significant act in the Senate prior
to his retirement. To be sure, there was more symbolism than reality behind the move. Helms had made no change in his position toward AIDS
and especially HIV-positive gays in the United States. Moreover, the AIDS
appropriation, perhaps because it lacked a healthy Helms behind it, languished in the Senate. Although in March 2002 Senate minority leader
Frist described AIDS as "the most devastating illness of modern time," in
June—immediately before the measure was scheduled for a Senate vote—
he reduced the appropriation to $200 million. Despite its earlier rhetoric,
the White House remained reluctant to support the measure, and Frist succeeded only in securing the administration's support for deferring an additional $300 million over three years. But soon after the measure passed the
Congress, the White House indicated that it would not spend any of the
money at all in 2002.[45]

FROM HELMS'S POINT of view, there were few regrets when the Clinton
presidency ended in January 2001. "Bill Clinton, let me say with great pleasure, is gone," he told the 28th annual meeting of the Conservative Political
Action Conference about three weeks after the inauguration of George W.
Bush. Referring to the furor over Clinton's last-minute pardons and
charges that he took White House belongings with him when he left—
which subsequently turned out to be inaccurate—Jesse described the president's last weeks in office as "an orgy of irresponsibility." But his dislike of
Clinton, though certainly related to his sexual improprieties, also reflected
what he called an "unwise, illegitimate and unconscionable" approach to
international relations. Clinton had inflicted "enormous damage—damage
that must be undone, and at best, that's going to take a while." There was
now, with Bush's election, an "unprecedented opportunity to set the policy
agenda again—especially in the realm of foreign affairs." Helms cited Clinton's support, on the eve of his retirement, for a new International Criminal
Court that would be empowered to try war criminals. Warning that U.S.
soldiers could be the victims of international show trials, Helms promised
to block the treaty: "We will never ratify it," he said, "if I have anything to
do with it." Clinton had been too cozy with Castro, he thought, who was
nothing more than a "mean-spirited, brutal dictator." Further, Clinton had
done little for a pet project of Helms's—ABM and missile defense. Anticipating one of the first actions of the new Bush administration, Helms had a
message for the Russians about missile defense: "It's going to happen. I
don't care whether they like it or not." Borrowing a saying from his favorite

leader, Winston Churchill, he promised that he would not retire until "I am a great deal worse or the country is a great deal better."[46]

George W. Bush's election in 2000 brought what Helms called a "president I can trust" to the White House. In the early months of Bush's presidency, Jesse cooperated with the new administration, and indeed his protégés occupied important positions in the new administration, especially regarding foreign policy. In 2001, two of his top Foreign Relations staffers, Steve Biegun, chief of staff, and Marc Thiessen, press secretary, joined the White House, Biegun as National Security Advisor Condoleezza Rice's chief of staff, and Thiessen as Secretary of Defense Donald Rumsfeld's chief speechwriter. Danielle Pletka, who had worked on Helms's Foreign Relations staff, joined the American Enterprise Institute as a vice president, and she became a leading voice supporting the eventual invasion of Iraq. Helms's ideas on foreign policy—the exertion of American sovereignty, opposition to United Nations multilateralism, and rejection of arms control—became standard features of Bush's foreign policy. The foreign policy initiatives of the post-9/11 Bush White House had a Helms flavor. This was an "intensely moral" foreign policy vision, said Thiessen, with the main goal to serve as a "strict guardian of American sovereignty" and the world's main bulwark against tyranny. Where the Clinton administration favored a web of treaties binding American power to the will of international organizations, Helms favored the free exercise of American global domination. Helms's ideas, which had been considered extreme in the previous decade, now "migrated to the center," according to Biegun.[47]

While he had opposed Clinton's nominations to the 4th Circuit on the grounds that additional judges were unnecessary, Helms helped to speed through Bush's nominations. When Bush nominated Massachusetts governor Paul Cellucci—like William Weld, a moderate Republican and supporter of abortion rights and gay rights—to be ambassador to Canada, Helms permitted the nomination to go through (although he voted against it in the end). As he had with other Republican presidents, however, Jesse soon proved an irritant. Shortly before Bush's inauguration, he urged that the Agency for International Development be abolished and its funds administered by a foundation working through private and church groups. By April 2001, the Bush administration had politely dismissed the suggestion.[48] In an appearance in May 2001 on the CNN talk show *Evans, Novak, Hunt, and Shields*, Helms announced that it was "perfectly outrageous" how China was "pushing us around." "We've got to straighten up and fly right about who's in charge of the United States' foreign policy, and I don't want it to be Beijing," he said. The United States, he believed, should oppose

China's bid to host the 2008 Olympics; the Bush administration was remaining neutral. In June, when President Bush described Russian president Vladimir Putin as "very straightforward and trustworthy" and a "remarkable leader" and then invited him to visit his Texas ranch, Helms criticized the president's "excessively personal endorsement." Putin was "far from deserving the powerful political prestige and influence" that comes from this language, he told Secretary of State Colin Powell when he visited the Foreign Relations Committee on June 20. *USA Today* described Helms's comments as a "stunning rebuke," while the *Times* of London declared that Jesse had "scorned" Bush. Still, his differences with the Bush White House were, like those with Reagan and the elder Bush, a matter of pressuring the president. "If I just pointed out the errors of judgment of people I [usually] don't agree with," he said, "I wouldn't be much of a senator."

Meanwhile, Helms continued to oppose gay rights. In May 2001, he introduced an amendment to Bush's No Child Left Behind education legislation prohibiting school districts from denying the Boy Scouts access to their facilities because of their anti-gay policies. Jesse asserted that the Boy Scouts had suffered "malicious assaults by homosexuals"; and he cited the instance of Chapel Hill, North Carolina, schools, which banned the Boy Scouts from using their facilities because they discriminated against gays. In March 2001, a Broward County, Florida, federal judge had already ruled that school districts could not exclude the organization, but Helms's legislation attempted to codify this decision. "Radical militants," Helms said in a Senate speech in May 2001, were attempting to subvert a recent Supreme Court decision that upheld the Scouts' policy that banned gays as Scouts or their leaders. "Everybody else's principles," he declared, "must be cast aside in order to protect the right of homosexual conduct." Jesse's amendment delayed passage of Bush's education bill in the Senate for months, and, when it passed in June with his Boy Scout amendment, Helms's opponents responded by successfully adding an amendment prohibiting schools from denying access to any group based on their attitudes toward sexual orientation.[49]

Helms's old methods of obstruction worked less effectively with the Bush White House, which was willing to use hard tactics, if necessary, to prevail. In May 2001, he stalled six Treasury Department appointments for a few months. In 2000, Congress had adopted the Africa-Caribbean trade law designed to benefit Third World economies with trade preferences, but Jesse was most concerned about the collapsing textile economy in North Carolina. The law had provided that American-made, "wholly formed" fabric could be assembled in Africa and the Caribbean, but Helms claimed that dyed, printed, and finished textiles were being imported in violation of the law. Jesse voiced his objections to the law to the outgoing Clinton administration and the incoming Bush White House, but both ignored him. Helms had little support from the Democrats in control of the Senate, who were unwilling to permit him to obstruct. Representative Bill Thomas, Republican chairman of the House Ways and Means Committee, resisted Helms's pressure tactics. "The whole idea of blackmailing an administration, either Republican or Democrat, has probably outlived its usefulness," Thomas declared. A single senator, he said, should not have the power to stop majority will. He opposed any compromise, and Jesse lifted the holds in August 2001 after obtaining only nominal and largely meaningless concessions; Treasury Secretary Paul O'Neill agreed to delay implementing the regulations until Congress could debate the matter, but the interim regulations permitting the textile imports remained in force. The senator "folded almost unconditionally," the *Washington Post* noted. There was a "rich absurdity" to Helms's efforts to sabotage a trade deal with poor countries when the Bush administration wanted to persuade poor nations to accept free trade. Although no other member of the Senate was "as contemptuous of the majority and as infatuated by his own will" and "no other is a bolder holder," the lesson seemed to be that Helms's old tactics would not survive in the Bush-dominated Republican Congress.[50]

AS JESSE MOVED into his fifth term in the Senate, the health problems that first began to emerge prominently in the early 1990s became more serious. In April 1998, he underwent surgery to repair a blocked carotid artery, and, a few months later, on July 27, he had knee replacement surgery performed by Dr. David Rendleman at Raleigh's Rex Hospital. The surgery, which replaced both knees with artificial joints, was considered successful, with the senator recovering for most of August and September, but this was, according to Jimmy Broughton, a "hard surgery" that did not succeed in restoring his mobility. Back in the Senate, Helms remained in his scooter, and he often used a four-pronged cane. For much of his last term, the scooter became his trademark, and he enjoyed zipping around the Capitol. He called his scooter "my Mercedes," and he would say that other senators were jealous "because they have to walk and I can run."[51] In October 1998, he felt well enough to campaign for Lauch Faircloth, then facing a re-election battle with John Edwards, and a reporter remembered that he arrived in a wheelchair and that "his voice lacked its old fire."[52] Jesse's problems with walking were complicated by his affliction with peripheral neuropathy, a nerve disease that was diagnosed during his knee replacement in

1998. The disease impaired his balance, caused numbness in his feet, and made walking difficult. It strikes the nervous system and damages the myelin sheath, which protects nerve endings. At the National Naval Medical Center in Bethesda, Maryland, Helms underwent an experimental therapy that was administered by the National Institutes of Health, involving multiple cycles of intravenenous immunoglobulin, which sought to replace lost antibodies and slow nerve deterioration.

By 2000, Helms was reporting that he had lost feeling below his knees, and he was unable to walk without a walker or scooter. Despite these health problems, Helms continued to hint that he might run for a sixth term in the Senate in 2002, saying that he "never felt better" and quipping that he might defy those people who were "praying that I won't run again." "If I feel good then, look out," he told a reporter.[53] In October 2000, he was hospitalized for three nights with pneumonia at Wake Medical Center and forced to stay home for about two weeks in Raleigh; though "no picnic," Helms quipped, "the nurses were pretty, and the doctors were Republicans, so it could have been worse."[54] Although the "liberal media" was circulating reports about him having pancreatic cancer, terminal prostate cancer, and other life-threatening afflictions, Helms declared in February 2001, he told the "guys and gals of the media" to put away their "balloons, champagne and party hats." "Old Jesse," he said, was "alive and kicking—and I plan to continue to be for a long time to come."[55]

He and his aides insisted that he was suffering from no physical deterioration, but the press continued to focus on the health issue after the national elections, when George W. Bush was narrowly elected and the Senate was evenly divided between the parties. The national media speculated about infirm Republican senators—including South Carolina's ninety-eight-year-old Strom Thurmond—who might soon be forced to retire. Both Helms and his aides considered these questions annoying. When asked about the implications of Jesse's health problems, chief of staff Jimmy Broughton declared that the North Carolina liberal press had been "speculating for a long time and hoping for a long time that they can get him." Pneumonia, he said, was not particularly unusual: "He had pneumonia. You recover from it."[56] In early December, press spokesman Marc Thiessen wrote a note to "our friends in the media": Helms was not sick, not hospitalized, not on life support, and was not suffering from prostate or pancreatic cancer. "He is absolutely fine and will (God willing) be around to torment you for a long time to come." "Relax and accept it," Thiessen said.[57]

The Helms staff dismissed rumors of health problems through early 2001, and they kept alive the notion that he might run again in 2002. But the prospect of another term effectively ended with the reoccurrence of his heart problems. On April 25, 2002, he had heart surgery to replace the pig valve that had replaced the mitral valve between the upper and lower chambers of his heart. The valve had worn out after his surgery of ten years earlier, in 1992; ordinarily, these valves last about a decade. Helms had recently complained of fatigue, and his aides noticed that he was not feeling well. Admitted into the hospital in late April, tests revealed that his liver and kidneys were no longer functioning adequately. Dr. Bert Coffer described him as "acutely sick" and on the verge of death, that his condition was "just awful, just really awful," while Broughton said that the situation was "touch and go." Hospitalized initially in Bethesda Naval Hospital, he was transferred to Inova Fairfax Hospital in Virginia, where Dr. Alan Speir performed the valve replacement surgery. The Helms family consulted constantly with Dr. Randy Chitwood, a heart expert at East Carolina Medical School whose daughter, Anne Chitwood, was the senator's scheduler. As had been true in 1992, the extent and seriousness of his illness was kept from the press. Although Dr. Coffer told reporters about two weeks after the surgery that Helms had made "remarkable progress," he remained in intensive care for over a month on a ventilator and had a temporary tracheostomy tube in order to facilitate breathing; it replaced an oral endotracheal tube that went down his throat.[58] At the end of May, Helms suffered a setback that put him temporarily back on the ventilator and delayed his departure from the hospital. On June 10, the senator finally left Inova after six weeks in the hospital, and he spent the next five weeks in rehabilitation facilities in northern Virginia. After returning to the Senate for one day when it was thought that they might need his vote, on June 26, Helms returned to North Carolina for further rehab at the local WakeMed facility. Meanwhile, Dot had open heart surgery to repair her mitral valve on July 1, 2002.[59] On July 16, Helms returned to his home in Raleigh for further recuperation and remained there until early September 2002, when he returned to the Senate.

Jesse's second valve replacement surgery was serious; although he returned to the Senate, according to Broughton, the health crisis "changed everything."[60] His recuperation marked a downward spiral in his health, as numerous observers noted a decided decline in his stamina and mental acuity after the middle of 2002. Thereafter, early signs of a larger problem—progressive dementia—began to manifest themselves, a disease that would in 2006 confine Helms to a convalescent home. *Charlotte Observer* reporter Jim Morrill, who had covered Helms's campaigns in the 1990s and often sparred with him and his staff, noticed a major personality change. In late

2002, he visited the senator as he was preparing to leave office. Helms greeted him as an old friend, putting his arm around him and insisting on a photograph. He was "avuncular, grandfatherly, and nice"—a side of Helms that Morrill had never seen. Helms, he concluded, "wasn't all there" and "wasn't the same person."[61]

THROUGH THE FIRST half of 2001, however, Helms kept the possibility of another campaign open. Jesse made a limited effort at organizing a 2002 campaign; by early 2001, he had raised under $20,000 and by August only $88,000. In early March 2001, he sent out a fund-raising letter telling supporters that he was undecided and might run, while campaign advisers were polling to determine his prospects. His political organization had been "running almost on idle," but now his "growing feeling" was that he and Dot should prepare for one more campaign. "I haven't made up my mind," he told an interviewer, "but more importantly, Mrs. Helms hasn't made up her mind." Nonetheless, he wanted enough money to "get the plane off the ground, if need be." At the Republican state convention in Raleigh in May 2001, he was equally equivocal. To an enthusiastic audience chanting "Run, Jesse, Run," he responded: "Let me give you an honest answer: I don't know." In this appearance, as in others, Jesse did not stand but sat in an armchair on stage and answered questions that were submitted in writing. He promised his audience a decision by September 2001. He and Dot would "make up our minds jointly," he promised. "I ain't saying I ain't running yet."[62]

Despite these public declarations, according to Jimmy Broughton, as early as the spring of 2001 Jesse had decided to retire from the Senate. In large part, Helms was determined not to stay too long in the Senate. "I'm not Strom Thurmond," he told one interviewer in February 2000.[63] Dot and the family opposed another run, and close friends such as physician Bert Coffer urged him to step aside. Spurred on by his family, Jesse reached this decision partly because of the Republicans' loss of control over the Senate, which passed into Democrats' hands after May 2001, when Jim Jeffords of Vermont defected from Republican ranks. Losing control of the Foreign Relations Committee chairmanship, Jesse also faced a GOP rule that imposed term limits and would require him to give up his ranking position on the committee after 2003. As potential aspirants to Helms's seat vied for position, Helms made a firm decision: at one point in the spring, he told Bob Dole that his wife, Elizabeth Dole, should "get her running shoes on." On August 17, he called Jim Goodmon, A. J. Fletcher's grandson and the president of Capitol Broadcasting, which owned WRAL. Helms told Goodmon that he wanted to broadcast a taped announcement on the 6:00 P.M. newscast. Goodmon immediately agreed, saying that he would make the broadcast widely available to the news media, and it was carried across the state, and nationally by C-SPAN and CNN. Writing his speech during the previous weeks, Jesse sent drafts by FedEx to Jimmy Broughton, who was vacationing at Morehead City, and Broughton retyped them; the office staff remained unaware of the senator's plans. Helms then returned to Raleigh on August 22, 2001, to videotape an eight-minute message on WRAL before an audience of family and friends, including his wife, daughters, and grandson Mike Stuart. When he was finished, he traveled to his Lake Gaston home and watched himself on TV. Invited to be present at the taping were senatorial candidates of both parties. Declaring his intention to spend more time with his family, Jesse announced his retirement. "I'm not running again," he announced, "and I thank you most sincerely from the bottom of my heart." He had, he admitted, faced the reality of aging and health problems. If reelected in 2002, he would finish his term at age eighty-eight, and this was something that "my family and I unanimously decided I should not do, and, ladies and gentlemen, I shall not." Quoting Sam Ervin, Helms declared that the "inescapable reality" was that "time takes a terrific toll." Noting that he had served longer than any other senator in North Carolina, Helms declared that "not in my wildest imagination did it ever occur to me that such a privilege would ever be mine." In a television interview aired immediately after his speech, Helms admitted that he had made this "very tough" decision after much indecision. Although he loved the Senate, "I had to choose between that and my family, and I made the right decision."[64]

Friends worried about what Helms, a dedicated workaholic with no hobbies, would do in retirement. Leaving the Senate would be "quite an awakening," said Tom Ellis. Although he had long said that he would return to Raleigh and play with his grandchildren, "I'm not sure how many he's got who are not grown. The ones I know are, and I don't know how he's going to play with them." Helms was a person who "loved being a United States senator 24 hours a day," said Bob Howison, who had participated in Helms's poker group in the 1950s and 1960s. He worried that "he's not going to know what to do once he's retired."[65] Jesse's retirement evoked numerous tributes, although his enemies welcomed his departure. Biden described him as "one of the most thoughtful, considerate and gracious senators I have ever served with." Others were more pointed. Harvey Gantt said that it would now be a "new day for us in North Carolina." Helms was, he thought, a "different kind of senator, a throwback to another time." "Nothing that Jesse Helms did in his entire career will enhance America's national security more than his retirement," added Robert Pastor, a Latin American expert whose nomination as ambassador to Panama Helms had blocked in 1994. Pastor asserted that Helms had "veered between the isolationist wing of his party and the unilateralist wing, but he has never accepted the tenets of cooperative multilateralism."[66]

For conservatives, Helms's departure was a major loss. In a statement, George W. Bush observed that the Senate had lost "an institution." Helms came to Washington, "but he never became a part of Washington." He "always remained true to his conservative principles and to the people of North Carolina." *Human Events* called Helms the "greatest U.S. senator of the last quarter of the 20th Century." On important issues, it asserted, he "sometimes stood alone," but he "never flinched or retreated." Helms maintained a grip on his belief in a transcendent order and a conviction that politics reflected morality. He supplied a "living, if lonely, link to the great souls of the American past" and the "permanent things that made America great."[67] The *Weekly Standard*'s William Kristol called Helms's departure "obviously the end of an era." Jesse "embodied the notion that there was an American conservative movement, a body of politicians and polemicists and grass-roots organizations that most of the time, on most issues, worked together" and had "a distinctive take on where the country was and where it should go."[68] Helms's departure, said *National Review,* was a more important development than Jeffords's departure from Republican ranks. Helms's decision would "almost certainly" make the Senate a less conservative institution.[69] Similarly, Gary Bauer, a leading conservative activist, asserted that Helms would be "irreplaceable." Jesse, he said, was "more than just right on the issues." He was also "a leader in every fight, ready to put his clout on the line for things he believed."[70]

Notes

INTRODUCTION

1. Rob Christensen, "Helms' Bold Voice Fades," *Raleigh News and Observer,* September 11, 2005; James Rosen, "Conservatives Gather to Pay Tribute to Helms," *Raleigh News and Observer,* September 21, 2005; Barnes interview, October 10, 2006.

2. R. Emmett Tyrrell, Jr., "Our Jesse," *American Spectator* 38 (October 2005).

3. Rob Christensen, "Helms Offers New Take on Segregation," *Raleigh News and Observer,* June 9, 2005; Rob Christensen, "Helms' Long-Held Views on Race Muted in Book," *Raleigh News and Observer,* June 10, 2005.

4. Barry Yeoman, "Whitewash," *Independent* Weekly, September 7, 2005.

5. "Debating Jesse: Does Sen. Helms' Memoir Whitewash His Past?" *Raleigh News and Observer,* September 11, 2005.

6. Bradley interview, December 18, 2006.

7. Ernest B. Furgurson, *Hard Right: The Rise of Jesse Helms* (New York: W. W. Norton, 1986). For recent work on modern conservatism, see Dan T. Carter, *The Politics of Rage: George Wallace, the Origins of the New Conservatism, and the Transformation of American Politics* (Baton Rouge: Louisiana State University Press, 1998); Lisa McGirr, *Suburban Warriors: The Origins of the New American Right* (Princeton: Princeton University Press, 2002); Matthew Lassiter, *The Silent Majority: Suburban Politics in the Sunbelt South* (Princeton: Princeton University Press, 2005); Kevin Kruse, *White Flight: Atlanta and the Making of Modern Conservatism* (Princeton: Princeton University Press, 2005); Donald T. Critchlow, *Phyllis Schlafly and Grassroots Conservatism: A Woman's Crusade* (Princeton: Princeton University

Press, 2005); and Joseph Crespino, *In Search of Another Country: Mississippi and the Conservative Counterrevolution* (Princeton: Princeton University Press, 2007).

8. Bruce J. Schulman, *The Seventies: The Great Shift in American Culture, Society, and Politics* (New York: Free Press, 2001).

PROLOGUE

1. Nidhi Agrawal, "Insider Poll Lists Helms among Nicest," *Durham Herald-Sun*, July 19, 1998.

2. Bill Arthur, "Tough or Mean? Helms Fights with Caustic Comments," *Charlotte Observer*, May 20, 1989.

3. Nickels interview, October 11, 2006.

4. Wilson interview, June 5, 2006.

5. "Washington Talk: Briefing: Helms at the Controls," *New York Times*, August 6, 1987; interview with Deborah DeMoss Fonseca, February 16, 2006.

6. Fonseca interview, February 16, 2006; Wilson interview, June 5, 2006; John Monk, "Who's Laughing Now? Long Written Off as a Noisy Blowhard, Jesse Helms Means to Be a Hard-Hitting Player," *Washingtonian*, November 1, 1995; JH interview (Tom Joyner), tape 34.

7. Nirenberg interview, June 7, 2006.

8. JH interview (Tom Joyner), tape 34; Scott Wilson interview (Tom Joyner); Nirenberg interview, June 7, 2006.

9. Interview with Jimmy Broughton, February 15, 2006; interviews with Marilynn Qurnell and Deborah DeMoss Fonseca, February 16, 2006; Babington interview, June 5, 2006.

10. Interview with Scott Wilson, June 5, 2006.

11. Monk interview, September 5, 2006.

12. Interview with Charles Babington, June 5, 2006.

13. Broughton interview, February 15, 2006; Monk interview, September 5, 2006; JH to Rolfe Neill, June 10, 1993, JH MSS. In another instance of how he sometimes offended Helms, Monk remembered writing a story about Nicaragua that was sympathetic to Violeta Chammoro. Jesse objected to his speaking with her and to his visit to Nicaragua, according to Monk.

14. Interview with Ken Eudy, September 7, 2006; Rosser interview, September 7, 2006.

15. Babington interview, June 5, 2006.

16. Jack Betts, "Helms Would Quit Senate after Second 6-Year Term," *Greensboro Daily News*, April 1, 1978; Betts, "Capitol Notebook," ibid., May 9, 1978; JH to Betts, April 17, May 1, 9, 1978; Betts to Ned Cline, October 1979; Gene Marlowe, "Helms May Seek Third Term," *Winston-Salem Journal*, October 16, 1979; "Helms Plans Race," *Raleigh News and Observer*, October 17, 1979; Betts, "Tar Heel Talk," *Greensboro Daily News*, February 15, 1984; Jack Betts, "The Indefatigable Jesse Helms for Some of the Senator's Detractors, the News That

He May Run for a Fifth Term Is Not Exactly Bad," *Charlotte Observer,* June 5, 1993; Clint Fuller to Betts, February 21, 1984; Betts interview, May 31, 2006. I am grateful to Jack Betts for sharing this correspondence with me.

17. Betts interview, May 31, 2006.

1. A BOLL WEEVIL IN THE COTTON PATCH

1. JH, speech at Monroe, North Carolina, October 17, 1992, the Papers of Jesse Helms Jesse Helms Center Archives, Wingate, N.C.; hereinafter cited as JH MSS.
2. Nance interview (by Jeffrey St. John), August 18, 1992; Robert Draper, "The Twilight of a Demagogue," *GQ,* February 1993, pp. 162–69, 207–9.
3. Ernest B. Furgurson, *Hard Right: The Rise of Jesse Helms* (New York: W. W. Norton, 1986), pp. 30–31; Virginia A. S. Kendrick, ed., *The Heritage of Union County, North Carolina* (Monroe, N.C.: Carolinas Genealogical Society, 1993), p. 4; Henson interview, August 10, 1992.
4. Furgurson, *Hard Right,* p. 31; Timothy B. Tyson, *Radio Free Dixie: Robert F. Williams and the Roots of Black Power* (Chapel Hill: University of North Carolina Press, 1999), pp. 4–6; Kendrick, ed., *Union County,* pp. 1–48; House interview (by St. John, July 7, 1992), JH MSS.
5. Jesse Helms, Sr., handwritten campaign description, March 6, 1950, Helms scrapbooks, JH MSS.
6. Unidentified clipping about Ethel Mae Helms, Helms scrapbooks; Kendrick, ed., *Union County,* p. 231.
7. "He's Still Handsome," *Monroe Journal,* October 5, 1945; "Sheriff Frank Niven Will Not Seek Re-Election in Primary," *Monroe Enquirer,* March 6, 1950; "Jesse Helms Made Permanent Chief Monroe Police Force," *Monroe Enquirer,* September 3, 1951, Helms scrapbooks.
8. Furgurson, *Hard Right,* p. 33; Jesse Helms, *Here's Where I Stand: A Memoir* (New York: Random House, 2005), p. 4; interview with Helms (by Ernest Furgurson) October 10, 1985, The Papers of Ernest Furgurson, folder 12, Southern Historical Collection, University of North Carolina at Chapel Hill Library; JH, speech, October 17, 1992, JH MSS; "Biographical Conversations with Jesse Helms," WUNC-TV broadcast, January 31, 2000; Nance interview (by St. John, August 18, 1992); Henson interview (by St. John, August 10, 1992); House interview (by St. John, July 7, 1992), JH MSS.
9. In 1945, Mr. Jesse became assistant chief of Monroe's police force, and in 1949 he began as deputy sheriff under longtime Union County sheriff B. Frank Niven. When Niven retired in 1950, Jesse ran for the office and narrowly lost.
10. Furgurson, *Hard Right,* pp. 30–32; interview with Helms (by Furgurson), October 10, 1985.
11. "Biographical Conversations with Jesse Helms," January 31, 2000.
12. Tyson, *Radio Free Dixie,* pp. 4–5, 83.
13. Young Jesse at the age of seven or eight would often sit at his front door "with

hands up to his face like he was afraid," while local black children made "faces at him as they went by." This observer concluded that young Jesse inherited his father's ways. Furgurson, *Hard Right*, pp. 38–40; interview with Mrs. Fullwood (by Furgurson), undated, Furgurson Papers, folder 25; Norman Gomlak and Kerry Prichard, "GQ Article Questions Helms' Memories of Monroe," *Charlotte Observer,* January 31, 1998.

14. JH interview (by Tom Joyner), tape 6, JH MSS; interview with Nathan Miller (by Furgurson), November 13, 1985, Furgurson Papers, folder 25, SHC.

15. The incident is recounted in Tyson, *Radio Free Dixie,* pp. 1–2. Williams referred to the white police officer in several of his writings, in some instances not identifying the person, in other specifically naming Mr. Jesse. See *Crusader* 9, no. 3 (December 1967): 3, and Robert F. Williams, "While God Lay Sleeping," unpublished autobiography. I am grateful to Tim Tyson for generously sharing these and other sources.

16. William D. Snider, *Helms and Hunt: The North Carolina Senate Pace, 1984* (Chapel Hill: University of North Carolina Press, 1985), p. 19; Tammy Joyner, "Jesse Helms Keeps Up with the Folks Back Home," *Union Observer,* June 23, 1983; "Biographical Conversations with Jesse Helms," February 11, 2000.

17. Eddie Yandle, "Jesse's Friends," *Monroe Enquirer-Journal,* February 20, 1983.

18. Marjorie Hunter, "Not So Vital Statistics on Mr. Helms," *New York Times,* January 5, 1982.

19. The Sunday School teacher was the mother of Monroe newspaper editor George Beasley, Jr. "Notes by the Wayside," *Monroe Enquirer,* February 21, 1972.

20. JH to Mrs. F. Ogburn Yates, February 24, 1961, JH MSS.

21. Jesse Glasgow interview (by Furgurson); Furgurson, *Hard Right,* pp. 38–40; Nance interview (by St. John), August 18, 1992.

22. JH, *Here's Where I Stand,* p. 4; JH interview (by Joyner), tape 6.

23. Furgurson, *Hard Right,* pp. 36–37; *VP* #921, August 25, 1964; JH, speech at Monroe, October 17, 1992, JH MSS.

24. "Former Student Fulfilling Promise Made to Miss Annie," Helms newsletter, *Monroe Enquirer-Journal,* October 15, 1980; JH, *Here's Where I Stand,* pp. 10–11; Nance interview (by St. John), August 18, 1992; Henson interview (by St. John), August 10, 1992; House interview, (by St. John), July 7, 1992.

25. JH, unidentified, undated [c. January 1943] article in the *Charlotte News,* Helms scrapbooks; Ray House to JH, January 29, 1943, JH MSS; Max F. Harris, "Bruce Snyder, Jr.," *Monroe Enquirer-Journal,* November 1, 1973; Max F. Harris, "Town and Country," *Monroe Enquirer-Journal,* September 2, 1975; JH interview (by Joyner), tape 2; Nance interview (by St. John), August 18, 1992; House interview (by St. John), July 7, 1992. JH MSS. Snyder roomed with Frank Sinatra. Henson interview (by St. John), August 10, 1992. JH MSS.

26. Furgurson, *Hard Right,* pp. 36–37; *VP* #1977, November 27, 1968; House interview (by St. John), July 7, 1992.

27. JH, *Here's Where I Stand,* pp. 4, 9; Eddie Yandle, "Jesse's Friends," *Monroe Enquirer-Journal,* February 20, 1983; Tammy Joyner, "Jesse Helms Keeps Up with the Folks Back Home," *Union Observer,* June 23, 1983; JH, speech at Monroe, North Carolina, October 17, 1992; Henson interview (by St. John), August 10, 1992.

28. JH to George M. Beasley, Jr., March 26, 1973, JH MSS.

29. House interview (by St. John), July 7, 1992; Eddie Yandle, "Jesse's Friends" *Monroe Enquirer-Journal,* February 20, 1983; George Beasley, Jr., "Notes by the Wayside," *Monroe Enquirer,* February 21, 1972; JH, "Monroe Pugs Lose," *Monroe Journal,* March 1, 1938; JH, "Pythons Uncoil," *Monroe Journal,* March 29, 1938; JH, "Waxhaw Record Clean," *Monroe Journal,* April 1, 1938; JH, "County Pugs Win," *Monroe Journal,* April 5, 1938; JH, "Pythons Deadly," *Monroe Journal,* April 15, 1938; JH, "Tortoise Again Beats the Hare," *Monroe Journal,* June 10, 1938, Helms scrapbooks.

30. House interview (by St. John), July 7, 1992.

31. He attended Wingate, writes Furgurson, "simply because he could not afford to go further." Furgurson, *Hard Right,* p. 38; JH, *Here's Where I Stand,* pp. 14–15.

32. Furgurson, notes about JH appearance on "North Carolina People," spring 1984, Furgurson Papers, folder 12, SHC; JH, *Here's Where I Stand,* pp. 15–16; JH to S. H. Hobbs, Jr., January 22, 1964, JH MSS.

33. Furgurson, notes about JH appearance on *North Carolina People,* spring 1984, Furgurson Papers, folder 12, SHC; Jack Crosswell, "Helms Controversial Councilman," *Raleigh News and Observer,* June 3, 1959.

34. The school yearbook makes no special mention of his presence; unlike many of his peers, he made little contribution to school either in his academic performance or in extracurricular activities—at least, activities outside of newspaper reporting. But the experience at Wake Forest—his first away from home—opened new doors. Jesse occasionally wrote about sports for the Wake Forest newspaper, the *Old Gold & Black.* JH, "Deacons Face Duke Today, Meet Carolina on Tuesday," *Old Gold & Black,* April 1940, Helms scrapbooks.

35. The *N&O*'s managing editor, Frank Smethurst, had visited Jesse's journalism class, and after class ended the ever impetuous Jesse approached him about a job. With a few weeks, he was hired. JH, "Deac Cagers Have Busy Week Ahead," *Raleigh Times,* February 12, 1940; same article appeared as "Deacons Face Tough Card During Week," *Henderson Daily Dispatch,* February 12, 1940, Helms scrapbooks; Jack Crosswell, "Helms Controversial Councilman," *Raleigh News and Observer,* June 3, 1959. On Helms's decision to leave Wake, see JH, *Here's Where I Stand,* pp. 15–17; Ferrel Guillory, "He Took That Advice, and It Took Him to the Senate," *Monroe Enquirer-Journal,* January 10, 1973.

36. Helms interview (by Furgurson), October 10, 1985; "Biographical Conversations with Jesse Helms," January 31, 2000; Furgurson, *Hard Right,* p. 43.

37. He occasionally wrote a human interest column, "Days of Daze," that appeared in a number of North Carolina newspapers, including the *Monroe Journal* and

the *Charlotte News.* During the fall of 1940 and spring of 1941, he worked as a stringer for Burke Davis, sports editor of the *Charlotte News,* and for the *Charlotte Observer.* See JH, "No Go with Deacon Ace," *Charlotte News,* October 7, 1940; JH, "Seat Sell-Out for Opening Battles," *Charlotte Observer,* February 26, 1941. See "Days of Daze," *Monroe Journal,* February 14, 1941.

38. "Staff Changes," *Raleigh Times,* c. November 1941, JH MSS.

39. See, for example, JH, "Bomber Crash Here Kills One," *Raleigh Times,* November 11, 1941; JH, "Bryan Expected to Remain Chief," *Raleigh Times,* November 27, 1941; JH, "Train Hits Truck; Raleigh Man Killed," *Raleigh Times,* January 15, 1942.

40. "Mrs. Helms—'Jesse Will Make a Good One,'" unidentified clipping from *Raleigh Times,* c. 1957, JH MSS; JH, *Here's Where I Stand,* pp. 19–21; "Biographical Conversations with Jesse Helms," January 31, 2000; "Dot Helms Pinch Hits for Husband Jesse," *Monroe Enquirer-Journal,* October 23, 1972.

41. John Wagner, "Helms' Reflections on War," *Raleigh News and Observer,* September 15, 2001. Working as a naval recruiter was not an entirely new notion. In November 1941, he had written about the appearance of former heavyweight boxer James J. "Gene" Tunney, who traveled to Raleigh on behalf of naval recruiters. Helms described Tunney as a "born and bred a fighter" who came to "make his nation a better fighting unit—and nobody could say that he didn't achieve his aim." JH, "Former Champion Tunney Here," *Raleigh Times,* November 21, 1941.

42. J. Melville Broughton to Sixth District Naval Commandant, January 28, 1942, Helms scrapbooks.

43. See certificate of graduation plus list of graduates, Naval Recruiter's School, April 25, 1943, Helms scrapbooks. See also Furgurson, *Hard Right,* p. 44.

44. Blanche Manoe, "Chatter," *Raleigh News and Observer,* August 23, 1942.

45. Melissa Browne Smith, "Newspapering Is Sometimes a Romantic Episode," *Raleigh News and Observer,* November 1, 1942; clipping from the *Sparkplug* (the *Raleigh Times* staff newsletter), October 1942, JH MSS; JH, *Here's Where I Stand,* pp. 20–21.

46. Macon Crowder Moore, "A Column Is Short Until the Times Comes to Fill It," *Raleigh News and Observer,* November 15, 1942.

47. JH to Caroline Wood, August 11, 1942, Helms scrapbooks.

48. "Navy Notes," *Wilmington Star,* August 1, 1942, clipping, JH MSS.

49. Furgurson, *Hard Right,* p. 45; JH, *Here's Where I Stand,* pp. 22–25.

50. They would have lived at the home of Fred M. Dearing. See Dearing to JH, July 1942, JH MSS.

51. Jesse's wartime movements are documented in Helms scrapbooks. See also "Dot Helms Pinch Hits for Husband Jesse," *Monroe Enquirer-Journal,* October 23, 1972. In one part of the scrapbook, Dot noted that in June 1943 the couple took a weekend vacation to the beach, staying at the Hotel Douglas MacArthur in Ocean Drive, South Carolina.

52. *Monroe Journal,* September 10, 1943; "Local Recruiter Given New Post," *Wilmington Star-News,* clipping, April 1944, JH MSS; *Monroe Journal,* September 8, 1944, February 13, 1945. On Jane's birth, see scrapbooks Helms.

53. "Helms Strikes Old Familiar Chords," *Charlotte Observer,* October 29, 1972.

54. JH, *Here's Where I Stand,* p. 26.

55. JH interview, May 14, 1999.

56. Clipping, Helms scrapbooks.

57. "Jesse Helms Takes WRNL [WRAL] Position," *Roanoke News,* January 1, 1948, Helms scrapbooks; JH, *Here's Where I Stand,* pp. 26–28.

58. "Variety Entertainment Is Offered Stunt Night Fri.," *Roanoke News,* March 27, 1947; "First Baptist Church Elects New Officers"; JH, "Martin Scouting in Florida Camps," *Raleigh News and Observer,* March 16, 1947; "Notables Praise Jays; Fans and Martin in Ceremonies," Helms scrapbooks; "Jays Look Ahead to Banner Year," *Raleigh News and Observer,* January 6, 1948.

59. "Helms Leaving as WCBT News, Program Chief," *Roanoke Rapids Herald,* January 1, 1948, Helms scrapbooks.

60. JH to C. D. Coburn, June 21, 1963, JH MSS.

61. "Ray Reeve, Jesse Helms to Be on Hand for Jays Opener Friday Night," *Roanoke Rapids Herald,* April 22, 1948, Helms scrapbooks.

62. Interview with Fred Fletcher (by Furgurson), May 23, 1985, Furgurson Papers, folder 16; JH, *Here's Where I Stand,* pp. 28–29.

63. See newspaper ad, "Hats Off! For a Topnotch Job, Jesse Helms," c. 1948, scrapbooks, JH MSS; "Biographical Conversations with Jesse Helms," January 31, 2000.

64. "Coley Trial Due Today"; "Schools Give Generously," c. 1948, clippings in Helms scrapbooks.

65. Faircloth interview, December 14, 2006.

66. Roy Parker, Jr., "Happenstance Along Helms' Political Journey," *Fayetteville Times,* October 2, 1978; Faircloth interview, December 14, 2006.

67. Parker interview, May 11, 2005; *VP* #346, April 16, 1962; Eddie Yandle, "Mr. Jesse Influenced His Son's Life," *Monroe Enquirer-Journal,* February 20, 1983; Pat Borden, "New Senator and Wife Discover 'Strange Town, Strange House,'" *Charlotte Observer,* January 16, 1973; JH, *Here's Where I Stand,* pp. 31–32.

68. Interview with Fred Fletcher (by Furgurson), May 23, 1985, Furgurson Papers, folder 16; Parker interview, May 11, 2005; Furgurson, *Hard Right,* pp. 45–46; Julian M. Pleasants and Augustus M. Burns III, *Frank Porter Graham and the 1950 Senate Race in North Carolina* (Chapel Hill: University of North Carolina Press, 1990), p. 95; Snider, *Helms and Hunt,* p. 24; A. J. Fletcher, "Incidents in the Life of A. J. Fletcher," September 23, 1966, JH MSS.

69. Jim Chaney, "Scott Asks Public Support in Road Bond Issue Drive," c. January 1949, clipping in Helms scrapbooks. Helms had a number of strong ties to the Scott administration. In one of Scott's many shake-ups, for example, he appointed his private secretary Charles Parker as director of the State Advertising

Division—thus bypassing the State Board of Conservation and Development, which had heretofore controlled the advertising contracts. To replace Parker, the governor appointed John Marshall, who had worked with Jesse on the *Times* and had been a groomsman at his wedding. "Parker Given News Post, Marshall Scott Secretary," undated, Helms scrapbooks.

70. Broughton had won a special election in 1948 which was held to fill the seat vacated by the death of longtime Senator (and New Deal opponent) Josiah William Bailey on December 15, 1946. The seat had been filled by W. B. Umstead, and Broughton defeated him in the special election.

71. In 1934, in a general strike that paralyzed the textile industry in the Carolinas, he offered to post bond when Alton Lawrence, a UNC graduate and socialist labor organizer, was arrested in High Point. Creating a furor, the Lawrence incident earned Graham the lasting enmity of the state's textile industrialists. Segregationists were especially suspicious of Graham's positions on race. Serving as president of the most liberal interracial organization of its day, the Southern Conference on Human Welfare, Graham remained associated with the organization even after its opponents publicized Communist involvement. A member of the Fair Employment Practices Committee (FEPC), which President Franklin Roosevelt established in 1940 to enforce nondiscrimination in defense contracts, Graham was also appointed to President Harry S Truman's Committee on Civil Rights, which published its landmark *To Secure These Rights* in 1947. Pleasants and Burns, *Frank Porter Graham*, ch. 1; Warren Ashby, *Frank Porter Graham: A Southern Liberal* (Winston-Salem: John F. Blair, 1980).

72. Parker interview, May 11, 2005.

73. Notes of an interview with Helms (by Julian Pleasants), December 11, 1984, in author's possession.

74. Herbert O'Keef, "Willis Smith—U.S. Senator," *Raleigh News and Observer,* July 2, 1950.

75. Helms interview (by Pleasants), December 11, 1984; Pleasants and Burns, *Frank Porter Graham*, pp. 72–74; interview with JH (by Furgurson). Helms recounted this story on a number of occasions over the years. See Bill Gilkeson, "Fabled Campaign of '50: Did Helms Get Bad Rap for His Part?," *Durham Morning Herald*, August 21, 1977; JH, *Here's Where I Stand*, pp. 32–34.

76. Helms interview by Pleasants, December 11, 1984; Ellis interview, July 14, 2005; Pleasants and Burns, *Frank Porter Graham*, pp. 88–89.

77. Ernest Furgurson calls the election the "most controversial" and "most formative" of Helms's young political life. Furgurson, *Hard Right*, p. 40.

78. "Willis Smith—U.S. Senator," *Raleigh News and Observer,* July 2, 1950.

79. Pleasants and Burns, *Frank Porter Graham*, pp. 174–87; Parker interview, May 11, 2005.

80. "Smith May Decide Today," *Raleigh News and Observer,* June 7, 1950; Bill Armstrong, "Smith Calls for a Run-off," *Raleigh Times,* June 7, 1950; Pleasants interview with JH, December 11, 1984; JH to Bill Sharpe, April 11, 1967, JH MSS;

Furgurson, *Hard Right*, p. 50; Ellis interview, July 14, 2005; JH, *Here's Where I Stand*, pp. 34–35; "Biographical Conversations with Jesse Helms," January 31, 2000.

81. Simmons Fentress, "Smith Ends Campaign with Rally," *Raleigh News and Observer*, June 24, 1950; Herbert O'Keef, "Smith Wins Senatorial Nomination," *Raleigh News and Observer*, June 25, 1950; Pleasants and Burns, *Frank Porter Graham*, pp. 221–22.

82. Daniel C. Hoover, "Helms Denies Roles in 'Dirty' 1950 Campaign," *Raleigh News and Observer*, August 9, 1981; JH, *Here's Where I Stand*, p. 34; "Biographical Conversations with Jesse Helms," January 31, 2000. Over time, Helms grew increasingly bitter about the accusations regarding his involvement in the 1950 campaign. In 1993, when Pleasants asked Helms to participate in a documentary about Frank Porter Graham, he refused because he was convinced that he would not be treated fairly about the 1950 Senate race. In the past, Helms wrote, "I have been so disappointed with others who have heretofore assured me that they would be objective, only to see them turn around and lie through their teeth." Participating in an interview would be "an exercise in futility" and a "trap." JH to Julian Pleasants, February 1, 1993, in author's possession. I am grateful to Professor Pleasants for sharing this letter with me.

83. *VP* #2492, January 4, 1971; Hoover Adams to Ernest Furgurson, March 21, 1986, Furgurson Papers, folder 1; "Biographical Conversations with Jesse Helms," January 31, 2000; Adams to JH, May 27, June 29, 1950, JH MSS.

84. "Helms, Ellis Roles in Dirtiest Campaign," no author, August 22, 1983, Furgurson Papers, folder 12.

85. Furgurson, *Hard Right*, pp. 54–55; Snider, *Helms and Hunt*, p. 25.

86. James H. Pou Bailey, "Raleigh Round-Up," clipping, Helms scrapbooks.

87. William B. White, "N. C. Penal Head Is Accused of Illegal Prison Labor Use," *Durham Morning Herald*, June 10, 1950; "Prisons Director Submits Report on Use of Labor," *Raleigh Times*, June 12, 1951; "S.B.I. to Make Complete Investigation of Charges Against Prison Director," *Durham Morning Herald*, June 13, 1950; "Moore Quits State Prisons Job," *Raleigh News and Observer*, July 1, 1950. Moore paid a $1,000 fine. "Court Assesses $1,000 Fine Against Former Prisons Head," clipping, Helms scrapbook.

88. *VP* #1910, August 22, 1968.

89. "Pou Bailey Says Jesse Helms Was Boll Weevil in Scott's Cotton Patch," *Monroe Journal*, clipping in Helms scrapbook; transcript of WRAL broadcast, February 15, 1951, JH MSS.

90. JH to E. L. Rankin, Jr., December 1, 1952, JH MSS.

91. JH to Josh L. Horne, November 10, 1952, JH MSS. See also JH to Sam Covington, November 10, 1952, JH MSS.

92. Helms interview (by Furgurson), October 10, 1985.

93. Clint Fuller interview (by Floyd Riddick), November 30, 1991, JH MSS; JH to M. A. Stroup, June 23, 1952, JH MSS; Faircloth interview, December 12, 2006.

94. JH to AJF, March 14, 1955, JH MSS.

95. JH to Bill Sharpe, July 4, 1952, JH MSS.

96. Alvin Wingfield to JH, February 5, 1954, JH MSS. See also Willis Smith to JH, c. January 1952, JH MSS.

97. Raymond Lowery, "Smith Backs Party Ticket, but He's Not Enthusiastic," *Raleigh News and Observer,* October 11, 1952. On Helms's hostility to Truman, see JH to Kathleen Lindsay, July 4, 1952, JH MSS.

98. JH to Richard Russell, June 11, 1957, JH MSS. See also JH to William J. Primm, September 1952; Russell to JH, November 6, 1953, JH MSS.

99. Furgurson, *Hard Right,* pp. 58–59.

100. JH to Willis Smith, August 12, 1952, JH MSS.

101. In September 1952, Helms attended a Young Democrats Club (YDC) state convention at Raleigh, and was appointed chair of the resolutions committee. But the committee was too liberal for Helms, and he voted against a resolution calling for a strengthening of the United Nations; he opposed pouring "more of our money, blood, and indeed lives" into the organization. He also clashed with other YDC members when a resolution came forward condemning Wisconsin senator Joseph R. McCarthy. By denouncing McCarthy, Helms said, the YDC risked interfering in national politics unnecessarily. When the *Raleigh News and Observer* reported Helms's comments, he complained that it had "completely misrepresented my position." JH, memo for the file, September 11, 1952, clipping from the *Raleigh News and Observer,* c. September 11, 1952, JH MSS.

102. JH, *Here's Where I Stand,* pp. 40–41.

103. JH to Thomas D. Blake, July 2, 1953, JH MSS.

104. "Jesse Helms, Jr., Named Secretary Bankers Assn.," *Monroe Journal,* September 15, 1953, clipping in JH MSS.

105. Wingfield to JH, February 5, 1954; JH to Wingfield, February 3, 1954; J. Winfield Crew, Jr., to JH, February 8, 1954; JH to Joseph R. McCarthy, January 28, 1954, JH to Crew, February 10, 1954, JH MSS. Helms, however, denied "running from a fight" in leaving Washington. JH to David J. Whichard, September 29, 1953, JH MSS.

106. "Helms Says He Gave Notice to Sen. Lennon," *Charlotte Observer,* September 22, 1953, clipping in JH MSS. See also "Sen. Lennon to Address Rotarians," *Winston-Salem Journal,* September 15, 1953; "Lennon Surprised by New Post of Aide," *Wilmington Star,* September 14, 1953, clippings in JH MSS. As late as July 30, Helms apparently was planning to move to Raleigh at the end of the congressional session to prepare for Lennon's senatorial campaign. John A. Park to JH, July 30, 1953, JH MSS.

107. Louis Sutton to JH, July 21, 1953; E. N. Pope to JH, July 22, 1953, JH MSS.

108. JH, "Twenty Years of Service," *Tarheel Banker* 35, no. 1 (July 1956): 24

109. Led by John P. Stedman, state treasurer during the 1930s and president of the Scottish Bank, the bankers wanted a new director who could defend their

interests more aggressively. The NCBA served primarily as a lobbying organization, and bankers were interested in revising North Carolina's state laws overseeing them. Stedman sought a youthful executive director who was well schooled in modern communication and mass media. "Gets Bankers' Post," *Monroe Enquirer,* September 14, 1953; Nisbet, "Helms' Resignation Was Expected," clippings in JH MSS.

110. "Helms Hits Truman, *N&O,*" *Raleigh News and Observer,* September 18, 1953; JH, speech, September 17, 1953, JH MSS.

111. JH to John P. Stedman, October 2, 1953, JH MSS.

112. Norman B. McCulloch, "This 'n' That," *Bladen Journal,* September 24, 1953.

113. *Hertford County Herald,* November 12, 1953; interview with Roy Parker, Jr., May 11, 2005. Helms's close friend and the NCBA's counsel, Pou Bailey, demanded a retraction and threatened a libel lawsuit, apparently without success. James H. Pou Bailey to JH, November 21, 1953, JH MSS.

114. JH, "Dot Thinks Flying Is Strictly for the Birds," *Tarheel Banker* 35, no. 4 (September 1956): 31.

115. Jack Crosswell, "Helms Controversial Councilman," *Raleigh News and Observer,* June 3, 1959, clipping in JH MSS; Ellis interview, July 14, 2005; Snider, *Helms and Hunt,* p. 27; David Perlmutt, "Friends Worry, but Family Relatives Say Helms Will Make the Tricky Transition from Life in Spotlight Man," *Charlotte Observer,* August 26, 2001.

116. After 1953, Helms promoted the organization's main legislative objective, the passage of a new banking bill, which required that state budget surpluses be deposited in state banks. Despite the opposition of Governor Luther Hodges and the *News and Observer*—and much of the state's political establishment—the law was enacted in 1957. JH, "Look Under the Sheet, Quick," *Tarheel Banker* 36, no. 1 (July 1957): 26.

117. "The Banker's Magazine," *Henderson Daily Dispatch,* September 29, 1955, clipping in JH MSS. The *Dispatch*'s editor, Henry A. Dennis, described himself as "one of your faithful followers." Henry A. Dennis to JH, March 12, 1958, JH MSS.

118. In the 1950s, Helms was especially close to assistant secretary of agriculture Earl Butz. During the Nixon and Ford administrations, Butz served as secretary of agriculture. However, in a conversation on Air Force One during Gerald Ford's 1976 reelection campaign, Butz told reporters that black people cared about three things: "first, a tight pussy; second, loose shoes; and third, a warm place to shit." He resigned under pressure on October 4, 1976. On the Butz-Helms relationship, see Butz to Helms, August 17, 1959, JH MSS.

119. "Now Wait a Minute," JH, *Tarheel Banker* 36, no. 8 (February 1958): 38.

120. "Hoover—A Fine American," JH, *Tarheel Banker* 33, no. 8 (February 1955): 30.

121. Quoted in "A Prophecy by Lenin," *Henderson Daily Dispatch,* March 1958, clipping in JH MSS.

122. JH to Thurman Sensing, April 9, 1958, JH MSS.

123. On another occasion, commenting on the *N&O's* anti-bank attitudes, Helms quoted a *N&O* editorial that described itself as "proud" of North Carolina banks. Helms, with some irony, then pointed out that the *N&O* editorial appeared on June 28, 1903. JH, "Truth vs. Half-Truth," *Tarheel Banker* 35, no. 9 (March 1957): 40; *Tarheel Banker* 35, no. 10 (April 1957): 34.

124. The *Observer,* Helms wrote, made him "sickest of all"; with McKnight at the helm and with reporter Jay Jenkins "wobbling around," he believed that the newspaper was a "sad sack." JH to Ralph Howland, January 13, 1956, JH MSS.

125. He recalled that Willis Smith once referred to a twenty-three-hour speech by Oregon senator Wayne Morse as a filibuster, and Morse "raised hell." That meant that "the distinguished Senator from Oregon would regard a twenty-three hour speech by a Southerner as a filibuster, but when the Senator from Oregon speaks that long he is merely educating the public." Conservatives, of necessity, were required to "stand up for our views" when facing such determined opponents as the *News and Observer.* JH to Bill Sharpe, March 11, 1958, JH MSS.

126. JH to Stella Barbee, June 23, 1961, JH MSS.

127. On Wingfield, see Furgurson, *Hard Right,* p. 46. Also see "Wingfield Defends Bricker Amendment," *Charlotte News,* January 29, 1954, enc in Wingfield to L. S. Drill, February 1, 1954 (cc to JH), and Alvin Wingfield to JH, February 5, 1954, JH MSS. For an example of Wingfield's ideological mentoring, see Wingfield to JH, December 8, 1953, JH MSS, in which he explains the distinctions between socialism and Communism.

128. Wingfield, statement announcing Senate candidacy, Alvin Wingfield, March 15, 1954, JH MSS.

129. Alvin Wingfield to JH, March 17, 1954; JH to Wingfield, March 18, 1954, JH MSS.

130. Miles Smith, Jr., to JH, March 17, 1954; JH to Smith, March 18, 1954, JH MSS.

131. JH to Alvin Wingfield, Jr., March 18, 1954, JH MSS.

132. "League Hears Senate Candidates," *Raleigh News and Observer,* May 12, 1954; "Wingfield Opposes Parties," *Raleigh News and Observer,* May 13, 1954; "Final Chapter in Odd Political Campaign to Be Written Saturday," *Raleigh News and Observer,* May 23, 1954.

133. Alvin Wingfield, Jr., to Dwight D. Eisenhower, December 28, 1959, JH MSS.

134. "Not that you have lost any of your forcefulness or attractiveness as a speaker," Fletcher wrote, "but simply because we feel that program-wise, it is better to have this spot filled occasionally by different people." AJF to Alvin Wingfield, March 1, 1960, JH MSS.

135. Bill Gilkeson, "Fabled Campaign of '50," *Durham Morning Herald,* August 21, 1977; JH to Bob Putnam, October 31, 1960; JH to Stella Barbee, December 5, 1960, June 23, 1961, JH MSS. Helms consoled himself by believing that Wingfield had "a great deal more faith than many people who plop down on the front pew every Sunday."

136. JH, "That Arkansas Farmer Is Plumb Confused," *Tarheel Banker* 36 no. 8 (February 1958): 39.

137. JH, "These Are Important Days for the South," *Tarheel Banker* 35, no. 2 (August 1956): 35.

138. JH to R. B. Carpenter, January 11, 1956, JH MSS.

139. William H. Chafe, *Civilities and Civil Rights: Greensboro, North Carolina, and the Black Struggle for Freedom* (New York: Oxford University Press, 1980), p. 67.

140. JH, "There is Another Way," *Tarheel Banker* 34, no. 3 (September 1955): 24. For an account of the editorial, see Bryan Hardin Thrift, "Jesse Helms, the New Right, and American Freedom" (Ph.D. diss., Boston University, 2005), pp. 42–44.

141. JH, "Let's Face the Issue," *Tarheel Banker* 34, no. 4 (October 1955): 28; "Bankers Know Better," editorial, *Greensboro Daily News,* September 7, 1955; JH to William Snider, September 9, 1955, JH MSS. For a more favorable response, see "Bankers Assn. Editorial Supports Private Schools," *Durham Herald,* September 6, 1955.

142. "Silliest School Suggestion Yet," editorial, *N&O,* September 6, 1955.

143. "Public Schools Belong to the People," editorial, *Asheville Citizen,* September 11, 1955.

144. "N. C. Has an Educational Choice, but It Isn't Logically 'Private,'" editorial, *Charlotte Observer,* September 7, 1955; JH to C. A. McKnight, September 9, 1955, JH MSS. On Lake's ideas, see I. Beverly Lake to Reed Surratt, September 9, 1955, JH MSS. For another editorial hostile to the Lake-Helms plan, see "'Private Enterprise Schools,'" *Winston-Salem Journal,* September 7, 1955.

145. JH, "Let's Face the Issue," *Tarheel Banker* 34, no. 4 (October 1955): 28. Nonetheless, many of Helms's publicity-shy bankers were reluctant to embroil themselves in a controversy. NCBA president John Stedman, who had hired Helms two years earlier, wrote that he regretted that Helms had written the *Tarheel Banker* editorial. Although Stedman admitted that Helms might be correct in his position, he reminded him that the *Tarheel Banker* was, after all, a trade magazine and that its pages should mainly concern banking. Helms disagreed, responding that his enemies at the *N&O* had inspired the controversy. Most bankers remained behind him, he claimed; Stedman's note was the first indication of any objections among bankers to the editorial. Helms questioned whether all of the *Tarheel Banker*'s contents should be devoted to banking. The magazine now enjoyed its "greatest readership in its history," he wrote, because he had "worked, and worked hard, to make it a vibrant publication." His editorials sought to be reasonable and accurate, but wanted to express, when necessary, a "two-fisted attitude about what I consider to be right." Although Helms offered to bring the issue to the NCBA membership, Stedman did not pursue the matter. John P. Stedman to JH, September 1955; JH to Stedman, September 9, 1955, JH MSS.

146. Jesse Helms to Mrs. Holmes Van Mater, March 30, 1956; JH to Frank J. Mackey, December 30, 1957, JH MSS.

147. JH to Mrs. E. H. Whinham, December 6, 1957, JH to Frank J. Mackey, December 30, 1957, JH MSS.

148. JH to Mrs. E. H. Whinham, December 6, 1957, JH MSS; Jesse Helms to Mrs. Holmes Van Mater, March 30, 1956, JH MSS.

149. JH to Thomas D. Collins, December 17, 1958, JH MSS. See also JH to Frank J. Mackey, December 30, 1957, JH MSS.

150. JH, "We Aren't Solving Anything," *Tarheel Banker* 36, no. 5 (November 1957): 32.

151. JH, excerpt from addresses to Western North Carolina Conference, National Association of Bank Auditors and Comptrollers, November 21, 1957, JH MSS; "Banker Asks Million for 'Truth Campaign,'" *Knoxville News-Sentinel,* November 22, 1957; "Bank Official Suggests 'Truth Drive' by South," unidentified clipping in JH MSS; JH to Wriston A. Helms, November 26, 1957, JH MSS.

152. Lillian Milla Mosseller to JH, November 23, 1957; JH to Mosseller, December 5, 1957; James E. Edmonds to JH, November 25, 1957; Mrs. W. W. Calhoun to JH, December 10, 1957, JH MSS.

153. JH to John U. Barr, January 6, 1958, JH MSS.

154. JH to W. H. Reedy, June 5, 1959, JH MSS.

155. JH to Garland B. Porter, December 4, 1957, JH MSS.

156. W. J. Simmons to JH, May 8, 1961, JH MSS; Furgurson, *Hard Right,* pp. 83–84. Helms later vehemently denied any ties with the White Citizens' Councils. JH to Sam Ervin, November 25, 1968, JH MSS.

157. "Helms Seeks Council Seat," *Raleigh News and Observer,* March 31, 1957.

158. JH, responses to questions about City Council election [April 1957], JH MSS; Richard B. Russell to Willis Smith, Jr., April 9, 1957, was reproduced in the Raleigh press. See clippings in JH MSS; JH, "Wherein a Fellow Muses About Politics," *Tarheel Banker* 35, no. 12 (June 1957): 31.

159. JH, "Wherein a Fellow Muses About Politics"; JH, responses to questions about City Council election, April 1957; JH to Richard Russell, June 11, 1957, JH MSS.

160. JH, "Wherein a Fellow Muses About Politics."

161. Paul Hoover, quoted in Furgurson, *Hard Right,* p. 63; JH to Fred H. Wheeler, May 15, 1957; JH to Thomas H. Woodard, May 22, 1957, JH MSS.

162. Jack Crosswell, "Helms Controversial Councilman," *Raleigh News and Observer,* June 3, 1959, clipping in JH MSS.

163. JH, "'Urban Redevelopment'—Phew," *Tarheel Banker* 36, no. 4 (October 1957): 31.

164. A. C. Snow, "Council Battle Lines Drawn in Urban Fight," *Raleigh Times,* April 3, 1958, JH MSS; "Mayor, Helms Clash on Urban Renewal," *Raleigh News and Observer,* April 3, 1958, clipping in JH MSS; Jack Crosswell, "Helms Controversial Councilman," *Raleigh News and Observer,* June 3, 1959, clipping in JH MSS.

165. JH, "Urban Renewal—Or Expedient Tyranny?," *Tarheel Banker* 38, no. 10 (April 1960): 36.

166. AJF to Bill Armstrong, January 27, 1958, JH MSS.

167. AFJ to JH, January 28, 1958, JH MSS.

168. JH to W. H. Carper, January 30, 1958, JH MSS.

169. "Institute's Speaker List Resented Here, Helms Says," *Raleigh News and Observer,* January 31, 1958; "Troubles Expected at Religious Meet," *Greensboro Daily News,* January 31, 1958, clipping in JH MSS.

170. Edward Watkins to the editor, *Raleigh News and Observer,* February 3, 1958, JH MSS.

171. "The 1958 Concern Somewhat Puzzling," editorial, *Raleigh Times,* undated, JH MSS.

172. "Pious Incitement," editorial, *Raleigh News and Observer,* February 1, 1958. For adverse reaction to this editorial, see R. M. Rothgeb to the editor, *Raleigh News and Observer,* February 1, 1958, ms letter, JH MSS.

173. JH to John M. Gibbs, Jr., February 3, 1958, JH to Henry A. Dennis, March 13, 1958, JH MSS. See also JH to Herbert O'Keef, January 31, 1958, JH MSS.

174. "Helms Criticizes N&O in Statement to Council," *Raleigh News and Observer,* February 4, 1958, clipping in JH MSS. The same story was also carried in *The Monroe Journal,* February 6, 1958, and "Vote Disturbs Councilmen," *Raleigh Times,* February 4, 1958.

175. Bill Sharpe to JH, March 10, 1958, JH MSS. Helms responded that he "would rather be right with Bill Sharpe than president of *The News and Observer.* . . . I've been mighty proud of the things you've written, Bill, and I'm certainly glad to be on the same side with you." JH to Bill Sharpe, March 11, 1958, JH MSS.

176. JH to Erwin A. Holt, February 10, 1958, JH MSS.

177. JH to James P. Dees, August 31, 1959, JH MSS.

178. "He Fought Urban Renewal in Raleigh," *Laurinburg Exchange,* June 5, 1959, clipping in JH MSS.

179. "Native Son Charges Apathy in Politics," *Monroe Journal,* May 29, 1959.

180. JH to Beatrice Summers, November 24, 1958, JH MSS.

181. JH to AJF, April 23, 1959, JH MSS.

182. A. C. Snow, "Helms Asks Council Seat," *Raleigh Times,* n.d., JH MSS.

183. JH, campaign letter, April 1959, JH MSS; A. C. Snow, "Helms Asks Council Seat," *Raleigh News and Observer,* clipping, April 1959, Helms scrapbook.

184. JH to Lenox Baker, February 12, 1963, JH MSS.

185. Furgurson, *Hard Right,* p. 63; JH to Gordon L. Jones, December 6, 1960, JH MSS.

186. JH to Mr. and Mrs. H. B. Brewer, April 16, 1961, JH MSS.

187. Mrs. V. F. Hobbs to JH, December 17, 1960; JH to Hobbs, December 20, 1960, JH MSS.

188. JH, press release, March 14, 1961, JH MSS; JH to Mr. and Mrs. H. B. Brewer, April 16, 1961, JH MSS.

189. Dot Crawford to JH, May 6, 1961; JH to Crawford, May 10, 1961, JH MSS. "I will certainly need your help and support," he wrote one supporter, "for, as you say, there are many who will devote considerable effort to making sure that I am defeated." JH to Mrs. W. A. Daniel, May 18, 1961, JH MSS.
190. JH to Patricia Van Camp, September 19, 1961, JH MSS.
191. JH, speech, Siler City Rotary Club, February 1, 1960, JH MSS.

2. TRAVELING THE LONG, DREARY ROAD

1. JH to B. T. Vance, January 17, 1958, JH MSS. Helms later observed that "knowing you [A. J. Fletcher] has been one of the real joys of my life, and our association has been most meaningful to me." JH to AJF, December 31, 1958, JH MSS.
2. JH, "He Was Billed for Office Rent Only Once," *Tarheel Banker* 36, no. 11 (May 1958): 33. Fletcher kept a close eye over costs. On occasion he questioned whether a WRAL mail clerk employee should be employed on Saturday, because A.J. worried about paying overtime. AJF to JH, July 10, 1961, JH MSS.
3. AJF to Everett Jordan, December 12, 1958, JH MSS.
4. AJF to JH, July 22, 1957, JH MSS.
5. JH, "He Was Billed for Office Rent Only Once," *Tarheel Banker* 36, no. 11 (May 1958): 33. On Helms's conservative networking, see J. W. Manning to George P. Geoghagan, February 10, 1958; Frank J. Mackey to JH, February 11, 1958, JH MSS.
6. JH to Joseph R. McCarthy, January 28, 1954, JH MSS.
7. JH to Sam Ervin, March 29, 1957, JH MSS. Ervin responded favorably. Sam Ervin, Jr., to JH, April 2, 1957.
8. JH to Robert L. King, March 29, 1957, JH MSS.
9. JH to Luther E. Barnhardt, April 30, 1957, JH MSS.
10. JH to AJF, February 7, 1958, JH MSS.
11. AJF to JH, July 17, September 4, 1957; JH to AJF, July 19, August 28, 1957, JH MSS.
12. JH to Charles M. Reeves, Jr., December 17, 1958, JH MSS.
13. Helms was paid $25 per broadcast. AJF to JH, July 2, 1958, JH MSS. See also JH, *Here's Where I Stand,* p. 44.
14. *FOM* transcript, July 20, 1958, JH MSS.
15. JH to Stephen H. Conger, October 31, 1960, JH MSS.
16. In this sense, Helms was ahead of his time. For an analysis of the importance of rights as whites defined them, see Kevin Kruse, *White Flight: Atlanta and the Making of Modern Conservatism* (Princeton: Princeton University Press, 2005).
17. *FOM,* October 19, December 14, 1958.
18. *FOM,* January 4, August 20, 1959.

19. JH, "What Fools We Mortals Be," *Tarheel Banker* 38, no. 9 (March 1960): 42; *FOM*, February 14, 1960.

20. *FOM*, February 14, March 6, 1960; JH to Jack Riley, March 15, 1960, JH MSS. Some of these "outside agitators" were black: Jesse would claim in a broadcast on March 13, 1960, that black sit-in leaders in Raleigh were actually from out of town. *FOM*, March 13, 1960.

21. *FOM*, March 27, 1960.

22. Earl LeBaron to JH, November 13, 1958, JH MSS.

23. A. Hartwell Campbell to JH, January 15, 1959, JH MSS.

24. Earl LeBaron to Sterling H. Booth, Jr., January 18, 1959, JH MSS.

25. JH to LeBaron, December 23, 1958, JH MSS.

26. JH to Earl LeBaron, November 17, 1958, JH MSS.

27. JH to Stella Barbee, June 23, 1961, JH MSS.

28. JH to W. H. Reedy, June 5, 1959, JH MSS. See also JH to Lake, June 9, 1959, JH MSS.

29. *FOM*, August 23, 1959.

30. Parker interview, May 11, 2005.

31. Ernest B. Furgurson, *Hard Right: The Rise of Jesse Helms* (New York: W. W. Norton, 1986), pp. 66–67; JH, "This Business of Being Neutral Is Dynamite," *Tarheel Banker* 39, no. 1 (July 1960): 29.

32. *VP* #479, November 8, 1962.

33. *VP* #8, December 1, 1960; JH to Billy Arthur, November 21, 1960, JH MSS.

34. AJF to Rudolph K. Scott, March 6, 1961, JH MSS.

35. AJF to Jim Goodmon, October 14, 1963, JH MSS; "Will North Carolina Save Us from Jesse Helms?," unidentifed clipping, May 1978, JH MSS.

36. JH to Preston A. Scott, December 21, 1960; Bill Gwaltney to JH, February 21, 1961; JH to Gwaltney, February 22, 1961; JH to Mrs. W. A. Daniel, May 18, 1961; JH to Katherine F. Murphy, June 29, 1961; J. B. Younts to AJF, June 27, 1961; JH to Younts, June 30, 1961, JH MSS. Helms also reached a number of radio stations via FM feeds later on during the 1960s. WRAL early on began the practice of sending hundreds of transcripts of the *Viewpoints* across North Carolina and the United States. The *Viewpoints* aired Monday through Friday, after the evening news, at 6:20, then were rebroadcast mornings at 7:25. The *Viewpoints* were the first daily TV editorials in North Carolina, the second in the South, and the fourth in the United States. Transcripts were sent across the country. In 1963, Helms estimated that twenty-five to thirty newspapers published the *Viewpoints* on a regular basis. JH to Lenox Baker, February 18, 1963, JH MSS.

37. JH to Harry C. Massey, Jr., June 6, 1961, JH MSS.

38. JH to Tom Anderson, November 23, 1960, JH MSS.

39. "Will North Carolina Save Us from Jesse Helms?," unidentifed clipping, May 1978, JH MSS.

40. JH to Stella Barbee, June 23, 1961, JH MSS.

41. JH to Mrs. Holland L. Robb, October 1, 1964, JH MSS.

42. Achieving the presidency after the "most liberal campaign in the history of this nation" and running on a party platform that was "so far to the left that hardly any Democrat...dared call attention to it during the campaign—much less endorse it," Helms observed that politics had forced a conservative Democrat, Luther Hodges, to join hands with Kennedy liberals. Hodges, who joined the Kennedy cabinet as secretary of commerce, had "indulged in some nimble footwork" and some "some rather interesting bed-fellowship." Kennedy and Hodges had not "seen eye to eye for almost ten years," and they disagreed about proposed legislation to assist the textile-producing areas of New England, legislation that Helms claimed would disadvantage the more efficient southern textile producers. If consistency was "a jewel," Luther Hodges faced a "tough time building a collection of politcal gems." *VP* #1, November 21, 1960.

43. *VP* #223, October 17, 1961. For a plea for lower taxes, see VP #104, April 18, 1961.

44. JH, speech, Benson Chamber of Commerce, January 23, 1964, JH MSS.

45. JH to James Dees, May 16, 1961, JH MSS.

46. *VP* #2, November 22, 1960. See also VP #27, December 18, 1960.

47. *VP* #22, December 21, 1960. See also VP #850. May 4, 1964.

48. *VP* #431, August 30, 1962; *VP* #208, September 26, 1961.

49. See also his position on Peru, where he approved a military coup. *VP* #416, July 25, 1962.

50. *VP* #283, January 12, 1962.

51. JH to Sam Ervin, June 13, 1961, JH MSS. Helms also developed a network of people who wrote with information about suspicious people. See Stella Barbee to JH, February 10, 1961; JH to Barbee, February 13, 1961, JH MSS, in which Barbee asserted the Communist connections of CBS television commentator Edward R. Murrow, and in which Jesse responded that he might "make good use" of this information.

52. *VP* #2008, January 10, 1969.

53. *VP* #274, December 29, 1961. Helms's associations with Hoover are mentioned in JH to J. Edgar Hoover, October 26, 1961; Hoover to JH, November 1, 1961, JH MSS.

54. David Burner, *Making Peace with the Sixties* (Princeton: Princeton University Press, 1996).

55. Jimmy Hunt to JH, May 22, 1961; JH to Hunt, May 24, 1961, JH MSS.

56. *VP* #62, February 17, 1961.

57. *VP* #219, October 11, 1961. Also see, on the same subject, *VP* #258, December 6, 1961.

58. *VP* #573, March 25, 1963.

59. JH to John T. Denny, June 3, 1963, JH MSS.

60. *VP* #693, September 19, 1963.

61. JH to Stella K. Barbee, June 30, 1964; JH to J. B. Jackson, September 23, 1963, JH MSS.

62. JH to Stella K. Barbee, June 30, 1964; JH to George C. Wallace, June 20, 1964, JH MSS; *VP* #1355, May 12, 1966. On Wallace, see Dan T. Carter, *The Politics of Rage: George Wallace, the Origins of the New Conservatism, and the Transformation of American Politics* (Baton Rouge: Louisiana State University Press, 2000).

63. *VP* #4, November 25, 1960; *VP* #92, March 31, 1961. When Senator Sam Ervin supported Kennedy in the debate about federal aid to education, Helms was bitterly disappointed. JH to Ervin, April 25, May 29, June 28, 1961; Ervin to JH, June 26, 1961; AJF to Ervin, August 29, 1961, JH MSS.

64. JH to Alton A. Lennon, January 31, 1961, JH MSS; *VP* #71, March 2, 1961; *VP* #38, #39, January 13, 16, 1961.

65. JH to Edwin P. Glenn, October 2, 1964, JH MSS.

66. JH to George M. Beasley, Jr., September 21, 1964, JH MSS.

67. JH to Kay Gary, September 21, 23, 1964; JH to R. J. Reavis, Jr., November 3, 1964; JH to Paul A. Jones, November 30, 1964, JH MSS.

68. Helms was especially concerned about sympathetic white ministers, especially those associated with the National Council of Churches. See, for example, JH to Eddie A. Daniels, Jr., December 10, 1960; *VP* #701, #705, #725, October, 1, 7, and November 5, 1963; Bill Sharpe to JH, April 7, 1964; JH to Sharpe, May 15, 1964.

69. *VP* #930, September 7, 1964.

70. *VP* #443, September 17, 1962.

71. *VP* #402, July 4, 1962.

72. *VP* #715, October 22, 1963.

73. *VP* #571, March 21, 1963.

74. *VP* #944, September 25, 1964.

75. *VP* #128, May 22, 1961.

76. JH to C. L. Green, Jr., June 24, 1963, JH MSS.

77. *VP* #1365, #1376, May 26, June 10, 1966; JH to Earle Elmore, January 7, 1964; JH to David W. Williams, January 20, 1964, JH MSS.

78. *VP* #909, August 7, 1964.

79. JH to William R. Easter, February 21, 1961, JH MSS.

80. JH to Bill Weidlick, March 8, 1961, JH MSS.

81. JH to P. F. Finley, June 14, 1961, JH MSS.

82. *VP* #98, April 10, 1961.

83. *VP* #819, March 20, 1964.

84. *VP* #989, December 4, 1964; JH to W. U. Lewis, Jr., July 12, 1963; JH to D. V. Andrew, July 12, 1963, JH MSS.

85. *VP* #193, #902, September 5, 1961, July 29, 1964. See also *VP* #187, August 28, 1961.

86. *VP* #659, August 1, 1963.

87. *VP* #736, November 20, 1963.

88. *VP* #1071, #1100, April 1, May 12, 1965. On Rustin, see John D'Emilio, *Lost Prophet: The and Times of Bayard Rustin* (Chicago: University of Chicago Press, 2003).

89. *VP* #1197, September 30, 1965; JH to Ed Cannon, September 25, 1964, JH MSS.

90. *VP* #672, #679, August 20, 29, 1963; D'Emilio, *Lost Prophet,* pp. 191–92. For a subsequent reference to Rustin, see *VP* #1656, August 4, 1967.

91. *VP* #761, December 30, 1963.

92. *VP* #794, February 14, 1964.

93. *VP* #814, March 13, 1964.

94. *VP* #843, April 23, 1964.

95. *VP* #114, May 2, 1961. Essentially the same language appeared in *VP* #573, March 25, 1963.

96. Henry T. Royall to JH, October 16, 21, 1961; JH to Royall, October 18, 1961. Helms commented on Scales's release in *VP* #349, April 19, 1962, *VP* #513, December 28, 1962, and *VP* #518, January 4, 1963.

97. See JH to Mrs. J. W. Ellis, October 26, 1961, JH MSS. For an example of Emery's correspondence, see Sarah Watson Emery to JH, March 22, 1962, JH MSS. Sarah Watson Emery to JH, December 16, 1960, January 17, 1961; JH to Emery, January 16, 1961, JH MSS.

98. Sarah Watson Emery, *Blood on the Old Well* (Dallas: Prospect House, 1963), pp. 100–103, 106. Emery also suggested that a number of mysterious deaths were related to the Communist conspiracy, as was the publication of books by subversives by the University of North Carolina Press.

99. JH to A. C. Jordan, August 20, 1963, JH MSS. See also JH to Paul A. Johnston, August 26, 1974, JH MSS.

100. Mary Jane Mann to JH, March 1, 1962, JH MSS.

101. Hoover Adams to Paul Sharp, September 19, 1965, JH MSS.

102. American Legion resolution, September 17, 1962, enclosed in Henry E. Royall to the General Assembly, January 5, 1963, JH MSS.

103. JH to Henry E. Royall, October 17, 1962, JH MSS.

104. Henry E. Royall to JH, January 7, 1963; JH to Royall, January 8, 1963, JH MSS.

105. *VP* #461, October 11, 1962.

106. *VP* #466, October 18, 1962.

107. *VP* #502, December 12, 1962. For one response, see "Jesse Helms and the DTH," December 14, 1962; JH to the editor of the DTH, December 17, 1962, JH MSS.

108. *VP* #582, April 5, 1963.

109. Henry E. Royall to JH, June 17, 1963, JH MSS, in which Royall wanted Helms to produce the "list." Helms called a "friend" at Chapel Hill and reported that "he did not think well of sending me the list" and that he would be "in real trouble if the adminstration were able to show that he had talked with me." JH to Royall, June 19, 1963, JH MSS.

110. *VP* #631, June 14, 1963.

111. *VP* #636, June 21, 1963.

112. William A. Link, *William Friday: Power, Purpose, and American Higher Education* (Chapel Hill: University of North Carolina Press, 1995), pp. 113–15.

113. *VP* #642, July 1, 1963; JH to Mrs. David W. Mascitelli, July 1, 1963, JH MSS.

114. *VP* #732, November 14, 1963; *VP* #642, July 1, 1963.

115. *VP* #692, September 17, 1963. "The communist-ban law," he wrote another time, "would never have been enacted unless there had been a very definite laxity." JH to Cheryle D. Smith, April 20, 1964, JH MSS.

116. *VP* #714, October 21, 1963.

117. JH to Philip P. Godwin, October 31, 1963, JH MSS. "The UNC people are really getting hot," he wrote soon thereafter. "The hotter they get, the more likely it becomes that they will fry themselves." JH to Barbara Hauser, November 13, 1962, JH MSS.

118. *VP* #722, October 31, 1963.

119. JH to James J. Kilpatrick, December 27, 1963; JJK to JH, December 28, 1963, JH MSS.

120. JH to Harris Purks, June 23, 1965, JH MSS.

121. *VP* #1001, December 22, 1964.

122. JH to Dan Moore, June 3, 1965, JH MSS.

123. *VP* #1118, June 7, 1965. On the SACS issue, see also *VP* #1099, May 11, 1965.

124. *VP* #1134, June 29, 1965; *VP* #1163, August 12, 1965.

125. *VP* #1178, September 2, 1965.

126. *VP* #1182, September 9, 1965.

127. *VP* #1233, November 23, 1965.

128. JH to Fred Hobson, February 15, 1966, JH MSS

129. *VP* #1285, February 3, 1966.

130. *VP* #1306, March 4, 1966.

131. *VP* #1286, 1290, February 4, 10, 1966. When Dickson's curfew violation first occurred, in September 1965, Helms criticized the "double standards" that were applied to the male and female students. He believed that this reflected the "alarming timidity of the University in grasping its responsibility of discipline." There was "too great a tendency" to see college students as "mature" without the need for "the protection and guidance which they were receiving at home only a year or so ago." College authorities should not abandon their "responsibility to serve as substitute parents as well as teachers." *VP* #1195, September 28, 1965.

132. *VP* #1976, November 26, 1968.

133. "UNC Class Assignment Seen 'Objectionable,'" *Durham Morning Herald,* October 18, 1966; report, Chancellor's Committee on Teaching and the Curriculum, October 18, 1966; Sitterson, statement, October 18, 1966, Sitterson Papers, box 11, SHC; "University Professor Reassigned in Furor Over 'Seduction' Theme," *Greensboro Daily News,* October 19, 1966; "Instructor Loses Teaching Duties," *Daily Tar Heel,* October 19, 1966; "Shift of Paull Reaffirmed at UNC," *Raleigh News and Observer,* October 22, 1966; Sitterson to Dr. Lytt I. Gardner, November 1, 1966, Sitterson Papers, box 11.

134. Paull interview, March 4, 2005; JH, "Instructor Loses Teaching Duties," *Daily Tar Heel,* October 19, 1966. See Paull's complete description of the sequence of events in Paull, "Chronology of the Events from Oct. 11, 1966," copy in author's possession.

135. "Students Support English Instructor, Draw Up Petition," *Greensboro Daily News,* October 20, 1966; student petition, October 20, 1966, Sitterson Papers, box 11.

136. JH to Bill Friday, October 3, 1966, JH MSS.

137. "The Seductive Groves of Academe," *Charlotte Observer,* editorial, October 25, 1966.

138. Paull interview, March 4, 2005; Pollitt interview, July 15, 2005.

139. Sitterson to JH, November 1, 1966, Sitterson Papers, box 11.

140. "Who's Afraid of Jesse Helms? The University—That's Who," editorial, *Daily Tar Heel,* October 20, 1966. At a meeting attended by three hundred people held on October 20, the Committee for Free Inquiry recommended that Paull be reinstated, that the English Department investigate the situation, and that the chancellor conduct an "immediate and open hearing" to deal with future procedures in similar cases. "Instructor Removal Subject of Meeting," *Daily Tar Heel,* October 20, 1966; "Statement of Policy," Committee for Free Inquiry, October 20, 1966, Sitterson Papers, box 11; "UNC Students to Hold Meeting to Protest Removal of Instructor," *Charlotte Observer,* October 20, 1966; "Group Seeks Reinstatement of UNC English Instructor," *Durham Morning Herald,* October 21, 1966.

141. "Score One for WRAL," *Greensboro Daily News,* editorial, October 20, 1966.

142. "Always a Nit to Pick," *Raleigh News and Observer,* editorial, October 25, 1966.

143. "Coyness All over the Place," *Southern Pines Pilot,* October 26, 1966, enclosed in Noval Neil Luxon to Sitterson, November 7, 1966, Sitterson Papers, box 11.

144. "25 English Instructors at UNC Threaten Walkout," *Raleigh News and Observer,* October 26, 1966; William A. West to Sitterson, October 21, 1966, Sitterson Papers, box 11; "Shift of Paull Reaffirmed at UNC," *Raleigh News and Observer,* October 22, 1966; "Chancellor Seeking Paull Case Advice," *Daily Tar Heel,* October 21, 1966; "English Department Receives Paull Case," *Daily Tar Heel,* October 22, 1966; "Chancellor's Position on Teacher Clairified," *Durham Morning Herald,* October 22, 1966; "Instructor's Case Is Reconsidered," *Charlotte Observer,* October 21, 1966.

145. "Teacher Who Assigned a Poem About Seduction Is Transferred," *New York Times,* October 23, 1966.

146. "English Prof's Case May Reach Chancellor," *Charlotte Observer,* October 26, 1966.

147. JH to Sitterson, October 25, 1966, Sitterson Papers, box 11; *VP* #1466, October 25, 1966.

148. JH to George F. Johnson, November 1, 1966, JH MSS.

149. *VP* #1473, November 3, 1966.

150. "Score One for Literature," *Greensboro Daily News,* editorial, November 12, 1966.
151. "Report of a Special Committee on a Disputed Theme Assignment in a Class Taught by Mr. Michael Paull," November 10, 1966, Sitterson Papers, box 11; Paull interview, March 4, 2005; "University Reinstates Suspended Instructor," *Greensboro Daily News,* November 11, 1966; "'Coy Mistress' Revisited," *Raleigh News and Observer,* November 14, 1966; Pollitt interview.
152. "The Rape of the Flock," editorial, *Raeford News-Journal,* October 1966; JH to Paul Dickson, October 31, 1966, JH MSS.
153. "The Coy Mistress Caper," *Life,* November 11, 1966.
154. Paull interview, March 4, 2005; Wallace Kaufman, *Coming Out of the Woods: The Solitary Life of a Maverick Naturalist* (Cambridge, Mass.: Perseus, 2000), p. 21.
155. "Michael Paull Stands Acquitted," *Durham Morning Herald,* November 12, 1966.
156. "Score One for Literature," *Greensboro Daily News,* editorial, November 12, 1966.
157. Gibson Prather, "The Week's Wash," *Fayetteville Observer,* November 20, 1966; Gordon F. Cooper to JH, November 21, 1966, JH MSS.
158. *VP* #1479, November 11, 1966.
159. *VP* #1480, November 14, 1966.
160. Edwin M. Yoder, Jr., "The Moral Majoritarian Platform," *Washington Star,* July 31, 1980; JH to the editor, *Washington Star,* August 17, 1980, Paull Papers. Yoder responded once more in "What Helms Really Said," *Greensboro Daily News,* September 7, 1980. Helms then declined to respond further. Gene Marlowe, "Who's the Kettle, Who's the Pot?," *Winston-Salem Journal,* October 5, 1980.

3. BLACK IS WHITE, AND WRONG IS RIGHT

1. Ferrel Guillory, "He Took That Advice, and It Took Him to the Senate," *Monroe Enquirer-Journal,* January 10, 1973.
2. M. Stanton Evans, "Sen. Jesse Helms: A New Kind of Politician," *Human Events,* August 5, 1978.
3. JH to Bill Sharpe, September 24, 1969, JH MSS.
4. Interview with Helms (by Furgurson).
5. JH to Lenox Baker, July 8, 1963, JH MSS; "Dot Helms Pinch Hits for Husband Jesse," *Monroe Enquirer-Journal,* October 23, 1972.
6. JH to Mrs. Carl Delamar, July 30, 1963, JH MSS.
7. JH to Lenox Baker, July 31, 1963, JH MSS; "The Helms Behind the Ogre Image," editorial, *Goldsboro News-Argus,* August 5, 1990.
8. JH to Lenox Baker, June 15, 1964, JH MSS.
9. Lenox Baker to Dan K. Moore, January 14, October 1, 1964; JH to Baker, October 6, 1964, July 3, 1967, JH MSS. In February, Jesse reported to Baker

that he was "delighted" by Charles's improvement. "From my own unprofessional observation, I think you have placed him in the position to do a great deal for himself. In any case, the blessings you have provided him are remarkable." He enrolled Charles in a summer camp, where Jesse hoped that he would benefit from "associations of a somewhat competitive nature with other schoolboys." JH to Lenox Baker, February 20, 1965, JH MSS.

10. JH to Lenox Baker, February 20, 1965, JH MSS.

11. Lenox Baker to JH, February 12, 1963, JH MSS.

12. Lenox Baker to JH, July 4, 1964, JH MSS.

13. Lenox Baker to Grier Martin, November 13, 1963, JH MSS.

14. Lenox Baker to JH, November 19, 1963; JH to Baker, November 25, 1963, JH MSS.

15. *VP* #1411, August 4, 1966.

16. *VP* #1005, December 29, 1964. For other studies about the rise of modern conservatism, see Kevin Kruse, *White Flight: Atlanta and the Making of American Conservatism* (Princeton: Princeton University Press, 2005); Matthew Lassiter, *The Silent Majority: Suburban Politics in the Sunbelt South* (Princeton: Princeton University Press, 2005). On conservatism in the West, see Lisa McGerr, *Suburban Warriors: The Origins of the New American Right* (Princeton: Princeton University Press, 2002).

17. Quoted in "Jesse Helms and 'the Whispers,'" editorial, *Charlotte Observer*, August 13, 1972.

18. *VP* #833, April 9, 1964.

19. *VP* #829, April 3, 1964.

20. *VP* #1674, August 30, 1967. See a similar theme in *VP* #1656, August 4, 1967.

21. *VP* #883, June 18, 1964.

22. *VP* #801, February 25, 1964.

23. *VP* #1086, April 22, 1965.

24. *VP* #899, July 24, 1964.

25. *VP* #1800, #1895, March 5 and July 30, 1968.

26. *VP* #1083, April 17, 1965.

27. *VP* #1350, #1390, May 5 and July 6, 1966. Helms entered into a small controversy about the Klan when Malcolm Seawell, head of the Governor's Committee on Law and Order (and the person responsible for conducting the anti-Klan campaign) favored revoking the Klan's state charter. Seawell eventually resigned. See Sam Beard to JH; JH to Beard, memos, c. May 5, 1966; Beard to JH, May 5, 1966; Sam Beard, news report, May 6, 1966; JH to Baker, July 22, 1966; *VP* # 1406, #1412, July 28, August 5, 1966, JH MSS.

28. *VP* #1539, February 9, 1967.

29. *VP* #1351, May 6, 1966.

30. *VP* #1433, September 8, 1966.

31. *VP* #1335, April 14, 1966.

32. *VP* #1835, #1968, April 30, November 14, 1968. On Hyde County, see

David S. Cecelski, *Along Freedom Road: Hyde County, North Carolina, and the Fate of Black Schools in the South* (Chapel Hill: University of North Carolina Press, 1994).

33. *VP* #1686, September 15, 1967. See also *VP* #1755, December 28, 1967. On Hyde County, see David S. Cecelski, *Along Freedom Road: Hyde County, North Carolina, and the Fate of Black Schools in the South* (Chapel Hill: University of North Carolina Press, 1994).

34. *VP* #2388, July 30, 1970.

35. *VP* #1455, October 10, 1966.

36. *VP* #1387, July 1, 1966.

37. *VP* #1491, December 2, 1966.

38. *VP* #1792, February 22, 1968.

39. *VP* #1847, May 16, 1968.

40. JH to H. F. Seawell, Jr., May 4, 1970, JH MSS.

41. JH to James J. Kilpatrick, September 9, 1964, JH MSS.

42. Helms noted that an "astute and generally well-informed political observer" told him that "much of our troubles" originated with the governor. According to one account, despite pressure from the Sanford administration, removing WRAL's license failed by one vote. Helms, for his part, engaged in a lobbying campaign on his own that relied on support from the state's two U.S. senators and much of its congressional delegation, spurred along by a vigorous letter-writing campaign. JH to William Jennings Dorn, August 12, 1963; JH to Barbara Hauser, January 6, 1964; JH to J. Warren Ellis, January 27, 1964; JH to Stella E. Barbee, March 31, 1964; JH to Lenox Baker, July 20, 1964; JH to Thurman Sensing, May 18, 1964, JH MSS; Parker interview. "After eight months of going over our operation with a fine-tooth comb," he wrote after the FCC renewed WRAL's license, "the two specific sins that they uncovered were our failure to implore two Negroes to appear on our station—both of them men with communist records and one of them a self-confessed homosexual." JH to J. W. Perry, Jr., August 3, 1964, JH MSS.

43. *VP* #906, August 4, 1964.

44. See JH to Thurman Sensing, August 29, 1963, JH MSS.

45. JH, memo for the files, October 31, 1966; Harold Cooley, transcript of news conference, November 7, 1966; Harold Cooley to Ben F. Waple, November 18, 1966, JH MSS.

46. JH, memo to the file, November 7, 1966, JH MSS.

47. *VP* #1476, November 7, 1966.

48. Harold Cooley to Ben F. Waple, November 18, 1966, JH MSS.

49. Abraham Holtzman to chairman, FCC, November 29, 1966, JH MSS.

50. Fred Fletcher, memo, c. December 16, 1966; Hoover Adams to JH, November 28, 1966; JH to Bill Sharpe, January 9, 1967, JH MSS.

51. "FCC Rules Stations Have Wide Freedom to Air Slurs if Those Assailed Can Reply," *Wall Street Journal,* June 20, 1966, clipping in JH MSS.

52. JH to Ben Waple, December 12, 1966, JH MSS. Holtzman claimed again that

he never received a copy of the editorial nor a letter inviting him to respond. Abraham Holtzman to JH, December 16, 1966, JH MSS.

53. Frank U. Fletcher to JH, June 20, 1967, JH MSS; Jack Batten, "FCC Rejects Cooley's Charge of Conspiracy," *Charlotte Observer,* July 8, 1967, clipping in JH MSS. See also "'Seab' Strikes Out," editorial, *Charleston Evening Post,* July 31, 1967, clipping in JH MSS.

54. See, for example, Glenn Dickson to JH, January 28, 1966; JH to Dickson, January 31, 1966; JH to Lenox Baker, January 14, February 2, 1966, JH to Hoover Adams, March 17, 1966, JH MSS.

55. *VP* #2220, November 24, 1969.

56. *VP* #2406, September 1, 1970. See also *VP* #2433, October 9, 1970.

57. Paletz later remembered that he found it "quite astonishing" that he completed his broadcast without ever once blinking. Paletz interview, March 3, 2005; Angela Davis to AJF, February 6, 1970; JH to David Paletz, February 9, May 28, August 24, 1970, January 18, February 10, 17, 22, 1971; Paletz to JH, May 22, August 28, December 31, 1970; January 15, February 8, 20, 1971; David Paletz, dissenting opinion to *Viewpoint* editorial, February 25, 1971, JH MSS.

58. Paletz to JH, March 16, 23, 1971, JH MSS.

59. Frank Fletcher to AJF, April 21, 1971, JH MSS.

60. JH to Paletz, March 25, 1971, JH MSS.

61. JH to Frank Fletcher, April 14, May 17, 1971; Frank Fletcher to AJF, April 21, 1971; Scott Lynch to William B. Ray, May 5, 26, 1971; JH to William B. Ray, June 11, 1971; William B. Ray to R. Scott Lynch, July 23, 1971, JH MSS.

62. Paletz interview, March 3, 2005.

63. Helms apparently brokered an arrangement in which Beverly Lake swung his support behind Moore in the second primary of 1964. JH to A. Paul Kitchin, June 9, 1964, JH MSS.

64. JH to Bill Sharpe, July 2, 1965, JH MSS.

65. JH to Bill Sharpe, April 11, 1967, JH MSS.

66. Earl Butz to JH, July 28, August 11, 1967, JH MSS.

67. JH to Earl Butz, August 1, 15, 1967; Butz to JH, July 28, August 11, 1967, JH MSS.

68. *VP* #1910, August 22, 1968.

69. *VP* #1966, November 12, 1968.

70. *VP* #2444, October 26, 1970.

71. *VP* #2428, #2431, October 2, 7, 1970. Bill Sharpe, Helms's conservative conscience, did not like Nixon and voted for Wallace in 1968. He described Nixon as "probably unfitted for the job." Bill Sharpe to JH, August 17, 1969, JH MSS.

72. Charles R. Jonas to T. Y. Milburn, July 18, 1969; Jonas to JH, July 31, 1969; JH to Jonas, July 21, 1969, JH MSS.

73. JH to Earl Butz, January 2, 1969; Butz to JH, January 1969, JH MSS.

74. Interview with JH, by Ben F. Bulla, May 25, 1989, SOHP; JH interview (Tom Joyner), tape 6; JH, *Here's Where I Stand,* p. 51.

75. JH to Richard Nixon, September 18, 1970, JH MSS. Nixon's assistant, Harry

Dent, responded: "it feels good, doesn't it?" Harry Dent to JH, September 28, 1970, JH MSS.

76. Helms interview (by Jack Bass), March 8, 1974, Southern Oral History Program, SHC.

77. Roy Thompson, "WRAL Chief Is Zealous in His Role," *Winston-Salem Journal,* December 2, 1966. JH to Jordan, November 26, 1971, JH MSS.

78. *VP* #2709, December 1, 1971; JH to Jordan, November 22, 26, 1971, JH MSS.

79. JH to B. Everett Jordan, December 3, 1971, JH MSS; interview with JH (Ben F. Bulla), May 25, 1989, SOHP.

80. Mrs. William C. McGee to JH, February 6, 1982; JH to McGee, February 9, 1962, JH MSS. He had decided against running by August 1963. See JH to Barbara Hauser, August 29, 1963, JH MSS.

81. Tom Ellis interview (by Joyner). A. J. Fletcher to JH, January 18, 1972, JH MSS, formalized these terms.

82. JH to B. Everett Jordan, February 1, 1972, JH MSS.

83. "Helms Close to Decision," *Charlotte News,* February 4, 1972, Helms clipping files.

84. "Helms Pledges to Seek Restoration of Sanity," unidentified clipping, February 18, 1972, JH MSS; "Helms Enters U.S. Senate Race," *Dunn Daily Record,* February 18, 1972.

85. JH, *Here's Where I Stand,* p. 52; Helms interview (by Bass), March 8, 1974, SOHP; Helms interview (by Joyner), tape 2; Fugurson, notes of interview with Tom Ellis, October 21, 1985, Furgurson Papers, folder 19, SHC; interview with Tom Ellis, July 14, 2005; John Kilgo, "Political Notebook," *Charlotte News,* February 4, 1972, Helms clipping files, Brent Hackney, "Helms' Alter Ego Has Put His Stamp on N.C. Politics," *Greensboro Daily News,* July 9, 1978; Ned Cline, "Helms: Conservative Lone Ranger," *Charlotte Observer,* November 20, 1977; Sharon Bond, "Ellis Is Mastermind Behind Conservatives," *Greensboro Daily News,* October 19, 1980; Elizabeth Drew, "Reporter at Large: Jesse Helms," *New Yorker,* July 20, 1981, p. 79. See also Ferguson, *Hard Right,* pp. 92–96.

86. JH interview (by Joyner), tape 2; Fuller interview (by Riddick), December 22, 1989, Helms Center.

87. *VP* #2762, February 21, 1972.

88. Dan T. Carter, *The Politics of Rage: George Wallace, the Origins of the New Conservatism, and the Transformation of American Politics* (Baton Rouge: Louisiana State University Press, 1998); Dan T. Carter, *From George Wallace to Newt Gingrich: Race in the Conservative Counterrevolution, 1963–1994* (Baton Rouge: Louisiana State University Press, 1999). For another look, see Thomas Byrne Edsall and Mary D. Edsall, *Chain Reaction: The Impact of Race, Rights, and Taxes on American Politics* (New York: W. W. Norton, 1991); Kruse, *White Flight;* Lassiter, *The Silent Majority.*

87. "Johnson Announces for Senate," *Charlotte News,* February 7, 1972; John Kilgo, "Political Notebook," *Charlotte News,* February 25, 1972; John Kilgo, "GOP Senate Race N.C.'s 'Meanest,'" *Charlotte News,* c. March 1972; Rick Gunter, "Johnson Says His Foes Too Conservative," *Asheville Times,* c. April 1972; "Candidates

Crisscross State as Campaign Temp Increases," unidentified clipping, c. April 1972, HCF. Ellis later admitted that the primary campaign "wasn't easy," and it was "a job" to defeat Johnson. Ellis interview, July 14, 2005.

90. "Rep. Jonas Backs Helms for Senate," *Winston-Salem Journal*, March 28, 1972.

91. John Kilgo, "Political Notebook," *Western Carolina Tribune*, March 5, 1972; Larry Tarleton, "Maverick GOP Legislator Seeking Senate Nomination," *Charlotte Observer*, undated; "DeLapp Joins Helms Campaign," *Winston-Salem Journal*, March 8, 1972.

92. "Incumbent Senator Defends Senate's Seniority System," *Durham Herald*, April 29, 1972.

93. "Henry Eichel, "Busing Is Biggest Issue Says Helms," *Greensboro Daily News*, April 30, 1972.

94. "Helms Scorns Kennedy," *Thomasville Times*, April 29, 1972.

95. Ken Irons, "Helms Targets East," unidentified clipping, c. April 1972, JH MSS.

96. "Helms States Stand on Election Issues," *Wilmington Star*, April 24, 1972.

97. "Helms Scorns Kennedy," *Thomasville Times*, April 29, 1972.

98. "Galifianakis Again Rips Jordan," *Winston-Salem Sentinel*, April 15, 1972.

99. Eddie Southards, "Helms: Schools Top Issue," unidentified clipping, c. April 1972, JH MSS.

100. Rick Gunter, "Helms Would Put 'Principles First,'" *Asheville Times*, April 14, 1972; "Skipper and Pat, Nick and Jordan, GOP's Jims Face Runoff Situations," *Greensboro Daily News*, c. May 1972.

101. Jack Scism, "'With a Name like Mine?,'" *Greensboro Daily News*, undated [c. October 1972]; Paul Clancy, "Galifianakis and Helms Have Avoided High Road," *Charlotte Observer*, November 5, 1972, HCF.

102. Black interview, February 15, 2006.

103. Daniel C. Hoover, "Mastermind of the Right," *Raleigh News and Observer*, November 25, 1979; Brent Hackney, "Helms' Alter Ego Has Put His Stamp on N.C. Politics," *Greensboro Daily News*, July 9, 1978; Ellis interview, July 14, 2005; interviews with Carter Wrenn (by Joe Mosnier), September 27, 1996, Southern Oral History Program; September 7, 2006; interview with Hamilton Horton, Jr. (by Mosnier), June 5, 1997, Southern Oral History Program; Guillory interview, February 2, 2006; Black interview, February 15, 2006; Stephens interview, June 6, 2006; Judy Sarasohn, "Ellis Not Interested in Running for Office," *Raleigh Times*, March 26, 1976; Judy Sarasohn, "GOP Win Engineered by Ellis and Helms," *Raleigh Times*, c. March 25, 1976; Brent Hackney, "Helms' Alter Ego Has Put His Stamp on N.C. Politics," *Greensboro Daily News*, July 9, 1978.

104. Wrenn interview, May 13, 2005; Sharon Bond, "Ellis Is Mastermind Behind Conservatives," *Greensboro Daily News*, October 19, 1980.

105. Ned Cline, "Helms: Conservative Lone Ranger," *Charlotte Observer*, November 20, 1977.

106. JH, speech to YAF meeting, April 14, 1973, in *CR*, May 8, 1973, floor speeches, JH MSS; Dunlop interview, June 5, 2006. See also JH, *Here's Where I Stand*, p.

54; Black interview, February 15, 2006. On the early history of YAF, see John A. Andrew, *The Other Side of the Sixties: The New Conservatism in American Thought and Politics* (New Brunswick: Rutgers University Press, 1997).

107. Guillory interview, February 2, 2006; Black interview, February 15, 2006; Charles Osolin, "'Outside' Money Flowing to Helms," *Winston-Salem Journal,* c. October 1972; Paul Clancy, "The People Who Run the Campaigns," *Charlotte Observer,* c. October 1972; Ned Cline, "Helms: Conservative Lone Ranger," *Charlotte Observer,* November 20, 1977, HCF; Wrenn interview, May 13, 2005; Ellis interview, July 14, 2005; Robin Toner, "New GOP Spokesman Ready for Battle with Democrats," *Raleigh News and Observer,* August 1, 1990. Helms received $40,000 from textile executives, according to one report. Pat Stith, "Textile Money Helping Helms," *Raleigh News and Observer,* October 27, 1972.

108. "Helms Says He Backs Most Wallace Aims," *Charlotte News,* October 24, 1972.

109. Paul Clancy, "Helms Shows Up at Convention, Praises Nixon," *Charlotte Observer,* August 2, 1972; Ellis interview, July 14, 2005; interview with Jack Lee (by Mosnier), November 15, 1996, Southern Oral History Program; Ellis interview, July 14, 2005; JH, *Here's Where I Stand,* p. 55.

110. Guillory interview, February 2, 2006.

111. Ellis interview, July 14, 2005; JH, *Here's Where I Stand,* pp. 53–54.

112. Paul Clancy, "Helms Strikes Old Familiar Chords," *Charlotte Observer,* October 20, 1972; Paul Clancy, "Galifianakis and Helms Have Avoided High Road," *Charlotte Observer,* November 5, 1972; Wingate Lassiter, "They Came Out to Hear Jesse Helms," *Smithfield Herald,* c. October 1972; "Helms Calls for a Return to 'Faith of Our Fathers,'" unidentified clipping, c. October 1972, JH MSS.

113. "Helms Says Spiritual Rebirth Needed," unidentified clipping, c. October 1972; JH, speech to the Concerned Christian Citizens for Political Action, Lynden, Washington, September 28, 1974, JH MSS; Dunlop interview (by Joyner), tape 26; Helms interview (by Joyner), tape 30. Helms described his born-again experience in an interview on Jim Bakker's televised *PTL Club* on October 18, 1978, and in JH, *Here's Where I Stand,* pp. 55–57. See "Helms Tells Audience of Christian Rebirth," *Raleigh News and Observer,* October 19, 1978.

114. JH interview (Tom Joyner), tape 30.

115. JH to Robert N. Sims, Jr., October 9, 1964; JH to J. E. Stancil, December 8, 1964, JH MSS; "Jesse Helms and the 'Whispers,'" *Charlotte Observer,* August 13, 1972; "Mr. Helms' Past Specifics Move Him to Generalities," editorial, *Charlotte Observer,* October 6, 1972; Paul Clancy and Howard Covington, "Galifianakis, Helms: Study in Contrasts," *Charlotte Observer,* October 7, 1972; "Helms: I Was Called 'Racist,'" *Charlotte Observer,* August 6, 1972; John Kilgo, "Political Notebook," unidentified clipping, August 11, 1972, JH MSS; Furgurson, *Hard Right,* p. 227.

116. "Voters Brush Aside Old-Line Favorites," *Monroe Enquirer-Journal,* June 5, 1972. See examples of Helms as the "citizen" candidate in the *Yancey Journal,* July 13, 27, August 10, 1972, JH MSS.

117. Bill Furlow, "Drug Ads Were Bought by Group Backing Helms," *Charlotte News*, September 2, 1972; Paul Clancy, "Helms Says Ads Lacked His OK," *Charlotte Observer*, September 27, 1972. See the ad in the *Yadkin Ripple*, September 21, 1972, JH MSS.

118. "Mr. Helms' Past Specifics Move Him to Generalities," editorial, *Charlotte Observer*, October 6, 1972; "Helms's Ad Hits Votes for Hospital, School 'Giveaway,'" *Charlotte Observer*, October 6, 1972; "McGovern-Galifianakis?," *Greensboro Daily News*, October 5, 1972.

119. John Kilgo, "Campaign for Senate Promises Hot Finale," October 11, 1972, "'One of Us,'" unidentified clipping, c. October 1972, HCF; Black interview, February 15, 2006; Chris Geis, "History Repeating?," *Winston-Salem Journal*, August 12, 1990.

120. Paul Clancy, "Helms Is Narrowing Gap in Campaign for Senate," *Charlotte Observer*, October 22, 1972; Ned Cline, "Helms and Galifianakis Neck and Neck—Pollster," *Greensboro Daily News*, November 2, 1972; Wrenn interview, May 13, 2005.

121. JH interview (by Joyner), tapes 2, 30; Covington interview, August 31, 2006; "Helms Wins Senate Seat," *Durham Herald*, November 6, 1972, HCF; newspaper ads in *Yadkin Ripple*, September 7, 28, 1972, *Yancey Journal*, October 26, 1972, JH MSS.

4. STANDING AGAINST THE PREVAILING WIND

1. Pat Borden, "New Senator and Wife Discover 'Strange Town, Strange House,'" *Charlotte Observer*, January 16, 1973; Ned Cline, "Helms: Conservative Lone Ranger," *Charlotte Observer*, November 20, 1977.

2. JH to Charles W. Lowry, January 12, 1973, JH MSS.

3. Wilson interview, June 5, 2006.

4. Ferrell Guillory, "He Took That Advice, and It Took Him to the Senate," *Monroe Enquirer-Journal*, January 10, 1973; "Sen. Helms: A Proud 'Classical Conservative,'" *Daily Tar Heel*, March 2, 1976; JH to Max F. Harris, December 21, 1972, JH MSS.

5. JH to Mrs. J. Melville Broughton, November 2, 1973, JH MSS.

6. Paul Clancy, "Sen. Helms Glimpses Former Glories," *Charlotte Observer*, April 7, 1974.

7. Fuller interview (by Riddick), December 21, 1989.

8. JH to A. J. Fletcher, December 18, 1974, JH MSS; Boney interview, June 1, 2006; Fuller interview (by Riddick), December 22, 1989.

9. Paul Clancy, "'Bless Your Heart' Helms Hits Town," *Charlotte Observer*, January 7, 1973; Paul Clancy, "Helms' Senate Career Taking Maverick Turn," *Charlotte Observer*, February 5, 1973; "Fuller Resigns as Times Editor to Join Helms Staff," *Franklin Times*, February 16, 1973; Paul Clancy, "Sen. Helms Shakes Up Staff," *Charlotte Observer*, February 5, 1974; Black interview, Febru-

ary 15, 2006; Scott Wilson interview, June 5, 2006; Fuller interview (by Riddick), November 20, 1991.

10. Dunlop interview, June 5, 2006.

11. Boney interview, June 1, 2006.

12. Guillory interview, February 2, 2006; Black interview, February 15, 2006; Paul Clancy, "You Always Know Where Helms Stands," *Charlotte Observer,* January 20, 1974.

13. JH to Aubrey H. Moore, Jr., January 10, 1973, JH MSS.

14. Polly Paddock, "Helms Tells YAF Convention He's 'Right-Wing Extremist,'" *Charlotte Observer,* August 17, 1973; Polly Paddock, "Helms Now a 'Pop Hero' to Young Right Wingers," *Charlotte Observer,* August 19, 1973. Helms disputed the *Charlotte Observer*'s charge that he described himself as an "extremist." According to his account, he related that, visiting Washington immediately after the election, a reporter asked him if he was "the right-wing extremist that they say you are." Define "they," Jesse responded; the reporter could not do so. Helms concluded with the comment: "Beauty is in the eye of the beholder." JH to H. Clifton Blue, September 4, 1973, JH MSS.

15. Don Hill, "Jesse Helms' Influence Makes Itself Felt," *Greensboro Daily News,* November 19, 1975.

16. "U.S. Senator Jesse Helms," Helms newsletter, *Monroe Enquirer-Journal,* September 10, 1974.

17. Helms newsletter, *Monroe Enquirer-Journal,* July 28, 1976.

18. Don Hill, "Jesse Helms' Influence Makes Itself Felt," *Greensboro Daily News,* November 19, 1975; Helms interview (by Joyner), tapes 2, 34; Furgurson, *Hard Right,* pp. 104–5.

19. "U.S. Senator Jesse Helms," Helms newsletter, *Monroe Enquirer-Journal,* August 7, 1973, and November 3, 1976; "Totally Principled Politician," *Conservative Digest,* October 1976, JH MSS; Helms interview (by Joyner), tape 34. During his first years, Jesse regularly presided over the Senate. After the 1950s, the vice president, though officially the Senate's presiding officer, appeared only occasionally, usually only when his vote was needed to break a tie. In the vice president's absence, the senior member of the majority party, the president pro tempore, presided. But during periods of routine speeches and debate, the Senate leadership permitted junior members (even of the minority party) to serve in this capacity. Beginning in the 1960s, the Senate majority leader created a Golden Gavel Award, to recognize senators who had presided more than one hundred hours. Jesse won the award twice—the first time this had ever occurred—in 1973 and 1974. "U.S. Senator Jesse Helms," Helms newsletter, *Monroe Enquirer-Journal,* September 4, 1974.

20. "Will North Carolina Save Us from Jesse Helms?," unidentified clipping, May 1978, JH MSS.

21. Bradley interview, December 18, 2006.

22. Steve Phillips interview (by Joyner), tape 32.

23. "Totally Principled Politician," *Conservative Digest,* October 1976.

24. JWP interview, May 14, 1999; Black interview, February 15, 2006; Ferrel Guillory, "Helms' Bills Lean Toward 'Making a Point,'" *Raleigh News and Observer,* March 12, 1978.

25. "Senator Helms Follows Busy Agenda," unidentified clipping, March 19, 1973, JH MSS. See also JH to Anne Morrison, February 1, 1974, JH MSS.

26. JH, speeches, January 29, 31, 1973, *CR,* JH floor speeches, JH MSS; Paul Clancy, "Helms' Senate Career Taking Maverick Turn," *Charlotte Observer,* February 5, 1973; Dolores Lavelle, "Senator Helms Calls for Return to Basics," *Monroe Enquirer-Journal,* March 5, 1973.

27. Unidentified clipping, September 24, 1973, JH MSS.

28. "Nominees Stymied by Sen. Helms," *Washington Post,* November 20, 1973; "Will North Carolina Save Us from Jesse Helms?," unidentified clipping, May 1978, JH MSS.

29. Paul Clancy, "You Always Know Where Helms Stands," *Charlotte Observer,* January 20, 1974; "U.S. Senator Jesse Helms," Helms newsletter, *Monroe Enquirer-Journal,* July 24, 1973.

30. "More Watergate (And Union County)," *Monroe Enquirer-Journal,* May 14, 1973. See also "Helms Rips Nixon Foes," *Charlotte News,* April 9, 1973, JH to Mrs. Rex R. Cockerham, April 18, 1973, JH MSS. Helms made another speech defending Nixon in July. "Monrovers in Limelight," *Monroe Enquirer-Journal,* August 3, 1973. On Helms and Watergate, see Furgurson, *Hard Right,* pp. 106–8.

31. JH to Allen P. Brantley, November 6, 1973, JH MSS.

32. "Helms Begrudges Watergate Expense," unidentified clipping, May 22, 1973, JH MSS; Polly Paddock, "Martin Bucks Carolinians on Hill over Nixon Tapes," *Charlotte Observer,* July 29, 1973; JH to T. Y. Milburn, May 2, 1973; JH to Frances Webb, May 29, 1973; JH to John R. Drummy, July 30, 1973; JH to George W. Birmingham, Jr., November 6, 1973, JH MSS. On the Senate Watergate hearings, Helms wrote: "I believe that the American people are able to see through the theatrics being presented during the televised Watergate hearings and evaluate these hearings for what they are worth." JH to Ethel F. Mann, August 13, 1973, JH MSS.

33. Elaine Shannon, "Helms' Conservatism Reflected," *Raleigh News and Observer,* March 22, 1973; "Sam, Jesse Roles Now Switched," unidentified clipping, August 10, 1973.

34. JH to William Loeb, August 1, 1973, JH MSS; Fuller interview (by Riddick), November 20, 1991.

35. Don Hill, "Helms Assails Buckley," typescript wire service report, March 19, 1974, in Seth Effron clippings collection, North Carolina Collection, University of North Carolina at Chapel Hill Library; speech, *CR,* March 19, 1974, floor speeches, JH MSS.

36. Don Hill, "Helms," typescript wire service report, May 8, 1974, Effron collec-

tion; Paul Clancy, "Conservatives See Liberal Conspiracy," *Charlotte Observer,* May 19, 1974.

37. Don Hill, typescript of wire service report, August 9, 1974, Effron collection; "U.S. Senator Jesse Helms," Helms newsletter, *Monroe Enquirer-Journal,* August 20, 1974; Paul Bernish, "Nixon 'Sounded Good' Helms Says of Call," *Charlotte Observer,* August 29, 1974; Rob Christensen, "Helms Reassured After Private Meeting with Reagan," *Raleigh News and Observer,* November 22, 1980; JH, *Here's Where I Stand,* pp. 79–80; "Biographical Conversations with Jesse Helms," WUNC-TV broadcast, February 7, 2000.

38. "Road Fund Fight Moves to House," *Charlotte News,* March 16, 1973; *Monroe Enquirer-Journal,* December 7, 1973.

39. Paul Clancy, "You Always Know Where Helms Stands," *Charlotte Observer,* January 10, 1974.

40. "Senate Restricts Debate Against Legal-Aid Plan," *Charlotte Observer,* January 31, 1974; Joe Hall, "Congressional Debate Opens on Legal Services Measure," unidentified clipping, January 28, 1974; Helms newsletter, January 29, 1974, JH MSS; "Helms Fought Bill Switching Legal Services to the Poor," unidentified clipping, July 19, 1974; Paul Clancy, "Legal Services Bill Irks N.C. Senators," *Charlotte Observer,* July 21, 1974; JH, speech, *CR,* July 16, 1974, floor speeches, JH MSS.

41. Waging a two-week battle over a labor bill that, he claimed, gave unions an advantage in work disputes, Helms lost a cloture vote. But his delaying tactics permitted time for anti-union forces, including the U.S. Chamber of Commerce, to regroup and organize opposition. "I'm exceedingly satisfied with the result," he told reporters. "Of course, I'd like to have won. But frankly I didn't think we had a chance." A month later, in December 1975, he also opposed the $2.3 billion federal bailout when New York City verged on bankruptcy, and, along with fellow Senators Allen and Byrd, mounted another unsuccessful filibuster attempt. Jack Betts, "Helms Leads Fight Against Aid to NYC," *Greensboro Daily News,* December 4, 1975.

42. Shirley Elder, "Helms Loses Cloture Vote on Labor Bill," *Raleigh News and Observer,* November 12, 1975; Shirley Elder, "Helms Filibuster Withstands Vote," *Raleigh News and Observer,* November 15, 1975; Shirley Elder, "Helms Courteously Unleashes Filibuster," *Raleigh News and Observer,* November 23, 1975.

43. Ferrel Guillory, "Helms' Forte: Senator Unafraid to Stand Alone," *Raleigh News and Observer,* August 6, 1977.

44. His fellow North Carolina senator, Robert Morgan, elected in 1974, was the antitrust bill's floor manager. As a former state attorney general, Morgan favored the provision of the bill that provided states with greater power to initiate antitrust suits. Morgan had handled one of biggest antitrust cases in North Carolina's history, a suit in which he joined with other states to sue five drug companies charging price-fixing. Although old friends and associates—Morgan was campaign manager for I. Beverly Lake's 1960 gubernatorial campaign—he

and Helms were at odds over this legislation. Shirley Elder, "Tar Heel Senators Face Off in Debate," *Raleigh News and Observer,* June 14, 1976; Ferrel Guillory, "Helms Backs Filibuster Curbs," *Raleigh News and Observer,* May 14, 1977. "The real important thing is the 60 votes," Helms said. When "cloture [debate cutoff] is voted, the ballgame is over anyway."

45. Don Hill, typescript of wire service report, August 9, 1974, Effron collection; Paul Clancy, "Helms Opposes 'Wife-Stealer,'" *Charlotte Observer,* August 15, 1974; Clancy, "Helms Denies Rockefeller Quote," *Charlotte Observer,* August 16, 1974; Nelson A. Rockefeller to JH, August 30, 1974, JH MSS. According to Clancy, Helms "may have thought he was talking off the record or in confidence, but I had no such understanding. I was taking notes and the interview was clearly on the record." Clancy, "Helms Denies Rockefeller Quote."

46. JH, speeches, *CR,* September 26, October 8, 9, 15, December 5, 1974, floor speeches, JH MSS. MSS; Paul Clancy, "Helms Rakes Rocky's Values," *Charlotte Observer,* September 27, 1974; "Helms Urges New Hearings to Examine Rocky's Gift," *Charlotte Observer,* October 9, 1974; "Senate Okays Rocky; Helms, 6 More Demur," *Charlotte Observer,* December 11, 1974.

47. JH, speech to the Peace Through Freedom Conference, London, in *CR,* September 10, 1973, floor speeches, JH MSS.

48. JH, speech to the Council Against Communist Aggression, Arlington, Virginia, June 15, 1974, JH MSS.

49. JH, speech, *CR,* December 18, 1975, floor speeches, JH MSS. See also Jesse Helms, *When Free Men Shall Stand* (Grand Rapids: Zondervan, 1976), ch. 18.

50. JH, speech, *CR,* September 21, 1973, floor speeches, JH MSS.

51. Don Hill, "'Protest,' Not Attack, Says Helms," *Greensboro Daily News,* November 19, 1975. Helms commented that Ford had "chosen the wrong man to fire": Kissinger, he said, had "fumbled détente with the Soviet Union ... had sealed the doom of the free Vietnamese, and ... had escalated tensions in the Middle East in the name of peace." JH, speech, *CR,* December 1, 1975, floor speeches, JH MSS.

52. "Helms Wants Full Disclosure of Sinai Agreements Terms," unidentified clipping, September 29, 1975, HCF. Despite Helms's opposition, the Senate voted 70–18 to station two hundred American technicians to monitor the peace. "Senators OK Sinai Peace Unit," unidentified clipping, October 10, 1975, JH MSS.

53. "U.S. Senator Jesse Helms," Helms newsletter, *Monroe Enquirer-Journal,* c. April 1975; JH, speeches, *CR,* February 18, April 1, October 4, 1974, March 20, 1975, floor speeches, JH MSS; Furgurson, *Hard Right,* pp. 113–14.

54. JH, speech, *CR,* July 7, 1975, floor speeches, JH MSS; "U.S. Senator Jesse Helms," Helms newsletter, *Monroe Enquirer-Journal,* July 16, 1975.

55. Ned Cline, "Helms Asked to Mediate Solzhenitsyn Snub," *Greensboro Daily News,* July 18, 1975.

56. Fred Barnes, "White House Eager to Satisfy Critics," *Washington Star,* July 16, 1975.

57. Ned Cline, "Helms Asked to Mediate Solzhenitsyn Snub," *Greensboro Daily News,* July 18, 1975; Shirley Elder, "Solzhenitsyn Flap Created Unwittingly," *Raleigh News and Observer,* July 24, 1975; Clint Fuller, "Solzhenitsyn Visit to Washington, June/July 1975," typewritten MS, in JH MSS; interview with Clint Fuller, December 21, 1989.

58. Ned Cline, "Helms Asked to Mediate Solzhenitsyn Snub," *Greensboro Daily News,* July 18, 1979; JH, speech, *CR,* July 16, 1975, floor speeches, JH MSS.

59. Rowland Evans and Robert Novak, "Snubbing Solzhenitsyn," *Washington Post,* July 17, 1975. See also Evans and Novak, "Henry's Problem," *Greensboro Daily News,* July 21, 1975; "Ford May Meet with Solzhenitsyn," *Winston-Salem Journal,* July 19, 1975.

60. JH to Don S. Holt, January 10, 1974, JH MSS.

61. Interview with Carter Wrenn, September 27, 1996, NCGOP; Wrenn interview, May 13, 2005; Ellis interview, July 14, 2005; John Monk and Jim Morrill, "Helms, Faircloth Split from Wrenn Camp," *Charlotte Observer,* October 2, 1994.

62. Interview with Carter Wrenn (by Mosnier), September 27, 1996.

63. "Buckley Praises Helms at 'Salute' Fete Here," *Raleigh News and Observer,* January 20, 1974; Max F. Harris, "Congressional Club Honors Citizen-Senator Jesse Helms," *Monroe Enquirer-Journal,* January 21, 1974.

64. Ned Cline, "A Lesson in Political Finance: Conservative Tar Heels Keep Helms Out of Red," *Greensboro Daily News,* July 20, 1975; "Big Reagan Crowd Expected," unidentified clipping, July 25, 1975, HCF; interview with Carter Wrenn (by Mosnier), September 27, 1996.

65. Viguerie interview, February 14, 2006.

66. Interview with Carter Wrenn (by Mosnier), September 27, 1996, May 13, 2005; Ellis interviews, July 14, 2005, February 3, 2006; Viguerie interview, February 14, 2006; Black interview, February 15, 2006; Eberle interview, June 6, 2006.

67. JH, "The Lasting Leadership of Ronald Reagan," Heritage Foundation talk, March 2, 2001, http://www.heritage.org/Research/PoliticalPhilosophy/HL700 .cfm, accessed June 9, 2004, Wrenn interview, May 13, 2005; Black interview, February 15, 2006; JH, *Here's Where I Stand,* p. 99; JH to Mrs. Thomas D. Wright, October 2, 1973, introduction of Reagan (speech), October 1, 1984, JH MSS.

68. JH, "The New American Majority: Time for a Political Realignment?," speech at Dean Manion testimonial dinner, May 15, 1974, JH MSS.

69. Paul Clancy, "Helms Would Create Conservative Party," *Charlotte Observer,* May 16, 1974; JH, speech to Conservative Action Conference, Washington, February 14, 1975, JH MSS; Jack Betts, typescript of wire service report, February 14, 1975, Effron clippings collection.

70. Meeting in February and June, COCA, whose ranks included elected leaders and a larger group of conservative activists, examined the process of putting candidates on the ballot in fifty states. It compiled fifteen loose-leaf binders of

material about the states' election laws; a *Human Events* reporter described this analysis as "very probably the best comprehensive overview of American election requirements in existence." "COCA Readying for Action in '76," *Human Events,* July 19, 1975; JH, "A Choice for America," speech at YAF convention, Chicago, August 15, 1975, JH MSS.

71. Daniel C. Hoover, "Helms Backs Reagan, Not Ford for '76 Race," *Raleigh News and Observer,* July 9, 1975; "Wrong Pew Again," editorial, *Newton Observer-News,* July 11, 1975; Jack Betts, "Senators Whittle at Victory Debts," *Charlotte Observer,* July 12, 1975; Wrenn interview, May 13, 2005; Helms interview (by Joyner), tape 6. Viguerie noted, in retrospect, that Helms had little "serious interest" in joining a third party. Viguerie interview, February 14, 2006.

72. Interview with Carter Wrenn (by Mosnier), September 27, 1996; Wrenn interview, May 13, 2005.

73. Interview with Carter Wrenn, September 27, 1996.

74. Tom Weaver, "Reagan Recommends 'New First Party,' " *Dunn Dispatch,* July 28, 1975; Paul Bernish, "Reagan Visits N.C for Helms," *Charlotte Observer,* undated; JH, speech, *CR,* July 24, 1975, floor speeches, JH MSS.

75. Interview with Carter Wrenn (by Mosnier), September 27, 1996; Ellis interview, July 14, 2005.

76. Cliff Blue, "People and Issues," unidentified clipping, June 27, 1973; John Kilgo, "Political Notebook," unidentified clippings, August 9, September 4, 1973, JH MSS; Daniel C. Hoover, "Helms-Holshouser Relations Strained," *Raleigh News and Observer,* February 10, 1974; Daniel C. Hoover, "Helms Preparing to Meet Senate Bid by Holshouser," *Raleigh News and Observer,* June 23, 1974; Ferrel Guillory, "N.C. GOP Drifts Without Defined Leadership," *Raleigh News and Observer,* February 23, 1975; Ellis interview, July 14, 2005; interview with David T. Flaherty (by Mosnier), September 27, 1996, Southern Oral History Program; interview with Frank Rouse (by Mosnier), November 14, 1996, Southern Oral History Program; interview with Gene Anderson (by Mosnier), November 15, 1996, Southern Oral History Program.

77. Tom Weaver, "Holshouser to Back Ford," *Dunn Dispatch,* August 7, 1975; "Holshouser Joins Ford Campaign," *Monroe Enquirer-Journal,* August 6, 1975.

78. Carl Stepp, "Helms Wishes Ford Would Drop Rocky in '76," *Charlotte Observer,* July 24, 1975.

79. Bob Poole, "Decision Pleases Helms," *Winston-Salem Journal,* November 4, 1975; "Helms Knew Rocky's Decision in July," *Henderson Daily Dispatch,* November 4, 1975.

80. Interview with Carter Wrenn (by Mosnier), September 27, 1996.

81. Howard Covington, "Fireworks Begin for State GOP," *Charlotte Observer,* November 16, 1975; Daniel C. Hoover, "GOP Leadership Debates Choices," *Raleigh News and Observer,* November 16, 1975.

82. Ned Cline, "Primary's GOP Vote to Test Efforts by Helms, Holshouser," *Greensboro Daily News,* March 22, 1976; Reynolds interview, April 4, 2006.

83. Daniel C. Hoover, "Holshouser, Helms Stake Prestige on N.C. Primary," *Raleigh News and Observer,* November 9, 1975.

84. Rip Woodin, "Helms Wing Swings at Stevens," *Greensboro Daily News,* July 11, 1974; "Helms Interested in a Cause, but Not G.O.P. Cause," *Raleigh News and Observer,* June 29, 1976.

85. "Ellis to Run Reagan Race," *Hanover Sun,* October 22, 1975; interview with Carter Wrenn, September 27, 1996; Wrenn interview, May 13, 2005; Fuller interview, November 30, 1991; Black interview, February 15, 2006; Dunlop interview, June 5, 2006; Craig Shirley, *Reagan's Revolution: The Untold Story of the Campaign That Started It All* (Nashville: Nelson Current, 2005), pp. 162–63; Ned Cline, "There's Feuding on Reagan Team," *Greensboro Daily News,* March 11, 1976; Brent Hackney, "Helms' Alter Ego Has Put His Stamp on N.C. Politics," *Greensboro Daily News,* July 9, 1978. On Reagan's 1976 campaign generally, see Matthew Dallek, *The Right Moment: Ronald Reagan's First Victory and the Decisive Turning Point in American Politics* (New York: Free Press, 2000), and Jules Tygiel, *Ronald Reagan and the Triumph of American Conservatism* (New York: Longman, 2005).

86. Don Hill, "Jesse Helms' Influence Makes Itself Felt," *Greensboro Daily News,* November 10, 1975.

87. Shirley, *Reagan's Revolution,* p. 163; "The Reagan-Helms Victory," editorial, *Raleigh Times,* March 24, 1976; Guillory interview, February 2, 2006; Black interview, February 15, 2006; Covington interview, August 31, 2006.

88. Shirley, *Reagan's Revolution,* pp. 164, 309; interview with Carter Wrenn (by Mosnier), September 27, 1996.

89. Rob Christensen, "How a Latino Morehead Scholar Saved Helms' Campaign," *Raleigh News and Observer,* July 24, 1995.

90. Reynolds interview, April 4, 2006; Fetzer interview, June 20, 2006.

91. David Keene to Reagan, November 20, 1975, Citizens for Reagan Collection, box 31, Hoover Institution Archives, Stanford University; interview with Carter Wrenn (by Mosnier), September 27, 1996; Ellis interview, July 14, 2005; Black interview, February 15, 2006; Shirley, *Reagan's Revolution,* pp. 169, 173.

92. Ken Plummer, "Helms Predicts Reagan Will Win," *Goldsboro News-Argus,* March 19, 1976; "Reagan Desperately Needs Florida Victory, Helms Says," *Charlotte Observer,* March 5, 1976; Ned Cline, "Reagan TV Spots, Backlash Won It,' *Greensboro Daily News,* March 25, 1976.

93. Judy Sarasohn, "GOP Win Engineered by Ellis and Helms," *Raleigh Times,* c. March 25, 1976; Ernest B. Furgurson, *Hard Right: The Rise of Jesse Helms* (New York: W. W. Norton, 1986), pp. 117–19.

94. Charles Sneed, "Helms Blasts Reagan Foes," *Wilmington Star,* March 19, 1976.

95. Black interview, February 15, 2006; JH, speech, *CR,* April 18, 1975, floor speeches, JH MSS. "We have learned how important it is to stand up for our rights," he said in another speech, "and we should do so in the Canal Zone." JH, speech, *CR,* May 15, 1975, JH MSS.

96. Dunlop interview, June 5, 2006.

97. Jesse Helms newsletter, *Monroe Enquirer-Journal*, April 21, 30, December 18, 1975; "Helms Cites Remark by President's Aide," *Fayetteville Observer*, March 6, 1976; "Panama Canal Lobby Grows," *Raleigh News and Observer*, November 9, 1975; Shirley, *Reagan's Revolution*, p. 174; Lou Cannon, quoted in Shirley, *Reagan's Revolution*, p. 176; Carl Stepp, "Politics and the Uses of Power," *Charlotte Observer*, March 14, 1976; Lou Cannon, "Reagan Winner in N.C. Primary; Carter Is Victor," *Washington Post*, March 24, 1976; Eberle interview, June 6, 2006.

98. "Nostalgia in North Carolina," editorial, *Washington Star*, March 26, 1976.

99. Ferrel Guillory, "Contrast in Campaign Style: Reagan Emotes, Ford Plods," *Raleigh News and Observer*, c. March 21, 1976.

100. Phyllis Schlafly to JH, March 24, 1976, JH MSS; Judy Sarasohn, "Reagan Rides Helms Appeal," *Raleigh Times*, March 25, 1976; "A Personal Rebuff," editorial, *Winston-Salem Journal*, March 28, 1976; Lou Cannon, "Reagan Stuck to Battle Plan for Victory," *Washington Post*, March 24, 1976.

101. Ellis interview, July 14, 2005; Horton interview (by Mosnier), June 5, 1997; Lee interview (by Mosnier), November 15, 1996; Ned Cline, "Helms Will Not Use Primary Win to Gain State GOP Control," *Greensboro Daily News*, March 29, 1976; Daniel C. Hoover, "Holshouser Mulls Delegate Decision," *Raleigh News and Observer*, May 13, 1976; "Under the Dome," *Raleigh News and Observer*, May 26, 1976; Ned Cline, "Won't Offer Trio Delegate Seats," *Greensboro Daily News*, June 16, 1976; Reese Cleghorn, "Sen. Helms Takes Control," *Charlotte Observer*, June 22, 1976; "Helms Interested in a Cause, but Not G.O.P. Cause," *Raleigh News and Observer*, June 29, 1976; Betts interview, May 31, 2006.

102. "Helms and Ellis, Pure or Impure?," editorial, *Richmond County Daily Journal*, July 20, 1976; Ned Cline, "Helms Says Reagan In It for the Country," *Greensboro Daily News*, July 21, 1976.

103. David A. Keene to James Holshouser, June 14, 1976, Citizens for Reagan Collection, box 31.

104. Ellis interview, July 14, 2005; interview with Carter Wrenn, September 27, 1996, NCGOP; Wrenn interview, February 1, 2006; Black interview, February 15, 2006; Shirley, *Reagan's Revolution*, p. 310; Jules Witcover, *Marathon: The Pursuit of the Presidency, 1972–76* (New York: Signet, 1977), p. 507.

105. Fuller interview (by Riddick), December 20, 1991.

106. Ned Cline, "Rocky Says Helms Leading Radical Right," *Greensboro Daily News*, c. August 16, 1976; James T. Wooten, "Rockefeller and Helms Avoid Each Other," *New York Times*, August 16, 1976; Shirley, *Reagan's Revolution*, p. 275; Fuller interview, November 20, 1991; Wrenn interview, February 1, 2006; Ellis interview, February 3, 2006; Black interview, February 15, 2006.

107. "North Carolina GOPs Irked by Reagan Pick," unidentified clipping, July 27, 1976, JH MSS; "Supporters Pushing Helms for VP Slot," *Chapel Hill Newspaper*, August 6, 1976; "Helms May Get Convention Honor," *Winston-Salem Journal*, August 7, 1976; "Right They Are," *Newsweek*, August 23, 1976.

108. "Platform Threatened by Reagan Supporters," unidentified clipping, August 9, 1976, JH MSS; "Helms Leading GOP Conservative Kansas City 'Revolt,'" *Winston-Salem Sentinel,* August 11, 1976; interview with Carter Wrenn (by Mosnier), September 26, 1996; Witcover, *Marathon,* p. 507.

109. Covington interview, August 31, 2006.

110. When one North Carolina delegate was asked why the Helms forces had not informed the Reagan team more fully of their plans, she responded: "Because he [Reagan] didn't call me about Schweiker." Jules Witcover, "Reagan Forces and Helms' 'Rebels' Get Together," *Washington Post,* August 12, 1976.

111. Helms statement, August 11, 1976, Citizens for Reagan Collection, box 58.

112. Spencer Rich, "Panel on Platform Won't Support ERA," *Washington Post,* August 12, 1976.

113. "Puzzle in Ranks of Right," *Raleigh Times,* August 12, 1976; Lou Cannon, "Buckley Hints He Would Run as 'Compromise,'" *Washington Post,* August 12, 1976; Shirley, *Reagan's Revolution,* p. 309.

114. Ned Cline, "Helms Reportedly Mulling Party Switch if Conservatives Fail," *Greensboro Daily News,* August 13, 1976; David S. Broder and Stephen Isaacs, "'Jesse Helms for President' Movement Is Under Way," *Winston-Salem Sentinel,* August 14, 1976.

115. "Helms Won't Take Federal Position," *Fayetteville Observer,* August 14, 1976; Mike Dembeck, "Helms Sticks with GOP," *Charlotte News,* August 16, 1976.

116. "Group to Seek Anti-Ford Plank," *Raleigh News and Observer,* August 16, 1976; "Foreign Policy; Appeasing the Right," *Economist,* August 21, 1976; interview with Carter Wrenn (by Mosnier), September 26, 1997; Ellis interviews, July 14, 2005, February 3, 2006; Shirley, *Reagan's Revolution,* p. 311; Wrenn interview, February 1, 2006.

117. Roger Simon, "Jesse Helms: Pulling Apart the Republican Wishbone," *Charlotte News,* August 16, 1976.

118. Luke West, "Helms Eyed as Leader of Right," *Fayetteville Times,* August 20, 1976. See also "Sen. Helms Views His V.P. Boomlet as Passing Fancy," *Durham Morning Herald,* August 19, 1976; Ken Friedlein, "Helms Declines Nomination," *Winston-Salem Journal,* August 20, 1976; "Helms Challenges GOP, Withdraws from Nomination," *Lexington Dispatch,* August 20, 1976; Wrenn interview, February 1, 2006.

119. "Helms Attempts to Stir Foreign Policy Fervor," *Raleigh News and Observer,* August 19, 1976; JH, speeches, August 18, 19, 1976, JH MSS.

120. Wrenn interview, February 1, 2006.

121. M. Stanton Evans, "Dark Horses," *National Review* 29, no. 1 (January 7, 1977): p. 43.

5. CONSERVATISM HAS COME OF AGE

1. Jesse Helms, "Helms: Conservatives Must Change Republicanism," *Charlotte Observer,* December 19, 1976. The Rockefeller pragmatism, he wrote, was "just a fancy way of saying that we should compromise in an effort to win the support of blacks, liberals and other bloc-voting pressure groups." JH to Spurille Braden, November 16, 1976, JH MSS. See also JH, speech to the Conservative Caucus, December 12, 1976, JH MSS.

2. Susan Harrigan, "An Old 'New Town' Hangs On, Sustained by Federal Money," *Wall Street Journal,* April 19, 1979; Harold Woodard, "Floyd McKissick: Portrait of a Leader" (M.A. thesis, University of North Carolina, 1981), pp. 40–46. On Soul City, see Christopher Strain, "Soul City, North Carolina: Black Power, Utopia, and the African American Dream," *Journal of African American History* 79 (Winter 2004): 57–74; Timothy Minchin, "'A Brand New Shining City': Floyd B. McKissick, Sr., and the Struggle to Build Soul City, North Carolina," *North Carolina Historical Review* 82 (April 2005): 125–55; Roger Biles, "The Rise and Fall of Soul City: Planning, Politics, and Race in Recent America," *Journal of Planning History* 4 (February 2005): 52–72.

3. VP #2013, January 17, 1969.

4. JH, speech, *CR,* July 26, 1976, floor speeches, JH MSS; Pat Stith, "HUD Cut Off Soul City Aid," *Raleigh News and Observer,* July 29, 1975; Ned Cline, "Soul City Dream Fades," *Charlotte Observer,* April 2, 1978.

5. JH, speech, *CR,* December 16, 1975, floor speeches, JH MSS.

6. Gary Pearce, "Review of Audit Urged by Helms," *Raleigh News and Observer,* December 17, 1975; Bob Poole, "GAO Report on Soul City Raises 'Serious Questions,'" *Winston-Salem Journal,* December 17, 1975.

7. Despite Helms's attack, federal support for Soul City continued. After HEW regional administrator G. A. Reich decided to close Soul City's public health clinic in December, giving them until March to cease operations, on January 20, 1976, HEW head Mathews countermanded the decision. At the same time, HUD secretary Hills wanted to continue funding. Mathews ordered another investigation, which confirmed the conclusions of the December 1975 GAO study. Soul City, HEW investigators concluded, had done "very little for the citizens in need." They found "little effort" by paid Soul City employees to work even full-time; asserting that fiscal management was "terrible," they also concluded that the entire project was dominated by McKissick. But HEW secretary Mathews ordered yet another study by the Bureau of Community Health Services, and on the basis of that study the grant was extended. Pat Stith, "Study Criticizes Soul City Clinic," *Raleigh News and Observer,* June 1, 1976.

8. "Congressmen Should Support Soul City, Its Developer Says," *Winston-Salem Journal,* May 29, 1979; "U.S. Cutting All Its Ties to Soul City," *Charlotte Observer,* June 29, 1979; "Soul City Gets Rebuff in Senate," *Greensboro Daily News,* July 14, 1979; Woodard, "Floyd McKissick," p. 43.

9. Minchin, "'A Brand New Shining City,'" makes the case for reassessing Soul City.

10. Jesse Helms, *When Free Men Shall Stand: A Sobering Look at the Supertaxing, Superspending Superbureaucracy in Washington* (Grand Rapids: Zondervan, 1975), pp. 100–102.

11. "Helms Offers Bill on Unitary Schools," unidentified clipping, August 4, 1973, JH MSS.

12. "North Carolina News Briefs," *Monroe Enquirer-Journal,* November 15, 1973; Helms newsletter, *Monroe Enquirer-Journal,* January 29, 1974.

13. "Helms's Antibusing Measure Okd; Foes See Little Impact," *Charlotte Observer,* September 18, 1974; JH, speech, *CR,* September 18, 1974, JH MSS; unidentified clipping, November 20, 1974, JH MSS.

14. JH, speech, *CR,* September 17, 1975, floor speeches, JH MSS; Shirley Elder, "Senate Battle Brews over Anti-Busing Measure," *Raleigh News and Observer,* September 19, 1975; Shirley Elder, "Sen. Helms Blocks Busing Vote," *Raleigh News and Observer,* September 20, 1975; "Senate's Busing Foes Win Vote to Restrict It," *Charlotte Observer,* September 25, 1975; "Busing: The Symbolic Issue," editorial, *Washington Star,* September 30, 1975; Richard L. Madden, "Senate Liberals Fail to Shut Off Debate on a Measure That Would Curb Busing," *New York Times,* September 24, 1975; "Jesse Helms Report: HEW Loses Skirmish, but Battle Continues," *Monroe Enquirer-Journal,* October 8, 1975.

15. Jesse Helms, "Jesse Helms Reports," *Monroe Enquirer-Journal,* March 11, 1976; Jack Betts, "Helms Launches New Attack on Busing," *Greensboro Daily News,* March 6, 1976.

16. JH, speech, *CR,* May 29, 1974, floor speeches, JH MSS.

17. JH, speech, *CR,* September 3, 1975, floor speeches, JH MSS; "Helms Introduces Bill to Ease Enforcement of Desegregation," *Winston-Salem Journal,* April 24, 1977. Helms's September 1975 speech referred to HEW's attempt to force UNC to locate a veterinarian school at N.C. State Agricultural and Technical University, rather than at the historically white N.C. State University. For further details about this complicated episode, see William A. Link, *William Friday: Power and Purpose in American Higher Education* (Chapel Hill: University of North Carolina Press, 1995), pp. 262–76.

18. Spencer Rich, "Senate Refuses to Ban 'Affirmative Action'; Senate Rejects 'Affirmative Action' Ban," *Washington Post,* June 29, 1977.

19. Although Helms's anti-quota bill achieved passage in both the Senate and House, in October 1978 to his chagrin it was abruptly dropped in conference. Gene Marlowe, "Anti-Quota Bill OK'd; Significance Questioned," *Winston-Salem Journal,* September 29, 1978; "Helms Loses Battle on UNC Race Quotas," *Durham Herald,* October 15, 1978.

20. "Helms Bill Aimed at Ending UNC Desegregation Problems," *Charlotte Observer,* August 3, 1977.

21. "Helms Blasts Califano; Would Cut HEW Funds," *Lumberton Robesonian,* February 13, 1978.

22. "War on Tobacco Is Without Precedent," *Henderson Daily Dispatch,* January 16, 1978.

23. Ned Cline, "Califano: N.C.'s Favorite Target," *Charlotte Observer,* January 15, 1978.

24. "Helms Blasts Califano; Would Cut HEW Funds," *Lumberton Robesonian,* February 13, 1978.

25. David Nivens, "Helms Bristles over HEW-UNC Rift," *Hickory Record,* February 23, 1978.

26. "Helms Says His Bill Would Protect Universities," editorial, *Greensboro Daily News,* March 3, 1979.

27. "Helms Quizzes HEW Nominee," *Raleigh News and Observer,* July 26, 1979; "Jesse and Patricia," editorial, *Fayetteville Observer,* July 28, 1979; "Sen. Helms Plans Delay on Harris," *Winston-Salem Journal,* July 27, 1979; Dan Haar, "Helms Angered by HEW Nominee," *Charlotte News,* July 27, 1979; "Helms Wants HEW's Harris to Visit N.C.," *Durham Sun,* July 28, 1979.

28. "Helms vs. Harris, Briefly," editorial, *Raleigh News and Observer,* July 29, 1979.

29. "Journal Says Helms Leads in Votes Against Carter," *Raleigh News and Observer,* January 19, 1980. Years later, when asked about Carter's presidency, Helms responded: "What presidency?" "Biographical Conversations with Jesse Helms," WUNC-TV broadcast, February 7, 2000.

30. Ferrel Guillory, "Helms Objects to 4 Carter Appointees," *Raleigh News and Observer,* January 25, 1977.

31. "Filibuster over Nominee Possible," *Raleigh News and Observer,* February 22, 1977.

32. "One Cheer for Jesse," editorial, *Greensboro Record,* May 9, 1980; "Helms Leading Opposition Against Top Military Chief," *Raleigh Times,* May 30, 1980; "Helms and General Quarrel over 'Agreement' to Resign," *Winston-Salem Journal,* June 5, 1980.

33. Obstructing nominations provided an opportunity to express his suspicions of career diplomats or administration policies. In April 1978, Helms put a hold on the nomination of the inspector general of the foreign service, Robert M. Sayre, as ambassador to Brazil, even thought Sayre was regarded as one of the State Department's most experienced Latin American specialists. Helms charged that Sayre had warned Pananamian leaders of the impending arrest of President Omar Torrijos's brother, Moises, on narcotics charges, and Helms objected to the nomination as part of his campaign against the Panama Canal treaties. State Department officials were appalled at these charges and convinced that this was only a personal vendetta. Despite Helms's objections, the Senate approved the nomination. Karen DeYoung and Marlise Simons, "Panama Embittered by Allegation of Torrijos Family Link to Drugs; Panama Embittered by Drug Allegations," *Washington Post,* November 13, 1977; Jeremih O'Leary, "Canal Pact Struggle Chalks Up a Casualty," *Washington Star,* April 26, 1978; "Senate Oks Envoy to Brazil," *Raleigh News and Observer,* April 28, 1971.

34. JH, *Where Free Men Shall Stand,* p. 108.

35. JH, speech, *CR,* June 15, 1973, floor speeches, JH MSS; "Helms Rider to Revive Prayer in School Fought by 8 Churches," *Greensboro Daily News,* August 6, 1978; "Surprise Prayer Vote Threatens Education Unit Bill," *Raleigh Times,* April 6, 1979; "At It Again!," editorial, *Sampson Independent,* April 6, 1979; "Helms Lobbying for Support to Allow Prayer in Schools," *Hickory Daily Record,* January 23, 1980.

36. In October 1978, Helms attached a rider that would remove the Court's jurisdiction over voluntary prayer laws passed by the states, and the measure passed the Senate but was buried in the House. In April 1979, he attached another amendment providing for voluntary school prayer to the bill establishing an independent Department of Education, and it was defeated only after heavy lobbying by the Carter administration. Then, in August 1980, he introduced another amendment that would abolish the Supreme Court's jurisdiction over state laws permitting voluntary school prayer. The amendment passed the Senate but failed in the House. Jesse Helms, "Jesse Helms Reports," *Monroe Enquirer-Journal,* November 26, 1975; Marjorie Hyer, "Church-State Wall Faces Senate Test," *Washington Post,* August 8, 1978; Gene Marlowe, "Senate Diverts Helms' Amendment on Prayer," *Winston-Salem Journal,* April 10, 1979; Marjorie Hunter, "Prayer Issue Has Encore in Congress," *New York Times,* reprinted in *Greensboro Daily News,* August 4, 1980; James J. Kilpatrick, "Helms Amendment Seeks Exercise in Tokenism," *Raleigh News and Observer,* August 8, 1980.

37. JH to H. Fleming Fuller, January 19, 1974, JH MSS. Helms, in 1964, told a correspondent that he favored criminal penalties for the parents of children born out of wedlock. "No one, in my judgment, has the 'right' or the 'freedom' to bring children into the world as a discard, as an unwanted creature, and as a burden on society." JH to George Stevens III, August 12, 1964, JH MSS.

38. Jesse Helms, "Abortion a Sign of Moral Decay," *Human Events,* September 13, 1975.

39. "Senate Kills Move to Ban Abortions," *Washington Star,* April 29, 1976; Paul Scott, "Senate Abortion Showdown," *Independent American,* April 14, 1976; JH, speech to the March for Life meeting, Washington, January 22, 1975, JH MSS. See also Helms's speeches on abortion in *CR,* June 29, October 1, December 5, 1973, January 17, March 3, 1975, March 15, April 28, June 28, 1976, in abortion notebook, JH MSS.

40. JH, Speech to the Concerned Christian Citizens for Political Action, Lynden, Washington, September 28, 1974, JH MSS.

41. JH, speech to the Bethel Christian Academy, Kinston, June 7, 1975, JH MSS.

42. Dennis Whittington, "Helms Suggests Spiritual Rebirth Needed in U.S.," *Winston-Salem Journal,* July 30, 1978.

43. "Helms Tells Audience of Christian Rebirth," *Raleigh News and Observer,* October 19, 1978.

44. Wrenn interview, February 1, 2006; Viguerie interview, February 14, 2006;

Weyrich interview, October 11, 2006. On the Moral Majority, see Steve Bruce, *The Rise and Fall of the New Christian Right: Conservative Protestant Politics in America, 1978–1988* (New York: Oxford University Press, 1988); Walter H. Capps, *The New Religious Right: Piety, Patriotism, and Politics* (Columbia: University of South Carolina Press, 1990).

45. "Decency Rally Planned," *Raleigh Times,* April 27, 1979.

46. A. L. May, "Fundamentalists' Effect on Politics Questioned," *Raleigh News and Observer,* August 31, 1980.

47. "Proposed IRS Regulations Threaten Private Schools," *Human Events,* October 7, 1978; "Private Schools Win Big Round Against IRS,"*Human Events,* September 15, 1979; Viguerie interview, February 14, 2006.

48. Godwin interview, June 1, 2006.

49. JH, *When Free Men Shall Stand,* pp. 25–28.

50. JH, speech, *CR,* November 30, 1979, floor speeches, JH MSS; Richard Whittle, "Humanist Values Upset Helms," *Raleigh News and Observer,* December 4, 1979; JH, speech to the Raleigh Board of Realtors Prayer Breakfast, April 21, 1981, JH MSS; Cole C. Campbell, "Aspen Institute Repudiates Helms's Charges," *Raleigh News and Observer,* December 5, 1979; John Alexander, "Three Cheers for Humanism," *Greensboro Daily News,* December 7, 1979; "Not Enough Humanism," editorial, *Greensboro Record,* December 11, 1979.

51. "Fundamentalism: New Outbreak of an Old Fever," editorial, *Charlotte Observer,* June 1, 1980.

52. "Sen. Helms Reiterates Stand Against Pornography, Ban on School Prayer," *Monroe Enquirer-Journal,* July 3, 1980.

53. Jesse Helms, "Jesse Helms Reports," *Monroe Enquirer-Journal,* March 16, 1977.

54. "Bryant Vows Battle Will Widen on Gays," *Raleigh News and Observer,* June 9, 1977.

55. Paul Clancy, "Helms Would Create Conservative Party," *Charlotte Observer,* May 16, 1974.

56. JH, speech, *CR,* October 1, 1974, JH MSS; Marty Gunther, "Women Will Be the Real Losers if Our Gov't. Continues to Give In to Libbers," *National Tattler,* October 26, 1975; Donald T. Critchlow, *Phyllis Schlafly and Grassroots Conservatism: A Woman's Crusade* (Princeton: Princeton University Press, 2005), pp. 244–48. For background, see Catherine E. Rymph, *Republican Women: Feminism and Conservatism from Suffrage Through the Rise of the New Right* (Chapel Hill: University of North Carolina Press, 2006).

57. Marjorie Julian Spruill, "'Women for God, Country, and Family': Religion, Politics, and Antifeminism in 1970s America" (unpublished paper in author's possession), p. 4; Jan Petersen to Margaret Costanza, September 7, 1977, White House Central File, holidays file (HO), Jimmy Carter Presidential Library, Atlanta.

58. "Women's Group Attacked," *Greensboro Record,* July 11, 1977; Susan Ades, "Helms Is All Wet, Local Women Say," *Charlotte News,* July 11, 1977.

59. JH, speech, *CR,* July 1, 1977, floor speeches, JH MSS; "Helms: Tactics Unfair at

Talks," *Raleigh News and Observer,* July 15, 1977; Jan Peterson to Margaret Costanza, July 28, 1977, White House Central File (WHCF), name file, Carter Library.

60. JH, speech, *CR,* July 21, 1977, floor speeches, JH MSS; Wendy Oglesby, "Helms Calls for IWY Investigation," *Greensboro Record,* July 26, 1977; Wendy Oglesby, "Cure for What Ails 'Em," *Greensboro Record,* August 1, 1977.

61. "Helms to Probe 'Women's Year,'" *Raleigh News and Observer,* September 8, 1977.

62. Robert Hodierne, "ERA Opponents Testify Feminists Left Them Out," *Charlotte Observer,* September 15, 1977; Polly Paddock, "IWY: Helms's Bad Dream?," *Charlotte Observer,* October 17, 1977.

63. Robert Hodierne, "ERA Opponents Testify Feminists Left Them Out," *Charlotte Observer,* September 15, 1977; Jack Betts, "N.C. Women Tell Helms IWY Convention Rigged," *Greensboro Daily News,* September 15, 1977; Ferrel Guillory, "'Stacked,' Says IWY of Helms' Hearings," *Raleigh News and Observer,* September 16, 1977.

64. Jack Betts, "Koontz Scolds Helms on IWY Hearing," *Greensboro Daily News,* September 30, 1977.

65. Jan Petersen to Margaret Costanza, September 7, 1977, WHCF, holidays file (HO), Carter Library.

66. "Exorcism, Not Stake, for IWY," editorial, *Raleigh News and Observer,* September 12, 1977.

67. "Helms and the Women," editorial, *Winston-Salem Sentinel,* September 19, 1977. Once the Houston conference completed its work and submitted a report to Congress, Helms continued to oppose it. See JH, speech, *CR,* February 7, 1978, floor speeches, JH MSS.

68. Polly Paddock, "IWY: Helms's Bad Dream?," *Charlotte Observer,* October 17, 1977.

69. JH, speech to the World Anti-Communist League General Conference, Rio de Janeiro, Brazil, April 24–25, 1975, JH MSS.

70. JH, speech, *CR,* June 17, 1975, March 22, 23, 1976, floor speeches, JH MSS. See also speech, September 4, 1975.

71. One embassy staff person, Wayne Smith, recalled that he and others were "puzzled" about why Helms was visiting. While the American embassy had been "bending over backwards to avoid giving rise to any impression that we endorsed what they were doing," Argentine military leaders concluded that Helms "was on their side and that with an important United States senator on their side, the military had won the battle of bringing the U.S. government around." Steven Livingston, "Jesse Helms's Friends," *Washington Post,* November 27, 1994.

72. JH, speech, *CR,* September 24, 1976, floor speeches, JH MSS. The evidence against the Chilean intelligence services in the Letelier assassination was compelling. See John Dinges, *The Condor Years: How Pinochet and His Allies Brought Terrorism to Three Continents* (New York: Free Press, 2004).

73. Jesse Helms, "Jesse Helms report," *Monroe Enquirer-Journal,* November 5, 1975,

July 21, 1976; JH, speech to the Americans for a Free Cuba, Miami, February 14, 1976, JH MSS; speech, *CR,* September 24, 1976, floor speeches, JH MSS. On the canal debate, see George D. Moffett III, *The Limits of Victory: The Ratification of the Panama Canal Treaties* (Ithaca: Cornell University Press, 1985).

74. JH, speeches, *CR,* July 19, 1973, March 4, 1975, floor speeches, JH MSS; Helms, press release, February 22, 1977, JH MSS; Ferrel Guillory, "Helms Fights Canal Move," *Raleigh News and Observer,* February 8, 1977; John F. Berry, "Panama Treaty Negotiator Quits N.Y. Bank Board," *Washington Post,* March 19, 1977; "High Court Rejects Helms' Suit on Canal," *Raleigh News and Observer,* June 21, 1977; Ferrel Guillory, "Helms Leads Suit Seeking House Say on Canal Pacts," *Raleigh News and Observer,* October 14, 1977; JH, testimony to the Separation of Powers Subcommittee, Senate Judiciary Committee, July 22, 1977, JH MSS.

75. Rowland Evans and Robert Novak, "Did Carter Retail the Panama Canal?," *Nashville Tennessean,* August 19, 1977.

76. "Helms Says He Didn't Call Baker a Squirming Worm," *Winston-Salem Journal,* July 13, 1977. Helms claimed that he was misquoted about Baker, but the only difference in the quote was, according to Jesse, that Baker "felt" like a "squirming worm." He also suggested that the reference to the moderate Republicans was misquoted because he spoke to the Florida group by a telephone hookup. Because the sound system failed to work, he said, some of what he said was misunderstood. See also JH to Jimmy Carter, June 15, 1977; Carter to JH, July 20, 1977, JH MSS.

77. JH, speech, *CR,* July 26, 1977, floor speeches, JH MSS; "U.S. and Panama Near Agreement," *Raleigh News and Observer,* August 10, 1977.

78. Murray Marder, "Accord Is Reached on Panama Canal," *Washington Post,* August 11, 1977.

79. JH, press release, August 11, 1977, JH MSS; JH to Jimmy Carter, August 12, 1977, WHCF, executive files (FO 3–1), JCL. See also Jimmy Carter to JH, June 30, 1977; JH to Carter, July 20, 1977, WHCF, name file (presidential), Carter Library.

80. Paul L. Krause, "Helms Fires Blast at Canal Proposal," *Raleigh Times,* August 17, 1977. See also Jim Schlosser, "Soviets to Gain from Peace—Helms," *Greensboro Record,* August 17, 1977, and David Nivens, "Helms to Fight Canal Treaty Proposal," *Hickory Daily Record,* August 17, 1977.

81. "Canal Treaty Scored as Peace Threat," *Raleigh Times,* August 12, 1977; "Treaty Method Praised," *Hickory Daily Record,* August 12, 1977; Martin Donsky, "Helms Hits Panama Canal Treaty," *Raleigh News and Observer,* August 12, 1977; "Helms Has Own Canal Plan," *Greensboro Daily News,* August 15, 1977; "Treaty Foes Plan Blitz," *Hickory Daily Record,* August 22, 1977.

82. "Helms Renews Attack," *Winston-Salem Journal,* September 2, 1977.

83. Ferrel Guillory, "Helms Says U.S. Agents Intercepted Canal Talks," *Raleigh News and Observer,* September 28, 1977.

84. JH, press release, May 15, 1976, JH MSS.

85. Graham Hovey, "Doubt Cast on 2 Republicans' Support of Canal Pacts," *New York Times,* August 22, 1977; Ferrel Guillory, *Raleigh News and Observer,* October 23, 1977.

86. Saul Friedman, "GOP Plans Total War Against Treaty," *Charlotte Observer,* August 12, 1977.

87. "Treaty Foes Plan Blitz," *Hickory Daily Record,* August 22, 1977; "Blitz on Canal: TV Program Attacks Panama Treaties," *Raleigh Times,* October 28, 1977.

88. " 'Truth Squad' on Canal," *Shelby Star,* January 18,1978; " 'Truth Squad,' Helms Marshal Treaty Foes," *Hickory Record,* January 18, 1978.

89. Harold Warren, "His Lyrics Plead, 'Keep Our Canal,' " *Charlotte Observer,* March 12, 1978.

90. JH, press release, January 17, 1978; JH to Cyrus Vance, December 8, 1977, JH MSS; Ferrel Guillory, "Helms Still Set Against Treaties," *Raleigh News and Observer,* January 24, 1978; "Move by Helms Slows Senators," *Winston-Salem Journal,* January 20, 1978.

91. JH, speech at North Carolina Congressional Club dinner, January 20, 1978, JH MSS; Brent Hackney, "Canal Fight May Be Lost, Helms Says," *Greensboro Daily News,* February 3, 1978. See similar pessimism by Helms in Ferrel Guillory, "Helms Says Chances Slim for Treaty Defeat," *Raleigh News and Observer,* March 15, 1978.

92. "Soap Opera Canal Talks: Slow Going," *Charlotte Observer,* March 5, 1978.

93. See JH speeches, February 20, 22, 1978, *Congressional Record, Proceedings and Debates of the 95th Congress, Second Session,* vol. 124, no. 20, pp. 1908–16, 4145; "Drug Issue Just a Scare Tactic," editorial, *Raleigh News and Observer,* February 23, 1978; "Panama Treaties Pass 1st Test Vote After Drug Debate," *Charlotte Observer,* February 23, 1978; "Canal Pact Foes Introduce First Crippling Amendment," *Raleigh News and Observer,* February 24, 1978; "Senators Continue Effort to Torpedo Canal Treaty," *Lenoir News Topic,* February 25, 1978; "Treaties Pass Crucial Test; Troops Vetoed," *Raleigh News and Observer,* February 28, 1978; Ferrel Guillory, "Senate Refuses to Pass Helms Canal Amendment," *Raleigh News and Observer,* March 8, 1978; "Senate Approves Canal Amendment Permitting U.S. Military Intervention," *Greensboro Daily News,* March 11, 1978. Attorney General Griffin Bell wrote to Helms earlier, saying that there would be no investigation of his charges of Panamanian drug involvement because it was based on hearsay evidence. Griffin Bell to JH, October 20, 1977, JH MSS.

94. Prior to the vote, in a last-minute effort, Helms and James Allen, his old Senate friend and hard-line treaty opponent, held hearings on March 11 in which they heard testimony from Doris McClellan, clerk of the U.S. District Court in the Canal Zone (and the daughter of Arkansas senator John McClellan), who testified that over 3,500 Americans purchased property in the Canal Zone between 1903 and 1914, paid for in gold. Another witness, James Luitweiler, had traveled to Panama as secretary of a joint land commission that negotiated

these purchases under the right of eminent domain. According to Luitweiler, "nobody ever complained" about unfair treatment. The witnesses produced two wooden crates of original land deeds, brought in under the guard of Capitol policemen, in order to make their point. "Crates 'Prove' U.S. Owns Canal Zone—Allen," *Greensboro Daily News,* March 12, 1978.

95. Ferrel Guillory, "One Loss Won't Stop Helms in Fight Against Canal Pacts," *Raleigh News and Observer,* March 17, 1978.

96. "Senate Leaders Seek Earlier Vote on Canal," *Morganton News Herald,* April 5, 1978; "Treaty Foes Concede Battle Lost," *Sanford Herald,* April 6, 1978; "Helms Gives Critical View of Panamanian Competence," *Winston-Salem Journal,* April 13, 1978; "Canal Pact Squeaks Past Senate," *Charlotte Observer,* April 19, 1978; "Sen. Morgan Backs Treaty as Sen. Helms Again Calls It Foreign Policy Retreat," *Durham Sun,* April 19, 1978.

97. Robert Hodierne, "Morgan Ignores Nightmares, Joins Senators Backing Canal Treaties," *Charlotte Observer,* January 28, 1978; Guillory interview, February 2, 2006.

98. Brent Hackney, "Morgan vs. the Critics: Now It's Canal Treaties," *Greensboro Daily News,* March 12, 1978.

99. Gene Marlowe, "Canal Votes Could End Senators' Careers," *Winston-Salem Journal,* April 23, 1978; Ellis interview, February 3, 2006.

100. Eberle interview, June 6, 2006.

101. Wrenn interviews, September 27, 1996 (by Mosnier), May 13, 2005; Viguerie interview, February 14, 2006.

102. Viguerie interview, February 14, 2006.

103. Daniel C. Hoover, "Helms Backers Ready for '78," *Raleigh News and Observer,* January 24, 1977; "New Right: Well Financed, Pragmatic Coalition Means Business," *Greensboro Daily News,* December 4, 1977; Wrenn interview, May 13, 2005, February 1, 2006; Elizabeth Drew, "Jesse Helms," *The New Yorker,* July 20, 1981; Viguerie interview, February 14, 2006.

104. Reynolds interview, April 4, 2006.

105. "Helms Heads for Fund-Raising Record," *Raleigh News and Observer,* July 13, 1977; Bob Poole, "Helms' Fund-Raising Plan Cost Him 80c for Every $1," *Winston-Salem Journal,* July 12, 1977; Wrenn interview, May 13, 2005.

106. Lenox Rawlings, "Helms Has Raised Nearly $1.8 Million," *Winston-Salem Journal,* October 11, 1977; Lenox Rawlings, "Mail Drive Pulls in Money for Helms," *Winston-Salem Journal,* October 16, 1977; "New Right: Well Financed, Pragmatic Coalition Means Business," *Greensboro Daily News,* December 4, 1977; Jack Betts, "Helms Re-Election Unit Gets, Spends Nearly $2.3 Million," *Greensboro Daily News,* March 3, 1978; Mike Dembeck, "Helms Has Collected $4.6 Million," *Charlotte News,* July 12, 1978; Ferrel Guillory, "Stalking the Political Dollar," *Raleigh News and Observer,* August 13, 1978; Ferrel Guillory, "Fund-Raising List a Factor in National Race," *Raleigh News and Observer,* September 29, 1978; Ned Cline, "Helms's $6 Million: What He's Buying," *Char-*

lotte Observer, October 23, 1978; Marquis Childs, "Campaign Spending '78: Big Becomes Bigger," *Washington Post,* November 14, 1978.

107. Wrenn interview, September 27, 1996 (by Mosnier); interview with Mike Dunne, June 21, 2006.

108. Wrenn interview, May 13, 2005. Ellis noted that during the 1970s Helms became less and less involved in matters of policy. Ellis interview, February 3, 2006.

109. "Landslide Jesse," *Greensboro Record,* November 18, 1977. See also "Poll Suggests Sen. Helms Faces Close Race," *Raleigh News and Observer,* February 27, 1978.

110. Ferrel Guillory, "Helms Modifying Image for '78 Race," *Raleigh News and Observer,* April 24, 1977; William D. Snider, "Looking Forward to Helms," *Greensboro Daily News,* May 15, 1977; Claude Sitton, "Fight for Helms' Seat Taking Shape," *Raleigh News and Observer,* May 22, 1977; interview with Hamilton Horton, Jr., June 5, 1997, NCGOP.

111. Vernon Loeb, "Helms Blasts Weaknesses of America," *Winston-Salem Journal,* June 25, 1967.

112. "It's No Joke for N.C.," editorial, *Raleigh News and Observer,* October 25, 1978; Christensen interview, April 4, 2006; Ernest B. Furgurson, *Hard Right: The Rise of Jesse Helms* (New York: W. W. Norton, 1986), p. 230.

113. Christensen interviews, September 27, 2005, April 4, 2006.

114. Brent Hackney, "Autopsy of Ingram Defeat: The Product Fell Short," *Greensboro Daily News,* November 9, 1978; interview with Clint Fuller, December 22, 1989.

115. Ned Cline, "Ingram: A Successful Puzzle," *Charlotte Observer,* October 1, 1978.

116. Phil Galley, "Populist Makes Helms Squirm on Fund-Raising," *Washington Star,* October 1, 1978.

117. "Jessecrats: It's a Party Now but Helms Later," *Greensboro Daily News,* March 9, 1978.

118. Brent Hackney, "Helms' Alter Ego Has Put His Stamp on N.C. Politics," *Greensboro Daily News,* July 9, 1978.

119. Jack Betts, "Helms Campaign Well Entrenched; Ingram Building," *Greensboro Daily News,* July 23, 1978; Daniel C. Hoover, "What Makes Helms Run Organization," *Raleigh News and Observer,* October 1, 1978; Bill Peterson, " 'The Six Million Dollar Man'; Record Kitty Sets Helms Contest Tone," *Washington Post,* October 31, 1978; Bob Harris interview, September 27, 2005; Reynolds interview, April 4, 2006.

120. Susan Jetton, "Helms Refuses All N.C. Money for Campaign," *Charlotte Observer,* July 20, 1978; "Jesse Doesn't Need Tar Heels' Money," editorial, *Sampson Independent,* July 27, 1978.

121. Daniel C. Hoover, "Helms Backers Ready for '78," *Raleigh News and Observer,* January 24, 1977.

122. Wrenn interviews, September 27, October 4, 1996 (by Mosnier), May 13,

2005, February 1, 2006; Ashe interview, July 15, 2005; Stephens interview, June 6, 2006; Fetzer interview, June 20, 2006.

123. "Helms Opens Massive Ad Campaign," *Wilmington Morning Star,* June 6, 1978; "Helms Ad Typifies Well-Known Campaign Tactics," editorial, *Lenoir News Topic,* June 7, 1978; "The First Low Blow," editorial, *Fayetteville Observer,* June 8, 1978.

124. Jack Betts, "TV Ad Plans for Senate Accelerated," *Greensboro Daily News,* September 21, 1978.

125. "Helms 'Doing Well' After Back Surgery," *Raleigh Times,* September 1, 1978; Wrenn interviews, September 27, 1996 (by Mosnier), May 13, 2005; Fuller interview (by Riddick), November 20, 1991.

126. Ned Cline, "Jesse Has a Private Hit List," *Charlotte Observer,* November 12, 1978; Paul L. Krause, "Helms: Ingram 'Too Liberal' for Tar Heels," *Raleigh Times,* November 17, 1978; "N.C. Poll Shows Helms-Ingram Race Close," *Winston-Salem Journal,* October 8, 1978; "Helms Shown in Lead," *Goldsboro News-Argus,* October 26, 1978; A. L. May, "Helms Lead Growing as Vote Nears, Poll Finds," *Raleigh News and Observer,* November 5, 1978; Stan Swofford, "Helms Supporters Didn't Wait Long for the News," *Greensboro Daily News,* November 8, 1978.

127. Brent Hackney, "Autopsy of Ingram Defeat: The Product Fell Short," *Greensboro Daily News,* November 9, 1978.

128. Ned Cline, "Is Gov. Hunt Really Backing Ingram?," *Charlotte Observer,* October 22, 1978; Daniel C. Hoover, "Gov. Hunt Says Helms Misrepresented Stand," *Raleigh News and Observer,* November 2, 1978.

129. Claude Sitton, "Senate Campaign Has Turned into a Farce," *Raleigh News and Observer,* October 22, 1978.

130. "For the Senate: We Regret It, but No Choice," editorial, *Charlotte Observer,* October 29, 1978; Covington interview, August 31, 2006.

131. Ned Cline, "The $7-Million Question: Why Didn't He Win Big?," *Charlotte Observer,* November 12, 1978; Marquis Childs, "Campaign Spending '78: Big Becomes Bigger," *Washington Post,* November 14, 1978; Wrenn interview, May 13, 2005. For another analysis, see "Swept Away," editorial, *Greensboro Daily News,* November 9, 1978.

131. Vermont Royster, "Explaining the Helms Phenomenon," *Wall Street Journal,* reprinted in *Winston-Salem Journal,* December 3, 1978.

133. "Helms: 1 More Term," *Gastonia Gazette,* April 2, 1978; Jack Betts, "Helms Reopens 3rd-Term Door," *Greensboro Daily News,* May 9, 1978; "Helms May Seek 3rd Term Despite 'Limit,'" *Greensboro Daily News,* October 17, 1979.

134. Wrenn interviews, September 27, 1996 (by Mosnier), February 1, 2006; Furgurson, *Hard Right,* p. 133.

135. Ned Cline, "Jesse Has a Private Hit List," *Charlotte Observer,* November 12, 1978; "Helms Campaign Raised $7 million, but Still in the Red," *Charlotte News,* December 2, 1978; Wrenn interview, February 1, 2006; Eberle interview, June 6, 2006; Fetzer interview, June 20, 2006.

6. ARCHANGEL OF THE RIGHT

1. Fred Barnes, "The Ascendancy of Jesse Helms," *Weekly Standard,* August 11, 1997; Helen Dewar and Dan Balz, "Ultimate Conservative Leaves Senate Without an Heir," *Washington Post,* August 23, 2001; Elizabeth Drew, "Reporter at Large: Jesse Helms," *New Yorker,* July 20, 1981, p. 78.

2. Guillory interview, February 2, 2006. On the rise of the American right, see Lisa McGirr, *Suburban Warriors: The Origins of the New American Right* (Princeton: Princeton University Press, 2001).

3. Brent Hackney, "Helms Seeking Panel Post," *Greensboro Daily News,* January 16, 1979; Gene Marlowe, "Helms Is Named to Liberal Panel," *Winston-Salem Journal,* January 19, 1979.

4. Saul Friedman, "Foreign Policy Conservatives Take Politics Past 'the Water's Edge,'" *Charlotte Observer,* January 25, 1979.

5. Brent Hackney, "Jesse Helms and His Foreign Policy 'Cabinet,'" *Greensboro Daily News,* August 5, 1979.

6. In June 1965, Lucier also wrote that the principle of majority rule was "alien" to American political tradition and ideals, and he declared that women's suffrage had "merely doubled the potential for irresponsible voting." Lucier later defended his writings as a journalist: "I was a young writer and that was a chance to experiment with creative styles." "I was trying to amuse, startle, exhort, encourage, and so forth.... It is probably not the mode I would write in today, in a different period." Richard Whittle, "Top Helms Lieutenants Stay Busy Building New Network of the Right," *Raleigh News and Observer,* November 25, 1979; Kathy Sawyer, "Two Helms Point Men: Locking Horns with the Liberals," *Washington Post,* November 27, 1979; Ernest B. Furgurson, *Hard Right: The Rise of Jesse Helms* (New York: W. W. Norton, 1986) pp. 191–92.

7. "The Helms Obstruction," *Economist,* April 18, 1981; Richard Whittle, "Top Helms Lieutenants Stay Busy Building New Network of the Right," *Raleigh News and Observer,* November 25, 1979; Kathy Sawyer, "Two Helms Point Men: Locking Horns with the Liberals," *Washington Post,* November 27, 1979; John M. Goshko, "'Vandal' on the Loose: Helms' Aide Transition Assignment Signals About-Face on U.S. Foreign Policy," *Raleigh Times,* November 24, 1980.

8. Gene Marlowe, "Helms' Think Tanks Feed Hungry Conservatives," *Winston-Salem Journal,* September 25, 1979; editorial, *Greensboro Record,* September 25, 1979; Richard Whittle, "Helms Aides Reimbursed $33,000 by Foundation," *Raleigh News and Observer,* September 26, 1979; "The Helms' 'Foundations,'" editorial, *Greensboro Daily News,* October 6, 1979; "Probe Sought of Think Tanks Linked to Helms," *Raleigh Times,* October 8, 1979; "Sen. Helms Builds a Machine of Interlinked Organizations to Shape Both Politics, Policy," *Congressional Quarterly* 40 (March 6, 1982), 499; Carbaugh interview (by John Wilson), September 3, 2003, in author's possession.

9. *Washington Post,* February 9, 1980.

10. JH, speech, *CR,* October 2, 1979, floor speeches, JH MSS.

11. "2 N.C. Senators at Odds on Cuba," *Winston-Salem Journal,* October 3, 1979.

12. Richard Whittle, "Salt II Pact Dead, Helms Contends," *Raleigh News and Observer,* January 4, 1980.

13. JH, speech, *CR,* December 13, 1973, floor speeches, JH MSS. On Rhodesia, see Andrew DeRoche, *Black, White & Chrome: The United States and Zimbabwe, 1953-1998* (Trenton, N. J. and Asmara, Eritrea: Africa World Press, 2001).

14. Tom Wicker, "Ian Smith and Jesse Helms: Soulmates," *Wilmington Star,* September 27, 1979; JH, speech, *CR,* July 26, 1978, floor speeches, JH MSS. Arthur R. Lewis, *Too Bright a Vision? African Adventures of an Anglican Rebel* (London: Covenant Books, 1992), pp. 232–33.

15. Helms's proposals would lift sanctions and permit trade; he proposed either a fifteen-month or six-month suspension. JH, speech, *CR,* July 19, 26, 1978, floor speeches, JH MSS; "Sen. Helms's Rhodesia Alternative," editorial, *Washington Post,* July 11, 1978; "Helms' Amendment Inviting Confusion," editorial, *Washington Post, Greensboro Daily News* (reprint), July 13, 1978; Phil Gailey, "Helms, Muzorewa Eyed Askance in Lobbying Effort," *Raleigh News and Observer,* July 20, 1978; Michael A. Samuels, "Can the Senate Aid a Rhodesian Settlement?," *Washington Post,* July 24, 1978; Richard Pyle, "Senate Focuses on Helms' Proposal to Lift Embargo Against Rhodesia," *Durham Sun,* July 26, 1978; "Senate Votes to Keep Rhodesian Trade Embargo," *Raleigh News and Observer,* July 27, 1978; Gene Marlowe, "Helms Calls Compromise on Rhodesia a Victory," *Winston-Salem Journal,* July 27, 1978; Jim Hoagland, "Helms-manship," *Washington Post,* August 1, 1978; Spencer Rich, "Rhodesian Chrome Embargo Restored in Senate Measure," *Washington Post,* March 16, 1977.

16. JH, speech, *CR,* April 24, June 6, 1979, floor speeches, JH MSS; Graham Hovey, "Helms Moves to Lift Rhodesia Sanctions," *New York Times,* April 25, 1979; "U.S. Retains Zimbabwe Sanctions," *Charlotte Observer,* June 8, 1979; "Senate Deals Setback to Carter on Rhodesia," *Greensboro Daily News,* June 13, 1979; "Momentum Gathers for Lifting Rhodesian Sanctions," *Human Events,* May 5, 1979.

17. JH, speech, *CR,* September 10, 1979, floor speeches, JH MSS; R. W. Apple, Jr., "British Accuse Senate Aide on Rhodesia," *New York Times,* September 20, 1979; Don Oberdorfer, "British Say Helms Aides Hurt Talks," *Washington Post,* September 20, 1979; Jim Hoagland, "Helms Denies His Aides Meddled in Negotiations on Zimbabwe-Rhodesia," *Washington Post,* September 21, 1979; Richard Whittle, "Helms' Aide Denies Zimbabwe Interference," *Raleigh News and Observer,* September 28, 1979; "Britain Raps Helms Aide's Advice to Rhodesia Whites," *Wilmington Star,* September 28, 1979; "Helms in a China Shop," editorial, *Raleigh News and Observer,* September 21, 1979. Carbaugh disclosed that he was the source of the original lead in "Under the Dome," *Raleigh News and Observer,* February 3, 1980.

18. JH, speech, *CR,* September 27, 1979, floor speeches, JH MSS.

19. Speech, *CR,* September 20, 1979; "Helms Claims That U.S. Circulated British Complaints as 'Dirty Trick,'" *Raleigh News and Observer,* September 27, 1979; "In-

terfering with Conferences," editorial, *Wall Street Journal*, September 24, 1979; "The Fabricated 'Leak,'" editorial, *Richmond Times-Dispatch*, September 26, 1979; Gene Marlowe, "An Unspecified Complaint," *Winston-Salem Journal*, October 7, 1979. In December 1979, Carter and the Senate Foreign Relations Committee agreed to a compromise in which Carter would lift sanctions promptly after the British governor arrived, or by January 31, 1980, whichever was sooner. Carter was permitted to extend sanctions, but it would be subject to a congressional veto. "Sanctions Agreement Reached," *Raleigh Times*, December 4, 1979.

20. "Jesse on the Vice Presidency," editorial, *Raleigh News and Observer*, July 15, 1979; "A Different Slant," editorial, *Fayetteville Observer*, July 6, 1979; Rob Christensen, "N.C. Group to Push Helms for Vice Presidential Post," *Raleigh News and Observer*, August 15, 1979; Rowland Evans and Robert Novak, "Helms Running for Vice President?," *Winston-Salem Sentinel*, August 14, 1979; "Helms Would Like a 'Safeguard' Choice," *Greensboro Daily News*, August 28, 1979; "Jesse Helms for Vice President," *Conservative Digest*, November 1979, pp. 6–8; Bob Rosser interview, September 7, 2006.

21. Charles Babington, "Helms Files in N.H.—For Vice President," *Greensboro Daily News*, December 28, 1979; "'Spectator': Helms Disavows Trying to Win Vice Presidency," unidentified clipping, undated, c. December 1979, JH MSS; "The Helms Candidacy," *Winston-Salem Journal*, January 2, 1980; Ellis interview, February 3, 2006; Fuller interview (by Riddick), November 30, 1991.

22. Dan Haar, "GOP Presidential Contenders Ignoring Helms—Publicly," *Charlotte News*, January 4, 1980; Wrenn interview, February 1, 2006.

23. Robert Hodierne, "Helms Gets Little Notice in Vice Presidential Push," *Charlotte Observer*, April 9, 1980; "Helms Prefers Senate Seat," *Greensboro Record*, May 5, 1980; Daniel C. Hoover, "Vice Presidential Strategy for Helms Still 'Fluid,'" *Raleigh News and Observer*, July 11, 1980.

24. "Helms Backs Off from Reagan," *Durham Morning Herald*, January 22, 1979; Rowland Evans and Robert Novak, "Connally Is Wooing Jesse Helms," *Durham Morning Herald*, September 5, 1979.

25. David S. Broder, "GOP Snubs Helms," *Washington Post*, July 6, 1980; William M. Welch, "Helms: Liberals Threatening to Take GOP Spot," *Hickory Daily Record*, July 7, 1980; "GOP Panel Hits Splinter in ERA Plank," *Charlotte Observer*, July 8, 1980; Paul West, "Helms Aims to Rescue GOP from Moderate Forces," *Raleigh Times*, July 8, 1980; "ERA Forces Rebuffed on GOP Plank," *Raleigh Times*, July 8, 1980; Daniel C. Hoover, "Helms Backs Maneuver to Defuse ERA Issue," *Raleigh News and Observer*, July 10, 1980.

26. Myra MacPherson, "Jesse Helms' Hour," *Washington Post*, July 17, 1980.

27. Gene Marlowe, "Helms Enjoying the Limelight as 'The Only Game in Town,'" *Winston-Salem Journal*, July 17, 1980.

28. Daniel C. Hoover, "Ellis' Quiet Efforts Draw Praise, Scorn," *Raleigh News and Observer*, July 18, 1980; James J. Kilpatrick, "GOP Doesn't Show a Rush to the Right," *Raleigh News and Observer*, July 18, 1980.

29. William R. Amlong, "GOP Moves to Helms," *Charlotte Observer,* July 12, 1980; Myra MacPherson, "Jesse Helms' Hour," *Washington Post,* July 17, 1980.

30. Jack W. Germond and Jules Witcover, "Helms Makes Reagan Look Reasonable," *Raleigh News and Observer,* July 14, 1980.

31. Gene Marlowe, "Helms Enjoying the Limelight as 'The Only Game in Town,'" *Winston-Salem Journal,* July 17, 1980.

32. Gene Marlowe, "Helms Thinks Reagan Could Pick Him," *Winston-Salem Journal,* July 2, 1980; William M. Welch, "Conservatives Still Pushing Helms for Vice President," *Charlotte News,* July 2, 1980; Jack Betts, "Helms Forces Plan to Make a Difference," *Greensboro Daily News,* July 6, 1980.

33. "Helms Forces Turn Bid into Stop-Bush Effort," *Greensboro Daily News,* July 17, 1980; "Helms Believed Ford Was Chosen," *Raleigh News and Observer,* July 17, 1980; Stephen R. Kelly "Helms Quietly Drops Vice Presidential Bid," *Charlotte Observer,* July 18, 1980; Stephen R. Kelly, "Why Helms Dropped Bid for VP Nomination," *Charlotte Observer;* Doug Smith, "Helms Backers Considering Bid to Knock Bush off GOP Ticket," *Charlotte News,* July 17, 1980; Gene Marlowe, "Helms Swallows Anger over Bush," *Winston-Salem Journal,* July 18, 1980; Jack Betts, "Helms Pulls Out, Places Second Anyway," *Greensboro Daily News,* July 17, 1980; Wrenn interview, February 1, 2006; Guillory interview, February 2, 2006. Bauman, a leading opponent of gay rights running for reelection to Congress, was arrested in October 1980 for soliciting sex with a sixteen-year-old male prostitute.

34. "Can It," editorial, *Greensboro Record,* July 18, 1980.

35. Wrenn interview, February 1, 2006; Ellis interview, February 3, 2006; Bill Cobey interview, September 6, 2006; "Helms Campaign Group Sponsors Television Ads Against Hunt," *Elizabeth City Daily Advance,* September 20, 1979; "Stations Refuse Ad Suggesting Payoffs," *Raleigh News and Observer,* September 21, 1979; "WECT-TV Alone in Airing Anti-Hunt Spot," *Wilmington Morning Star,* September 22, 1979; "Ads Preview '80 Campaign," *Hickory Daily Record,* October 1, 1979; Allan J. Mayer and James Doyle, "The GOP Money Game," *Newsweek,* July 14, 1980.

36. Brent Hackney, "East Considering GOP Senate Bid," *Greensboro Daily News,* August 3, 1979; Ellis interview, February 3, 2006.

37. Wrenn interview, February 1, 2006.

38. Jack Betts, "Morgan Defends Helms," *Greensboro Daily News,* September 1, 1978; Ashe interview, July 15, 2005; Wrenn interviews, May 13, 2005, February 1, 2006; Stephens interview, June 6, 2006; Furgurson, *Hard Right,* pp. 140–43.

39. Wrenn interview, February 1, 2006; Stephen R. Kelly, "Staff Makes Morgan Realize Helms Hankers for His Scalp," *Charlotte Observer,* September 12, 1980.

40. For example, one East ad claimed that Morgan voted to permit unions to use dues for political purposes. What he had actually voted on was an amendment, offered by Helms, that would have banned union dues to be used for political purposes while it would have permitted corporate donations (the law prohibited both). Stephen R. Kelly, "East Triples Foes in Funds Raised During Summer," *Charlotte Observer,* October 17, 1980; "Morgan's 'Attack' Is Criticized,"

Winston-Salem Journal, October 17, 1980; Robert Hodierne, "Morgan Charges Challenger East Has Spread Lies," *Charlotte Observer,* October 24, 1980; Kathleen Curry, "Polls Give Morgan Strong Lead but Still He Campaigns for Votes," *Charlotte News,* October 25, 1980; Gene Marlowe, "East's New Ads Criticize Morgan on Textiles, Leaf," *Winston-Salem Journal,* October 31, 1980; Harris interview, September 27, 2005.

41. Stephen R. Kelly and Mae Israel, "TV Blitz Gave East Victory," *Charlotte Observer,* November 22, 1980.

42. "Morgan, Helms Clash Head-on in Senate," *Charlotte News,* November 13, 1980; "Morgan's Speech 'Appalls' Helms," *Raleigh News and Observer,* November 14, 1980; Robert Hodierne, "Morgan Bids Senate a Harsh Farewell," *Charlotte Observer,* December 10, 1980; "Helms Flustered by Morgan's Barbs," in "Under the Dome," *Raleigh News and Observer,* September 29, 1981.

43. Marjorie Hunter, "Not So Vital Statistics on Mr. Helms," *New York Times,* January 5, 1982; Rob Christensen, "Helms Socializes with the Best of Them in Washington," *Raleigh News and Observer,* February 28, 1981; Albert Hunt and James M. Perry, "Despite Courtly Ways, Sen. Jesse Helms Is One Shrewd Operator," *Wall Street Journal,* July 16, 1981.

44. The senator, according to one reporter, was unhappy with the *Time* story, and he later told an interviewer that it was a "cheap shot." Alfred Leslie, the artist who did the cover portrait, painted Jesse after two sittings in seven hours in the senator's Washington office. Although most of the subjects of *Time*'s covers refused to give that much time, Helms was eager to sit for the portrait. But, once completed, his likeness made Helms appear, according to the reporter, as if he was "peering mournfully into an empty refrigerator." With the light throwing "sinister-looking shadows across his face," Jesse's eyes were "both determined and mournful"; he resembled "an exasperated school principal who is slightly put out with the rest of us." Although some of Helms's supporters suspected that Leslie was a liberal, he reported that he had no idea who Helms was and had not voted in fifteen or twenty years. "Helms' Time Has Come and He's on the Cover," *Greensboro Daily News,* September 10, 1981; Gene Marlowe, "You Can't Judge a Senator by His Cover," *Winston-Salem Journal,* September 20, 1981.

45. Albert Hunt and James M. Perry, "Despite Courtly Ways," *Wall Street Journal,* July 16, 1981.

46. Rudy Abramson, "Jesse Helms: Right Arms of New Right," *Los Angeles Times,* August 17, 1981; Peter Ross Range, "Thunder from the Right," *New York Times Magazine,* January 25, 1981.

47. Jim Schlosser, "Jesse Helms: Love Him or Hate Him," *Greensboro Record,* February 23, 1981.

48. Peter Ross Range, "Thunder from the Right," *New York Times Magazine,* January 25, 1981.

49. JH interview (Tom Joyner), tape 30; interview with Jade West, April 19, 2006;

Nickles interview, October 11, 2006; Weyrich interview, October 11, 2006; Irwin B. Arieff, "Obscure Conservative Group Bolsters Senate GOP Power," *Congressional Quarterly Weekly Report,* May 12, 1979, p. 903; Furgurson, *Hard Right,* p. 109.

50. William D. Snider, *Helms and Hunt: The North Carolina Senate Race, 1984* (Chapel Hill: University of North Carolina Press, 1985), p. 58; Black interview, February 15, 2006.

51. Lynn Rosellini, "North Carolina Republican, Mark II," *New York Times,* February 16, 1982.

52. Rob Christensen, *Raleigh News and Observer,* February 1, 1981; Jim Schlosser, "Jesse Helms," *Greensboro Record,* February 23, 1981.

53. Rob Christensen, "Helms Reassured After Private Meeting with Reagan, *Raleigh News and Observer,* November 22, 1980.

54. "The Senate's Mr. Right," *Newsweek,* March 16, 1981.

55. Rudy Abramson, "Jesse Helms: Right Arm of New Right," *Los Angeles Times,* August 17, 1981; Helen Dewar, "The Senate's Archangel of the Right," *Washington Post,* February 15, 1981; Weyrich interview, October 11, 2006.

56. "A Program That Works," editorial, *Fayetteville Times,* March 5, 1981.

57. Ellis interview, February 3, 2006.

58. Helen Dewar, "Spending Cuts Just Fine—in Other Districts; Spending Restraint Has Limits Despite Zeal in Budget-Cutting," *Washington Post,* February 25, 1981.

59. Don Nelson to William Brock, January 23, 1981; Craig Fuller to Martin Anderson, January 28, 1981; Brock to Ronald Reagan, c. January 28, 1981, Benedict Cohen Papers, box 3, case file OA7974, Ronald Reagan Presidential Library, Simi Valley, California.

60. Rob Christensen, "Helms Asks Reagan to Delay Probe of Leaf Import Quota," *Raleigh News and Observer,* January 31, 1981; Rob Christensen, "Political Rivalries at Center of Battle on 'Scrap Tobacco,'" *Raleigh News and Observer,* February 1, 1981; "Helms Wants Politics Left Out of Tobacco Issue," *Charlotte News,* February 9, 1981; Rob Christensen, "Helms Says His Tobacco Stance Misunderstood," *Raleigh News and Observer,* February 9, 1981; Mary McGrory, "Tobacco Stains the New Reagan Budget," *Greensboro Record,* February 28, 1981; "Tobacco as a Football," editorial, *Raleigh News and Observer,* March 25, 1981; Fred Barnes, "Jesse Helms and the (Non-Existent) Tobacco Subsidy," *Chapel Hill Newspaper* (from the *Baltimore Sun*), April 5, 1981; Ward Sinclair, "Probe of Tobacco Imports Threatens to Run Away with Its Backers," *Washington Post,* May 27, 1981; Ward Sinclair, "Imports, Dissent Undercut Tobacco Price Supports," *Charlotte Observer* (from *Washington Post*), July 7, 1981.

61. Boney interview, June 1, 2006.

62. Patrick McDonnell, "Helms Confident on Tobacco Program," *Durham Morning Sun,* February 28, 1981.

63. Rob Christensen, "Tobacco Cut OK, Helms Says," *Raleigh News and Observer,* March 2, 1981; Rob Christensen, "Helms Backs Earlier Cutoff of Leaf Funds," *Raleigh News and Observer,* April 17, 1981.

64. *CR,* March 3, 1981, floor speeches, JH MSS; Miles Benson, "Tobacco Interests Claim Supports Aren't Subsidy," *Chapel Hill Newspaper,* March 4, 1981; "No One Exempt from Budget Ax, Senator Warns," *Wilmington Morning Star,* March 21, 1981; Fred Barnes, "Jesse Helms and the (Non-Existent) Tobacco Subsidy."

65. Helen Dewar, "Helms Maneuvers Senate Democrats into Voting to Cut Foreign Aid," *Washington Post,* March 28, 1981; "Famine and Games," *Greensboro Daily News,* March 30, 1981.

66. "Senate Panel Votes Not to Increase Milk Price Supports," *Charlotte Observer,* March 5, 1981; Rob Christensen, "Helms' Tale of Food Stamp Abuse Only Partially Correct," *Raleigh News and Observer,* March 28, 1981; Reagan telephone call memo, March 4, 1981, presidential handwriting file, Ronald Reagan Library (RRL).

67. "Senate Hearing Opens on Farm Bill," *New York Times,* March 3, 1981.

68. Seth S. King, "Senator Helms Offers a Farm Bill at Odds with Reagan Proposals," *New York Times,* April 8, 1981.

69. Robert G. Kaiser, "Senate's Multibillion Farm Bill Still Sprouting," *Washington Post,* May 1, 1981.

70. Seth S. King, "Reagan Will Face Early Decision on Cost of Food Stamp Problem," *New York Times,* December 7, 1980.

71. "Helms Pledges He Will Attempt to Trim Food Stamp Program," *Durham Morning Herald,* November 6, 1980; "Helms Eager to Trim Food Stamps Program," *Winston-Salem Journal,* November 7, 1980; "N.C. Official Says Helms Is Wrong on Food Stamps," *Greensboro Daily News,* November 11, 1980; Ward Sinclair, "Ascendancy of Helms Puts the Food Stamp Program Under the Gun," *Washington Post,* November 12, 1980; Gordon Borrell, "Food Stamps: Sen. Helms Getting Cutting Equipment in Order," *Norfolk Virginian-Pilot,* November 23, 1980.

72. Robert Hodierne, "Helms Power: Senator in Life to Head Panel Affecting Food Stamps, Wilderness," *Charlotte Observer,* November 6, 1980; Ward Sinclair, "Budget Plan Calls for Cut of About One-Fourth in Food Stamp Aid," *Washington Post,* January 28, 1981.

73. Harry Rosenthal, "Food Stamps Likely to Be Bloodiest Fight," *Greensboro Record,* February 18, 1981.

74. Rob Christensen, "Helms' Food Stamp Fight Spurs Leaf Worries," *Raleigh News and Observer,* November 30, 1980; Ward Sinclair, "Budget Plan Calls for Cut of About One-Fourth in Stamp Aid," *Washington Post,* January 28, 1981.

75. The *News and Observer* portrayed him as supporting a 40 percent cut; Helms claimed that it would be somewhere between 10 and 40 percent. "Helms Calls N&O Report Contrived," *Raleigh News and Observer,* January 4, 1981; Fugurson, *Hard Right,* pp. 156–58.

76. Phil Swann, "Helms Loses Fight over Stamp Cuts," *Durham Morning Herald,* February 19, 1981; Patrick McDonnell, "Helms Wants Leaner Food Stamp Budget," *Wilmington Morning Star,* February 21, 1981; Daniel C. Hoover, "Food Stamps Will Require New Clipping, Helms Says," *Raleigh News and Observer,*

February 22, 1981; Rob Christensen, "Helms Cites Food Stamp Fraud; Others Cite Hunger," *Raleigh News and Observer,* March 20, 1981.

77. Miles Benson, "Helms Not as Effective Inside the Senate," *Durham Sun,* February 19, 1981.

78. Ward Sinclair, "Food Stamps Fuel Helms' Money Machine; But Some 'Abuses' Already Corrected," *Washington Post,* October 11, 1981.

79. "More on Food Stamp Cuts," editorial, *Washington Post,* May 4, 1981.

80. Ward Sinclair, "Panel Thwarts Helms in Food-Stamp Debate," *Washington Post,* May 8, 1981.

81. Robert Hodierne and David Bartel, "Helms's Panel Rebuffs Him on Food Stamps," *Charlotte Observer,* May 13, 1981; Ward Sinclair, "Senate Approves Food Stamp Program After Rejecting Further Benefit Cuts," *Washington Post,* June 11, 1981.

82. Francis X. Clines, "Helms Takes Aim at 'Secular Humanism,'" *New York Times,* June 28, 1981.

83. Ward Sinclair, "Probe of Tobacco Imports Threatens to Run Away with Its Backers," *Washington Post,* May 27, 1981; Robert Hodierne, "Helms Foes Think of Tobacco as Revenge," *Charlotte Observer,* July 23, 1981.

84. Don Graff, "The Jesse Helms Show in D. C.," *Hendersonville Times News,* May 20, 1981; Rob Christensen, "Anti-Helms Backlash Jeopardizes Leaf Supports," *Raleigh News and Observer,* July 26, 1981. See also "Helms Hurts Tobacco," editorial, *Fayetteville Observer,* July 24, 1981.

85. "Helms Denies Backlash Claims," *Winston-Salem Journal,* August 3, 1981; Terry Martin, "Editor Plots Against Him, Helms Says," *Winston-Salem Journal,* August 14, 1981.

86. Daniel C. Hoover, "Helms Reassures N. C. Tobacco Farmers," *Raleigh News and Observer,* September 2, 1981.

87. "Helms Assails Brooklyn Rep., Other Critics," *Durham Morning Herald,* August 10, 1981; Furgurson, *Hard Right,* pp. 156–57.

88. *Winston-Salem Journal,* September 2, 1981; Ward Sinclair, "Tobacco Smoke; N.C. Senators Personally Attack Two Critics of U.S. Price Supports," *Washington Post,* September 14, 1981.

89. "Helms and East Go Too Far for Tobacco," editorial, *Asheville Citizen,* September 3, 1981; editorial, *Raleigh News and Observer,* September 3, 1981.

90. "East-Helms Personal Attacks Indefensible," editorial, *Durham Sun,* September 4, 1981.

91. Sinclair, "Tobacco Smoke"; "Helms Regrets Recent Remark About New York Representative," *Charlotte Observer,* September 7, 1981.

92. "East Sends Apology to Eagleton," *Charlotte Observer,* September 11, 1981.

93. "Sen. Tom Eagleton, Pricked by Barb, Uses It to Needle East," *Charlotte Observer,* September 17, 1981.

94. A compromise measure continued peanut quotas and price supports. Robert Hodierne, "Helms Loses Fight as Senate Alters Peanut Program," *Charlotte*

Observer, September 17, 1981. See also "The Helms Peanut Rule," editorial, *Washington Post,* September 18, 1981; Furgurson, *Hard Right,* pp. 157–58.

95. According to *Newsweek,* "bad blood" had developed between Helms and Hatfield, although both were born-again Christians. Bill Roeder, "The Hatfield-Helms Feud," *Newsweek,* October 15, 1981.

96. Jack Betts, "Leaf Program Saved from Ax," *Greensboro Daily News,* September 18, 1981; "Tobacco Support Plan Wins," *Fayetteville Times,* September 18, 1981; Rob Christensen, "Close Vote Saves Leaf Supports," *Raleigh News and Observer,* September 19, 1981; Jack Betts, "Who Saved Leaf Program from Demise?" *Greensboro News & Record,* September 20, 1981; Ward Sinclair, "Reagan Adds to Pressure on Farm Bill Conferees," *Washington Post,* December 3, 1981.

97. Ward Sinclair, "Not a Good Week; Helms Takes the Spotlight but Falters in Leading Farm Bill Through Senate," *Washington Post,* September 19, 1981; Ward Sinclair, "By Close Vote, Discontented Senate Adopts Battered, Austere Farm Bill," *Washington Post,* September 19, 1981.

98. JH, speech to Grove City College commencement, May 15, 1982, JH MSS.

99. Bill Peterson and David S. Broder, "Split in the Senate; Senate GOP Divided on 'Social Issues' Timing," *Washington Post,* March 27, 1981; "Helms Says Senate May Consider Some Social Measures This Year," *New York Times,* March 27, 1981; Furgurson, *Hard Right,* pp. 159–60.

100. Jesse Helms, "Filibuster Designed to Stop Busing Measure," JH newsletter, July 1, 1981.

101. Robert Hodierne, "It's a New Day for Helms's Anti-Busing Bill," *Charlotte Observer,* April 28, 1981.

102. Rob Christensen, "Filibuster Hits Helms' Anti-Busing Measure," *Raleigh News and Observer,* June 17, 1981; Richard L. Lyons, "Weicker Fights Helms Proposal Against Busing," *Washington Post,* June 17, 1981; Richard L. Lyons, "Conservatives in Senate Broaden Anti-Busing Bill," *Washington Post,* June 23, 1981.

103. Richard L. Lyons, *Washington Post,* June 19, 1981.

104. Bill Peterson, "11 Senators Join Weicker in Fight on Busing Curbs," *Washington Post,* July 1, 1981. The group also included Senators Edward M. Kennedy (Massachusetts), Daniel Patrick Moynihan (New York), Gary Hart (Colorado), Bill Bradley (New Jersey), George J. Mitchell (Maine), and Spark M. Matsunaga (Hawaii).

105. Bill Peterson, "Foes of Busing Fail Again to Break Senate Filibuster," *Washington Post,* September 11, 1981; Bill Peterson, "Senate Breaks 3-Month Busing Filibuster, Delays Final Action," *Washington Post,* September 17, 1981; "Senate Conservatives Break Busing Filibuster," *Durham Sun,* September 17, 1981; "Anti-Busing Backers End Senate Filibuster," *Durham Morning Herald,* December 11, 1981; Steven V. Roberts, "Bill to Ban Busing Delayed in Senate," *New York Times,* December 11, 1981; "O'Neill to Sit on Anti-Busing Rider," *Raleigh Times,* March 4, 1982.

106. "Senior Staff Meeting Action Items," subject files, FG006–1, case file 061280, Reagan Library.

107. "Helms Wins, Then Withdraws a Senate Busing Restriction," *New York Times,* October 22, 1983.

108. One indicator of the power of this coalition came with the nomination of C. Everett Koop, Jr., for surgeon general, whom Jesse enthusiastically endorsed because of his anti-abortion views. Because Koop, at age sixty-four, was approaching federal retirement, Helms attached a rider that revised the law in his case. Rob Christensen, "Helms Takes a Second Route in Battle over Abortion," *Raleigh News and Observer,* January 25, 1981; T. R. Reid, "Hill Abortion Opponents Seek New Law to Nullify '73 Supreme Court," *Washington Post,* February 7, 1981; Jesse Helms, "Innocent Lives Can't Be Destroyed," JH newsletter, March 25, 1981; A. O. Sulzberger, Jr., "Reagan Says Ban on Abortion May Not Be Needed," *New York Times,* March 6, 1981; "Abortion Becoming a Top Priority Issue in Congress," *New York Times,* March 13, 1981.

109. "Senate Begins Hearings on Bill to Outlaw Abortions," *New York Times,* April 24, 1981; Robert Hodierne, "Sen. East Wields New Power,"*Charlotte Observer,* April 26, 1981.

110. "A Question of Fairness," editorial, *Raleigh News and Observer,* April 27, 1981.

111. "The Abortion Issue," *Washington Post,* September 1, 1982.

112. "A Bad Piece of Legislation," editorial, *Wilson Daily Times,* May 9, 1981.

113. Rob Christensen, "Bill by Helms Pitched Aside in Anti-Abortion Crusade," *Raleigh News and Observer,* July 19, 1981; "Anti-Abortion Bill Voted, 4–0," *New York Times,* December 16, 1981; Nick Thimmesch, "Pro-Life Forces Feud over Helms and Hatch Bills," *Winston-Salem Sentinel* (from the *Los Angeles Times*), January 27, 1982; Patricia O'Brien, "Right Pushes for Action on Busing, Abortion," *Asheboro Courier Tribune,* January 31, 1982. See also JH to the Pro-Life Caucus (which was drafted by James Lucier), October 15, 1981, JH MSS, which lays out the argument in favor of a Human Life bill and against the Hatch-sponsored constitutional amendment.

114. Bill Peterson, "Worries for New Right; Group Thwarted on Social Policy, Badly Split over Abortion Tactics," *Washington Post,* February 16, 1982.

115. "Helms Introduces Anti-Abortion Bill," *New Bern Journal,* March 2, 1982; Rob Christensen, "New Helms Bill Revives Effort to Restrict Abortion," *Raleigh News and Observer,* March 2, 1982; "Helms Introduces Bill to Bar Federal Money for Abortions," *New York Times,* March 3, 1982.

116. Ellen Goodman, "Abortion and the '3-H Club,'" *Washington Post,* May 8, 1982. Packwood's filibuster had support from Senators Lowell Weicker, Jr., of Connecticut, Arlen Specter of Pennsylvania, Paul Tsongas of Massachusetts, Howard Metzenbaum of Ohio, and Max Baucus of Montana. It continued into September 1982, and, despite lobbying by Reagan on Helms's behalf, three attempts at cloture failed. Ironically, pro-choice forces had defeated the measure by Helms's favorite method of obstruction. Rob Christensen, "Helms

Offers Anti-Abortion Amendment," *Raleigh News and Observer,* August 17, 1982; Robert Pear, "Filibuster Starts Abortion Debate," *New York Times,* August 17, 1982; Rob Christensen, "Helms Loses Test Vote on Social Issues Bill," *Raleigh News and Observer,* August 19, 1982; Bill Peterson, "Liberals Predict Abortion Issue Dead for Year; Helms Disagrees," *Washington Post,* August 19, 1982; "Efforts to End Abortion Impasse in Senate Collapse," *Raleigh Times,* August 20, 1982; Robert Pear, "Baker Sets Vote After Labor Day on Ending Filibuster on Abortion and School Prayer," *New York Times,* August 21, 1982; Bill Peterson, "Abortion Foes Again Fail to Halt Filibuster," *Washington Post,* September 14, 1982; Bill Peterson, "New Right Defeated on Abortion; Senate Kills Bill as 3d Move to Halt Filibuster Fails," *Washington Post,* September 16, 1982; Reagan to Helms, September 7, 1982, Pamela Turner files, Reagan Library; Morton C. Blackwell to Diana Lozano, August 20, 1982, Stephen Galebach files, Reagan Library.

117. Bill Peterson, "Backers of Legalized Abortion, in Switch, Adopt Hardball Tactics," *Washington Post,* August 24, 1982.

118. Joe Brown, "Helms, on the March; Preaching and Pledging to Abortion Foes," *Washington Post,* January 24, 1983.

119. Helen Dewar, "Senate Sets Back Anti-Abortion Cause," *Washington Post,* June 29, 1983.

120. JH, speech, *CR,* February 16, 1981, floor speeches, JH MSS; "Senators Submit School Prayer Bill," *Raleigh News and Observer,* February 19, 1981; "Neutral Against the Courts," editorial, *New York Times,* September 11, 1982; Herbert H. Denton and Marjorie Hyer, "Reagan to Ask Hill for Prayer Amendment," *Washington Post,* May 7, 1982; Steven R. Weisman, "Reagan Neutral on Bid to Curb Court on Prayer," *New York Times,* September 9, 1982.

121. Steven V. Roberts, "School Prayer Bill Brings New Filibuster in Senate," *New York Times,* September 17, 1982; Bill Peterson, "Helms Fails to Stop Filibuster in Senate Against Prayer Bill," *Washington Post,* September 21, 1982. After the cloture amendment failed for a third time, on September 23, Moynihan called the successful filibuster an "emphatic and final rejection of the New Right." Barry Goldwater's motion to table Helms's rider was then narrowly defeated. With Helms tying up Senate business for five weeks, Goldwater complained that Helms had aided conservatism "not one bit"; even a liberal such as Teddy Kennedy, he believed, would not have employed Helms's tactics. "We've got enough trouble in this country without worrying about social issues," said Goldwater, and he described himself as "just an old-fashioned conservative" and an "old, old son of a bitch." "Senate Conservatives Fail to Curtail Prayer Filibuster," *Durham Morning Herald,* September 21, 1982; Steven V. Roberts, "Prayer Filibuster Wins Senate Test," *New York Times,* September 21, 1982; Bill Peterson, "Second Attempt Fails to Halt Filibuster on School Prayer Issue," *Washington Post,* September 22, 1982; "Goldwater: Helms Hasn't Helped," *Durham Morning Herald,* September 23, 1982.

122. Bill Peterson, "Tempers Flare on Prayer Filibuster," *Washington Post*, September 23, 1982; Steven V. Roberts, "School Prayer Advocates Lose Third Vote in Senate," *New York Times*, September 23, 1982.

123. Rob Christensen, "Prayer Bill Fight Lost in the Senate," *Raleigh News and Observer*, September 24, 1982.

124. Bill Peterson, "Senate Kills School Prayer Legislation for Session," *Washington Post*, September 24, 1982; Steven V. Roberts, "Senate Makeup on Social Issues: 'Conservative It Ain't,'" *New York Times*, September 24, 1982.

125. Rob Christensen, "Helms Scoffs at Idea Defeats Tarnish His Leadership," *Raleigh News and Observer*, September 26, 1982; JH, speech to School Prayer Day, September 25, 1982, JH MSS.

126. T. R. Reid, "Helms to Offer Alternatives; Prayer Backers Plan New Drive," *Washington Post*, March 23, 1984.

7. A PURE GOSPEL OF CONSERVATISM

1. John Osborne, "Helms Taking a Mean Dog Stance in Reagan Junkyard," *New Republic*, in the *Raleigh News and Observer*, February 14, 1981.

2. Judith Miller, "Reagan's Shift to Center Brings Attacks from Right," *New York Times*, January 24, 1981.

3. Hedrick Smith, "Conservatives Cite Gains in Top Posts," *New York Times*, March 7, 1981; Rob Christensen, "Helms Courting Latin Right 'To Keep Communism Out,'" *Raleigh News and Observer*, April 25, 1982.

4. Rob Christensen, "Helms and East Shun N.C. Man for Federal Post," *Raleigh News and Observer*, October 3, 1981; Carla Hall, "Bradford's Boosters; Bradford's GOP Boosters; 16 GOP Senators Push Texan for NEH Chair," *Washington Post*, October 20, 1981.

5. Carla Hall, "The Amazing Endowment Scramble; When Politics and Professors Meet, the Fracas Is Anything but Academic," *Washington Post*, December 13, 1981; Will, quoted in "Good Choice at NEH," *New Republic*, December 16, 1981.

6. Carla Hall, "The Amazing Endowment Scramble," *Washington Post*, December 13, 1981.

7. Carla Hall, "Bradford Speaks Out: NEH Chair Candidate on His Program Plans," *Washington Post*, October 28, 1981.

8. Pat Buchanan, "Another Plum to 'Neo-Cons'?,'" *Chicago Tribune*, November 7, 1981.

9. Jim McClellan to John East, November 9, 1981, JH MSS.

10. JH to Max Friedersdorf, November 23, 1981, subject files, FG203–3, case file 051804, Reagan Library.

11. James P. Lucier to the Editor, *Raleigh News and Observer*, December 2, 1981. Lucier was a particularly vigorous opponent of Bennett's nomination, and he strenuously argued his case with Helms. See Lucier to JH, November 20, December 12, 1981, JH MSS.

12. "Unfair Test for Bennett," editorial, *Raleigh News and Observer,* December 2, 1981.

13. "Helms May Not Back Bennett for U.S. Post," *Durham Morning Herald,* December 1, 1981; "Bennett Rebuts Helms' Charge," *Kinston Daily Free Press,* December 2, 1981.

14. "Helms May Not Back Bennett for U.S. Post," *Durham Morning Herald,* December 1, 1981; "Bennett Rebuts Helms' Charge," *Kinston Daily Free Press,* December 2, 1981; "Bennett Chosen New Chairman of Humanities," *Raleigh News and Observer,* December 23, 1981; Rob Christensen, "Helms, East Back Bennett for Humanities Chairman," *Raleigh News and Observer,* February 3, 1982.

15. John M. Goshko, "Transition's Carbaugh Alarms State Dept.," *Washington Post,* November 23, 1980.

16. John Osborne, "Helms Taking a Mean Dog Stance in Reagan Junkyard"; Jesse Helms, "Gen. Haig Will Make America a Stronger Nation," JH newsletter, February 4, 1981; Don Oberdorfer, "On Surface, Helms Has Won Little in Challenge to Reagan Diplomacy," *Washington Post,* June 10, 1981.

17. Robert J. Wagman, "Senator Helms Wants Assurances from Haig," *Goldsboro News-Argus,* January 11, 1981; John M. Goshko, "'Vicar' Haig Takes Oath, Taps Policy Mainstream," *Washington Post,* January 23, 1981; Robert Hornig, "Helms Is Blocking One Post, Threatens Others," *Greensboro Record* (from the *Washington Star*), January 22, 1981.

18. Jack Betts, "Helms, East Stand Alone in Vote Against Weinberger," *Greensboro Daily News,* January 21, 1981; Helen Dewar and Margot Hornblower, "Two Republican Senators Vote Against Weinberger," *Washington Post,* January 21, 1981; "Helms Protests Defense Secretary," *Charlotte News,* January 21, 1981; Robert Hodierne, "Sen. Helms Flashes His Old (Bulldog) Form," *Charlotte Observer,* January 23, 1981; Jesse Helms, "Doubts About Weinberger Raised," Helms newsletter, February 18, 1981; Rob Christensen, "Helms Fights Some Nominees, Fears Reagan Move to the Middle," *Raleigh News and Observer,* January 23, 1981; Peter Ross Range, "Thunder from the Right," *New York Times Magazine,* January 25, 1981; Helen Dewar, "The Senate's Archangel of the Right," *Washington Post,* February 15, 1981.

19. Robert Hornig, "Helms Is Blocking One Post, Threatens Others," *Greensboro Record* (from the *Washington Star*), January 22, 1981; JH to Reagan, January 22, 1981; Bill Gribbin to Reagan, January 24, 1981, Turner files, Reagan Library; Rob Christensen, "Helms Says He Is Content with Subcabinet Nominees," *Raleigh News and Observer,* January 27, 1981.

20. Gene Marlowe, "Helms' Right-Wing Revolt Fails," *Winston-Salem Journal,* February 4, 1981; Rob Christensen, "Helms, East Vote Against Confirmation," *Raleigh News and Observer,* February 4, 1981; "Senator No to Friend and Foe," editorial, *Raleigh News and Observer,* February 8, 1981.

21. The nominees included Lawrence Eagleburger, formerly Kissinger's deputy and Haig's choice to serve as assistant secretary for European affairs. Helms also objected to the rumored nominations for assistant secretaries of John

Holdridge, for East Asian and Pacific affairs, and Chester Crocker, for African affairs; both were also holdovers from the Kissinger era. Helms opposed the prospective appointment of Thomas Enders to the Latin American desk; instead, he was reportedly promoting Carbaugh for that position.

22. In early March, Eagleburger, Crocker, and Holdridge were nominated, along with Robert Hormats as assistant secretary for economic affairs and Myer Rashish as undersecretary for economic affairs. Helms was skeptical of all these choices, and, placing holds on eight of the nominations, delayed their consideration. "Helms, Allies Ready for Nominee Fight,"*Raleigh News and Observer*, February 14, 1981; James McCartney, "Helms Blocking Haig's Key Appointments," *Charlotte Observer*, February 24, 1981; "Knight-Ridder Helms Story Is Denied," *Charlotte Observer*, February 26, 1981; "Helms Denies Blocking Haig Appointees," *Charlotte News*, February 26, 1981; Rob Christensen, "Helms Socializes with the Best of Them in Washington," *Raleigh News and Observer*, February 28, 1981; Jeremiah O'Leary, "Helms' Price," *Greensboro Record* (from *Washington Star*), March 4, 1981; "Former Aide to Kissinger Selected," *Charlotte News*, March 5, 1981; Jesse Helms, "There's Reason for Being Cautious," Helms newsletter, March 18, 1981; Elizabeth Drew, "Reporter at Large," *New Yorker*, March 16, 1981, p. 90.

23. Howell Raines, "White House Headhunter Feels the Heat," *New York Times*, May 3, 1981.

24. Rob Christensen, "Helms Aide Wielding Foreign Policy Influence," *Raleigh News and Observer*, January 5, 1981; Judith Miller, "Behind Senator Helms: A Cherubic Assistant Reigns," *New York Times*, April 20, 1981; Rob Christensen, "Haig's Job Offer to Helms Adviser Rouses Suspicions," *Raleigh News and Observer*, April 25, 1981; Albert Hunt and James M. Perry, "Despite Courtly Ways, Sen. Jesse Helms Is One Shrewd Operator," *Wall Street Journal*, July 16, 1981.

25. Helms also wondered whether Rashish, nominated for undersecretary of state for economic affairs, shared the president's views, and he suspected that he might have posssessed "mixed loyalties" because he had previously worked as a lobbyist for West Germany and France. Bill Peterson, "Helms' Doubts on Reagan Nominees Place Several Key Officials on 'Hold'; Sen. Helms Describes His Doubts About Nominees," *Washington Post*, April 26, 1981; "Helms Letter Explains His Strategy," *Charlotte Observer*, April 26, 1981.

26. "Senator Helms Pledges Note to Block Nominees," *New York Times*, April 29, 1981; Gene Marlowe, "Helms Simmers Down," *Winston-Salem Journal*, May 3, 1981; "Helms Silent as Nomination Logjam Breaks," *Raleigh Times*, May 6, 1981.

27. Eagleburger, whom Helms originally had vehemently opposed because of his close connections to Kissinger, enjoyed unqualified White House support, and this deflated Helms's opposition. Hormats enjoyed enough support from business leaders to persuade Helms, while Enders persuaded him because of his

anti-Cuban approach to Latin American policy. Focusing his attack on the Holdridge and Crocker nominations, Helms insisted that both areas of the State Department, Asia and Latin America, include lower-level appointees of Helms's choosing. In Holdridge's case, Helms demanded that two deputies be transferred and replaced with Helms protégés. Holdridge's dealings with Helms were largely irrelevant: the transfers were going to occur anyway, and Helms's choices were not interested in the positions. Although the arrangement with Helms resulted in his lifting the hold on Holdridge's nomination, after it was leaked from Congress, the State Department was embarrassed. Don Oberdorfer, "On Surface, Helms Has Won Little in Challenge to Reagan Diplomacy," *Washington Post,* June 10, 1981. Helms focused especially on Crocker's nomination. To counterbalance Crocker, Helms urged the appointment, as Crocker's deputy, of Clifford A. Kiracofe, Jr. A research associate at the Boston-based Institute for Foreign Policy Analysis, Inc., Kiracofe was described by one unnamed source as a "far-right hardliner, very articulate and activist." Crocker, however, wanted nothing to do with Kiracofe, and he insisted on keeping Lannon Walker, a holdover from the Carter administration. When the Foreign Relations Committee approved Crocker's nomination by a 16–0 vote in Helms's absence, the senator responded with a twelve-page minority report that asserted that Crocker advocated policies that were unchanged from the positions of Jimmy Carter. The matter then ended when Majority Leader Howard Baker in early June intervened by removing the hold on Crocker's nomination, and he was approved by the full Senate by an 84–7 vote. " 'Helms Deal' May End Diplomats' Jobs," *Durham Morning Herald,* May 23, 1981; E. Michael Myers, "Helms Ended Fight of Nominee for 2 Aides' Firing, Sources Say," *Raleigh News and Observer,* May 24, 1981; Don Oberdorfer, "Helms Offers Nomination Swap; Helms Offers White House a Tradeoff on Appointments; Crocker Appointment at Stake," *Washington Post,* June 3, 1961; Don Oberdorfer, "Sen. Helms to Allow Votes on State Dept. Nominees," *Washington Post,* June 9, 1981; "Crocker Clears Senate Despite Fight by Helms," *Raleigh News and Observer,* June 10, 1981.

28. Don Oberdorfer, "On Surface, Helms Has Won Little in Challenge to Reagan Diplomacy," *Washington Post,* June 10, 1981.

29. Joel Brinkley, "Helms and Rightists: Long History of Friendship," *New York Times,* August 1, 1984; Claude Sitton, "Helms' Dual Role Raises Vexing Question," *Raleigh News and Observer,* August 22, 1982; Rob Christensen, "Helms Courting Latin Right 'To Keep Communism Out,' " *Raleigh News and Observer,* April 25, 1982; Steven Livingston, "Jesse Helms's Friends," *Washington Post,* November 27, 1994.

30. Helms's support for Argentina was a "philosophical sellout to the jackbooted Argentinian junta," said the *Raleigh News and Observer,* and the North Carolina senator "ought to be ashamed to keep such company so openly." For too long, Helms had been "cozy with these gaucho fascists," said Claude Sitton, because

he saw them "as just the fellows to block any communist takeover of the Western Hemisphere." "Helms Adrift on Falklands," *Raleigh News and Observer,* April 9, 1982; Claude Sitton, "Falklands Dispute Disturbs Old Friendships," *Raleigh News and Observer,* April 11, 1982.

31. Rob Christensen, "Helms Defends Endorsement of Argentina's Claim to Islands," *Raleigh News and Observer,* April 9, 1982; "Give Up Falkland Islands, Helms Urges Great Britain," *Greensboro Daily News,* April 8, 1982.

32. *CR,* April 21, 1982, floor speeches, JH MSS: Richard Oppel, "Helms Aiding Falklands Negotiations?," *Charlotte Observer,* April 10, 1982; "Helms' Aid Is Sought During Falklands Crisis," in "Under the Dome," *Raleigh News and Observer,* April 20, 1982; "Helms Offers Falklands Compromise," *Greensboro Daily News,* April 23, 1982; Rob Christensen, "Helms Proposes British Laws, Argentine Sovereignty in Islands," *Raleigh News and Observer,* April 23, 1982; Jesse Helms, "Report from U.S. Senator Jesse Helms," JH newsletter, April 29, 1982; DeMoss Fonseca interview, October 10, 2006.

33. Helms did manage to dilute the resolution significantly. Biden's resolution endorsed U.N. Security Council Resolution 502, which required Argentine withdrawal and recognized the "right of the United Kingdom and all other nations' right of self-defense under the United Nations Charter." But the original resolution urging the administration to employ "all appropriate means to assist the British government" was removed, as was language stating that the United States would support the principle of self-determination (the Falkland islanders overwhelmingly wanted to remain British). Margot Hornblower, "Senate Resolution Sides with Britain," *Washington Post,* April 30, 1982; "Helms Fails to Block Senate's Pro-British Resolution," *Durham Sun,* April 30, 1982; *CR,* April 29, 1982, floor speeches, JH MSS.

34. *CR,* May 3, 1982, floor speeches, JH MSS; Rob Christensen, "Helms Calls Haig's Role in Falklands a Mistake," *Raleigh News and Observer,* May 4, 1982.

35. Keith Upchurch, "Helms Promises Fight if U.S. Sends Troops to Falklands," *Durham Sun,* June 14, 1982; "Helms Says British Victory Wasn't Worth Bloodshed," *Durham Morning Herald,* June 16, 1982.

36. "Helms: U.S. Cuts Off Aid to Nicaragua," *Winston-Salem Journal,* March 3, 1981; "Helms Says Administration Has Cut Off Nicaraguan Aid," *New York Times,* March 2, 1981; "U.S. Halts Economic Aid to Nicaragua," *New York Times,* April 2, 1981; "Nicaragua: The Wrong Move," editorial, *Washington Post,* April 5, 1981.

37. Bill Peterson, "Reagan Plea Rejected, Senate Votes Terms for Salvadoran Aid," *Washington Post,* September 25, 1981.

38. Rob Christensen, "Helms Fights Report Requirement on Progress in Salvadoran Probe," *Raleigh News and Observer,* July 22, 1982; Rob Christensen, "Helms, East Take Stand Against Salvadoran Legislation," *Raleigh News and Observer,* July 31, 1982.

39. "Salvador Policy Takes Beating," *Durham Morning Herald,* February 28, 1982;

Rob Christensen, "Helms Says Media, 'Careerists' Hurt Salvadoran Aim,'" *Raleigh News and Observer,* February 28, 1982; Ferrel Guillory, "Right-Wing President Assailed from Right," *Raleigh News and Observer,* March 6, 1982.

40. *From Madness to Hope: The 12-Year War in El Salvador* (U.N. Truth Commission report), at http://www.usip.org/library/tc/doc/reports/el_salvador/tc_es_03151993_casesD1_2.html#D1 (accessed November 30, 2006).

41. Rob Christensen, "Helms Courting Latin Right 'To Keep Communism Out,'" *Raleigh News and Observer,* April 25, 1982; Joanne Omang, "Hill Panel Says Helms' Charges Are 'Overstated,'" *Washington Post,* May 10, 1984; "Biographical Conversations with Jesse Helms," WUNC-TV, February 11, 2000.

42. *CR,* January 27, 1984; Joanne Omang, "D'Aubuisson Is Promoted Here," *Washington Post,* February 23, 1984; A. L. May, "Report Links Helms Aides, Salvadoran Rightist Party," *Raleigh News and Observer,* February 26, 1984; "El Salvador Meddling," editorial, *Raleigh News and Observer,* February 29, 1984; Joanne Omang, "State Department Denies Entry Visa to El Salvador's D'Aubuisson," *Washington Post,* March 6, 1984; John Monk, "Helms' Secret Weapon," *Charlotte Observer,* May 1, 1994; DeMoss Fonseca interview, October 10, 2006; "Report from Senator Jesse Helms," June 11, 1984, no. 547.

43. JH to Reagan, May 1, 1984, subject files, FO002, case file 224902, Reagan Library; Cliff Kiracofe to JH, May 8, 1984, JH MSS; Lydia Chavez, "Helms Bids Envoy to Salvador Quit," *New York Times,* May 3, 1984; Robert J. McCartney, "Helms Said to Demand Envoy Pickering's Ouster," *Washington Post,* May 3, 1984.

44. Kenneth Duberstein to William Clark, c. July 26, 1983, subject files, FO002, case file 160174, Reagan Library.

45. (DeMoss) Fonseca interview, October 10, 2006.

46. Steven V. Roberts, "Reagan Defends Aide in Salvador Assailed by Helms," *New York Times,* May 4, 1984; Helen Dewar, "Helms Resumes Attacks on Centrist Foreign Policy," *Washington Post,* May 5, 1984; *CR,* May 8, 1984, floor speeches, JH MSS; John Felton, "CIA Role Casts Doubt on Salvador Election," *Congressional Quarterly Weekly Report,* May 12, 1984, p. 1091.

47. DeMoss Fonseca interview, October 10, 2006.

48. Edward Cody, "Rightist Candidate Claims Victory in El Salvador," *Washington Post,* May 10, 1984.

49. "Washington at Work; Man with His Own Foreign Policy," *New York Times,* December 7, 1994.

50. "U.S. Confirms a Rightist Plot in El Salvador to Murder Envoy," *New York Times,* June 23, 1984; John Monk, "Helms' Secret Weapon," *Charlotte Observer,* May 1, 1994; DeMoss Fonseca interview, October 10, 2006.

51. A. L. May, "Salvador's D'Aubuisson to Visit U.S., Helms Says," *Raleigh News and Observer,* June 5, 1984; "Salvadoran Rightist Tied to Murder Plot Will Meet Senators," *New York Times,* June 25, 1984; Hedrick Smith, "Salvadoran's Visa Tied to His Help," *New York Times,* June 26, 1984; Bill Arthur, "Rightist Greeted Coolly," *Charlotte Observer,* June 28, 1984.

52. Reagan telephone call memo, with RR notation, July 22, 1982, Pamela Turner files, Reagan Library; Reagan telephone call memo, with RR notation, August 12, 1982, presidential handwriting file, Reagan Library; Ernest B. Furgurson, *Hard Right: The Rise of Jesse Helms* (New York: W. W. Norton, 1986), pp. 162–63.

53. "Helms, East Under Fire on Votes for Tax Boost," *Hickory Daily Record,* July 24, 1982; Charles Jeffries, "Switch in Votes by Helms, East Shakes Tobacco Interests," *Raleigh News and Observer,* July 24, 1982; "Helms Changes Mind in Tax Vote," *Monroe Enquirer-Journal,* July 25, 1982; "Hunt Aide: Votes Hurt East, Helms," *Hickory Daily Record,* July 27, 1982; William M. Welch, "Democrats Attack Senators' Votes on Tobacco Tax," *Greensboro Daily News,* August 6, 1962; " 'Tobacco Tax Twins' Ad Draws Club's Ire," in "Under the Dome," *Raleigh News and Observer,* August 7, 1982; David Maraniss, "Filibuster's Helmsman Sails Home to a State Buffeted by Winds of '84," *Washington Post,* January 2, 1983; Wrenn interview, February 1, 2006; Ellis interview, February 3, 2006; Furgurson, *Hard Right,* pp. 162–63.

54. Wrenn interview, February 1, 2006; Pearce interview, February 3, 2006; Alston interview, October 12, 2006; Stephens interviews, June 6, October 10, 2006; Black interview, February 15, 2006; Bill Peterson, "Democrats Claim Rout of the Commandos of New Right Once and for All," *Washington Post,* November 5, 1982. For North Carolina reaction, see "Congressional Club a Loser," *Charlotte News,* November 3, 1982; Ken Eudy, " 'Ultraliberal' Media Blamed for Losses," *Charlotte Observer,* November 4, 1982; Daniel C. Hoover and A. L. May, "Hunt Emerges as a Big Winner from GOP Congressional Losses," *Raleigh News and Observer,* November 4, 1982; Chuck Alston, "Club Tactics Boomeranged?," *Greensboro Daily News,* November 4, 1982; Miles Benson, "Manatt Says Helms Reduced to 'Most Vulnerable,' " *Winston-Salem Journal,* November 6, 1982.

55. Reagan telephone call memo, with RR notation, December 14, 1982, Pamela Turner files, Reagan Library; Wilson interview, June 5, 2006; "Report from U. S. Senator Jesse Helms," nos. 471 and 472, December 27, 1982, January 3, 1983, JH MSS.

56. Nickles interview, October 11, 2006.

57. Bill Arthur, "Will Colleagues' Anger Hurt Helms?," *Charlotte Observer,* December 23, 1982; David Maraniss, "Sen. Helms: An Outcast in Senate," *Washington Post,* December 23, 1982; "Democrats Exploit Helms's Filibuster Tactics," *New York Times,* January 2, 1983; Helms interview (by Joyner), tape 34; Furgurson, *Hard Right,* pp. 163–64.

58. Claude Sitton, "Sens. No and No-No Draw Nation's Jeers," *Raleigh News and Observer,* December 26, 1982.

59. Robert Hodierne, "Helms Faces the 2nd Act of Power Play," *Charlotte Observer,* May 2, 1981.

60. Bill Peterson, "New-Right Knight Dulls His Senate Sword," *Washington Post,* September 21, 1982; Helen Dewar, "GOP's 'Old Center' Holds, Despite New Right Senators," *Washington Post,* August 23, 1982.

61. "Stand By for Jesse," editorial, *Greensboro News & Record,* September 26, 1982.

62. David Maraniss, "Filibuster's Helmsman Sails Home to a State Buffeted by Winds of '84," *Washington Post,* January 2, 1983; "Report from U.S. Senator Jesse Helms," no. 473, January 10, 1983, JH MSS.

63. Bill Peterson, "New-Right Knight Dulls His Senate Sword," *Washington Post,* September 21, 1982; Elizabeth Drew, "Reporter at Large," *The New Yorker,* July 20, 1981, p. 81.

64. Michael Whiteley, "Helms, Others Were Scheduled for Downed Jet," *Raleigh Times,* September 1, 1983; Helen Dewar and Vivian Aplin-Brownlee, "Rep. McDonald Hailed as Right-Wing Martyr," *Washington Post,* September 2, 1983; "Washington Notebook," *Winston-Salem Journal,* September 18, 1983. On the KAL 007 shoot-down, see Alexander Dallin, *Black Box: KAL 007 and the Super-powers* (Berkeley: University of California Press, 1985); Seymour M. Hersh, *The Target Is Destroyed: What Really Happened to Flight 007 and What America Knew About It* (London: Faber, 1986).

65. Meredith Barkley and Chuck Alston, "Helms Condemns Soviet Action as 'Barbarity,'" *Greensboro Daily News,* September 2, 1983; Todd Cohen, "Helms Cites Rumor Lawmakers Were Soviets' Targets," *Raleigh News and Observer,* September 2, 1983; Todd Cohen, "Helms Possible Target of Soviets, Ellis Says," *Raleigh News and Observer,* September 3, 1983.

66. Ken Allen and Bill Arthur, "Jesse Helms Urges Reagan to Limit Ties with Soviets," *Charlotte Observer,* September 7, 1983; Helen Dewar, "Conservatives Seek Tougher Soviet Sanctions," *Washington Post,* September 14, 1983.

67. *CR,* September 15, 1983, floor speeches, JH MSS; Martin Tolchin, "Senate 95–0, Condemns Moscow; Sanctions Rejected," *New York Times,* September 16, 1983; A. L. May, "Senate Rejects Helms' Proposals for Tougher Action on Soviets," *Raleigh News and Observer,* September 16, 1983; "Senator Lashes Senate Rejection of Amendments," *Durham Herald,* September 17, 1983.

68. Chuck Alston, "Helms' Foes Change, but His Issues Don't," *Greensboro News & Record,* September 18, 1983.

69. *CR,* September 15, 1983, floor speeches, JH MSS; "The Jesse Helms Few People Know...," editorial, *Goldsboro News-Argus,* September 11, 1983; A. L. May, "Helms Adds New Detail as He Relates Meeting Jet Victims," *Raleigh News and Observer,* September 17, 1983; Paul T. O'Connor, "Helms' Letter Draws Criticism," *Raleigh Times,* December 2, 1983; Ferrel Guillory, "Helms Seizes New Issue, Thanks to Soviets," *Raleigh News and Observer,* September 23, 1983; Bill Peterson, "A Battle of the Titans Shaping Up in Carolina," *Washington Post,* September 24, 1983. Some of his supporters considered Helms's use of the doomed family on KAL 007 in bad taste, especially a reproduction of a family photograph.

70. JH to William Loeb, July 17, 1973, JH MSS.

71. "Biographical Conversations with Jesse Helms," WUNC-TV, February 11, 2000.

72. Betts interview, May 31, 2006.

73. Francis X. Clines, "Helms Takes Aim at 'Secular Humanism,'" *New York Times,* June 28, 1981; "Helms Earns Criticism," editorial, *Durham Sun,* June 11, 1982.

74. William D. Snider, *Helms and Hunt: The North Carolina Senate Race, 1984* (Chapel Hill: University of North Carolina Press, 1985), pp. 26–27.

75. Pearce interview, February 3, 2006.

76. JH to David Mascitelli, August 14, 1963; JH to Joseph M. Lalley, Jr., August 14, 1964, JH MSS.

77. "Helms Hires Black as Campaign Spokesman," in "Under the Dome," *Raleigh News and Observer,* July 12, 1983. Allen would later join the George W. Bush administration as domestic policy adviser. In 2006, Allen resigned after an arrest and subsequent plea for shoplifting at a Gaithersburg, Maryland, Target store. Holli Chmela, "Ex-Bush Aide Admits Shoplifting and Is Fined," *New York Times,* August 5, 2006.

78. Robert Hodierne, "Helms Feels He's a Walking Target for 'Cheap Shots' in News Media," *Charlotte Observer,* July 18, 1981; Gene Marlowe, "Helms Scoffs at Mounting Criticism," *Winston-Salem Journal,* July 20, 1981; "Helms Cries Foul," editorial, *Hickory Daily Record,* July 21, 1981; Jesse Helms, *Here's Where I Stand: A Memoir* (New York: Random House, 2005), pp. 158–64 (quotation on p. 159).

79. Stephen R. Kelly, "Helms Stalls Possible Voting Rights Act Renewal," *Charlotte Observer,* April 28, 1982; Stephen R. Kelly, "Voting Act Discussion Kept Short," *Charlotte Observer,* April 30, 1982; *CR,* May 5, 1982, floor speeches, JH MSS.

80. "Voting Bill Delay Irks Thurmond," *Hickory Daily Record,* April 28, 1982; Michael Wright and Caroline Rand Herron, "The Nation in Summary: Voting Rights Stuck in Senate," *New York Times,* May 2, 1982; Mike Shanahan, "Helms, Thurmond Wage Quiet War in Senate," *Greensboro Daily News and Record,* May 2, 1982.

81. The bill would enable covered jurisdictions to "bail out" of preclearance if they could prove a decade of nondiscriminatory behavior along with a pattern of increasing minority participation. According to one estimate, a quarter of all the jurisdictions in 1982 would meet this test immediately. "Voting Rights Plan Is Worked Out," *Winston-Salem Journal,* May 4, 1982; Stephen R. Kelly, "Senate Compromise Breaks Voting Rights Impasse," *Charlotte Observer,* May 4, 1982; Steven V. Roberts, "Senators Debate Voting Rights Act," *New York Times,* June 10, 1982.

82. Dennis Whittington, "Voting Rights Bill Advances; East Dissents," *Winston-Salem Journal,* May 5, 1982.

83. "Helms Said Ready to Fight Voting Act," *Greensboro Record,* May 25, 1982; *CR,* June 9, 10, 1982, floor speeches, JH MSS; Mary Thornton, "Helms Threatens to Stall Voting Rights Act," *Washington Post,* June 10, 1982; "Senator No Rises Again," editorial, *Raleigh News and Observer,* May 28, 1982.

84. Keith Upchurch, "Helms Criticizes Rights Bill," *Durham Sun,* June 15, 1982.

85. Steven V. Roberts, "Senators Debate Voting Rights Act," *New York Times,* June 10, 1982.

86. "Helms Outvoted; Senate Discusses Voting Rights Bill," *Raleigh News and Observer,* June 16, 1982; "Helms Ends First Filibuster Against Voting Rights Act," *Durham Morning Herald,* June 18, 1982; Rob Christensen, "Fiery Helms Sees Senate Shut Off First Part of Voting Rights Filibuster," *Raleigh News and Observer,* June 18, 1982.

87. "Voting Rights Bill Passes a Key Test," *New York Times,* June 16, 1982; Steven V. Roberts, "Filibuster Ends on Voting Rights; Senate Rejects Weakening Clauses," *New York Times,* June 18, 1982; Joanne Omang, "Senate Chokes Off Voting Rights Act Filibuster, 97–0; Series of Weakening Amendments Defeated, but Effort to Pass the Measure Quickly Is Unsuccessful," *Washington Post,* June 18, 1982; Rob Christensen, "Senate Pressured into Voting Rights Act, Helms Says," *Raleigh News and Observer,* June 19, 1982; "The Nation in Summary: Senate Uncorks Voting Rights," *New York Times,* June 20, 1982.

88. A. L. May, "Helms Cites Cost Factor in Fighting King Holiday," *Raleigh News and Observer,* September 13, 1983.

89. "Helms Will Filibuster King-Holiday Bill," *Winston-Salem Journal,* October 3, 1983. On Helms's Martin Luther King filibuster, see Furgurson, *Hard Right,* pp. 176–78.

90. *CR,* October 3, 1983, floor speeches, JH MSS; Helen Dewar, "Helms Stalls King's Day in Senate," *Washington Post,* October 4, 1983; Paul Houston, "Helms Launches Filibuster Against Holiday for King," *Greensboro Record,* October 4, 1983; Dave Doubrava, "Helms Moves to Head Off Vote on Bill Creating King Holiday," *Washington Times,* October 4, 1983; Steven V. Roberts, "King Holiday Bill Faces a Filibuster," *New York Times,* October 4, 1983. Helms, in his weekly newspaper column, told constituents that creating a King holiday was "not merely wrong—it is a debasement of our nation and a perversion of those truths which we proclaim to be self-evident." "Report from U.S. Senator Jesse Helms," October 17, 1983, no. 513.

91. Fred G. Folson, "The File on Martin Luther King Jr.," *Washington Post,* November 2, 1983.

92. John Alexander, "Sen. Helms' Smear Against King," *Greensboro Daily News,* October 9, 1983.

93. "Jesse the Wonder," editorial, *Fayetteville Observer,* October 5, 1983.

94. "Helms Revives Smear," editorial, *Raleigh News and Observer,* October 5, 1983.

95. Edwin M. Yoder, Jr., "Helms v. the Holiday," *Washington Post,* October 6, 1983.

96. Julia Malone, "As Helms Cries 'Marxism,' GOP Maneuvers to Back King Holiday," *Christian Science Monitor,* October 5, 1983.

97. *CR,* October 3, 1983, floor speeches, JH MSS; Helen Dewar, "Helms Stalls King's Day in Senate," *Washington Post,* October 4, 1983; Steven V. Roberts, "King Holiday Bill Faces a Filibuster," *New York Times,* October 4, 1983.

98. "Report from U.S. Senator Jesse Helms," October 17, 1983.

99. A. L. May, "Helms End King Filibuster Threat," *Raleigh News and Observer,* October 5, 1983; Richard Whittle, "Helms: King-Holiday Action Paid Off," *Greensboro Daily News,* October 9, 1983.

100. "Biographical Conversations with Jesse Helms," February 11, 2000.

101. Sandy Grady, "The King Holiday: Opponents Try Reviving FBI Smear," *Charlotte Observer,* October 1, 1983.

102. George Lardner, Jr., and Howard Kurtz, "Hearing Set on Helms' Request to Unseal FBI's Tapes on King," *Washington Post,* October 14, 1983; Bill Arthur, "Conservative Caucus Joins Suit Seeking Records on Rev. King," *Charlotte Observer,* October 14, 1983; "SCLC Leader Calls Helms' Effort to Open King Files 'Racist Ploy,'" *Winston-Salem Journal,* October 15, 1983; A. L. May, "Government Opposes Helms' Suit Seeking King Surveillance Tapes," *Raleigh News and Observer,* October 18, 1983; "Hearing on King Tapes Sought by Sen. Helms Is Reset for Tuesday," *Washington Post,* October 15, 1983; George Lardner, Jr., "White House Fights Release of King's File," *Washington Post,* October 18, 1983; Claude Sitton, "King Debate Followed Old Dixie Pattern," *Raleigh News and Observer,* October 23, 1983.

103. *CR,* October 18, 1983, floor speeches, JH MSS; Dwight Cunningham and Dave Doubrava, "Helms Strategy to Block King Bill Fails on Two Fronts," *Washington Times,* October 19, 1983; Bill Arthur, "Kennedy, Helms Trade Barbs in Debate over King," *Charlotte Observer,* October 19, 1983; George Lardner, Jr, "Judge Denies Helms Access to King Data," *Washington Post,* October 19, 1983; Steven V. Roberts, "Senators Are Firm on King Holiday," *New York Times,* October 19, 1983.

104. *CR,* October 19, 1983, floor speeches, JH MSS; Steven R. Weisman, "U.S. Will Create Holiday to Mark Dr. King's Birth," *New York Times,* October 20, 1983; Bill Arthur, "Senate Approves King Holiday," *Charlotte Observer,* October 20, 1983; Juan Williams, "President Reluctantly Promises to Sign the King Birthday Bill; Declines to Differ with Helms," *Washington Post,* October 20, 1983; Francis X. Clines, "Reagan's Doubts on Dr. King Disclosed," *New York Times,* October 22, 1983; David Hoffman, "King Is Saluted as President Signs Holiday into Law," *Washington Post,* November 3, 1983. Bradley later noted that Jesse's King holiday filibuster was nothing more than him "playing to his racist base." Otherwise, he said, "it was incomprehensible." Bradley interview, December 18, 2006.

105. Helen Dewar, "Solemn Senate Votes for National Holiday Honoring Rev. King," *Washington Post,* October 20, 1983.

106. Bill Arthur, "Capital Muses Impact of Helms's Remarks," *Charlotte Observer,* October 5, 1983; Will Campbell, "Even Today, the Issue Is Race," *Charlotte Observer,* October 16, 1983.

107. JH to Ray W. House, October 14, 1986, JH MSS.

108. JH, *Here's Where I Stand,* pp. 161–63.

109. Rob Christensen and A. L. May, "Impact Uncertain over Helms' Stand on King Holiday," *Raleigh News and Observer,* October 20, 1983.

110. Pearce interview, February 3, 2006.

111. James R. Dickenson and Paul Taylor, "Helms in Trouble," *Washington Post,*

April 19, 1983; Mike McLaughlin, "King Holiday Issue May Have Aided Helms," *Chapel Hill Newspaper,* July 5, 1984; Wrenn interview, February 1, 2006.

112. Guillory interview, February 2, 2006.

113. Tyson to Ellis and Wrenn, February 20, 1984, JH MSS.

114. Wrenn interview, February 1, 2006.

8. A Lionhearted Leader of a Great and Growing Army

1. Reagan, speech at JH fund-raiser, Washington, June 16, 1983, speech files, SP 773, Reagan Library.

2. Stephens interview, June 6, 2006. For the context of the election of 1984, see Paul Luebke, *Tar Heel Politics 2000* (Chapel Hill: University of North Carolina Press, 1998), pp. 161–88.

3. Fetzer interview, June 20, 2006.

4. Gwen Ifill, "Bush Camp Plans Negative Campaign; Objective Is to Transfer High 'Unfavorable' Ratings to Dukakis," *Washington Post,* August 13, 1988.

5. Wrenn interview, October 4, 1996, May 14, 2005; Eudy interview, September 7, 2006; Stephens interview, June 6, 2006; Rosser interview, September 7, 2006; "Word for Word / Jesse Helms; The North Carolinian Has Enemies, but No One Calls Him Vague," *New York Times,* November 27, 1994.

6. Hickman interview, April 21, 2006.

7. Rosser interview, September 7, 2006; Pearce interview, February 3, 2006.

8. The teachers ad asserted that Hunt supported legislation authorizing payroll deductions for teachers belonging to the North Carolina Association of Educators—legislation that was then before the State Senate. "Hunt's plan will represent a giant step toward unionization," the ad charged, with the "calling of strikes and general disruption of the education of our children." "Helms Ads Take Early Shots at Hun" in "Under the Dome," *Raleigh News and Observer,* May 6, 1983; paid political ad, "What North Carolina Newspapers Say About Voter Registration," *Goldsboro News-Argus,* June 8, 1983; Ken Eudy, "Ads Signal Helms-Hunt Race Is On," *Charlotte Observer,* June 9, 1983; Dennis Whittington, "Helms Ads Preheat 1984 Race Against Hunt," *Winston-Salem Journal,* June 12, 1983; Bill Peterson, "A Battle of the Titans' Shaping Up in Carolina," *Washington Post,* September 24, 1983.

9. Art Eisenstadt, "Helms' Spending Tops $1.5 Million," *Winston-Salem Journal,* August 2, 1983; Rob Christensen, "Helms, Hunt Prepare for All-Out Battle," *Raleigh News and Observer,* November 6, 1983.

10. Helms political ads, 1984, JH MSS; Fetzer interview, June 20, 2006.

11. "Senate Democratic Incumbents Leading in Funds for 1984 Election," *New York Times,* November 7, 1983; Art Eisenstadt, "Helms' Spending Tops $1.5 Million," *Winston-Salem Journal,* August 2, 1983; Ken Allen, "Anti-Helms Association Disbanding," *Charlotte Observer,* July 2, 1983; Rob Christensen, "FEC

Ruling Killed Fund, State Democrats Contend," *Raleigh News and Observer,* July 10, 1983; interview with Carter Wrenn (by Mosnier), October 4, 1996.

12. Ellis interview, February 3, 2006; Pearce interview, February 3, 2006.

13. Thomas B. Edsall, Dan Balz, and Bill Peterson, "Tea Leaves," *Washington Post,* November 17, 1983.

14. Chuck Alston, "Hunt's Ad Drive Against Helms Has Rocky Start," *Greensboro Daily News,* November 30, 1983; Rob Christensen, "Helms Committee Threatens Suit over Radio Ads," *Raleigh News and Observer,* December 1, 1983; Mary Anne Rhyne, "Helms Unveils TV Ads," *Wilson Daily Times,* December 3, 1983.

15. JH to Jim Hunt, November 28, 1983, *Raleigh News and Observer,* December 1, 1983.

16. Stephens interview, June 6, 2006; Tyson interview, December 7, 2006.

17. Ernest B. Furgurson, *Hard Right: The Rise of Jesse Helms* (New York: W. W. Norton, 1986), pp. 179–80; Harris interview, September 27, 2005; Reynolds interview, April 4, 2006; "Low-Profile Idea Man Gets Credit for Helms Victory," *New Bern Sun Journal,* September 12, 1985.

18. Thomas B. Edsall, "Partners in Political PR Firm Typify Republican New Breed; Operatives in Demand by Candidates, Corporations, Governments," *Washington Post,* April 7, 1985.

19. Hickman interview, April 21, 2006; Furgurson, *Hard Right,* p. 180.

20. Mary Anne Rhyne, "Helms Unveils TV Ads," *Wilson Daily Times,* December 3, 1983; Ken Eudy and Katherine White, "Helms Camp Launches Ads in Duel with N.C. Democrats," *Charlotte Observer,* December 3, 1983; Wrenn interview, February 1, 2006; Harris interview, September 27, 2005.

21. Helms political ads, 1984, JH MSS.

22. Ken Eudy, "Tug-of-War for Voters' Attention," *Charlotte Observer,* February 7, 1984; Daniel C. Hoover, "Helms, Hunt Pitch Battle over Airwaves," *Raleigh News and Observer,* February 10, 1984; Christensen interview, April 4, 2006; Hickman interview, April 21, 2006.

23. A. L. May, "Hunt Assails Helms at D. C. Dinner," *Raleigh News and Observer,* February 25, 1984; Daniel C. Hoover, "Helms Describes Hunt as a Demagogue Running Scared," *Raleigh News and Observer,* February 26, 1984; Ken Eudy, "Smoke Rising in Hunt-Helms Tobacco War," *Charlotte Observer,* February 28, 1984; Edmondson interview, October 24, 2006.

24. Ken Eudy, "Tug-of-War for Voters' Attention," *Charlotte Observer,* February 7, 1984.

25. A. L. May, "Hunt Votes for Plan to Increase Taxes, Prompting Quick Criticism from Helms," *Raleigh News and Observer,* February 29, 1984; Tom Wicker, "The Other Jesse," *New York Times,* April 17, 1984.

26. "Hunt Raises $130,000 in NYC for Campaign," *Winston-Salem Journal,* March 1, 1984.

27. Ken Eudy, "Helms, Hunt Hike Volume of Blasts in Radio Ad War," *Charlotte Observer,* March 7, 1984; Tim Pittman, "Helms, Hunt Trade Charges over TV

Spots," *Greensboro News and Record,* March 24, 1984; Ashe interview, July 15, 2005; Wrenn interview, February 1, 2006.

28. Two Fayetteville natives and UNC graduates, Don Baer and Harriet Sugar, had organized the event, and the steering committee included ten people who were either North Carolina natives or their spouses. Helms political ads, 1984, JH MSS; "Hunt Unveils Campaign Ad," *Winston-Salem Journal,* March 20, 1984; Tim Pittman, "Helms, Hunt Trade Charges over TV Spots," *Greensboro News and Record,* March 24, 1984; Rob Christensen, "New Helms Ads Attack Hunt's N.Y. Fund-Raiser," *Raleigh News and Observer,* March 28, 1984; Chuck Alston, "Helms' Latest Ads Take Jab at Hunt's Credibility," *Greensboro News and Record,* March 29, 1984.

29. Rob Christensen, "Helms, Hunt Spend $3.4 Million for TV Spots," *Raleigh News and Observer,* August 19, 1984.

30. Helen Dewar, "Black Vote One Target of N.C. 'Mud Fight'; The Senate Races," *Washington Post,* June 15, 1984.

31. Helen Dewar, "Hunt, Helms in $21 Million Dead Heat," *Washington Post,* October 28, 1984.

32. Bill Arthur, "Questions Surround Congressional Club's Ties with Firm," *Charlotte Observer,* February 20, 1984; "Helms Supporters Admit 'Dumb' Move," *Wilson Daily Times,* February 20, 1984; Rob Christensen, "Political Associates Innocent, Helms Says," *Raleigh News and Observer,* February 24, 1984; Ferrel Guillory, "Many Pieces Add Up to One Helms Empire," *Raleigh News and Observer,* February 24, 1984; Michael Whiteley, "FEC Sues Groups Linked to Helms," *Raleigh Times,* February 8, 1985. The suit was eventually settled. The Congressional Club paid a fine of $10,000 and agreed to a formal disengagement between Jefferson Marketing and the National Congressional Club. But the effectiveness of the Helms political empire remained intact. "Club Settles Lawsuit over Campaign," *Wilmington Morning Star,* May 16, 1986; Rob Christensen and A. L. May, "Congressional Club Stands Intact with FEC Suit Settled," *Raleigh News and Observer,* May 18, 1986.

33. "Hunt Hits Helms," *Washington Post,* May 12, 1984.

34. "Helms Is Assailed by Rival on Foreign Stands," *New York Times,* May 27, 1984.

35. Guillory interview, February 2, 2006.

36. Eudy interview, September 7, 2006.

37. Christensen interview, April 4, 2006.

38. "A Close-Minded Club," editorial, *Raleigh News and Observer,* June 26, 1984; "Reporters Expelled," *Washington Post,* June 26, 1984; "Mob Reaction Replaced Judgment at Convention," editorial, *Durham Morning Herald,* June 28,1984; J. Earl Danieley to the Editor, *Greensboro News & Record,* July 4, 1984; William D. Snider, *Helms and Hunt: The North Carolina Senate Race, 1984* (Chapel Hill: University of North Carolina Press, 1985), p. 127; Christensen interview, September 27, 2005; Wrenn interview, February 1, 2006; Christensen interview, April 4, 2006; Betts interview, May 31, 2006.

39. "Hunt Airs TV Ad Linking Helms to D'Aubuisson," *Charlotte Observer,* June 29, 1984.

40. Pearce interview, February 3, 2006.

41. Helen Dewar, "Senate Race in North Carolina Is a Southern-Fried Alley Fight," *Washington Post,* July 6, 1984.

42. Helms political ads, 1984, JH MSS.

43. Pearce interview, February 3, 2006.

44. Stephens interview, June 6, 2006; Hickman interview, April 21, 2006.

45. "Helms Draws Fire for Targeting Jackson," in "Under the Dome," *Raleigh News and Observer,* March 8, 1984; Helen Dewar, "Black Vote One Target of N.C. 'Mud Fight,'" *Washington Post,* June 15, 1984; Haynes Johnson, "Despite Progress, South Sees This Election in Black and White," *Washington Post,* September 30, 1984.

46. "Fundraising Letter Called 'Race Baiting,'" *Charlotte Observer,* August 16, 1984; Haynes Johnson and Thomas B. Edsall, "North Carolina Contests Spark Registration War," *Washington Post,* September 20, 1984; interview with David Flaherty (by Mosnier), September 27, 1996, Southern Oral History Program.

47. Katherine White and Ken Eudy, "Helms's Campaign by Mail Against Hunt," *Charlotte Observer,* October 23, 1984.

48. Helms interview (by Furgurson), October 10, 1985, Furgurson Papers.

49. Jim Schlosser, "Helms Promises Blacks Better Communication," *Greensboro News and Record,* January 16, 1984; Fuller interview (by Riddick), November 20, 1991.

50. Wrenn interview, February 1, 2006; Guillory interview, February 2, 2006. Jack Betts reflected that this was an attempt by Helms to convince the public that he had an "undeserved and misunderstood" position on race. Betts interview, May 31, 2006.

51. Chuck Alston, "Helms Receives Cold Shoulder from Black Students at College," *Greensboro News and Record,* October 18, 1984; Elizabeth Leland, "Many Blacks Don't Listen to Helms' College Talk," *Raleigh News and Observer,* October 18, 1984; "Blacks Boycott Helms's Talk on His Visit to Their Campus," *New York Times,* October 18, 1984.

52. Wrenn interview, February 1, 2006.

53. Jack Betts, "Cold, Cold Campus," *Greensboro News and Record,* October 20, 1984.

54. "Eloquent Record," editorial, *Fayetteville Times,* October 17, 1984.

55. Wrenn interview, February 1, 2006.

56. Stephens interview, June 6, 2006.

57. JH, speech to the Freedom Council, Washington, D.C., February 18, 1984, JH MSS.

58. JH, speech to the Baptist Fundamentalism Conference, April 13, 1984, JH MSS.

59. JH to John S. Crews, July 7, 1982, JH MSS.

60. JH, speech at the Northside Baptist Church, September 9, 1984, JH MSS; Chuck Alston, "Fundamentalist Baptists Hear Helms Speak in Charlotte Pulpit," *Greensboro News and Record,* September 10, 1984.

61. "Falwell, Helms to Launch Tour Here,"*Asheville Citizen,* July 1, 1983; Martin Tolchin, "Helms and Anti-Helms Campaigns Going Strong," *New York Times,* July 9, 1983.

62. Furgurson, *Hard Right,* pp. 168–71; Haynes Johnson and Thomas B. Edsall, "North Carolina Contests Spark Registration War," *Washington Post,* September 20, 1984; Wrenn interview, February 1, 2006; Ellis interview, February 3, 2006; Viguerie interview, February 14, 2006; Godwin interview, June 1, 2006.

63. Cecile Holmes-White, "Helms' Tactic Questioned by Baptists," *Greensboro News and Record,* August 25, 1984; "What Price Privette?," editorial, *Raleigh Times,* August 29, 1984; John Herbers, "Senate Race in North Carolina Proving a Bitter Mix of Politics and Religion," *New York Times,* October 6, 1984; Godwin interview, June 1, 2006; Eudy interview, September 7, 2006; Stephens interview, June 6, 2006.

64. Wrenn interview, February 1, 2006.

65. Haynes Johnson and Thomas B. Edsall, "North Carolina Contests Spark Registration War," *Washington Post,* September 20, 1984; Ginny Carroll, "N.C. Voters Increase 18 percent Since '80," *Raleigh News and Observer,* October 20, 1984; Stephens interview, June 6, 2006.

66. Rob Christensen, "Helms, East Fight to Keep Laws Against Certain Sex Acts," *Raleigh News and Observer,* September 12, 1981.

67. Snider, *Helms and Hunt,* p. 136; Michael B. Bobrow to JH, April 3, 1984, JH MSS.

68. "Jesse Helms Makes a Tasteless Remark," editorial, *Asheville Citizen,* March 3, 1984; JH, speech to the Conservative Political Action Conference, March 1, 1984, JH MSS.

69. JH, speech to the Baptist Fundamentalism Conference, Washington, April 13, 1974, JH MSS.

70. "Report From U.S. Senator Jesse Helms," May 1, 1984, JH MSS.

71. Helen Dewar, "Black Vote One Target of N.C. 'Mud Fight'; The Senate Races," *Washington Post,* June 15, 1984.

72. "Quotes from Hunt's New York City's Fundraisers," *Landmark,* March 29, 1984; Daniel C. Hoover, "Pro-Helms Newspaper Publishes Rumor That Hunt Had Gay Lover," *Raleigh News and Observer,* July 6, 1984.

73. "Republican Asks in Ad if Hunt Got Funds from Gays; Aide for Campaign Says No," *Raleigh News and Observer,* June 6, 1984.

74. "Jim Hunt Is Sissy, Prissy, Girlish and Effeminate," *Landmark,* July 5, 1984; "Hunt Demand Letter to Windsor Paid by Taxpayer Money," *Landmark,* July 19, 1984; "State by Editor Bob Windsor," *Landmark,* July 19, 1984; Daniel C. Hoover, "Pro-Helms Newspaper Publishes Rumor that Hunt Had Gay Lover," *Raleigh News and Observer,* June 6, 1984; Ramona Jones, "Hunt Prepared to Sue Weekly Edi-

tor," *Raleigh Times,* July 6, 1984; Ken Eudy, "Helms Disavows Paper's Attack," *Charlotte Observer,* July 7, 1984; "Hunt Blames Helms for 'Scurrilous Lies,'" *Asheville Citizen-Times,* July 7, 1984; Joel Brinkley, "Article Stirs New Charges in Carolina Senate Race," *New York Times,* July 7, 1984.

75. "Jim Hunt Received Contributions from Gay Activists," *Landmark,* January 5, 1984.

76. "Jim Hunt Visits Limp Wrist Set Fund Raiser in N.Y.," *Landmark,* March 1, 1984.

77. "Faggots Dominate Fourth Congressional District Convention," *Landmark,* June 7, 1984; "Gay Rights Plank in Democratic Party Platform," *Landmark,* June 21,1984.

78. Wrenn interview, February 1, 2006; Eudy interview, September 7, 2006.

79. Ken Eudy, "Helms Disavows Paper's Attack," *Charlotte Observer,* July 7, 1984; "Issues, Fair and Unfair," editorial, *Raleigh News and Observer,* July 11, 1984; Christensen interview, April 4, 2006; Eudy interview, September 7, 2006.

80. Daniel C. Hoover, "Editor Says He Was 'Dead Wrong' to Publish,'" *Raleigh News and Observer,* July 8, 1984. Hunt initially pursued a lawsuit against Windsor; he dropped it about a year later. "Under the Dome," *Raleigh News and Observer,* July 6, 1985.

81. "Issues, Fair and Unfair," editoral, *Raleigh News and Observer.*

82. Interview with David Flaherty (by Mosnier), October 4, 1996.

83. "Brutal Attack on Hunt," editorial, *Raleigh News and Observer,* July 7, 1984.

84. Claude Sitton, "The Week Ends Hope for Clean Campaign," *Raleigh News and Observer,* July 8, 1984.

85. "Clerk Says Windsor Okd Mailings," *Raleigh Times,* July 19, 1984.

86. "'Queer' Statements Called an Indiscretion," in "Under the Dome," *Raleigh News and Observer,* October 13, 1984; "Poison-Pen Climate," editorial, *Salisbury Post,* October 20, 1984; Alston interview, October 12, 2006.

87. Mike McFarland, "Extremist Mailings Circulating in Area," *Chapel Hill Newspaper,* October 18, 1984; "Helms' Camp Denies Link to Letter on Homosexuality," *Raleigh Times,* October 20, 1984; "UNC President Friday Says Threatening Letter 'Forged,'" *Fayetteville Observer,* October 20, 1984.

88. Alston interview, October 12, 2006.

89. Bill Arthur, "Hunt Agrees to Debates with Helms," *Charlotte Observer,* May 3, 1984.

90. Hickman interview, April 21, 2006.

91. Pearce interview, February 3, 2006.

92. Pearce interview, February 3, 2006; Wrenn interview, February 1, 2006; Fetzer interview, June 20, 2006; Ellis interview, February 3, 2006; Rosser interview, September 7, 2006; Wilson interview, June 5, 2006; Stephens interview, June 6, 2006.

93. Helen Dewar, "Hunt Goes on Offensive in Debate with Helms," *Washington Post,* July 30, 1984; "Helms and Hunt Debate in Carolina Senate Race," *New*

York Times, July 30, 1984; Ken Eudy and Ken Allen, "Hunt Controlled Debate, Experts Say," *Charlotte Observer,* July 31, 1984; Rob Christensen, "Helms, Hunt Lively, Biting in 1st Debate," *Raleigh News and Observer,* July 30, 1984; Ginny Carroll, "Political Experts Give Hunt Edge in Debate," *Raleigh News and Observer,* July 20, 1984; "First Round to Hunt," editorial, *Greensboro News and Record,* July 31, 1984; Mary Burch, "Hunt-Helms Ad War Intensifies," *Raleigh Times,* August 8, 1984; Rob Christensen, "Helms, Hunt Spend $3.4 Million for TV Spots," *Raleigh News and Observer,* August 19, 1984; Wrenn interviews, May 13, 2005, February 1, 2006; Harris interview, September 27, 2005; Ellis interview, February 3, 2006; Christensen interview, April 4, 2006; Scott Wilson interview (Tom Joyner); Stephens interview, June 6, 2006; Fetzer interview, June 20, 2006.

94. "Candidates Clash in Carolina Race," *New York Times,* September 10, 1984; Elizabeth Leland, "Helms, Hunt Renew Attacks," *Raleigh News and Observer,* September 10, 1984; Wrenn interview, February 1, 2006; Ellis interview, February 3, 2006; Wilson interview, June 5, 2006.

95. Pearce interview, February 3, 2006.

96. "Mondale an Issue in Carolina Race," *New York Times,* September 24, 1984; Martin Tolchin, "Ads Debated in North Carolina Race," *New York Times,* October 15, 1984; "Debates: Hunt-Helms," editorial, *Greensboro News and Record,* October 16, 1984; Wrenn interview, February 1, 2006; Ellis interview, February 3, 2006; Scott Wilson interview (by Joyner); Fetzer interview, June 20, 2006.

97. Robert McG. Thomas, Jr., "Sports World Specials; The Catfish Switches," *New York Times,* April 16, 1984; Trip Purcell, "Andy Griffith Says 'I'm for Hunt,'" *Wilson Daily Times,* August 13, 1984; "Helms Goes Hollywood," *New York Times,* September 17, 1984.

98. "Helms Aide: 'Here Goes Hunt Again with His Flip-Flop,'" *Winston-Salem Sentinel,* September 4, 1984; Wrenn interview, February 1, 2006.

99. "Helms TV Commercial Warned of Another Recession if Hunts Wins," *Greensboro News and Record,* October 19, 1984; Hickman interview, April 21, 2006.

100. "Textiles Become an Issue in the Hunt-Helms Race," *Raleigh News and Observer,* October 19, 1984; Rob Christensen, "Social Security a Focal Issue in Senate Battle," *Raleigh News and Observer,* October 23, 1984; Chuck Alston, "Hunt Criticizes Helms' Social Security Tactics," *Greensboro News and Record,* October 23, 1984; William E. Schmidt, "Caustic North Carolina Senate Race Is Ending Up in a Dead Heat," *New York Times,* November 4, 1984; Bill Peterson, "Jesse Helms' Lesson for Washington; Big Bucks, Streetfighter's Skills, Racist Appeals and Charisma Still Work," *Washington Post,* November 18, 1984.

101. Babington interview, June 5, 2006; Eudy interview, September 7, 2006.

102. Pearce interview, February 3, 2006; Stephens interview, June 6, 2006; Wrenn

interview, February 1, 2006; Ellis interview, February 3, 2006; Black interview, February 16, 2006; Fetzer interview, June 20, 2006; Bill Peterson and Don Oberdorfer, "Tension Mounts in North Carolina; Charges, Countercharges Escalate in Costly Senate Race," *Washington Post,* November 2, 1984; Bill Peterson, "Jesse Helms' Lesson for Washington; Big Bucks, Streetfighter's Skills, Racist Appeals and Charisma Still Work," *Washington Post,* November 18, 1984; Hickman interview, April 21, 2006. For the proposed Reagan letter, see Reagan to JH [letter drafted by Helms campaign], October 30, 1984; Frank Donatelli to Richard Darman, October 30, 1984, Peter Rusthoven files, Reagan Library. White House counsel Fred Fielding argued that there was insufficient evidence that the White House had, along with Helms, made the distinction between abortion and birth control in proposing anti-abortion legislation. Fielding to Darman, October 31, 1984, Peter Rusthoven files, Reagan Library.

103. "Helms Links Hunt to Mondale; Hunt Denies," *Monroe Enquirer-Journal,* October 23, 1984.

104. Bill Peterson, "Helms' Religion Stand Rallies Christian Group," *Washington Post,* November 3, 1984.

105. Bill Peterson, "Election '84: Mudslinging Escalates Helms-Hunt Senate Race; Candidates Play Down Polls in Final Days," *Washington Post,* November 4, 1984.

106. Bill Peterson, "North Carolina Race Ends in Bitterness; Hunt Calls Helms 'Right-Wing Extremist'; Senator Says His Opponent Is Desperate," *Washington Post,* November 6, 1984; "The 1984 Elections: Hard-Fought Contests for the Senate; Helms Beats Hunt to Stay in Senate," *New York Times,* November 7, 1984; Bill Peterson, "Jesse Helms' Lesson for Washington; Big Bucks, Streetfighter's Skills, Racist Appeals and Charisma Still Work," *Washington Post,* November 18, 1984.

107. Bill Peterson, "Helms Defeats Gov. Hunt; Rockefeller Cuts Voting-Day Dollars; New Right Leader Heralds Victory of Conservatism," *Washington Post,* November 7, 1984.

108. Christensen interview, April 4, 2006; Pearce interview, February 3, 2006; Bill Peterson, "Helms Savors Victory over Hunt; Senator Says 'Cruel Hoax of Liberal Politicians Has Run Its Course,'" *Washington Post,* November 8, 1984; Hickman interview, April 21, 2006.

109. Wrenn interview, September 7, 2006; Eudy interview, September 7, 2006.

110. Wrenn interviews, February 1, September 7, 2006; Guillory interview, February 2, 2006; Pearce interview, February 3, 2006; Black interview, February 15, 2006; Ferrel Guillory, "Hunt-Helms Race Gives Birth to Myth," *Raleigh News and Observer,* March 22, 1985; Hickman interview, April 21, 2006; Betts interview, May 31, 2006.

111. Hickman interview, April 21, 2006; Betts interview, May 31, 2006; Eudy interview, September 7, 2006.

112. Jack Betts, "Race, Religion, Patriotism," *Charlotte Observer,* September 25, 1994; Rosser interview, September 7, 2006; Eudy interview, September 7, 2006; Alston interview, October 12, 2006.

9. I AM BEYOND YOUR REACH

1. On the Saturday before election day, he told a Greenville crowd at a tobacco warehouse that "this Senator is going to continue to be the chairman of the Senate Agriculture Committee, not the Foreign Relations Committee." But he also made clear that he would eventually seek the Foreign Relations chairmanship. Although his campaign pledge cost him "something I sincerely wanted," he told the Conservative Caucus in late November, he suggested that this might change during the next Congress. Joanne Omang and John M. Goshko, "Shifts on Capitol Hill Could Cause Foreign Policy Problems for Reagan," *Washington Post,* November 8, 1984; "The Vote on Foreign Policy," *Washington Post,* November 8, 1984; "Who's Hot and Who's Not About a Second Term; State Dept. in a Dither over Helms," *New York Times,* November 8, 1984; Helen Dewar, "Race for Majority Leader Turns Byzantine; Chain Reaction Could Put Liberal Senators in Powerful Spots," *Washington Post,* November 11, 1984; A. L. May, "Odds Against Helms Ousting Lugar in '86, Observers Say," *Raleigh News and Observer,* December 1, 1984.

2. Ward Sinclair, "Farm Bill's Progress Stunted in Senate and House," *Washington Post,* July 31, 1985; Ward Sinclair, "GOP Effort to Force Vote on Farm Bill Collapses; Dole Drops Threat to Open Floor Debate," *Washington Post,* August 1, 1985; Ward Sinclair, "Agriculture Panels Quit Without Bills; Work to Resume Next Month," *Washington Post,* August 2, 1985; Ward Sinclair, "Congress Readies for Farm-Bill Fight; House, Senate Staging Standoff over Who Cuts Spending First," *Washington Post,* September 10, 1985. In late July, the committee voted 9–8 for a Democratic-supported proposal to enact a four-year freeze maintaining the current levels of payments and adding $4 billion to the agriculture bill. Helms instead favored a one-year freeze, but was willing to accept a two-year freeze, followed by reductions. Bob Dole, a wheat-state senator and a member himself of the Agriculture Committee, badly wanted a bill that would help wheat farmers before they planted their winter crop. Dole threatened to bypass the committee and introduce his own bill on the Senate floor, but he was able to persuade the committee to accept his own version of a two-year freeze. On August 1, Senator Tom Harkin (D-IA), referring to Dole's defiance of Helms, asked who the "real" chairman of the committee was. Jesse responded by telling him to "watch his tongue." "I'm still chairman and I don't plan to be deposed," he told committee members on another occasion. It was "very difficult to run a committee under such circumstances," Helms told a reporter in late July. "We've played games up and down the road. I think the message I'm getting is that we don't want no farm bill." Ward Sinclair, "Farm

Bill Writers Dig in Hard Ground; All but One Price-Support Proposal Weeded Out," *Washington Post,* July 25, 1985; A. L. May, "Wrangle over Farm Bill Angers Helms," *Raleigh News and Observer,* August 2, 1985.

3. A. L. May, "Helms, Allies Offer Compromise on Cigarette Tax," *Raleigh News and Observer,* September 19, 1985; Spencer Rich, "Senate Panel Approves Expanding Medicare Tax, Erupts over Tobacco Plan," *Washington Post,* September 19, 1985.

4. Spencer Rich, "Guarding Social Security; Congress Moves to Free It from Budget," *Washington Post,* September 20, 1985; Ward Sinclair, "Senate Rejects One-Year Freeze on Farm Subsidies; Republicans Team with Democrats to Hand Administration a Major Setback," *Washington Post,* October 31, 1985; Ward Sinclair, "Sen. Melcher Is Smiling Again; Enigmatic Montanan Draws GOP Ire for Thwarting Farm Bill," *Washington Post,* November 2, 1985; Ward Sinclair, "Farm Bill Conferees Disagree on Key Points; Administration Pressure Called Misplaced," *Washington Post,* December 6, 1985; Ward Sinclair, "Income Supports Mire Conferees on Farm Bill; Final Action This Week Seems Unlikely," *Washington Post,* December 12, 1985; "Budget Accords on the Military and on Tobacco," *New York Times,* December 14, 1985; Ward Sinclair, "Hill Conference Approves Major Farm Legislation; Measure Could Abruptly Shift Agricultural Policy," *Washington Post,* December 15, 1985.

5. Within the Helms camp, there were, Wrenn recalled, three distinct views of the media. Tom Ellis detested the press, considered them the enemy, and believed that the only way to overcome liberal bias was through massive amounts of paid media. Arthur Finkelstein, in contrast, believed that the media was "maybe a little biased" but their motives were to present stories that would attract and expand their audience. If one could provide stories to the media, they were happy; the classic example of Finkelstein's approach occurred in the 1976 North Carolina Republican primary, when he persuaded Ellis to tell Helms to demand that President Ford fire Henry Kissinger. That, recalled Wrenn, attracted media in a way that benefited the Reagan campaign. Finally, there was Helms's approach to the media. Jesse also considered them the enemy, but he chose his battles carefully, and where he did battle with the media—for example in school busing or the King holiday—he used issues where he knew he had strong public support. Helms's approach with the media was what Wrenn called the "Br'er Rabbit in the Briar Patch" approach. The issue of a CBS takeover did not arise during the 1984 election: "we didn't think about anything," said Wrenn, "except survival." But somehow Ellis became intrigued with the idea of a direct, attention-getting strike at the liberal media fortress. "In an attack of hubris," Wrenn recalled, in the days immediately after the election the Helms political organization became convinced that it could take on the media, and the Ellis view and Helms view converged. Wrenn interview, April 5, 2006; Babington interview, June 5, 2006.

6. Wrenn interview, April 5, 2006.

7. "Text of Helms Letter," January 11, 1985, *Raleigh News and Observer,* January 11, 1985. Babington found the letter in a trash bin. Christensen interview, April 4, 2006; Babington interview, June 5, 2006. See also Charles Babington, "Helms & Co.: Plotting to Unseat Dan Rather," *Columbia Journalism Review* 24 (July/August 1985): 47–51, and Ernest B. Furgurson, *Hard Right: The Rise of Jesse Helms* (New York: W. W. Norton, 1986), pp. 262–69.

8. Fairness in Media was an organization that attracted widespread conservative support: on January 11, Terry Dolan of Nicpac promised $100,000 toward the purchase of CBS stock, while Jerry Falwell suggested that the Moral Majority might join the campaign. On behalf of FIM, Wrenn and Cain briefed the weekly luncheon meeting of the Senate Steering Committee on Capitol Hill. On February 4, Representative Philip Crane (R-IL) filed a Federal Election Commission statement announcing that he would join the FIM campaign because it was the "best chance conservatives have ever had to end the liberal bias in media. "Stock Analyst: Helms Won't Influence CBS Very Much," *Raleigh Times,* January 11, 1985; A. L. May and Charles Babington, "Helms Files Papers Outlining Stock Plan," *Raleigh News and Observer,* January 11, 1985; "Money Pledged to Help Helms Get CBS Stock," *Rocky Mount Telegram,* January 12, 1985; "Falwell: Moral Majority Might Join CBS Efforts," *Asheville Citizen,* January 12, 1985; JH, speech at Helms for Senate Victory Dinner, Washington, January 18, 1985, JH MSS; Bill Arthur, "Helms 'Encouraged' over CBS Buyout Effort," *Charlotte Observer,* January 19, 1985; A. L. May, "Conservative Senators Briefed on CBS Stock-Buying Plan," *Raleigh News and Observer,* February 2, 1985; Chuck Alston and Sarah Avery, "Helms Pursues New CBS Options," *Greensboro News and Record,* February 9, 1985; "'End Liberal Bias' Is CBS Takeover Aim; Network Calls Helms-Led Effort a Bid to Intimidate Media," *Washington Post,* February 17, 1985; David A. Vise, "Wall Street Sharks Watch Helms-CBS Fight," *Washington Post,* February 17, 1985; David Boul, "Taking on CBS Is Nothing New for Hoover Adams," *Greensboro Daily News,* February 23, 1985; Thomas B. Edsall and David A. Vise, "CBS Fight a Litmus Test for Conservatives; Helms Group Faces Legal Hurdles in Ideological Takeover Bid," *Washington Post,* March 31, 1985; Wrenn interview, April 5, 2006.

9. JH, speech, CPAC convention, March 1, 1985, JH MSS; Bill Peterson, "Helms Says 'Elite Media' Out of Step with People; Conservative Conference Addressed," *Washington Post,* March 2, 1985. Many in the media took Helms's attack personally. CBS correspondent Bob Schieffer, who was present at Helms's speech, said that Jesse's attack reminded him of the days of Spiro Agnew, who had launched a full-scale assault on the liberal media. Schieffer also noted that the audience made "catcalls" at reporters, and some of them derisively pointed out CBS reporters. "I haven't heard a speech like that in that kind of an atmosphere in a long time," Schieffer declared. Tom Shales, "Takeover Talk: All Eyes on CBS; Inside the Network, There's Apprehension over Helms, Turner and What Happens Next," *Washington Post,* March 4, 1985. See also, for another

perspective, William F. Buckley, Jr., "On the Right," *National Review* 37, no. 4 (March 8, 1985): 54.

10. "Helms Says Group Got CBS Biting Nails," *Washington* (N.C) *Daily News,* March 7, 1985.

11. "Helms to CBS: Make My Day," *Lincolnton Times News,* March 25, 1985.

12. Lloyd Little, "CBS Chairman Says Buyout Won't Work," *Durham Herald,* February 6, 1985; Larry Kaplow, "CBS Chairman Says Network Unchanged by Takeover Threat," *Charlotte Observer,* February 6, 1985; James Dutra, "CBS President Says Takeover Effort Not a Threat," *Raleigh News and Observer,* February 6, 1985; "Proxy Battle Considered for CBS Seats," *Washington Post,* February 12, 1985; "CBS Sues to Block Takeover," *New York Times,* February 15, 1985; David A. Vise, "CBS Gives Fairness in Media a List of Its Shareholders," *Washington Post,* March 27, 1985.

13. There were already some connections between Turner and Helms: in August 1982, Turner donated two and a half hours of time on WTBS for a documentary entitled *KGB: The Lie . . . and the Truth,* which the Coalition for Freedom, an organization that was part of the Helms empire, had produced and which included appearances by Helms and East. Thomas B. Edsall and David A. Vise, "CBS Fight a Litmus Test for Conservatives; Helms Group Faces Legal Hurdles in Ideological Takeover Bid," *Washington Post,* March 31, 1985; Elizabeth Tucker and Mark Potts, "CBS Subpoenas Turner on Possible Helms Link; Seen Lacking Cash for Takeover," *Washington Post,* March 6, 1985; David A. Vise, "CBS Attacks Group Seeking to Control It," *Washington Post,* March 13, 1985.

14. Bill Arthur, "Helms: Turner Shows Interest in Network," *Charlotte Observer,* March 2, 1985; A. L. May, "Turner, Helms Talk About CBS Takeover," *Raleigh News and Observer,* March 2, 1985.

15. David A. Vise, "CBS Denies Rumors of Buyout Plan," *Washington Post,* March 22, 1985.

16. Marion A. Ellis and Miriam Durkin, "A Few Heeding Helms's Call to Buy CBS," *Charlotte Observer,* February 4, 1985.

17. David A. Vise, "Arbitrageur Boesky Acquires 8.7% of CBS; Pays $247 Million for Stake in Company," *Washington Post,* April 2, 1985.

18. David A. Vise, "CBS Chief Slams Turner; Says Broadcaster Lacks 'Conscience' to Own a Network," *Washington Post,* March 14, 1985; David A. Vise, "Turner Discussed CBS Bid with Sen. Helms," *Washington Post,* March 20, 1985; David A. Vise, "Capital Cities to Sell 2 TV Stations; Turner Indicates That He's Still Interested," *Washington Post,* March 21, 1985.

19. David A. Vise, "Capital Cities to Sell 2 TV Stations," *Washington Post,* March 21, 1985.

20. David A. Vise, "CBS Meets Amid Takeover Rumors; E.F. Hutton Said to Be Raising Funds for Ted Turner," *Washington Post,* April 17, 1985.

21. David A. Vise, "FIM Targets CBS Stock with Ads," *Washington Post,* June 21, 1985; Stephens interview, October 10, 2006.

22. Joanne Omang, "Helms Retains His Hold on Nominations; State Department Furious, Helpless," *Washington Post,* July 5, 1985.

23. The conservatives supposedly to be purged included Richard T. McCormack, who worked for Helms and then became assistant secretary for economic affairs; Gregory J. Newell, assistant secretary for international organization affairs and a former White House assistant; and James L. Malone, assistant secretary for oceans and international environmental and scientific affairs. John M. Goshko and Lou Cannon, "State Intelligence Chief Replaced; Conservatives Fear Shultz Launching Departmental Purge," *Washington Post,* December 20, 1984.

24. Philip Geyelin, "Right-Wing Knock," *Washington Post,* June 2, 1985.

25. Helms complained about the nomination of Rozanne L. Ridgway, the ambassador to East Germany, whom Shultz nominated to replace Richard R. Burt as assistant secretary of state for European and Canadian affairs. Helms threatened to delay the appointment of the American ambassador to Honduras, John D. Negroponte, as assistant secretary of state for scientific and environmental affairs unless conservative James L. Malone—whom Negroponte was replacing— was given another position of importance. Lou Cannon, "Reagan Hears GOP Senators' Complaints; Reservations Aired on Budget, SALT," *Washington Post,* June 13, 1985.

26. Helms threatened to place holds on the nominations of Ridgway, along with that of Elliott Abrams, as assistant secretary for inter-American affairs. Helms also opposed the ambassadorial nomination of Richard R. Burt to West Germany. Helms engaged in other tactics to stall the nominations. Near the end of the Foreign Relations Committee testimony of Thomas Pickering, who was nominated as ambassador to Israel, Helms submitted 150 written questions regarding his experience as ambassador to El Salvador. If Pickering could provide answers by the time the committee reconvened the next day, the senator suggested, he might be confirmed. Five people at the State Department worked into the early morning hours, but, despite their labors, the next day Helms refused to remove the hold. Joanne Omang, "Helms Retains His Hold on Nominations; State Department Furious, Helpless," *Washington Post,* July 5, 1985; John M. Goshko, "9 GOP Senators Block Action on Envoy Nominees," *Washington Post,* June 21, 1985. Eight senators supporting Helms in his anti-Shultz campaign were James McClure (Idaho), Strom Thurmond (South Carolina), Steve Symms (Idaho), Paula Hawkins (Florida), Chic Hecht (Nevada), Orrin Hatch (Utah), Phil Gramm (Texas), and Mitch McConnell (Kentucky).

27. "'Serving Notice': Helms Fights Reagan's Diplomatic 'Careerism,'" *Sanford Herald,* June 15, 1985; Lucier to JH, June 21, 1985, JH MSS.

28. Moving from a post as assistant secretary for economic affairs, McCormack was named ambassador to the Organization of American States; conservative ideologue Lewis A. Tambs became ambassador to Costa Rica; and J. William Middendorf moved from the OAS ambassadorship to become ambassador to

the European Economic Community. John M. Goshko, "Shultz Wins Battle over U.S. Envoy; Career Diplomat Tapped by President," *Washington Post,* June 12, 1985.

29. Joanne Omang, "Panel Approves 7 Diplomat Nominees; Senate Unit Delays Action on Others Until After Recess," *Washington Post,* June 26, 1985.

30. Joanne Omang, "Conservatives Torpedo Deal with White House on Envoys; Helms Faction Wants Job Security for Six," *Washington Post,* June 28, 1985; "Deadlock on Diplomatic Nominees Eases Slightly," *New York Times,* June 28, 1985; A. L. May, "Helms Continues to Stall Confirmations," *Raleigh News and Observer,* June 28, 1985.

31. "Helms' Stalling Hurting U.S.," editorial, *Atlanta Constitution,* reprinted in *Raleigh News and Observer,* July 4, 1985.

32. "Helms' Ideological Blackmail," editorial, *Los Angeles Times,* reprinted in the *Greensboro Daily News,* July 5, 1985.

33. Helms acquiesced in the confirmation of John Whitehead as deputy secretary of state, and the next day the Senate approved twenty-four more diplomatic appointees, including Pickering and Abrams, while Burt's and Ridgway's nominations remained on hold, as did Edwin G. Corr's, Pickering's replacement as ambassador to El Salvador, and John A. Ferch's, nominated as ambassador to Honduras. A. L. May, "Conservatives End Delay on Nominations," *Raleigh News and Observer,* July 12, 1985; "Senate Confirms Aide for Post at State Department," *Washington Post,* July 9, 1985; Joanne Omang, "Senate Confirms 24; 'Hold' on Most State Dept. Nominees Lifted," *Washington Post,* July 12, 1985; "Senate Votes Confirmation of 23 for Diplomatic Posts," *New York Times,* July 12, 1985.

34. When Reagan nominated one of the six conservative diplomats that Helms was trying to protect, James L. Malone, as ambassador to Belize, the nomination encountered opposition in the Foreign Relations Committee. On April 10, 1986, the committee, by a close 9–7 vote, rejected the nomination, after Edward Zorinsky, Democrat of Nebraska, made the case that he was an "inadequate" manager, had "questionable" judgment, and had a record of job performance that was "less than satisfactory." The committee's rejection of Malone was the first time in American history that an ambassadorial nomination had been rejected at the committee level. Although Malone was criticized for mismanagement of the State Department's Bureau of Oceans and International Environmental and Scientific Affairs—as well as filling it with outside consultants—Helms remained determined to protect him. Insisting on a reconsideration, Helms held up votes on ten ambassadorial nominations and the promotion of Edwin Corr, ambassador to El Salvador, until the Malone nomination was reconsidered. The most important of these nominations was that of Morton I. Abramowitz as assistant secretary of state for intelligence and research, and although the committee approved his nomination by a 16–1 vote (with Helms voting negative), Helms put a hold on the nomination. He op-

posed the Abramowitz nomination because, he charged, he was a weak supporter of Taiwan, but his overall objective was to force through Malone's appointment. Republican senator Charles McC. Mathias, Jr., of Maryland, who had voted with the majority to reject Malone's nomination, agreed to reconsider if Helms permitted Abramowitz to go forward. But after Abramowitz was confirmed, Democrats on the Foreign Relations Committee boycotted the meeting in which Malone was reconsidered. When the committee then unanimously sent Malone's nomination to the Senate floor, Zorinsky led an effort to obstruct the vote. Some seventeen diplomatic nominations were stalled in the dispute. Joanne Omang, "Helms' Protege Rejected as U.S. Envoy; Foreign Relations Panel Defeats Ambassadorial Bid for First Time," *Washington Post*, April 12, 1986; Marjorie Williams, "Democrats Turn Tactic on Helms," *Washington Post*, September 24, 1986; "The Politics of End-of-Session Nominations," *New York Times*, October 15, 1986.

35. JH to Robert Dole, July 11, 1985, subject files, FG011, case file 334268, Reagan Library; Robert S. Greenberger, "Shultz Faces Another Test of Diplomacy in Fight with Jesse Helms over State Department Posts," *Wall Street Journal*, July 9, 1985.

36. Rowland Evans and Robert Novak, "Shultz Still Feuding with Helms," *Rocky Mount Telegram*, January 4, 1986.

37. "An Inquisition Ends," editorial, *Raleigh News and Observer*, July 20, 1985; Bill Arthur, "Helms's War on State Department Takes Personal Tone," *Charlotte Observer*, July 20, 1985; "Shultz as Scapegoat," editorial, *Greensboro News and Record*, August 16, 1985.

38. Transcript of Winston Lord testimony, Senate Foreign Relations Committee, September 30, 1985, JH MSS: "Helms Blocks Reagan," editorial, *Raleigh News and Observer*, November 3, 1985; Philip Geyelin, "A Vote of 16-to-Helms," *Washington Post*, November 3, 1985; Joanne Omang, "Nominee Beset on 2 Sides; Lord Delayed by Democrats, Barred by GOP," *Washington Post*, October 9, 1985; Lars-Erik Nelson, "Helms' 1-Man China Policy," *Charlotte Observer*, November 24, 1985; JH et al. to Reagan, October 2, 1985; JH to Reagan, November 4, 1985, Turner files, Reagan Library; "The Abortion Network at A.I.D. under the Reagan Administration," c. 1983; Tom Ashcraft to JH, June 6, 1983, JH MSS.

39. JH et al. to Ronald Reagan, April 2, 1985; Tom Ashcraft to JH, March 29, April 4, 1985, JH MSS; George Archibald, "AID Seeks to Cut UN Population Agency's Funding," *Washington Times*, April 1, 1985; George Archibald, "New Right Leaders Enraged During Talk with AID Chief," *Washington Times*, April 9, 1985; Philip Shenon, "A.I.D. Chief's Ouster Urged," *New York Times*, April 10, 1985; Bill Peterson, "AID's Peace Mission to Conservatives Backfires," *Washington Post*, April 11, 1985; Herbert L. Beckington to JH, September 11, 1985, JH MSS. On the charges regarding population planning in China, see "Paying for Abortions," editorial, *Wall Street Journal*, April 9, 1984.

40. Lionel Barber, "Shultz to Resolve Dispute over Support for UN Population Fund," *Washington Post*, September 18, 1985.

41. JH et al. to Donald T. Regan, September 12, 1985; Tom Ashcraft to JH, October 10, 1985; JH to Kemp, October 21, 1985; JH to Reagan, November 4, 1985, JH MSS; JH, floor speech, November 5, 1985, *CR*, A. L. May, "Senate OKs Lord as Envoy to China as Helms' Effort to Delay Action Ends," *Raleigh News and Observer*, November 6, 1985; "Helms Puts in Active Week on His Foreign Policy," *New York Times*, November 11, 1985; "Senate, Ending Impasse, Approves Envoy to China," *New York Times*, November 11, 1985.

42. "Helms Bars Envoy, Demanding Reagan Halt Abortion Aid," *New York Times*, November 1, 1985; "Sen. Helms's Hostage," editorial, *Washington Post*, November 3, 1985; M. Peter McPherson to Jesse Helms, November 4, 1985, JH MSS; presidential telephone call memo, November 5, 1985, presidential handwriting file; Reagan to JH, October 6, 1985, subject files, FO002, case file 348177, Reagan Library.

43. "Foreign Affairs; The Survival Question," editorial, *New York Times*, December 13, 1985. Helms subsequently objected to AID's program in Bangladesh. See Tom Ashcraft to JH, March 13, 1986; McPherson to JH, April 1, 1986, JH MSS.

44. JH, speech to CPAC, February 1, 1986, JH MSS.

45. Bill Arthur, "Sen. Helms Vents Ire on Shultz," *Charlotte Observer*, October 19, 1985; Lawrence L. Knutson, "Conservatives Accuse Shultz of Undermining Star Wars' Plan," *Charlotte Observer*, October 21, 1985.

46. A. L. May, "Helms Denies Plans to Attend Summit, but Adviser Says He May Go to Geneva," *Raleigh News and Observer*, November 6, 1985; Rowland Evans and Robert Novak, "Helms Should Stay Away from Geneva," (Marion, N.C.) *McDowell News*, November 12, 1985.

47. Loretta Tofani, "Senate Leaders Move to Subpoena Soviet Sailor; U.S. Judge in New Orleans Refuses to Block Ship's Departure, Due Friday or Saturday," *Washington Post*, November 7, 1985; "Politics-Free Political Asylum," *New York Times*, November 20, 1985; "Medvid's Fate," editorial, *Greensboro News & Record*, November 9, 1985; "Beyond One Sailor's Fate," editorial, *Raleigh News and Observer*, November 9, 1985; Thiessen interview, June 6, 2006.

48. Mary Thornton and Ward Sinclair, "Medvid Case Agents Face Punishment; Meese, INS Chief Evaluate Handling of Defection Attempt," *Washington Post*, November 13, 1985; "Did 'Agreement' Let Sailor Go? Helms Asks," *Winston-Salem Journal*, November 13, 1985.

49. "State Dept. Denies Soviet Seaman Was Impostor," *Washington Post*, March 4, 1986; A. L. May, "Helms Is Holding Hearing on Handling of Medvid Affair," *Raleigh News and Observer*, November 12, 1985; JH speech, November 12, 1985, *CR*; A. L. May, "Helms Criticizes State Department," (Marshall, N.C.) *News Record*, November 14, 1985. For the official explanation, see Robert M. Smalley to Walter Chopiwskyj, December 3, 1985, subject files, IM, case file 351239, Reagan Library.

50. "For Medvid, a Happier Return; Refused Asylum in 1985, Ex-Soviet Sailor Savors Trip Back," *Washington Post*, February 6, 2001; "Jesse Helms, Vindicated," *Weekly Standard*, February 12, 2001; Thiessen interview, June 6, 2006.

51. JH, speech at Northside Baptist Church, October 6, 1985, JH MSS.

52. Nirenberg later suggested that Helms's approach toward Israel was consistent: prior to the mid-1980s, he maintained, Helms had opposed policies that were perceived to be pro-Israel, especially his opposition to foreign aid to the Israeli government (as opposed to private organizations and individuals). Helms had also supported economic and military aid for moderate Arab regimes such as Egypt and Saudi Arabia. After the mid-1980s, Nirenberg now asserts, Helms helped to "redefine what it meant to be pro-Israel" by insisting that American policy oppose any form of terrorism, by supporting Israel's shift of its capital to Jerusalem, and by expanding defense cooperation with the Israeli military. As a result of Helms's effort, moreover, Nirenberg maintains, support for Israel was now more broadly bipartisan because it contained significant conservative participation. Nirenberg interview, June 7, 2006.

53. A. L. May, "Helms' Action Shows Shift Toward Israel," *Raleigh News and Observer,* October 20, 1985; Claude Sitton, "Helms' Shift Shows How Mideast Hopes Die," *Raleigh News and Observer,* January 26, 1986.

54. "Helms Changes His Mind About West Bank," *Asheville Citizen,* January 24, 1986; Furgurson, *Hard Right,* pp. 196–97.

55. Margaret Shapiro, Howard Kurtz, and Ward Sinclair, "House Democrats Endorse Sanctions Against South Africa," *Washington Post,* April 4, 1985.

56. Bill Arthur, "Helms Claims Tactical Win in Defeat of Bill," *Charlotte Observer,* July 13, 1985.

57. "Senate Panel Backs Anti-Apartheid Bill," *New York Times,* June 5, 1985; David B. Ottaway and Margaret Shapiro, "Senate Panel Votes S. Africa Sanctions; Foreign Relations Committee Would End Bank Loans to Pretoria," *Washington Post,* June 5, 1985.

58. Bill Arthur, "Helms's Filibuster Thwarts Passage of S. Africa Sanctions," *Charlotte Observer,* July 9, 1985; A. L. May, "Helms Threatens Filibuster on S. Africa Bill," *Raleigh News and Observer,* July 9, 1985; Joanne Omang, "Senate Votes to Limit Debate of S. Africa Sanctions; 88-to-8 Approval Indicates Wide Support for New Measures Against Apartheid," *Washington Post,* July 11, 1985; Paul Haskins, "Senate Squelches Helms' Filibuster, 88–8," *Winston-Salem Journal,* July 11, 1985; "Senate Approves Economic Moves Against S. Africa," *New York Times,* July 12, 1985.

59. "Reagan Shifts Policy, Calls for Sanctions," *Greensboro News and Record,* September 10, 1985; Bill Arthur, "Senate Democrats Fail to Force Vote on Sanctions Bill," *Charlotte Observer,* September 10, 1985.

60. Edward Walsh, "Senate Panel Votes Sanctions on Pretoria; Measure Would Ban New U.S. Investment," *Washington Post,* August 2, 1986.

61. Edward Walsh, "S. Africa Minister Warns of Grain Purchase Cutoff; Threat over Sanctions Phoned to Senators," *Washington Post,* October 2, 1986; Edward Walsh, "Sanctions Imposed on S. Africa as Senate Overrides Veto, 78–21," *Washington Post,* October 3, 1986.

62. "Mexico Under Stress," editorial, *Washington Post,* June 11, 1986; "The Worth of Mexico," editorial, *Winston-Salem Journal,* June 20, 1986.

63. Philip Geyelin, "Message to Mexico," *Washington Post,* May 29, 1986.

64. On May 22, Attorney General Edwin Meese telephoned Mexican attorney general Sergio García Ramírez to deny that the Reagan administration believed that the government of President Miguel de la Madrid was tainted by drug corruption. Neither von Raab nor Abrams, Meese said, represented the Reagan administration. Treasury Department officials also backed up the White House position. In addition, in June 1986, assistant secretary of the Treasury for international affairs David C. Mulford, in testimony before Helms's subcommittee, emphasized that the Mexican government was now exercising appropriate budget discipline and had taken "difficult steps" that had not received "the recognition they deserve." Edward Cody, "Mexican Governor Gets U.S. Apology; No Evidence Found to Support Charge of Involvement with Drugs," *Washington Post,* May 29, 1986; JH, "U.S. Can't Tolerate Mexican Drug Traffic," *Charlotte Observer,* May 25, 1986.

65. "Mexico Under Stress," editorial, *Washington Post,* June 11, 1986.

66. A. L. May, "Senators Critical of Helms' Stance on Mexico," *Raleigh News and Observer,* June 20, 1986.

67. Bill Arthur, "Helms Waves Aside Mexican Protests, Continues Hearings," *Charlotte Observer,* June 8, 1986.

68. In an interview, Helms contended that he was responding to a *Newsweek* report describing a Mexican journalist's description of Helms as a "pot-smoking gringo tourist who complained about Mexican corruption while smuggling in cocaine himself." Helms told the *Observer* reporter that "the Latin"—meaning the Mexican reporter—was "volatile." John Alexander, "Helms, Mexico-Bashing and Bruised Relations," *Greensboro News and Record,* June 22, 1986.

69. "Hispanics Want Helms Censured," Greenville (N.C.) *Daily Reflector,* June 19, 1986.

70. "Insulting the Latins," editorial, *Washington Post,* June 17, 1986. See also "Helms' Remarks Cloud Work on Drug Problem," editorial, *Durham Sun,* June 13, 1986.

71. Dana Walker, "Meese Conciliatory on Mexico's Drug Problem," *Reidsville Review,* July 4, 1986.

72. "Mr. Meese's Phone Call," editorial, *Washington Post,* May 28, 1986; Edward Cody, "Mexican Governor Gets U.S. Apology; No Evidence Found to Support Charge of Involvement with Drugs," *Washington Post,* May 29, 1986; Edward Cody, "Mexico Reacts with Anger to U.S. Charges; Some Say Country Sensitive to History of Foreign Intervention," *Washington Post,* June 1, 1986; "Helms Says Hearings Averted U.S. Bailout of Mexico Debts," *Henderson Dispatch,* June 20, 1986.

73. "Roundhouse Right for Mexico," editorial, *Raleigh News and Observer,* June 16, 1986.

74. Former ambassador to Mexico John Gavin then testified. Gavin, a former actor who had become ambassador because of an old friendship with Reagan, was reportedly forced out of the job by the White House once the Mexican crisis heated up. Helms asked Gavin whether these assertions were correct. Gavin refused to answer, saying that the information was classified and that "it would be improper to comment." Gavin defended Rodolfo Félix Valdez, the Sonoran governor that Helms accused of drug trafficking, but he claimed that two Mexican governors whom he refused to name were "up to their elbows in the [drug] trade." One of the governors provided "shelter, comfort and protection" to a person that Gavin described as the most important "drug overlord of Mexico." "2 Mexicans Linked to Drugs by Helms," *New York Times,* June 27, 1986; "Helms Says Hearings Averted U.S. Bailout," *Henderson Dispatch,* June 20, 1986; A. L. May, "Helms Tries to Bring Deaver into Mexican Controversy," *Raleigh News and Observer,* June 28, 1986.

75. Mary Thornton and Joanne Omang, "Mexican Chief's Election Fraudulent, Helms Says; Embassy Denies Senator's Allegations," *Washington Post,* June 18, 1986; David Maraniss, "On Both Sides of the Border, Laredo's Alienation Runs Deep; Rhetoric from Washington Stirs Anger," *Washington Post,* June 29, 1986; Bill Arthur, "2 Governors Blast Helms' Attacks on Mexican Government," *Charlotte Observer,* June 27, 1986. For Rogers's views, see William D. Rogers, "Mexico-Bashing in Washington," *Washington Post,* June 19, 1986.

76. Although President de la Madrid, also interviewed on *Meet the Press,* said that American officials testifying before Helms's subcommittee had "acted very frivolously" and had slandered Mexican officials, Helms defended their testimony. The senator's objective over the long term, said Jim Lucier, was to foster greater social and political stability in Mexico "so that we no longer have the pressure of immigration." "Helms Urges Caution on Mexico Aid," *Charlotte Observer,* June 23, 1986.

77. "Helms Says Mexicans Won't Put Up with Fraud by Their Government," *Winston-Salem Journal,* August 15, 1986; Bill Krueger, "Helms Lets de la Madrid Foes Speak Out," *Raleigh News and Observer,* August 15, 1986.

78. Joe Pichirallo, "Antidrug Tactic Targets Aid; Helms, Kerry Seek to Penalize 3 Countries," *Washington Post,* March 24, 1987; Gil Klein, "Latin Failure to Stem Drugs Angers Senators," *Winston-Salem Journal,* March 24, 1987.

79. Elaine Sciolino, "Draft U.S. Report on Drugs Urges No Penalty for Panama or Mexico," *New York Times,* February 20, 1988; Helen Dewar, "Senate Slaps Mexico over Antidrug Assistance; Economic Curbs Approved for Failure to Cooperate Fully with War Against Trafficking," *Washington Post,* April 15, 1988.

80. John Dinges, *Our Man in Panama: How General Noriega Used the United States— and Made Millions in Drugs and Arms* (New York: Random House, 1990), pp. 236–37; Frederick Kempe, *Divorcing the Dictator: America's Bungled Affair with Noriega* (New York: G. P. Putnam's Sons, 1990), p. 176; Kevin Buckley, *Panama: The Whole Story* (New York: Simon and Schuster, 1991), pp. 42–43, 47–48.

81. Buckley, *Panama*, pp. 51–52.

82. Kempe, *Divorcing the Dictator*, pp. 176–77; Dinges, *Our Man in Panama*, pp. 236–39; Buckley, *Panama*, pp. 54–56; Seymour Hersh, "Panama Strongman Said to Trade in Drugs, Arms and Illicit Money," *New York Times*, June 12, 1986; Seymour Hersh, "U.S. Aides in '72 Weighed Killing Officer Who Now Leads Panama," *New York Times*, June 13, 1986; Seymour Hersh, "Panama General Said to Have Told Army to Rig Vote," *New York Times*, June 21, 1986; John Herbers, "Panama General Accused by Helms," *New York Times*, June 23, 1986; "Helms Ties Official to Drug Trafficking," *Jacksonville Daily News*, June 23, 1986. See also "Helms Unsung Hero in Noriega Ouster," *Human Events*, January 20, 1990; JH speech, July 30, 1986, *CR*.

83. Kempe, *Divorcing the Dictator*, pp. 179–80. Helms's struggle with Casey was wrapped up in a larger conflict with the CIA over Latin America.

84. Dennis Volman, "Top 'Contras' Under Scrutiny for Corruption," *Christian Science Monitor*, April 11, 1986; Buckley, *Panama*, pp. 108–9; DeMoss Fonseca interview, January 3, 2007; JH speech, February 4, 1988. At the Senate hearings, former Panamanian consul José Blandon testified that U.S. intelligence had provided information to Noriega about Helms and Kennedy, including information about their top staffers DeMoss and Gregory Craig. Joe Pichirallo, "Noriega Got CIA Data, Panel Told; Reports Are Said to Include Details on Kennedy, Helms," *Washington Post*, February 10, 1988.

85. "Helms Unsung Hero in Noriega Ouster," *Human Events*, January 20, 1990.

86. Buckley, *Panama*, p. 204.

87. Dinges, *Our Man in Panama*, pp. 304–5; Buckley, *Panama*, pp. 204–5; Bob Woodward and Joe Pichirallo, "U.S. Move on Noriega Was Option; Rebellion in Panama Ended as Commander Was Receiving Orders," *Washington Post*, October 8, 1989; Bob Woodward, "The Conversion of Gen. Powell; Incidents Led JCS Chief to Reverse Opposition to Use of Force," *Washington Post*, December 21, 1989.

88. Buckley, *Panama*, pp. 207–8.

89. Kempe, *Divorcing the Dictator*, p. 371. Curiously, Kempe has no recounting of Helms's role in the Giroldi coup, although he provides the longest and most detailed account available. See ch. 21.

90. Buckley, *Panama*, pp. 214–15.

91. Buckley, *Panama*, pp. 214–15; Kempe, *Divorcing the Dictator*, p. 393.

92. Molly Moore and Joe Pichirallo, "Cheney: U.S. Was Willing to Take Custody of Noriega," *Washington Post*, October 6, 1989; David Hoffman and Joe Pichirallo, "Rebels Held Noriega for Hours; General's Fate Was Discussed with U.S. Officer During Coup Attempt," *Washington Post*, October 5, 1989.

93. "Central American Policy Clearly in Disarray" and "Helms Scores Administration on Failed Panama Coup," *Human Events*, October 14, 1989; DeMoss Fonseca interviews, February 16, 2006, January 3, 2007.

94. "Helms Unsung Hero in Noriega Ouster," *Human Events*, January 20, 1990.

95. "Man Burned in Chile Strike Dies," *New York Times,* July 7, 1986; David K. Shipler, "Proper Medical Care Reportedly Denied Man Burned In Chile," *New York Times,* July 8, 1986; Mark Honigsbaum, "Pinochet's Men Burnt My Son—And I Want Justice," *Guardian,* January 17, 1999; Helms speech, *CR,* August 7, 1986; Ken Eudy, "Helms Says Tape Shows Dead Man's Communist Ties," *Charlotte Observer,* September 30, 1986. For background, see Cathy Lisa Schneider, *Shantytown Protest in Pinochet's Chile* (Philadelphia: Temple University Press, 1995); Lois Hecht Oppenheim, *Politics in Chile: Democracy, Authoritarianism, and the Search for Development* (Boulder: Westview, 1999). On the Rojas case, see Mary Helen Spooner, *Soldiers in a Narrow Land: The Pinochet Regime in Chile* (Berkeley: University of California Press, 1994), pp. 209–15.

96. "Chile's Military Government Is Praised by Jesse Helms," *Winston-Salem Journal,* July 12, 1986.

97. "U.S., Keeping Pressure on Chile, Sends Official to Urge Transition," *New York Times,* July 12, 1986; Michael Specter, " 'I Know How Much My Son Suffered'; Mother of Slain Activist Returns from Chile, Tells of His Death," *Washington Post,* July 13, 1986; "Jesse Helms on Chile," editorial, *Washington Post,* July 16, 1986; Marjorie Williams, "Talking Points; Career Diplomat Being Chosen for Lebanon Hot Seat," *Washington Post,* July 18, 1986; Lisa Pullen, "Ambassador to Chile Strikes Back at Helms," *Charlotte Observer,* March 24, 1987.

98. The Helms-Barnes conversation was the subject of declassified documents discussed in Jon Elliston, "Deadly Alliance: New Evidence Shows How Far Jesse Helms Went to Support Chilean Dictator Augusto Pinochet," *Independent Weekly,* May 23, 2001; DeMoss Fonseca interview, October 10, 2006.

99. "Hear the Screams," editorial, *Raleigh Times,* July 17, 1986.

100. John M. Goshko, "Players; Elliott Abrams: 'Tough Guy' of Convictions on Reagan's Team at State," *Washington Post,* July 21, 1986.

101. Jon Elliston, "Deadly Alliance," *Independent Weekly,* May 23, 2001.

102. A. L. May, "Helms Defends Hold on Senate Resolution on Chile," *Raleigh News and Observer,* July 16, 1986.

103. Jay Elliston, "Deadly Alliance," *Independent Weekly,* May 23, 2001. "I'm taking a lot of heat these days," he wrote *Washington Inquirer* columnist Marx Lewis, "but not nearly enough to bother me." JH to Marx Lewis, August 25, 1986, Marx Lewis Papers, box 1, Hoover Institution Archives.

104. Elliott Abrams had taken Helms on publicly when he charged that Helms's involvement in Chile was "indefensible." Now Abrams was also involved in exposing Helms's security breach. In a statement issued on the same day, August 4, the chairman and vice chairman of the Senate Intelligence Committee, David Durenberger (R-MN) and Patrick Leahy (D-VT), announced that they had received information about an unauthorized disclosure of classified information through Abrams, who had "mentioned" the violation to Durenberger at "a chance encounter" at a social event. Durenberger, according to Senate rules, then felt compelled to report the leak to the Justice

Department for investigation. Abrams was subsequently quoted as saying that there was "no indication Helms was personally responsible for any breach of security," but he did not eliminate the possibility of a leak from a staffer. Joanne Omang, "Helms, Aide Probed on Security Leak; Intelligence Panel Sought FBI Inquiry; Senator Denies Charge," *Washington Post*, August 5, 1986.

105. Stephen Engelberg, "Helms Is Facing Inquiry on Chile and U.S. Spying," *New York Times*, August 3, 1986; Joanne Omang, "Helms, Aide Probed on Security Leak," *Washington Post*, August 5, 1986.

106. A. L. May, "Helms Denies Leaking CIA Information," *Raleigh News and Observer*, August 4, 1986. See also "Helms Under Scrutiny," editorial, *Greensboro News and Record*, August 5, 1986.

107. Steven V. Roberts, "Helms Declares Officials Harass Him," *New York Times*, August 5, 1986; "Helms Aide Said to Be the Focus of Inquiry on Disclosure of Data," *New York Times*, August 6, 1986. On August 6, it was reported that a Chilean government official had officially complained to Ambassador Barnes about "spies" stealing military secrets. When Barnes asked him for details, he said that the information had come from Helms's office. The Chileans were objecting to a secret Chilean army report that American intelligence had obtained; the report verified the involvement of the Chilean army in Rojas's burning and death. Intelligence officials, according to a National Public Radio report broadcast on August 6, made the report available at a congressional intelligence briefing that Helms's aide Chris Manion attended. Within hours of the briefing, the Chilean government protested to Barnes. According to an intelligence official, the details of the report provided "almost a road map to how we got the information," and after the exposure of the information, the Chileans shut down a very useful CIA intelligence source. It was on this basis that suspicion focused on Manion and Helms. "That's why we were upset," the official told a reporter. Joanne Omang, "Chilean Was Source in Helms Inquiry; Santiago Aide Complained to U.S. Envoy of 'Spies' Stealing Secrets," *Washington Post*, August 7, 1986.

108. Joanne Omang, "Chilean Was Source in Helms Inquiry," *Washington Post*, August 7, 1986.

109. In September, meanwhile, the National Congressional Club spent $715,000 nationwide on television ads presenting Jesse's version of the squabble with the State Department about Latin American policy. Rowland Evans and Robert Novak, "Helms Mounts Attack on the CIA," *Asheville Citizen*, August 10, 1986; Steven V. Roberts, "Helms Says Intelligence Agencies May Have Spied on Him in Chile," *New York Times*, August 11, 1986; "Helms Says Probe Shifting Focus on Chile Leak," *Charlotte Observer*, September 11, 1986; "TV Ads to Give Helms' View on Chilean Controversy," *Winston-Salem Journal*, September 11, 1986.

110. Fonseca interview, February 16, 2006.

111. Paul Haskins, "Singlaub Did Not Make Trip as My 'Envoy,' Helms Says,"

Winston-Salem Journal, June 10, 1987; JH, speech to CPAC, February 20, 1987, JH MSS.

112. Steven V. Roberts, "Helms Assails Many over Chile," *New York Times,* August 8, 1986; Helms speech, *CR,* August 7, 1986.

113. "Helms Says Probe Shifting Focus on Chile Leak," *Charlotte Observer,* September 11, 1986.

114. Stephen Engelberg, "Vote in Senate Supports Helms on C.I.A. Curb," *New York Times,* September 26, 1986.

115. "East Seemed High Spirited Before Death," *Asheboro Courier-Tribune,* June 30, 1986; Todd Cohen, "Helms Says He Was Unaware That East Possibly Was Troubled," *Raleigh News and Observer,* June 30, 1986; Jim Schlosser, "Colleagues Mourn Loss of 'Patriot,' " *Greensboro News and Record,* June 30, 1986.

116. James R. Dickenson, "Sanford Switches, Decides to Run," *Washington Post,* January 14, 1986; Wrenn interview, April 5, 2006.

117. John Flesher, "Helms Declares Neutrality," *Watauga Democrat,* October 18, 1985.

118. Stan Swofford, "Sen. Helms Eyes Foreign Relations Minority Post," *Greensboro News & Record,* November 6, 1986; "Washington Talk: Briefing; Helms vs. Lugar," *New York Times,* November 10, 1986; Bill Arthur, "Helms Planning to Challenge Lugar for Post," *Charlotte Observer,* November 13, 1986; Stan Swofford, "Helms in Battle for Top Seat," *Greensboro News and Record,* November 14, 1986; "Helms to Battle Lugar for Senate Panel Post," *New York Times,* November 15, 1986.

119. Pat Buchanan to Donald T. Regan and Will Ball, November 17, 1986, subject files, FG036–10, case file 455796, Reagan Library; Stan Swofford, "Helms in Battle for Top Seat," *Greensboro News & Record,* November 14, 1986; Rob Christensen, "Helms Defends Against a 'Full-Court Press,' " *Raleigh News and Observer,* November 14, 1986; "Washington Talk: Congress; A Contretemps Among Republicans," *New York Times,* December 3, 1986; "Republicans Pick Helms over Lugar for a Senate Job," *New York Times,* January 21, 1987; Nirenberg interview, June 7, 2006.

120. "Either we'll have Senator Helms in the position of fighting for a strong anti-Communist policy," said one Conservative Caucus mailing, "or we'll have Republicans disregarding the long-standing rules of their party in order to exclude a conservative from a position to which he was entitled." This choice might well "determine the fate of freedom fighters around the world." If Helms were defeated, then conservatives might abandon their "blind fidelity" to the Republicans. Ferrell Guillory, "Helms Plans Pressure for His GOP Colleagues," *Raleigh News and Observer,* December 19, 1986; "Washington Talk: Briefing: The Helms-Weicker Tie," *New York Times,* December 24, 1986; "Lugar Defeats Helms in Race for G.O.P. Job," *New York Times,* January 7, 1987; Tom Kenworthy, "Helms Loses Preliminary Round; Foreign Relations' Republicans Endorse Lugar's Bid to Lead Them," *Washington Post,* January 7, 1987; DeMoss Fonseca interview, February 16, 2006.

121. Bill Krueger, "Helms-Lugar Contest Creates Strange Bedfellows in Senate," *Raleigh News and Observer,* December 13, 1986; "Washington Talk: Briefing: The Helms-Weicker Tie," *New York Times,* December 24, 1986; David S. Broder, "Maverick Lives Up to Label; Weicker Puts Himself in Helms' Corner," *Washington Post,* January 1, 1987.

122. Bill Arthur and Jeff Nesbitt, "Sen. Helms Beats Lugar for Post," *Charlotte Observer,* January 21, 1987; Jim Schlosser, "Helms Wins Post on Foreign Affairs," *Greensboro News & Record,* January 21, 1987; "Republicans Pick Helms over Lugar for a Senate Job," *New York Times,* January 21, 1987; Helen Dewar, "Helms Wins Seniority Dispute; Lugar Loses Ranking as Top Republican on Foreign Relations," *Washington Post,* January 21, 1987.

123. Fonseca interview, February 16, 2006.

124. JH, speech to CPAC, February 20, 1987, JH MSS.

125. "Role for Helms Dismays U.S. Officials," *New York Times,* January 22, 1987; "Helms, Shultz Sign No Truce," *Asheville Citizen,* January 25, 1987; "Jesse Helms Returns," editorial, *Washington Post,* January 21, 1987; "Seniority Boosts Helms," editorial, *Raleigh News and Observer,* January 22, 1987; "A Challenge for Helms," editorial, *Greensboro News and Record,* January 22, 1987.

126. Claude Sitton, "Helms' Senate Switch Means Trouble Ahead," *Raleigh News and Observer,* January 25, 1987.

10. JESSE'S SPIDERWEB

1. JH, speech to Congressional Club, Raleigh, February 25, 1989, JH MSS.

2. JH, "Who Will Pay for Perestroika," speech at CPAC meeting, February 24, 1989, JH MSS.

3. "Senator Alms," *New Republic,* May 28, 1990; interview with Wilkie, April 21, 2006.

4. Helms had certainly noticed the young Maupin. "Would you put a young conservative who's doing a column for the *Daily Tar Heel* on your mailing list?" he wrote to a fellow southern conservative. "He's the first conservative in years who has cracked through the shell of liberalism on that campus journal." JH to Thurman Sensing, October 29, 1962, JH MSS.

5. Maupin interview, December 27, 2006; Charles Salter, Jr., "*Tales of the City* Raleigh Writer Armistead Maupin Looks Homeward and Reflects on His Colorful Coming of Age," *Raleigh News and Observer,* November 29, 1992. In February 1971, Helms wrote Maupin about the "fine work" he was doing for the *News and Courier,* "so obviously my wish for your success has come true." JH to Armistead Maupin, Jr., February 9, 1971, in author's possession. I appreciate Armistead Maupin's generosity in sharing a copy of this letter with me.

6. Maupin interview, December 27, 2006. Maupin later attracted attention when *Tales of the City* was televised as a PBS series. See Charles Salter, Jr., "*Tales of the City* Raleigh Writer Armistead Maupin Looks Homeward and Reflects on

His Colorful Coming of Age," *Raleigh News and Observer,* November 29, 1992; Tim Funk, "Ex-Carolinian Maupin Worked for Jesse Helms," *Charlotte Observer,* January 8, 1994.

7. Maupin interview, December 27, 2006; David Fellerath, "Armistead Maupin's Jesse Years," *Independent Weekly,* August 9, 2006.

8. Helms's moral crusading also focused on an effort to curb "dial-a-porn." The pornography industry had proved remarkably resilient, and in the late 1980s a new, highly profitable side of the industry emerged: subscribers called telephone numbers, with a per-call charge, and received either a taped or live sexually explicit message. Although existing legislation banned children from listening to pornography on the telephone, these restrictions proved ineffective. In October 1986, Helms offered an amendment prohibiting dial-a-porn to a Senate anti-drug bill; his amendment focused on prohibiting access for children. Helms's amendment was buried in a House-Senate conference, but in December 1987 he brought the issue up again, in an amendment to an $8.3 billion education bill that would criminalize "any obscene or indecent communication" made over the telephone. It was "time for the Senate to say, forcefully, emphatically, that enough is enough," Helms declared. He described how a nine-year-old boy, thinking he was calling the talking bear Teddy Ruxpin, heard a pornographic message instead. Helms's dial-a-porn amendment attracted little opposition, and it passed easily; no one wanted to be, as the *Washington Post* put it, "the senator from the pornography industry." After the Senate enacted the ban in April 1987, the House responded by passing it in April 1988. "True Obscenity," editorial, *Washington Post,* April 21, 1988; "Senate Approves School Programs," *New York Times,* December 2, 1987; JH to Howard Baker, September 17, 1987, subject files, FG006–1, case file 515433, Reagan Library; "Games with the First Amendment," editorial, *Washington Post,* April 14, 1988; Tom Kenworthy, "House Votes to Ban 'Dial-a-Porn' Phone Services," *Washington Post,* April 20, 1988; "House OKs Bill Banning 'Dial-a-Porn' Services," *Winston-Salem Journal,* April 20, 1988. In August 1990, New York federal district court judge Robert P. Patterson struck down the law—two days before it was to take effect—ruling that it was too broad and vague and that it threatened "irreparable harm" to First Amendment freedoms. The Supreme Court subsequently upheld Patterson's decision. But Helms was undeterred, and, in 1989, he sponsored yet another amendment strictly limiting dial-a-porn, and in a 1992 decision the Supreme Court upheld the law. Michael Specter, "Judge Blocks Anti-Porn Amendment; Helms-Backed Law Targets Phone Services," *Washington Post,* August 14, 1990; Ruth Marcus, "Justices Clear the Way for 'Dial-a-Porn' Shield," *Washington Post,* January 28, 1992.

9. Interview with Mary Potter Summa, April 7, 2006; Wilkie interview, April 21, 2006.

10. JH, Senate speech, June 1986, JH MSS; Bill Arthur, "Helms Fights AIDS Law Barring Insurance Bias," *Charlotte Observer,* June 20, 1986; Arthur S. Brisbane,

"D.C. AIDS Bill Draws Challenge in Congress; City 'Snookered' on Insurance, Says Helms," *Washington Post,* June 20, 1986; *CR,* June 19, 1986.

11. "AIDS Insurance Bill," *Washington Post,* July 2, 1986; Sandra Evans, "D.C. AIDS Law Fails Senate Test; Helms Bid to Repeal Measure Angers Home Rule Backers," *Washington Post,* August 2, 1986; Margaret Engel, "Insurance Groups Sue to Block D.C. AIDS Law," *Washington Post,* August 6, 1986; Sandra Evans, "Senate Votes Second Time to Repeal D.C. AIDS Law," *Washington Post,* October 4, 1986; Sandra Evans, "Conferees Drop Threat to D.C. Insurance Law; Act Covers Those Exposed to AIDS Virus," *Washington Post,* October 11, 1986.

12. William Allegar, "AIDS Law Prompts Major Insurers to Quit Selling," *Washington Times,* January 15, 1987; "Senate Votes to Let Insurers in Capital Reject AIDS Clients," *New York Times,* October 2, 1987; Lawrence Feinberg, "Bill Would Ease Denying Insurance in AIDS Cases," *Washington Post,* November 24, 1987; Sandra G. Boodman, "Sen. Helms May Stymie AIDS Measure; Republican Opposes Secrecy in Testing," *Washington Post,* October 7, 1988.

13. "Dangerous Moves at HHS," *CR,* May 7, 1990; Helen Dewar and Sandra G. Boodman, "Reagan Leans Toward Requiring AIDS Tests for Some, Aide Says; Senate Rejects Move to Check Marriage Applicants, Immigrants," *Washington Post,* May 22, 1987; Steve Taravella, "AIDS Removed from Immigration Restrictions," *Modern Healthcare,* January 14, 1991.

14. Wilkie interview, April 21, 2006; *CR,* June 10, 1987; Bill Krueger, "Helms Submits Bill for Broader AIDS Testing," *Raleigh News and Observer,* June 11, 1987.

15. Earlier, in September 1987, the materials had been supplied to Helms's office by John P. Hale, who represented the Roman Catholic archdiocese of New York City. Hale sent a copy of the comic to Mary Potter, who urged Helms to take action. Howard Phillips also forwarded GMHC materials to Jesse's office. JH to James O. Mason, October 7, 1987; John P. Hale to JH, September 18, 1987, enc. "Safer Sex Comix #4"; Howard Phillips to JH, September 30, 1987, JH MSS; *CR,* October 14, 1987; "Limit Voted on AIDS Funds," *New York Times,* October 15, 1987; Edward I. Koch, "Senator Helms's Callousness Toward AIDS Victims," *New York Times,* November 7, 1987; Spencer Rich, "Anti-AIDS Comics Used No U.S. Funds; HHS Report Agrees That N.Y. Gay Group Is Playing by the Book," *Washington Post,* November 20, 1987.

16. "Ads Attack Helms AIDS-Education Amendment," *Raleigh Times,* October 26, 1987.

17. Edward I. Koch, "Senator Helms' Callousness Toward AIDS Victims," *New York Times,* November 7, 1987; JH to the Editor, *New York Times,* November 23, 1987.

18. "The Senate Debate: A Battle Plan Against Aids," *Washington Post,* May 2, 1988; Josh Getlin, "Senate Curbs Use of Anti-AIDS Funds; Programs That 'Promote' Homosexuality Would Be Ruled Out," *Washington Post,* April 29, 1988; Bill Arthur, "Helms Delays AIDS Debate," *Charlotte Observer,* April 29, 1988.

19. "Senate Votes to Require Test of Aliens for AIDS Virus," *New York Times,* June 3, 1987; "Senate Approves AIDS Testing," *Raleigh Times,* June 3, 1987.

20. "Senator Helms and the Guilty Victims," editorial, *New York Times,* June 17, 1987; JH, Senate speech, June 1987, JH MSS.

21. Insisting that confidentiality protections be eliminated, Helms favored restoring provisions of the Senate bill that provided for mandatory spousal notification of AIDS infection. After about a week of Helms's obstruction, the bill's supporters gave in and dropped the confidentiality provisions. The law provided $1 billion in federal funding for research and education, but its main sponsor in the House, Democrat Henry Waxman of California, described its passage as "bittersweet" because he believed that the elimination of confidentiality provisions would lower participation. Although Helms won on the confidentiality issue, he failed to block $105 million for education and $100 million for anonymous testing. Waxman sponsored legislation that provided an extensive program of education and research, and his bill enjoyed widespread support in Congress and the medical community, and among civil liberties groups. Waxman opposed any federally supported education that did not provide for confidential testing, and the result was an impasse in which Waxman and the chief Senate sponsor, Edward Kennedy, would send a bill that provided for research but no education programs. "If we get any bill less than the whole package," said one supporter, "we have to make it clear to people that that's because of one person: Sen. Helms." Sandra G. Boodman, "Sen. Helms May Stymie AIDS Measure; Republican Opposes Secrecy in Testing," *Washington Post,* October 7, 1988; "Congress Passes Compromise AIDS Bill," *New York Times,* October 14, 1988; Michael Specter, "Hill Approves $1 Billion AIDS Bill; Compromise Adds Researchers, Omits Confidentiality Safeguards," *Washington Post,* October 14, 1988.

22. "$2.9 Billion Bill for AIDS Relief Gains in Senate," *New York Times,* May 16, 1990; *CR,* May 14, 15, 16, 1990; "Word for Word / Jesse Helms; The North Carolinian Has Enemies, but No One Calls Him Vague," *New York Times,* November 27, 1994.

23. "6 Gay-Rights Activists Arrested," *Washington Post,* July 18, 1990; Lisa M. Keen, "Six Activists Hold Kiss-in in Helms' Office," *Washington Blade,* July 20, 1990.

24. In the same speech, he attacked gay rights demonstrators who "had slithered into" New York City's St. Patrick's Cathedral to denounce "5,000 years of Judeo-Christian teachings against the sin of sodomy." Although he was a Baptist, "I resent the hell out of what they did at St. Patrick's." Helms further criticized the "homosexual apologists in the media and in politics" such as New York governor Mario Cuomo, who had, he claimed, taken a weak position on the St. Patrick's demonstrators. Cuomo had claimed that the gay protesters were provoked. "Bullfeathers, I say to the Governor of New York." "Senate, 92 to 4, Wants U.S. Data on Crimes That Spring from Hate," *New York Times,* February 9, 1990; Jon Healey, "Helms Loses Battle to Beat Bill on Information on Hate Crimes," *Winston-Salem Journal,* February 9, 1990; Mike Robinson, "Senate Approves Crime Bill," *Greensboro News and Record,* February 9, 1990; Charles

Babington, "Senate Rebuffs Helms on Hate-Crimes Count," *Raleigh News and Observer,* February 9, 1990; Helen Dewar, "Senate Passes Bill Requiring Data on 'Hate Crimes,'" *Washington Post,* February 9, 1990.

25. "Senate, 92 to 4, Wants U.S. Data on Crimes That Spring from Hate," *New York Times,* February 9, 1990.

26. *CR,* June 23, 1989.

27. William H. Honan, "Congressional Anger Threatens Arts Endowment's Budget," *New York Times,* June 20, 1989; Dennis Szakacs, "The NEA Controversy: The Last Temptation," *Independent,* July 27, 1989.

28. Wilkie interview, April 21, 2006.

29. Mashburn interview, April 19, 2006; Wilkie interview, April 21, 2006; John Monk, "Who's Laughing Now? Long Written Off as a Noisy Blowhard, Jesse Helms Means to Be a Hard-Hitting Player," *Washingtonian,* November 1, 1995.

30. *CR,* May 18, 1989.

31. Mashburn to JH, June 7, 1989, JH MSS; Blaine Harden, "As Reelection Curtain Time Nears, Senator from New York Changes Tune on NEA," *Washington Post,* July 2, 1997; Wilkie interview, April 21, 2006. When he ran unsuccessfully for reelection in 1998, D'Amato was described by Hillary Rodham Clinton as "a clone of Jesse Helms." *Washington Post,* September 24, 1998.

32. "Where is the catalogue?," asked Helms. Pointing to D'Amato, Mashburn responded: "In his hands!" Following D'Amato's speech, Mashburn retrieved the photo plate from the catalogue containing *Piss Christ,* which had survived the catalogue's destruction. Mashburn interview, April 19, 2006.

33. Mashburn interview, April 19, 2006; *CR,* May 18, 1989; John Monk, "Who's Laughing Now?," *Washingtonian,* November 1, 1995.

34. "Helms Vows to Fight on Arts Funds," *New York Times,* October 23, 1990.

35. "Congressional Anger"; Barbara Gamarekian, "Corcoran, to Foil Dispute, Drops Mapplethorpe Show," *New York Times,* June 14, 1989; Barbara Gamarekian, "Mapplethorpe Backers Picket the Corcoran and Plan New Shows," *New York Times,* June 17, 1989; Peggy Phelan, "Serrano, Mapplethorpe, the NEA and You: 'Money Talks': October 1989," *TDR* 34 (Spring 1990): 4–15; Elizabeth Kastor, "The Broad Sweep of Helms' Arts Amendment; NEA Not Only Agency Proposal Would Affect," *Washington Post,* August 2, 1989; Elizabeth Kastor, "Corcoran's Orr-Cahall Resigns After 6-Month Arts Battle," *Washington Post,* December 19, 1989.

36. Mashburn interview, April 19, 2006.

37. *CR,* June 19, 1989.

38. Elizabeth Kastor, "Arts Supporters Denounce Helms; Senator's NEA Amendment Causes Unease on the Hill," *Washington Post,* July 28, 1989; Mashburn to JH, June 7, 1989; Bob Friedlander to JH, August 3, 1989, JH MSS.

39. Helms criticized the NEA's inability to manage itself. On June 6, NEA director Hugh Southern, responding to D'Amato's letter of May 18, agreed that he found Serrano's art offensive but that he was prevented by the endowment's authorizing language from intervening. The NEA relied on review panels to

ensure the integrity of grant decisions, and Southern promised to review NEA processes. That Southern's answer was completely deficient became evident in the furor over Mapplethorpe's photographs. His "sick art" slipped through the panel review system, Helms claimed, suggesting that the system was flawed and requiring that the Senate intervene. His amendment would prevent the NEA from using federal money to "fund filth" and to guarantee that the "sensitivities of all groups" were respected. Americans, Helms said, were "moral, decent people and they have a right not to be denigrated, offended, or mocked with their own tax dollars." *CR,* July 26, 1989.

40. Elizabeth Kastor, "Senate Votes to Expand NEA Grant Ban; Helms Amendment Targets 'Obscene' Art," *Washington Post,* July 27, 1989; Maureen Dowd, "Unruffled Helms Basks in Eye of Arts Storm," *New York Times,* July 28, 1989; "More on Arts Funding," editorial, *Washington Post,* July 20, 1989; "Helmsian Aesthetics," editorial, *Greensboro News and Record,* July 28, 1989. In JH to Mashburn, May 2, 1990, JH MSS, Helms described possible anti-NEA amendments that he suggested to Mashburn. "I feel we should settle on *at most* two," he wrote, "and let me take 'em to Byrd."

41. Jonathan Yardley, "Helms and the Art of Pragmatism," *Washington Post,* July 31, 1989. For another view, see Ed Yoder, "Helms Revives Eternal Dilemma of Subsidized Art," *Raleigh News and Observer,* August 2, 1989.

42. Maureen Dowd, "Unruffled Helms Basks in Eye of Arts Storm," *New York Times,* July 28, 1989; Kara Swisher, "Helms's 'Indecent' Sampler; Senator Sends Photos to Sway Conferees," *Washington Post,* August 8, 1989.

43. "More on Arts Funding," editorial, *Washington Post,* July 20, 1989.

44. Broughton interview, February 15, 2006.

45. Elizabeth Kastor, "Students on the March," *Washington Post,* September 21, 1989; Todd Allan Yasui, "A Jarring Protest Against Helms," *Washington Post,* September 18, 1989; Grace Glueck, "Whitney Sponsors an Ad Against Helms Amendment," *New York Times,* September 7, 1989.

46. "A Giant Artistic Gibe at Jesse Helms," *New York Times,* April 20, 1990; "Sounds Around Town," *New York Times,* July 13, 1990.

47. The Senate defeated Helms's attempts to restore his amendment with a "sense of the Senate" resolution, despite Helms's impassioned speech on September 28. Waving copies of the Mapplethorpe photographs, Helms described them as "garbage" and called their creator "a known homosexual who died of AIDS." Senators should not be persuaded by the major media and those who had "been so careless with the truth." Instead, he said, "Look at the pictures." Before he displayed Mapplethorpe's photographs, he called for women, pages, and some staff to leave the Senate, because of the inappropriate nature of the material, but most remained. In the end, Congress enacted legislation that prohibited the NEA from supporting "obscene" art in the future. Incorporating the Supreme Court's definition of obscenity (that obscene works lacked literary, artistic, political, or scientific merit), the new legislation created a twelve-person commission

to oversee the development of obscenity standards for NEA. Elizabeth Kastor, "Art Wars; Battling Helms; Hill Conferees Besieged in Lobbying Effort," *Washington Post,* September 8, 1989; Elizabeth Kastor, "Corcoran's Damage Control; Mending Fences with the Arts Community," *Washington Post,* September 12, 1989; William H. Honan, "Helms Amendment Is Facing a Major Test in Congress," *New York Times,* September 13, 1989; Don Phillips and Elizabeth Kastor, "House Votes to Restrict Lobbyists; Helms-Backed Curb on 'Indecent' Art Loses Key Round," *Washington Post,* September 14, 1989; "No to the Helms Amendment," *Washington Post,* September 16, 1989; William H. Honan, "Compromise Is Proposed on Helms Amendment," *New York Times,* September 28, 1989; William Hohan, "Senate Debating Helms Amendment," *New York Times,* September 29, 1989; Charles Babington, "Helms Art-Fund Limits Rejected by U.S. Senate," *Raleigh Times,* September 29, 1989; Elizabeth Kastor, "Senate Defeats Helms Move to Revive Arts Amendment," *Washington Post,* September 29, 1989.

48. Elizabeth Kastor, "Obscenity Measure Approved; Conference Panel Agrees on Diluted Helms Amendment," *Washington Post,* September 30, 1989; Helen Dewar, "Exasperated Senators Rebuff Helms; His Arts, Internee Amendments Lose," *Washington Post,* September 30, 1989; "Congress Passes Bill Curbing Art Financing," *New York Times,* October 8, 1989.

49. Elizabeth Kastor, "Congress Bars Funding for 'Obscene' Art; Senate Vote Sends Measure to Bush," *Washington Post,* October 8, 1989; "Liberals Gut Amendment to Stop Porno Funding," *Human Events,* October 14, 1989; "Helms Loses Latest Round on Arts Funding," *Human Events,* October 21, 1989.

50. Tom Wicker, "In the Nation; Art and Indecency," *New York Times,* July 28, 1989. See also Anthony Lewis, "Who Will Decide What Is Art? The Know Nothings?," *Greensboro News and Record,* June 11, 1990.

51. Clarence Page, "Helms Should Stay Out of the Arts," *Lexington Dispatch,* August 16, 1989.

52. Edwin Yoder, "Sen. Helms, Thy Middle Name Is 'Repression,'" *Winston-Salem Journal,* November 2, 1990.

53. Joseph Spear, "Columnist Rips Helms, Chides Voters," *Goldsboro News-Argus,* August 17, 1989.

54. Larry McMurtry, "Sex, Art and Jesse Helms," *Washington Post,* December 10, 1989.

55. JH to John Frohnmayer, November 7, 1989, JH MSS.

56. JH to Charles A. Bowsher, March 6, May 14, 1990; John Mashburn to JH, April 6, 1990, April 29, 1991; Bowsher to JH, May 31, 1990, JH MSS; "Mr. Frohnmayer's Fumble," editorial, *New York Times,* November 17, 1989; "White House Opposes Restrictions on Arts Grants," *New York Times,* March 22, 1990; "Whose Business?," editorial, *New York Times,* September 15, 1990.

57. Howard Reich, "NEA at the Center of a Morality Play," *Asheville Times,* June 28, 1990.

58. "NEA Panel Votes to Kill Anti-Obscenity Pledge," *Winston-Salem Journal*, August 4, 1990.

59. Kim Masters, "House Passes Compromise Arts Bill; Endowment Limits Overwhelmingly Rejected," *Washington Post*, October 12, 1990.

60. John Mashburn to JH, May 2, 1990, JH MSS.

61. JH to Closs Peace Wardlaw, May 22, 1990, JH MSS; "Senate Passes Compromise on Arts Endowment," *New York Times*, October 25, 1990; *CR*, October 24, 1990; John Monk, "Helms Loses Opening Round as Senate Debates Arts Funding," *Charlotte Observer*, October 25, 1990; Broughton interview, February 15, 2006.

62. "Senate Passes Compromise on Arts Endowment," *New York Times*, October 25, 1990; Kim Masters, "Senate Passes Arts Bill, Defeats Obscenity Curbs; Last-Minute Helms Amendment Bars Federal Funding of Works That Denigrate Religion," *Washington Post*, October 25, 1990; "Last-Minute Save for the NEA," editorial, *Washington Post*, October 27, 1990; "Congress Removes Restrictions on Federal Arts Funding," *New York Times*, October 27, 1990; Stephen Salisbury, "NEA Has Money, but Path Leading to It Could Be Tricky," *Charlotte Observer*, October 31, 1990.

63. JH to John Frohnmayer, March 26, 1990, JH MSS; "Jesse Helms on Offense," *U.S. News & World Report*, May 14, 1990.

64. "The Right Wing's Cultural Warrior," *New York Times*, July 7, 1990.

65. "Helms Loads Up for Election," editorial, *Durham Morning Herald*, August 3, 1989.

66. In 1996, a Boston magazine would out Finkelstein when it revealed that he and his partner (whom he later married) had adopted two children and lived with them in Massachusetts's North Shore. Frank Rich, "The Gay G.O.P.," *New York Times*, September 29, 1996; "GOP Consultant's Strategy: Label Opponents Liberally; D'Amato Ally Setting Theme in Senate Races," *Washington Post*, October 22, 1996.

67. Wrenn interview, September 7, 2006.

68. Wrenn interview, April 5, 2006; Rosser interview, September 7, 2006. One poll found in late May 1990 that Helms had a 35 percent unfavorable rating and a 44 percent favorable rating. Seth Effron, "Helms Softens Image in Public," *Greensboro News and Record*, July 2, 1990.

69. Steve Riley and Bill Krueger, "Hunt Says No to Senate Race," *Raleigh Times*, August 16, 1989; E. J. Dionne, Jr., "Hunt Declines to Enter Race Against Helms," *New York Times*, August 17, 1989; Thomas B. Edsall, "Hunt Won't Challenge Helms in '90; Democrats Stumbling as Strong Challengers Turn Down Senate Races," *Washington Post*, August 17, 1989.

70. Wrenn interview, April 5, 2006; Paul Taylor, "Gantt Leads Race to Challenge Helms; North Carolina Democrat Wants to Break Party Color Line in Senate," *Washington Post*, May 5, 1990; Paul Taylor, "North Carolina Runoff Comes Alive in Final Days," *Washington Post*, June 1, 1990; John Drescher, "Ads Aims

at Pair," *Charlotte Observer,* June 1, 1990; Rob Christensen, "Helms Ads Take Harder Shot at Easley," *Raleigh News and Observer,* June 1, 1990; Kevin Ellis, "Easley Says Helms Would Rather Face Gantt in November," *Morganton News Herald,* June 4, 1990.

71. Rob Christensen, "Gantt Courting Swing Vote," and Charles Babington, "Helms Plays Coy on Strategy," *Raleigh News and Observer,* June 7, 1990; Christensen, "Gantt Tale Is One of Luck and Pluck," *Raleigh News and Observer,* June 11, 1990.

72. "The Race in Black and White," *U.S. News & World Report,* July 23, 1990; Stephens interview, October 10, 2006.

73. "Great to Go with Gantt," editorial, *Raleigh News and Observer,* June 7, 1990; Jim Morrill and John Drescher, "Nation's Eyes on Gantt-Helms Match," *Charlotte Observer,* June 7, 1990; Garland L. Thompson, "Is North Carolina Ready to Elect Harvey Gantt?," *Baltimore Sun,* reprinted in *Charlotte Observer,* June 23, 1990; "AIDS Activist Urges Boycott of Helms' Allies and Tourism," *Greenville Daily Reflector,* June 10, 1990; Ruth Sheehan, "Media Lining Up for Helms-Gantt Election Stories," *Burlington Daily Times News,* June 10, 1990; Seth Effron, "Nation Looking at Helms, Gantt," *Greensboro News and Record,* June 10, 1990.

74. Robin Toner, "Unseating Helms: Rival Charts His Uphill Climb," *New York Times,* July 16, 1990; Robin Toner, "In North Carolina's Senate Race, A Divisive TV Fight over 'Values,' " *New York Times,* September 23, 1990.

75. Seth Effron, "Gantt Wins Battle, but War?," *Greensboro News and Record,* June 7, 1990; "A Convincing Win for Gantt," editorial, *Winston-Salem Journal,* June 7, 1990; Ronald Smothers, "The 1990 Elections; North Carolina Democrat Sets Strategy in Taking on Helms," *New York Times,* June 7, 1990, June 6, 1990.

76. Jane Gross, "Gantt Speaks to NOW," *Charlotte Observer,* July 1, 1990.

77. Peter Applebome, "Carolina Race Is Winning the Wallets of America," *New York Times,* October 13, 1990.

78. Matthew Davis, "Gay Activists Demonstrate at Helms' Election Dinner," *Wilmington Morning Star,* June 15, 1990.

79. Doug Clark, "Helms Loves This Kind of Parade," *High Point Enterprise,* June 26, 1990; Jon Healey, "Boycott Effort to Defeat Helms May Turn Out to Be Beer Down the Drain," *Winston-Salem Journal,* August 6, 1990. The Helms campaign subsequently filed a Federal Election Commission complaint charging that ACT UP's boycott was acting as a political action group and hence violated election law. "Helms Camp Protests Gay Boycott," *Greensboro News and Record,* August 15, 1990.

80. "Faxman! (In Full Context)," editorial, *Charlotte Observer,* September 11, 1990; Morrill interview, September 5, 2006.

81. Rob Christensen, "Slow Start by Gantt Stirs Worry," *Raleigh News and Observer,* August 2, 1990.

82. Jim Morrill, "Gantt and Helms Both Like Poll," *Charlotte Observer,* June 16, 1990.

83. Rob Christensen, "Gantt Opens Attack on Helms," *Raleigh News and Observer,*

June 17, 1990; Seth Effron, "Gantt Rallies Troops," *Greensboro News and Record,* June 17, 1990.

84. Bernie Woodall, "Gantt Dares Helms to Debate Issues," *Greensboro News and Record,* June 8, 1990; Seth Effron, "Helms Hits Airwaves in Senate Election Bid," *Greensboro News and Record,* July 3, 1990; Ruth Sheehan, "Gantt, Helms Girding Up for Senate Campaign," *Gastonia Gazette,* August 11, 1990; John Drescher, "Helms Is Difficult to Spot, Except in TV Ads," *Charlotte Observer,* August 19, 1990.

85. John Drescher and Jim Morrill, "Gantt Tries to Counter Tax Attack," *Charlotte Observer,* August 15, 1990; "Gantt Campaign Says Helms Ads Distort Record, but They Won't Say How," *Jacksonville Daily News,* August 15, 1990; Ken Otterbourg, "Gantt and Abortion-Rights Group Are in Collusion on Ads, GOP Says," *Winston-Salem Journal,* August 14, 1990; "Why Is Helms So Hot?," editorial, *Charlotte Observer,* August 15, 1990; "The Truth Stalks Helms," editorial, *Raleigh News and Observer,* August 16, 1990; Hickman interview, April 21, 2006.

86. Wrenn interview, April 5, 2006.

87. Matthew Davis, "Helms Tells Senators Abortion Rights Groups 'Invading My State,'" *Charlotte Observer,* September 12, 1990.

88. Rob Christensen, "New Ads by Helms Spur Gantt Camp into the Airwaves," *Raleigh News and Observer,* August 15, 1990; Steve Riley, "Gantt Campaign Calls Helms Ads on Taxes Distorted," *Raleigh News and Observer,* August 15, 1990; "Helms on Television" and "Helms on Radio," *Winston-Salem Journal,* August 21, 1990.

89. Rob Christensen, "Gantt Says Helms Ad on Abortion 'A Lie,' Demands Withdrawal," *Raleigh News and Observer,* September 7, 1990; Rob Christensen, "Ignore 'Whiny Woman,' Gantt Urges N.C. Voters," *Raleigh News and Observer,* September 16, 1990; Ken Otterbourg and Chris Geis, "Gantt Criticizes Helms' Commercial on Abortion," *Winston-Salem Journal,* September 19, 1990; Wrenn interview, April 5, 2006; Kathleen Hall Jamieson, *Dirty Politics: Deception, Distraction, and Democracy* (New York: Oxford University Press, 1992), pp. 94–95.

90. Bart Ritner, "Meredith's Exploits Generate Interest," *Rocky Mount Evening Telegram,* October 25, 1990.

91. James Meredith, speech in Miami, December 9, 1988; letter to members of Congress, c. 1989, JH MSS; Hal Sieber, "Helms Aide Rebukes Civil Rights Groups," *Carolina Peacemaker,* October 28, 1989; "We Can't Remain Neutral," *CR,* vol. 136, no.12, February 20, 1990; Joseph Berryhill, "Meredith Criticizes Affirmative Action," *Raleigh News and Observer,* March 27, 1990; David Jrolf, "Rights Leader's Hub Speech Laced with Controversy," *Boston Herald,* March 29, 1990; "A Historic Race Down South," *Newsweek,* July 20, 1990; "Meredith: No Mistake," editorial, *Raleigh News and Observer,* October 10, 1990; interview with Clint Fuller (by Riddick), November 30, 1991; Helms interview (Tom Joyner), tape 9; Steve Phillips interview (Tom Joyner), tape 31; DeMoss Fonseca interview, February 16, 2006; "Biographical Conversations with Jesse Helms," WUNC-TV, February 11, 2000.

92. Charles Babington, "Former Civil-Rights Leader Ranks 12th in Pay Among Helms Aides," *Raleigh News and Observer,* June 24, 1990; "Meredith Invitation Withdrawn," *Raleigh News and Observer,* August 13, 1990; Jim Morrill, "Parties Argue: Who Injected Race Issue into Campaign?," *Charlotte Observer,* August 17, 1990; Ferrel Guillory, "When Looking Ahead, Does Helms Have Vision," *Raleigh News and Observer,* October 26, 1990; "Under the Dome," *Raleigh News and Observer,* August 23, 1990; Rob Christensen, "Gantt Charges 'Racism,'" *Raleigh News and Observer,* August 25, 1990; Seth Effron, "Helms Laughs at Racism Charge," *Greensboro News & Record,* August 26, 1990.

93. "Right, Wrong and Helms," editorial, *Raleigh News and Observer,* September 8, 1990.

94. Charles Babington, "Helms Denies Claim He Dozed Off on Saudi King," *Raleigh News and Observer,* October 26, 1990; Jack Betts, "Look Out, 1996," *Charlotte Observer,* December 11, 1993.

95. John Monk, "Helms Stays Put in Washington," *Charlotte Observer,* October 19, 1990; Peter Applebome, "Pit Bull Politician," *New York Times,* October 28, 1990.

96. Edwin Yoder, "Sen. Helms, Thy Middle Name Is 'Repression,'" *Winston-Salem Journal,* November 2, 1990.

97. Jim Morrill, "'Wilder Factor' Has Sent Wrong Signals to Pollsters Before," "Poll: Gantt Leading 49%–41%," *Charlotte Observer,* October 20, 1990; Foon Rhee, "Gantt Says Momentum's on His Side," *Charlotte Observer,* October 21, 1990; Ken Otterbourg, "Gantt Raised Nearly $100,000 a Day in Early October, Report Says," *Winston-Salem Journal,* October 25, 1990; Seth Effron, "Gantt's Fund Raising Passes Helms," *Greensboro News and Record,* October 27, 1990; Rob Christensen and Steve Riley, "Helms Attacks Gantt Role in TV Deal," *Raleigh News and Observer,* October 20, 1990; "The 1992 Campaign; Helms Campaign Signs Decree on Racial Postcards," *New York Times,* February 28, 1992; Stephens interview, October 10, 2006.

98. JH, speech at Helms for Senate dinner, Rocky Mount, September 29, 1990, JH MSS.

99. John Drescher, "Helms: No Racism in Money Appeals," *Charlotte Observer,* August 26, 1990; JH, speech, c. August 25, 1990, JH MSS; John Gizzi, "Senator Helms in the Fight of His Life," *Human Events,* October 20, 1990.

100. Elizabeth Leland, "Helms Rips Gantt's Acceptance of Funds from Homosexuals," and Hunter Kome, "No Comment from Gantt," *Wilmington Morning Star,* October 23, 1990.

101. "Ad Attacks Ties to Gays," *Winston-Salem Journal,* October 25, 1990; full-page newspaper ad, *Roanoke Rapids Herald,* October 25, 1990; "Word for Word / Jesse Helms; The North Carolinian Has Enemies, but No One Calls Him Vague," *New York Times,* November 27, 1994.

102. JH, speech at the American Association of Christian Schools, February 21, 1989, JH MSS.

103. Hawke interview (by Mosnier), December 3, 1996.

104. John Monk, "Christian Group's Role in Helms Campaign Questioned," *Charlotte Observer,* June 7, 1994; Stephens interview, October 10, 2006.

105. Seth Effron, "Helms Radio Ad Angers Gantt," *Greensboro News and Record,* October 26, 1990.

106. Rob Christensen and Steve Riley, "Helms Attacks Gantt Role in TV Deal," *Raleigh News and Observer,* October 20, 1990; "Helms Ad: Gantt Got Quick Buck," *Winston-Salem Journal,* October 30, 1990. The Helms campaign also ran radio ads criticizing Gantt for his involvement in Floyd McKissick's Soul City project. Rob Christensen, "Gantt Stops Short of Charging Racism," *Raleigh News and Observer,* November 1, 1990.

107. F. Alan Boyce, "Helms Again Charges Gantt Injected Race into Campaign," *Durham Herald,* October 31, 1990; Rob Christensen, "Senator Assails Civil Rights Bill," *Raleigh News and Observer,* October 31, 1990; Steve Riley, "Gantt, Helms Keep Attacks at a Fast Boil," *Raleigh News and Observer,* November 1, 1990; Ken Otterbourg, "Helms Questions Gantt's Honesty in Deals," *Winston-Salem Journal,* November 1, 1990; Charles Babington, "Racial Themes Arise in Senate Campaign," *Raleigh News and Observer,* November 1, 1990.

108. Peter Applebome, "The 1990 Campaign; Subtly and Not, Race Bubbles Up as Issue in North Carolina Contest," *New York Times,* November 2, 1990.

109. Peter Applebome, "Racial Politics in South's Contests: Hot Wind of Hate or a Last Gasp?," *New York Times,* November 5, 1990.

110. Jon Healey, "Helms' Ad Is Overtly Racial, Some Say," *Winston-Salem Journal,* November 1, 1990; Jamieson, *Dirty Politics,* pp. 96–99.

111. Rob Christensen, "How a Latino Morehead Scholar Saved Helms' Campaign," *Raleigh News and Observer,* July 24, 1995; Wrenn interview, April 5, 2006; Stephens interview, October 10, 2006.

112. Morrill interview, September 5, 2006.

113. Seth Effron, "Gantt, Helms View Civil Rights Veto Differently," *Greensboro News and Record,* October 24, 1990; Wrenn interview, April 5, 2006; Ellis interview, April 4, 2006; "The Race Card," *New Republic,* December 17, 1990.

114. "U.S. Settles N. Carolina Vote Charge," *Washington Post,* February 27, 1992; Jane Ruffin and Bill Krueger, "Helms, Aides Deny Voter Intimidation Suit Settled to Avoid Costly Court Fight," *Raleigh News and Observer,* February 28, 1992; John Monk, "Helms Says He Didn't Know About Voter Postcards," *Charlotte Observer,* February 28, 1992; "What the Files Don't Say ...," editorial, *Winston-Salem Journal,* March 6, 1992; "Complaint for Declaratory Relief," and "Consent Decree," February 26, 27, 1992, *US v. North Carolina Republican Party et al.,* case # 92–161-cv-5, accession # 021 98 0279, box 20, National Archives Records Center, Atlanta.

115. Rob Urban, "GOP Mailing Under Fresh Fire," *Charlotte Observer,* November 2, 1990; Thomas B. Edsall, "Helms Makes Race an Issue; Carolina GOP Also Pushes 'Ballot Security,'" *Washington Post,* November 1, 1990; Michael Isikoff, "Justice Dept. Investigates GOP Mailing to Voters," *Washington Post,* November

6, 1990; Thomas B. Edsall, "Bush Takes No Stand on Ballot Plan; Program Targeted N.C. Black Voters," *Washington Post,* November 9, 1990; "The 1992 Campaign; Helms Campaign Signs Decree on Racial Postcards," *New York Times,* February 28, 1992; "NC Republicans Settle Complaint," *Congressional Quarterly Weekly Report,* February 29, 1992; Jane Ruffin and Bill Krueger, "Helms, Aides Deny Voter Intimidation Suit Settled to Avoid Costly Court Fight," *Raleigh News and Observer,* February 28, 1992.

116. Wrenn interview, September 7, 2006; Hawke interview (by Mosnier), December 3, 1996; Stephens interview, October 12, 2006; "Complaint for Declaratory Relief," and "Consent Decree," *US v. North Carolina Republican Party et al.*

117. Hawke interview (by Mosnier), December 3, 1996.

118. Peter Applebome, "The 1990 Elections: Congress—North Carolina; Helms, Basking in Victory, Taunts 'Ultra-Liberal' Foes," *New York Times,* November 7, 1990; Peter Applebome, "The 1990 Elections: North Carolina; Helms Kindled Anger in Campaign, and May Have Set Tone for Others," *New York Times,* November 8, 1990; "The Race Card," *New Republic,* December 17, 1990; JH, victory speech, November 6, 1990, JH MSS.

119. Rob Christensen, "Helms, Gantt Spending Near-Record $24.7 Million," *Raleigh News and Observer,* February 6, 1991.

11. THE CONSERVATIVE LION IN HIS WINTER

1. Rob Christensen, "Helms' Wife in Raleigh Hospital," *Raleigh News and Observer,* August 28, 1991; John Monk, "Voting Record Slips," *Charlotte Observer,* January 12, 1992.

2. Rob Christensen, "Helms Being Treated for Prostate Cancer, Senator, Doctor Predicting Full Recovery," *Raleigh News and Observer,* September 24, 1991; "Senator Helms Says Doctors Are Treating Him for Cancer," *New York Times,* September 24, 1991; John Monk and David Perlmutt, "Sen. Helms Has Prostate Cancer, but Complete Recovery Predicted," *Charlotte Observer,* Setember 24, 1991.

3. John Monk, "Bone Disease Hasn't Taken Helms' Sense of Humor," *Charlotte Observer,* July 25, 1991; Jane Ruffin, "Ill Helms Asked to Lend a Hand," *Raleigh News and Observer,* July 26, 1991; "Helms Gets Clean Bill of Health," *Raleigh News and Observer,* November 23, 1991; John Monk, " 'Best I've Felt in Years,' Helms Says, Senator Optimistic After Treatment," *Charlotte Observer,* November 24, 1991; Broughton interview, February 15, 2006; Coffer interview, September 7, 2006.

4. Coffer interview, July 14, 2005; House interview (by St. John), July 7, 1992.

5. Coffer interview, July 14, 2005.

6. Jim Morrill, "Helms Set for Bypass Surgery Senate Return Likely 3 to 6 Weeks Later," *Charlotte Observer,* May 8, 1992; John Monk, "Helms Confident on Surgery," *Charlotte Observer,* May 14, 1992; Rachele Kanigel, "Helms Upbeat

About Surgery, Senator Typical of Heart Patients," *Raleigh News and Observer,* May 30, 1992; Monk interview, September 5, 2006; "Biographical Conversations with Jesse Helms," WUNC-TV, February 11, 2000.

7. Coffer interview, July 14, 2005.

8. Kim Masters, "Big Bird Meets the Right Wing; Senate Critics Take Aim at Public TV," *Washington Post,* March 4, 1992; Charles Trueheart, "Senate Backs Big Bird; Conservative Effort to Freeze CPB Funds Is Overturned," *Washington Post,* June 4, 1992; John Monk and Greg Trevor, "Sen. Helms Resting After Quadruple Heart Bypass," *Charlotte Observer,* June 4, 1992; "Helms Doing Well, Doctor Says; Concern, Prayers Touch Family," *Raleigh News and Observer,* June 5, 1992; John Conway, "Helms 'Resting' After His Surgery," *Greensboro News and Record,* June 5, 1992.

9. Rachele Kanigel and Bill Krueger, "Helms Put on Respirator After His Breathing Stops, Longer Hospital Stay Expected After Setback," *Raleigh News and Observer,* June 8, 1992; Coffer interview, September 7, 2006.

10. Rachele Kanigel, "Sen. Helms off Respirator After Frightening Setback," *Raleigh News and Observer,* June 9, 1992.

11. "Helms Walking and in Good Shape at Rex," *Raleigh News and Observer,* June 12, 1992; Rachele Kanigel, "Helms Leaves Intensive Care, Progress Good," *Raleigh News and Observer,* June 13, 1992; Rachele Kanigel, "Helms Leaves Hospital After Heart Surgery," *Raleigh News and Observer,* June 18, 1992.

12. Kim R. Kenneson, "Helms Dismisses Reports He's Planning to Retire from Senate," *Raleigh News and Observer,* July 27, 1992; John Monk, "Washington Feels a Void with Helms Hospitalized," *Charlotte Observer,* June 10, 1992; John Monk, "Rumors That Helms Will Resign Denied," *Charlotte Observer,* December 20, 1992; John Monk, "Helms, Democrats Spar over Long Hours Despite Doctor's Orders, Republican Said He'd Stay Up Late to Question Nominees," *Charlotte Observer,* January 17, 1993.

13. Betts interview, May 31, 2006; Coffer interview, September 7, 2006. For another variation of the pork barbecue/pig valve joke, see Jim Morrill, "Helms: Less Money, More Openness in '96," *Charlotte Observer,* May 21, 1995.

14. Stephen Hoar, "Congressional Club Sheds Name but Keeps Identity," *Raleigh News and Observer,* February 6, 1994.

15. Rob Christensen, "Mail-Driven Money Machine Produces Millions for Helms," *Raleigh News and Observer,* April 28, 1991; Stephens interview, October 10, 2006.

16. Stephens interviews, June 6, October 10, 2006; Wrenn interview, September 7, 2006; Wilson interview, June 5, 2006; Fetzer interview, June 20, 2006.

17. Morrill interview, September 5, 2006.

18. John Monk and Jim Morrill, "Helms, Faircloth Split from Wrenn Camp," *Charlotte Observer,* October 2, 1994; Ned Cline, "Jesse Helms' Split with Conservative Club Is More Personal than Political," *Greensboro News and Record,* October 9, 1994; Stephens interview, June 6, 2006; Wrenn interviews, April 5,

September 7, 2006; Betts interview, May 31, 2006; Wilson interview, June 5, 2006.

19. John Monk, "IRS Gives Deadline to Fund-Raising Group Once Linked to Helms," *Charlotte Observer,* September 7, 1994; John Monk and Jim Morrill, Staff Writers, "Rift in Helms Network May Rattle N.C. Politics; Faircloth Also Breaks Off with Wrenn," *Charlotte Observer,* October 2, 1994; Rosser interview, September 7, 2006. PEM Management was named for Wrenn's wife, Page, and his daughter, Emily.

20. Wrenn interview, September 7, 2006; Jacqueline Bueno, "Conservative PAC Is Struggling to Survive After Rift with Helms," *Wall Street Journal,* May 17, 1995.

21. Stephens interview, June 6, 2006; Bob Rosser interview, September 7, 2006.

22. Wrenn interview, September 7, 2006.

23. Scott Wilson interview, June 5, 2006; Fetzer interview, June 20, 2006.

24. Wrenn interviews, April 5, 2006, September 7, 2006; Carter Wrenn, press release, April 19, 1995, JH MSS; Ellis interview, April 4, 2006; Ellis interview (by Joyner); Lorraine Ahearn, "Helms-PAC Split No Shock," *Greensboro News and Record,* August 7, 1994; Rob Christensen, "The Lion in Winter: The North Carolina Senator Has Just Come Through His Toughest Period. But Helms Shows Signs of Once Again Becoming the Old Jesse the Public Loves—Or Loves to Hate," *Raleigh News and Observer,* November 21, 1993; Ned Cline, "Jesse Helms' Split with Conservative Club Is More Personal than Political," *Greensboro News and Record,* October 9, 1994.

25. Bill Krueger, "Faircloth Seeking New Home in GOP," *Raleigh News and Observer,* April 21, 1992; interview with Fuller (by Riddick), November 20, 1991; Faircloth interview, December 14, 2006.

26. Ellis interview, April 4, 2006; Wrenn interview, April 5, 2006; Rob Christensen, "Faircloth Joins GOP, Scouts Senate Race; Helms Organization Appears to Back Him," *Raleigh News and Observer,* February 22, 1991; Faircloth interview, December 14, 2006.

27. Wrenn interview, April 5, 2006; Rob Christensen, "Faircloth Announces Bid for Sanford's Senate Seat," *Raleigh News and Observer,* April 19, 1991.

28. Jim Morrill, "Congressional Club Gets Early Start for Faircloth," *Charlotte Observer,* May 5, 1991; Rob Christensen, "Senate Race Ads Begin," *Raleigh News and Observer,* August 13, 1991.

29. In April 1992, about a month before the primary, Myrick charged that she was not the club's preferred candidate because, unlike Faircloth, she did not have $1 million of her own money to spend. Wrenn responded by claiming that Myrick's hostility dated to the 1990 campaign, when the club turned down a proposal from her consulting firm, Myrick Advertising, Marketing & Public Relations, to work against Harvey Gantt in exchange for $50,000. "Her anger with us goes back to then," Wrenn told a reporter; her "ill will" had persisted. Bill Krueger, "Helms Aide Brushes Off Myrick Attack," *Raleigh News and Observer,* April 11, 1992.

30. John Drescher, "Sen. Helms Asserts Primary Neutrality," *Charlotte Observer,* December 5, 1991. Myrick later distanced herself from Helms. Jim Morrill, "Myrick Points to Differences with Helms," *Charlotte Observer,* January 10, 1992.

31. Rob Christensen, "Faircloth Remains a Mystery," *Raleigh News and Observer,* March 22, 1993. This was "totally about Carter Wrenn," according to Faircloth. Faircloth interview, December 14, 2006.

32. Bill Krueger, "Faircloth Provides GOP Cheer on Otherwise Dismal Evening," *Raleigh News and Observer,* November 4, 1992.

33. Donna Seese, "Board Fires Priest Who Founded Hale High School," *Raleigh News and Observer,* March 30, 1994; Donna Seese, "Hale's Ouster Followed Other School Firings," *Raleigh News and Observer,* March 31, 1994, Wrenn interviews, April 5, September 7, 2006.

34. Ellis interview, April 4, 2006; Ellis interview (by Joyner).

35. Wrenn interview, September 7, 2006.

36. For the FEC case and its relationship to the split with the Congressional Club, see FEC to Elizabeth Smith, April 7, 1994; FEC to Margaret Currin, June 24, 1994; Carter Wrenn to Darryl Nirenberg, May 10, June 14, 1994; Wrenn to Margaret Currin, July 7, 1994; Wrenn to JH and Jack Bailey, August 2, 1994; Thomas A. Farr to Nirenberg, June 7, 1994; Farr, memo to file, June 6, 1994; Farr to JH, June 14, 1994; Nirenberg, notes of conversation with Farr, June 9, 1994; Nirenberg to JH, June 8, 10, 1994; JH to Elizabeth Smith, June 17, July 1, 1994; Margaret Currin to Anne A. Weissenborn, July 5, August 1, 1994, all in JH MSS. On Wrenn's attitude toward the split, see Nirenberg, notes of conversation with Wrenn, c. July 26, 1994, JH MSS.

37. John Monk, "Wrenn Says Net Worth $152,532, Longtime Helms Fund-Raiser Denies Senator's Suggestion He's Profited from Connection," *Charlotte Observer,* October 5, 1994; Jacqueline Bueno, "Conservative PAC Is Struggling to Survive After Rift with Helms," *Wall Street Journal,* May 17, 1995.

38. Nirenberg to JH, April 25, 1995, Margaret Currin to FEC, April 26, 1995; James Rosen, "FEC Rules Against Former Helms Adviser," *Raleigh News and Observer,* April 28, 1995; Samuel T. Currin to Joe Knott, April 28, 1995, FEC advisory opinion, April 27, 1995, JH MSS.

39. Lorraine Ahearn, "Helms-PAC Split No Shock," *Greensboro News and Record,* August 7, 1994; David Droschak, "Helms Divorces Fund-Raising Committee," *Hickory Record,* August 6, 1994; Bill Krueger, "Helms Breaks 20-Year Connection with Congressional Club," *Raleigh News and Observer,* August 6, 1994; Bob Harris to JH, August 19, 1994; JH to Harris, August 25, 1994, JH MSS.

40. Christensen interview, April 4, 2006; Rosser interview, September 7, 2006; Jack Betts, "Successful Partners Call It Quits; Sen. Helms Splits with His Longtime Political Allies Once Called the Congressional Club," *Charlotte Observer,* August 13, 1994.

41. Jerry Shinn, "A Political Marriage on the Rocks," *Charlotte Observer,* October 7, 1994.

42. Stephens interview, October 10, 2006.

43. Barnes interview, October 10, 2006.

44. "Interim Report on POW/MIA's," *CR,* October 27, 1990; Monika Jensen-Stevenson and William Stevenson, "What Is the Military Hiding? A Hill Report Asks Hard Questions," *Washington Post,* October 28, 1990; "Slow-Fading Hope," *Economist,* November 24, 1990; "Helms Says POW Issue Haunts Him, Prompted Report," *Raleigh News and Observer,* October 29, 1990; "Jesse's World," *Newsweek,* December 5, 1994. See also "Mock Burial of MIA's," *CR,* October 5, 1990; "Temporary Select Committee on POW," *CR,* August 2, 1991.

45. Thomas W. Lippman, "Senate Panel Finds 'No Compelling Evidence' of POWs in Indochina," *Washington Post,* January 14, 1993.

46. "POW Group Threatens to Promote Helms' Defeat," *Charlotte Observer,* February 6, 1995.

47. Berry interview, June 6, 2006.

48. Charles Babington, "Va. Police File Assault Warrant Against Ex-Aide for Helms, East," *Raleigh News and Observer,* April 1, 1989; Bill Arthur, "Ex-Senate Aide Charged with Attempted Sodomy," *Charlotte Observer,* April 1, 1989; John F. Harris, "Hill Aide Sought in Sex Crimes; Police in Arlington Expect Surrender," *Washington Post,* April 1, 1989; Dana Priest, "Assault by Ex-Senate Aide Left Woman with Flashbacks of Fear," *Washington Post,* July 24, 1989; Rob Christensen, "Faircloth Remains a Mystery," *Raleigh News and Observer,* March 22, 1993; John Monk, "Jesse's Secret Weapon," *Washingtonian,* February 1994; Boney interview, June 1, 2006.

49. Berry interview, June 6, 2006.

50. Rob Christensen and Ferrel Guillory, "Longtime Helms Aide, 6 Others Fired by Senator," *Raleigh News and Observer,* January 8, 1992; "Helms Shakes Up Foreign Affairs Panel," *Human Events,* January 18, 1992; Charles Babington, "Helms Makes Familiar Cost-Cutting Call," *Raleigh News and Observer,* March 3, 1991; "Helms Sweeps Through Panel, Fires Nine GOP Staff Aides," *Congressional Quarterly Weekly Report,* January 11, 1992; Rob Christensen, "Jesse & Bud: Monroe Boys Still Travel Conservative Road," *Raleigh News and Observer,* March 13, 1995; Boney interview, June 1, 2006.

51. Rob Christensen and Ferrel Guillory, "Longtime Helms Aide, 6 Others Fired by Senator," *Raleigh News and Observer,* January 8, 1992; "Panel's Top G.O.P. Staff Is Dismissed by Helms," *New York Times,* January 8, 1992; "Helms Sweeps Through Panel, Fires Nine GOP Staff Aides", *Congressional Quarterly Weekly Report,* January 11, 1992; Helen Dewar, "Sen. Helms Purges 'Combative' Staff from Committee," *Washington Post,* January 8, 1992; Michael Ross, "Helms Fires 11 from Panel's GOP Staff, Policy Divisions Had Surfaced to Upset Foreign Relations Colleagues," *Charlotte Observer,* January 8, 1992; Craig Winneker, "Helms Fires Nine; Veteran Foreign Relations Aides Purged," *Roll Call,* January 9, 1992; John Monk, "Longtime Ally Guided Helms' Staff Purge,"

Charlotte Observer, January 20, 1992; Rob Christensen, "Did the Purge Dull the Foreign Policy Staff's Ideological Edge?," *Raleigh News and Observer,* November 21, 1993; interview with Garrett Grigsby, April 20, 2006; Monk interview, September 5, 2006; Nance interview, August 18, 1992.

52. Taft Wireback, "Helms Aide Stunned by the Firings but Still Admires the Boss," *Greensboro News and Record,* January 9, 1992; Jon Healey, "Helms Fires Staff Members," *Winston-Salem Journal,* January 8, 1992; "Inside the Beltway," *Washington Times,* January 10, 1992; "Jesse Helms," *U.S. News & World Report,* January 20, 1992; Rob Christensen, "The Lion in Winter: The North Carolina Senator Has Just Come Through His Toughest Period. But Helms Shows Signs of Once Again Becoming the Old Jesse the Public Loves—Or Loves to Hate," *Raleigh News and Observer,* November 21, 1993; Rob Christensen, "Did the Purge Dull the Foreign Policy Staff's Ideological Edge?," *Raleigh News and Observer,* November 21, 1993; John Monk, "Conservatives Replacing Fired Staff, Helms Says," *Charlotte Observer,* January 10, 1992; John Monk, "Longtime Ally Guided Helms' Staff Purge," *Charlotte Observer,* January 20, 1992; Christensen interview, April 4, 2006.

53. Martha Quillin, "Clint Fuller, Ex-Aide to Helms," *Raleigh News and Observer,* February 8, 1993; interview with Fuller (by Riddick), November 30, 1991.

54. John Monk, "Voting Record Slips," *Charlotte Observer,* January 12, 1992; John Monk, "Helms Shrugs at Challenges, Outlines Goals," *Charlotte Observer,* February 16, 1992; Coffer interviews, July 14, 2005, September 7, 2006; interview with Fuller (by Riddick), November 30, 1991.

55. Coffer interview, September 7, 2006.

56. Rob Christensen, "The Lion in Winter: The North Carolina Senator Has Just Come Through His Toughest Period," *Raleigh News and Observer,* November 21, 1993; Jack Betts, "Look Out, 1996," *Charlotte Observer,* December 11, 1993; Nirenberg interview, June 7, 2006.

57. Much of Keating's success lay in cultivating political support for his attempt to influence regulators. In April 1989, federal regulators seized Keating's S&L, and its collapse eventually cost taxpayers $2 billion, while Keating was charged with fraud. By February 1991, the committee's investigation had concluded that Senators John Glenn of Ohio and John McCain of Arizona exercised poor judgment and that Senators Dennis DeConcini of Arizona and Donald Reigle of Michigan had engaged in activities that "gave the appearance of being improper." The case focused especially on Alan Cranston of California, who had received $1 million in campaign contributions from Keating. In a brief, twelve-page summary, the committee found "substantial credible evidence" that he had "engaged in an impermissible pattern of conduct in which fund-raising and official activities were substantially linked" in his relationship with Keating. After a political action committee controlled by Cranston made a contribution to Harvey Gantt's campaign in 1990, Helms had called the California senator "the leading water carrier in Congress for that S.&L. kingpin Charles Keating."

Cranston's lawyers attempted unsuccessfully to have Helms removed from the Senate Ethics Committee; Helms remained Cranston's most dogged pursuer. But the release of the full Ethics Committee report and a decision about what sanctions should be applied to Cranston were delayed by partisan differences, with Democrats on the committee reluctant to act against Cranston.

58. "Offering No Apologies, Cranston Faces Judges," *New York Times,* November 17, 1990; Helen Dewar, "Sanctions Vote Seen in Keating Case; Lott: Panel to Act Against 1 or More," *Washington Post,* January 9, 1991; Helen Dewar, "Panel Finds 'Credible Evidence' Cranston Violated Ethics Rules; No Further Action Sought Against 4 Other Senators in Keating Case," *Washington Post,* February 28, 1991; Helen Dewar, "Partisan Divisions Reemerge on Ethics Panel over Cranston Conduct Case," *Washington Post,* July 23, 1991; "Cranston Censure Urged by Counsel," *New York Times,* August 5, 1991; Charles R. Babcock, "Helms Report Urges Censure of Cranston in 'Keating 5' Case," *Washington Post,* August 5, 1991; Helen Dewar, "Ethics Panel Chiefs Ask Probe of Report Release; Helms Assailed for Disclosure on 'Keating 5,'" *Washington Post,* August 6, 1991; "Helms Lobs Hot-Potato Report into Cranston Deliberations," *Congressional Quarterly Weekly Report,* August 10, 1991; "Helms Fires Back at Ethics Panel," *Human Events,* August 17, 1991; "Helms Report Exposes Cranston's Bold Misdeeds," *Human Events,* August 24, 1991; Helen Dewar, "Cranston Accepts Reprimand; 'Keating 5' Senator Angers Colleagues by Denying Misconduct," *Washington Post,* November 21, 1991; "As Keating Case Comes to a Close, Confusion over Ethics Rules Remains," *New York Times,* November 24, 1991.

59. Steven Thomma, "Senate Hears Plea, Rebuffs Helms on Confederate Symbol," *Charlotte Observer,* July 23, 1993; Robert Naylor, Jr., "Senate Rejects Helms Amendment over Confederate Symbol," *Charlotte Observer,* July 23, 1993; "Daughter of Slavery Hushes Senate," *New York Times,* July 23, 1993; Jonathan Yardley, "Rebels Without a Clue," *Washington Post,* July 26, 1993.

60. "Ms. Moseley Braun's Majestic Moment," editorial, *New York Times,* July 24, 1993; Ferrel Guillory, "A Symbol of Change?," *Raleigh News and Observer,* July 24, 1993; Helen Dewar, "Senate Bows to Braun on Symbol of Confederacy," *Washington Post,* July 23, 1993.

61. Ferrel Guillory, "A Symbol of Change?," *Raleigh News and Observer,* July 24, 1993.

62. John Monk, "Elevator 'Dixie' Stirs Talk Helms Intones Song to Make Colleague Cry, but Moseley-Braun Says His Singing Anything Could Make Her Weep," *Charlotte Observer,* August 6, 1993; "Senator's Barb Stings Tuneful Helms," *Greensboro News and Record,* August 6, 1993; John Monk, "In Elevator, Helms Wasn't Singing Her Song," *Charlotte Observer,* August 8, 1993; "Senate Must Censure Helms for Harassment," Mark Gorman to the editor, *New York Times,* August 12, 1993; Roxanne Roberts, "In a League of Her Own; Sen. Moseley-Braun Is Conquering Hero at Dinner," *Washington Post,* August 5,

1993; Broughton interview, February 15, 2006. "Any gentlemanly white person would never do that," said South Carolina congressman James Clyburn, who is black. "Most gentlemanly white people would not intentionally antagonize or harass a woman, be she black or white, and what he was doing was harassing that woman." "Helms Serenades Moseley-Braun with 'Dixie,'" *Knight Ridder/Tribune News Service*, August 5, 1993; John Monk, "Who's Laughing Now? Long Written Off as a Noisy Blowhard, Jesse Helms Means to Be a Hard-Hitting Player," *Washingtonian*, November 1, 1995.

63. "Helms Attack Given Silent Treatment; Sen. Moseley-Braun Won't Bite on Aspersions," *Charlotte Observer*, August 24, 1993.

64. *CR*, July 22, 1993; "Raw Racism Gets a Black Eye in the Senate," *National Catholic Reporter*, August 13, 1993.

65. "In the Nation; Riding the Quota Wave," editorial, *New York Times*, July 4, 1991; R. A. Zaldivar and Alexis Moore, "Senate Passes Rights Bill in Hard-Won Compromise," *Charlotte Observer*, October 31, 1991.

66. John Monk, "Helms to Propose Cuts in Affirmative Action," *Charlotte Observer*, March 3, 1995; "Helms Attacks Hiring Rules," *Raleigh News and Observer*, March 4, 1995.

67. "Smithsonian Project: Helms Blocks Plans for Black Museum," *Raleigh News and Observer*, December 2, 1993; Lorraine Ahearn, "Squashed Two Projects; Minorities Question Helms' Recent Votes," *Greensboro News & Record*, October 11, 1994; Jacqueline Trescott, "Museum Bill Dies in Senate; Helms Opposed Afro-American Facility," *Washington Post*, October 8, 1994; John Monk, "Helms Kills African American Museum," *Charlotte Observer*, October 9, 1994.

68. Monk interview, September 5, 2006.

69. Barry Saunders, "Uh, Senator, Larry's 'Little Lady Friend' Has Another Name," *Raleigh News and Observer*, November 21, 1994.

70. John Monk, "Helms Decries Caller's Bad Word," *Charlotte Observer*, September 13, 1995; John Monk, "Should Helms Have Responded to Alabama Caller's Racial Slur?," *Charlotte Observer*, September 14, 1995; John Monk, "Infamous Call Continuing to Haunt Helms," *Charlotte Observer*, September 17, 1995; "Some of Their Best Friends," *Time*, September 25, 1995; David Menconi, "Randy Newman's Latest Devilry," *Raleigh News and Observer*, September 29, 1995; Broughton interview, October 25, 2006.

71. Fuller interview, November 20, 1991.

72. Greg Ring, "Controversial Aide Leaves Helms' Staff," *Charlotte Observer*, January 27, 1991; Charles Babington, "Meredith 'Has Departed' from Helms' Staff," *Raleigh News and Observer*, January 26, 1991; JH interview (Tom Joyner), tape 9; Bill Krueger, "Meredith on New Political Tack: Helms' Former Aide Endorses Former Klan Leader in Louisiana," *Raleigh News and Observer*, October 12, 1991.

73. JH, introductory remarks about amendment, JH MSS; "Department of the Interior," *CR*, vol. 137, no.130, September 19, 1991; Gwen Ifill, "Senate Votes to

Limit Arts Grants," *New York Times,* September 20, 1991; Eric Pianin, "Helms Wins Senate Vote to Restrict NEA Funds; Action Targets 'Offensive' Materials," *Washington Post,* September 20, 1991.

74. "House Backs Restrictions on Arts Grants," *New York Times,* October 17, 1991; Kim Masters, "Congress's Shaky Arts Fund Bargain," *Washington Post,* October 17, 1991; Matt Yancey, "House Backs Helms on NEA Money Patently Offensive Works Are Target," *Charlotte Observer,* October 17, 1991; "Interior Conference Makes a Deal: 'Corn for Porn,'" *Congressional Quarterly Weekly Report,* October 19, 1991; Kim Masters, "'Corn for Porn' Victory; NEA Funds Okayed Without Helms Proposal," *Washington Post,* October 25, 1991; "Conference Deal on Interior Wins House Acceptance," *Congressional Quarterly Weekly Report,* October 26, 1991; "Lawmakers Reject Helms' Obscenity Restrictions on Art," *Raleigh News and Observer,* November 1, 1991.

75. "Corn, Porn and the N.E.A.," editorial, *New York Times,* October 27, 1991.

76. John Monk, "Sex Study Debate Rancorous; U.S. Senate Holds Money Until Review," *Charlotte Observer,* April 3, 1992; "Sex, American Style," editorial, *New York Times,* October 8, 1994.

77. Angela Wright, "Helms' Home Scene of Protest by Aids Group," *Charlotte Observer,* September 6, 1991; *Washington Post,* September 6, 1991; John Monk, "Who's Laughing Now?," *Washingtonian,* November 1, 1995.

78. John Monk, "Helms: Punish Groups That Push for Gay Scouts," *Charlotte Observer,* September 17, 1992; "Department of Defense," *CR,* September 22, 1992.

79. Linda Greenhouse, "Senate, 96–3, Easily Affirms Judge Ginsburg as a Justice," *New York Times,* August 4, 1993.

80. John Monk, "Man's Transfer After Remark on Gays Angers Helms," *Charlotte Observer,* July 17, 1994; "Senate Passes Agriculture Bill After Detour into Gay Rights," *Congressional Quarterly Weekly Report,* July 23, 1994; John Monk, "Helms Keeps Trying to Get Usda Official Re-Instated," *Charlotte Observer,* July 24, 1994; "Showdown on Gay Agenda at USDA," *Human Events,* August 5, 1994.

81. "USDA Agrees to Reinstate," *CR,* October 4, 1994; John Monk, "Helms Gives a Lesson in the Rules," *Charlotte Observer,* October 16, 1994.

82. Edward Kennedy then introduced another amendment, which, like Dale Bumpers's amendment regarding the USDA, introduced more general language banning the use of federal funds that promoted any form of sexual activity. Katharine Q. Seelye, "Senate Backs Cuts for Schools That Endorse Homosexuality," *New York Times,* August 2, 1994; "Sex, Education and the Senate," editorial, *Washington Post,* August 3, 1994; "A 'Flogging' by Helms," editorial, *Raleigh News and Observer,* August 6, 1994. As early as 1992, Helms had raised the issue of federally supported programs that seemed to promote homosexuality. "Higher Education Amendments of 1991," *CR,* February 20, 1992.

83. Jim Abrams, "Helms Leads Call for Cuts over Group," *Charlotte Observer,* Janu-

ary 27, 1994; John Monk, "Gays Say Helms Is Exploiting a Dead Issue," *Charlotte Observer*, January 30, 1994; "State Department Resorts to Misleading Comment," *CR*, February 1, 1994; Berry interview, June 6, 2006.

84. John Monk, "Helms Might Fight Clinton on Allowing Gays in Military," *Charlotte Observer*, November 15, 1992; John Monk, "Helms Denies He Made Deal on Gays in Military," *Charlotte Observer*, January 24, 1993.

85. Steven A. Holmes, "Helms Seeks Law to Restrict Gay Groups in Government," *New York Times*, February 3, 1995.

86. "A 'Flogging' by Helms," editorial, *Raleigh News and Observer*, August 6, 1994.

87. Gary Bauer to Donald Riegle, April 27, 1993; Family Research Council, "Forestry Report Reveals HUD Nominee Robert Achtenberg's Radical Agenda," c. April 1993, JH MSS; "Helms on Nominee: 'She's a Damn Lesbian,'" *Washington Post*, May 7, 1993; "Housing Nominee Is Attacked," *New York Times*, May 21, 1993; "Lesbian Confirmed in Housing Position with Votes to Spare," *New York Times*, May 25, 1993; "Jesse Helms, Loser," *Progressive*, July 1993; "Mean Lesbians and Fever Swamps," *Humanist*, August 1993.

88. Helen Dewar, "Impasse on Clinton Nominees Eases; 8 Confirmed After Mitchell Chides Senators for Delaying Tactics," *Washington Post*, May 19, 1983; Helen Dewar, "Achtenberg Floor Debate Intensifies; Vote on Nomination Planned for Monday," *Washington Post*, May 21, 1983; "Nomination of Roberta Achtenberg," *CR*, May 20, 1993; John Monk, "Helms Denounces Nominee; Backers of Lesbian Official Rip Attack," *Charlotte Observer*, May 20, 1993; "That Famous Parade in San Francisco," *CR*, May 24, 1993; Kristin Huckshorn, "Lesbian Nominee Gets Post," *Charlotte Observer*, May 25, 1993; David W. Dunlap, "Nomination of Gay Man Is Dropped," *New York Times*, January 1, 1995. Later, Helms described Achtenberg as a "boastful lesbian who was Parade Marshal for a disgusting homosexual parade through the streets of San Francisco." JH, commencement address at Liberty University, May 14, 1994, JH MSS. Notably, when Republicans captured control of Congress in 1994, the White House withdrew its nomination of James Hormel, a gay leader from San Francisco, as ambassador to Fiji, for fear of Helms's opposition.

89. Rob Christensen, "Helms Keeps His Fists Flying from the Right," *Raleigh News and Observer*, August 4, 1991.

90. Elizabeth Siefert to JH, May 2, 1995; "Talking Points on Ryan White," c. May 1995, JH MSS.

91. John Monk, "Helms Bottles Up Money for Aids Treatment," *Charlotte Observer*, May 31, 1995; "Helms' AIDS Game," editorial, *Raleigh News and Observer*, June 2, 1995; Katharine Q. Seelye, "Helms Puts the Brakes to a Bill Financing AIDS Treatment," *New York Times*, July 5, 1995; John Monk, "Helms Stirs Controversy with Remarks About Aids," *Charlotte Observer*, July 7, 1995; David W. Dunlap, "Different Faces of AIDS Are Conjured Up by Politicians," *New York Times*, July 8, 1995. Helms later said that Ryan White was exploited by gay activists. He

had been infected, Helms asserted, by gay people who had "knowingly" given infected blood. "Biographical Conversations with Jesse Helms," WUNC-TV broadcast, February 11, 2000.

92. John Monk, "Helms Stands by Remarks but Says Stance on AIDS Bill Misinterpreted," *Charlotte Observer,* July 12, 1995.

93. John Monk, "Backers Not Bothered by Helms' Blunt Talk—Or His Foes' Reaction," *Charlotte Observer,* July 9, 1995.

94. Gary L. Bauer to JH, July 27, 1995, JH MSS: "Clinton Calls for Tolerance; Top GOP Official Distances Self from Helms' AIDS Comment," *Raleigh News and Observer,* July 7, 1995.

95. "Congressional Roundup; Vote on AIDS Act," *New York Times,* July 28, 1995; James Rosen, "Senate Approves Aids Bill over Helms' Fierce Objections," *Raleigh News and Observer,* July 28, 1995; "Hometown Paper Belittles Helms on AIDS Stance," *Human Events,* August 11, 1995.

96. As part of his strategy, he directly attacked a liberal/gay alliance that was transforming a public health matter into a civil rights issue. Gay activists, he said on July 21, had exploited Ryan White, who "died of AIDS, and now his name is being exploited as if the homosexuals didn't have anything to do with the tainted blood he got." AIDS was receiving special treatment at the expense of other diseases, he said, and a "great bunch" of federal funds would go to gay groups. President Clinton was guilty of "kowtowing to the homosexual lobby at every turn." The *New York Times,* he believed, was deliberately trying to embarrass him. "I've been putting up with this kind of treatment" from the *Times* and "other self-appointed guardians of the liberal establishment for 23 years, and I understand politics when I see it." "Talking Points on Ryan White," July 7, 1995, JH MSS; James Rosen, "Helms Vows He'll Fight AIDS Bill," *Raleigh News and Observer,* July 22, 1995; James Rosen, "Helms Tries to Restrict AIDS Treatment Bill," *Raleigh News and Observer,* July 27, 1995; *CR,* July 26, 1995; John Monk, "Aids Bill Passes in Senate; Sen. Jesse Helms' Violent Opposition Made Media Waves, but Didn't Sway the 97–3 Vote," *Charlotte Observer,* July 28, 1995.

97. The Senate enacted one of his amendments—which prohibited any use of Ryan White funds to promote and encourage homosexuality—but a substitute amendment then watered this down. Lisa Rhodes to JH, July 21, 1995, JH MSS; "Sen Helms Battles Gay Activist Lobby, GOP Moderates on AIDS Funding," *Human Events,* August 11, 1995.

98. "Don't Let Bigotry Kill Ryan White," *Blood Weekly,* July 24, 1995; Helen Dewar, "Senate Votes to Continue AIDS Program; Helms Fails in Bid to Freeze Funding," *Washington Post,* July 28, 1995.

99. Nicole Brodeur, "Mothers Aim Card at Helms," *Raleigh News and Observer,* May 5, 1996; "Recovering Republicans Against Helms," *Progressive,* July 1996; Nicole Brodeur, "Helms Has United These Moms," *Raleigh News and Observer,* October 26, 1996; Derrick Z. Jackson, "AIDS Mothers Target Helms," *Wilmington Star* (reprinted from *Boston Globe*), September 10, 1996; Patsy Clarke and

Eloise Vaughn, with Nicole Brodeur, *Keep Singing: Two Mothers, Two Sons, and Their Fight Against Jesse Helms* (Los Angeles and New York: Alyson Books, 2001), pp. 77–78.

12. A BIG ROCK IN A RIVER

1. John Monk, "Helms Plans to Stop Bills Too Liberal," *Charlotte Observer*, November 8, 1992.
2. Jack Betts, "The Indefatigable Jesse Helms: For Some of the Senator's Detractors, the News That He May Run for a Fifth Term Is Not Exactly Bad," *Charlotte Observer*, June 5, 1993.
3. *Washingtonian*, November 1993.
4. In July 1993, the nomination received the unanimous approval of the Judiciary Committee, which sent it to the Senate floor. Claiming that the Clinton administration had violated Senate protocols in which senators should approve nominees from their home states, Helms also objected to Dellinger because he advised Senate Democrats in their successful attempt in 1987 to block Robert Bork's nomination to the Supreme Court. Helms told a reporter that he would "go to my grave regretting that Judge Bork was denied a seat on the U.S. Supreme Court." Dellinger had also advised Jim Hunt during the 1984 campaign. The larger point of the fight over Dellinger had more to do with obstructing the Clinton White House and discrediting, according to the *Raleigh News and Observer*, a potential Supreme Court nominee. During the first week of October, Helms and Faircloth filibustered the nomination; on October 7, a cloture vote failed by one vote. Although the two North Carolina senators subsequently abandoned the filibuster, and the nomination went through, the fight over the Dellinger nomination apparently eliminated him as a future Supreme Court nominee. John Monk, "Helms Holds Up Approval of N.C. Native for Post," *Charlotte Observer*, September 19, 1993; "Petty Delay on Dellinger," editorial, *Raleigh News and Observer*, September 23, 1993; "Nomination of Walter Dellinger," *CR*, October 6, 1993; "Helms Filibusters Against a Nominee," *New York Times*, October 8, 1993; John Monk, "Senators Win Their Point, Then Agree to End Filibuster," *Charlotte Observer*, October 8, 1993; Al Kamen, "No More Talk Against Nominee," *Washington Post*, October 8, 1993; "Dellinger Near Confirmation for Legal Counsel Job," *Congressional Quarterly Weekly Report*, October 9, 1993.
5. John Monk, "Helms Is No Fan of Clinton's New Surgeon General," *Charlotte Observer*, September 12, 1993.
6. John Monk, "Shalala's Not Biting After Helms' Remark," *Charlotte Observer*, February 6, 1994.
7. "Managed Competition Is Socialized Medicine," *CR*, June 23, 1993; JH, commencement address at Liberty University, May 14, 1994, JH MSS; John Monk, "Helms Loses Bid to Put Health Care Vote on Hold," *Charlotte Observer*, August

11, 1994; "Helms vs. Health Reform," editorial, *Raleigh News and Observer,* August 26, 1993 ; "Liberals Won't Delay Health Care Vote," *Human Events,* August 19, 1994.

8. Howard Schneider, "Judge Met Sen. Faircloth Before Fiske Was Ousted; Sentelle Says Special Counsel Wasn't Discussed," *Washington Post,* August 12, 1994; "Judge in Whitewater Dispute Rewards Faith of His Patron," *New York Times,* August 17, 1994; Saundra Torry, "The Judge's Lunch That Didn't Go Down Well," *Washington Post,* August 22, 1994; Toni Locy and Marilyn W. Thompson, "Lunch Among 'Old Friends' Causes Latest Whitewater Ripple," *Washington Post,* August 24, 1994; Toni Locy, "Complaints on Judge's Contacts Dismissed," *Washington Post,* November 2, 1994; Faircloth interview, December 14, 2006.

9. In September 1994, he successfully blocked the appointment of Robert Pastor as ambassador to Panama because Pastor had served as Jimmy Carter's chief Latin American adviser when the hated Panama Canal treaties were adopted and ratified. Pastor was, Helms said, a "man whose career has been punctuated by troubling decisions." Helms put a hold on Pastor's nomination and, when it reached the Foreign Relations Committee, he delayed committee approval. When Pastor's nomination was sent out of committee, Helms used Senate rules to prevent it from reaching consideration on the Senate floor. James Rosen, "Wily Helms Trips Up Nomination," *Raleigh News and Observer,* September 30, 1994; Al Kamen, "Time Waits for No Nominee," *Washington Post,* September 30, 1994; Ferrel Guillory, "Panama Envoy Nominee Gets Bipartisan Support," *Raleigh News and Observer,* October 1, 1994; "Helms Prevents Action on Panama Nominee," *Congressional Quarterly Weekly Report,* October 1, 1994; Monk, "Helms Gives a Lesson in the Rules"; "Helms Finally Bags Pastor," *Human Events,* February 10, 1995. Helms succeeded in delaying Pastor's nomination for thirteen months by first requesting large quantities of documents from over a seventeen-year period. When the documents failed to turn up anything incriminating, Helms filibustered his own committee and succeeded in delaying the nomination until the congressional session expired on October 8. With the Republican sweep of November 1994, Pastor's nomination was doomed. "Delay and Obstruct; My Nomination Is Dead, and Jesse Helms Is Still Fighting the Panama Canal Treaties," *Washington Post,* February 1, 1995.

10. John Monk, "'The Time to Get Out Is Now,' Helms Says," *Charlotte Observer,* October 7, 1993.

11. Ann Devroy and John M. Goshko, "U.S. Pressed Malval for Changes; Broadening of Haitian Cabinet Rejected After Veto by Aristide," *Washington Post,* October 21, 1993; Helen Dewar, "Senators Approve Troop Compromise; Clinton Authority Is Left Unrestricted," *Washington Post,* October 21, 1993; Helen Dewar, "Clinton and Congress Cease Fire; Senate Refuses to Limit President's Powers to Send Troops to Haiti," *Washington Post,* October 22, 1993; R. Jeffrey Smith and John M. Goshko, "CIA's Aristide Profile Spurs Hill Concern,"

Washington Post, October 22, 1993; John Monk, "Helms, Democratic Senators Trade Barbs over Aristide," *Charlotte Observer,* October 24, 1993; "Images of Aristide," *Congressional Quarterly Weekly Report,* January 23, 1993; John Monk, "Jesse's Secret Weapon," *Washingtonian,* February 1994; (DeMoss) Fonseca interview, October 10, 2006.

12. "Sunday's Nicaraguan Elections," *CR,* February 22, 1990; "The Nicaragua Elections," *CR,* February 28, 1990.

13. "On Nicaragua's Back," editorial, *Washington Post,* September 2, 1992.

14. Edward Cody, "Managua's Reconciliation Effort Nurtures Enmities," *Washington Post,* June 23, 1992; "Nicaragua; At the Helm," *Economist,* August 22, 1992; John M. Goshko, "Nicaraguan Government Criticized; President Chamorro Reduced to Figurehead, Senate Report Says," *Washington Post,* September 1, 1992; "U.S. Cooling Toward Sandinistas' Successors," *New York Times,* September 3, 1992; Douglas Farah, "Chamorro Replaces Sandinista Police Chief, 11 Others," *Washington Post,* September 6, 1992l; "Managua Seesaw: U.S. vs. Sandinistas," *New York Times,* September 8, 1992; Tim Padgett and Marcus Mabry, "Swatted by Hurricane Jesse," *Newsweek,* September 14, 1992; Linda Robinson, "Uncle Sam Puts Nicaragua's President Between a Rock and Hard Place," *U.S. News & World Report,* September 21, 1992; John Monk, "Helms Rebuffs Bush Request Nicaragua Aid Still Frozen," *Charlotte Observer,* October 3, 1992; John Monk, "When Sen. Jesse Helms Froze U.S. Aid to President Violeta Chamorro's Government, He Said He Was Safeguarding U.S. Interests," *Charlotte Observer,* October 25, 1992. It was later reported that Ernesto Palazio, Nicaragua's ambassador to the United States, was a source for DeMoss's report and was forced to resign his position when this was discovered in early 1993. John Monk, "Helms, Democrats Spar over Long Hours Despite Doctor's Orders, Republican Said He'd Stay Up Late to Question Nominees," *Charlotte Observer,* January 17, 1993; John Monk, "Jesse's Secret Weapon," *Washingtonian,* February 1994.

15. John M. Goshko, "U.S. to Free $50 Million for Managua; Nicaraguan Progress on Rights Rewarded," *Washington Post,* April 3, 1993; "Not Another Cent for Nicaragua," *CR,* vol. 139, no. 45, April 2, 1993.

16. John Monk, "Bush Frees Aid to Nicaragua, over Helms' Objections," *Charlotte Observer,* December 4, 1992; John Monk, "Clinton Order Deflates Helms Clout Nicaragua's $50 Million in Aid Freed," *Charlotte Observer,* April 3, 1993; John Monk, "Helms Threatens to Hold Up Appointment over Nicaragua Aid," *Charlotte Observer,* May 6, 1993; "Helms Denounces Nicaragua for Guerrilla Arms Cache," *Congressional Quarterly Weekly Report,* July 24, 1993; John Monk, "Sen. Helms Is Gaining Unlikely Support to Stop U.S. Aid to Nicaragua," *Charlotte Observer,* August 1, 1993; John M. Goshko, "State Department Assails Chamorro; Charge That Nicaraguan Is Moving Too Slowly on Reform Is to Be Probed," *Washington Post,* September 2, 1992; Rodolfo Garcia, "Sandinistas Rail at Chamorro Move," *Charlotte Observer,* September 4, 1993; Tim Johnson, "Senate Vote Bad News for Nicaragua," *Charlotte Observer,* September 24, 1993.

17. Wilkie interview, April 21, 2006.

18. John Monk, "Immigration Bill Places Helms in a Difficult Position," *Charlotte Observer,* August 22, 1993; John Monk, "Helms Stakes Claim to Chairmanship of Foreign Relations," *Charlotte Observer,* October 2, 1994.

19. "Helms: Aid, State Dept. to Be Under Microscope," *Durham Herald-Sun,* November 10, 1994; Rosen interview, December 7, 2006; Thiessen interview, June 6, 2006; Berry interview, June 6, 2006.

20. John Monk, "Helms Stands His Ground, Grills Nominee," *Charlotte Observer,* January 15, 1993; John Monk, "Helms Still Dives into Foreign Policy," *Charlotte Observer,* January 17, 1993. Danielle Pletka described Christopher as "not a warm man." Pletka interview, October 12, 2006.

21. Elaine Sciolino, "Christopher Spells Out New Priorities," *New York Times,* November 5, 1993; John Monk, "Helms Lambastes Clinton's Top Diplomat, Handling of Haiti in Hearing on Policy," *Charlotte Observer,* November 5, 1993; John M. Goshko, Daniel Williams, "U.S. Policy Faces Review by Helms; State Dept. Nemesis to Flex Muscle as Chairman of Foreign Relations," *Washington Post,* November 13, 1994.

22. Jay Euban, "Helms Prepares to Make Big Changes," *Greensboro News & Record,* November 10, 1994; "Republicans Plan to Guide Foreign Policy by Purse String," *New York Times,* November 13, 1994; "Helmsmanship," *Economist,* November 19, 1994; "The Picture Abroad: Grave New World," *U.S. News & World Report,* November 28, 1994.

23. David E. Sanger, "The New Congress: Trade; Helms Requests a Delay in Vote on Trade Accord," *New York Times,* November 16, 1994; James Rosen, "Helms' Letter Spurs Effort to Bolster Support for GATT," *Raleigh News and Observer,* November 17, 1994; Peter Behr and Helen Dewar, "Dole Wants Vote This Year on Trade Pact; but Republican Leader Seeks Changes in Measure," *Washington Post,* November 17, 1994; "Helms Weighs in Against WTO," *Human Events,* November 25, 1994.

24. JH interview (Tom Joyner), tape 9.

25. Helms might have picked up the commander in chief theme from a comment by Oliver North, a Reagan administration official and a central figure in the Iran-contra scandal. In 1994, North was mounting an aggressive and ultimately unsuccessful campaign to unseat incumbent Democratic senator Charles Robb of Virginia. When asked about Clinton, North had quipped that he was "not my commander in chief." "The New Congress: Confrontation; Helms Voices Doubts on Clinton as Commander," *New York Times,* November 19, 1994; John M. Goshko, "Helms Questions Clinton's Ability to Hold Commander-in-Chief Post; GOP Senator Criticizes U.S. Military Intervention in Haiti," *Washington Post,* November 19, 1994; Bradley Graham and Dan Morgan, "Shalikashvili Rebuts Helms on Clinton's Ability as Commander," *Washington Post,* November 20, 1994; James Rosen, "Helms Stands by Statement," *Raleigh News and Observer,* November 22, 1994; "Helms Takes New

Swipe at Clinton, Then Calls It Mistake," *New York Times,* November 23, 1994; Helen Dewar, "Helms Rekindles a Furor Trying to Put One Out; Senator Says Clinton Should Fear Bases," *Washington Post,* November 23, 1994; "What's on Jesse's Mind?," *Time,* December 5, 1994; Wilkie interview, April 21, 2006.

26. "Raleigh Publisher Rejects Charges of Helms' Liberal Critics," *Human Events,* December 9, 1994.

27. "Giving 'Em Helms," editorial, *Charlotte Observer,* November 23, 1994; " 'Hail' to the Chief," editorial, *Raleigh News and Observer,* November 22, 1994; "Welcome, Mr. President," editorial, *Raleigh News and Observer,* November 23, 1994; "Mr. Helms Must Step Aside," editorial, *New York Times,* November 23, 1994; "2 Democrats Urging Dole to Avoid Helms as Leader," *New York Times,* November 25, 1994; James Rosen, "New Role Puts Helms on Hot Seat Foreign Policy Post Constant Test of Candor," *Raleigh News and Observer,* November 27, 1994; Bill Krueger, "Helms Still in Line to Head Key Committee," *Raleigh News and Observer,* November 24, 1994; "What's on Jesse's Mind?," *Time,* December 5, 1994; Kenneth T. Walsh, "Aiming for the Center," *U.S. News & World Report,* December 5, 1994.

28. Michael Ruby, "Rethinking America's Role," *U.S. News & World Report,* December 5, 1994.

29. R. Jeffrey Smith and Ann Devroy, "Panetta Answers Attack on Clinton, Describing Helms as an Extremist; Senate GOP Colleagues Decline to Back Incoming Chairman's Remarks," *Washington Post,* November 21, 1994; Helen Dewar, "Saying Helms Vows to Hold His Tongue, Dole Won't Deny Him Chairmanship," *Washington Post,* November 24, 1994; "Jesse's World," *New Republic,* December 12, 1994. See also "Nuts at the Helms," *Progressive,* January 1, 1995; "Indulging Mr. Helms," editorial, *Washington Post,* November 27, 1994; David S. Broder, "Pit Bulls; Jesse Helms Is Just a Symptom of What You Might Call the GOP's Meanness Problem," *Washington Post,* November 29, 1994. See also "Bitter Beginning," editorial, *Charlotte Observer,* November 22, 1994; John Monk, "Jesse Helms Put Under News Media Microscope, Magazines Dissect N.C. Senator, His Record," *Charlotte Observer,* November 29, 1994.

30. Steven V. Roberts and Gloria Borger et al., "Jesse Helms Still Rattles the Saber," *U.S. News & World Report,* December 5, 1994.

31. James Rosen, "Helms Says He Made 'Mistake,' " *Raleigh News and Observer,* November 23, 1994; "Helms Takes New Swipe at Clinton, Then Calls It Mistake," *New York Times,* November 23, 1994; "Raleigh Publisher Rejects Charges of Helms' Liberal Critics," *Human Events,* December 9, 1994.

32. "Raleigh Publisher Rejects Charges of Helms' Liberal Critics," *Human Events,* December 9, 1994; Broughton interview, Februrary 15, 2006; Nirenberg interview, June 7, 2006. Helms later called the "bodyguard" incident a "manufactured fight." "Biographical Conversations with Jesse Helms," WUNC-TV broadcast, February 11, 2000.

33. Rosen interview, December 7, 2006.

34. Rob Christensen, "Remark Didn't Hurt Helms Poll: Comment on Clinton Left N.C. Views Unaltered," *Raleigh News and Observer,* December 18, 1994; "Remark About Clinton Didn't Hurt at Home," *Charlotte Observer,* December 19, 1994. Rosen later observed that he tried repeatedly to get the names of military people that Helms claimed had written to him complaining about Clinton, but the senator remained evasive. Rosen interview, December 7, 2006.

35. "Senator Breaks His Silence Helms Berates News Media," *Raleigh News and Observer,* December 7, 1994; Paul Nowell, "Helms Challenges Media over Reporting on Remark," *Charlotte Observer,* December 7, 1994; Howard Kurtz, "Helms Maintains Media Distorted Clinton Remark," *Washington Post,* December 7, 1994. Thiessen later described the "bodyguard" comment as a "throwaside" that was the product of press distortion. Thiessen interview, June 6, 2006. Rosen remembered the story about the sheriff, but it was a "very long, shaggy dog story" that did not diminish his point—which was to question Clinton's ability to lead the military. Rosen interview, December 7, 2006.

36. James Rosen, "Pursued by Media Pack, Helms Buttons His Lip," *Raleigh News and Observer,* December 2, 1994; John Monk, "Helms Declines to take Questions from Press," *Charlotte Observer,* December 2, 1994.

37. John Monk, "Helms Holds Own Talk with Post," *Charlotte Observer,* January 22, 1995.

38. James Rosen, "Senate Panel's New Helmsman Relishes His First Day of Power," *Raleigh News and Observer,* January 12, 1995.

39. John Monk, "Chairman Helms: Soft Style, but No Soft Touch," *Charlotte Observer,* January 29, 1995.

40. John Monk, "More Influence, More Scrutiny Ahead for Helms," *Charlotte Observer,* January 5, 1995.

41. Jesse Helms, *When Free Men Shall Stand: A Sobering Look at the Supertaxing, Superspending Superbureaucracy in Washington* (Grand Rapids, Michigan: Zondervan Publishing, 1975), pp. 81–83.

42. JH et al. to Reagan, September 18, 1985, subject files, FG003–02, case file 396859, Reagan Library.

43. Berry interview, June 6, 2006.

44. "G.O.P. Backs Merging Foreign Policy Agencies," *New York Times,* February 15, 1995. Gore explained his reasons for rejecting State Department reorganization in Gore to Helms, February 21, 1995, JH MSS; Thiessen interview, June 6, 2006.

45. Thomas W. Lippman, "Helms's Praise Has Christopher Explaining," *Washington Post,* February 15, 1995.

46. Thomas W. Lippman, "Helms Outlines Foreign Policy Reorganization; Prolonged Hill Battle Expected over Agency Merger Proposal," *Washington Post,* March 16, 1995.

47. James Rosen, "Diplomacy Reigns at Senate Foreign Relations Committee; Helms Mixes Sugar and Spice," *Raleigh News and Observer,* February 15, 1995; "The Real Foreign Aid Debate," editorial, *Washington Post,* February 18, 1995; "Helms Puts His Own Stamp on Cuts Gore Rejected," *Congressional Quarterly Weekly Report,* February 18, 1995; James Rosen, "Helms Seeks Overhaul of Foreign Aid," *Raleigh News and Observer,* March 12, 1995; John Monk, "Helms to Submit Bills to His Panel," *Charlotte Observer,* May 14, 1995.

48. "A Flap over Privatizing Foreign Aid," *Christian Science Monitor,* February 27, 1995; James Rosen, "Helms Hopes to Score with Interceptions," *Raleigh News and Observer,* May 10, 1995; James Rosen, "Veto Threat Looms over Helms' Plan to Slash Foreign Aid," *Raleigh News and Observer,* May 24, 1995.

49. JH, "Christopher Is Right," *Washington Post,* February 14, 1995; "Helms's Praise Has Christopher Explaining; Merger Plan Sounds a Lot Like the One Gore Rejected," *Washington Post,* February 15, 1995.

50. "Helms Aides Show Aid Agency's Plans to Battle Cutbacks," *Charlotte Observer,* May 11, 1995; Thiessen interview, June 6, 2006.

51. John Monk, "Democrats Stall Helms' Effort to Reshape Policy, Agencies," *Charlotte Observer,* August 2, 1995; John Monk, " 'Senator No,' Aka 'Senator Art of the Deal,' " *Charlotte Observer,* August 13, 1995; Eric Pianin and Helen Dewar, "Senate Democrats Stymie Helms's Bid to Kill Three Foreign Policy Agencies," *Washington Post,* August 2, 1995; "Helms' Reorganization Plan Stymied by Democrats," *Congressional Quarterly Weekly Report,* August 5, 1995; "Senator Helms's Bargaining Chips," editorial, *New York Times,* August 28, 1995; "Awaiting Call, Helms Puts Foreign Policy on Hold," *New York Times,* September 24, 1995; Berry interview, June 6, 2006.

52. "Helms, White House Back at Square One," *Congressional Quarterly Weekly Report,* September 23, 1995; "Helms Apparently to Get Vote on Agency Elimination," *Congressional Quarterly Weekly Report,* September 30, 1995.

53. "Helms Reports Compromise," *Congressional Quarterly Weekly Report,* November 18, 1995; "Reformation of the Foreign Affairs," *CR,* December 7, 1995; Helen Dewar, "Senate Deal on Foreign Policy Agencies Ends Impasse on Envoys, Treaties," *Washington Post,* December 8, 1995; John Monk, "Standoff Is Over," *Charlotte Observer,* December 12, 1995; James Rosen, "Senate OKs Helms Bill, Standoff Ends," *Raleigh News and Observer,* December 15, 1995; "Held for Ransom," editorial, *Washington Post,* December 17, 1995.

54. JH to Bruce Eberle, October 5, 1995, JH MSS.

55. Rob Christensen and Bill Krueger, "Helms Shows He Can Still Raise Lots of Money," *Raleigh News and Observer,* January 27, 1996; Lorraine Ahearn, "Sen. Helms Files to Seek Fourth Term," *Greensboro News and Record,* January 30, 1996; "Big Money for Big Senate Races," *Washington Post,* August 15, 1996; Bill Krueger, "Wrenn Says Helms Knew Fund-Raising Letters Vital," *Raleigh News and Observer,* October 12, 1996; Bill Krueger, "Helms Gets Down to Business,"

Raleigh News and Observer, November 1, 1996; Coffer interview, September 7, 2006; Wrenn interview, September 7, 2006; Edmondson interview, October 24, 2006.

56. Edmondson interview, October 24, 2006; Broughton interview, October 25, 2006.

57. Rob Christensen, "Democratic Senate Candidates Hold Debate, Castigate Helms," *Raleigh News and Observer,* March 24, 1996; Jim Morrill, "Ad Watch," *Charlotte Observer,* April 11, 1996; Rob Christensen, "Race Heats Up as Gantt and Sanders Tussle, Helms Drops Aide," *Raleigh News and Observer,* April 18, 1996; Jim Morrill, "Helms' Ads Expected to Take On New Look," *Charlotte Observer,* April 18, 1996; John Hoeffell, "Helms Pulls TV Ad, Cuts Ties with Consultant," *Winston-Salem Journal,* April 18,1996; Rob Christensen, "Surveying the Political Battlefield in Wake of Primary," *Raleigh News and Observer,* May 13, 1996; James Rosen, " 'New' Helms Keeps People Guessing," *Raleigh News and Observer,* May 15, 1996; Fred Barnes, "Jesse Helms Gets Cuddly," *The Weekly Standard,* November 4, 1996; Edmondson interview, October 24, 2006.

58. Danny Lineberry, "Gantt Gets 2nd Shot at Helms; Former Charlotte Mayor Easily Defeats Sanders," *Durham Herald-Sun,* May 8, 1996; "The Second Time Around," editorial, *Chapel Hill Herald,* May 10, 1996; "Politics; Round Two," *Newsweek,* May 20, 1996; Bill Lee, Helms campaign 1996 plan, November 15, 1995, JH MSS.

59. Helms campaign plan, 1996, JH MSS; Rob Christensen, "Gantt, Hayes Ready for Next Test 6 Years Later, Helms Still a Tough Foe," *Raleigh News and Observer,* May 9, 1996; Helen Dewar, "Gantt Hopes Centrist Message Will Attract 'Jessecrats' in Rematch," *Washington Post,* November 1, 1996.

60. "The North Carolina Senate Race," *Economist,* June 1, 1996; Jim Morrill, "Helms, Gantt Unknown to Many, N.C. Electorate's Changed Since '90 Vote," *Charlotte Observer,* October 1, 1996.

61. Rob Christensen, "Helms Turns Down Challenge to Debate Gantt," *Raleigh News and Observer,* June 5, 1996; Noah Kotch, " 'Only Jesse Can Save Our Nation'; Helms Rallies Johnston Faithful," *Raleigh News and Observer,* August 12, 1996; "In North Carolina, a Senate Rematch on a Changed Playing Field," *Washington Post,* September 23, 1996; Danny Lineberry, "Poll: Helms Holding Lead, More Popular Than in 1990," *Durham Herald-Sun,* October 18, 1996; Bill Krueger, "Gantt's Little Gifts Say a Lot," *Raleigh News and Observer,* November 1, 1996; Helen Dewar, "Gantt Hopes Centrist Message Will Attract 'Jessecrats' in Rematch," *Washington Post,* November 1, 1996; Danny Lineberry, "Poll: Helms Holding 6-Point Lead over Gantt," *Durham Herald-Sun,* November 1, 1996; Rob Christensen and James Rosen, "Helms, Gantt Slug and Plug," *Raleigh News and Observer,* November 3, 1996; Morrill interview, September 5, 2006; Nancy E. Roman, "Gantt Has Twice Helms' War Chest," *Washington Times,* October 23, 1996.

62. Helms campaign plan, 1996, November 15, 1995, JH MSS.

63. Bob Geary, "Whistlestop, HelmsWatch," *Independent,* September 11–17, 1996; Edmondson interview, October 24, 2006.

64. Rob Christensen, "Helms Eases View of 'Choice,'" *Raleigh News and Observer,* August 6, 1996; Emery P. Dalesio, "Helms Says His World Role Benefits State," *Charlotte Observer,* August 18, 1996; "In North Carolina, a Senate Rematch on a Changed Playing Field," *Washington Post,* September 23, 1996; "Nightmare on Helms Street," *In These Times,* September 30, 1996.

65. Tyson interview, December 7, 2006; Jim Morrill, "Jesse Helms Senate Campaign," *Charlotte Observer,* September 10, 1996; Lorraine Ahearn, "Senate Race Ads Contrast Styles of Candidates," *Greensboro News and Record,* September 12, 1996; Rob Christensen, "Tried-and-True GOP Strategy: Using Homosexuality as a Wedge Issue," *Raleigh News and Observer,* October 7, 1996.

66. Rob Christensen, "Gantt, Helms Exchange Barbs," *Raleigh News and Observer,* October 1, 1996; Jim Morrill, "Helms Senate Campaign," *Charlotte Observer,* October 2, 1996; Jena Heath, "A Side Helping of Foreign Affairs: Helms Campaign Enlists Kissinger," *Raleigh News and Observer,* October 20, 1996; "Politics," *Washington Post,* October 5, 1996; "Helms Campaign Is Heading to the Gutter," editorial, *Greensboro News and Record,* October 12, 1996.

67. Edmondson interview, October 24, 2006; "Gantt, Helms Target Senior Citizens," *Greensboro News and Record,* October 19, 1996.

68. Jane Stancill, "Storm Touches Politics," *Raleigh News and Observer,* September 13, 1996.

69. Lynn Pearsall Williams, "They Came for 'Vintage Jesse,'" *Mount Olive Tribune,* October 18, 1996; Broughton interview, October 25, 2006.

70. Bob Geary, "Whistlestop, HelmsWatch," *Independent,* September 11–17, 1996; Jim Morrill, "Helms Says He Will Not Debate Gantt," *Charlotte Observer,* October 4, 1996; Fred Barnes, "Jesse Helms Gets Cuddly," *The Weekly Standard,* November 4, 1996.

71. Jim Morrill, "Helms Charms Backers," *Charlotte Observer,* October 15, 1996; Rob Christensen, "It's Always a Good Show When Helms Takes to the Stage to Wage War on Evil," *Raleigh News and Observer,* October 21, 1996; "Helms Mixes Homily, Attack," *Raleigh News and Observer,* October 24, 1996.

72. Edmondson interview, October 24, 2006.

73. John Hoeffel, "With Heat Turned Up, Senatorial Races Takes Turns," *Winston-Salem Journal,* October 18, 1996; "CBS Says Gantt Is Leading Helms by Two Points," *Winston-Salem Journal,* October 19, 1996; "Helms Injects Race Issue into Rematch with Gantt," *Washington Post,* October 23, 1996; Jim Morrill, "Jesse Helms Senate Campaign," *Charlotte Observer,* October 23, 1996; John Hoeffel, "Helms Pulls His Latest Ad from '90s Strategy Bag," *Winston-Salem Journal,* October 23, 1996; Helen Dewar, "Gantt Hopes Centrist Message Will Attract 'Jessecrats' in Rematch," *Washington Post,* November 1, 1996; Jim Morrill, "Race Emerges as Issue Late in Senate Battle," *Charlotte Observer,* November 2, 1996.

74. Joseph Neff, "Helms, Wife Underreport Real Estate Holdings," *Raleigh News and Observer,* October 9, 1996; Scott Moneyham, "Helms Family Rents Houses

Lacking Heat," *Asheville Citizen-Times,* October 10, 1996; Joseph Neff, "Reviews of Helmses' Houses Mixed," *Raleigh News and Observer,* October 11, 1996; Dianne Whitacre and Jim Morrill, "Ethics Probe Sought on Helms Finance Reports," *Charlotte Observer,* October 11, 1996; Helen Dewar and David Maraniss, "North Carolina Democrats Seek Helms Ethics Probe," *Washington Post,* October 11, 1996.

75. Ruth Marcus, "Foundation for Special Interests; Sen. Helms's Charity Gets Large Gifts from Taiwan, Kuwait, Tobacco," *Washington Post,* October 26, 1996; Estes Thompson, "Helms Says Article on Center 'Typical,'" *Charlotte Observer,* October 27, 1996; Rob Christensen, "Gantt, Helms Pitch for Jessecrats' Support," *Raleigh News and Observer,* October 27, 1996; Carol D. Leonnig, John Monk, and Tim Funk, "Gantt Urges Helms to Give Back Foreign Contributions," *Charlotte Observer,* October 30, 1996; Jim Morrill, "Race Emerges as Issue Late in Senate Battle," *Charlotte Observer,* November 2, 1996; Rob Christensen and James Rosen, "Helms, Gantt Slug and Plug," *Raleigh News and Observer,* November 3, 1996.

76. Rob Christensen, "Senator Handed 5th Term," *Raleigh News and Observer,* November 6, 1996; Danny Lineberry, "Helms Fends Off Gantt for 2nd Time," *Durham Herald-Sun,* November 6, 1996; Stan Swofford, "Basking in Victory, Feisty Helms Gears Up for a Fifth Senate Term," *Greensboro News and Record,* November 7, 1996; Coffer interview, September 7, 2006.

77. John F. Harris, "U.S. Bases Join Education Test Effort; Military-Run Schools Enlist in National Standards Plan, Clinton Says," *Washington Post,* March 14, 1997; Broughton interview, February 15, 2006.

78. Thomas B. Edsall and Ceci Connolly, "Helms and Clinton: An Unlikely Couple," *Washington Post,* September 27, 1997. Helms's Foreign Relations staff director, Steve Biegun, described Clinton as a person who often "turned on the charm" and was "very charismatic." Biegun interview, October 10, 2006. According to another staffer, Helms found Clinton "very charismatic," although he "deeply disapproved" of his behavior. Pletka interview, October 12, 2006.

79. Parker Lee Nash, "Helms, Edwards Mum on Vote," *Greensboro News and Record,* December 23, 1998; Broughton interview, February 15, 2006.

80. JH, speech at CPAC, January 31, 1998, JH MSS.

81. After Hillary Rodham Clinton included Helms and Faircloth in a "vast right-wing conspiracy" to topple the president, Helms was aghast. There was "absolutely no truth" to Hillary's charges, and he sent word that he "thought our relationship was better." He recalled that he and Hillary "kid a lot," and he regarded her as a "very personable lady" whose experience now "must be a frustrating time for her." Later, in a receiving line at a state dinner at the White House, he told her that the "right-wing conspiracy is here." "Well, welcome," she responded. Carol D. Leonnig, "Helms Taking Fast Lane Back from Surgery," *Charlotte Observer,* September 26, 1998; James Rosen, "Helms: Clinton Scandal Makes U.S. Look Silly," *Raleigh News and Observer,* February 1, 1998;

"Biographical Conversations with Jesse Helms," WUNC-TV broadcast, February 11, 2000.

82. James Rosen, "Helms Supports Removing Clinton," *Raleigh News and Observer,* January 7, 1999.

83. Beth McNichol, "Historical Votes: N.C. Senators Felt Weight of Impeachment Trial Roles; Helms Berates Media; Edwards Reveals Angst of Decision," *Durham Herald-Sun.* February 13, 1999; JH, statement about Clinton impeachment trial, February 11, 1999, JH MSS.

84. Helle Bering-Jensen, "Dissing Albright," *Weekly Standard,* December 23, 1996; JH, introduction of Madeleine Albright, Wingate College, March 25, 1997, JH MSS.

85. "Ambassador Albright on the Hill," editorial, *Washington Post,* January 8, 1997; Madeleine Albright, *Madam Secretary* (New York: Miramax, 2003), p. 227.

86. Albright, *Madam Secretary,* pp. 133–34. Carol D. Leonnig, "Helms Welcomes, Warns Nominee," *Charlotte Observer,* January 9, 1997; "Lexington: Albright's Perch," *Economist,* January 11, 1997; Broughton interview, October 25, 2006. Albright recalled that her daughter Katie felt patronized by Helms's courtliness. At a White House dinner, when he referred to Katie as a "lady lawyer," she and mother laughed on the way home at what Helms's reaction might have been if she had responded: "a lawyer, but no lady." Albright, *Madam Secretary,* p. 134.

87. Thiessen interview, June 6, 2006.

88. Richard L. Berke and Steven Lee Myers, "In Washington, Few Trifle with Jesse Helms," *New York Times,* August 2, 1997; Joie Lapolla, Jim Morrill, and Ted Reed, "Day of Mutual Compliments for Albright, Helms," *Charlotte Observer,* March 26, 1997; Rosemary Roberts, "'Madeleine and Jesse Show' Plays Well in Helms Country," *Greensboro News and Record,* March 28, 1997; Broughton interviews, February 15, October 25, 2006; Albright, *Madam Secretary,* p. 225.

89. Thomas W. Lippman, "At Albright's Confirmation Hearing, Differences Are Smoothed Over," *Washington Post,* January 9, 1997. Helms made the same point at a speech at CPAC, March 8, 1997, JH MSS.

90. James Rosen, "Helms Issues Policy Warning," *Raleigh News and Observer,* January 23, 1997.

91. Thiessen interview, June 6, 2006.

92. Biegun interview, October 10, 2006; John Monk, "Helms Aide Doesn't Mind Making Points Forcefully,'" *Charlotte Observer,* November 2, 1995; Pletka interview, October 12, 2006.

93. "AID in Motion," editorial, *Washington Post,* April 18, 1999; "A Nomination Crashed," editorial, *Washington Post,* May 21, 1999.

94. Wilkie interview, April 21, 2006; "A Bare-Knuckled Brawl," *Newsweek,* August 4, 1997; Al Kamen, "Lip Sink," *Washington Post,* June 4, 1997; James Rosen, "Helms Opposes Clinton's Choice for Mexico Envoy," *Raleigh News and Observer,* June 4, 1997; Steven Lee Myers, "Helms to Oppose Weld as Nominee for Ambassador," *New York Times,* June 4, 1997; "The Weld Nomination," editorial, *Washington Post,*

June 5, 1997; Richard L. Berke, "White House Stands by Weld Despite Opposition of Helms," *New York Times,* June 5, 1997; Helen Dewar, "Clinton Standing by Weld as Choice for Mexico Post; Helms's Objections Could Block Approval," *Washington Post,* June 6, 1997; Carol D. Leonnig, "Nominee's Gop Credentials Not Enough for Helms," *Charlotte Observer,* June 8, 1997; "Chairman Helms," editorial, *New York Times,* June 7, 1997; "What Does Jesse Want?," *Newsweek,* June 16, 1997; Sara Rimer, "Weld, Seeking Mexico Post, Challenges White House to Stand Up to Helms," *New York Times,* July 16, 1997; Peter Baker, Ceci Connolly, and John F. Harris, "A Think Tank's Divide on Weld," *Washington Post,* August 6, 1997; Denise Dresser, "Why Mexico Wants Weld," *New York Times,* August 2, 1997; "Weld, Crusading for Confirmation, May Have Eyes on Another Prize," *Congressional Quarterly Weekly Report,* August 2, 1997; Carol D. Leonnig, "Donation Adds Fuel to Helms-Weld Fire," *Charlotte Observer,* August 6, 1997. For conservative sentiment about Weld, see "Jesse Helms Is Right to Oppose Weld," *Human Events,* August 15, 1997; Joe Battenfeld, "Right Set to Slam Weld—Conservatives Take Helms' Side in Fight," *Boston Globe,* August 21, 1997; Broughton interview, February 15, 2006.

95. Frank Phillips and Scot Lehigh, " 'I Intend to Stand and Fight'; Weld Blasts Helms, Urges Clinton to Back Nomination," *Boston Globe,* July 16, 1997; Peter Baker and Helen Dewar, "Clinton Taps Weld for Post Despite Helms Objection; Mexico Ambassadorship Caught in GOP Divisions," *Washington Post,* July 24, 1997.

96. Peter Baker and Helen Dewar, "Clinton Taps Weld for Post Despite Helms Objection," *Washington Post,* July 24, 1997; Peter Baker, "Weld to Resign as Governor to Pursue Post; Mass. Republican Is Battling for Mexico Ambassadorship," *Washington Post,* July 28, 1997; Blaine Harden, "Weld Quits Statehouse to Tackle 'Washington Rules'; Governor Will Seek National Spotlight in Clash with Helms over Envoy's Post," *Washington Post,* July 29, 1997; Tucker Carlson, "What Is Weld up To?," *Weekly Standard,* August 11, 1997; "Helms Holds the Line on Weld," *Human Events,* August 8, 1997.

97. Carolyn Ryan, "A Diplomatic Weld: Helms 'Misinformed,' " *Boston Globe,* August 2, 1997; Wilkie interview, April 21, 2006.

98. Susan Schmidt, "Lugar May Defy Helms, Push for Hearing on Weld," *Washington Post,* August 4, 1997; Peter Baker, Ceci Connolly, and John F. Harris, "A Think Tank's Divide on Weld," *Washington Post,* August 6, 1997; Lizette Alvarez, "Lugar Vows Trouble for Helms if He Balks on Hearing for Weld," *New York Times,* August 8, 1997; Carol D. Leonnig, "Tobacco a Hostage in Helms-Weld Standoff?," *Charlotte Observer,* August 8, 1997; Terry M. Neal and Ceci Connolly, "Lugar Challenges Helms on Weld Hearing; One Senate Chairman Tests Another's Refusal to Act on Nomination," *Washington Post,* August 9, 1997; Matthew Cooper and Howard Fineman, "A Summer Squall," *Newsweek,* August 18, 1997; Carolyn Ryan, "Lugar Says Helms Risks Tobacco Clout Stonewalling Weld," *Boston Globe,* August 8, 1997; Broughton interview, October 25, 2006.

99. "Lugar to Helms: 'Loosen Up' on Weld," *Charlotte Observer,* August 11, 1997; Jim Hoagland, "Lugar's Larger Campaign," *Washington Post,* August 14, 1997.

100. Notably, Albright remained out of the fray. "She and I have never discussed Mr. Weld—never," Helms explained in an interview. "She has brought up a number of nominations of particular interest to her. She's come to see me, and I've gone down and had a sandwich with her." Al Kamen, "No Temporary Weld," *Washington Post,* September 5, 1997; Andrew Miga, "4 Senators Launch Bid to Force Weld Hearing," *Boston Globe,* September 6, 1997; Thomas B. Edsall, "Weld Says Most Want 'A Fair Hearing,'" *Washington Post,* September 8, 1997; "The Way of the Weld," *Weekly Standard,* September 8, 1997; James Rosen, "Helms Will Not Budge on Weld," *Raleigh News and Observer,* September 10, 1997; Peter Baker, "Lott Urges Withdrawal of Weld's Nomination," *Washington Post,* September 12, 1997.

101. Joe Battenfeld, "Weld Will Go Public with Attack on Helms," *Boston Globe,* August 25, 1997; Helen Dewar, "Sen. Helms's Gavel Leaves Weld Nomination in Limbo; Chairman Thwarts Majority Call for Hearing," *Washington Post,* September 13, 1997; James Rosen, "Helms Unyielding in Weld Hearing," *Raleigh News and Observer,* September 13, 1997; "Helms Lashes Back at Critics, Holds Firm on Blocking Weld," *Congressional Quarterly Weekly Report,* September 13, 1997; Carol D. Leonnig, "Helms Silences Weld's Backers, Refuses Hearing," *Charlotte Observer,* September 13, 1997; Thiessen interview, June 6, 2006; Broughton interviews, February 15, October 25, 2006; Wilkie interview, April 21, 2006.

102. George Lardner, Jr., "Nomination Declared 'Dead,' but Weld Vows to Fight On," *Washington Post,* September 15, 1997.

103. James Rosen, "Weld Gives Up Fight for Post," *Raleigh News and Observer,* September 16, 1997; John F. Harris, "Weld Ends Bid to Be Ambassador; Blasting Helms, Mexico Nominee Refuses to 'Go on Bended Knee,'" *Washington Post,* September 16, 1997; Katharine Q. Seelye, "Weld Ends Fight over Nomination by Withdrawing," *New York Times,* September 16, 1997; Andrew Miga, "Weld Says Adios to Mexico Envoy Job; He Hints at Run for Higher Office," *Boston Globe,* September 16, 1997.

104. Thiessen interview, June 6, 2006.

105. Carol D. Leonnig, "Federal Judgeships Could Be Dropped; Helms Tactic Kept 2 of 3 N.C. Seats Open," *Charlotte Observer,* February 18, 1997; "Unpacking the Court," editorial, *Washington Post,* June 13, 1998; James Rosen, "Helms Raises Ire with Court Bill," *Raleigh News and Observer,* March 28, 1999; Wade Rawlins, "Helms Still Adamant on Wynn," *Raleigh News and Observer,* September 1, 1999; John Minter, "And Justice for All?," *Charlotte Post,* January 27, 2000; John Wagner, "Clinton Takes Helms to Task," *Raleigh News and Observer,* July 14, 2000; Jim Morrill, "Clinton Bypasses Helms on Judge," *Charlotte Observer,* December 28, 2000; John Wagner, "Clinton Taps N.C. Judge for 4th Circuit," *Raleigh News and Observer,* January 4, 2001; John Wagner, "Judge's Approval Hinges on

Helms' Support," *Raleigh News and Observer,* January 5, 2001; Nirenberg interview, June 7, 2006; Broughton interview, October 25, 2006.

106. Michelle Cottle, "Undiplomatic," *New Republic,* November 15, 1999.

107. Helen Dewar, "Helms v. Moseley-Braun, Again; Flag Fight, Ethics Concerns Snag Ex-Senator's Nomination," *Washington Post,* October 19, 1999; James Rosen, "Blame Piles Up on Helms," *Raleigh News and Observer,* October 20, 1999; Eric Schmitt, "Nominee as Ambassador Runs into Adversary," *New York Times,* October 19, 1999.

108. Alison Mitchell, "Parties Trade Accusations over Race and Nominations," *New York Times,* October 21, 1999; "A Few Words from a Freewheeling Helms," *Washington Post,* October 25, 1999; Rosen interview, December 7, 2006.

109. "World View: Noteworthy," *Congressional Quarterly Weekly Report,* October 20, 1999; Eric Schmitt, "Helms Would Act on Nominee in Return for Sensitive Papers," *New York Times,* October 27, 1999; Helen Dewar, "Moseley-Braun Gets a Hearing; Panel Gives Nominee Warm Reception; Chief Accuser Absent," *Washington Post,* November 6, 1999; Helen Dewar, "Senate Committee Approves Moseley-Braun," *Washington Post,* November 9, 1999; "Washington in Brief," *Washington Post,* November 10, 1999; "Senate Confirms Moseley-Braun, Ambassadors to China and Israel," *Congressional Quarterly Weekly Report,* November 13, 1999; Michelle Cottle, "Undiplomatic," *New Republic,* November 15, 1999; Kate O'Beirne, "Madame Ambassador? Yech!," *National Review,* November 22, 1999; JH, speech, *CR,* November 9, 1999.

110. "Statesmanship vs Helmsmanship," *Nation,* February 5, 1996.

13. Time Takes a Terrific Toll

1. John Wagner, "Helms Still Talks the Talk," *Raleigh News and Observer,* July 4, 2000.

2. "Clinton Support for War Crimes Court Sparks Barrage of Criticism," *Global News Wire,* January 1, 2001; Jesse Helms, "Slay This Monster," *Empire for Liberty: A Sovereign America and Her Moral Mission,* edited by Marc Thiessen (Wingate, N.C.: Jesse Helms Center, 2001), pp. 10–14.

3. Daniel Williams, "Helms Offers Tough Anti-Castro Bill; Bipartisan Effort Seeks to Tighten Economic Sanctions Against Cuba," *Washington Post,* February 10, 1995; Jesse Helms, "Castro Needs a Final Push," *Washington Post,* May 4, 1995; Thomas W. Lippman, "Sanctions Move Reignites Volatile Debate on Cuba; White House, Hill in Policy Confrontation," *Washington Post,* October 7, 1995; Stephen Lisio, "Helms-Burton and the Point of Diminishing Returns," *International Affairs* 72, no. 4 (1996): 691–711.

4. John Monk, "Helms' Cuba Bill Revived by Shootdown," *Charlotte Observer,* February 28, 1996; "Senate Approves Compromise Bill Tightening Curbs on Cuba," *New York Times,* March 6, 1996; John Monk, "Helms Savors Win on

Cuba; Clinton Did the Right Thing with Sanctions, Senator Says," *Charlotte Observer,* March 13, 1996.

5. Clinton Delays but Allows Suits over Confiscated Property," *Congressional Quarterly Weekly Report,* July 20, 1996; Biegun interview, October 10, 2006.

6. "One Key Element in Anti-Cuba Law Postponed Again," *New York Times,* January 4, 1997.

7. Thomas W. Lippman, "Helms Cordiality Cracks; Conflicts Arise over Cuba, Weld, U.N.," *Washington Post,* July 20, 1997; "Helms Demands Documents on Cuba Sanctions," *Congressional Quarterly Weekly Report,* October 11, 1997.

8. Thomas W. Lippman, "It's a Smaller World After Budget Shrinkage," *Washington Post,* March 21, 1996.

9. Douglas Stanglin and Bruce B. Auster et al., "Wooing the Great Helmsman," *U.S. News & World Report,* February 24, 1997; Thomas W. Lippman, "Helms to Delay Vote on Chemical Arms Pact; Panel Chairman Puts GOP 'Priorities' First," *Washington Post,* February 4, 1997; Jesse Helms, "The Flaws in the Chemical Weapons Treaty," *USA Today,* September 12, 1996, JH, *Empire for Liberty: A Sovereign America and Her Moral Mission* (Washington: Regnery Publishing, 2001), p. 86; Carol D. Leonnig, "Helms Opposes Treaty Banning Chemical Arms Many in GOP Back," *Charlotte Observer,* February 13, 1997; John F. Harris, "Administration Considers Moving Foreign Affairs Agencies to State Dept.," *Washington Post,* March 23, 1997; James Rosen, "Helms May Win Fight over Agencies," *Raleigh News and Observer,* March 24, 1997; Thomas W. Lippman, "Helms Signals Vote Likely on Chemical Weapons Pact; Senator, Albright Warm to an Unlikely Alliance," *Washington Post,* March 26, 1997; Albright to JH, March 28, 1997, JH MSS; Peter Slevin, "There's Method in the Gladness for Unlikely Allies Helms, Albright," *Charlotte Observer,* March 29, 1997; "Taking Helms' Word," editorial, *Raleigh News and Observer,* March 28, 1997; James Rosen, "Clinton Lobbies for Treaty," *Raleigh News and Observer,* April 5, 1997; Carol D. Leonnig, "Doing the Chemical Weapons Ban Two-Step," *Charlotte Observer,* April 6, 1997; "Who Muscled Jesse Helms?," *Weekly Standard,* April 7, 1997; "Chemical Treaty, at a Price ...," editorial, *Washington Post,* April 27, 1997; Madeleine Albright, *Madam Secretary* (New York: Miramax, 2003), pp. 231, 331–32.

10. James Rosen, "Senate Oks Chemical Arms Treaty," *Raleigh News and Observer,* April 25, 1997; Helen Dewar, "Senate Approves Chemical Arms Pact After Clinton Pledge," *Washington Post,* April 25, 1997; Thiessen interview, June 6, 2006.

11. Stephen Barr, "Foreign Affairs Plan Doesn't Aim to Cut Jobs, Budgets," *Washington Post,* April 18, 1997; "More Than Turf," editorial, *Washington Post,* April 20, 1997; Thomas W. Lippman and Peter Baker, "Bipartisanship, but at a Price; President Trades Foreign Policy Concessions for GOP Support of Treaty," *Washington Post,* April 25, 1997; JH, Senate speech, June 15, 1997; Albright to JH, November 13, 1998, JH MSS; Pletka interview, October 12, 2006.

12. Michael Dobbs, "Senate Removes a Barrier to European Troop Pact; White House Objects to Link with ABM Treaty," *Washington Post,* May 15, 1997; Bill Clinton to JH, October 30, 1997, May 27, 1998, February 22, 1999, JH MSS; Bernie Quigley, "Helms May Carry Peace Mantle on Issue of NATO expansion," *Durham Herald-Sun,* August 10, 1997; James Rosen, "Helms, Albright See Eye to Eye on NATO," *Raleigh News and Observer,* October 8, 1997; Helen Dewar, "Senate Giving NATO Expansion a Virtual Free Ride," *Washington Post,* March 8, 1998; JH to Bill Clinton, January 21, 1998, *CR,* September 30, 1999; Thiessen interview, June 6, 2006; Biegun interview, October 10, 2006; JH, speech at CPAC, January 31, 1998, JH MSS.

13. Thomas W. Lippman and Bradley Graham, "Helms Offers Bill to Force U.S. out of ABM Treaty; Aides Give Measure Little Chance of Approval," *Washington Post,* February 8, 1996; Carol D. Leonnig, "Helms: Test Ban Treaty Shown Up as Sham," *Charlotte Observer,* May 14, 1998; James Rosen, "Helms Still Balking as Clinton Pushes Test-Ban Treaty," *Raleigh News and Observer,* June 4, 1998; Geneva Overholser, "Treaty in a Bottle," *Washington Post,* July 29, 1999.

14. "...And a Captive Treaty," editorial, *Washington Post,* July 25, 1999.

15. Biegun interview, October 6, 2006.

16. James Rosen, "Helms Gets Serious over Treaty," *Raleigh News and Observer,* October 2, 1999; James Rosen, "Helms to Clinton: Pull Treaty or It Fails," *Raleigh News and Observer,* October 7, 1999.

17. Biegun interview, October 10, 2006.

18. Biegun interview, October 10, 2006; Helen Dewar and Roberto Suro, "Senate Conservatives to Demand Vote on Test Ban Treaty," *Washington Post,* October 7, 1999; Helen Dewar, "As Debate Starts, Clinton Asks Senate to Delay Test Ban Vote; Democrats Threaten to Cut Off Treaty if Lott Doesn't Withdraw It," *Washington Post,* October 9, 1999; William Claiborne, "Clinton: Test Ban Treaty Is Essential; Rejection Would Be 'Dangerous U-turn,'" *Washington Post,* October 10, 1999; Charles Babington and Michael Grunwald, "President Requests Treaty Vote Deferral; But GOP Seeks a Delay Until at Least 2001," *Washington Post,* October 12, 1999.

19. Helen Dewar, "Democrats Push Delay on Treaty; Compromise Offered by Daschle Would Block Vote Until After Elections," *Washington Post,* October 13, 1999; Biegun interview, October 10, 2006.

20. Charles Babington, "Clinton Campaigns for Senate Passage of Test Ban Treaty," *Washington Post,* October 5, 1999; Jim Hoagland, "Sorting Out the Blame," *Washington Post,* October 15, 1999; Michael Elliott, Michael Hirsh, and John Barry, "All Bets Are Off," *Newsweek,* October 25, 1999; Matthew Rees, "'The Right Thing for Our Country'; How Jon Kyl and a Handful of His Republican Colleagues in the Senate Engineered the Defeat of the Comprehensive Test Ban Treaty," *Weekly Standard,* October 25, 1999; Jesse Helms, "Why the Senate Said No to the Nuclear Test Ban Treaty," *Wall Street Journal,* October 18, 1999, in *Empire for Liberty,* pp. 72–73; Richard Lowry, "Test-Ban Ban,"

National Review, November 8, 1999; JH speech, *CR,* October 13, 1999; Carol D. Leonnig, "Clinton Lashes Out at Helms for Treaty Defeat," *Charlotte Observer,* October 15, 1999; "A Reckless Rejection," editorial, *Washington Post,* October 14, 1999; John Harris, "White House's Berger Assails the Hill's 'Isolationist Right,'" *Washington Post,* October 22, 1999; Broughton interview, October 25, 2006.

21. Biegun interview, October 10, 2006; Jesse Helms, "Mr. Boutros-Ghali Has to Change His Tune," JH, *Empire for Liberty,* 2001), pp. 25–29. On Bosnia, see, *Empire for Liberty,* ch. 8.

22. Thomas W. Lippman, "A Contributing Writer in the Enemy's Pages; Helms Blasts U.N. in Establishment Journal," *Washington Post,* August 20, 1996; Broughton interview, February 15, 2006.

23. John M. Goshko, "In Shift, U.N. Chief Meets with Helms on Reforms," *Washington Post,* January 24, 1997; "Secretary General Annan's Visit," editorial, *Washington Post,* January 26, 1997; Kofi Annan to JH, January 7, February 3, 1997, JH MSS; John M. Goshko, "U.N.'s New Leader Outlines Personnel, Budget Cutbacks; Conservatives in Congress Express Skepticism," *Washington Post,* March 18, 1997; Thiessen interview, June 6, 2006.

24. "The U.N. and Sen. Helms," editorial, *Washington Post,* March 26, 1997.

25. Thomas W. Lippman, "Helms Backs Bill to Pay U.N. Debt; Other Key Senators Agree on Foreign Affairs Reorganization," *Washington Post,* June 11, 1997; James Rosen, "Helms Revels in U.N. Revamp," *Raleigh News and Observer,* June 13, 1997.

26. "Don't Ask for More, Mr. Annan," *Economist,* November 20, 1999; Derek Chollet and Robert Orr, "Carpe Diem: Reclaiming Success at the United Nations," *Washington Quarterly* 24, no. 4 (Autumn 2001): 13; Thiessen interview, June 6, 2006.

27. James Rosen, "Helms to Make History, Address UN Security Council," *Raleigh News and Observer,* January 19, 2000; Taft Wireback, "Helms to UN to Be First for Senator," *Greensboro News and Record,* January 20, 2000; Robert Novak, "Slandering Jesse Helms," *Daily Southerner* (Tarboro, N.C.), August 30, 2001; Biegun interview, October 10, 2006.

28. Thiessen interview, June 6, 2006.

29. Alison Vekshin, "Helms Gets First Opportunity to Address U.N," *Durham Herald-Sun,* January 16, 2000; "Washington in Brief," *Washington Post,* January 19, 2000; James Rosen, "Helms to Make History, Address U.N. Security Council," *Raleigh News and Observer,* January 19, 2000; Taft Wireback; "Helms Address to U.N. to Be First for a Senator," *Greensboro News and Record,* January 20, 2000.

30. Thiessen interview, June 6, 2006; Biegun interview, October 10, 2006.

31. Lauren Markoe, "Helms Chides UN Members," *Charlotte Observer,* January 21, 2000; Helms's speech can be found at http://www.sovereignty.net/center/helms.htm (accessed August 27, 2006).

32. James Rosen, "Heed U.S., Helms says," *Raleigh News and Observer,* January 21, 2000; Colum Lynch, "Sen. Helms Offers Cooperation, Then Castigates United Nations," *Washington Post,* January 21, 2000; Richard Holbrooke to JH, January 22, 2000, JH MSS.

33. Thiessen interview, June 6, 2006; Colum Lynch, "Helms's View Is Not U.S.'s, Albright Tells U.N.," *Washington Post,* January 25, 2000.

34. John Wagner, "Helms Will Lead Mission to Mexico," *Raleigh News and Observer,* April 4, 2001; Peter Wallsten, "Helms Will Lead Delegation to Mexico; Trip Plan Enhances His Reinvigorated Image," *Charlotte Observer,* April 4, 2001; John Wagner, "Helms Traveling First Class," *Raleigh News and Observer,* April 14, 2001; John Wagner, "Critic Helms Seeks New Role in Mexico City Trip," *Durham Herald-Sun,* April 16, 2001; Peter Wallsten, "Helms Packs New Approach for Today's Trip to Mexico," *Charlotte Observer,* April 16, 2001; "Longtime Critic Helms Arrives in Mexico; Senator's Visit for Talks with New President Met with Surprise, Skepticism," *Washington Post,* April 17, 2001; John Wagner, "Helms Meetings Touch on Drug Traffic, Cuba," *Raleigh News and Observer,* April 18, 2001; "Visit by Helms Begins Warmly; Mexico Offered 'Friendship,'" *Washington Post,* April 18, 2001; Peter Wallsten, "Helms, Mexican Leaders Tackle Thorny Issues," *Charlotte Observer,* April 18, 2001.

35. "Gentle Jesse," *National Journal,* May 19, 2001.

36. John Wagner, "In Helms, Bono Finds the Ally He's Looking For," *Raleigh News and Observer,* September 21, 2000; John Cassidy, "They Are the World," *New Yorker,* October 9, 2000; John Wagner, "Aides Find Helms Tale Perplexing," *Raleigh News and Observer,* October 14, 2000; "Bono Seeks Helms' Help for Needy Nations," editorial, *Charlotte Observer,* October 19, 2000; "Can Debt Relief Make a Difference?," *Economist,* November 18, 2000; Rob Christensen, "Explaining the 2 Faces of Jesse," *Raleigh News and Observer,* February 23, 2001; Dorothy Rompalske, "Rock Star to the Rescue," *Biography* 6 (October 2002): 56; Albert Eisele and Betsy Rothstein, "Helms: I'd Quit the Senate to Help Starving Kids," *Hill,* October 11, 2000; Joseph Kahn, "A Star Close to the Heart of Aid Policy," *New York Times,* March 15, 2002; Gersh Kuntzman, "American Beat: The Unforgettable Friendship," *Newsweek,* July 2, 2001; Don O'Briant, "The Newsstand," *Atlanta Journal-Constitution,* February 26, 2002; Madeleine Bunting and Oliver Burkeman, "Pro Bono: When George Bush Announced a Hike in US Aid Last Week, Many Were Surprised by the Figure at His Side," *Guardian* (London), March 18, 2002; Mary Jacoby, "Singing Bono's Praises," *St. Petersburg Times,* June 2, 2002; Broughton interview, February 15, 2006; Bono to JH, September 29, 2000, JH MSS. For Helms's version, see JH, *Here's Where I Stand: A Memoir* (New York: Random House, 2005), pp. 144–49.

37. John Wagner, "Holbrooke Deplores U.N. Peacekeeping in Africa," *Raleigh News and Observer,* July 13, 2000; "Helms Surprises Foreign-Aid Advocates by Work on African Debt Relief," AP wire service, October 28, 2000.

38. Bono to JH, May 2, 2001, JH MSS. In February 2002, Helms met with Secretary of State Colin L. Powell and National Security Adviser Condoleezza Rice, both of whom supported increased aid. In May 2002, Bono hosted a visit to Africa with Treasury Secretary Paul H. O'Neill; the trip changed O'Neill's mind about Africa.

39. Elisabeth Bumiller, "Bush Plans to Raise Foreign Aid and Tie It to Reforms," *New York Times,* March 15, 2002.

40. John Wagner, " 'Senator No' Shows He's Pro Bono," *Raleigh News and Observer,* June 16, 2001; "American Beat: The Unforgettable Friendship," *Newsweek,* June 2, 2001; Broughton interview, February 15, 2006.

41. John Wagner, "Helms Admits 'Shame' over Inaction on AIDS," *Raleigh News and Observer,* February 21, 2002; "Helms' Candor on AIDS," editorial, *Raleigh News and Observer,* February 21, 2002; Broughton interview, February 15, 2006.

42. Kevin Begos and John Railey, "Helms Clarifies His Views on AIDS," *Winston-Salem Journal,* March 6, 2002; Raju Chebium, "Graham Gets Helms to Back AIDS Fight," *Asheville Citizen-Times,* February 21, 2002; John Wagner, "Views on AIDS Unchanged, Helms Says," *Raleigh News and Observer,* March 6, 2002; Bono to JH, February 21, 2002.

43. "Senator Hosts Meeting with Rock Star, Actor," AP wire service, March 14, 2002; Charles Hurt, "Helms Brings Hollywood to the Hill Bono Discusses Strategy for New AIDS Activism with GOP Senators," *Charlotte Observer,* March 14, 2002.

44. JH, "We Cannot Turn Away," *Washington Post,* March 24, 2002; Adam Clymer, "Helms Reverses Opposition to Help on AIDS," *New York Times,* March 25, 2002; John Donnelly, "Helms's Reversal on US Aid Reverberates; Senator Seeks $500m to Help Stamp Out AIDS Transmission in Africa," *Boston Globe,* March 27, 2002; Al Kamen, "Helms Leads Bid to Boost U.S. Contribution to AIDS Fight," *Washington Post,* March 24, 2002.

45. "Sen. Frist Backs Down," editorial, *Washington Post,* June 12, 2002; "Retreat on AIDS," editorial, *Washington Post,* September 12, 2002.

46. John Wagner, "Helms Bids Clinton Good Riddance," *Raleigh News and Observer,* February 16, 2001; JH, speech at CPAC, February 15, 2001, JH MSS.

47. Thiessen interview, June 6, 2006; Biegun interview, October 10, 2006; Pletka interview, October 12, 2006.

48. "White House Says It Won't Abolish AID," *Congressional Quarterly Weekly Report,* April 28, 2001.

49. John Wagner, "Helms Links School Funds to Scouts," *Raleigh News and Observer,* May 15, 2001; John Wagner, "Helms Puts Hold on Bush Nominees," *Raleigh News and Observer,* June 13, 2001; "Scouting for Votes," *Washington Post,* June 15, 2001; Helen Dewar, "Senate Passes Major Revamp of Education; Fight over Funding Gap Looms," *Washington Post,* June 15, 2001; John Wagner, "Helms Opposes Bush's Getting Chummy with Putin," *Raleigh News and Observer,* June 21, 2001; John Wagner, "Trouble in Paradise: Helms Spars

with Bush Administration," *Raleigh News and Observer,* July 2, 2001; John Wagner, "Helms Lifts Nominee 'Holds,'" *Raleigh News and Observer,* August 4, 2001.

50. Bill Clinton to JH, October 25, 1999, JH MSS; David Espo, "Helms Holds Up Bush over Textiles; Treasury Nominees Held Hostage in Effort to Shape Trade Rules to Save Jobs," *Charlotte Observer,* July 23, 2001; David Espo, "Senate Confirms Treasury Appointees as Helms Relents; N.C. Senator Hoped to Delay Rules He Says Would Hurt Textile Industry," *Charlotte Observer,* August 4, 2001; "Bush vs. Helms," *Washington Post,* August 6, 2001.

51. "Helms Has Surgery to Replace Knees," *Raleigh News and Observer,* July 28, 1998; Carol D. Leonnig, "Helms Taking Fast Lane Back from Surgery," *Charlotte Observer,* September 26, 1998; "Control of Senate Hangs by a Thread; Health of Thurmond, Helms Is Focus of Attention in Evenly Divided Chamber," *Washington Post,* December 12, 2000; Taft Wireback, "Will Age, Health Finally Sideline 'Senator No'?," *Greensboro News and Record,* September 3, 2000; Broughton interview, October 25, 2006.

52. Hal Tarleton, "Oh Yeah, Jesse Helms and I Go Back a Long Way, Surprisingly," *Wilson Daily Times,* September 1, 2001.

53. James Rosen, "Helms Is Dealing with Nerve Disease," *Raleigh News and Observer,* April 1, 2000; "An Update on Helms' Health," *Raleigh News and Observer,* September 23, 2000; Coffer interview, September 7, 2006.

54. John Wagner, "Helms Recovering from Case of Pneumonia," *Raleigh News and Observer,* October 25, 2000; Peter Wallsten, "Helms' 3-Day Hospital Stay Over; Senator Is Working at Home, Aides Say," *Charlotte Observer,* October 25, 2000.

55. JH, speech to CPAC, February 15, 2001, JH MSS.

56. "Helms Staying in N.C. After Falling Ill," *Durham Herald-Sun,* October 26, 2000; Suzanne Smalley, "Helms' Health Watched with Possible Senate Split," *Durham Herald-Sun,* November 14, 2000; John Wagner, "Republican Majority Is Fragile," *Raleigh News and Observer,* November 19, 2000.

57. Amy Gardner, "Media Get Scolding over Helms," *Raleigh News and Observer,* December 8, 2000.

58. Coffer interview, September 7, 2006; John Wagner, "Helms Clears First Hurdle," *Raleigh News and Observer,* April 26, 2002; Jackie Koszczuk, "'Remarkable Progress' for Helms," *Charlotte Observer,* May 8, 2002; Kevin Begos, "Helms Doing Well, Might Go Home in Two Weeks, Doctor Says," *Winston-Salem Journal,* May 8, 2002; Rob Christensen, "Helms Not Likely to Return to the Senate Soon," *Raleigh News and Observer,* May 8, 2002.

59. John Wagner, "Helms Faces Slow Healing," *Raleigh News and Observer,* May 1, 2002; Sarah Avery, "Helms Gaining Strength but Remains on Ventilator," *Raleigh News and Observer,* May 4, 2002; Charles Hurt, "Helms to Move Soon to Rehab Center," *Charlotte Observer,* May 17, 2002; John Wagner, "Helms May Leave Hospital Soon," *Raleigh News and Observer,* May 31, 2002; "Helms Moves

to Rehab Unit," *High Point Enterprise,* June 11, 2002; April Bethea, "Helms Leaves Hospital; In Rehab," *Raleigh News and Observer,* June 11, 2002; John Wagner, "Helms, on Mend, Pays Visit to Capitol," *Raleigh News and Observer,* June 26, 2002; Amy Gardner, "Mrs. Helms in Good Condition After Heart Surgery," *Raleigh News and Observer,* July 2, 2002; "Names & Faces," *Washington Post,* July 17, 2002; Broughton interview, October 25, 2006.

60. Broughton interview, February 15, 2006.

61. "Helms Makes First Washington Appearance Since His Open-Heart Surgery," *Congress Daily,* June 26, 2002; "Ailing Helms May Be out Until July or August," *Congressional Quarterly Weekly,* May 11, 2002; John Wagner, "Helms Goes Home; Eyes D.C. Return," *Raleigh News and Observer,* July 17, 2002; "Helms Expected to Return to Senate Just in Time for Year-End Push," *Congressional Quarterly Weekly Report,* August 31, 2002; Jesse J. Holland, "Helms Returns to D.C. to Finish Senate Term," *Charlotte Observer,* September 4, 2002; Coffer interview, September 7, 2006; Morrill interview, September 5, 2006.

62. John Wagner, "Weak Fund Raising Not Helms Retirement Sign, Aides Say," *Raleigh News and Observer,* February 7, 2001; John Wagner, "Helms Keeps Options Open with Fund-Raising Letter," *Raleigh News and Observer,* March 1, 2001; Rob Christensen, " 'Will Jesse Run?' On Everyone's Lips at GOP Meeting," *Raleigh News and Observer,* May 20, 2001; Mark Johnson, "Helms to Decide by September," *Charlotte Observer,* May 20, 2001; Rob Christensen, "Helms Keeping Us Guessing," *Raleigh News and Observer,* June 13, 2001; Kevin Sack, "Watching for the Sunset of a Senate Legend," *New York Times,* August 12, 2001.

63. "Biographical Conversations with Jesse Helms," WUNC-TV broadcast, February 11, 2000.

64. Jim Morrill, "Switch Would End Helms' Chairmanship," *Charlotte Observer,* May 24, 2001; Jim Morrill, "Signs Look like Helms off Ballot; Many Republicans Think Age, Health Rule Out 6th Campaign," *Charlotte Observer,* August 18, 2001; John Wagner, "Helms Expected to Retire in 2003," *Raleigh News and Observer,* August 22, 2001; John Sullivan, "Senator's Decision Puts WRAL in a Bind," *Raleigh News and Observer,* August 23, 2001; Taft Wireback, "Aging Helms Bows Out; Senator Cites 'Toll of Time' in Decision to Retire," *Greensboro News and Record,* August 23, 2001; "Helms Confirms He'll Retire in 2003," *Washington Post,* August 23, 2001; John Wagner, " 'Thank You, Dear Friends,' " *Raleigh News and Observer,* August 23, 2001; Broughton interviews, February 15, October 25, 2006.

65. David Perlmutt, "Friends Worry, but Family Doesn't; Relatives Say Helms Will Make the Tricky Transition from Life in Spotlight," *Charlotte Observer,* August 26, 2001.

66. Kevin Sack, "The Jockeying Starts as Helms Yields to Time," *New York Times,* August 23, 2001.

67. "Greatest Senator of Our Time," *Human Events,* August 27, 2001. See also "Conservatives Hail Jesse Helms," *Human Events,* August 27, 2001.
68. "Helms to Retire from the Senate; Decision Colors 2002 Race for Control," *Washington Post,* August 22, 2001.
69. "Helms Deep," *National Review,* August 22, 2001.
70. John Wagner, " 'Thank You, Dear Friends,' " *Raleigh News and Observer,* August 23, 2001.

Acknowledgments

I n researching and writing this book, I have become indebted to a number of individuals and institutions. In 2004, after many years at the University of North Carolina at Greensboro, I moved to the University of Florida, where I discovered an exceptionally welcoming environment. I am grateful to department chairs Brian Ward and Joe Spillane for their unflagging support. The research and writing of this book would have been impossible without the support of the Richard J. Milbauer Eminent Scholar endowment. At an early stage of the book's conception, Glenda Gilmore provided very helpful advice. I relied on a number of colleagues for suggestions: Charles Bolton, Robert Calhoun, Peter Carmichael, Joseph Crespino, Davison M. Douglas, Christine R. Flood, J. Matthew Gallman, Charles Holden, Steven Lawson, Watson Jennison, Tom Jackson, Cheryl Junk, Kevin Kruse, Louise Newman, Julian Pleasant, and Luise White. I appreciate their advice, even though I may not have taken it in every instance. Tim Tyson very generously opened up his research materials about Robert F. Williams and Monroe, North Carolina. John Wilson, while working on a film documentary about Helms, made available his interview materials, research notes, and photographic images. Rob Christensen was very helpful in sharing his vast knowledge about North Carolina politics and assisting me when I needed to track down people. Jack Betts generously photocopied some correspondence with Helms.

I have relied on the help of student assistants James Broomall, Heather

Bryson, Stephen Jackson, and Courtney Moore. Heather was especially helpful in arranging interviews and managing a complex schedule for me, while Jim was a great help with the last stages of the manuscript preparation. I also appreciate the intellectual interaction of an undergraduate research seminar that I taught at the University of Florida in the spring of 2006 about Helms and his legacy, and I thank the students for their ideas and enthusiasm. I presented portions of the book at Southern Historians of the Piedmont Seminar, the Milbauer Seminar, and the British Association of American Studies, and participants supplied very useful ideas and suggestions.

I have benefited from the useful advice and experience of my literary agent, Wendy Strothman, who not only guided me through the processes of publication but provided very helpful editorial and substantive comments on an early book proposal. Michael Flamini, my editor at St. Martin's Press, has been encouraging and supportive, and I am grateful for his abilities as an editor. I am also grateful for Vicki Lame's assistance in shepherding the manuscript toward publication. Heather Florence provided an exceptionally thorough reading of the manuscript, and Fred Chase was a skillful copy editor.

Various libraries and archives provided substantial assistance, including the Southern Historical Collection and the North Carolina Collection at the University of North Carolina at Chapel Hill, the North Carolina State Archives, the Jimmy Carter Presidential Library, the Ronald Reagan Presidential Library, and the Hoover Institution Archives. Kim Cumber of the State Archives was especially helpful with photographic research. The staff of the Jesse Helms Center generously opened their doors to me, and I appreciate their many kindnesses. Jo Jackson has skillfully organized a major collection about Helms and late- twentieth-century America, and she has been unflaggingly helpful in assisting me. The director of the center, John Dodd, shared his knowledge about Helms in numerous conversations, and he contributed his considerable insights about the senator's career and made numerous suggestions about research leads. John was very generous in extending the hospitality of the center and making it a welcoming place to conduct research. We diverge on major interpretive points regarding Helms; it is my hope, however, that he will find much here that is valuable. Deborah DeMoss Fonseca, longtime aide and friend to Senator Helms, has been very generous in providing help, not only by sharing her extensive knowledge of Helms's long career but also encouraging other former staffers to speak with me.

As always, I appreciate the support of friends and family. For their cheerful hospitality, I am grateful to Bob and Mandy Avery, Pete and Beth Carmichael, Kathy Franz and Brendon Danaher, Paul and Nicole Mazgaj, Bruce Ragsdale and Rick Scobey, and Amy and Joe Thompson. My sister Peggy and my brother Stan both put me up during extended stays in North Carolina, and both expressed a constant interest in my subject. My three daughters offered their usual intelligent skepticism: Maggie helped with the research and explored leads, and she didn't hesitate to offer some interpretive suggestions; Percy and Josie were curious observers with regard to Helms and American politics in general. Susannah, my life partner, supported the project from its inception with cheerfulness, encouragement, and wisdom. She read the manuscript sympathetically but rigorously, and subjected it to her usual critical eye. As always, I'm in her debt for everything, the least of which is this book.

The dedication is for Steven Lawson and Nancy Hewitt, friends, mentors, cheerful critics, and constant supporters over the past two decades.

Index